TWO CENT...
OF A GREA...

"There is a whol... ...ting in sociology, comprehension and enjoyment of which does not require specialized training. It is a tradition in which acuteness of perception, stylistic grace, and humane significance are joined in an endeavor to bring at once enlightenment and pleasure. Works in this vein are indeed a pleasure to read. It is this tradition I wish to highlight."

—from the Introduction by Lewis A. Coser

ABOUT THE EDITOR:
LEWIS A. COSER, co-founder of *Dissent*, is Distinguished Professor of Sociology at the State University of New York at Stony Brook and past President of the American Sociological Association. His many books include *The Functions of Social Conflict, Men of Ideas,* and *Masters of Sociological Thought*. With Irving Howe, he edited *The New Conservatives,* available in a Meridian edition.

THE PLEASURES OF SOCIOLOGY

EDITED AND
WITH AN INTRODUCTION
AND NOTES BY

Lewis A. Coser

A MENTOR BOOK
NEW AMERICAN LIBRARY

TIMES MIRROR
NEW YORK AND SCARBOROUGH, ONTARIO

NAL BOOKS ARE AVAILABLE AT QUANTITY DISCOUNTS
WHEN USED TO PROMOTE PRODUCTS OR SERVICES. FOR
INFORMATION PLEASE WRITE TO PREMIUM MARKETING DIVISION,
THE NEW AMERICAN LIBRARY, INC., 1633 BROADWAY,
NEW YORK, NEW YORK 10019.

Copyright © 1980 by Lewis A. Coser

Library of Congress Catalog Card Number: 79-91057

Ⓜ

MENTOR TRADEMARK REG. U.S. PAT. OFF. AND FOREIGN COUNTRIES
REGISTERED TRADEMARK—MARCA REGISTRADA
HECHO EN WINNIPEG, CANADA

SIGNET, SIGNET CLASSIC, MENTOR, PLUME, MERIDIAN AND NAL BOOKS
are published *in the United States* by The New American Library, Inc.,
1633 Broadway, New York, New York 10019,
in Canada by The New American Library of Canada Limited,
81 Mack Avenue, Scarborough, Ontario M1L 1M8

First Printing, March, 1980

3   4   5   6   7   8   9

PRINTED IN CANADA

CONTENTS

Contents

VII. CRIME AND DEVIANCE 413

VIII. SOCIOLOGICAL WORKS 455

INTRODUCTION

SOCIOLOGY, WHICH MIGHT be broadly described as an attempt to elucidate how human beings and their fate on this earth are affected by the position they occupy in different social structures and cultural milieus, and how interaction between people largely determines their joys and their sorrows, is a fairly new discipline. The ancient Egyptians and Babylonians already studied the skies with a measure of sophistication, and the natural sciences began to assume their modern shape in the sixteenth century. But the disciplined and methodical study of humans in society is only some two hundred years old. For many centuries the human race was concerned with penetrating the secrets of nature, but it is only fairly recently—specifically since the Enlightenment of the eighteenth century—that it has turned its gaze inward to discover the complicated ways in which men and women construct a social world which, in its turn, determines in large part their own destiny.

Like all newcomers, sociology faces the derision, skepticism, and even contempt of those who occupied the scientific territory before sociologists began to make their claims. Philosophers, humanists and literary people have been known to react to invading sociologists much as, say, old-time Brahmins in Boston reacted to the invading Irish in the last century. Both groups were said to be crude barbarians, incapable of appreciating, or of living up to, the genteel life-styles of older elites.

Economics was long known as "the dismal science." Sociology has often not had a much better reputation. It uses an elaborate and unwieldy terminology, it is alleged; a set of highly complicated conceptualizations to document "what everyone knows." Its jargon is said to be as impenetrable as its techniques are unwieldy. Sociologists are reputed to be unable to use the resources of the English language with elegance and grace. Their style is said to be leaden, their findings boring, and their conclusions obvious. Far from illuminating the human condition in novel ways, their labors are said to obfuscate central human problems by burying them in statistical tables, correlational analyses, and intolerable "newspeak."

As the old saying goes, where there is smoke there is likely to be some fire. It would be silly to deny that some sociologists write badly, that some are insensitive to human problems, and that others never manage to move from the trivial to the significant. But it is hard to believe that sociologists have a corner on such faults. Many—perhaps most—economists are addicted to the building of mathematical models that bear only a faint resemblance to what in fact happens in economic life. They sometimes operate with assumptions about "rational behavior" that have little relation to the actual behavior of human beings. Some anthropologists spend a lifetime investigating the minutiae of primitive societies that interest only a few fellow researchers. And while many great historians of the past did indeed use the resources of the English language in impressive ways, most contemporary historical works would hardly please the ghosts of Gibbon or Macaulay. One might go on. The fact is that every academic discipline has its share of sheep and goats, its esoteric jargon, its tribal customs, and its special foolishness.

But that said, it must also be recognized that every specialized human endeavor, be it in the arts or the sciences, must use specialized tools of inquiry that may seem strange and even threatening to the layperson. Most of us have made our peace with the fact that even though our lives are deeply affected by modern science, few among us have more than an acquaintance with, as opposed to knowledge of, the principles and findings on which it is based. But when it comes to human affairs, people seem to feel that common sense suffices to understand them. We are hence inclined to look at the findings of sociology with a great measure of ambivalence, if not hostility. And yet it is hardly intuitively obvious that, say, demographic trends should be more easily explained by common sense than molecular movements.

Anti-sociological Yahoos' contrary opinions notwithstanding, there *is* a place for highly technical investigations, research methods, and mathematical models in the social sciences. To master these requires a long period of specialized training and their arduous application to the specialized tasks at hand. It would be a sign of sociology's impoverishment if any layperson were able to read all the research papers in the *American Sociological Review*.

Yet there is also a whole tradition of writing in sociology, comprehension and enjoyment of which does not require specialized training. It is a tradition in which acuteness of perception, stylistic grace, and humane significance are joined in an endeavor to bring at once enlightenment and pleasure. Works in this vein are indeed a pleasure to read. It is this tradition I wish to highlight in the present volume.

The papers in this volume attempt to give the reader some preliminary access to many of the great intellectual achievements of the past, from Marx to Simmel, from Saint-Simon to Tönnies, even as they also attempt to provide a good sample of more contemporary work. By such a mixed offering of the old and the new, I hope to illustrate how themes and problems first adumbrated by our intellectual ancestors have continued to inspire contemporary investigators who have pushed the frontiers of knowledge beyond what the pioneers could possibly accomplish. By standing on the shoulders of the giants of the past, we have been able to see further than they. Just as it would be foolish not to read Saul Bellow because Proust or Balzac supposedly said it all, so it would be foolish not to read Erving Goffman because Georg Simmel broke open the paths on which Goffman travels.

The papers in this volume have been grouped under eight chapter headings, from Social Types to Social Interaction, from Social Definitions to Sociological Whimsy, from Crime and Deviance to Work and Leisure, from Social Groups to Age and Sex. These are only primitive ordering devices; many of the papers overlap formal categories of classification. Most of the writers and scholars represented here possess a sociological imagination that could hardly be kept in formal bounds. Much of the pleasure of reading them, I believe, will come from the fact that a paper ostensibly devoted to one particular topic will open new vistas on a number of others. Richly suggestive as many of these papers are, they are meant to provide for their readers what my former teacher the late Paul Lazarsfeld called an "Aha! experience." That is, they will suggest insights into human and personal experiences that are not always formally addressed in the main theme of the paper. The varied texture of the fare offered here may provide illumination for the modern reader that was unanticipated by the author. I hope that these readings will provide for the reader the joy of discovery as well as the light of new understanding.

Peter Berger, in the most graceful and charming introduction to the discipline, *Invitation to Sociology*, argues that sociology may be an individual pastime, a form of consciousness and a new perspective, as well as a humanistic discipline. I hope that the readings here provided lend themselves to all these uses, though obviously in unequal measure. It will largely depend on the readers which morsels of this alluring feast are more particularly to their taste. This is as it should be.

"There is no impression of life, no manner of feeling it or of seeing it," Henry James once wrote, "to which the plan of the novelist may not offer a place." I do not think that it is immodest to suggest that this holds true also for the sociologist. Just like the novelists, the sociologist provides readers with a large variety of richly textured commentaries on life in society and people's involvement with their fellows. Sociologists, however, tend to be a little more systematic and methodical about this than are their literary brothers and sisters. Sociologists have contributed to the self-interpretation of men and women in their societies and to the ancient injunction to "know thyself." The great traditions of sociology are humanistic. And attempts to penetrate to the roots of the behavior of the human animal, while often arduous and painstaking, can also be a great deal of fun. We should not take ourselves too seriously. After all, only humans among all the animal kingdom have the capacity to smile.

Lewis A. Coser

I.

WHAT IS OBVIOUS?

SOCIAL AND SOCIOLOGICAL DEFINITIONS

about American soldiers in World War II that seem as contrary to common sense. I venture that this attempt will show that the actual findings were the opposite of what common sense would have suggested. Hereafter, with mention of those that what appears to be obvious play this common in specimen in specialist's country to evidence logical analysis asks the claim of sociologists with their appearance in changing life part of social reality that another much more complex and confusing than common sense will do.

Certainly some see little, but it problematic in features of social phenomena. That is, it would suggest, that somebody while one there and then report your findings, but some common sense turns out to be wrong. The data be not simply wall to be caught at the very moment the second, but in its. Nobody is able to report all the data that were found in any particular setting, so some choices must be made. Such choices will reflect the researcher's theoretical concerns, over-all assumptions and analytical notions. The way of studying the lifeworld of the human being around a while and its standing way or not seeing. Thus, as Dennis Wrong suggests in his paper, "The Oversocialized Conception of Man in Modern Sociology," it may be that much modern sociologists, conscious of having downgraded the importance of socialization in the making of the human animal, have tended to prison varieties of over-socialized being and neglected motivation and the social determinant as human behavior. Wrong attempts to redress the balance by insisting that humans are social but nonetheless conflicted, conscious creatures, and so cannot be

COMMON SENSE can hardly go wrong—or so people believe. In fact, as an excerpt from a famous review by the late Paul Lazarsfeld of the classic study *The American Soldier* by Samuel Stouffer et al. shows, common sense can often lead us down a garden path. Listing a series of purported "findings" about American soldiers in World War II that seem indeed to conform to common sense, Lazarsfeld then turns around and shows that the *actual* findings were the opposite of what common sense would have suggested. He shows with peculiar force that what appears to be obvious may turn out upon inspection to be clearly contrary to evidence; hence, he vindicates the claim of sociologists that their offices are needed to interpret a social reality that is often much more complex and opaque than common sense will allow.

Common sense sees little that is problematic in regard to social phenomena. Just go, it would suggest, and study the world out there and then report your findings. But again, common sense turns out to be wrong. The data do not simply wait to be caught in the researcher's net like so many butterflies. Nobody is able to report all the data that were found in any particular setting, so some choice must be made. Such choices will reflect the researcher's theoretical concern, overall orientation, and particular interest. "A way of seeing," the literary critic Kenneth Burke argued a while ago, "is always a way of not seeing." Thus, as Dennis Wrong suggests in his paper "The Oversocialized Conception of Man in Modern Sociology," it may be that many modern sociologists, justifiably proud of having discovered the importance of socialization in the making of the human animal, have tended to present man as a fully socialized being and neglected instinctual and biological determinants of human behavior. Wrong attempts to redress the balance by insisting that humans are surely social, but never completely socialized creatures; and so a dialecti-

2

cal, rather than a one-sided, conception of human nature is required and should inform research efforts.

There is still another complication in the study of human societies to which common sense tends to be oblivious. The human beings the social scientist studies are not just inert "material." They are continuously involved in structuring their experiences, in imposing meanings on their interactions with others. They live in a symbolic universe, and their responses to each other are influenced by the symbolic meanings they discern in their encounters. A puny little man might not impress us very much, but if we learn that he is a prophet or a king, we will respond to him with awe and respect. As William Isaac Thomas, one of the fathers of American sociology states in his famous discussion of "the definition of the situation," "If men define situations as real, they are real in their consequences." When, for example, some people define certain old women as witches, even though these definitions are "obviously" nonsense to the modern observer, they may have major consequences in that people holding such beliefs might attempt to kill such "witches." Each culture provides for its members such standardized definitions of the situation and, hence, largely structures their ways of perceiving, and therefore their ways of responding to, persons and events.

In the next selection, the leading contemporary sociologist Robert K. Merton extends Thomas' seminal insight by suggesting, among other things, that human beings are often involved in making self-fulfilling prophecies by providing initially false definitions of a situation and then acting on such false definitions, so that—and this is the crucial irony— the originally falsely defined event comes to be true in fact. When we proclaim that women or blacks are inferior and hence deem it "a waste of taxpayers' money" to provide equal educational opportunities for them, we can then turn around and proclaim that these categories of people, having fewer achievements to their credit as a result of lack of resources, are, in fact, inferior. In similar ways, Merton suggests, we are inclined to count as virtues patterns of behavior that we attribute to in-groups, but blame out-groups when they exhibit objectively similar behavior. Things are never only what they may be described as in objective terms; they are defined by the context in which they are variously perceived and interpreted.

Merton alludes in his paper to Robert and Helen Lynd's

classic community study *Middletown in Transition* and to its famous chapter "The Middletown Spirit." Major parts of this chapter are reprinted here to illustrate the imaginative manner in which the Lynds were able to show the many contradictions and distortions that were involved in the definitions of the situations that were perceived as the American Way of Life. The Lynds show how Middletowners act on various cultural premises that may seem contradictory to the outsider, but are not so perceived by the insiders. Here again, what seems "obvious" to the insider may not seem so to the outsider. Only disciplined inquiry will increase our understanding.

What Is Obvious?

by
Paul F. Lazarsfeld

The limitations of survey methods are obvious. They do not use experimental techniques; they rely primarily on what people say, and rarely include objective observations; they deal with aggregates of individuals rather than with integrated communities; they are restricted to contemporary problems—history can be studied only by the use of documents remaining from earlier periods.

In spite of these limitations survey methods provide one of the foundations upon which social science is being built. The finding of regularities is the beginning of any science, and surveys can make an important contribution in this respect. For it is necessary that we know what people usually do under many and different circumstances if we are to develop theories explaining their behavior. Furthermore, before we can devise an experiment we must know what problems are worthwhile; which should be investigated in greater detail. Here again surveys can be of service.

Finding regularities and determining criteria of significance are concerns the social sciences have in common with the natural sciences. But there are crucial differences between the two fields of inquiry. The world of social events is much less "visible" than the realm of nature. That bodies fall to the ground, that things are hot or cold, that iron becomes rusty, are all immediately obvious. It is much more difficult to realize that ideas of right and wrong vary in different cultures; that customs may serve a different function from the one which the people practising them believe they are serving; that the same person may show marked contrasts in his behavior as a member of a family and as a member of an occupational group. The mere description of human behavior, of its variation from group to group and of its changes in different situations, is a vast and difficult undertaking. It is this

From *Public Opinion Quarterly*, Vol. 13 (Fall 1949), pp. 378–80. Reprinted with permission of Elsevier North Holland, Inc., publishers.

task of describing, sifting and ferreting out interrelationships which surveys perform for us. And yet this very function often leads to serious misunderstandings. For it is hard to find a form of human behavior that has not already been observed somewhere. Consequently, if a study reports a prevailing regularity, many readers respond to it by thinking "of course that is the way things are." Thus, from time to time, the argument is advanced that surveys only put into complicated form observations which are already obvious to everyone.

Understanding the origin of this point of view is of importance far beyond the limits of the present discussion. The reader may be helped in recognizing this attitude if he looks over a few statements which are typical of many survey findings and carefully observes his own reaction. A short list of these, with brief interpretive comments, will be given here in order to bring into sharper focus probable reactions of many readers.

1. Better educated men showed more psycho-neurotic symptoms than those with less education. (The mental instability of the intellectual as compared to the more impassive psychology of the-man-in-the-street has often been commented on.)

2. Men from rural backgrounds were usually in better spirits during their Army life than soldiers from city backgrounds. (After all, they are more accustomed to hardships.)

3. Southern soldiers were better able to stand the climate in the hot South Sea Islands than Northern soldiers (of course, Southerners are more accustomed to hot weather).

4. White privates were more eager to become non-coms than Negroes. (The lack of ambition among Negroes is almost proverbial.)

5. Southern Negroes preferred Southern to Northern white officers. (Isn't it well known that Southern whites have a more fatherly attitude toward their "darkies"?)

6. As long as the fighting continued, men were more eager to be returned to the States than they were after the German surrender. (You cannot blame people for not wanting to be killed.)

We have in these examples a sample list of the simplest type of interrelationships which provide the "bricks" from which our empirical social science is being built. But why, since they are so obvious, is so much money and energy given to establish such findings? Would it not be wiser to take them for granted and proceed directly to a more sophisticated type of analysis? This might be so except for one interesting point about the list. *Every one of these statements is the direct opposite of what actually was found.* Poorly educated soldiers were more neurotic than those with high education; Southerners showed no greater ability than Northerners to adjust to a tropical climate; Negroes were more eager for promotion than whites; and so on. . . .

If we had mentioned the actual results of the investigation first, the reader would have labelled these "obvious" also. Obviously something is wrong with the entire argument of "obviousness." It should really be turned on its head. Since every kind of human reaction is conceivable, it is of great importance to know which reactions actually occur most frequently and under what conditions; only then will a more advanced social science develop.

The Oversocialized Conception of Man in Modern Sociology

by
Dennis H. Wrong

Gertrude Stein, bed-ridden with a fatal illness, is reported to have suddenly muttered, "What, then, is the answer?" Pausing, she raised her head, murmured, "But what is the question?" and died. Miss Stein presumably was pondering the ultimate meaning of human life, but her brief final soliloquy has a broader and humbler relevance. Its point is that answers are meaningless apart from questions. If we forget the questions, even while remembering the answers, our knowledge of them will subtly deteriorate, becoming rigid, formal, and catechistic as the sense of indeterminacy, of rival possibilities, implied by the very putting of a question is lost.

Social theory must be seen primarily as a set of answers to questions we ask of social reality. If the initiating questions are forgotten, we readily misconstrue the task of theory and the answers previous thinkers have given become narrowly confining conceptual prisons, degenerating into little more than a special, professional vocabulary applied to situations and events that can be described with equal or greater precision in ordinary language. Forgetfulness of the questions that are the starting points of inquiry leads us to ignore the substantive assumptions "buried" in our concepts and commits us to a one-sided view of reality.

Perhaps this is simply an elaborate way of saying that sociological theory can never afford to lose what is usually called a "sense of significance"; or, as it is sometimes put, that sociological theory must be "problem-conscious." I choose instead to speak of theory as a set of answers to questions because reference to "problems" may seem to suggest too close a linkage with social criticism or reform. My primary reason for

Reprinted from *American Sociological Review*, Vol. 26, No. 2 (April 1961), pp. 183–93, with permission of the American Sociological Association and the author.

insisting on the necessity of holding constantly in mind the questions that our concepts and theories are designed to answer is to preclude defining the goal of sociological theory as the creation of a formal body of knowledge satisfying the logical criteria of scientific theory set up by philosophers and methodologists of natural science. Needless to say, this is the way theory is often defined by contemporary sociologists.

Yet to speak of theory as interrogatory may suggest too self-sufficiently intellectual an enterprise. Cannot questions be satisfactorily answered and then forgotten, the answers becoming the assumptions from which we start in framing new questions? It may convey my view of theory more adequately to say that sociological theory concerns itself with questions arising out of problems that are inherent in the very existence of human societies and that cannot therefore be finally "solved" in the way that particular social problems perhaps can be. The "problems" theory concerns itself with are problems *for* human societies which, because of their universality, become intellectually problematic for sociological theorists.

Essentially, the historicist conception of sociological knowledge that is central to the thought of Max Weber and has recently been ably restated by Barrington Moore, Jr. and C. Wright Mills[1] is a sound one. The most fruitful questions for sociology are always questions referring to the realities of a particular historical situation. Yet both of these writers, especially Mills, have a tendency to underemphasize the degree to which we genuinely wish and seek answers to trans-historical and universal questions about the nature of man and society. I do not, let it be clear, have in mind the formalistic quest for social "laws" or "universal propositions," nor the even more formalistic effort to construct all-encompassing "conceptual schemes." Moore and Mills are rightly critical of such efforts. I am thinking of such questions as, "How are men capable of uniting to form enduring societies in the first place?"; "Why and to what degree is change inherent in human societies and what are the sources of change?"; "How is man's animal nature domesticated by society?"

Such questions—and they are existential as well as intellectual questions—are the *raison d'être* of social theory. They were asked by men long before the rise of sociology. Sociology itself is an effort, under new and unprecedented historical

[1] Barrington Moore, Jr., *Political Power and Social Theory,* Cambridge: Harvard University Press, 1958; C. Wright Mills, *The Sociological Imagination,* New York: Oxford University Press, 1959.

conditions, to find novel answers to them. They are not questions which lend themselves to successively more precise answers as a result of cumulative empirical research, for they remain eternally problematic. Social theory is necessarily an interminable dialogue. "True understanding," Hannah Arendt has written, "does not tire of interminable dialogue and 'vicious circles' because it trusts that imagination will eventually catch at least a glimpse of the always frightening light of truth."[2]

I wish briefly to review the answers modern sociological theory offers to one such question, or rather to one aspect of one question. The question may be variously phrased as, "What are the sources of social cohesion?"; "How is social order possible?"; or, stated in social-psychological terms, "How is it that man becomes tractable to social discipline?" I shall call this question in its social-psychological aspect the "Hobbesian question" and in its more strictly sociological aspect the "Marxist question." The Hobbesian question asks how men are capable of the guidance by social norms and goals that makes possible an enduring society, while the Marxist question asks how, assuming this capability, complex societies manage to regulate and restrain destructive conflicts between groups. Much of our current theory offers an oversocialized view of man in answering the Hobbesian question and an overintegrated view of society in answering the Marxist question.

A number of writers have recently challenged the overintegrated view of society in contemporary theory. In addition to Moore and Mills, the names of Bendix, Coser, Dahrendorf, and Lockwood come to mind.[3] My intention, therefore, is to concentrate on the answers to the Hobbesian question in an

[2] Hannah Arendt, "Understanding and Politics," *Partisan Review*, 20 (July–August, 1953), p. 392 For a view of social theory close to the one adumbrated in the present paper, see Theodore Abel, "The Present Status of Social Theory," *American Sociological Review*, 17 (April, 1952), pp. 156–164.

[3] Reinhard Bendix and Bennett Berger, "Images of Society and Problems of Concept Formation in Sociology," in Llewellyn Gross, editor, *Symposium on Sociological Theory*. Evanston, Ill.: Row, Petersen & Co., 1959, pp. 92–118; Lewis A. Coser, *The Functions of Social Conflict*, Glencoe, Ill.: The Free Press, 1956; Ralf Dahrendorf, "Out of Utopia: Towards a Re-Orientation of Sociological Analysis," *American Journal of Sociology*, 64 (September, 1958), pp. 115–127; and *Class and Class Conflict in Industrial Society*, Stanford, Calif.: Stanford University Press, 1959; David Lockwood, "Some remarks on "The Social System'," *British Journal of Sociology*, 7 (June, 1956), pp. 134–146.

effort to disclose the oversocialized view of man which they seem to imply.

Since my view of theory is obviously very different from that of Talcott Parsons and has, in fact, been developed in opposition to his, let me pay tribute to his recognition of the importance of the Hobbesian question—the "problem of order," as he calls it—at the very beginning of his first book, *The Structure of Social Action.*[4] Parsons correctly credits Hobbes with being the first thinker to see the necessity of explaining why human society is not a "war of all against all"; why, if man is simply a gifted animal, men refrain from unlimited resort to fraud and violence in pursuit of their ends and maintain a stable society at all. There is even a sense in which, as Coser and Mills have both noted,[5] Parsons' entire work represents an effort to solve the Hobbesian problem of order. His solution, however, has tended to become precisely the kind of elaboration of a set of answers, in abstraction from questions, that is so characteristic of contemporary sociological theory.

We need not be greatly concerned with Hobbes' own solution to the problem of order he saw with such unsurpassed clarity. Whatever interest his famous theory of the origin of the state may still hold for political scientists, it is clearly inadequate as an explanation of the origin of society. Yet the pattern as opposed to the details of Hobbes' thought bears closer examination.

The polar terms in Hobbes' theory are the state of nature, where the war of all against all prevails, and the authority of Leviathan, created by social contract. But the war of all against all is not simply effaced with the creation of political authority: it remains an ever-present potentiality in human society, at times quiescent, at times erupting into open violence. Whether Hobbes believed that the state of nature and the social contract were ever historical realities—and there is evidence that he was not that simple-minded and unsociological, even in the seventeenth century—is unimportant; the whole tenor of his thought is to see the war of all against all and Leviathan dialectically, as coexisting and interacting opposites.[6] As R. G. Collingwood has observed, "According to

[4] Talcott Parsons, *The Structure of Social Action*, New York: McGraw-Hill Book Co., 1937, pp. 89–94.

[5] Coser, *op. cit.*, p. 21; Mills, *op. cit.*, p. 44.

[6] A recent critic of Parsons follows Hobbes in seeing the relations between the normative order in society and what he calls "the sub-

Hobbes . . . *a body politic is a dialectical thing,* a Heraclitean world in which at any given time there is a negative element."[7] The first secular social theorist in the history of Western thought, and one of the first clearly to discern and define the problem of order in human society long before Darwinism made awareness of it a commonplace, Hobbes was a dialectical thinker who refused to separate answers from questions, solutions to society's enduring problems from the conditions creating the problems.

What is the answer of contemporary sociological theory to the Hobbesian question? There are two main answers, each of which has come to be understood in a way that denies the reality and meaningfulness of the question. Together they constitute a model of human nature, sometimes clearly stated, more often implicit in accepted concepts, that pervades modern sociology. The first answer is summed up in the notion of the "internalization of social norms." The second, more commonly employed or assumed in empirical research, is the view that man is essentially motivated by the desire to achieve a positive image of self by winning acceptance or status in the eyes of others.

The following statement represents, briefly and broadly, what is probably the most influential contemporary sociological conception—and dismissal—of the Hobbesian problem: "To a modern sociologist imbued with the conception that action follows institutionalized patterns, opposition of individual and common interests has only a very limited relevance or is thoroughly unsound."[8] From this writer's perspective, the

---

stratum of social action" and other sociologists have called the "factual order" as similar to the relation between the war of all against all and the authority of the state. David Lockwood writes: "The existence of the normative order . . . is in one very important sense inextricably bound up with potential conflicts of interest over scarce resources . . . ; the very existence of a normative order mirrors the continual potentiality of conflict." Lockwood, *op. cit.,* p. 137.

[7] R. G. Collingwood, *The New Leviathan,* Oxford: The Clarendon Press, 1942, p. 183.

[8] Francis X. Sutton and others, *The American Business Creed,* Cambridge: Harvard University Press, 1956, p. 304. I have cited this study and, on several occasions, textbooks and fugitive articles rather than better-known and directly theoretical writings because I am just as concerned with what sociological concepts and theories are taken to mean when they are actually used in research, teaching, and introductory exposition as with their elaboration in more self-conscious and explicitly theoretical discourse. Since the model of human nature I am criticizing is partially implicit and "buried" in our concepts, cruder and less qual-

problem is an unreal one: human conduct is totally shaped by common norms or "institutionalized patterns." Sheer ignorance must have led people who were unfortunate enough not to be modern sociologists to ask, "How is order possible?" A thoughtful bee or ant would never inquire, "How is the social order of the hive or ant-hill possible?" for the opposite of that order is unimaginable when the instinctive endowment of the insects ensures its stability and built-in harmony between "individual and common interests." Human society, we are assured, is not essentially different, although conformity and stability are there maintained by non-instinctive processes. Modern sociologists believe that they have understood these processes and that they have not merely answered but disposed of the Hobbesian question, showing that, far from expressing a valid intimation of the tensions and possibilities of social life, it can only be asked out of ignorance.

It would be hard to find a better illustration of what Collingwood, following Plato, calls *eristical* as opposed to dialectical thinking:[9] the answer destroys the question, or rather destroys the awareness of rival possibilities suggested by the question which accounts for its having been asked in the first place. A reversal of perspective now takes place and we are moved to ask the opposite question: "How is it that violence, conflict, revolution, and the individual's sense of coercion by society manage to exist at all, if this view is correct?"[10] Whenever a one-sided answer to a question compels us to raise the opposite question, we are caught up in a dialectic of concepts which reflects a dialectic in things. But let us examine the particular processes sociologists appeal to in order to account for the elimination from human society of the war of all against all.

---

ified illustrations are as relevant as the formulations of leading theorists. I am also aware that some older theorists, notably Cooley and MacIver, were shrewd and worldly-wise enough to reject the implication that man is ever fully socialized. Yet they failed to develop competing images of man which were concise and systematic enough to counter the appeal of the oversocialized models.

[9]Collingwood, *op. cit.*, pp. 181–182.

[10]*Cf.* Mills, *op. cit.*, pp. 32–33, 42. While Mills does not discuss the use of the concept of internalization by Parsonian theorists, I have argued elsewhere that his view of the relation between power and values is insufficiently dialectical. See Dennis H. Wrong, "The Failure of American Sociology," *Commentary*, 28 (November, 1950), p. 378.

THE CHANGING MEANING OF INTERNALIZATION

A well-known section of *The Structure of Social Action*, devoted to the interpretation of Durkheim's thought, is entitled "The Changing Meaning of Constraint."[11] Parsons argues that Durkheim originally conceived of society as controlling the individual from the outside by imposing constraints on him through sanctions, best illustrated by codes of law. But in Durkheim's later work he began to see that social rules do not "merely regulate 'externally' . . . they enter directly into the constitution of the actor's ends themselves."[12] Constraint, therefore, is more than an environmental obstacle which the actor must take into account in pursuit of his goals in the same way that he takes into account physical laws: it becomes internal, psychological, and self-imposed as well. Parsons developed this view that social norms are constitutive rather than merely regulative of human nature before he was influenced by psychoanalytic theory, but Freud's theory of the superego has become the source and model for the conception of the internalization of social norms that today plays so important a part in sociological thinking. The use some sociologists have made of Freud's idea, however, might well inspire an essay entitled, "The Changing Meaning of Internalization," although, in contrast to the shift in Durkheim's view of constraint, this change has been a change for the worse.

What has happened is that internalization has imperceptibly been equated with "learning," or even with "habit-formation" in the simplest sense. Thus when a norm is said to have been "internalized" by an individual, what is frequently meant is that he habitually both affirms it and conforms to it in his conduct. The whole stress on inner conflict, on the tension between powerful impulses and superego controls the behavioral outcome of which cannot be prejudged, drops out of the picture. And it is this that is central to Freud's view, for in psychoanalytic terms to say that a norm has been internalized, or introjected to become part of the superego, is to say no more than that a person will suffer guilt-feelings if he fails to live up to it, not that he will in fact live up to it in his behavior.

[11]Parsons, *op. cit.*, pp. 378–390.
[12]*Ibid.*, p. 382.

The relation between internalization and conformity assumed by most sociologists is suggested by the following passage from a recent, highly-praised advanced textbook: "Conformity to institutionalized norms is, of course, 'normal.' The actor, having internalized the norms, feels something like a need to conform. His conscience would bother him if he did not."[13] What is overlooked here is that the person who conforms may be even more "bothered," that is, subject to guilt and neurosis, than the person who violates what are not only society's norms but his own as well. To Freud, it is precisely the man with the strictest superego, he who has most thoroughly internalized and conformed to the norms of his society, who is most wracked with guilt and anxiety.[14]

Paul Kecskemeti, to whose discussion I owe initial recognition of the erroneous view of internalization held by sociologists, argues that the relations between social norms, the individual's selection from them, his conduct, and his feelings about his conduct are far from self-evident. "It is by no means true," he writes, "to say that acting counter to one's own norms always or almost always leads to neurosis. One might assume that neurosis develops even more easily in persons who *never* violate the moral code they recognize as valid but repress and frustrate some strong instinctual motive. A person who 'succumbs to temptation,' feels guilt, and then 'purges himself' of his guilt in some reliable way (e.g., by confession) may achieve in this way a better balance, and be less neurotic, than a person who never violates his 'norms' and never feels conscious guilt."[15]

Recent discussions of "deviant behavior" have been compelled to recognize these distinctions between social demands, personal attitudes towards them, and actual conduct, although they have done so in a laboriously taxonomic fashion.[16] They represent, however, largely the rediscovery of what was always central to the Freudian concept of the superego. The main explanatory function of the concept is to show how people repress themselves, imposing checks on their own

[13] Harry M. Johnson, *Sociology: A Systematic Introduction*, New York: Harcourt, Brace and Co., 1960, p. 22.

[14] Sigmund Freud, *Civilization and Its Discontents*, New York: Doubleday Anchor Books, 1958, pp. 80–81.

[15] Paul Kecskemeti, *Meaning, Communication, and Value*, Chicago: University of Chicago Press, 1952, pp. 244–245.

[16] Robert Dubin, "Deviant Behavior and Social Structure: Continuities in Social Theory," *American Sociological Review*, 24 (April, 1959), pp. 147–164; Robert K. Merton, "Social Conformity, Deviation, and

desires and thus turning the inner life into a battlefield of conflicting motives, no matter which side "wins," by successfully dictating overt action. So far as behavior is concerned, the psychoanalytic view of man is less deterministic than the sociological. For psychoanalysis is primarily concerned with the inner life, not with overt behavior, and its most fundamental insight is that the wish, the emotion, and the fantasy are as important as the act in man's experience.

Sociologists have appropriated the superego concept, but have separated it from any equivalent of the Freudian id. So long as most individuals are "socialized," that is, internalize the norms and conform to them in conduct, the Hobbesian problem is not even perceived as a latent reality. Deviant behavior is accounted for by special circumstances: ambiguous norms, anomie, role conflict, or greater cultural stress on valued goals than on the approved means for attaining them. Tendencies to deviant behavior are not seen as dialectically related to conformity. The presence in man of motivational forces bucking against the hold social discipline has over him is denied.

Nor does the assumption that internalization of norms and roles is the essence of socialization allow for sufficient range of motives underlying conformity. It fails to allow for variable "tonicity of the superego," in Kardiner's phrase.[17] The degree to which conformity is frequently the result of coercion rather than conviction is minimized.[18] Either someone has internalized the norms, or he is "unsocialized," a feral or socially isolated child, or a psychopath. Yet Freud recognized that many people, conceivably a majority, fail to acquire superegos. "Such people," he wrote, "habitually permit themselves to do any bad deed that procures them something they want, if only they are sure that no authority will discover it or make them suffer for it; their anxiety relates only to the possibility of detection. Present-day society has to take into account the prevalence of this state of mind."[19] The last sentence suggests that Freud was aware of the decline of "inner-direction," of the Protestant conscience, about which we have heard so much lately. So let us turn to the other elements of

Opportunity Structures: A Comment on the Contributions of Dubin and Cloward," *Ibid.*, pp. 178–189.

[17] Abram Kardiner, *The Individual and His Society*, New York: Columbia University Press, 1930, pp. 65, 72–75

[18] Mills, *op. cit.*, pp. 39–41; Dahrendorf, *Class and Class Conflict in Industrial Society*, pp. 157–165.

[19] Freud, *op. cit.*, pp. 78–79.

human nature that sociologists appeal to in order to explain, or rather explain away, the Hobbesian problem.

MAN THE ACCEPTANCE-SEEKER[20]

The superego concept is too inflexible, too bound to the past and to individual biography, to be of service in relating conduct to the pressures of the immediate situation in which it takes place. Sociologists rely more heavily therefore on an alternative notion, here stated—or, to be fair, overstated—in its baldest form: "People are so profoundly sensitive to the expectations of others that all action is inevitably guided by these expectations."[21]

Parsons' model of the "complementarity of expectations," the view that in social interaction men mutually seek approval from one another by conforming to shared norms, is a formalized version of what has tended to become a distinctive sociological perspective on human motivation. Ralph Linton states it in explicit psychological terms: "The need for eliciting favorable responses from others is an almost constant component of [personality]. Indeed, it is not too much to say

[20]In many ways I should prefer to use the neater, more alliterative phrase "status-seeker." However, it has acquired a narrower meaning than I intend, particularly since Vance Packard appropriated it, suggesting primarily efforts, which are often consciously deceptive, to give the appearance of personal achievements or qualities worthy of deference. "Status-seeking" in this sense is, as Veblen perceived, necessarily confined to relatively impersonal and segmental social relationships. "Acceptance" or "approval" convey more adequately what all men are held to seek in both intimate and impersonal relations according to the conception of the self and of motivation dominating contemporary sociology and social psychology. I have, nevertheless, been unable to resist the occasional temptation to use the term "status" in this broader sense.

[21]Sutton and others, *op. cit.*, p. 264. Robert Cooley Angell, in *Free Society and Moral Crisis*, Ann Arbor: University of Michigan Press, 1958, p. 34, points out the ambiguity of the term "expectations." It is used, he notes, to mean both a factual prediction and a moral imperative, e.g. "England expects every man to do his duty." But this very ambiguity is instructive, for it suggests the process by which behavior that is non-normative and perhaps even "deviant" but nevertheless "expected" in the sense of being predictable, acquires over time a normative aura and becomes "expected" in the second sense of being socially approved or demanded. Thus Parsons' "interaction paradigm" provides leads to the understanding of social change and need not be confined, as in his use of it, to the explanation of conformity and stability. But this is the subject of another paper I hope to complete shortly.

that there is very little organized human behavior which is not directed toward its satisfaction in at least some degree"[22]

The insistence of sociologists on the importance of "social factors" easily leads them to stress the priority of such socialized or socializing motives in human behavior.[23] It is frequently the task of the sociologist to call attention to the intensity with which men desire and strive for the good opinion of their immediate associates in a variety of situations, particularly those where received theories or ideologies have unduly emphasized other motives such as financial gain, commitment to ideals, or the effects on energies and aspirations of arduous physical conditions. Thus sociologists have shown that factory workers are more sensitive to the attitudes of

[22]Ralph Linton, *The Cultural Background of Personality*, New York: Appleton-Century Co., 1945, p. 91.

[23] When values are "inferred" from this emphasis and then popularized, it becomes the basis of the ideology of "groupism" extolling the virtues of "togetherness" and "belongingness" that have been attacked and satirized so savagely in recent social criticism. David Riesman and W. H. Whyte, the pioneers of this current of criticism in its contemporary guise, are both aware, as their imitators and epigoni usually are not, of the extent to which the social phenomenon they have described is the result of the diffusion and popularization of sociology itself. See on this point Robert Gutman and Dennis H. Wrong, "Riesman's Typology of Character" (forthcoming in a symposium on Riesman's work to be edited by Leo Lowenthal and Seymour Martin Lipset), and William H. Whyte, *The Organization Man*, New York: Simon and Schuster, 1956, Chapters 3–5. As a matter of fact, Riesman's "inner-direction" and "other-direction" correspond rather closely to the notions of "internalization" and "acceptance-seeking" in contemporary sociology as I have described them. Riesman even refers to his concepts initially as characterizations of "modes of conformity," although he then makes the mistake, as Robert Gutman and I have argued, of calling them character types. But his view that all men are to some degree both inner-directed and other-directed, a qualification that has been somewhat neglected by critics who have understandably concentrated on his empirical and historical use of his typology, suggests the more generalized conception of forces making for conformity found in current theory. See David Riesman, Nathan Glazer, and Reuel Denny, *The Lonely Crowd*, New York: Doubleday Anchor Books, 1953, pp. 17 ff. However, as Gutman and I have observed: "In some respects Riesman's conception of character is Freudian rather than neo-Freudian: character is defined by superego mechanisms and, like Freud in *Civilization and Its Discontents*, the socialized individual is defined by what is forbidden him rather than by what society stimulates him to do. Thus in spite of Riesman's generally sanguine attitude towards modern America, implicit in his typology is a view of society as the enemy both of individuality and of basic drive gratification, a view that contrasts with the at least potentially benign role assigned it by neo-Freudian thinkers like Fromm and Horney." Gutman and Wrong, "Riesman's Typology of Character," p. 4 (typescript).

their fellow-workers than to purely economic incentives; that voters are more influenced by the preferences of their relatives and friends than by campaign debates on the "issues"; that soldiers, whatever their ideological commitment to their nation's cause, fight more bravely when their platoons are intact and they stand side by side with their "buddies."

It is certainly not my intention to criticize the findings of such studies. My objection is that their particular selective emphasis is generalized—explicitly, or, more often, implicitly—to provide apparent empirical support for an extremely one-sided view of human nature. Although sociologists have criticized past efforts to single out one fundamental motive in human conduct, the desire to achieve a favorable self-image by winning approval from others frequently occupies such a position in their own thinking. The following "theorem" has been, in fact, openly put forward by Hans Zetterberg as "a strong contender for the position as the major Motivational Theorem in sociology":[24]

> An actor's actions have a tendency to become dispositions that are related to the occurrence of favored uniform evaluations of the actor and-or his actions in his action system.[25]

Now Zetterberg is not necessarily maintaining that this theorem is an accurate factual statement of the basic psychological roots of social behavior. He is, characteristically, far too self-conscious about the logic of theorizing and "concept formation" for that. He goes on to remark that "the maximization of favorable attitudes from others would thus be the counterpart in sociological theory to the maximization of profit in economic theory."[26] If by this it is meant that the theorem is to be understood as a heuristic rather than an empirical assumption, that sociology has a selective point of view which is just as abstract and partial as that of economics and the other social sciences, and if his view of theory as a set of logically connected formal propositions is granted provisional acceptance, I am in agreement. (Actually, the view of theory suggested at the beginning of this paper is a quite different one.)

But there is a further point to be made. Ralf Dahrendorf

[24]Hans L. Zetterberg, "Compliant Actions," *Acta Sociologica,* 2 (1957) p. 189.
[25]*Ibid.,* p. 188.
[26]*Ibid.,* p. 189.

has observed that structural-functional theorists do not "claim that order *is based on* a general consensus of values, but that it *can be conceived of in terms of* such consensus and that, if it is conceived of in these terms, certain propositions follow which are subject to the test of specific observations."[27] The same may be said of the assumption that people seek to maximize favorable evaluations by others; indeed this assumption has already fathered such additional concepts as "reference group" and "circle of significant others." Yet the question must be raised as to whether we really wish to, in effect, define sociology by such partial perspectives. The assumption of the maximization of approval from others is the psychological complement to the sociological assumption of a general value consensus. And the former is as selective and one-sided a way of looking at motivation as Dahrendorf and others have argued the latter to be when it determines our way looking at social structure. The oversocialized view of man of the one is a counterpart of the overintegrated view of society of the other.

Modern sociology, after all, originated as a protest against the partial views of man contained in such doctrines as utilitarianism, classical economics, social Darwinism, and vulgar Marxism. All of the great nineteenth and early twentieth century sociologists[28] saw it as one of their major tasks to expose the unreality of such abstractions as economic man, the gain-seeker of the classical economists; political man, the power-seeker of the Machiavellian tradition in political science; self-preserving man, the security-seeker of Hobbes and Darwin; sexual or libidinal man, the pleasure-seeker of doctrinaire Freudianism; and even religious man, the God-

---

[27] Dahrendorf, *Class and Class Conflict in Industrial Society*, p. 158.

[28] Much of the work of Thorstein Veblen, now generally regarded as a sociologist (perhaps the greatest America has yet produced), was, of course, a polemic against the rational, calculating *homo economicus* of classical economics and a documentation of the importance in economic life of the quest for status measured by conformity to arbitrary and shifting conventional standards. Early in his first and most famous book Veblen made an observation on human nature resembling that which looms so large in contemporary sociological thinking: "The usual basis of self-respect," he wrote, "is the respect accorded by one's neighbors. Only individuals with an aberrant temperament can in the long run retain their self-esteem in the face of the disesteem of their fellows." *The Theory of the Leisure Class*, New York: Mentor Books, 1953, p. 38. Whatever the inadequacies of his psychological assumptions, Veblen did not, however, overlook other motivations to which he frequently gave equal or greater weight.

seeker of the theologians. It would be ironical if it should turn out that they have merely contributed to the creation of yet another reified abstraction in socialized man, the status-seeker of our contemporary sociologists.

Of course, such an image of man is, like all the others mentioned, valuable for limited purposes so long as it is not taken for the whole truth. What are some of its deficiencies? To begin with, it neglects the other half of the model of human nature presupposed by current theory: moral man, guided by his built-in superego and beckoning ego-ideal.[29] In recent years sociologists have been less interested than they once were in culture and national character as backgrounds to conduct, partly because stress on the concept of "role" as the crucial link between the individual and the social structure has directed their attention to the immediate situation in which social interaction takes place. Man is increasingly seen as a "role-playing" creature, responding eagerly or anxiously to the expectations of other role-players in the multiple group settings in which he finds himself. Such an approach, while valuable in helping us grasp the complexity of a highly differentiated social structure such as our own, is far too often generalized to serve as a kind of *ad hoc* social psychology, easily adaptable to particular sociological purposes.

But it is not enough to concede that men often pursue "internalized values" remaining indifferent to what others think of them, particularly when, as I have previously argued, the idea of internalization has been "hollowed out" to make it more useful as an explanation of conformity. What of desire for material and sensual satisfactions? Can we really dispense with the venerable notion of material "interests" and invariably replace it with the blander, more integrative "social values"? And what of striving for power, not necessarily for its own sake—that may be rare and pathological—but as a means by which men are able to *impose* a normative definition of reality on others? That material interests, sexual drives, and the quest for power have often been over-estimated as

[29]Robin M. Williams. Jr. writes: "At the present time, the literature of sociology and social psychology contains many references to 'Conformity'—conforming to norms, 'yielding to social pressure,' or 'adjusting to the requirements of the reference group.' . . . ; the implication is easily drawn that the actors in question are *motivated* solely in terms of conformity or non-conformity, rather than in terms of 'expressing' or 'affirming' internalized values . . ." (his italics). "Continuity and Change in Sociological Study," *American Sociological Review,* 23 (December, 1958), p. 630.

human motives is no reason to deny their reality. To do so is to suppress one term of the dialectic between conformity and rebellion, social norms and their violation, man and social order, as completely as the other term is suppressed by those who deny the reality of man's "normative orientation" or reduce it to the effect of coercion, rational calculation, or mechanical conditioning.

The view that man is invariably pushed by internalized norms or pulled by the lure of self-validation by others ignores—to speak archaically for a moment—both the highest and the lowest, both beast and angel, in his nature. Durkheim, from whom so much of the modern sociological point of view derives, recognized that the very existence of a social norm implies and even creates the possibility of its violation. This is the meaning of his famous dictum that crime is a "normal phenomenon." He maintained that "for the originality of the idealist whose dreams transcend his century to find expression, it is necessary that the originality of the criminal, who is below the level of his time, shall also be possible. One does not occur without the other."[30] Yet Durkheim lacked an adequate psychology and formulated his insight in terms of the actor's cognitive awareness rather than in motivational terms. We do not have Durkheim's excuse for falling back on what Homans has called a "social mold theory" of human nature.[31]

SOCIAL BUT NOT ENTIRELY SOCIALIZED

I have referred to forces in man that are resistant to socialization. It is not my purpose to explore the nature of these forces or to suggest how we ought best conceive of them as sociologists—that would be a most ambitious undertaking. A few remarks will have to suffice. I think we must start with the recognition that *in the beginning there is the body*. As soon as the body is mentioned the specter of "biological determinism" raises its head and sociologists draw back in fright. And certainly their view of man is sufficiently disembodied and non-materialistic to satisfy Bishop Berkeley, as well as being de-sexualized enough to please Mrs. Grundy.

[30]Emile Durkheim, *The Rules of Sociological Method*, Chicago: University of Chicago Press, 1938, p. 71.

[31]George C. Homans, *The Human Group*, New York: Harcourt, Brace and Company, 1950, pp. 317–319.

Am I, then, urging us to return to the older view of a human nature divided between a "social man" and a "natural man" who is either benevolent, Rousseau's Noble Savage, or sinister and destructive, as Hobbes regarded him? Freud is usually represented, or misrepresented, as the chief modern proponent of this dualistic conception which assigns to the social order the purely negative role of blocking and redirecting man's "imperious biological drives."[32] I say "misrepresented" because, although Freud often said things supporting such an interpretation, other and more fundamental strains in his thinking suggest a different conclusion. John Dollard, certainly not a writer who is oblivious to social and cultural "factors," saw this twenty-five years ago: "It is quite clear," he wrote, ". . . that he (Freud) does not regard the instincts as having a fixed social goal; rather, indeed, in the case of the sexual instinct he has stressed the vague but powerful and impulsive nature of the drive and has emphasized that its proper social object is not picked out in advance. His seems to be a drive concept which is not at variance with our knowledge from comparative cultural studies, since his theory does not demand that the 'instinct' work itself out with mechanical certainty alike in every varying culture."[33]

So much for Freud's "imperious biological drives"! When Freud defined psychoanalysis as the study of the "vicissitudes of the instincts," he was confirming, not denying, the "plasticity" of human nature insisted on by social scientists. The drives or "instincts" of psychoanalysis, far from being fixed dispositions to behave in a particular way, are utterly subject to social channelling and transformation and could not even reveal themselves in behavior without social modling any more than our vocal chords can produce articulate speech if we have not learned a language. To psychoanalysis man is

[32]Robert K. Merton, *Social Theory and Social Structure,* Revised and Enlarged Edition, Glencoe, Ill.: The Free Press, 1957, p. 131. Merton's view is representative of that of most contemporary sociologists. See also Hans Gerth and C. Wright Mills, *Character and Social Structure,* New York: Harcourt, Brace and Company, 1953, pp. 112–113. For a similar view by a "neo-Freudian," see Erich Fromm, *The Sane Society,* New York: Rinehart and Company, 1955, pp. 74–77.

[33]John Dollard, *Criteria for the Life History,* New Haven: Yale University Press, 1935, P. 120. This valuable book has been neglected, presumably because it appears to be a purely methodological effort to set up standards for judging the adequacy of biographical and autobiographical data. Actually, the standards serve as well to evaluate the adequacy of general theories of personality or human nature and even to prescribe in part what a sound theory ought to include.

indeed a social animal; his social nature is profoundly reflected in his bodily structure.[34]

But there is a difference between the Freudian view on the one hand and both sociological and neo-Freudian conceptions of man on the other. To Freud man is a *social* animal without being entirely a *socialized* animal. His very social nature is the source of conflicts and antagonisms that create resistance to socialization by the norms of any of the societies which have existed in the course of human history. "Socialization" may mean two quite distinct things; when they are confused an oversocialized view of man is the result. On the one hand socialization means the "transmission of the culture," the particular culture of the society an individual enters at birth; on the other hand the term is used to mean the "process of becoming human," of acquiring uniquely human attributes from interaction with others.[35] All men are socialized in the latter sense, but this does not mean that they have been completely molded by the particular norms and values of their culture. All cultures, as Freud contended, do violence to man's socialized bodily drives, but this in no sense means that men could possibly exist without culture or independently of society.[36] From such a standpoint, man may properly be called as Norman Brown has called him, the

[34]One of the few attempts by a social scientist to relate systematically man's anatomical structure and biological history to his social nature and his unique cultural creativity is Weston La Barre's *The Human Animal*, Chicago: University of Chicago Press, 1954. See especially Chapters 4–6, but the entire book is relevant. It is one of the few exceptions to Paul Goodman's observation that anthropologists nowadays "commence with a chapter on Physical Anthropology and then forget the whole topic and go on to Culture." See his "Growing up Absurd," *Dissent*, 7 (Spring, 1960), p. 121.

[35]Paul Goodman has developed a similar distinction. *Op. cit.,* pp. 123–125.

[36]Whether it might be possible to create a society that does not repress the bodily drives is a separate question. See Herbert Marcuse, *Eros and Civilization*, Boston: The Beacon Press, 1955; and Norman O. Brown, *Life Against Death*, New York: Random House, Modern Library Paperbacks, 1960. Neither Marcuse nor Brown are guilty in their brilliant, provocative, and visionary books of assuming a "natural man" who awaits liberation from social bonds. They differ from such sociological Utopians as Fromm, *op cit.*, in their lack of sympathy for the de-sexualized man of the neo-Freudians. For the more traditional Freudian view, see Walter A. Weisskopf, "The 'Socialization' of Psychoanalysis in Contemporary America," in Benjamin Nelson, editor, *Psychoanalysis and the Future*, New York: National Psychological Association for Psychoanalysis 1957, pp. 51–56; Hans Meyerhoff, "Freud and the Ambiguity of Culture," *Partisan Review*, 24 (Winter, 1957), pp. 117–130.

"neurotic" or the "discontented" animal and repression may be seen as the main characteristic of human nature as we have known it in history.[37]

But isn't this psychology and haven't sociologists been taught to foreswear psychology, to look with suspicion on what are called "psychological variables" in contradistinction to the institutional and historical forces with which they are properly concerned? There is, indeed, as recent critics have complained, too much "psychologism" in contemporary sociology, largely, I think, because of the bias inherent in our favored research techniques. But I do not see how, at the level of theory, sociologists can fail to make assumptions about human nature.[38] If our assumptions are left implicit, we will inevitably presuppose of a view of man that is tailor-made to our special needs; when our sociological theory over-stresses the stability and integration of society we will end up imagining that man is the disembodied, conscience-driven, status-seeking phantom of current theory. We must do better if we really wish to win credit outside of our ranks for special understanding of man, that plausible creature[39] whose wagging tongue so often hides the despair and darkness in his heart.

[37]Brown, *op. cit.*, pp. 3–19.

[38]"I would assert that very little sociological analysis is ever done without using at least an implicit psychological theory." Alex Inkeles, "Personality and Social Structure," in Robert K. Merton and others, editors, *Sociology Today,* New York: Basic Books, 1959, p. 250.

[39]Harry Stack Sullivan once remarked that the most outstanding characteristic of human beings was their "plausibility."

The Definition of the Situation

by
William Isaac Thomas

One of the most important powers gained during the evolution of animal life is the ability to make decisions from within instead of having them imposed from without. Very low forms of life do not make decisions, as we understand this term, but are pushed and pulled by chemical substances, heat, light, etc., much as iron filings are attracted or repelled by a magnet. They do tend to behave properly in given conditions—a group of small crustaceans will flee as in a panic if a bit of strychnia is placed in the basin containing them and will rush toward a drop of beef juice like hogs crowding around swill—but they do this as an expression of organic affinity for the one substance and repugnance for the other, and not as an expression of choice or "free will." There are, so to speak, rules of behavior but these represent a sort of fortunate mechanistic adjustment of the organism to typically recurring situations, and the organism cannot change the rule.

On the other hand, the higher animals, and above all man, have the power of refusing to obey a stimulation which they followed at an earlier time. Response to the earlier stimulation may have had painful consequences and so the rule of habit in this situation is changed. We call this ability the power of inhibition, and it is dependent on the fact that the nervous system carries memories or records of past experiences. At this point the determination of action no longer comes exclusively from outside sources but is located within the organism itself.

Preliminary to any self-determined act of behavior there is always a stage of examination and deliberation which we may call *the definition of the situation*. And actually not only concrete acts are dependent on the definition of the situation,

Reprinted from *The Unadjusted Girl* by William Isaac Thomas, by permission of Little, Brown and Co., copyright 1923 by Little, Brown and Co., © renewed 1951 by Little, Brown and Co.

but gradually a whole life-policy and the personality of the individual himself follow from a series of such definitions.

But the child is always born into a group of people among whom all the general types of situation which may arise have already been defined and corresponding rules of conduct developed, and where he has not the slightest chance of making his definitions and following his wishes without interference. Men have always lived together in groups. Whether mankind has a true herd instinct or whether groups are held together because this has worked out to advantage is of no importance. Certainly the wishes in general . . . can be satisfied only in a society. But we have only to refer to the criminal code to appreciate the variety of ways in which the wishes of the individual may conflict with the wishes of society. And the criminal code takes no account of the many unsanctioned expressions of the wishes which society attempts to regulate by persuasion and gossip.

There is therefore always a rivalry between the spontaneous definitions of the situation made by the member of an organized society and the definitions which his society has provided for him. The individual tends to a hedonistic selection of activity, pleasure first; and society to a utilitarian selection, safety first. Society wishes its member to be laborious, dependable, regular, sober, orderly, self sacrificing; while the individual wishes less of this and more of new experience. And organized society seeks also to regulate the conflict and competition inevitable between its members in the pursuit of their wishes. The desire to have wealth, for example, or any other socially sanctioned wish, may not be accomplished at the expense of another member of the society—by murder, theft, lying, swindling, blackmail, etc.

It is in this connection that a moral code arises, which is a set of rules or behavior norms, regulating the expression of the wishes, and which is built up by successive definitions of the situation. In practice the abuse arises first and the rule is made to prevent its recurrence. Morality is thus the generally accepted definition of the situation, whether expressed in public opinion and the unwritten law, in a formal legal code, or in religious commandments and prohibitions.

The family is the smallest social unit and the primary defining agency. As soon as the child has free motion and begins to pull, tear, pry, meddle, and prowl, the parents begin to define the situation through speech and other signs and pressures: "Be quiet," "Sit up straight," "Blow your nose,"

"Wash your face," "Mind your mother," "Be kind to sister,"
etc. This is the real significance of Wordsworth's phrase,
"Shades of the prison house begin to close upon the growing
child." His wishes and activities begin to be inhibited, and
gradually, by definitions within the family, by playmates, in
the school, in the Sunday school, in the community, through
reading, by formal instruction, by informal signs of approval
and disapproval, the growing member learns the code of his
society.

In addition to the family we have the community as a defining agency. At present the community is so weak and
vague that it gives us no idea of the former power of the local group in regulating behavior. Originally the community
was practically the whole world of its members. It was composed of families related by blood and marriage and was not
so large that all the members could not come together; it was
a face-to-face group. I asked a Polish peasant what was the
extent of an "*okolica*" or neighborhood—how far it reached.
"It reaches," he said, "as far as the report of a man
reaches—as far as a man is talked about." And it was in
communities of this kind that the moral code which we now
recognize as valid originated. The customs of the community
are "folkways," and both state and church have in their more
formal codes mainly recognized and incorporated these folkways.

The typical community is vanishing and it would be neither possible nor desirable to restore it in its old form. It does
not correspond with the present direction of social evolution
and it would now be a distressing condition in which to live.
But in the immediacy of relationships and the participation of
everybody in everything, it represents an element which we
have lost and which we shall probably have to restore in
some form of cooperation in order to secure a balanced and
normal society—some arrangement corresponding with human nature.

The Self-Fulfilling Prophecy

by
Robert K. Merton

In a series of works seldom consulted outside the academic fraternity, W. I. Thomas, the dean of American sociologists, set forth a theorem basic to the social sciences: "If men define situations as real, they are real in their consequences." Were the Thomas theorem and its implications more widely known more men would understand more of the workings of our society. Though it lacks the sweep and precision of a Newtonian theorem, it possesses the same gift to relevance, being instructively applicable to many, if indeed not most, social processes.

THE THOMAS THEOREM

"If men define situations as real, they are real in their consequences," wrote Professor Thomas. The suspicion that he was driving at a crucial point becomes all the more insistent when we note that essentially the same theorem had been repeatedly set forth by disciplined and observant minds long before Thomas.

When we find such otherwise discrepant minds as the redoubtable Biship Bossuet in his passionate seventeenth-century defense of Catholic orthodoxy, the ironic Mandeville in his eighteenth-century allegory honeycombed with observations on the paradoxes of human society, the irascible genius Marx in his revision of Hegel's theory of historical change, the seminal Freud in works which have perhaps gone further than any others of his day toward modifying man's outlook on man, and the erudite, dogmatic, and occasionally sound

Reprinted with permission of Macmillan Publishing Co., Inc., from *Social Theory and Social Structure* by Robert K. Merton, Copyright © 1967, 1968, Robert K. Merton.

Yale professor, William Graham Sumner, who lives on as the Karl Marx of the middle classes—when we find this mixed company (and I select from a longer if less distinguished list) agreeing on the truth and the pertinence of what is substantially the Thomas theorem, we may conclude that perhaps it is worth our attention as well.

To what, then, are Thomas and Bossuet, Mandeville, Marx, Freud and Sumner directing our attention?

The first part of the theorem provides an unceasing reminder that men respond not only to the objective features of a situation, but also, and at times primarily, to the meaning this situation has for them. And once they have assigned some meaning to the situation, their consequent behavior and some of the consequences of that behavior are determined by the ascribed meaning. But this is still rather abstract, and abstractions have a way of becoming unintelligible if they are not occasionally tied to concrete data. What is a case in point?

A SOCIOLOGICAL PARABLE

It is the year 1932. The Last National Bank is a flourishing institution. A large part of its resources is liquid without being watered. Cartwright Millingville has ample reason to be proud of the banking institution over which he presides. Until Black Wednesday. As he enters his bank, he notices that business is unusually brisk. A little odd, that, since the men at the A.M.O.K. steel plant and the K.O.M.A. mattress factory are not usually paid until Saturday. Yet here are two dozen men, obviously from the factories, queued up in front of the tellers' cages. As he turns into his private office, the president muses rather compassionately: "Hope they haven't been laid off in midweek. They should be in the shop at this hour."

But speculations of this sort have never made for a thriving bank, and Millingville turns to the pile of documents upon his desk. His precise signature is affixed to fewer than a score of papers when he is disturbed by the absence of something familiar and the intrusion of something alien. The low discreet hum of bank business has given way to a strange and annoying stridency of many voices. A situation has been defined as real. And that is the beginning of what ends as Black

Wednesday—the last Wednesday, it might be noted, of the Last National Bank.

Cartwright Millingville had never heard of the Thomas theorem. But he had no difficulty in recognizing its workings. He knew that, despite the comparative liquidity of the bank's assets, a rumor of insolvency, once believed by enough depositors, would result in the insolvency of the bank. And by the close of Black Wednesday—and Blacker Thursday—when the long lines of anxious depositors, each frantically seeking to salvage his own, grew to longer lines of even more anxious depositors, it turned out that he was right.

The stable financial structure of the bank had depended upon one set of definitions on the situation: belief in the validity of the interlocking system of economic promises men live by. Once depositors had defined the situation otherwise, once they questioned the possibility of having these promises fulfilled, the consequences of this unreal definition were real enough.

A familiar type-case this, and one doesn't need the Thomas theorem to understand how it happened—not, at least, if one is old enough to have voted for Franklin Roosevelt in 1932. But with the aid of the theorem the tragic history of Millingville's bank can perhaps be converted into a sociological parable which may help us understand not only what happened to hundreds of banks in the '30's but also what happens to the relations between Negro and white, between Protestant and Catholic and Jew in these days.

The parable tells us that public definitions of a situation (prophecies or predictions) become an integral part of the situation and thus affect subsequent developments. This is peculiar to human affairs. It is not found in the world of nature, untouched by human hands. Predictions of the return of Halley's comet do not influence its orbit. But the rumored insolvency of Millingville's bank did affect the actual outcome. The prophecy of collapse led to its own fulfillment.

So common is the pattern of the self-fulfilling prophecy that each of us has his favored specimen. Consider the case of the examination neurosis. Convinced that he is destined to fail, the anxious student devotes more time to worry than to study and then turns in a poor examination. The initially fallacious anxiety is transformed into an entirely justified fear. Or it is believed that war between two nations is inevitable. Actuated by this conviction, representatives of the two nations become progressively alienated, apprehensively countering each "offensive" move of the other with a "defensive" move of their own. Stockpiles of armaments, raw materials, and armed men grow larger and eventually the anticipation of war helps create the actuality.

The self-fulfilling prophecy is, in the beginning, a *false* definition of the situation evoking a new behavior which makes the originally false conception come *true*. The specious validity of the self-fulfilling prophecy perpetuates a reign of error. For the prophet will cite the actual course of events as proof that he was right from the very beginning. (Yet we know that Millingville's bank was solvent, that it would have survived for many years had not the misleading rumor *created* the very conditions of its own fulfillment. Such are the perversities of social logic.)

It is the self-fulfilling prophecy which goes far toward explaining the dynamics of ethnic and racial conflict in the America of today. That this is the case, at least for relations between Negroes and whites, may be gathered from the fifteen hundred pages which make up Gunnar Myrdal's *An American Dilemma*. That the self-fulfilling prophecy may have even more general bearing upon the relations between ethnic groups than Myrdal has indicated is the thesis of the considerably briefer discussion that follows.[1]

SOCIAL BELIEFS AND SOCIAL REALITY

As a result of their failure to comprehend the operation of the self-fulfilling prophecy, many Americans of good will (sometimes reluctantly) retain enduring ethnic and racial prejudices. They experience these beliefs, not as prejudices, not as prejudgments, but as irresistible products of their own observation. "The facts of the case" permit them no other conclusion.

Thus our fair-minded white citizen strongly supports a pol-

---

[1]Counterpart of the self-fulfilling prophecy is the "suicidal prophecy" which so alters human behavior from what would have been its course had the prophecy not been made, that it *fails* to be borne out. The prophecy destroys itself. This important type is not considered here. For examples of both types of social prophecy, see R. M. MacIver, *The More Perfect Union* (New York: Macmillan, 1948); for a general statement, see Merton, "The unanticipated consequences of purposive social action," *op. cit.*

icy of excluding Negroes from his labor union. His views are, of course, based not upon prejudice, but upon the cold hard facts. And the facts seem clear enough. Negroes, "lately from the nonindustrial South, are undisciplined in traditions of trade unionism and the art of collective bargaining." The Negro is a strikebreaker. The Negro, with his "low standard of living," rushes in to take jobs at less than prevailing wages. The Negro is, in short, "a traitor to the working class," and should manifestly be excluded from union organizations. So run the facts of the case as seen by our tolerant but hardheaded union member, innocent of any understanding of the self-fulfilling prophecy as a basic process of society.

Our unionist fails to see, of course, that he and his kind have produced the very "facts" which he observes. For by defining the situation as one in which Negroes are held to be incorrigibly at odds with principles of unionism and by excluding Negroes from unions, he invited a series of consequences which indeed made it difficult if not impossible for many Negroes to avoid the role of scab. Out of work after World War I, and kept out of unions, thousands of Negroes could not resist strikebound employers who held a door invitingly open upon a world of jobs from which they were otherwise excluded.

History creates its own test of the theory of self-fulfilling prophecies. That Negroes were strikebreakers because they were excluded from unions (and from a wide range of jobs) rather than excluded because they were strikebreakers can be seen from the virtual disappearance of Negroes as scabs in industries where they have gained admission to unions in the last decades.

The application of the Thomas theorem also suggests how the tragic, often vicious, circle of self-fulfilling prophecies can be broken. The initial definition of the situation which has set the circle in motion must be abandoned. Only when the original assumption is questioned and a new definition of the situation introduced, does the consequent flow of events give the lie to the assumption. Only then does the belief no longer father the reality.

But to question these deep-rooted definitions of the situation is no simple act of the will. The will, or for that matter, good will, cannot be turned on and off like a faucet. Social intelligence and good will are themselves *products* of distinct social forces. They are not brought into being by mass propaganda and mass education, in the usual sense of these terms so dear to the sociological panaceans. In the social realm, no more than in the psychological realm, do false ideas quietly vanish when confronted with the truth. One does not expect a paranoiac to abandon his hard-won distortions and delusions upon being informed that they are altogether groundless. If psychic ills could be cured merely by the dissemination of truth, the psychiatrists of this country would be suffering from technological unemployment rather than from over-work. Nor will a continuing "educational campaign" itself destroy racial prejudice and discrimination.

This is not a particularly popular position. The appeal to education as a cure-all for the most varied social problems is rooted deep in the mores of America. Yet it is nonetheless illusory for all that. For how would this program of racial education proceed? Who is to do the educating? The teachers in our communities? But, in some measure like many other Americans, the teachers share the same prejudices they are being urged to combat. And when they don't, aren't they being asked to serve as conscientious martyrs in the cause of educational utopianism? How long the tenure of an elementary school teacher in Alabama or Mississippi or Georgia who attempted meticulously to disabuse his young pupils of the racial beliefs they acquired at home? Education may serve as an operational adjunct but not as the chief basis for any but excruciatingly slow change in the prevailing patterns of race relations.

To understand further why educational campaigns cannot be counted on to eliminate prevailing ethnic hostilities, we must examine the operation of in-groups and out-groups in our society. Ethnic out-groups, to adopt Sumner's useful bit of sociological jargon, consist of all those who are believed to differ significantly from "ourselves" in terms of nationality, race, or religion. Counterpart of the ethnic out-group is of course the ethnic in-group, constituted by those who "belong." There is nothing fixed or eternal about the lines separating the in-group from out-groups. As situations change, the lines of separation change. For a large number of white Americans, Joe Louis is a member of an out-group—when the situation is defined in racial terms. On another occasion, when Louis defeated the nazified Schmeling, many of these same white Americans acclaimed him as a member of the (national) in-group. National loyalty took precedence over racial separatism. These abrupt shifts in group boundaries sometimes prove embarrassing. Thus, when Negro-Americans ran away with the honors in the Olympic games held in Berlin, the Nazis, pointing to the second-class citizenship assigned Negroes in various regions of this country, denied that the United States had really won the games, since the Negro athletes were by our own admission "not full-fledged" Americans. And what could Bilbo or Rankin say to that?

Under the benevolent guidance of the dominant in-group, ethnic out-groups are continuously subjected to a lively process of prejudice which, I think, goes far toward vitiating mass education and mass propaganda for ethnic tolerance. This is the process whereby "in-group virtues become out-group vices," to paraphrase a remark by the sociologist Donald Young. Or, more colloquially and perhaps more instructively, it may be called the "damned-if-you-do and damned-if-you-don't" process in ethnic and racial relations.

IN-GROUP VIRTUES AND OUT-GROUP VICES

To discover that ethnic out-groups are damned if they do embrace the values of white Protestant society and damned if they don't, we have first to turn to one of the in-group culture heroes, examine the qualities with which he is endowed by biographers and popular belief, and thus distill the qualities of mind and action and character which are generally regarded as altogether admirable.

Periodic public opinion polls are not needed to justify the selection of Abe Lincoln as the culture hero who most fully embodies the cardinal American virtues. As the Lynds point out in *Middletown*, the people of that typical small city allow George Washington alone to join Lincoln as the greatest of Americans. He is claimed as their very own by almost as many well-to-do Republicans as by less well-to-do Democrats.[2]

[2]On Lincoln as culture hero, see the perceptive essay, "Getting Right with Lincoln," by David Donald, *Lincoln Reconsidered* (New York: Alfred A. Knopf, 1956), 3–18.

Though Lincoln nominally remains of course, the symbolic leader of the Republicans, this may be just another paradox of political history of the same kind which Lincoln noted in his day with regard to Jefferson and the Democrats.

"Remembering, too, that the Jefferson party was formed upon its supposed superior devotion to the personal rights of men, holding the rights of property to be secondary only, and greatly inferior, and as-

Even the inevitable schoolboy knows that Lincoln was thrifty, hard-working, eager for knowledge, ambitious, devoted to the rights of the average man, and eminently successful in climbing the ladder of opportunity from the lowermost rung of laborer to the respectable heights of merchant and lawyer. (We need follow his dizzying ascent no further.)

If one did not know that these attributes and achievements are numbered high among the values of middle-class America, one would soon discover it by glancing through the Lynds' account of "The Middletown Spirit." For there we find the image of the Great Emancipator fully reflected in the values in which Middletown believes. And since these are their values, it is not surprising to find the Middletowns of America condemning and disparaging those individuals and groups who fail, presumably, to exhibit these virtues. If it appears to the white in-group that Negroes are *not* educated in the same measure as themselves, that they have an "unduly" high proportion of unskilled workers and an "unduly" low proportion of successful business and professional men, that they are thriftless, and so on through the catalogue of middle-class virtue and sin, it is not difficult to understand the charge that the Negro is "inferior" to the white.

Sensitized to the workings of the self-fulfilling prophecy, we should be prepared to find that the anti-Negro charges which are not patently false are only speciously true. The allegations are true in the Pickwickian sense that we have found self-fulfilling prophecies in general to be true. Thus, if the dominant in-group believes that Negroes are inferior, and sees to it that funds for education are not "wasted on these

suming that the so-called Democrats of to-day are the Jefferson, and their opponents the anti-Jefferson, party, it will be equally interesting to note how completely the two have changed hands as to the principle upon which they were originally supposed to be divided. The Democrats of to-day hold the liberty of one man to be absolutely nothing, when in conflict with another man's right of property; Republicans, on the contrary, are for both the man and the dollar, but in case of conflict the man before the dollar.

"I remember being once much amused at seeing two partially intoxicated men engaged in a fight with their great-coats on, which fight, after a long and rather harmless contest, ended in each having fought himself out of his own coat and into that of the other. If the two leading parties of this day are really identical with the two in the days of Jefferson and Adams, they have performed the same feat as the two drunken men."

Abraham Lincoln, in a letter to H. L. Pierce and others, April 6, 1859, in *Complete Works of Abraham Lincoln*, edited by John G. Nicolay and John Hay, (New York, 1894), V, 125–126.

incompetents" and then proclaims as final evidence of this inferiority that Negroes have proportionately "only" one-fifth as many college graduates as white, one can scarcely be amazed by this transparent bit of social legerdemain. Having seen the rabbit carefully though not too adroitly placed in the hat, we can only look askance at the triumphant air with which it is finally produced. (In fact, it is a little embarassing to note that a larger proportion of Negro than of white high school graduates have gone on to college; apparently, the Negroes who are hardy enough to scale the high walls of discrimination represent an even more highly selected group than the run-of-the-high-school white population.)

So, too, when the gentleman from Mississippi (a state which spends five times as much on the average white pupil as on the average Negro pupil) proclaims the essential inferiority of the Negro by pointing to the per capita ratio of physicians among Negroes as less than one-fourth that of whites, we are impressed more by his scrambled logic than by his profound prejudices. So plain is the mechanism of the self-fulfilling prophecy in these instances that only those forever devoted to the victory of sentiment over fact can take these specious evidences seriously. Yet the spurious evidence often creates a genuine belief. Self-hypnosis through one's own propaganda is a not infrequent phase of the self-fulfilling prophecy.

So much for out-groups being damned if they don't (apparently) manifest in-group virtues. It is a tasteless bit of ethnocentrism, seasoned with self-interest. But what of the second phase of this process? Can one seriously mean that out-groups are also damned if they *do* possess these virtues? One can.

Through a faultlessly bisymmetrical prejudice, ethnic and racial out-groups get it coming and going. The systematic condemnation of the out-grouper continues largely *irrespective of what he does*. More: through a freakish exercise of capricious judicial logic, the victim is punished for the crime. Superficial appearances notwithstanding, prejudice and discrimination aimed at the out-group are not a result of what the out-group does, but are rooted deep in the structure of our society and the social psychology of its members.

To understand how this happens, we must examine the moral alchemy through which the in-group readily transmutes virtue into vice and vice into virtue, as the occasion may demand. Our studies will proceed by the case-method.

We begin with the engagingly simple formula of moral alchemy: the same behavior must be differently evaluated according to the person who exhibits it. For example, the proficient alchemist will at once know that the word "firm" is properly declined as follows:

> I am firm,
> Thou art obstinate,
> He is pigheaded.

There are some, unversed in the skills of this science, who will tell you that one and the same term should be applied to all three instances of identical behavior. Such unalchemical nonsense should simply be ignored.

With this experiment in mind, we are prepared to observe how the very same behavior undergoes a complete change of evaluation in its transition from the in-group Abe Lincoln to the out-group Abe Cohen or Abe Kurokawa. We proceed systematically. Did Lincoln work far into the night? This testifies that he was industrious, resolute, perseverant, and eager to realize his capacities to the full. Do the out-group Jews or Japanese keep these same hours? This only bears witness to their sweatshop mentality, their ruthless undercutting of American standards, their unfair competitive practices. Is the in-group hero frugal, thrifty, and sparing? Then the out-group villain is stingy, miserly and pennypinching. All honor is due the in-group Abe for his having been smart, shrewd, and intelligent and, by the same token, all contempt is owing the out-group Abes for their being sharp, cunning, crafty, and too clever by far. Did the indomitable Lincoln refuse to remain content with a life of work with the hands? Did he prefer to make use of his brain? Then, all praise for his plucky climb up the shaky ladder of opportunity. But, of course, the eschewing of manual work for brain work among the merchants and lawyers of the out-group deserves nothing but censure for a parasitic way of life. Was Abe Lincoln eager to learn the accumulated wisdom of the ages by unending study? The trouble with the Jew is that he's a greasy grind, with his head always in a book, while decent people are going to a show or a ball game. Was the resolute Lincoln unwilling to limit his standards to those of his provincial community? That is what we should expect of a man of vision. And if the out-groupers criticize the vulnerable areas in our society, then send 'em back where they came from. Did Lincoln, rising high above his origins, never forget the rights of the common man and applaud the right of workers to strike? This testifies only that, like all real Americans, this greatest of Americans was deathlessly devoted to the cause of freedom. But, as you examine the statistics on strikes, remember that these un-American practices are the result of out-groupers pursuing their evil agitation among otherwise contented workers.

Once stated, the classical formula of moral alchemy is clear enough. Through the adroit use of these rich vocabularies of encomium and opprobrium, the in-group readily transmutes its own virtues into others' vices. But why do so many in-groupers qualify as moral alchemists? Why are so many in the dominant in-group so fully devoted to this continuing experiment in moral transmutation?

An explanation may be found by putting ourselves at some distance from this country and following the anthropologist Malinowski to the Trobriand Islands. For there we find an instructively similar pattern. Among the Trobrianders, to a degree which Americans, despite Hollywood and the confession magazines, have apparently not yet approximated, success with women confers honor and prestige on a man. Sexual prowess is a positive value, a moral virtue. But if a rank-and-file Trobriander has "too much" sexual success, if he achieves "too many" triumphs of the heart, an achievement which should of course be limited to the elite, the chiefs or men of power, then this glorious record becomes a scandal and an abomination. The chiefs are quick *to resent any personal achievement not warranted by social position.* The moral virtues remain virtues only so long as they are jealously confined to the proper in-group. The right activity by the wrong people becomes a thing of contempt, not of honor. For clearly, only in this way, by holding these virtues exclusively to themselves, can the men of power retain their distinction, their prestige, and their power. No wiser procedure could be devised to hold intact a system of social stratification and social power.

The Trobrianders could teach us more. For it seems clear that the chiefs have not calculatingly devised this program of entrenchment. Their behavior is spontaneous, unthinking, and immediate. Their resentment of "too much" ambition or "too much" success in the ordinary Trobriander is not contrived, it is genuine. It just happens that this prompt emotional response to the "misplaced" manifestation of in-group virtues also serves the useful expedient of reinforcing the chiefs' special claims to the good things of Trobriand life. Nothing could be more remote from the truth and more distorted a reading of the facts than to assume that this conversion of in-group virtues into out-group vices is part of a calculated deliberate plot of Trobriand chiefs to keep Trobriand commoners in their place. It is merely that the chiefs have been indoctrinated with an appreciation of the proper order of things, and see it as their heavy burden to enforce the mediocrity of others.

Nor, in quick revulsion from the culpabilities of the moral alchemists, need we succumb to the equivalent error of simply upending the moral status of the in-group and the outgroups. It is not that Jews and Negroes are one and all angelic while Gentiles and whites are one and all fiendish. It is not that individual virtue will now be found exclusively on the wrong side of the ethnic-racial tracks and individual viciousness on the right side. It is conceivable even that there are as many corrupt and vicious men and women among Negroes and Jews as among Gentile whites. It is only that the ugly fence which encloses the in-group happens to exclude the people who make up the out-groups from being treated with the decency ordinarily accorded human beings.

SOCIAL FUNCTIONS AND DYSFUNCTIONS

We have only to look at the consequences of this peculiar moral alchemy to see that there is no paradox at all in damning out-groupers when they do and when they don't exhibit in-group virtues. Condemnation on these two scores performs one and the same social function. Seeming opposites coalesce. When Negroes are tagged as incorrigibly inferior because they (apparently) don't manifest these virtues, this confirms the natural rightness of their being assigned an inferior status in society. And when Jews or Japanese are tagged as having too many of the in-group values, it becomes plain that they must be securely contained by the high walls of discrimination. In both cases, the special status assigned the several out-groups can be seen to be eminently reasonable.

Yet this distinctly reasonable arrangement persists in having most unreasonable consequences, both logical and social. Consider only a few of these.

In some contexts, the limitations enforced upon the out-group—say, rationing the number of Jews permitted to enter colleges and professional schools—logically imply a fear of the alleged superiority of the out-group. Were it otherwise, no discrimination need be practiced. The unyielding, impersonal forces of academic competition would soon trim down the number of Jewish (or Japanese or Negro) students to an "appropriate" size.

This implied belief in the superiority of the out-group seems premature. There is simply not enough scientific evidence to demonstrate Jewish or Japanese or Negro superiority. The effort of the in-group discriminator to supplant the myth of Aryan superiority with the myth of non-Aryan superiority is condemned to failure by science. Moreover, such myths are ill-advised. Eventually, life in a world of myth must collide with fact in the world of reality. As a matter of simple self-interest and social therapy, therefore, it might be wise for the in-group to abandon the myth and cling to the reality.

The pattern of being damned-if-you-do and damned-if-you-don't has further consequences—among the out-groups themselves. The response to alleged deficiencies is as clear as it is predictable. If one is repeatedly told that one is inferior, that one lacks any positive accomplishments, it is all too human to seize upon every bit of evidence on the contrary. The in-group definitions force upon the allegedly inferior out-group a defensive tendency to magnify and exalt "race accomplishments." As the distinguished Negro sociologist, Franklin Frazier, has noted, the Negro newspapers are "intensely race conscious and exhibit considerable pride in the achievements of the Negro, most of which are meagre performances as measured by broader standards." Self-glorification, found in some measure among all groups, becomes a frequent counter-response to persistent belittlement from without.

It is the damnation of out-groups for excessive achievement, however, which gives rise to truly bizarre behavior. For, after a time and often as a matter of self-defense, these out-groups become persuaded that their virtues really are vices. And this provides the final episode in a tragi-comedy of inverted values.

Let us try to follow the plot through its intricate maze of self-contradictions. Respectful admiration for the arduous climb from office boy to president is rooted deep in American culture. This long and strenuous ascent carries with it a two-

fold testimonial: it testifies that careers are abundantly open
to genuine talent in American society and it testifies to the
worth of the man who has distinguished himself by his heroic
rise. It would be invidious to choose among the many stalwart figures who have fought their way up, against all odds,
until they have reached the pinnacle, there to sit at the head
of the long conference table in the longer conference room of
The Board. Taken at random, the saga of Frederick H. Ecker,
chairman of the board of one of the largest privately managed corporations in the world, the Metropolitan Life Insurance Company, will suffice as the prototype. From a menial
and poorly paid job, he rose to a position of eminence. Appropriately enough, an unceasing flow of honors has come to
this man of large power and large achievement. It so happens, though it is a matter personal to this eminent man of
finance, that Mr. Ecker is a Presbyterian. Yet at last report,
no elder of the Presbyterian church has risen publicly to announce that Mr. Ecker's successful career should not be
taken too seriously, that, after all, relatively few Presbyterians
have risen from rags to riches and that Presbyterians do not
actually "control" the world of finance—or life insurance, or
investment housing. Rather, one would suppose, Presbyterian
elders join with other Americans imbued with middle-class
standards of success to felicitate the eminently successful Mr.
Ecker and to acclaim other sons of the faith who have risen
to almost equal heights. Secure in their in-group status, they
point the finger of pride rather than the finger of dismay at
individual success.

Prompted by the practice of moral alchemy, noteworthy
achievements by out-groupers elicit other responses. Patently,
if achievement is a vice, the achievements must be dis-
claimed—or at least, discounted. Under these conditions,
what is an occasion for Presbyterian pride must become an
occasion for Jewish dismay. If the Jew is condemned for his
educational or professional or scientific or economic success,
then, understandably enough, many Jews will come to feel
that these accomplishments must be minimized in simple
self-defense. Thus is the circle of paradox closed by out-
groupers busily engaged in assuring the powerful in-group that
they have not, in fact, been guilty of inordinate contributions
to science, the professions, the arts, the government, and the
economy.

In a society which ordinarily looks upon wealth as a warrant of ability, an out-group is compelled by the inverted atti-

tudes of the dominant in-group to deny that many men of wealth are among its members. "Among the 200 largest non-banking corporations . . . only ten have a Jew as president or chairman of the board." Is this an observation of an anti-Semite, intent on proving the incapacity and inferiority of Jews who have done so little "to build the corporations which have built America?" No; it is a retort of the Anti-Defamation League of B'nai B'rith to anti-Semitic propaganda.

In a society where, as a recent survey by the National Opinion Research Center has shown, the profession of medicine ranks higher in social prestige than any other of ninety occupations (save that of United States Supreme Court Justice), we find some Jewish spokesmen manoeuvred by the attacking in-group into the fantastic position of announcing their "deep concern" over the number of Jews in medical practice, which is "disproportionate to the number of Jews in other occupations." In a nation suffering from a notorious undersupply of physicians, the Jewish doctor becomes a deplorable occasion for deep concern, rather than receiving applause for his hard-won acquisition of knowledge and skills and for his social utility. Only when the New York Yankees publicly announce deep concern over their numerous World Series titles, so disproportionate to the number of triumphs achieved by other major league teams, will this self-abnegation seem part of the normal order of things.

In a culture which consistently judges the professionals higher in social value than even the most skilled hewers of wood and drawers of water, the out-group finds itself in the anomalous position of pointing with defensive relief to the large number of Jewish painters and paper hangers, plasterers and electricians, plumbers and sheet-metal workers.

But the ultimate reversal of values is yet to be noted. Each succeeding census finds more and more Americans in the city and its suburbs. Americans have travelled the road to urbanization until fewer than one-fifth of the nations population live on farms. Plainly, it is high time for the Methodist and the Catholic, the Baptist and the Episcopalian to recognize the iniquity of this trek of their coreligionists to the city. For, as is well known, one of the central accusations levelled against the Jew is his heinous tendency to live in cities. Jewish leaders, therefore, find themselves in the incredible position of defensively urging their people to move into the very farm areas being hastily vacated by city-bound hordes of Christians. Perhaps this is not altogether necessary. As the Jewish crime of urbanism becomes ever more popular among the in-group, it may be reshaped into transcendent virtue. But, admittedly, one can't be certain. For in this daft confusion of inverted values, it soon becomes impossible to determine when virtue is sin and sin, moral perfection.

Amid this confusion, one fact remains unambiguous. The Jews, like other peoples, have made distinguished contributions to world culture. Consider only an abbreviated catalogue. In the field of creative literature (and with acknowledgment of large variations in the calibre of achievement), Jewish authors include Heine, Karl Kraus, Börne, Hofmannsthal, Schnitzler, Kafka. In the realm of musical composition, there are Meyerbeer, Felix Mendelssohn, Offenbach, Mahler, and Schönberg. Among the musical virtuosi, consider only Rosenthal, Schnabel, Godowsky, Pachmann, Kreisler, Hubermann, Milstein, Elman, Heifetz, Joachim, and Menuhin. And among scientists of a stature sufficient to merit the Nobel prize, examine the familiar list which includes Beranyi, Mayerhof, Ehrlich, Michelson, Lippmann, Haber, Willstätter, and Einstein. Or in the esoteric and imaginative universe of mathematical invention, take note only of Kronecker, the creator of the modern theory of numbers; Hermann Minkowski,[3] who supplied the mathematical foundations of the special theory of relativity; or Jacobi, with his basic work in the theory of elliptical functions. And so through each special province of cultural achievement, we are supplied with a list of pre-eminent men and women who happened to be Jews.

And who is thus busily engaged in singing the praises of the Jews? Who has so assiduously compiled the list of many hundreds of distinguished Jews who contributed so notably to science, literature and the arts—a list from which these few cases were excerpted? A philo-Semite, eager to demonstrate that his people have contributed their due share to world culture? No, by now we should know better than that. The complete list will be found in the thirty-sixth edition of the anti-Semitic handbook by the racist Fritsch. In accord with the alchemical formula for transmuting in-group virtues into out-group vices, he presents this as a roll call of sinister spir-

---

[3]Obviously, the forename must be explicitly mentioned here, else Hermann Minkowski, the mathematician, may be confused with Eugen Minkowski, who contributed so notably to our knowledge of schizophrenia, or with Mieczyslaw Minkowski, high in the ranks of brain anatomists, or even with Oskar Minkowski, discoverer of pancreatic diabetes.

its who have usurped the accomplishments properly owing the Aryan in-group.

Once we comprehend the predominant role of the in-group in defining the situation, the further paradox of the seemingly opposed behavior of the Negro out-group and the Jewish out-group falls away. The behavior of both minority groups is in response to the majority-group allegations.

If the Negroes are accused of inferiority, and their alleged failure to contribute to world culture is cited in support of this accusation, the human urge for self-respect and a concern for security often leads them *defensively* to magnify each and every achievement by members of the race. If Jews are accused of excessive achievements and excessive ambitions, and lists of pre-eminent Jews are compiled in support of this accusation, then the urge for security leads them *defensively* to minimize the actual achievements of members of the group. Apparently opposed types of behavior have the same psychological and social functions. Self-assertion and self-effacement become the devices for seeking to cope with condemnation for alleged group deficiency and condemnation for alleged group excesses, respectively. And with a fine sense of moral superiority, the secure in-group looks on these curious performances by the out-groups with mingled derision and contempt.

ENACTED INSTITUTIONAL CHANGE

Will this desolate tragi-comedy run on and on, marked only by minor changes in the cast? Not necessarily.

Were moral scruples and a sense of decency the only bases for bringing the play to an end, one would indeed expect it to continue an indefinitely long run. In and of themselves, moral sentiments are not much more effective in curing social ills than in curing physical ills. Moral sentiments no doubt help to motivate efforts for change, but they are no substitute for hard-headed instrumentalities for achieving the objective, as the thickly populated graveyard of soft-headed utopias bears witness.

There are ample indications that a deliberate and planned halt can be put to the workings of the self-fulfilling prophecy and the vicious circle in society. The sequel to our sociological parable of the Last National Bank provides one clue to the way in which this can be achieved. During the fabulous '20's, when Coolidge undoubtedly caused a Republican era of lush prosperity, an average of 635 banks a year quietly suspended operations. And during the four years immediately before and after The Crash, when Hoover undoubtedly did not cause a Republican era of sluggish depression, this zoomed to the more spectacular average of 2,276 bank suspensions annually. But, interestingly enough, in the twelve years following the establishment of the Federal Deposit Insurance Corporation and the enactment of other banking legislation while Roosevelt presided over Democratic depression and revival, recession and boom, bank suspensions dropped to a niggardly average of 28 a year. Perhaps money panics have not been institutionally exorcized by legislation. Nevertheless, millions of depositors no longer have occasion to give way to panic-motivated runs on banks simply because deliberate institutional change has removed the grounds for panic. Occasions for racial hostility are no more inborn psychological constants than are occasions for panic. Despite the teachings of amateur psychologists, blind panic and racial aggression are not rooted in human nature. These patterns of human behavior are largely a product of the modifiable structure of society.

For a further clue, return to our instance of widespread hostility of white unionists toward the Negro strikebreakers brought into industry by employers after the close of the very first World War. Once the initial definition of Negroes as not deserving of union membership had largely broken down, the Negro, with a wider range of work opportunities, no longer found it necessary to enter industry through the doors held open by strike-bound employers. Again, appropriate institutional change broke through the tragic circle of the self-fulfilling prophecy. Deliberate social change gave the lie to the firm conviction that "it just ain't in the nature of the nigra" to join co-operatively with his white fellows in trade unions.

A final instance is drawn from a study of a bi-racial housing project. Located in Pittsburgh, this community of Hilltown is made up of fifty per cent Negro families and fifty per cent white. It is not a twentieth-century utopia. There is some interpersonal friction here as elsewhere. But in a community made up of equal numbers of the two races, fewer than a fifth of the whites and less than a third of the Negroes report that this friction occurs between members of *different* races. By their own testimony, it is very largely confined to disagreements *within* each racial group. Yet only one in every twenty-five whites initially *expected* relations between the races in this community to run smoothly, whereas five times as many expected serious trouble, the remainder anticipating a tolerable, if not altogether pleasant, situation. So much for expectations. Upon reviewing their actual experience, three of every four of the most apprehensive whites subsequently found that the "races get along fairly well" after all. This is not the place to report the findings of this study in detail, but substantially these demonstrate anew that under *appropriate institutional and administrative conditions,* the experience of interracial amity can supplant the fear of interracial conflict.

These changes, and others of the same kind, do not occur automatically. *The self-fulfilling prophecy, whereby fears are translated into reality, operates only in the absence of deliberate institutional controls.* And it is only with the rejection of social fatalism implied in the notion of unchangeable human nature that the tragic circle of fear, social disaster, and reinforced fear can be broken.

Ethnic prejudices do die—but slowly. They can be helped over the threshold of oblivion, not by insisting that it is unreasonable and unworthy of them to survive, but by cutting off the sustenance now provided them by certain institutions of our society.

If we find ourselves doubting man's capacity to control man and his society, if we persist in our tendency to find in the patterns of the past the chart of the future, it is perhaps time to take up anew the wisdom of Tocqueville's century-old remark: "I am tempted to believe that what we call necessary institutions are often no more than institutions to which we have grown accustomed, and that in matters of social constitution the field of possibilities is much more extensive than men living in their various societies are ready to imagine."

Nor can widespread, even typical, failures in planning human relations between ethnic groups be cited as evidence for pessimism. In the world laboratory of the sociologist, as in the more secluded laboratories of the physicist and chemist, it is the successful experiment which is decisive and not the thousand-and-one failures which preceded it. More is learned from the single success than from the multiple failures. A single success proves it can be done. Thereafter, it is necessary only to learn what made it work. This, at least, is what I take to be the sociological sense of those revealing words of Thomas Love Peacock: "Whatever is, is possible."

The Middletown Spirit

by
Robert and Helen Lynd

One cannot talk about "what Middletown thinks" or "feels" or "is" without a large amount of distortion. As many qualifications must be noted in speaking of a "typical" Middletown citizen as in speaking of Middletown as a "typical" American inland city. Some of these qualifications, distinguishing attitudes of different racial groups, business class and working class, men and women, parents and children, as well as differing attitudes of individuals, have been noted in the preceding pages, and others will be discussed in this chapter.

And yet, Middletown can be lived in and described only because of the presence of large elements of repetition and coherence in the culture. As one moves about the city one encounters in the city government, in the church, the press, and the civic clubs, and in the folk talk on the streets and about family dinner tables points of view so familiar and so commonly taken for granted that they represent the intellectual and emotional shorthands of understanding and agreement among a large share of the people. These are the things that one does and feels and says so naturally that mentioning them in Middletown implies an "of course." Individual differences at these points have become rubbed away, and thought and sentiment pass from person to person like smooth familiar coins which everyone accepts and no one examines with fresh eyes. Just as surely, too, there are other things that one does not ordinarily say or think or do. Around these patterns of customary acceptance and rejection certain types of personality develop. Those persons who most nearly exemplify the local stereotypes thrive, are "successful," and "belong"; while dropping away behind them are others who embody less adequately the values by which Middletown lives, down to the community misfits who live meagerly in the shadow of frustration and unpopularity. These latter deviant types often labor under pressures and lack of support in Middletown which they might not experience in other communities— larger communities, communities harboring a wider range of types, where one's life does not lie so open to one's neighbors or where one's dissident ideas or actions are not taken so personally as threats to one's neighbor's accepted ways of life, or even where certain types which are out of the ordinary in Middletown are normal rather than deviant.

It is the purpose of this chapter to attempt to uncover the patterns of life and of personality which are of the "of-course" type accepted by the mass of Middletown people, as well as modifications of these patterns among different groups in the population during the span of the last ten years.

These accepted regularities in Middletown tend to appear in each significant area of living. They tend also to form a design of some rough continuity,[1] so that if one picks up the life of a Middletown citizen anywhere throughout the web, one can go on familiarly throughout the rest of the pattern without meeting many unexpected knots. This is what gives some rough unity to Middletown culture, and enables one to speak, as did the title of the local newspaper editorial set at the head of this chapter, of "the [Middletown] spirit." This by no means implies that in carrying on its daily operations of living Middletown acts necessarily according to these values which it affirms. Often quite the contrary is the case. But these are the values *in the name of which* it acts, the symbols which can be counted upon to secure emotional response, the banners under which it marches.

The following suggest the rough pattern of things Middletown is *for* and *against*—in short, its values.

By and large Middletown believes:

In being honest.
In being kind.[2]

---

[1] See *Middletown*, pp. 492–93.
[2] A favorite quotation from Ella Wheeler Wilcox still appears in Middletown's club programs:

> "So many gods, so many creeds,
>   So many paths that wind and wind,
> While just the art of being kind,
>   Is all the sad world needs."

In being friendly,[3] a "good neighbor," and a "good fellow."[4]

In being loyal, and a "booster, not a knocker."

In being successful.

In being an average man. "Practically all of us realize that
we are common men, and we are prone to distrust and
hate those whom we regard as uncommon."[5]

In having character as more important than "having
brains."

In being simple and unpretentious and never "putting on
airs" or being a snob.[6]

A resident of twenty-five years in Middletown, describing the
launching of the first Christmas campaign for helping the poor some
years ago, writes: "Within three days the [newspaper] office was so piled
with contributions that the reporters couldn't find their desks. Middletown people may have no culture, but when appealed to in the right
way there is no limit to their sympathy."

[3]Willis Fisher presents an excellent picture of the mellow friendliness
of the small community in the Middle West in his chapter, "Small-
Town Middle-Westerner," in *Who Owns America?* edited by Herbert
Agar and Allen Tate. (Boston; Houghton Mifflin, 1936.)

[4]The quoted words and phrases scattered through this list of things
Middletown believes are from local editorials, club programs, civic-club
and other addresses and papers, and from conversations. All are included because, in the experience of the writers, they represent widely-
held Middletown attitudes. For the sake of brevity, the many sources
are not always identified in this long listing.

[5]Middletown business people for the most part think of themselves as
being a city of "small businessmen" and make a virtue of it. A note of
editorial comment in November, 1935; stated: "Several persons were
asked how many people in [Middletown] in their opinion have a weekly
income of $100 or better, and the top estimate was 1,000. Most of
them believed half that number would be more nearly correct. A few
thought 200 would be about right. The right answer probably is somewhere between these last two extremes."

[6]Such "folksy" jingles as the following in Edgar Guest's daily "Just
Folks" in Middletown's morning paper evoke a comforting chuckle of
agreement at the breakfast table:

> My overcoat, when winds blow cold,
>   Is stout enough to keep me warm,
> This year it will be three years old
>   And sag a trifle round my form,
> But what of that? I shall not freeze
>   Nor feel the weather more than they
> Who bought their garments overseas
>   At prices I could never pay;
> Comparisons are relative
>   When everything is said and done,
> Though on a lesser plain I live,
>   I get my share of honest fun.

In prizing all things that are common and "real" and "wholesome."

"There are beauties at your own doorstep comparable to those you find on long journeys."

In having "common sense."

In being "sound" and "steady."

In being a good sport and making friends with one's opponents. "It doesn't help to harbor grudges."[7]

In being courageous and good-natured in the face of trouble and "making friends with one's luck."[8]

In being, when in doubt, like other people.

In adhering, when problems arise, to tried practices that have "worked" in the past.

That "progress is the law of life," and therefore:

That evolution in society is "from the base and inferior to the beautiful and good."

That, since "progress means growth," increasing size indicates progress. In this connection Middletown tends to emphasize quantitative rather than qualitative changes, and absolute rather than relative numbers or size.

That "the natural and orderly processes of progress" should be followed.

That change is slow, and abrupt changes or the speeding

My friends are neither rich nor great,
  But I am fond of them, and they
Are fond of me, I dare to state.
  What more can pomp and fortune say?

[7] Elections evoke this prevalent mood of friendly and good-natured acceptance of victory or defeat in characteristic form. The day after the 1936 election an editorial in the local Republican press remarked simply: "After an election we must get together and support everybody who has been elected. In [Middletown] this thing does not hurt at all, because those who were elected are our own folks, regardless of politics."

Another editorial stated that anyone wishing to protest the 1936 election could do so before November 15, and added, "But you don't contest earthquakes and landslides." The same editor commented in his column on an attorney who was looking for a community in which to hang out his shingle, who described himself as "an honest lawyer and a Republican": "He was told by a friend, 'It doesn't make any difference where you go, for if you are an honest lawyer you will have no competition, and if you are a Republican the game laws will protect you.'"

[8] Despite Middletown's general faith in the forward movement of things in America, its personal goals tend to be moderate, and adversity is not a total stranger when it visits most of these families. Under the brave exterior of confidence, a common mood is that "It isn't a good thing to expect too much of life."

up of changes through planning or revolution is unnatural.

That "radicals" ("reds," "communists," "socialists," "atheists"—the terms are fairly interchangeable in Middletown) want to interfere with things and "wreck American civilization." "We condemn agitators who masquerade under the ideals guaranteed by our Constitution. We demand the deportation of alien Communists and Anarchists."

That "in the end those who follow the middle course prove to be the wisest. It's better to stick close to the middle of the road, to move slowly, and to avoid extremes."

That evils are inevitably present at many points but will largely cure themselves. "In the end all things will mend."

That no one can solve all his problems, and consequently it is a good rule not to dwell on them too much and not to worry. "It's better to avoid worry and to expect that things will come out all right." "The pendulum will swing back soon."

That good will solve most problems.

That optimism on our part helps the orderly forces making for progress. "The year 1936 will be a banner year because people believe it will be."

That within this process the individual must fend for himself and will in the long run get what he deserves, and therefore:

That character, honesty, and ability will tell.

That one should be enterprising; one should try to get ahead of one's fellows, but not "in an underhand way."

That one should be practical and efficient.

That one should be hard-working and persevering. "Hard work is the key to success." "Until a man has his family financially established, he should not go in for frills and isms."

That one should be thrifty and "deny oneself" reasonably. "If a man will not learn to save his own money, nobody will save for him."

That a man owes it to himself, to his family, and to society to "succeed."

That "the school of hard knocks is a good teacher," and one should learn to "grin and bear" temporary setbacks. "It took an early defeat to turn many a man into a success." "After all, hardship never hurts anyone who has the stuff in him."

That social welfare, in Middletown and elsewhere, is the result of the two preceding factors working together—the natural law of progress and the individual law of initiative, hard work, and thrift—and therefore:

That any interference with either of the two is undesirable. "The Lord helps him who helps himself." "Congress," an editorial remarked sarcastically, "is now preparing for farm relief, while the wise farmer is out in the field relieving himself."

That society should not coddle the man who does not work hard and save, for if a man does not "get on" it is his own fault. "There is no such thing as a 'youth problem.' It is up to every boy and girl to solve his own problem in his own way."

That "the strongest and best should survive, for that is the law of nature, after all."

That people should have community spirit.

That they should be loyal, placing *their* family, *their* community,[9] *their* state, and *their* nation first. "The best American foreign policy is any policy that places America first." "America first is merely common sense."

That "American ways" are better than "foreign ways."

That "big-city life" is inferior to Middletown life and undesirable.[10] "Saturday-night crowds on [Middletown] streets," comments an editorial, "are radiantly clean as to person and clothes. . . . Saturday-night shopping becomes a holiday affair after they have bathed and put on their best garments at home. . . . [Middletown] is still a 'Saturday-night town,' and if big cities call us 'hicks' for that reason, let 'em."

[9]A recently arrived new resident in Middletown remarked: "Beauty in any form seems to be conspicuous by its absence, and yet seemingly intelligent people praise the town as the most desirable possible place in which to live."

[10]There is in Middletown's press an undertone of disparagement of New York and other big cities, as noted in Ch. X. A shrewd observer of long residence in the city, describing her first years there, says: "I was quite unconscious at first of the fact that people from New York and other big cities are looked on with suspicion."

That most foreigners are "inferior." "There is something to this Japanese menace. Let's have no argument about it, but just send those Japs back where they came from."

That Negroes are inferior.

That individual Jews may be all right but that as a race one doesn't care to mix too much with them.

That Middletown will always grow bigger and better.

That the fact that people live together in Middletown makes them a unit with common interests, and they should, therefore, all work together.

That American business will always lead the world. "Here in the United States, as nowhere else in the world, the little business and the big business exist side by side and are a testimonial to the soundness of the American way of life."

That the small businessman is the backbone of American business. "In no country in the world are there so many opportunities open to the little fellow as in the United States. . . . These small businesses are succeeding . . . because they meet a public need." "A wise [Middletown] banker once said: 'I like to patronize a peanut stand because you only have one man to deal with and his only business is to sell peanuts.'"

That economic conditions are the result of a natural order which cannot be changed by man-made laws. "Henry Ford says that wages ought to be higher and goods cheaper. We agree with this, and let us add that we think it ought to be cooler in the summer and warmer in winter."[11]

That depressions are regrettable but nevertheless a normal aspect of business. "Nothing can be done to stop de-

[11]The above is from a Middletown editorial comment of January, 1930. Another editorial states: "It never is safe to tamper with natural laws—and that of supply and demand is one of them. So to a student of economics or even one who is not a student but has some slight knowledge of them, such schemes as 'pools' and holding companies for grains have slight appeal because, essentially, they are attempting to do something by sheer economic pressure that natural causes and their inevitable results cannot sustain. Of course this sounds like rank heresy to those who believe, notwithstanding the long history of failure, that man-made laws really are of some consequence when opposed to Nature-made ones."

And still another comment in the same vein: "The advancing price of farm products [is] not due to any kind of legislation, but to natural causes which are always responsible for prices whether high or low."

pressions. It's just like a person who feels good one day and rotten the next."

That business can run its own affairs best and the government should keep its hands off business. "All these big schemes for planning by experts brought to Washington won't work."

That every man for himself is the right and necessary law of the business world, "tempered, of course, with judgment and fair dealing."

That competition is what makes progress and has made the United States great.

That the chance to grow rich is necessary to keep intiative alive. "Young folks today are seeking material advantage, which is just exactly what all of us have been seeking all our lives."

That "men won't work if they don't have to." "Work isn't fun. None of us would do a lick of work if he didn't have to."

That the poor-boy-to-president way is the American way to get ahead.

That ordinarily any man willing to work can get a job.[12]

That a man "really gets what is coming to him in the United States."

That "any man who is willing to work hard and to be thrifty and improve his spare time can get to the top. That's the American way, and it's as true today as it ever was."

That it is a man's own fault if he is dependent in old age.

That the reason wages are not higher is because industry cannot afford to pay them. "Employers want to pay as high wages as they can, and they can be counted on to do so just as soon as they are able."

That the rich are, by and large, more intelligent and industrious than the poor. "That's why they are where they are."

That the captains of industry are social benefactors because they create employment. "Where'd all our jobs be if it wasn't for them?"

That capital is simply the accumulated savings of these people with foresight.

---

[12]This, like some of the other assumptions regarding economic matters in this section, is a commoner business-class than working-class point of view.

That if you "make it too easy" for the unemployed and people like that they will impose on you.

That nobody is really starving in the depression.

That capital and labor are partners and have basically the same interests. "It is a safe bet that if the average worker and employer could sit down calmly together and discuss their differences, a great deal more would be done to solve their difficulties than will be accomplished by politics or by extremists on either side."

That "the open shop is the American way."

That labor organization is unwise and un-American in that it takes away the worker's freedom and initiative, puts him under the control of outsiders, and seeks to point a gun at the head of business. "We wouldn't mind so much if our own people here would form their own unions without any of these outsiders coming in to stir up trouble."

That strikes are due to troublemakers' leading American workers astray.

That Middletown people should shop in Middletown. "Buy where you earn your money."

That the family is a sacred institution and the fundamental institution of our society.

That the monogamous family is the outcome of evolution from lower forms of life and is the final, divinely ordained form.

That sex was "given" to man for purposes of procreation, not for personal enjoyment.

That sexual relations before or outside of marriage are immoral.

That "men should behave like men, and women like women."

That women are better ("purer") than men.

That a married woman's place is first of all in the home, and any other activities should be secondary to "making a good home for her husband and children."

That men are more practical and efficient than women.

That most women cannot be expected to understand public problems as well as men.

That men tend to be tactless in personal relations and women are "better at such things."

That everybody loves children, and a woman who does not want children is "unnatural."

That married people owe it to society to have children.

That it is normal for parents to want their children to be "better off," to "have an easier time," than they themselves have had.

That childhood should be a happy time, "for after that, one's problems and worries begin." "Everyone with a drop of humanitarian blood believes that children are entitled to every possible happiness."

That parents should "give up things for their children," but "should maintain discipline and not spoil them."

That it is pleasant and desirable to "do things as a family."

That fathers do not understand children as well as mothers do.

That children should think on essential matters as their parents do.

That young people are often rebellious ("have queer ideas") but they "get over these things and settle down."

That home ownership is a good thing for the family and also makes for good citizenship.

That schools should teach the facts of past experience about which "sound, intelligent people agree."

That it is dangerous to acquaint children with points of view that question "the fundamentals."

That an education should be "practical," but at the same time, it is chiefly important as "broadening" one.

That too much education and contact with books and big ideas unfits a person for practical life.

That a college education is "a good thing."

But that a college man is no better than a non-college man and is likely to be less practical, and that college men must learn "life" to counteract their concentration on theory.

That girls who do not plan to be teachers do not ordinarily need as much education as boys.

That "you forget most of the things you learn in school." "Looking back over the years, it seems to me that at least half of the friends of my schoolday youth who have made good were dumbunnies. . . . Anyway they could not pile up points for honors unless it was an honor to sit someplace between the middle and the foot of the class."

That schoolteachers are usually people who couldn't make good in business.

That teaching school, particularly in the lower grades, is women's business.

That schools nowadays go in for too many frills.

That leisure is a fine thing, but work comes first.

That "all of us hope we'll get to the place sometime where we can work less and have more time to play."

But that it is wrong for a man to retire when he is still able to work. "What will he do with his time?"

That having a hobby is "all very well if a person has time for that sort of thing and it doesn't interfere with his job."

That "red-blooded" physical sports are more normal recreations for a man than art, music, and literature.

That "culture and things like that" are more the business of women than of men.

That leisure is something you spend with people and a person is "queer" who enjoys solitary leisure.

That a person doesn't want to spend his leisure doing "heavy" things or things that remind him of the "unpleasant" side of life. "There are enough hard things in real life—books and plays should have a pleasant ending that leaves you feeling better."

But that leisure should be spent in wholesomely "worthwhile" things and not be just idle or frivolous.

That it is better to be appreciative than discriminating. "If a person knows too much or is too critical it makes him a kill-joy or a snob not able to enjoy the things most people enjoy."

That anything widely acclaimed is pretty apt to be good; it is safer to trust the taste and judgment of the common man in most things rather than that of the specialist.

That Middletown wants to keep abreast of the good new things in the arts and literature, but it is not interested in anything freakish.

That "being artistic doesn't justify being immoral."

That smoking and drinking are more appropriate leisure activities for men than for women.

That it is more appropriate for well-to-do people to have automobiles and radios and to spend money on liquor than for poor people.

That it is a good thing for everyone to enjoy the fine, simple pleasures of life.[13]

[13]Characteristic is the article which first appeared in the editor's personal column, *Comment*, on the first page of the afternoon paper in

That "we folks out here dislike in our social life formality, society manners, delicate food, and the effete things of rich Eastern people."

That the American democratic form of government is the final and ideal form of government.

That the Constitution should not be fundamentally changed.

That Americans are the freest people in the world.

That America will always be the land of opportunity and the greatest and richest country in the world.

That England is the finest country in Europe.

That Washington and Lincoln were the greatest Americans. (Edison is sometimes linked with these two as the third great American.)

That only unpatriotic dreamers would think of changing the form of government that was "good enough for" Washington and Lincoln.[14]

1933. In response to many requests, it has been reprinted every year since then:

"WHEN THERE MAY NEVER BE ANOTHER?

"I hate to sleep, these summer nights. I may never have another summer, and this one is fleeting as a bird on wing. I only have this summer hour, this summer minute, but today summer is mine, if I will take it—summer with verdant grass dew-besprent in the early morning and birds at dawn singing their matin songs; summer with the glory of its sunsets of mackerel and gold night approaches; summer with its mellow moons and its chirpings and plaintive calls of little wild creatures from out the dark. . . .

"And so I like to crowd into life in summer time all the hours that I can summon. Hot winds may sweep across the land, but they are summer winds and betimes they cool; flitting insects may annoy, but they express the life that is of summer's essence; the sun may beat down upon us, but it is summer's sun that makes the flowers to give us their radiance, the trees to rear their leaf-crowned heads in majesty against the cerulean blue and shadow in fine traceries the white fleece of the clouds.

"Sleep? In summer? When there may never be another?"

[14]Middletown is wont to invoke old leaders against new leaders who threaten to leave the "safe and tried middle of the road." Such innovations as its Revolutionary founding fathers and the other heroes in its pantheon stood for are forgotten; their revolts were but the orderly work of natural progress; their conservatism was their essential contribution as persons. Thus, a recent editorial on "Lincoln the Conservative" urges that "Lincoln's name has been taken in vain by radicals. . . . He was a political fundamentalist and knew his Constitution" and did not believe in "tearing out the foundations of government in the attempt to rebuild it on the blueprints of Utopians. . . . He kept the middle of the road."

That socialism, communism, and facism are disreputable and un-American.

That socialists and communists believe in dividing up existing wealth on a per-capita basis. "This is unworkable because within a year a comparatively few able persons would have the money again."

That radicalism makes for the destruction of the church and family, looseness of morals, and the stifling of individual initiative.

That only foreigners and long-haired troublemakers are radicals.

That the voters, in the main, really control the operation of the American government.

That newspapers give citizens "the facts."

That the two-party system is the "American way."

That it does not pay to throw away one's vote on a minority party.

That government ownership is inefficient and more costly than private enterprise.

That the government should leave things to private initiative. "More business in government and less government in business." (Events since 1933 have been causing large numbers of people in the lower income brackets in Middletown to question this formerly widely held assumption, though the upper income brackets hold to it as tenaciously as ever.)

That high tariffs are desirable. "Secretary Hull's tariff policy is putting the American producer in the city and in the country in competition with the peasant and serf in Europe and Asia."

That taxes should be kept down.

That our government should leave Europe and the rest of the world alone.

That the United States should have large military and naval defenses to protect itself, but should not mix in European wars.

That pacifism is disreputable and un-American. "We're militaristic rather than pacifist out here—though of course we don't want wars."

That many public problems are too big for the voter to solve but that Congress can solve them.

That "experts" just "gum up" the working of democracy.

That national problems can be solved by "letting nature take its course" or by passing laws.

That problems such as corruption in public office can be largely solved by electing better men to office.

That local problems such as crime can be ameliorated by putting people in jail and by imposing heavier sentences.

That, human nature being what it is, there will always be some graft in government but that despite this we are the best-governed nation in the world.

That organizations such as the American Legion and the D.A.R. represent a high order of Americanism.

That because of "poor, weak human nature" there will always be some people too lazy to work, too spendthrift to save, too shortsighted to plan. "Doesn't the Bible prove this when it says. 'The poor ye have always with you'?"

That charity will always be necessary. "For you wouldn't let a dog starve."

That in a real emergency anyone with any human feeling will "share his shirt with an unfortunate who needs it."[15]

But that a "government dole" on a large scale is an entirely different thing from charity to an individual, and that "a paternalistic system which prescribes an exact

[15]This mood of human kindliness to people in distress is met with everywhere in the talk of Middletown. It is conspicuously met with among the people who protest most loudly against public relief. One may suspect that the indignation of many of Middletown's business class over the existence of such a broad policy of public relief as has existed in the depression derives in part from their knowledge that they, in common with people generally in Middletown, have this deep, neighborly attitude towards "anyone really in dire need." It is significant of the contradictions into which Middletown's thought and emotions run in matters involving the specific single cases of need and generalized policies for handling need as a social problem that the same editor, quoted in Ch. IV as writing in his paper that there are so many down-and-outers on relief in Middletown that it would be a boon to everyone if a plague would come and wipe them all out, also sprinkles his column with such mellow human comment as the following:

"Do you know how much the average waitress is being paid in [Middletown]? Neither do I, but it's something scandalous. They are expected to remain virtuous on eight dollars a week. Your tip might help a bit."

"He slithered into the restaurant early in the morning. He was not so old in years as he was in appearance. . . . The world had beaten him down. He was unlovely to behold, as degenerate age always is. . . . 'I'd like to have a cup of coffee,' he said, and his glance was sidewise. He fumbled about for a nickel and finally laid it on the counter. 'We don't charge for coffee today,' said the waitress. I hope she won't be fired. I hope she has a chair in Heaven."

method of aiding our unfortunate brothers and sisters is demoralizing."

That idleness and thriftlessness are only encouraged by making charity too easy.

That it "undermines a man's character" for him to get what he doesn't earn.

That it is a fine thing for rich people to be philanthropic.

That recipients of charity should be grateful.

That relief from public funds during the depression is a purely emergency matter to be abandoned as soon as possible, and that it is unthinkable for the United States to have anything resembling a permanent "dole."

That things like unemployment insurance are unnecessary because "in ordinary times any man willing to work can get a job"; and that they are demoralizing both to the recipient and to the businessman taxed to support them.

That Christianity is the final form of religion and all other religions are inferior to it.

But that what you believe is not so important as the kind of person you are.

That nobody would want to live in a community without churches, and everybody should, therefore, support the churches.

That churchgoing is sometimes a kind of nuisance, one of the things you do as a duty, but that the habit of churchgoing is a good thing and makes people better.

That there isn't much difference any longer between the different Protestant denominations.

But that Protestantism is superior to Catholicism.

That having a Pope is un-American and a Catholic should not be elected President of the United States.

That Jesus is the Son of God and what he said is true for all time.

That Jesus was the most perfect man who ever lived.

That God exists and runs the universe.

That there is a "hereafter." "It is unthinkable that people should just die and that be the end."[16]

---

[16]The related belief in reward or punishment after death is less bluntly held by Middletown's Presbyterians, Episcopalians, Universalists, and Friends, who are for the most part business-class folk, than by other denominations. Emotionally, a vague, uneasy belief in a hereafter where there will be some sort of accounting lingers deep in the lives of a very large share of Middletown's population. It is characteristic of a

That God cannot be expected to intercede in the small
   things of life, but that through faith and prayer one may
   rely upon His assistance in the most important concerns
   of life.[17]

That preachers are rather impractical people who wouldn't
   be likely to make really good in business.[18]

That I wouldn't want my son to go into the ministry.[19]

That preachers should stick to religion and not try to talk
   about business, public affairs, and other things "they
   don't know anything about."

Middletown is *against* the reverse of the things it is for.
These need not be listed here, but they may be summarized
by saying that Middletown is *against:*

Any strikingly divergent type of personality, especially the
   nonoptimist, the non-joiner, the unfriendly person, and
   the pretentious person.[20]

Any striking innovations in art, ideas, literature, though it
   tolerates these more if they are spectacular, episodic in-

---

culture sure of its rightness in the best of all possible nations that the
pleasant idea of "immortality" is strong while the idea of "punishment"
is receding.

[17]Middletown people vary widely in the literalness of their belief in
prayer. In general, women believe in it more than men and the South
Side more than the North Side. While only the women in a South Side
church might ordinarily pledge themselves to pray for a piece of legislation, as did one group in the case of the Eighteenth Amendment, in
times of great personal or familial emergency even many businessmen
will admit to close friends that they "prayed" over it. "Not," as one of
them explained, "that I exactly thought it would make any difference,
but my wife was so sick I just wasn't going to leave any stone un-
turned."

[18]This is the male attitude. Women tend to accept the minister more
on the latter's own terms.

[19]This again is more a male attitude. Women would be more apt to
feel secret pride in a son in the ministry.

[20]In a poem by a local poet entitled "Middletown," in a column
headed "Our Own Poets" in the local press in 1935, the following lines
occur:

> "There she lies, by fear prostrated
> Fear of doing aught unusual,
> Fear of thinking, fear of doubting,
> Fear of frankness, fear of gossip,
> Fear of those in higher places,
> Fear of those who are the lowly,
> Fear of herself and others
> Fearing 'twill be known she's fearing."

trusions from without than if they are practiced within Middletown.

Any striking innovations in government, religion, education, the family.

Centralized government, bureaucracy, large-scale planning by government. "It's impossible to plan on a large scale. There are too many factors involved. It is best to leave it to individuals, who are likely to take a more normal or more natural course."

Anything that curtails money making.

Anybody who criticizes any fundamental institution.

People engaged in thinking about or working for change: social planners, intellectuals, professors, highbrows, radicals, Russians, pacifists, anybody who knows too much.

Foreigners, internationalists, and international bankers.

People who are not patriots—for city, state, and nation.

Non-Protestants, Jews, Negroes—as "not quite our sort."

People who stress the importance of sex, including those who favor the general dissemination of information about birth control.

People who buy things, do things, live in ways not customary for one of that income level.

Frills, notions, and anything fancy.

People and things that are fragile or sensitive rather than robust.

II.

SOCIAL INTERACTION

Human beings, as social animals, realize their aspirations often through interactions with others of their kind. Indeed it is found to tinstanc influence behavior, before human beings that is studied within the influence contexts in which they work and move. The interplay between the action of self and that of others and social function of one or many others acquire the sense of the human stage. Not solitary but there, interacting actions mutually influencing each other, behavior are the matter of social acts, acquiant than personal conduct.

Claude Levi Strauss, the foremost French anthropologer, though he was mystified here that a specific term of social evolution which he call "reciprocity" is of peculiar human importance. Choosing exaggeration a primitive culture, the case from contemporary French life he illustrates in further to indicate that reciprocal exchange between human beings renders much of the cement for human bonds and bonds those human beings in the society of their fellows. Through such exchanges and exchanges, human beings overcome isolation and are enmeshed in social acts that sustain and ener their own individual lives.

Erving Goffman in the next selection shows how humor and laughter, which might seem at first blush to be purely individual phenomena, are in fact patterned in social actions and even socially controlled. Laughter, the author suggests, is not merely expected to occur only in specific and structured social situations. It is socially patterned and can best be understood in terms of the interactive contexts in which it occurs. Far from being a private experience, it may entertain a group, reassure its members, relieve tensions, convey information, and draw people more closely into the interactive process in which they are all involved.

Erving Goffman, perhaps the most prominent current analyst of interactive processes, shows in the next pas

HUMAN BEINGS, as social animals, realize their aspirations largely through interactions with others of their kind. Nobody is an island to himself or herself, hence human beings must be studied within the interactive contexts in which they variously move. The interplay between the action of self and the expected or actual reaction of one or many others occupies the center of the human stage. Not solitary individuals, but interacting persons mutually influencing each other's behavior are the center of sociological, as distant from psychological, inquiry.

Claude Levi-Strauss, the foremost French anthropologist, suggests in the essay reprinted here that a specific form of interaction, which he calls "reciprocity," is of peculiar human significance. Choosing examples from primitive cultures and also from contemporary French life, he illustrates in instructive detail that reciprocal exchange between human actors provides much of the cement for human bonds and hence binds human beings to the society of their fellows. Through such reciprocities and exchanges, human beings overcome isolation and are enmeshed in social ties that sustain and energize their individual lives.

Rose Laub Coser, in the next selection, shows how humor and laughter, which might seem at first blush to be purely individual phenomena, are in fact patterned in social actions and hence socially controlled. Laughter, the author suggests, occurs, or is expected to occur, only in specific and structured social situations. It is socially patterned and can best be understood in terms of the interactive context in which it occurs. Far from being a private experience, it may entertain a group, reassure its members, release tensions, convey information, and draw people more closely into the interactive process in which they are all involved.

Erving Goffman, perhaps the most prominent contemporary student of interactive processes, shows in the next paper how people may adapt to failures with the help of others who "cool them out." He uses the example of the con game in which the "mark" or "sucker" is consoled about his financial losses by being given an explanation by some of the confederates that allows him to keep his self-esteem. By being shown that the loss does not reflect on the loser, the latter is allowed to keep face. Goffman uses the con game as a convenient springboard for considering phenomena of wider sociological significance. What he describes here is meant to give privileged sociological access to the many interactive settings in which losers will have to come to terms with failure. Goffman highlights situations in which, say, bossess have to assuage the wounds they have inflicted by refusing a promotion or by outright firing. Goffman's insightful paper on the adaptations to loss suggests the many defenses, consolations, mitigations, and compensations that interactive partners may provide so that people may learn to adapt to loss without permanent psychic scars. Coping with failure is not left to the individual alone, but also to others—often to those very partners who have helped cause the failure.

William J. Goode in his "The Protection of the Inept" follows a line of inquiry opened up by Goffman. He suggests that all human organizations, if they are to function effectively, must provide ways in which those that do not measure up to expectations—the inept—are provided with positions in which they can serve honorably even though they do not make a significant contribution. They must be protected, but, at the same time, the group or organization must be protected from them. Productivity in modern organizations, Goode suggests, may be the result of more efficient utilization of the inept than was possible in the past. By having found more humane ways of protecting the inept, modern organizations have also found more efficient ways of keeping them from doing great harm.

The final paper in this chapter presents an ambitious and ingenious attempt to move into an area where most sociologists have feared to tread. Theodore Caplow's "The Motives of Hamlet" suggests that sociological studies of interactions, especially of triadic patterns, may throw light on certain difficulties of interpretation that humanistic Hamlet scholars have failed to solve over the centuries. Most humanistic scholars have tended to regard sociological interpretations as illegitimate invasions of their territory by uncouth barbarians, while most sociologists have regarded the world of the humanists as alien territory best not entered by men and women trained in the scientific method. Caplow shows that this separation between the "two cultures" is unwarranted and counterproductive. Humanists and sociologists can learn from each other; their endeavors are complementary rather than antagonistic.

Reciprocity, the Essence of Social Life

by
Claude Levi-Strauss

The conclusions of the famous *Essay on the Gift* are well known. In this study which is considered a classic today, Mauss intended to show first of all, that in primitive societies exchange consists less frequently of economic transactions than of reciprocal gifts; secondly, that these reciprocal gifts have a much more important function in these societies than in ours; finally, that this primitive form of exchange is not wholly nor essentially of an economic character but is what he calls "a total social fact," i.e., an event which has at the same time social and religious, magic and economic, utilitarian and sentimental, legal and moral significance. It is known that in numerous primitive societies, and particularly in those of the Pacific Islands and those of the Northwest Pacific coast of Canada and of Alaska, all the ceremonies observed on important occasions are accompanied by a distribution of valued objects. Thus in New Zealand the ceremonial offering of clothes, jewels, arms, food and various furnishings was a common characteristic of the social life of the Maori. These gifts were presented in the event of births, marriages, deaths, exhumations, peace treaties and misdemeanors, and incidents too numerous to be recorded. Similarly, Firth lists the occasions of ceremonial exchange in Polynesia: "birth, initiation, marriage, sickness, death and other social events . . ."[1] Another observer cites the following occasions for ceremonial exchange in a section of the same region: betrothal, marriage, pregnancy, birth and death; and he describes the presents offered by the father of the young man at the celebration of the betrothal: ten baskets of dry fish, ten

Reprinted with the permission of the publisher from *Sociological Theory*, Coser and Rosenberg, eds., New York: The Macmillan Co., 1957, pp. 84–94.

[1]Raymond Firth, *Primitive Polynesian Economy*, London, 1939, p. 321.

thousand ripe and six thousand green coconuts, the boy himself receiving in exchange two large cakes.[2]

Such gifts are either exchanged immediately for equivalent gifts, or received by the beneficiaries on the condition that on a subsequent occasion they will return the gesture with other gifts whose value often exceeds that of the first, but which bring about in their turn a right to receive later new gifts which themselves surpass the magnificence of those previously given. The most characteristic of these institutions is the potlatch of the Indians in Alaska and in the region of Vancouver. These ceremonies have a triple function: to give back with proper "interest" gifts formerly received; to establish publicly the claim of a family or social group to a title or privilege, or to announce a change of status; finally, to surpass a rival in generosity, to crush him if possible under future obligations which it is hoped he cannot meet, thus taking from him privileges, titles, rank, authority and prestige.

Doubtless the system of reciprocal gifts only reaches such vast proportions with the Indians of the Northwest Pacific, a people who show a genius and exceptional temperament in their treatment of the fundamental themes of a primitive culture. But Mauss has been able to establish the existence of similar institutions in Melanesia and Polynesia. The main function of the food celebrations of many tribes in New Guinea is to obtain recognition of the new "pangua" through a gathering of witnesses, that is to say, the function which in Alaska, according to Barnett, is served by potlatch. . . . Gift exchange and potlatch is a universal mode of culture, although not equally developed everywhere.

But we must insist that this primitive conception of the exchange of goods is not only expressed in well-defined and localized institutions. It permeates all transactions, ritual or secular, in the course of which objects or produce are given or received. Everywhere we find again and again this double assumption, implicit or explicit, that reciprocal gifts constitute a means of transmission of goods; and that these goods are not offered principally or essentially, in order to gain a profit or advantage of an economic nature: "After celebrations of birth," writes Turner of the Samoan culture, "after having received and given the *oloa* and the *tonga* (that is the masculine gifts and the feminine gifts) the husband and the wife are not any richer than they were before."

[2]H. Ian Hogbin, "Sexual life of the natives of Ongton Java," *Journal of the Polynesian Society*, Vol. 40, p. 28.

Exchange does not bring a tangible result as is the case in the commercial transactions in our society. Profit is neither direct, nor is it inherent in the objects exchanged as in the case of monetary profit or consumption values. Or rather, profit does not have the meaning which we assign to it because in primitive culture, there is something else in what we call a "commodity" than that which renders it commodious to its owner or to its merchant. Goods are not only economic commodities but vehicles and instruments for realities of another order: influence, power, sympathy, status, emotion; and the skillful game of exchange consists of a complex totality of maneuvers, conscious or unconscious, in order to gain security and to fortify one's self against risks incurred through alliances and rivalry.

Writing about the Andaman Islanders, Radcliffe-Brown states: "The purpose of the exchange is primarily a moral one; to bring about a friendly feeling between the two persons who participate." The best proof of the supra-economic character of these exchanges is that, in the potlatch, one does not hesitate sometime to destroy considerable wealth by breaking a "copper" or throwing it in the sea and that greater prestige results from the destruction of riches than from its distribution; for distribution, although it may be generous, demands a similar act in return. The economic character exists, however, although it is always limited and qualified by the other aspects of the institution of exchange. "It is not simply the possession of riches which brings prestige, it is rather their distribution. One does not gather riches except in order to rise in the social hierarchy. . . . However, even when pigs are exchanged for pigs, and food for food, the transactions do not lose all economic significance for they encourage work and stimulate a need for cooperation."[3]

The idea that a mysterious advantage is attached to the obtainment of commodities or at least certain commodities by means of reciprocal gifts, rather than by production or by individual acquisition is not limited to primitive societies.

In modern society, there are certain kinds of objects which are especially well suited for presents, precisely because of their nonutilitarian qualities. In some Iberian countries these objects can only be found, in all their luxury and diversity, in stores especially set up for this purpose and which are similar

[3]A. B. Deacon, *Malekula . . . A Vanishing People in the New Hebrides,* London, 1934, p. 637.

to the Anglo-Saxon "gift shops." It is hardly necessary to note that these gifts, like invitations (which, though not exclusively, are also free distributions of food and drink) are "returned"; this is an instance in our society of the principle of reciprocity. It is commonly understood in our society that certain goods of a non-essential consumption value, but to which we attach a great psychological aesthetic or sensual value, such as flowers, candies and luxury articles, are obtainable in the form of reciprocal gifts rather than in the form of purchases or individual consumption.

Certain ceremonies and festivals in our society also regulate the periodic return and traditional style of vast operations of exchange. The exchange of presents at Christmas, during one month each year, to which all the social classes apply themselves with a sort of sacred ardor, is nothing else than a gigantic potlatch, which implicates millions of individuals, and at the end of which many family budgets are confronted by lasting disequilibrium. Christmas cards, richly decorated, certainly do not attain the value of the "coppers"; but the refinement of selection, their outstanding designs, their price, the quantity sent or received, give evidence (ritually exhibited on the mantelpiece during the week of celebration), of the recipient's social bonds and the degree of his prestige. We may also mention the subtle techniques which govern the wrapping of the presents and which express in their own way the personal bond between the giver and the receiver: special stickers, paper, ribbon, etc. Through the vanity of gifts, their frequent duplication resulting from the limited range of selection, these exchanges also take the form of a vast and collective destruction of wealth. There are many little facts in this example to remind one that even in our society the destruction of wealth is a way to gain prestige. Isn't it true that the capable merchant knows that a way to attract customers is by advertising that certain high-priced goods must be "sacrificed"? The move is economic but the terminology retains a sense of the sacred tradition.

In the significant sphere of the offering of food, for which banquets, teas, and evening parties are the modern customs, the language itself, e.g., "to give a reception," shows that for us as in Alaska or Oceania, "to receive is to give." One offers dinner to a person whom one wishes to honor, or in order to return a "kindness." The more the social aspect takes precedence over the strictly alimentary, the more emphasis is given to style both of food and of the way in which it is presented: the fine porcelain, the silverware, the embroidered table cloths which ordinarily are carefully put away in the family cabinets and buffets, are a striking counterpart of the ceremonial bowls and spoons of Alaska brought out on similar occasions from painted and decorated chests. Above all, the attitudes towards food are revealing: what the natives of the Northwest coast call "rich food" connotes also among ourselves something else than the mere satisfaction of physiological needs. One does not serve the daily menu when one gives a dinner party. Moreover, if the occasion calls for certain types of food defined by tradition, their apparition alone, through a significant recurrence, calls for shared consumption. A bottle of old wine, a rare liqueur, bothers the conscience of the owner; these are delicacies which one would not buy and consume alone without a vague feeling of guilt. Indeed, the group judges with singular harshness the person who does this. This is reminiscent of the Polynesian ceremonial exchanges, in which goods must as much as possible not be exchanged within the group of paternal relations, but must go to other groups and into other villages. To fail at this duty is called "sori tana"—"to eat from one's own basket." And at the village dances, convention demands that neither of the two local groups consume the food which they have brought but that they exchange their provisions and that each eat the food of the other. The action of the person who, as the woman in the Maori proverb *Kai Kino ana Te Arahe,* would secretly eat the ceremonial food, without offering a part of it, would provoke from his or her relations sentiments which would range, according to circumstances, from irony, mocking and disgust to sentiments of dislike and even rage. It seems that the group confusedly sees in the individual accomplishment of an act which normally requires collective participation a sort of social incest.

But the ritual of exchange does not only take place in the ceremonial meal. Politeness requires that one offer the salt, the butter, the bread, and that one present one's neighbor with a plate before serving oneself. We have often noticed the ceremonial aspect of the meal in the lower-priced restaurants in the south of France; above all in those regions where wine is the main industry, it is surrounded by a sort of mystical respect which makes it "rich food." In those little restaurants where wine is included in the price of the meal each guest finds in front of his plate a modest bottle of a wine more than often very bad. This bottle is similar to that of the person's neighbor, as are the portions of meat and vegetables, which a waiter passes around. However, a peculiar difference of attitude immediately manifests itself in regard to the liquid nourishment and the solid nourishment: the latter serves the needs of the body and the former its luxury, the one serves first of all to feed, the other to honor. Each guest eats, so to speak, for himself. But when it comes to the wine, a new situation arises; if a bottle should be insufficiently filled, its owner would call good-naturedly for the neighbor to testify. And the proprietor would face, not the anger of an individual victim, but a community complaint. Indeed, the wine is a social commodity whereas the *plat du jour* is a personal commodity. The small bottle can hold just one glass, its contents will be poured not in the glass of the owner, but in that of his neighbor. And the latter will make a corresponding gesture of reciprocity.

What has happened? The two bottles are identical in size, their contents similar in quality. Each participant in this revealing scene, when the final count is made, has not received more than if he had consumed his own wine. From an economic point of view, no one has gained and no one has lost. But there is much more in the exchange itself than in the things exchanged.

The situation of two strangers who face each other, less than a yard apart, from two sides of a table in an inexpensive restaurant (to obtain an individual table is a privilege which one must pay for, and which cannot be awarded below a certain price) is commonplace and episodical. However, it is very revealing, because it offers an example, rare in our society (but prevalent in primitive societies) of the formation of a group for which, doubtless because of its temporary character, no ready formula of integration exists. The custom in French society is to ignore persons whose name, occupation and social rank are unknown. But in the little restaurant, such people find themselves placed for two or three half-hours in a fairly intimate relationship, and momentarily united by a similarity of preoccupations. There is conflict, doubtless not very sharp, but real, which is sufficient to create a state of tension between the norm of "privacy" and the fact of community. They feel at the same time alone and together, compelled to the habitual reserve between strangers, while their respective positions in physical space and their relationships to the objects and utensils of the meal, suggest and to a certain degree call for intimacy. These two strangers are exposed for a short period of time to living together. Without doubt not for as long a time nor as intimately as when one shares a sleeping car, or a cabin on a transatlantic crossing, but for this reason also no clear cultural procedure has been established. An almost imperceptible anxiety is likely to arise in the minds of the two guests with the prospect of small disagreements that the meeting could bring forth. When social distance is maintained, even if it is not accompanied by any manifestation of disdain, insolence or aggression, it is in itself a cause of suffering; for such social distance is at variance with the fact that all social contact carries with it an appeal and that this appeal is at the same time a hope for response. Opportunity for escape from this trying yet ephemeral situation is provided by an exchange of wine. It is an affirmation of good grace which dispels the reciprocal uncertainty; it substitutes a social bond for mere physical juxtaposition. But it is also more than that; the partner who had the right to maintain reserve is called upon to give it up; wine offered calls for wine returned, cordiality demands cordiality. The relationship of indifference which has lasted until one of the guests had decided to give it up can never be brought back. From now on it must become a relationship either of cordiality or hostility. There is no possibility of refusing the neighbor's offer of his glass of wine without appearing insulting. Moreover, the acceptance of the offer authorizes another offer, that of conversation: Thus a number of minute social bonds are established by a series of alternating oscillations, in which a right is established in the offering and an obligation in the receiving.

And there is still more. The person who begins the cycle has taken the initiative, and the greater social ease which he has proved becomes an advantage for him. However, the opening always carried with it a risk, namely that the partner will answer the offered libation with a less generous drink, or, on the contrary, that he will prove to be a higher bidder thus forcing the person who offered the wine first to sacrifice a second bottle for the sake of his prestige. We are, therefore, on a microscopic scale, it is true, in the presence of a "total social fact" whose implications are at the same time social, psychological and economic.

This drama, which on the surface seems futile and to which, perhaps, the reader will find that we have awarded a disproportionate importance, seems to us on the contrary to offer material for inexhaustible sociological reflection. We have already pointed out the interest with which we view the non-crystallized forms of social life: the spontaneous aggregations arising from crises, or (as in the example just discussed) simple sub-products of collective life, provide us with vestiges which are still fresh, of very primitive social psychological experiences. In this sense the attitudes of the strangers in the restaurant appear to be an infinitely distant projection, scarcely perceptible but nonetheless recognizable, of a fundamental situation; that in which individuals of primitive tribes find themselves for the first time entering into contact with each other or with strangers. The primitives know only two ways of classifying strangers; strangers are either "good" or "bad." But one must not be misled by a naive translation of the native terms. A "good" group is that to which, without hesitating, one grants hospitality, the one for which one deprives oneself of most precious goods; while the "bad" group is that from which one expects and to which one inflicts, at the first opportunity, suffering or death. With the latter one fights, with the former one exchanges goods.

The general phenomenon of exchange is first of all a total exchange, including food, manufactured objects, as well as those most precious items: women. Doubtlessly we are a long way from the strangers in the restaurant and perhaps it seems startling to suggest that the reluctance of the French peasant to drink his own bottle of wine gives a clue for the explanation of the incest taboo. Indeed, we believe that both phenomena have the same sociological and cultural meaning.

The prohibition of incest is a rule of reciprocity. It means: I will only give up my daughter or my sister if my neighbor will give up his also. The violent reaction of the community towards incest is the reaction of a community wronged. The fact that I can obtain a wife is, in the last analysis, the consequence of the fact that a brother or a father has given up a woman.

In Polynesia Firth distinguishes three spheres of exchange according to the relative mobility of the articles concerned. The first sphere concerns food in its diverse forms; the second, rope and fabrics made of bark; the third, hooks, cables, turmeric cakes and canoes. He adds: "Apart from the three spheres of exchange mentioned a fourth may be recognized in cases where goods of unique quality are handed over. Such for instance was the transfer of women by the man who could not otherwise pay for his canoe. Transfers of land might be put into the same category. Women and land are given in satisfaction of unique obligations. . . ."[4]

It is necessary to anticipate the objection that we are relating two phenomena which are not of the same type; it might be argued that indeed gifts may be regarded even in our own culture as a primitive form of exchange but that this kind of reciprocal interaction has been replaced in our society by exchange for profit except for a few remaining instances such as invitations, celebrations and gifts: that in our society the number of goods that are being transferred according to these archaic patterns represents only a small proportion of the objects of commerce and merchandising, and that reciprocal gifts are merely amusing vestiges which can retain the curiosity of the antiquary; and that it is not possible to say that the prohibition of incest, which is as important in our own society as in any other, has been derived from a type of phenomenon which is abnormal today and of purely anecdotal interest. In other words, we will be accused, as we ourselves have accused Mc'Lennan, Spencer, Avebury and Durkheim, of deriving the function from the survival and the general case from the existence of an exceptional one.

This objection can be answered by distinguishing between two interpretations of the term "archaic." The survival of a custom or of a belief can be accounted for in different ways; the custom or belief may be a vestige, without any other significance than that of an historical residue which has been spared by chance; but it may also continue throughout the centuries to have a specific function which does not differ essentially from the original one. An institution can be archaic because it has lost its reason for existing or on the contrary because this reason for existing is so fundamental that its transformation has been neither possible nor necessary.

Such is the case of exchange. Its function in primitive society is essential because it encompasses at the same time material objects, social values and women, while in our culture the original function of exchange of goods has gradually been reduced in importance as other means of acquisition have developed; reciprocity as the basis of getting a spouse, however, has maintained its fundamental function; for one thing because women are the most precious property, and above all because women are not in the first place a sign of social value, but a natural stimulant; and the stimulant of the

[4] Firth, *op. cit.*, p. 344.

only instinct whose satisfaction can be postponed, the only one consequently, for which, in the act of exchange and through the awareness of reciprocity, the transformation can occur from the stimulant to the sign and, thereby, give way to an institution; this is the fundamental process of transformation from the conditions of nature to cultural life.

The inclusion of women in the number of reciprocal transactions from group to group and from tribe to tribe is such a general custom that a volume would not suffice to enumerate the instances in which it occurs. Let us note first of all that marriage is everywhere considered as a particularly favorable occasion for opening a cycle of exchanges. The "wedding presents" in our society evidently enter again into the group of phenomena which we have studied above.

In Alaska and in British Columbia, the marriage of a girl is necessarily accompanied by a potlatch; to such a point that the Comox aristocrats organize mock-marriage ceremonies, where there is no bride, for the sole purpose of acquiring privileges in the course of the exchange ritual. But the relation which exists between marriage and gifts is not arbitrary; marriage is itself an inherent part of as well as a central motive for the accompanying reciprocal gifts. Not so long ago it was the custom in our society to "ask for" a young girl in marriage; the father of the betrothed woman "gave" his daughter in marriage; in English the phrase is still used, "to give up the bride." And in regard to the woman who takes a lover, it is also said that she "gives herself." The Arabic word, *sadaqa*, signifies the alm, the bride's price, law and tax. In this last case, the meaning of the word can be explained by the custom of wife buying. But marriage through purchase is an institution which is special in form only; in reality it is only a modality of the fundamental system as analyzed by Mauss, according to which, in primitive society and still somewhat in ours, rights, goods and persons circulate within a group according to a continual mechanism of services and counter-services. Malinowski has shown that in the Trobriand Islands, even after marriage, the payment of mapula represents, on the part of the man, a counter-service destined to compensate for the services furnished by the wife in the form of sexual gratifications.

Even marriage through capture does not contradict the law of reciprocity; it is rather one of the possible institutionalized ways of putting it into practice. In Tikopia the abduction of the betrothed woman expresses in a dramatic fashion the obligation of the detaining group to give up the girls. The fact that they are "available" is thus made evident.

It would then be false to say that one exchanges or gives gifts at the same time that one exchanges or gives women. Because the woman herself is nothing else than one of these gifts, she is the supreme gift amongst those that can only be obtained in the form of reciprocal gifts. The first stage of our analysis has been directed towards bringing to light this fundamental characteristic of the gift, represented by the woman in primitive society, and to explain the reasons for it. It should not be suprising then to see that women are included among a number of other reciprocal prestations.

The small nomadic bands of the Nambikwara Indians of western Brazil are in constant fear of each other and avoid each other; but at the same time they desire contact because it is the only way in which they are able to exchange, and thereby obtain articles which they are lacking. There is a bond, a continuity between the hostile relations and the provision of reciprocal presentations: exchanges are peacefully resolved wars, wars are the outcome of unsuccessful transactions. This characteristic is evidenced by the fact that the passing of war into peace or at least of hostility into cordiality operates through the intermediary of ritual gestures: the adversaries feel each other out, and with gestures which still retain something of the attitudes of combat, inspect the necklaces, earrings, bracelets, and feathered ornaments of one another with admiring comments.

And from battle they pass immediately to the gifts; gifts are received, gifts are given, but silently, without bargaining, without complaint, and apparently without linking that which is given to that which is obtained. These are, indeed, reciprocal gifts, not commercial operations. But the relationship may be given yet an additional meaning: two tribes who have thus come to establish lasting cordial relations, can decide in a deliberate manner, to join by setting up an artificial kinship relation between the male members of the two tribes: the relationship of brothers-in-law. According to the matrimonial system of the Nambikwara, the immediate consequence of this innovation is that all the children of one group become the potential spouses of the children of the other group and vice-versa; thus a continuous transition exists from war to ex-

change and from exchange to intermarriage; and the exchange of betrothed women is merely the termination of an
uninterrupted process of reciprocal gifts, which brings about
the transition from hostility to alliance, from anxiety to confidence and from fear to friendship.

Some Social Functions of Laughter[1]

by
Rose Laub Coser

Laughter is a peculiarly human trait. Animals do not laugh—*vide* the interesting German idiom *tierischer Ernst* (animal earnestness). No wonder that this distinctively human activity has preoccupied philosophers ever since antiquity and that psychology and especially psychoanalysis, following Freud's lead, have devoted much attention to its interpretation.[2] Yet there have been few attempts at a sociological analysis of humor. The literature contains mainly discussions of specific types of humor in some social settings[3] but hardly any generalizations about the social functions of humor.[4] The relative neglect of humor and laughter on the part of sociologists is the more suprising since, as many a philosopher has remarked, laughter is a peculiarly social activity.

Laughter, like all other expressions of emotions, as well as most other physiological reactions, is regulated by society. It is expected to remain under control: 'mad laughter', 'hysterical laughter', are disapproved. This is to say that laughter is socially patterned, like yawning, for example; but it is not so much that which makes laughter similar to other physiological reactions but rather what makes it dissimilar from them that requires sociological inquiry.

Laughter, unlike many other human activities, occurs—or is expected to occur—only within patterns of interaction.

Reprinted from *Human Relations,* Vol.12, No.2, pp. 171–182, with permission of Plenum Publishing Corporation and the author.

[1]Revised version of a paper read at the meetings of the Eastern Sociological Society, New York, March 1956. I am indebted to Warren Bennis for a critical reading of this paper.

[2]See the bibliographical article by J. C. Flügel (12).

[3]Of outstanding importance is, of course, Radcliffe-Brown's work (27). Other anthropologists, among them Margaret Mead and Gregory Bateson (3), have also dealt with joking relationships and comic representations. Some sociological writings have also appeared on the subject (2, 7, 8, 22, 24).

[4]On some social functions of humor, see the writing of Blau (6), Burns (9), and Fox (14).

This seemingly most spontaneous means of individual release
and self-expression is not expected to be used by a person
who is alone. The man who laughs or chuckles to himself is
looked at as 'probably crazy'. He is granted an exemption
from this stigma only if it can be observed that he responds
to the symbolic stimulus of an interactive pattern, as when he
reads a comic book or responds to a comic incident on a
movie screen.[5] Laughter, like language, is supposed to function within a communicative relationship and the man who
laughs to himself, like the man who talks to himself or the
man who hoards his goods or his daughters, is considered an
asocial man. He who laughs in isolation calls forth a social
disapproval that may be compared to the disapproval that
greets the miser or the incestuous father. Laughter must be
shared; it is socially defined as a prime part of the interactive
process, of the give and take of social life. As Francis Jeanson has remarked: 'Even your joys must be quoted on the
market, you are not allowed a satisfaction which is not listed
on the exchange—and if you refrain from saying why you
laugh and if the reason is not apparent, you will soon be told
that "you laugh like an idiot" [that is, to go back to the root
sense of the term, like a peculiar, a dis-sociated man]'. Jeanson continues: 'Your laughter is supposed only to express the
reactions of the "collective consciousness": in any other case
it is absurd to the extent that it signifies maladaptation' (20,
p. 152).

To laugh in the company of others presupposes a minimum of common 'definition of the situation'. Those who refuse to join in common laughter are frowned upon, they are
'bad sports'; on the other hand, if an invitation to laugh is not
accepted by the group, the incipient humorist feels 'out of
place'. In laughter one must share and share alike.

To laugh, or to occasion laughter through humor and wit,
is to invite those present to come close. Laughter and humor
are indeed like an invitation, be it an invitation for dinner, or
an invitation to start a conversation: it aims at decreasing social distance. What Levi-Strauss has said about the social
meaning of an exchange of table wine among strangers seated
at the same table in a French restaurant applies to the uses of
humor: 'The partner who had the right to maintain reserve is

[5]Even in the marginal case of a person laughing because he sees a
stranger stumble, the laughter establishes an interactive relationship
with a symbolic other in that he rejoices over his own good fortune in
comparison with the victim.

called upon to give it up; . . . cordiality demands cordiality. . . . There is no possibility of refusing the neighbor's offer . . . without appearing insulting. Moreover, the acceptance of the offer authorizes another offer, that of conversation. Thus a number of minute social bonds are established in the offering and an obligation in the receiving. And there is still more. The person who begins the cycle has taken the initiative, and the greater social ease which he has proved becomes an advantage for him. However, the opening always carries with it a risk, namely that the partner will answer the offered libation with a less generous drink . . .' (23, pp. 84–94).

Laughter always involves an element of reciprocity. This is why it would be impossible to analyse the functions of laughter without discussing humor, that is without discussing what elicits laughter. Thus Bergson, who entitles his famous essay *Laughter,* proceeds to analyse the comic. Humor and laughter are instrinsically linked because a situation is defined as humorous by the laughing response that it elicits. 'The comic,' writes Baudelaire 'the power of laughter, lies in the man who laughs, not in the object of laughter' (4, p. 370).

Hence, humor and laughter can be understood only in terms of the common concerns of the participants. 'To understand laughter', writes Bergson, 'we must put it back into its natural environment, which is society, and above all must we determine that utility of its function which is a social one . . . Laughter must answer to certain requirements of life in common. It must have *social* signification' (5, pp. 8–9; emphasis in the original).

From what has been said so far it would appear that different degrees or frequencies of laughter, and different types of humor, prevail in different types of group structure. It is well known that different nationalities as well as ethnic groups have their peculiar types of humor. There is Jewish humor, British humor, Irish humor. Certain types of humor are peculiar to particular status positions: there is the humor of the underdog as well as the humor of the top dog. Specific types of humor flourish under different political conditions: there is totalitarian humor as there is democratic humor.

A social group or subgroup, as it is differentially located within the social structure, produces and sanctions variant forms of humor. And since, within particular groups, structures of authority and systems of role allocation differ, the specific types of interaction that accompany such variations will also encourage specific types of humorous interaction. The present paper will explore in detail some of the social mechanisms of humor in one subgroup of a complex organization: the ward patients of a general hospital.

The writer has been engaged recently in a study of the social structure of a hospital ward. Although this study was primarily concerned with other problems, it has been possible to make a series of observations on the use of humor and jocular talk within this setting which lend themselves to the formulation of some hypotheses. The interpretations presented here are meant as suggestions for stimulating further research.

This report will be limited to jocular talk among patients, i.e. among peers, and will not discuss any humor between patients and staff; it has to be remembered that humor across status lines may well take other forms and have other functions than humor among status equals.

During daily observations in the ward for a period of three months, the researcher was impressed by the jocular tone of conversation among patients. Although some patients were more gifted than others in highlighting comic elements of their experiences, most of them, when they were together in the sitting-room or when they were conversing in the ward, tended to fall into jocular conversation. Much of their jocular talk consisted of jocular griping. The humorous intent was discernible in the tone of voice, in facial expression, but above all in the laughing responses that it elicited. If much of what will be quoted will not appear humorous to the reader, this will be evidence for the main point of this paper, namely that humor is an expression of the collective experience of the participants, and receives response only from those who share common concerns.

Jocular talk and laughter of hospital patients can be understood in reference to three main characteristics: anxiety about self, submission to a rigid authority structure, and, related to this, adjustment to rigid routine.

Hospital patients are likely to be subject to a high degree of insecurity and generalized anxiety. As Michael M. Davis has stated in his introduction to R. Rorem's book, to the sick person '. . . the hospital is a battlefield between life and death, the focus of intense anxieties and hopes' (28, p. vii). The very fact of hospitalization is an indication that there is some measure of danger. Patients report:

'I'm not afraid of being alone in the hospital, but it's just the uncertainty.'

'I was very apprehensive. I was frightened to death. I didn't know what to expect.'

'[A good doctor is] a good speaker to you who explains you very good, explains everything what happens to you and what's going to happen, that's what I call a good doctor.'

The insecurity of patients not only derives from their physical condition but is enhanced by the peculiar type of authority relation to which they are submitted. A patient's loss of control over his body is matched by his loss of control over his physical environment and over his own actions. Everything is planned for him—his meals, his intake of medication, etc. Even his body temperature is no longer his concern, but that of nurses who insist on removing the thermometer immediately after its use. The total control by hospital staff is justified in terms of a sick person's helplessness and lack of competence (25, pp. 439–46).

To patients the authority of the hospital staff seems to be unlimited. Whereas in the society at large people are under the authority of one set of persons for a limited amount of time, say from nine till five, a patient has to submit to the authority of hospital staff twenty-four hours a day. He is under continuous supervision and his full day is scheduled for him.[6]

Authority relations in the hospital are symbolized by the sharp contrast in dress: while patients are deprived of most body symbols—not only of clothes but also of other intimate belongings such as jewelry—which constitutes a loss of identity of the social self, the staff, nurses as well as doctors, dispose of elaborate body extensions for the sake of status recognition and role symbolization.

Related to authority relations is the strict routine of the hospital. It would seem that hardly anywhere is the term 'routinized emergency', which Everett C. Hughes has coined (19), more applicable than to the hospital. 'In many occupa-

[6]For a brilliant statement of these authority relations and of the split between staff and patients, see Erving Goffman's work on 'Total Institutions' (17). For a formulation of the problem of patients' deprivation of decision-making, see the remarks by Leo W. Simmons and Harold G. Wolff (29, pp. 176–87).

tions', says Hughes, 'the workers or practitioners deal routinely with what are emergencies to the people who receive the services.' For the staff the term points to the functional importance of discipline in emergency situations. But since the definitions of 'emergency' and 'routine' emerge from the staff,[7] a patient is soon impressed with the fact that he is a 'routine case', and senses that many of the hospital's rules and regulations may be extrinsic to his own treatment, that they serve to maintain the organization as a going concern.

The patient's need of security, their low position in the hospital hierarchy, and the need to preserve their moral self against the pressure of physical routine—these are three main aspects of the status of patients in a hospital. Though it is true that these three factors are not peculiar to hospitals only but may be variously distributed in society, they seem to occur simultaneously and perhaps in a more dramatic way in organizations set up to deal routinely with the emergency of physical threat.

The following example, a patient's jocular report of a significant event in the ward, will illustrate the combination of the three themes:

> 'Did you hear what happened yesterday? I'm telling ye, it was a riot, the funniest thing. There were two Mrs. Broseman admitted here yesterday with the identical first name. So, Mrs. Broseman from our ward [i.e. medical] was sitting here with us, and up comes Dr B. [from the surgical ward] and asks for Mrs. Ann Broseman. Out she goes. When she walks to the left to the medical ward, he says. "No, this way, please," and takes her to the other side to give her a physical. In the meantime, the nurses in the medical ward were looking for Mrs. Broseman. They were all excited and worried because they are responsible for the patients, you know. Well, finally they got her. She was raving mad and red as a beet. She came here for high blood-pressure in the first place. Well, it must have gone sky-high after that!'

[7] Cf. '. . . The institutional plant and name come to be identified by both staff and inmates as somehow belonging to staff, so that when either grouping refers to the views of interests of the "institution", by implication they are referring to the views and concerns of the staff' (17, p. 7).

The patient who reported the incident reinterpreted it in such a way that it became stripped of its threatening aspects. This recalls Freud's observation that humor serves as a means of allaying anxiety: 'The principal thing is the intention which humor fulfils. Its meaning is: "Look here! This is all this seemingly dangerous world amounts to. Child's play, the very thing to jest about"' (15, p. 220). The humorous reporter modified reality by denying the objective justification of the fears common to all, namely that some confusion in administering medication might occur. By making the story sound funny and by implicitly contrasting, through ridicule, the plight of the victim to the good luck of those present, this patient implied that such fears are not grounded in reality, that even if a confusion occurs it is simply 'the very thing to jest about'.[8]

Moreover, the jocular wording of the report provided an opportunity for talker and listeners to get back at the nurses.[9] Note that the nurses and not the patients were 'excited and worried'. Such a reversal of roles is a frequent element in comic representations, as Bergson has shown.[10] This type of humor is referred to by Freud as 'tendency wit' which 'is used with special preference as a weapon of attack or criticism of superiors who claim to be in authority' (16, p. 699).

The main 'funny' element of the story, however, consists in the confusion resulting from a mechanical way of dealing with individual persons. Bergson speaks of the comic element contained in the 'complete automatism . . . in the official, for instance, who performs his duty like a mere machine.' The story illustrates his point, that an incident is comic 'that calls

[8]On the safety-producing functions of humor, see also the writings of Donald Hayworth (18) and Renée Fox (14).

[9]This is a frequent device. It is a type of 'rebellion' that promises immunity from retaliation by the 'powerful', which is especially important in a dependency situation. To give one other example: Patient at the eve of a repeated operation, taking bobby pins out of her hair: 'I may as well do this now. They'd do that to me tomorrow anyhow. This keeps me one step ahead of the nurses.' The four patients present laugh heartily.

[10]Bergson has stressed the fact that reversal of roles is a frequent element in comedies (5, p. 95). The psychoanalyst Ludwig Jekels (21) remarks that whereas in tragedies the theme is usually the hostility of the son against the father, in comedies the theme is reversed: the father is being deprived of his 'fatherly' attributes and invested with the weaknesses of the son. Gregory Bateson (3) writes about a reversal of roles in the ceremonials of primitive tribes, through buffoonery for the man and magnificent ceremony for the woman, in a society which glorifies masculinity in everyday life and assigns a passive role to women.

our attention to the physical in a person when it is the moral side that is concerned' (5, pp. 90–1).

This type of humor, then, serves as a means of warding off danger; as a means of rebellion against authority; and as a relief from mechanical routine. It is important to note that these themes are conveyed to persons who have the same worries and anxieties and that the humorist invites the listeners to join with her in a 'triumph of invincibility'.

The very process of communication, moreover, consists in the jocular talk through which the speaker conveys information: the other patients are told, in this story, that the nurses protect patients because 'they are responsible, you know', and 'they finally got her'. Again, there is reassurance that there is no real danger; this time the security comes, according to the report, from the social organization of the hospital. Thus the jocular report is, as Donald Hayworth has pointed out, a 'communication to other members in the group that they may relax with safety' (18).

In her jocular report, this patient *taught* the other patients, through jocular interaction with them rather than through a moralizing speech, to adapt to hospital society. Thus, in addition to its *safety-producing* functions, jocular talk serves the *socialization* of patients. This is even more obvious in cases where the use of humor permits the transformation of individual complaints into collective pleasure.

The need to abstain from complaining was well expressed by one patient:

'I never complain. What good would it be anyhow? No use complainen . . . Got to take things as they are. Take life as it is. Some people magnify things. Others make them smaller. That's the better way.'

This patient stated that she intentionally 'makes things smaller', and indeed in her jocular talk with other patients she fashioned reality herself, *for* herself and *for* the other patients as well. Conversations like the following are rather typical for the ward:

'I couldn't sleep all night. The lady next to me had a nightmare and was shrieking. Across the hall there was one who had gotten a needle and she yelled that the ceiling came down, I'm telling ye. So, I walked out to have a smoke and there in the television room there was the family of one who had died across the hall. They were crying and lamenting. I'll be glad to get home to get some rest. If I stay here longer, I'm going to get sick.'

Patients laugh, nod, exclaim: 'Yeah, that's how it is.' Another patient joins in: 'Yeah, just like me, I came in as a lion and am going out as a lamb. I came in for three days, have been here for two weeks now.'

Third patient: 'Sure you can't get no rest. At 6 o'clock they wake you up. So I thought I'll sleep after breakfast. I dozed off, and there I hear the doctor: "Are you sleeping?" Of course I said, "Not anymore." I went to sleep after they left, so the nurse comes up with a pill.'
Everybody laughs.

In this conversation there are some jokes that have become standard in hospital life: that in the hospital you get sick, that you cannot get any rest; the story of the nurse who wakes you up to give you a sleeping pill is not a new one. These jokes are part of the hospital folklore. They all imply rebellion against the routine,[11] against the 'mechanical encrusted upon the living', and against the staff who on the basis of their authority may intrude any time they wish on the privacy of the patient. It is to be noted also that shrieking patients and laments over death are stripped of their threatening quality.

Again, the content of the jocular talk consists in the three themes that were stated at the start. But there is more: the mechanism consists in transforming a personal experience into one that can be shared by all. *The jocular gripe is the collective expression of an individual complaint.*

Peter Blau in his recent *Dynamics of Bureaucracy*, observes that complaints are nearly always made to a single person whereas jokes are often told to a group (6, p. 92). What Blau says about jokes applies also to the jocular gripe. What is more, the jocular gripe performs the functions of both complaint and joke, but differs from both.

[11]The following remarks of patients provide additional illustration of this type of jocular talk: 'All night patients in, patients out, nurses running around. At home a sick man can get some rest.' Or again: Patient A, opening the newspaper: 'They shot the President of Panama.' Patient B: 'They go on shooting these days just like they shoot needles into you. It's true, all they do is shoot needles into you, a dime a dozen.'

A patient told the observer: 'Dinner was no good, what I cook is better.' Ten minutes later, in the sitting-room, she told the other patients:

> 'Those hamburgers today were as hard as rocks, if I'd bounced them against the wall they'd come right back' (breaks out in laughter about her own good joke and other patients join in).

The contrast between these two negative statements is remarkable.

(i) The patient talked about herself when she was alone with the observer, but when several patients were present she chose to transform her personal experience into a general one. Her humorous image let all participate imaginatively in the appraisal of the meat's quality, while in her remark to the observer she had pointed to her own superior cooking ability as a basis for judgement.

(ii) The image the patient used permitted all to join in liberating laughter. It is not necessary here to labor what has become obvious since Freud's writing on the subject, namely that this feeling of liberation consists in a release of tension and aggression (16, pp. 733 ff.). But the comparison between the complaint and the jocular gripe can be carried a step further by drawing upon one other insight by Freud in his analysis of humor: 'What is fine about [humor] is the ego's victorious assertion of its own invulnerability' (15, p. 217). In the complaint the patient admits his vulnerability; in the jocular gripe, as in humor generally, he overcomes it and allows his listeners to participate in his triumph over weakness. In addition to the humorist's triumph over his own weakness—the peculiar quality of gallows humor—there is here the added gratification in the *collective* character of the triumph.

The jocular gripe is peculiarly fit as a mechanism of adaptation to the hospital for it helps patients to regain their identity through collective triumph over their weakness and at the same time to release their grudges in 'substitute complaints'.

(iii) The liberating effect of joined laughter consists also in the consensus that it brings about in a brief span of time.[12] Stanton and Schwartz point out that real consensus brings with it an element of delight about its achievement (31, p. 196). They join Bergson, who saw that the liberating amuse-

---

[12] Cf. 'The joke is a shortcut to consensus' (9, p. 657).

ment indicates a feeling that 'only we' know what it means. It strengthens the boundaries between the group of laughters and the outsiders (5, p. 6), between the patients and those who are in authority, doctors and nurses. One only has to think of the annoyance that overcomes us sometimes when we hear people laugh in the next room, a feeling of being 'left out.' Thus not only do the patients achieve consensus, but through this consensus nurses and doctors, who otherwise have access to the most intimate parts of the patients' bodies, are denied access.

(iv) Jokes and jocular talk are the fare of sociability. As a patient said, 'We are full of jokes. My sister asked me, "How do you feel?" I said, "I'm enjoying myself; we're chatting around; it's a pleasure".' Personal complaints are tabooed on the ward because, as Simmel remarked, 'the purely and deeply personal traits of one's life, character, mood and fate must . . . be eliminated as factors in sociability. It is tactless . . . to display merely personal moods of depression, excitement, despondency—in brief, the light and darkness of one's most intimate life.' When Simmel goes on to say that in sociability 'each individual ought to have as much satisfaction . . . as is compatible with [the] satisfaction on the part of all others' (29, pp. 46–7), he seems to mean that each participant must present his piece of conversation in such a manner that it becomes meaningful to all other participants.

The patient who complains considers himself more important than others and thereby violates the 'democratic structure of sociability' of which Simmel speaks. Corroborative evidence comes from a patient who said: 'There's always one who's crabbing. He thinks he's better than others, but he isn't more than a patient. A patient is a patient in the hospital . . . Even when you're a doctor and you're a patient, you're just another patient.'

Unlike the complainer, the patient who invites others to laugh with him creates or strengthens the feeling of equality in the participants. Hence jocular griping brings about a social relationship in its simplest and purest form: that of reciprocity. There are many different ways of saying the same thing, depending on the social situation; one only has to consider the difference in implication between 'I cannot sleep' and 'a hospital is no place to rest'. Although both phrases denote the same experience, the first is, in Piaget's terms, an egocentric statement that does not take account of the point of view of the other person (26).

The jocular gripe differs not only from the complaint but to some extent from the joke also. Like all jocular talk, it is more akin to humor in that it contributes more than the pure joke to the reinterpretation of events and to the solidarity of the participants. Fowler's differential definition may serve well here: whereas the joke has its comic quality in the sur-prise element of the punch line and makes a demand upon the intelligence of the listener, the humor contained in jocular talk is based on observation of actual events and relies on the sympathy of the listener (13, p. 241). Unlike the pure joke, jocular talk, especially the jocular gripe, is based on shared experience; it unites the group by allowing it to reinterpret to-gether an experience that previously was individual to each. Although, like the joke, it permits all to join in laughter which in itself strengthens social cohesion, it cannot be resorted to in the complete absense of social cohesion for it presupposes a common experience between speaker and listener that is the basis of the sympathy that it elicits. A patient's different ac-counts of the same experience—one to those who are 'in the know' and another one to a newcomer—will make this clear:

> Patient, to a group of women in the sitting-room, all of whom had been in the ward for several days, at least, and who were griping about the commotion on the ward: 'They never let you sleep here. One thing you can't get is sleep. At 6 o'clock it's temperature, at 6:30 it's blood pressure, at 7 it's washing and at 7:30 it's breakfast, and so it goes all day. They never leave you alone. Not even right after my operation. Four nurses would stand around me and come up all the time asking, "Do you feel all right?" "Do you have any pain?" "Do you want a pill?" "Do you want some water?" when all you want is sleep.'
> Other patients nodded, smiled, and laughed.

A little later that same afternoon, the same patient sat in the sitting-room again, and also present was a newcomer, ad-mitted a few hours previously.

> Newcomer: 'I wonder what they're going to do to me.'
> Patient: 'They're really nice here, you know. Like af-ter my operation, four nurses were standing around me asking if I wanted something and they kept coming asking if I was in pain or was there anything I wanted. I

didn't want anything, but it felt good just the same, to know they care. You don't have to worry around here.'

The newcomer might have been more perturbed than relieved had she learned that 'they never leave you alone', for she could not have interpreted this patient's gripe in the same way as the initiated. To participate in jocular talk one has to have overcome one's worst fears and be somewhat detached, and what is more, participation in jocular talk presupposes some common experiences about which consensus is sought. Jocular talk and especially jocular griping is not being shared with a stranger.

In summary: unlike the joke which calls for a listener, the jocular gripe calls for a participant. It transforms a personal experience into a collective one; by generalizing it and making it the property of all, the individual sufferer is 'dispossessed' of his own suffering. This type of behavior stresses the equality of all patients within a social structure otherwise characterized by its rigid hierarchy; it brings about consensus and strengthens group identification among persons whose relationships are only transitory.

The different accounts that a patient gave about her experience with nurses after her operation raises the problem of the role of the jocular griper.

Though it is obvious that in her serious reassurance of the newcomer the 'veteran' patient had acted as an agent of socialization, she acted in a similar role when talking in jocular fashion to the initiated. There is reason to believe that this patient enjoyed the care and reassurance of the nurses when she woke up after the operation, and that she somehow 'put up an act' in her jocular criticism of hospital routine. There is, indeed, a performance quality in jocular talk. In Flügel's words, 'at least one of the most important functions [of laughter] is to attract the attention of our fellow beings and to elicit an appropriate reaction from them' (12, p. 730). Just as in an artistic creation,[13] there is a make-believe element: the term 'make-believe' expresses well the bond that the act creates between speaker and listener (1, p. 153). Moreover, as Freud, Baldwin, and others have suggested, make-believe gives a sense of exaggerated self.

The self-aggrandizement of the speaker, far from being egocentric, is a means of establishing a bond with his audi-

[13]Cf. 'The funny story is an artistic thing even as is the novel, the movie or the drama . . .' (18, p. 379).

ence. When the patient was griping in humorous fashion
about the nurses' busyness around her, she did not merely
overcome her own fear and wretchedness, which must have
overwhelmed her when waking up from the operation, and
she did not only oppose the institutionalized, routinized care
that she was given. She also exaggerated her own self with regard to the other persons in the audience. Not only did she
make an assertion of invulnerability, but she adopted toward
her listeners, as Freud remarked, 'the attitude of an adult
towards a child, recognizing and smiling at the triviality of
the interests and sufferings which seem to the child so big.
Thus the humorist acquires his superiority by assuming the
role of the grown-up . . . while he reduces the other people
to the position of children' (15, p. 218).

It is to a large extent through jocular griping that a patient
assumes the role of a socializing agent with respect to other
patients. Bergson's remark, 'the humorist is a disguised moralist' (5, p. 28), is appropriate here. In her account of her waking after the operation, this patient acted as a socializing
agent in two ways. With the newcomer she manifestly took
the role of adult toward a child; with the initiated she
concealed her socializing role in a performance that had, at
the same time, an 'equalizing' function in bringing about collective pleasure and elation in consensus about common experiences.

So far some functions of jocular talk for the participants
have been considered as well as the role of the jocular griper.
It will now be seen that jocular griping performs integrative
functions for the social structure of the ward.

The tendency to reduce complaints through the taboo enforced by the patients themselves and through their substitution by jocular griping, helps to shape the behavior of
patients according to the expectations of doctors and nurses,
and is thus an integrating element among these three groups
in the ward. The patients themselves, by teaching and helping
each other to suppress complaints through laughter, help to
enforce the norms of the hospital community. Through laughter, 'we internalize a community attitude toward the self. We
learn in great laughter that it is possible to love those we
laugh at, as well as those we laugh with' (11, p. 54).

Moreover, by referring in jocular fashion to incidents that
ordinarily would call forth complaints, the patients effect
what Bergson calls a 'corrective for an imperfection' (5,
p. 87). The undesirable situation is being remedied, in the

minds of those who are exposed to it, through its humorous interpretation. The patients themselves, by bringing about a change in the definition of the situation, transform the undesirable into the harmless, the frightening into amusement, and thereby make the hospital ward acceptable, *as it is*.

This points to a possible dysfunctional consequence of humor: by effecting a 'corrective for an imperfection' only in the *perception* of the patients, an unsatisfactory situation may remain unaltered and continue to be a source of concern.[14] The early waking of patients is one example that stands for many.

Humor is a 'safety-valve', i.e. it provides institutionalized outlets for hostilities and for discontent ordinarily suppressed by the group. Thus, as Lewis A. Coser has remarked, it reduces the 'pressure for modifying the system to meet changing conditions'. 'Wit may not bring about a change in the relations between one person and another, especially if the target of the aggressive wit is not aware of the source and intention of the witticism . . . [Wit] may afford expression to the weaker member without changing the terms of the relationship' (10, pp. 48 and 43 respectively).

In conclusion: humor allows the participants, in a brief span of time and with a minimum of effort, mutually to reinterpret their experiences, to entertain, reassure, and communicate; to convey their interest in one another, to pull the group together by transforming what is individual into collective experience, and to strengthen the social structure within which the group functions. Whereas Freud has pointed to the *psychic economy* that humor makes possible for the individual (15, 16),[15] the contribution it makes to *social economy* should be stressed—a contribution that should not be underestimated in groups whose membership is continuously changing, and especially in the transient little subgroups that are formed for short spans of time each day in wards and sitting-rooms. In such a shifting and threatening milieu, a story well told, which, in a few minutes, entertains, reassures, conveys information, releases tension, and draws people more closely together, may have more to contribute than carefully planned lectures and discussions toward the security of the frightened sick.

[14] Cf. '[Humor] transforms reality without any efficacious material intervention and even makes such intervention unnecessary. In this respect the social function of laughter in modern societies is comparable to that of magic in pre-literate societies' (32, p. 166).

[15] On this point, see also Victoroff's work (32, Ch. V).

REFERENCES

1. Baldwin, James. *Mental Development*. New York: The Macmillan Co., p. 153, 1897.

2. Barron, Milton L. 'A Content Analysis of Intergroup Humor.' *Amer. Sociol. Rev.*, Vol. XV, pp. 88–94, 1950.

3. Bateson, Gregory. *Naven*. 1936.

4. Baudelaire, Charles. 'De l'essence du rire.' In *Curiosités Esthétiques*, Paris: Calmann-Levy, II, 1884.

5. Bergson, Henri. *Laughter*. London: Macmillan & Co., 1911.

6. Bleau, Peter. *Dynamics of Bureaucracy*. Chicago: University of Chicago Press, 1955.

7. Bradney, Pamela. 'The Joking Relationship in Industry.' *Hum. Rela.*, Vol. X, pp. 179–87, 1957.

8. Burma, John H. 'Humor as a Technique in Race Conflict.' *Amer. Sociol. Rev.*, Vol XI, pp. 710–15, 1946.

9. Burns, Tom. 'Friends, Enemies and Polite Fiction.' *Amer. Sociol. Rev.*, Vol. XVIII, pp. 654–62, 1953.

10. Coser, Lewis A. *The Functions of Social Conflict*. Glencoe, Ill.: The Free Press, 1956.

11. Duncan, Hugh Dalziel. *Language and Literature in Society*. Chicago: University of Chicago Press, 1953.

12. Flügel, J. C. 'Humor and Laughter.' In Gardner Lindzey (Ed.). *Handbook of Social Psychology*. Cambridge, Mass.: Addison-Wesley, Vol. II, pp. 709–34, 1954.

13. Fowler. *A Dictionary of Modern English Usage*. Oxford: Clarendon Press, 1952.

14. Fox, Renée. *Ward F-Second and The Research Physician*. Unpubl. Ph.D. Dissertation. Harvard University, 1953.

15. Freud, Sigmund. 'Humor.' in *Collected Papers*. London: Hogarth Press, pp. 215–21, 1950.

16. Freud, Sigmund. *Wit and Its Relation to the Unconscious*. New York: Moffat Yard, 1916.

17. Goffman, Erving. *On the Characteristics of Total Institutions*. To appear in the Proceedings of the Symposium on Preventive and Social Psychiatry, Walter Reed Army Institute of Research, Washington, D.C., 15–17 April, 1957 (Mimeo.).

18. Hayworth, Donald. 'The Origin and Function of Laughter.' *Psychol. Rev.*, Vol. XXXV, pp. 367–84, 1928.

19. Hughes, Everett C. 'Work and Self.' In John H. Rohrer and Muzafer Sherif (Eds.), *Social Psychology at the Crossroads*. New York: Harper, pp. 313–23, 1951.

20. Jeanson, Francis. *Signification humaine du rire*. Paris: Editions du Seuil, 1950.

21. Jekels, Ludwig, 'Zur Psychologie der Komoedie.' A. J. Storfer

(Ed.), *Almanach des Internationalen Psychoanalytischen Verlags.* pp. 190–8, 1927.

22. Klapp, Orrin E. 'The Fool as a Social Type.' *Amer. J. Sociol.*, Vol. LIV, pp. 135–41, 1948, and Vol. LV, pp. 157–62, 1949.

23. Levi-Strauss, Claude. 'The Principle of Reciprocity.' In Lewis A. Coser and Bernard Rosenberg (Eds.), *Sociological Theory.* New York: The Macmillan Co., pp. 84–94, 1957.

24. Obrdlik, Antonin J. 'Gallow's Humor—A Sociological Phenomenon.' *Amer. J. Sociol.*, Vol. XXXXVII, pp. 709–16, 1942.

25. Parsons, Talcott. *The Social System.* Glencoe, Ill.: The Free Press, 1951; London: Tavistock Publications, 1952.

26. Piaget, Jean. *The Moral Judgment of the Child.* Glencoe, Ill.: The Free Press, 1948.

27. Radcliffe-Brown, A. R. 'On Joking Relationships' and 'A Further Note on Joking Relationships'. In *Structure and Function in Primitive Society.* Glencoe, Ill.: The Free Press, Chapters IV and V, 1952.

28. Rorem, C. Rufus. *The Public's Investment in Hospitals.* Chicago: University of Chicago Press, 1930.

29. Simmel, Georg. *The Sociology of Georg Simmel.* Trans. Kurt H. Wolff. Glencoe, Ill.: The Free Press, 1950.

30. Simmons, Leo W., and Wolff, Harold G. *Social Science in Medicine.* New York: Russel Sage Foundations, 1954.

31. Stanton, Alfred H., and Schwartz, Morris S. *The Mental Hospital.* New York: Basic Books, 1954; London: Tavistock Publications.

32. Victoroff, D. *Le rire et le risible.* Paris: Presses Universitaires de France. 1953.

On Cooling the Mark Out:
Some Aspects of Adaptation to Failure

by
Erving Goffman

In cases of criminal fraud, victims find they must suddenly
adapt themselves to the loss of sources of security and status
which they had taken for granted. A consideration of this
adaptation to loss can lead us to an understanding of some
relations in our society between involvements and the selves
that are involved.

In the argot of the criminal world, the term "mark" refers
to any individual who is a victim or prospective victim of
certain forms of planned illegal exploitation. The mark is the
sucker—the person who is taken in. An instance of the operation of any particular racket, taken through the full cycle of
its steps or phases, is sometimes called a play. The persons
who operate the racket and "take" the mark are occasionally
called operators.

The confidence game—the con, as its practitioners call
it—is a way of obtaining money under false pretenses by the
exercise of fraud and deceit. The con differs from politer
forms of financial deceit in important ways. The con is practiced on private persons by talented actors who methodically
and regularly build up informal social relationships just for
the purpose of abusing them; white-collar crime is practiced
on organizations by persons who learn to abuse positions of
trust which they once filled faithfully. The one exploits poise;
the other, position. Further, a con man is someone who accepts a social role in the underworld community; he is part of
a brotherhood whose members make no pretense to one an-

Reprinted by special permission of the William Alanson White Psychiatric Foundation, Inc., from *Psychiatry*, Vol.15, 1952, pp. 451–63,
copyright © 1952 by the William Alanson White Psychiatric Foundation,
Inc.

other of being "legit." A white-collar criminal, on the other hand, has no colleagues, although he may have an associate with whom he plans his crime and a wife to whom he confesses it.

The con is said to be a good racket in the United States only because most Americans are willing, nay eager, to make easy money, and will engage in action that is less than legal in order to do so. The typical play has typical phases. The potential sucker is first spotted, and one member of the working team (called the outside man, steerer, or roper) arranges to make social contact with him. The confidence of the mark is won, and he is given an opportunity to invest his money in a gambling venture which he understands to have been fixed in his favor. The venture, of course, is fixed, but not in his favor. The mark is permitted to win some and then persuaded to invest more. There is an "accident" or "mistake," and the mark loses his total investment. The operators then depart in a ceremony that is called the blowoff or sting. They leave the mark but take his money. The mark is expected to go on his way, a little wiser and a lot poorer.

Sometimes, however, a mark is not quite prepared to accept his loss as a gain in experience and to say and do nothing about his venture. He may feel moved to complain to the police or to chase after the operators. In the terminology of the trade, the mark may squawk, beef, or come through. From the operators' point of view, this kind of behavior is bad for business. It gives the members of the mob a bad reputation with such police as have not yet been fixed and with marks who have not yet been taken. In order to avoid this adverse publicity, an additional phase is sometimes added at the end of the play. It is called cooling the mark out. After the blowoff has occurred, one of the operators stays with the mark and makes an effort to keep the anger of the mark within manageable and sensible proportions. The operator stays behind his team-mates in the capacity of what might be called a cooler and exercises upon the mark the art of consolation. An attempt is made to define the situation for the mark in a way that makes it easy for him to accept the inevitable and quietly go home. The mark is given instruction in the philosophy of taking a loss.

When we call to mind the image of a mark who has just been separated from his money, we sometimes attempt to account for the greatness of his anger by the greatness of his financial loss. This is a narrow view. In many cases, especially in America, the mark's image of himself is built up on the belief that he is a pretty shrewd person when it comes to making deals and that he is not the sort of person who is taken in by anything. The mark's readiness to participate in a sure thing is based on more than avarice; it is based on a feeling that he will now be able to prove to himself that he is the sort of person who can "turn a fast buck." For many, this capacity for high finance comes near to being a sign of masculinity and a test of fulfilling the male role.

It is well known that persons protect themselves with all kinds of rationalizations when they have a buried image of themselves which the facts of their status do not support. A person may tell himself many things; that he has not been given a fair chance; that he is not really interested in becoming something else; that the time for showing his mettle has not yet come; that the usual means of realizing his desires are personally or morally distasteful, or require too much dull effort. By means of such defenses, a person saves himself from committing a cardinal social sin—the sin of defining oneself in terms of a status while lacking the qualifications which an incumbent of that status is supposed to possess.

A mark's participation in a play, and his investment in it, clearly commit him in his own eyes to the proposition that he is a smart man. The process by which he comes to believe that he cannot lose is also the process by which he drops the defenses and compensations that previously protected him from defeats. When the blowoff comes, the mark finds that he has no defense for not being a shrewd man. He has defined himself as a shrewd man and must face the fact that he is only another easy mark. He has defined himself as possessing a certain set of qualities and then proven to himself that he is miserably lacking in them. This is a process of self-destruction of the self. It is no wonder that the mark needs to be cooled out and that it is good business policy for one of the operators to stay with the mark in order to talk him into a point of view from which it is possible to accept a loss.

In essence, then, the cooler has the job of handling persons who have been caught out on a limb—persons whose expectations and self-conceptions have been built up and then shattered. The mark is a person who has compromised himself, in his own eyes if not in the eyes of others.

Although the term, mark, is commonly applied to a person who is given short-lived expectations by operators who have intentionally misrepresented the facts, a less restricted definition is desirable in analyzing the larger social scene. An expectation may finally prove false, even though it has been possible to sustain it for a long time and even though the operators acted in good faith. So, too, the disappointment of reasonable expectations, as well as misguided ones, creates a need for consolation. Persons who participate in what is recognized as a confidence game are found in only a few social settings, but persons who have to be cooled out are found in many. Cooling the mark out is one theme in a very basic social story.

For purposes of analysis, one may think of an individual in reference to the values or attributes of a socially recognized character which he possesses. Psychologists speak of a value as a personal involvement. Sociologists speak of a value as a status, role, or relationship. In either case, the character of the value that is possessed is taken in a certain way as the character of the person who possesses it. An alteration in the kinds of attributes possessed brings an alteration to the self-conception of the person who possesses them.

The process by which someone acquires a value is the process by which he surrenders the claim he had to what he was and commits himself to the conception of self which the new value requires or allows him to have. It is the process that persons who fall in love or take dope call getting hooked. After a person is hooked, he must go through another process by which his new involvement finds its proper place, in space and time, relative to the other calls, demands, and commitments that he has upon himself. At this point certain other persons suddenly begin to play an important part in the individual's story; they impinge upon him by virtue of the relationship they happen to have to the value in which he has become involved. This is not the place to consider the general kinds of impingement that are institutionalized in our society and the general social relationships that arise: the personal relationship, the professional relationship, and the business relationship. Here we are concerned only with the end of the story, the way in which a person becomes disengaged from one of his involvements.

In our society, the story of a person's involvement can end in one of three general ways. According to one type of ending, he may withdraw from one of his involvements or roles in order to acquire a sequentially related one that is considered better. This is the case when a youth becomes a man, when a student becomes a practitioner, or when a man from the ranks is given a commission.

Of course, the person who must change his self at any one of these points of promotion may have profound misgivings. He may feel disloyal to the way of life that must be left behind and to the persons who do not leave it with him. His new role may require action that seems insincere, dishonest, or unfriendly. This he may experience as a loss in moral cleanliness. His new role may require him to forgo the kinds of risk-taking and exertion that he previously enjoyed, and yet his new role may not provide the kind of heroic and exalted action that he expected to find in it.[1] This he may experience as a loss in moral strength.

There is no doubt that certain kinds of role success require certain kinds of moral failure. It may therefore be necessary, in a sense, to cool the dubious neophyte in rather than out. He may have to be convinced that his doubts are a matter of sentimentality. The adult social view will be impressed upon him. He will be required to understand that a promotional change in status is voluntary, desirable, and natural, and that loss of one's role in these circumstances is the ultimate test of having fulfilled it properly.

It has been suggested that a person may leave a role under circumstances that reflect favorably upon the way in which he performed it. In theory, at least, a related possibility must be considered. A person may leave a role and at the same time leave behind him the standards by which such roles are judged. The new thing that he becomes may be so different from the thing he was that criteria such as success or failure cannot be easily applied to the change which has occurred. He becomes lost to others that he may find himself; he is of the twice-born. In our society, perhaps the most obvious example of this kind of termination occurs when a woman voluntarily gives up a prestigeful profession in order to become a wife and a mother. It is to be noted that this illustrates an institutionalized movement; those who make it to do not make news. In America most other examples of this kind of termination are more a matter of talk than of occurrence. For example, one of the culture heroes of our dinner-table mythology is the man who walks out on an established calling

---

[1]Mr. Hughes has lectured on this kind of disappointment, and one of his students has undertaken a special study of it. See Miriam Wagenschein, " 'Reality Shock': A Study of Beginning School Teachers," M.A. thesis, Dept. of Sociology, Univ. of Chicago, 1950.

in order to write or paint or live in the country. In other societies, the kind of abdication being considered here seems to have played a more important role. In medieval China, for instance, anchoretic withdrawal apparently gave to persons of quite different station a way of retreating from the occupational struggle while managing the retreat in an orderly, face-saving fashion.[2]

Two basic ways in which a person can lose a role have been considered; he can be promoted out of it or abdicate from it. There is, of course, a third basic ending to the status story. A person may be involuntarily deprived of his position or involvement and made in return something that is considered a lesser thing to be. It is mainly in this third ending to a person's role that occasions arise for cooling him out. It is here that one deals in the full sense with the problem of persons losing their roles.

Involuntary loss seems itself to be of two kinds. First, a person may lose a status in such a way that the loss is not taken as a reflection upon the loser. The loss of a loved one, either because of an accident that could not have been prevented or because of a disease that could not have been halted, is a case in point. Occupational retirement because of old age is another. Of course, the loss will inevitably alter the conception the loser has of himself and the conception others have of him, but the alteration itself will not be treated as a symbol of the fate he deserves to receive. No insult is added to injury. It may be necessary, none the less, to pacify the loser and resign him to his loss. The loser who is not held responsible for his loss may even find himself taking the mystical view that all involvements are part of a wider con game, for the more one takes pleasure in a particular role the more one must suffer when it is time to leave it. He may find little comfort in the fact that the play has provided him with an illusion that has lasted a lifetime. He may find little comfort in the fact that the operators had not meant to deceive him.

Secondly, a person may be involuntarily deprived of a role under circumstances which reflect unfavorably on his capacity for it. The lost role may be one that he had already acquired or one that he had openly committed himself to preparing for. In either case the loss is more than a matter of ceasing to act in a given capacity; it is ultimate proof of an incapacity. And in many cases it is even more than this. The

[2] See, for example, Max Weber, *The Religion of China* (H. H. Gerth, tr.): Glencoe, Ill, Free Press, 1951; p. 178.

moment of failure often catches a person acting as one who feels that he is an appropriate sort of person for the role in question. Assumption becomes presumption, and failure becomes fraud. To loss of substance is thereby added loss of face. Of the many themes that can occur in the natural history of an involvement, this seems to be the most melancholy. Here it will be quite essential and quite difficult to cool the mark out. I shall be particularly concerned with this second kind of loss—the kind that involves humiliation.

It should be noted, parenthetically, that one circle of persons may define a particular loss as the kind that casts no reflection on the loser, and that a different circle of persons may treat the same loss as a symbol of what the loser deserves. One must also note that there is a tendency today to shift certain losses of status from the category of those that reflect upon the loser to the category of those that do not. When persons lose their jobs, their courage, or their minds, we tend more and more to take a clinical or naturalistic view of the loss and a nonmoral view of their failure. We want to define a person as something that is not destroyed by the destruction of one of his selves. This benevolent attitude is in line with the effort today to publicize the view that occupational retirement is not the end of all active capacities but the beginning of new and different ones.

A consideration of consolation as a social process leads to four general problems having to do with the self in society, First, where in modern life does one find persons conducting themselves as though they were entitled to the rights of a particular status and then having to face up to the fact that they do not possess the qualification for the status? In other words, at what points in the structures of our social life are persons likely to compromise themselves or find themselves compromised? When is it likely that a person will have to disengage himself or become disengaged from one of his involvements? Secondly, what are the typical ways in which persons who find themselves in this difficult position can be cooled out; how can they be made to accept the great injury that has been done to their image of themselves, regroup their defenses, and carry on without raising a squawk? Thirdly, what, in general, can happen when a person refuses to be cooled out, that is, when he refuses to be pacified by the cooler? Fourthly, what arrangements are made by operators and marks to avoid entirely the process of consolation?

In all personal-service organizations customers or clients sometimes make complaints. A customer may feel that he has been given service in a way that is unacceptable to him—a way that he interprets as an offense to the conception he has of who and what he is. The management therefore has the problem of cooling the mark out. Frequently this function is allotted to specialists within the organization. In restaurants of some size, for example, one of the crucial functions of the hostess is to pacify customers whose self-conceptions have been injured by waitresses or by the food. In large stores the complaint department and the floorwalker perform a similar function.

One may note that a service organization does not operate in an anonymous world, as does a con mob, and is therefore strongly obliged to make some effort to cool the mark out. An institution, after all, cannot take it on the lam; it must pacify its marks.

One may also note that coolers in service organizations tend to view their own activity in a light that softens the harsher details of the situation. The cooler protects himself from feelings of guilt by arguing that the customer is not really in need of the service he expected to receive, that bad service is not really deprivational, and that beefs and complaints are a sign of bile, not a sign of injury. In a similar way, the con man protects himself from remorseful images of bankrupt marks by arguing that the mark is a fool and not a full-fledged person, possessing an inclination towards illegal gain but not the decency to admit it or the capacity to succeed at it.

In organizations patterned after a bureaucratic model, it is customary for personnel to expect rewards of a specified kind upon fulfilling requirements of a specified nature. Personnel come to define their career line in terms of a sequence of legitimate expectations and to base their self-conceptions on the assumption that in due course they will be what the institution allows persons to become. Sometimes, however, a member of an organization may fulfill some of the requirements for a particular status, especially the requirements concerning technical proficiency and seniority, but not other requirements, especially the less codified ones having to do with the proper handling of social relationships at work. It must fall to someone to break the bad news to the victim; someone must tell him that he has been fired, or that he has failed his examinations, or that he has been by-passed in promotion. And after the blowoff, someone has to cool the mark out. The necessity of disappointing the expectations that a person has taken for granted may be infrequent in some organizations, but in others, such as training institutions, it occurs all the time. The process of personnel selection requires that many trainees be called but that few be chosen.

When one turns from places of work to other scenes in our social life, one finds that each has its own occasions for cooling the mark out. During informal social intercourse it is well understood that an effort on the part of one person (ego) to decrease his social distance from another person (alter) must be graciously accepted by alter or, if rejected, rejected tactfully so that the initiator of the move can save his social face. This rule is codified in books on etiquette and is followed in actual behavior. A friendly movement in the direction of alter is a movement outward on a limb; ego communicates his belief that he has defined himself as worthy of alter's society, while at the same time he places alter in the strategic position of being able to discredit this conception.

The problem of cooling persons out in informal social intercourse is seen most clearly, perhaps, in courting situations and in what might be called de-courting situations. A proposal of marriage in our society tends to be a way in which a man sums up his social attributes and suggests to a woman that hers are not so much better as to preclude a merger or partnership in these matters. Refusal on the part of the woman, or refusal on the part of the man to propose when he is clearly in a position to do so, is a serious reflection on the rejected suitor. Courtship is a way not only of presenting oneself to alter for approval but also of saying that the opinion of alter in this matter is the opinion one is most concerned with. Refusing a proposal, or refusing to propose, is therefore a difficult operation. The mark must be carefully cooled out. The act of breaking a date or of refusing one, and the task of discouraging a "steady" can also be seen in this light, although in these cases great delicacy and tact may not be required, since the mark may not be deeply involved or openly committed. Just as it is harder to refuse a proposal than to refuse a date, so it is more difficult to reject a spouse than to reject a suitor. The process of de-courting by which one person in a marriage maneuvers the other into accepting a divorce without fuss or undue rancor requires extreme finesse in the art of cooling the mark out.

In all of these cases where a person constructs a conception of himself which cannot be sustained, there is a possibility that he has not invested that which is most important to him in the soon-to-be-denied status. In the current idiom, there is a possibility that when he is hit, he will not be hit where he really lives. There is a set of cases, however, where the blowoff cannot help but strike a vital spot; these cases arise, of course, when a person must be dissuaded from life itself. The man with a fatal sickness or fatal injury, the criminal with a death sentence, the soldier with a hopeless objective—these persons must be persuaded to accept quietly the loss of life itself, the loss of all one's earthly involvements. Here, certainly, it will be difficult to cool the mark out. It is a reflection on the conceptions men have—as cooler and mark —that it is possible to do so.

I have mentioned a few of the areas of social life where it becomes necessary, upon occasion, to cool a mark out. Attention may now be directed to some of the common ways in which individuals are cooled out in all of these areas of life.

For the mark, cooling represents a process of adjustment to an impossible situation—a situation arising from having defined himself in a way which the social facts come to contradict. The mark must therefore be supplied with a new set of apologies for himself, a new framework in which to see himself and judge himself. A process of redefining the self along defensible lines must be instigated and carried along; since the mark himself is frequently in too weakened a condition to do this, the cooler must initially do it for him.

One general way of handling the problem of cooling the mark out is to give the task to someone whose status relative to the mark will serve to ease the situation in some way. In formal organizations, frequently, someone who is two or three levels above the mark in line of command will do the hatchet work, on the assumption that words of consolation and redirection will have a greater power to convince if they come from high places. There also seems to be a feeling that persons of high status are better able to withstand the moral danger of having hate directed at them. Incidentally, persons protected by high office do not like to face this issue, and frequently attempt to define themselves as merely the agents of the deed and not the source of it. In some cases, on the other hand, the task of cooling the mark out is given to a friend and peer of the mark, on the assumption that such a person will know best how to hit upon a suitable rationalization for the mark and will know best how to control the mark should the need for this arise. In some cases, as in those pertaining to death, the role of cooler is given to doctors or priests. Doctors must frequently help a family, and the member who is leaving it, to manage the leave-taking with tact and a minimum of emotional fuss.[3] A priest must not so much save a soul as create one that is consistent with what is about to become of it.

A second general solution to the problem of cooling the mark out consists of offering him a status which differs from the one he has lost or failed to gain but which provides at least a something or a somebody for him to become. Usually the alternative presented to the mark is a compromise of some kind, providing him with some of the trappings of his lost status as well as with some of its spirit. A lover may be asked to become a friend; a student of medicine may be asked to switch to the study of dentistry;[4] a boxer may become a trainer; a dying person may be asked to broaden and empty his worldly loves so as to embrace the All-Father that is about to receive him. Sometimes the mark is allowed to retain his status but is required to fulfill it in a different environment; the honest policeman is transferred to a lonely beat; the too zealous priest is encouraged to enter a monastery; an unsatisfactory plant manager is shipped off to another branch. Sometimes the mark is "kicked upstairs" and given a courtesy status such as "Vice President." In the game for social roles, transfer up, down, or away may all be consolation prizes.

A related way of handling the mark is to offer him another chance to qualify for the role at which he has failed. After his fall from grace, he is allowed to retrace his steps and try again. Officer selection programs in the army, for example, often provide for possiblities of this kind. In general, it seems that third and fourth chances are seldom given to marks, and that second chances, while often given, are seldom taken. Failure at a role removes a person from the company of those who have succeeded, but it does not bring him back—in spirit, anyway—to the society of those who have not tried or are in the process of trying. The person who has failed in a role is a constant source of embarrassment, for

---

[3] This role of the doctor has been stressed by W. L. Warner in his lectures at the University of Chicago on symbolic roles in "Yankee City."

[4] In his seminar, Mr. Hughes has used the term "second choice" professions to refer to cases of this kind.

none of the standard patterns of treatment is quite applicable to him. Instead of taking a second chance, he usually goes away to another place where his past does not bring confusion to his present.

Another standard method of cooling the mark out—one which is frequently employed in conjunction with other methods—is to allow the mark to explode, to break down, to cause a scene, to give full vent to his reactions and feelings, to "blow his top." If this release of emotions does not find a target, then it at least serves a cathartic function. If it does find a target, as in "telling off the boss," it gives the mark a last-minute chance to re-erect his defenses and prove to himself and others that he had not really cared about the status all along. When a blow-up of this kind occurs, friends of the mark or psychotherapists are frequently brought in. Friends are willing to take responsibility for the mark because their relationship to him is not limited to the role he has failed in. This, incidentally, provides one of the less obvious reasons why the cooler in a con mob must cultivate the friendship of the mark; friendship provides the cooler with an acceptable reason for staying around while the mark is cooled out. Psychotherapists, on the other hand, are willing to take responsibility for the mark because it is their business to offer a relationship to those who have failed in a relationship to others.

It has been suggested that a mark may be cooled out by allowing him, under suitable guidance, to give full vent to his initial shock. Thus the manager of a commercial organization may listen with patience and understanding to the complaints of a customer, knowing that the full expression of a complaint is likely to weaken it. This possibility lies behind the role of a whole series of buffers in our society—janitors, restaurant hostesses, grievance committees, floorwalkers, and so on—who listen in silence, with apparent sympathy, until the mark has simmered down. Similarly, in the case of criminal trials, the defending lawyer may find it profitable to allow the public to simmer down before he brings his client to court.

A related procedure for cooling the mark out is found in what is called stalling. The feelings of the mark are not brought to a head because he is given no target at which to direct them. The operator may manage to avoid the presence of the mark or may convince the mark that there is still a slight chance that the loss has not really occurred. When the mark is stalled, he is given a chance to become familiar with the new conception of self he will have to accept before he is absolutely sure that he will have to accept it.

As another cooling procedure, there is the possibility that the operator and the mark may enter into a tacit understanding according to which the mark agrees to act as if he were leaving of his own accord, and the operator agrees to preserve the illusion that this was the case. It is a form of bribery. In this way the mark may fall in his own eyes but prevent others from discovering the failure. The mark gives up his role but saves his face. This, after all, is one of the reasons why persons who are fleeced by con men are often willing to remain silent about their adventure. The same strategy is at work in the romantic custom of allowing a guilty officer to take his own life in a private way before it is taken from him publicly, and in the less romantic custom of allowing a person to resign for delicate reasons instead of firing him for indelicate ones.

Bribery is, of course, a form of exchange. In this case, the mark guarantees to leave quickly and quietly, and in exchange is allowed to leave under a cloud of his own choosing. A more important variation on the same theme is found in the practice of financial compensation. A man can say to himself and others that he is happy to retire from his job and say this with more conviction if he is able to point to a comfortable pension. In this sense, pensions are automatic devices for providing consolation. So, too, a person who has been injured because of another's criminal or marital neglect can compensate for the loss by means of a court settlement.

I have suggested some general ways in which the mark is cooled out. The question now arises: what happens if the mark refuses to be cooled out? What are the possible lines of action he can take if he refuses to be cooled? Attempts to answer these questions will show more clearly why, in general, the operator is so anxious to pacify the mark.

It has been suggested that a mark may be cooled by allowing him to blow his top. If the blow-up is too drastic or prolonged, however, difficulties may arise. We say that the mark becomes "disturbed mentally" or "personally disorganized." Instead of merely telling his boss off, the mark may go so far as to commit criminal violence against him. Instead of merely blaming himself for failure, the mark may inflict great punishment upon himself by attempting suicide, or by acting so as to make it necessary for him to be cooled out in other areas of his social life.

Sustained personal disorganization is one way in which a mark can refuse to cool out. Another standard way is for the individual to raise a' squawk, that is, to make a formal complaint to higher authorities obliged to take notice of such matters. The con mob worries lest the mark appeal to the police. The plant manager must make sure that the disgruntled department head does not carry a formal complaint to the general manager or, worse still, to the Board of Directors. The teacher worries lest the child's parent complain to the principal. Similarly, a woman who communicates her evaluation of self by accepting a proposal of marriage can sometimes protect her exposed position—should the necessity of doing so arise—by threatening her disaffected fiancé with a breach-of-promise suit. So, also, a woman who is de-courting her husband must fear lest he contest the divorce or sue her lover for alienation of affection. In much the same way, a customer who is angered by a salesperson can refuse to be mollified by the floorwalker and demand to see the manager. It is interesting to note that associations dedicated to the rights and the honor of minority groups may sometimes encourage a mark to register a formal squawk; politically it may be more advantageous to provide a test case than to allow the mark to be cooled out.

Another line of action which a mark who refuses to be cooled can pursue is that of turning "sour." The term derives from the argot of industry but the behavior it refers to occurs everywhere. The mark outwardly accepts his loss but withdraws all enthusiasm, good will, and vitality from whatever role he is allowed to maintain. He complies with the formal requirements of the role that is left him, but he withdraws his spirit and identification from it. When an employee turns sour, the interests of the organization suffer; every executive, therefore, has the problem of "sweetening" his workers. They must not come to feel that they are slowly being cooled out. This is one of the functions of granting periodic advancements in salary and status, of schemes such as profit-sharing, or of giving the "employee" at home an anniversay present. A similar view can be taken of the problem that a government faces in times of crisis when it must maintain the enthusiastic support of the nation's disadvantaged minorities, for whole groupings of the population can feel they are being cooled out and react by turning sour.

Finally, there is the possibility that the mark may, in a manner of speaking, go into business for himself. He can try to gather about him the persons and facilities required to establish a status similar to the one he has lost, albeit in relation to a different set of persons. This way of refusing to be cooled is often rehearsed in phantasies of the "I'll show them" kind, but sometimes it is actually realized in practice. The rejected marriage partner may make a better remarriage. A social stratum that has lost its status may decide to create its own social system. A leader who fails in a political party may establish his own splinter group.

All these ways in which a mark can refuse to be cooled out have consequences for other persons. There is, of course, a kind of refusal that has little consequence for others. Marks of all kinds may develop explanations and excuses to account in a creditable way for their loss. It is, perhaps, in this region of phantasy that the defeated self makes its last stand.

The process of cooling is a difficult one, both for the operator who cools the mark out and for the person who receives this treatment. Safeguards and strategies are therefore employed to ensure that the process itself need not and does not occur. One deals here with strategies of prevention, not strategies of cure.

From the point of view of the operator, there are two chief ways of avoiding the difficulties of cooling the mark out. First, devices are commonly employed to weed out those applicants for a role, office, or relationship who might later prove to be unsuitable and require removal. The applicant is not given a chance to invest his self unwisely. A variation of this technique, that provides, in a way, a built-in mechanism for cooling the mark out, is found in the institution of probationary period and "temporory" staff. These definitions of the situation make it clear to the person that he must maintain his ego in readiness for the loss of his job, or, better still, that he ought not to think of himself as really having the job, If these safety measures fail, however, a second strategy is often employed. Operators of all kinds seem to be ready, to a suprising degree, to put up with or "carry" persons who have failed but who have not yet been treated as failures. This is especially true where the involvement of the mark is deep and where his conception of self had been publicly committed. Business offices, government agencies, spouses, and other kinds of operators are often careful to make a place for the mark, so that dissolution of the bond will not be necessary. Here, perhaps, is the most important source of private charity in our society.

A consideration of these preventive strategies brings to attention an interesting functional relationship among age-grading, recruitment, and the structure of the self. In our society, as in most others, the young in years are defined as not-yet-persons. To a certain degree, they are not subject to success and failure. A child can throw himself completely into a task, and fail at it, and by and large he will not be destroyed by his failure; it is only necessary to play at cooling him out. An adolescent can be bitterly disappointed in love, and yet he will not thereby become, at least for others, a broken person. A youth can spend a certain amount of time shopping around for a congenial job or a congenial training course, because he is still thought to be able to change his mind without changing his self. And, should he fail at something to which he has tried to commit himself, no permanent damage may be done to his self. If many are to be called and few chosen, then it is more convenient for everyone concerned to call individuals who are not fully persons and cannot be destroyed by failing to be chosen. As the individual grows older, he becomes defined as someone who must not be engaged in a role for which he is unsuited. He becomes defined as something that must not fail, while at the same time arrangements are made to decrease the chances of his failing. Of course, when the mark reaches old age, he must remove himself or be removed from each of his roles, one by one, and participate in the problem of later maturity.

The strategies that are employed by operators to avoid the necessity of cooling the mark out have a counterpart in the strategies that are employed by the mark himself for the same purpose.

There is the strategy of hedging, by which a person makes sure that he is not completely committed. There is the strategy of secrecy, by which a person conceals from others and even from himself the facts of his commitment; there is also the practice of keeping two irons in the fire and the more delicate practice of maintaining a joking or unserious relationship to one's involvement. All of these strategies give the mark an out; in case of failure he can act as if the self that has failed is not one that is important to him. Here we must also consider the function of being quick to take offense and of taking hints quickly, for in these ways the mark can actively cooperate in the task of saving his face. There is also the strategy of playing it safe, as in cases where a calling is chosen because tenure is assured in it, or where a plain woman is married for much the same reason.

It has been suggested that preventive strategies are employed by operator and mark in order to reduce the chance of failing or to minimize the consequences of failure. The less importance one finds it necessary to give to the problem of cooling, the more importance one may have given to the application of preventive strategies.

I have considered some of the situations in our society in which the necessity for cooling the mark out is likely to arise. I have also considered the standard ways in which a mark can be cooled out, the lines of action he can pursue if he refuses to be cooled, and the ways in which the whole problem can be avoided. Attention can now be turned to some very general questions concerning the self in society.

First, an attempt must be made to draw together what has been implied about the structure of persons. From the point of view of this paper, a person is an individual who becomes involved in a value of some kind—a role, a status, a relationship, an ideology—and then makes a public claim that he is to be defined and treated as someone who possesses the value or property in question. The limits to his claims, and hence the limits to his self, are primarily determined by the objective facts of his social life and secondarily determined by the degree to which a sympathetic interpretation of these facts can bend them in his favor. Any event which demonstrates that someone has made a false claim, defining himself as something which he is not, tends to destroy him. If others realize that the person's conception of self has been contradicted and discredited, then the person tends to be destroyed in the eyes of others. If the person can keep the contradiction a secret, he may succeed in keeping everyone but himself from treating him as a failure.

Secondly, one must take note of what is implied by the fact that it is possible for a person to be cooled out. Difficult as this may be, persons regularly define themselves in terms of a set of attributes and then have to accept the fact that they do not possess them—and do this about-face with relatively little fuss or trouble for the operators. This implies that there is a norm in our society persuading persons to keep their chins up and make the best of it—a sort of social sanitation enjoining torn and tattered persons to keep themselves packaged up. More important still, the capacity of a person to sustain these profound embarrassments implies a certain looseness and lack of interpenetration in the organization of his several life activities. A man may fail in his job, yet go on succeeding with his wife. His wife may ask him for a divorce, or refuse to grant him one, and yet he may push his way onto the same streetcar at the usual time on the way to the same job. He may know that he is shortly going to have to leave the status of the living, but still march with the other prisoners, or eat breakfast with his family at their usual time and from behind his usual paper. He may be conned of his life's savings on an eastbound train but return to his home town and succeed in acting as if nothing of interest had happened.

Lack of rigid integration of a person's social roles allows for compensation; he can seek comfort in one role for injuries incurred in others. There are always cases of course, in which the mark cannot sustain the injury to his ego and cannot act like a "good scout." On these occasions the shattering experience in one area of social life may spread out to all the sectors of his activity. He may define away the barriers between his several social roles and become a source of difficulty in all of them. In such cases the play is the mark's entire social life, and the operators, really, are the society. In an increasing number of these cases, the mark is given psychological guidance by professionals of some kind. The psychotherapist is, in this sense, the society's cooler. His job is to pacify and reorient the disorganized person; his job is to send the patient back to an old world or a new one, and to send him back in a condition in which he can no longer cause trouble to others or can no longer make a fuss. In short, if one takes the society, and not the person as the unit, the psychotherapist has the basic task of cooling the mark out.

A third point of interest arises if one views all of social life from the perspective of this paper. It has been argued that a person must not openly or even privately commit himself to a conception of himself which the flow of events is likely to discredit. He must not put himself in a position of having to be cooled out. Conversely, however, he must make sure that none of the persons with whom he has dealings are of the sort who may prove unsuitable and need to be cooled out. He must make doubly sure that should it become necessary to cool his associates out, they will be the sort who allow themselves to be gotten rid of. The con man who wants the mark to go home quietly and absorb a loss, the restaurant hostess who wants a customer to eat quietly and go away without causing trouble, and, if this is not possible, quietly to take his patronage elsewhere—these are the persons and these are the relationships which set the tone of some of our social life. Underlying this tone there is the assumption that persons are institutionally related to each other in such a way that if a mark allows himself to be cooled out, then the cooler need have no further concern with him; but if the mark refuses to be cooled out, he can put institutional machinery into action against the cooler. Underlying this tone there is also the assumption that persons are sentimentally related to each other in such a way that if a person allows himself to be cooled out, however great the loss he has sustained, then the cooler withdraws all emotional identification from him; but if the mark cannot absorb the injury to his self and if he becomes personally disorganized in some way, then the cooler cannot help but feel guilt and concern over the predicament. It is this feeling of guilt—this small measure of involvement in the feelings of others—which helps to make the job of cooling the mark out distasteful, wherever it appears. It is this incapacity to be insensitive to the suffering of another person when he brings his suffering right to your door which tends to make the job of cooling a species of dirty work.

One must not, of course, make too much of the margin of sympathy connecting operator and mark. For one thing, the operator may rid himself of the mark by application or threat of pure force or open insult.[5] In Chicago in the 1920's small businessmen who suffered a loss in profits and in independence because of the "protection" services that racketeers gave to them were cooled out in this way. No doubt it is frivolous to suggest that Freud's notion of castration threat has something to do with the efforts of fathers to cool their sons out of oedipal involvements. Furthermore, there are many occasions when operators of different kinds must act as middlemen, with two marks on their hands; the calculated use of one mark as a sacrifice or fall guy may be the only way of cooling the other mark out. Finally, there are barbarous ceremonies in our society, such as criminal trials and the drumming-out ritual employed in court-martial procedures, that are expressly designed to prevent the mark from saving his face. And even in those cases where the cooler makes an

[5] Suggested by Saul Mendlovitz in conversation.

effort to make things easier for the person he is getting rid of, we often find that there are bystanders who have no such scruples.[6] Onlookers who are close enough to observe the blowoff but who are not obliged to assist in the dirty work often enjoy the scene, taking pleasure in the discomfiture of the cooler and in the destruction of the mark. What is trouble for some is Schadenfreude for others.

This paper has dealt chiefly with adaptations to loss; with defenses, strategies, consolations, mitigations, compensations, and the like. The kinds of sugar-coating have been examined, and not the pill. I would like to close this paper by referring briefly to the sort of thing that would be studied if one were interested in loss as such, and not in adaptations to it.

A mark who requires cooling out is a person who can no longer sustain one of his social roles and is about to be removed from it; he is a person who is losing one of his social lives and is about to die one of the deaths that are possible for him. This leads one to consider the ways in which we can go or be sent to our death in each of our social capacities, the ways, in other words, of handling the passage from the role that we had to a state of having it no longer. One might consider the social processes of firing and laying off; or resigning and being asked to resign; of farewell and departure; of deportation, excommunication, and going to jail; of defeat at games, contests, and wars; of being dropped from a circle of friends or an intimate social relationship; of corporate dissolution; of retirement in old age; and, lastly, of the deaths that heirs are interested in.

And, finally, attention must be directed to the things we become after we have died in one of the many social senses and capacities in which death can come to us. As one might expect, a process of sifting and sorting occurs by which the socially dead come to be effectively hidden from us. This movement of ex-persons throughout the social structure proceeds in more than one direction.

There is, first of all, the dramatic process by which persons who have died in important ways come gradually to be brought together into a common graveyard that is separated ecologically from the living community.[7] For the dead, this is at once a punishment and a defense. Jails and mental institu-

[6]Suggested by Howard S. Becker in conversation.
[7]Suggested by lectures of and a personal conversation with Mr. Hughes.

tions are, perhaps, the most familiar examples, but other important ones exist. In America today, there is the interesting tendency to set aside certain regions and towns in California as asylums for those who have died in their capacity as workers and as parents but who are still alive financially.[8] For the old in America who have also died financially, there are old-folks homes and rooming-house areas. And, of course, large cities have their Skid Rows which are, as Park put it, ". . . . full of junk, much of it human, i.e., men and women who, for some reason or other, have fallen out of line in the march of industrial progress and have been scrapped by the industrial organization of which they were once a part."[9] Hobo jungles, located near freight yards on the outskirts of towns, provide another case in point.

Just as a residential area may become a graveyard, so also certain institutions and occupational roles may take on a similar function. The ministry in Britain, for example, has sometimes served as a limbo for the occupational stillborn of better families, as have British universities. Mayhew, writing of London in the mid-nineteenth-century, provides another example; artisans of different kinds, who had failed to maintain a position in the practice of their trade, could be found working as dustmen.[10] In the United States, the jobs of waitress, cab driver, and night watchman, and the profession of prostitution, tend to be ending places where persons of certain kinds, starting from different places, can come to rest.

But perhaps the most important movement of those who fail is one we never see. Where roles are ranked and somewhat related, persons who have been rejected from the one above may be difficult to distinguish from persons who have risen from the one below. For example, in America, upper-class women who fail to make a marriage in their own circle

[8]Some early writers on caste report a like situation in India at the turn of the nineteenth century. Hindus who were taken to the Ganges to die, and who then recovered, were apparently denied all legal rights and all social relations with the living. Apparently these excluded persons found it necessary to congregate in a few villages of their own. In California, of course, settlements of the old have a voluntary character, and members maintain ceremonial contact with younger kin by the exchange of periodic visits and letters.

[9]R. E. Park, *Human Communities;* Glencoe, Ill; Free Press, 1952; p. 60.

[10]Henry Mayhew, *London Labour and the London Poor;* London, Grimn, Bohn, 1861; Vol. II, pp. 177–178.

may follow the recognized route of marrying an upper-middle class professional. Successful lower-middle class women may arrive at the same station in life, coming from the other direction. Similarly, among those who mingle with one another as colleagues in the profession of dentistry, it is possible to find some who have failed to become physicians and others who have succeeded at not becoming pharmacists or optometrists. No doubt there are few positions in life that do not throw together some persons who are there by virtue of failure and other persons who are there by virtue of success. In this sense, the dead are sorted but not segregated, and continue to walk among the living.

The Protection of the Inept

by
William J. Goode

The dissident have throughout history voiced a suspicion that the highly placed have not earned their mace, orb, and scepter. Plato designed a city in which the ablest would rule, but this was accomplished only in his imagination. Leaders in the Wat Tyler Rebellion expressed their doubts that lords were of finer quality than the peasants they ruled. Against the grandiloquent assertion of kings that they were divinely appointed, both court jesters and the masses have sometimes laughed, and asked, where were their virtue and wisdom? In more recent times, this skepticism about their merit has culminated in the dethronement or weakening of practically every ascriptive ruler in the world.

Nor has the end of kings by birth stifled this doubt that the elite are indeed the ablest, that the inept may be protected in high position. Jefferson spoke of a "natural aristocracy," but he did not suppose the members of the ruling class necessarily belonged to it. In our less heroic epoch, we are assured that we live in an achievement-oriented society, and the norm is to place individuals in their occupations by merit. Nevertheless, the inquiries of sociologists and psychologists demonstrate that as the child passes through the successive gateways to higher position, the cumulative effect of class, race, sex, and other readily ascribed traits grows rather than lessens. For example, lower class or Negro children who could perform well by comparison with their more advantaged peers in the first few grades drop farther and farther behind. The gap between them widens.[1]

Of course, not all talent at any class level would be trans-

Reprinted from *American Sociological Review*, Vol. 32, No. 1, February 1967, pp. 5–19, with permission of the American Sociological Association and the author.

[1] Allen H. Barton and David E. Wilder, "Research and Practice in the Teaching of Reading: A Progress Report," in Matthew B. Miles (ed.), *Innovation in Education*, New York: Teachers College, Columbia University, 1964, pp. 361–398.

muted into skill, even in the best of *possible* worlds. However the privileged (at all levels of privilege) do try systematically to prevent the talent of the less privileged from being recognized or developed. And though analysts of stratification assume that social mobility is an index of open competition, ample if unsystematic evidence suggests that both the able and the inept may move into high position.

These comments should not be interpreted as the jaundiced complaints of the misanthrope, or as a call for destruction of the stratification system. Such common observations from Ecclesiastes (". . . the race is not to the swift . . .") and Plato onward describe arrangements which every social system exhibits, and which cope with a universal *system problem:* How to utilize the services of the less able?

The social responses to this problem are the resultant of two sets of factors in tension: protection *of* the inept; and protection of the group *from* the inept. In almost all collectivities, for reasons to be explored later, the arrangements for protecting the less able seem to be more pervasive, common, and effective than those for protecting the group from ineptitude. Industrial society is highly effective at production not so much because it allows the most able to assume positions of high leadership, but because it has developed two great techniques (bureaucracy and machinery) for both using the inept and limiting the range of their potential destructiveness.[2]

Adequate proof of this rather laconic theoretical statement, and a full exposition of its implications, is not possible within the brief compass of a single paper. In subsequent sections we shall consider these issues:

1. Does the evidence suggest there is a widespread pattern of protecting the less competent?
2. In supposedly achievement-oriented societies, is this protection merely an evasion of widely accepted achievement norms, i.e., is it "real," as contrasted with "ideal," behavior, or do people in fact accept many norms contrary to achievement?

[2]More cautiously, the chances that the chief of a bureaucracy may be able to act irresponsibly and destructively are probably reduced. However, (1) the bureaucracy itself generates power, so that his usually limited range of action may nevertheless be more destructive than that of a feudal chieftain could be; and (2) in the event that the chief (Stalin, Hitler) *can* really capture the bureaucracy, his range of destructiveness is multiplied greatly.

3. What are the specific or general processes and patterns protecting the less able?
4. Presumably, different social structures handle the problem of ineptitude differently. What consequences flow from these differences?

One can at least imagine, even if one will never find, a society in which the division of labor in every type of group allots tasks and rewards entirely on the basis of achievement, or one in which those allotments are made without regard for achievement. All societies fall between those two extremes. Leaders within industrial societies assert, in part as a defense of the system they lead, that the lowly able will rise, and that the highly placed deserve their rank. Even if such statements are classified as exhortations or hopes, evidence can be adduced to show that on the average the successful are more talented or skilled than the less successful, e.g., the research productivity of Nobel Prize winners *vs.* that of nonwinners.[3]

Yet such averages are, after all, derived from *distributions*. These distributions always reveal that *some* of the less successful seem equal or superior to the more successful. Far more important for our present inquiry, all such individuals live and work in *groups*, so that the relevant comparison is not with all other individuals in the same aggregate, such as all full professors, but with other members of the same group, such as the *department*. The protection of the inept is a *group* phenomenon, an aspect of a collectivity.

Let us, then, consider briefly some of the wide array of evidence that groups do not typically expose or expel their members for lesser achievement or talent. The following findings are only a reminder of how widespread our research has shown such social arrangements to be.

Almost every inquiry into the productivity of workers has shown that the informal work group protects its members by setting a standard which everyone can meet, and they develop techniques for preventing a supervisor from measuring accurately the output of each man.[4] Higher level management has

[3] See Harriet Zuckerman, "Nobel Laureates in Science: Patterns of Productivity, Collaboration, and Authorship," presented at the 61st Annual Meeting of the American Sociological Association, August 31, 1966, especially the comments on the "uncrowned Laureates."

[4] As a contrary case, because its members did not form a real group, see William J. Goode and Irving Fowler, "Incentive Factors in a Low Morale Plant," *American Sociological Review*, 14 (October, 1949), pp. 618–624.

for the most part evaded such scrutiny, but industrial sociologists have reported comparable behavior there, too.[5] The protection of one another by lower-level workers might be due to less commitment; the fact that higher-level men do the same suggests the need for a more general explanation.

All professions, while claiming to be the sole competent judges of their members' skills, and the guardians of their clients' welfare, refuse to divulge information about how competent any of them are, and under most circumstances their rules assert it is unethical to criticize the work of fellow members to laymen.[6] Wall Street law firms try to find good positions in other firms for those employees they decide are not partnership material.[7] When a new profession is organized, grandfather clauses permit older practitioners with less training to continue in practice without being tested. When hospitals begin to demand a higher performance standard from those who enjoy staff privileges, inevitably rejecting some, both patients and physicians object.[8] One study of a group of physicians showed that there was little relationship between an M.D.'s income and the quality of medical care he gave to his patients.[9]

Wherever unions are strong, foremen know that promotion by merit rather than by seniority is unwise, and in any event

[5] For one such comment, see Julius A. Roth, "Hired Hand Research," *The American Sociologist*, 1 (August, 1966), pp. 192–193. See also Melville Dalton, *Men Who Manage*, New York: Wiley, 1959, Chs. 7–9. Most analyses of management make such comments implicitly or explicitly.

[6] It is noteworthy that, when such ratings are made, it is typically "outsiders" who make them. See, for example, the Teamsters' study of hospital care in New York City: *The Quantity, Quality and Costs of Medical and Hospital Care Secured by a Sample of Teamster Families in the New York Area*, Columbia University, School of Public Health and Administrative Medicine, n.d.

[7] Erwin O. Smigel, *The Wall Street Lawyer: Professional Organization Man?*, New York: The Free Press, 1964, Chap. 4.

[8] For related comments see Jules Henry, "The GI Syndrome," *Trans-Action*, 1 (May, 1964), pp. 8–9, 30; and Eliot Freidson, "The Professional Mystique," *ibid.*, pp. 18–20. For a broader analysis, see my "Community Within a Community: The Professions," *American Sociological Review*, 22 (April, 1957), pp. 195–200; and "Encroachment, Charlatanism, and the Emerging Profession: Psychology, Sociology, and Medicine," *American Sociological Review*, 25 (December, 1960), pp. 902–914.

[9] O. L. Peterson, *et al.*, "An analytical Study of North Carolina General Practice," *Journal of Medical Education*, 31 (1956), p. 130.

unusual.[10] Many corporations do not fire their managers; they find or create other posts for them.[11] Employees are close students of promotion behavior, and are "notoriously suspicious and cynical" about management claims that promotion is through merit.[12] Many are not convinced the best men are at the top.[13] More generally, members of what Goffman calls "teams" (army officers, parents, policemen, managers, nurses, and so forth) protect each other from any exposure of their errors.[14]

In all societies—if present psychological testing may be extrapolated—there are more talented, in absolute numbers, born into the lower social strata than into the upper; every detailed study of a class system describes how the upper strata prevent the lower from acquiring the skills appropriate for higher level jobs. This effort alone is a good indicator that the upper strata include many who are less talented. For example, the Southerner as well as the Northerner would not even *need* to discriminate against the Negro child or man, if in fact he were always untalented; performance alone would demonstrate his inferiority. The same proposition holds for the poor generally, for Jews (as in banking or heavy industry), for women, and (in some circles) for Catholics.[15]

[10]Ely Chinoy, "The Tradition of Opportunity and the Aspirations of Automobile Workers," in Philip Olson, editor, *America as a Mass Society*, New York: The Free Press, 1963, pp. 506, 508, 512 and especially footnote 17; John W. Gardner, *Excellence*, New York: Harper & Row, 1961, p. 110; Melville Dalton, *op. cit.*, pp. 5–6, 128; and his "Economic Incentives and Human Relations," in *Industrial Productivity*, Publication No. 7 of Industrial Relations Research Association, Madison, Wisconsin, 1951, pp. 130–145; as well as Michel Crozier, *The Bureaucratic Phenomenon*, Chicago: University of Chicago Press, 1964, Ch. 3.

[11]For example, see the revealing article in the *Wall Street Journal*, January 24, 1966, "Obsolete Executives," as well as Fred Goldner, "Demotion in Industrial Management," *American Sociological Review*, 30 (October, 1965), pp. 714–724. Consider, too, the perceptive essay by one of our more imaginative social theorists, C. Northcote Parkinson, "Pension Point or the Age of Retirement," in his *Parkinson's Law*, Boston: Houghton Mifflin, 1962, pp. 101–113.

[12]James G. March and Herbert A. Simon, *Organizations*, New York: Wiley, 1963, p. 62.

[13]For some evidence that they are right, see Dalton, *op. cit.*, Ch. 6, and his "Unofficial Union-Management Relations," *American Sociological Review*, 15 (October, 1950), especially p. 615.

[14]Erving Goffman, *The Presentation of Self in Everyday Life*, New York: Doubleday Anchor, 1959, Chap. 2.

[15]It is hardly necessary here to cite from the voluminous literature on discrimination of various types. See, however, E. Digby Baltzell, *The*

Few are fired for incompetence, especially if they last long enough to become members of their work group. One consequence is that, in craft or white collar jobs, higher standards are set for obtaining a job than for performance. The result is that a high level of formal education is often necessary for jobs that any average eighth-grader could learn to perform rather quickly. Once the person enters his work group, however, the social arrangements do not permit much overt discrimination between the less able and the rest. Thus we observe the irony in our generation that the middle classes, with their greater access to education, continue to have the advantage in getting jobs, though the standards, i.e., formal education, are ostensibly universalistic and achievement-based.

As Galbraith has pointed out, the greatest source of insecurity for both individuals and companies has been competition; business men "have addressed themselves to the elimination or mitigation of this source of insecurity."[16] Cartels, price and production agreements, tariffs, price fixing by law, and quiet understandings are among the techniques used to prevent the less able from being pushed to the wall. The "development of the modern business enterprise can be understood only as a comprehensive effort to reduce risk . . . (and) in no other terms."[17]

Analysts have reported such behavior most often from work groups, but similar patterns are observable if we look instead at the operation of any type of collectivity. All groups are creating *some* type of output, whether the socialization of a child or sheer entertainment. On the other hand, as we shall note later, the *degree* of protection may vary from one type of activity to another.

In examining the protection of ineptitude, we are considering the division of labor from a different perspective. For our limited purposes, the inept are made up of two classes of people in any collectivity: (1) with reference to one or more tasks, some are likely to be less skilled than others who do not enjoy the rewards of membership in that group; (2) in

Protestant Establishment, New York: Random House, 1964; Melvin M. Tumin, *Inventory and Appraisal of Research on American Anti-Semitism*, New York: B'nai Brith, 1961; C. Northcote Parkinson should not be overlooked: "The Short List or Principles of Selection," *op. cit.*, pp. 45–48; and George E. Simpson and J. Milton Yinger, *Racial and Cultural Minorities*, 3rd ed., New York: Harper & Row, 1965.

[16]John K. Galbraith, *The Affluent Society*, Harmondsworth: Penguin, 1965, pp. 90–91.

[17]*Ibid.*, p. 91.

addition, some in that collectivity will be considerably less skilled than others. Clearly the group does not typically expel these less competent members. Instead, in each collectivity there are structures or processes which protect them.

ACHIEVEMENT NORMS VS. BEHAVIOR

Even so brief a selection from the evidence confirms the impression from daily experience that some social behavior protects the less able from open competition. Is this, however, simply one more instance of action counter to a norm? Perhaps all these cases are only violations of the well-accepted norm of achievement. Let us, then, examine the possibility that people are only partially committed to the criterion of achievement as the basis for reward, and also accept other opposing norms.

The current sociological tradition, following Linton and Parsons, views industrial society as achievement-based, i.e., stratified by achievement criteria, in contrast to most other social systems, in which statuses are mostly ascribed.[18] However, we may question such descriptions, and assert instead that people in our own type of society feel committed to many criteria of ranking that run counter to achievement, and that in the so-called ascriptive societies the principle of placement by birth is in turn qualified a good deal by achievement norms. That is, let us consider whether *both* behavior and norms in all societies prevent the exposure of the less competent and productive.

I have not been able to locate an adequate empirical study of even the American population—the one most studied by sociologists—concerning its commitment to the notion of ranking by achievement, but I shall venture several armchair descriptions of some value patterns that I believe are now observable.

In the so-called achievement societies—the most conspicuous being traditional China and the industrial West—the norm of free competition has been accepted for other

[18]See, for example, Ralph Linton, *The Study of Man*, New York: Appleton-Century-Crofts, 1936, pp. 115, 127–129; Talcott Parsons, *The Social System*, Glencoe, Ill.: The Free Press, 1951, pp. 151–200; Leonard Broom and Philip Selznick, *Sociology*, second ed., White Plains: Row, Peterson, 1959, p. 191.

people's sons, but most parents have believed their own sons deserved somewhat better than that. On the other hand, I doubt that even a majority of people in ascriptive societies (Western or not) have believed it was right for those *above* them to have been placed there by birth, although of course a majority might have affirmed their right by birth to be *above* others.[19]

Even in relatively "ascriptive" societies, the norm is that those who inherit their place should also validate it by both training and later adequate performance, e.g., knighthood. Almost never is there a norm denying any importance to achievement. Similarly, myths and legends recount with approval the ascent of the lowly to high position through merit.

In our presumably achievement-based society, few whites will fail to sense a twinge of the injustice of it all, when a superior Negro is made their boss. Few men believe that a woman should be promoted over them, even if by the criterion of merit she has earned it. Men with seniority believe it should count for more than achievement; and so on. Note, I am not stating merely that they are resentful, but that their value affirmations are in favor of other norms than performance when by those other norms they can lay claim to preferment.

Similarly, not only do the analyses of class membership, kinship, or friendship ties show the advantages or disadvantages of these non-achievement factors, but most individuals will, if pressed, admit they believe these factors should be used as norms, too. At a minimum, for example, if kinship or friendship is rejected in favor of merit as a norm, most will feel they are obliged either to give an additional justification of such a decision (thus demonstrating their lack of strong belief in the norm of achievement itself), or perhaps to help their role partner in some other way.

In an ongoing work group, both supervisors and members affirm a wide variety of other norms than achievement—seniority, the man's need, loyalty,—to justify the retention of all but the most flagrantly inept and non-contributing members.

In all industrial countries, and perhaps especially in the

[19]Joseph W. Elder found that 44 percent of the Mill Elite and 58 percent of the Brahmins believed that lower caste persons in that status were there because of sins committed in a previous life. "Industrialization in Hindu Society," Ph.D. dissertation (Harvard University, 1959), pp. 411, 415, 439.

Communist countries, whether industrial or industrializing, the *rhetoric* of placement by achievement is insistent. It has a strong political appeal. It is like a handful of other such normative positions as hard work, opposition to sin, or an open mind: people do not publicly deny their worth, but they do believe they are much better when used to measure the worth of the other fellow.

The appeal of this rhetoric is illustrated well by the vociferous objection in the 1870's and 1880's to the introduction of merit placement in the United States Civil Service. People did not, after all, argue much against merit itself. On the other hand, they did introduce different standards, e.g., humanistic and anti-intellectual ones,[20] so as to avoid asserting that jobs should be given to the less able. In short, even in a society which is widely described as adhering to the rule of placement by achievement, not only does this norm not determine action consistently, but the commitment itself is highly qualified or weakened by belief in a wide range of other criteria as bases for rewards. Doubtless, one may argue nevertheless that members of an industrial society are somewhat more committed to this norm than are members of most other societies, but the contrast does not seem so great as contemporary sociology has asserted.

So persistent a phenomenon, even in a society whose rhetoric is permeated by achievement norms, cannot be interpreted as simply the usual failure of any society to implement its own values fully; in fact, people are committed to competing values as well.

The social arrangements (both behavioral and normative) that I have labeled "the protection of the inept" comprise a range of answers to a universal resource problem, which grows from the tension between the challenges of the external environment and the internal resources of the social system. Specifically, these arrangements comprise a partial answer to the question of what to do with that inevitable segment of a group that is relatively less productive or competent? How can the group utilize them, how gain from them that smaller, but measurable, amount of marginal productivity the group believes their efforts can contribute?

More generally, given the existence of the relatively inept in nearly all groups, what are the patterns or processes which will on the one hand protect them from the rigors of untram-

[20]Richard Hofstadter, *Anti-Intellectualism in American Life*, New York: Knopf, 1963, especially pp. 181 ff.

meled competition (and thus gain their support and contribution), and on the other hand protect the group from the potentially destructive consequences of their ineptitude? Needless to say, there is no evidence that the social arrangements now observable are the most productive possible, whether of material goods or human satisfaction.

Having broadly reviewed some of the widespread evidence that such protective patterns exist, and that the norms in favor of reward by achievement are not unchallenged, let us now examine more closely the factors that create or support such patterns.[21]

FACTORS THAT INCREASE OR DECREASE THE PROTECTION OF INEPTITUDE

These factors can be classified by whether they are *mainly* generated in the outside environment, as high or low demands are made on the collectivity for its output; or whether they largely originate in connection with internal social processes of the collectivity.

External Factors. (1) Perhaps the simplest formulation is that when there is a very high demand for a given type of group output or performance, the pressures on the group to fire, expel, or downgrade a member will be low. That is, the collectivity prospers in such an environment without demanding a higher performance from its members, or without recruiting more effective members. This principle is perhaps most clearly illustrated by the extraordinary current expansion of the college and university system in this and several other countries, and particularly by the expansion of graduate education. We do not create high-level men merely by announcing that a department will henceforth grant graduate degrees. Similarly, the increasing contemporary demand in business and government for expertise in a wide range of subjects offers new and increased rewards, and will doubtless eventually produce more skilled men. However, at present the expansion of opportunities occurs faster than that of skills,

[21] As will be seen, several of these have been adapted from H. M. Blalock, "Occupational Discrimination: Some Theoretical Propositions," *Social Problems,* 9 (Winter, 1962), pp. 240–247.

with the consequent protection of ineptitude in many places.[22]

(2) We may also derive from this relation a secondary formulation, that, when the supply of services, outputs, or candidates is relatively low, a similar result is produced: a higher tolerance of ineptitude.[23] The best illustrations can be found at the lower job levels, where few people actively *want* that kind of work. However, at such levels those who hire cannot easily find substitutes, such as machines, or a new source of labor. This type of work is ranked as socially necessary but not important. Thus, though the demand may not be high, it will not drop to meet a low supply. The typical result in most societies seems to be the same: people decide they would rather pay little and tolerate ineptitude than pay good wages and thus be able to demand a high level of performance.

This formulation applies to most slave labor, to domestic work in almost all countries past or present, to nearly all dirty, unskilled tasks, to K.P. in the armed services, and of course by and large to the performance of family role obligations.

By a structural peculiarity of the recruitment process this principle may be observed in the academic world—though instances in other spheres are doubtless to be uncovered. Here the administrative jobs pay relatively well, but the most desirable recruits are likely to be professors who rank that type of job as somewhat of a comedown. Thus, there is a relatively low supply of the highly competent, with the same result, a greater protection of ineptitude than would otherwise occur. This type of recruitment may also be observed in the selection of adminstrative personnel in foundations.

(3) Demand may be *deliberately* kept low by the sociopolitical structure. Here again there is little pressure on the group or collectivity to expose or punish the less productive. It is especially in government that one may locate such sub-

[22]Though numerically less important, it should not be forgotten, on the other hand, that jobs in this environment may be given to *some* talented and skilled men who would in a tighter market be classified by personnel men as "inept," i.e., "socially unacceptable," or too innovative or deviant, and so on.

[23]Space does not permit me to go into the matter, but there are technical and theoretical reasons for considering high demand and low supply separately. Although occupational and other outputs do operate through market processes, I believe that a wide variety of such demands—such as love, emotional support, household and "dirty" types of work—have a high inelasticity, especially at the lower demand levels. At a cautious minimum, there are some obvious sociological factors that limit the *range* within which both supply and demand *can* respond swiftly.

units, although perhaps they are common in all organizations large enough to confront the whole society on many fronts, e.g., General Motors or the Catholic Church.

In the recent past, examples have included such agencies as the Office of Civil Defense, numerous antidiscrimination units, vice squads and gambling squads, agencies to reduce or prevent water and air pollution, or to beautify and develop parks and highways, and so on. Safety research in the automobile industry is another such instance. A high level of performance by this type of sub-unit would produce strong political opposition. As a consequence, a fairly low, often ritual, level of output is tolerated, and thus there are few pressures to evaluate the personnel by reference to the supposed target performance.

In general, of course, where clients do not demand high quality in performance, whether in Civil Defense or American cooking, the inept are relatively better protected than in other types of situations.

(4) A variant formulation of the basic supply-demand relation is that there will be less or more protection of ineptitude, depending on its consequences for the power or prestige of the person who heads the collectivity. For example, if the subordinate's ineptitude reduces the chief's power, the latter is unlikely to tolerate low competence. This type of case may occur when the subordinate's action is highly visible, or has a public dimension, e.g., the messenger boys of the House of Representatives. An employee whose function it is to move between social systems or sub-systems will be under greater pressure to perform well, if a poor performance would reduce the authority of his chief.

Internal Processes. Of course, such environmental factors can operate only through group processes, but the collectivity also generates protective measures because of its own internal needs as well. Among these, the following may be noted. The first is that the inept create a "floor," a lowest permissible level of competence. To fire them is to raise that level, so that those who are now comfortably above it might be threatened. To some degree, the mediocre "need" the really inept. The Southern White, in this sense, has needed the Negro. Consequently, in perhaps most collectivities the thoroughgoing application of achievement criteria would be viewed as a threat.

Second, even the less competent have powers of bargaining, resources, pelf, contracts to give. Or they can make their fellow members feel guilty of inhumane conduct, thus invoking an alternate set of standards. In any given set of performance measurements, the costs of firing or downgrading the less able, or replacing them by better men, are weighted against the costs of permitting them to remain in the collectivity. This is simply another application of the general theory of role bargaining.[24]

Third, collectivities also assent to patterned exemptions from role obligations,[25] by which inevitable dips in performance are tolerated. These dips may be of short duration or not. Some permit the relaxing of standards because of another role obligation of high urgency or priority, e.g., the child of a working mother is ill, accidents, death in the family, and so on. Others express the tolerance of the group for individual fluctuations in personal integration, e.g., a man is going through a difficult marital crisis, has a work block, or becomes a heavy drinker for a while.

Another rule recognizes with compassion that the individual has entered on the normal declining curve in productivity with advancing age. What that age is will depend on the kind of activity the man performs. It is low among physical scientists, perhaps highest in politics and the law. In the occupational world, various structural solutions for this problem have been found, such as transferring a man to an essentially honorary or symbolic position, giving him easy physical work in a factory, handing over tasks of an essentially "human relations" type, or making him a representative of the organization in dealing with outside groups. More often, no formal changes are made, but less production is expected of him.[26]

A fourth internal factor is the complex problem of evaluation. That shrewd contemporary social analyst, Peter Ustinov, has noted that if the Secretary of State were to pass himself off as a comic, the observer would know within a few minutes that this is not his *métier*, but if a comic were to become Secretary of State, we would not at once discern any failure. The performance of the university president is especially difficult to measure, because of the complex relations between what the president does and the responses of his professors. Rewards are paid to the effective professor himself,

[24]See William J. Goode, "A Theory of Role Strain," *American Sociological Review*, 25 (August, 1960), pp. 483–496; and Peter M. Blau, *Exchange and Power in Social Life*, New York: Wiley, 1964, especially Ch. 4.

[25]Robert K. Merton, *Social Theory and Social Structure* (revised and enlarged edition), Glencoe, Ill.: The Free Press, 1957, pp. 368–384.

[26]See Goldner, *op. cit.*, pp. 714–724.

but the prestige of professors may also be used as a measure of the president's achievement (at the levels where presidents are evaluated) even if in fact he has hindered their work. That is, the professor is motivated to work hard for himself, but his achievement may be viewed as proof of the president's competence. By contrast, the president of a municipal university may be given a lower evaluation because he fails to attract creative professors, when it is the low achievement of the tenured men which makes the university unattractive to potential recruits.

In any event, the less able are protected more in those types of performances that are difficult to evaluate. Parenthood, religious behavior, and administration are conspicuous examples. When war included hand-to-hand combat, performance could of course be evaluated much more easily than it is today. Similarly, sports offer an especially clear set of standards by which to evaluate performance, though here too some protection of weaker members by their teams can be observed. To some degree, the adversary system in Anglo-Saxon law tests competence in a public way. The higher levels of basic research constitute another area in which the less able are more likely to be exposed, and their lower performance made known.

These instances are notable because they *do* permit ready evaluation of performance. Granted that measurement is difficult, the interesting sociological question remains: Why do people (who after all constantly measure each other as individuals) not create group techniques for evaluating and making known the individual's performance level? Throughout this analysis, I am, of course suggesting that, in spite of some achievement rhetoric, people do not really want such a measurement system built into the social structure. We can, however, take note of several main *types* of answers to the measurement problem.

Perhaps the most difficult performances to measure are those of interpersonal skills or personal interaction. It is especially in such activities and occupations that the less able have a greater chance of avoiding exposure and—as social commentators have reminded us for centuries—of obtaining a desired post. Of course, people do weigh one another with respect to these skills. However, the individual who can create a friendly atmosphere about himself may be able to escape any exposure of his inability to elicit a high performance from his subordinates, or to execute a bureaucratic task skillfully. He may make friends, but contribute little to the main task or target performance.

In such tasks, one common pattern of avoiding open competition is to assume that the problem of measurement can be skirted by refusing the position to people in low-ranking statuses, such as Negroes, Jews, and women, even when these traits are not important for the task, and some available candidates with those characteristics might conceivably manage the job well.

This pattern of "insulation" protects the less able by preventing competition with all but a limited number of preselected people. Essentially, then, the group selects an *irrelevant* trait, which can be a status or a performance that makes little or no contribution to the main task. The collectivity may alternatively focus instead on only *part* of the target performance. For example, a man may elicit loyalty among his crew, but cannot persuade them to work hard; the group ranks him by the loyalty of his crew.

A focus on the irrelevant status may combine with insulation to produce a lower skill level among those whose competition might otherwise be feared. If the group or stratum can command the *gateways* to training, insulating their own sons from open competition, then the *ultimate* result is that their own sons can indeed outperform those who were kept from acquiring those skills. The protection of ineptitude, then, begins much earlier, so that at the end point those who receive the training may well be superior. This complex process may be observed among the lower social strata, Negroes, Mexican-Americans, women, and so on.

This pattern is most strikingly illustrated in music. The less able can be less easily protected when a conspicuously inborn talent makes a difference, i.e., when measurement is easier. Thus, a goodly number of Negroes have achieved great success in popular music, though they were nearly autodidacts. By contrast, concert performance of standard music requires both high talent and a long and costly training. It is notable. but to be expected, that Negroes are rare in the latter field.[27]

---

[27]Perhaps the popular stereotype that "Negroes have rhythm" and are "musical" arose in part because it is one of the few areas in which it would be difficult to overlook a great talent. Until recently in the South, Whites sometimes visited Negro churches to listen to their choirs. One result was that a handful of Negro female singers *did* get the long and expensive education necessary to become concert performers of the standard repertoire.

These "answers" to the problem of measurement—focusing on an irrelevant trait, seizing on an irrelevant performance, insulating members from outside competition. barring the gateways to training—protect the less talented or less skillful. That evaluation of performance may be difficult goes without saying, but it is equally noteworthy that collectivities make few sustained moves toward solving the problem in the direction of rewarding on the basis of achievement. The work of a clergyman is especially hard to measure, in part because there has been little agreement on what the performance ought to achieve. However, both his superiors and clients are more likely to measure his work by, say, an increase in church attendance rather than by the parishioners' increased rejection of sin.

CONSEQUENCES OF PROTECTING THE LESS ABLE

Although we have by implication considered some of the consequences of these forms of protection, let us now examine them directly. One question must be faced at the outset. Does the protection of the less productive result in much inefficiency, so that the sub-system or collectivity (family, church, sports team) might fall or be destroyed?

Three important theoretical principles bear on this question. First, if I am correct in arguing that nearly all groups have social arrangements for protecting their inept, then that fact alone would not necessarily handicap any particular group. The soldier or sailor, observing the general disorganization, unwise recruitment, and misapplication of personnel resources during a war, may suppose that his side is bound to lose. However, since the opposing forces are similarly crippled, it is likely that other factors than the protection of the inept will decide the war. In blunt terms, most organizations and individuals do not have to perform at peak capacity in order to survive, because the competition is not doing so either.

At a somewhat broader level of generality, as I have elsewhere argued, social systems can operate with considerable anomie and incompetence.[28] This is especially true for socie-

[28]See especially my "Illegitimacy, Anomie, and Cultural Penetration," *American Sociological Review*, 26 (December, 1961), pp. 910–925; and

ties. Except in the case of war, which measures only one kind of performance, the threat of the environment is almost never so great as to destroy the advantages of human intelligence and organization.[29] Nearly always there is a sufficient surplus of manpower and resources to absorb almost any attack from the environment.

A second principle to be considered, in weighing the costs of protecting the less able, is that in fact some collectivities probably do go under because they protect their members too well. Organizations and sub-units compete primarily with others performing the same type of task, rather than with other social units in general. Upper-class families, for example, face their harshest competition for the available power, pelf, and prestige from other families in their own stratum, not from families at lower social ranks. For several generations their margin of safety may be great, but eventually they may fail. Other upper-class families are a more direct political threat. They are eligible for all the lucrative posts any given elite family possesses. Until the advent of the mass army, the elite fought each other in war.

The irony of the universal family pattern of protecting the less able children from open competition is that to the very extent that they succeed in this effort, they risk the diminution of their own family rank, because the next generation will be unable to survive the *intra*-elite contest—or even, possibly, the threat from men who rise from still lower ranks. Moreover, there is some evidence that the chances of revolution increase when a set of elite families succeeds too well in excluding the able who seek to rise.

CONSEQUENCES OF NOT PROTECTING THE LESS ABLE

At a still deeper level of theoretical analysis, even for maximum efficiency the system-needs of any social unit *require*

also "Social Mobility and Revolution," Camelot Conference, Airlee House, Virginia, June 4–6, 1965; and "Family Patterns and Human Rights," *International Social Science Journal*, XVIII (No. 1, 1966), pp. 41–54.

[29]This is one reason for the sterility of the search for the "requisites for the continuation of a society." Far too few societies have totally failed at all, and perhaps none has failed because it lacked any of these requisites. Lacking negative cases, it is difficult to test such requisites, and they are therefore to be viewed as a way of defining a society.

some protection of the inept, no matter what the goals of the group are, from the socialization of the child to the manufacture of transistor radios. The rigorous application of the norm of performance to the actions of all members of a collectivity would under most circumstances destroy both its social structure and its productivity.

It is, however, rare that any measurement of this kind has been carried out. Two of my first inquiries in the sociology of work ascertained: (a) that when sales performance was measured by individual success with the customer, salesmen engaged in several kinds of behavior that lowered *group* totals—holding customers who might have been waited on by others, refusing to replenish stock, and so on; and (b) that when management could prevent the formation of a genuine group, workers might have low morale but high individual productivity.[30] Also Blau outlined the consequences of the objective appraisal of performance in a clerical agency, some of which included falsifying records, undermining of the supervisor's authority, inconveniencing clients, and so on.[31] More recently, people doing industrial research have questioned the general assumption that an objective appraisal process would increase individual production.[32]

The sociological view is that placement, or punishment and reward, on the basis of performance alone, would essentially create a Hobbesian jungle, the undermining of group structure, the loss of the usual benefits of organization and cooperation, and the dissolution of group loyalties. Gouldner expresses this theoretical position effectively in his analysis of the contest system in Athenian society.[33] That system, he argues, "disposes individuals to make decisions that are often at variance with the needs and interests of the group." The type of open competition represented by the Greek contest system leads to bitterness, lowers the individual's commitment to group cooperation, creates strains in interpersonal relations, reduces conformity to established morality, and undermines

---

[30] Nicholas Babchuk and William J. Goode, "Work Incentives in a Self-Determined Group," *American Sociological Review*, 16 (October, 1951), pp. 679–687; and Goode and Fowler, *op. cit.* In the latter case, fortunately for the manager-owner, productivity depended very little on the maintenance of a group structure.

[31] Peter M. Blau, *The Dynamics of Bureaucracy*, Chicago: University of Chicago Press, 1955, pp. 44–47, 162–167, 208–213.

[32] Alvin Zander, editor, *Performance Appraisals*, Ann Arbor, Mich.: The Foundation for Research on Human Behavior, 1963.

[33] Alvin W. Gouldner, *Enter Plato*, New York: Basic Books, 1965, pp. 52 ff.

the stability of the *polis*. The failure to protect the inept would also, then, lower the output of the group.

Needless to say, I am omitting from this sketch the primarily psychodynamic consequences of appraisal by merit. These may include feelings of being threatened, responses of distrust and hostility toward those doing the appraising, aversion of superiors to communicate those appraisals to their subordinates, resistance mechanisms of individuals who receive low appraisals, lowering of the individual's performance because of his diminished esteem after receiving a low appraisal, and so on.[34]

Structures With Less Protection of Ineptitude. The laconic assertion that not protecting the inept would lower group output needs further analysis, since clearly there are types of activities and groups in which a close approximation of appraisal and reward by merit occurs, without a destructive outcome. Perhaps the closest approximations, as noted earlier, are sports and the basic scientific research in a university department or corporation. The cases may be instructive.

The relevant relationships can be sketched briefly. On a sports team, when an individual does very well, the system of measurement makes this known, but the rewards of the less able are *increased*, while their work load is decreased. This is also true of the basic research team, though less so. In the university department engaged in scientific research, this relationship is somewhat weaker—because what one individual first discovers, another cannot. Nevertheless: (a) if the more able do reduce their work output, this will not raise the relative standing of the less able, since performance is measured by reference to achievement in the field as a whole; (b) in addition, men in the same department usually work on different problems; and (c) if all reduce their production in order to protect the less able, all individuals lose somewhat because the prestige of their department drops,[35] and work becomes less fun for the participants.

[34]Most of these are noted by Alvin Zander, in "Research on Self-Evaluation, Feedback and Threats of Self-Esteem," in Zander, *op. cit.*, pp. 5–17. See also T. Whisler and S. Harper, editors, *Performance Appraisal: Research and Practice*, New York: Holt, Rinehart, and Winston, 1962; and Arthur R. Cohen, "Situational Structure, Self-Esteem and Threat-Oriented Reactions to Power," in Dorwin Cartwright, editor, *Studies in Social Power*, Ann Arbor, Mich.: Institute for Social Research, 1959.

[35]That individuals gain from being in the more successful departments is shown by Diane Crane, "Scientists at Major and Minor Universities," *American Sociological Review*, 30 (1965), pp. 699–714.

Cooperation and Output. These relationships do not hold in most work situations, although the more skilled corporation managers try to achieve such a structure where possible. If an individual does his best, knowing that achievement criteria alone will determine his advancement, the less able will drop relatively in the esteem of their supervisors, and possibly the level of required production from each member will rise. The less able members may, in fact, be squeezed out because they do not meet the new standard. Moreover, if each individual is rewarded only for his own performance, then in effect the group has given him nothing; whether his achievement level is high or low, he will feel no loyalty to the group.

If, as is now generally true of work systems, production does in fact partly depend on the efficiency of group organization and cooperation, the end result is likely to be less output, not more. By contrast, if the individual knows that when he needs it he will be protected somewhat by the group, he enjoys his personal relations with its members more, feels more securely identified with them, protects himself less from them, and is willing for the sake of the group to cooperate even when it will not raise his individual standing on the achievement scale.

Of course the professions, for all their emphasis on the rhetoric of individualism and achievement, illustrate the structural pattern common to most work situations, especially those with a strong union: the loss to all members would be greater, if the organizational structure failed, than would be the gain to a few highly able individuals if unrestricted public measurement of skill and effectiveness were permitted.[36]

Even the actual combat situation in war illustrates once more the dependence of organizational effectiveness on some protection of the inept. Without it, the competent will be killed along with the incompetent, for the former need the firepower and the loyalty of the latter. Such loyalty would not be so freely given if the inept could not count on being protected themselves. As implied earlier, the treatment of the demoted in management is an index of the judgment that the

[36]This is pointed out in my two articles, "Community Within a Community: the Professions," *op. cit.*, and "Encroachment, Charlatanism, and the Emerging Profession: Psychology, Sociology, and Medicine," *op. cit.;* and in more detail in *The Professions in Modern Society,* by William J. Goode, Mary Jean Huntington, and Robert K. Merton, unpub. Mimeo., Russell Sage Foundation, 1956, "Code of Ethics."

less able must be protected, to increase the effectiveness of the larger group.[37]

UTILIZATION OF THE INEPT UNDER INDUSTRIALIZATION

The preceding relationships merit further testing, but it is also worthwhile here to consider how they should be qualified on theoretical grounds. For even if all societies, and nearly all collectivities do protect the less able, and even if failure to protect them will usually reduce output, it is equally clear that the protection of ineptitude can also *reduce* the effectiveness of the group. Certainly the evidence from societies with a high protection of the inept, such as caste or feudal systems, suggests that a high degree of protection is typically associated with low production. How does the utilization of the inept affect output?

The earlier sections of this paper anticipated that question by offering the hypothesis that social structures embody a tension between two factors, the protection *of* the inept and the protection of the group *from* the inept. At the psychological level this may be viewed as a tension between the frustration of the more able, and the degradation of the less able. Social structures vary in their solutions to this tension. For example, as noted earlier, family systems are far toward the extreme of placing little emphasis on achievement in ranking people, while sports (especially individual competition) fall toward the opposite extreme.

Social analysts have noted these differences, and have generally asserted that, for psychological integration, the individual cannot operate solely in activities whose criteria for reward are mainly those of performance. Everyone must at times retreat to other areas, such as friendship or the family, or perhaps religion and recreation, in which people are somewhat more protected from group downgrading or expulsion

[37]Fred H. Goldner interprets the varied solutions to this problem as ways of avoiding the "dysfunctions" of demotion, in his "Demotion in Industrial Management," *op. cit.* He also introduces the useful fact that demotion is psychologically easier for some, because the costs of high responsibility are thought to be great: weighed against these costs, demotion can sometimes be palatable.

by a relatively lower frequency of public rankings, and the lack of refined ranks.[88]

This paper has focused, however, on the social structures which support nonachievement behavior *and* values even in groups or organizations whose rhetoric emphasizes achievement criteria. Some of the resulting protection of the inept is necessary if the collectivity is to produce effectively.

Yet such a hypothesis does not answer the question of how *much* protection of the inept is necessary for the highest efficiency or output. It is obvious, however, as a partial answer, that the modern industrial system outproduces all prior social systems. Is this the result, as so many have claimed, of giving freer scope to the highest talent and skill, and from rewarding more by merit than other societies have done?

That possibility cannot now be rejected, but I wish to suggest an alternative hypothesis, which emerges from the basic focus of this inquiry—how social structures handle the problem of what to do with the less competent. My alternative hypothesis is that the modern system is more productive because its social structures *utilize the inept more efficiently*, rather than because it gives greater opportunity and reward to the more able.

At one level this alternative explanation is merely self-evident. The two most significant tools of industrial society are the rationalized bureaucracy and the factory; their relation to ineptitude is the same. Both are based on a high division of labor, with fairly precise definitions of the task. As a consequence, a wide range of talent can acquire the skill necessary to carry out most jobs. Within any job level, some people will be much less competent than others, or than others whose job levels are lower, but they *can* do the job. Both the machine and the bureaucratic system lower the chances of catastrophic individual failure by the inept. They embody a control system which diminishes the range of possible error on the part of the individual worker. And, as so many essayists have noted, they also diminish the advantages that high talent would create, by narrowing the scope of free action. Then too, mod-

---

[88] In Talcott Parsons' formulation, each sub-system must go through the "latency phase" of the AGIL sequence from time to time, but other sub-systems (notably the family) may have as a *primary* activity (its "output") the latency function, thus restoring the individual to a healthier state for further effective participation in, say, an "instrumental" system such as the factory. See "An Outline of the Social System," in Talcott Parsons *et al.*, editors, *Theories of Society*, New York: The Free Press, 1961, Vol. 1, pp. 30–79.

ern egalitarian ideology encourages men to feel valued as persons, providing motivation to all.

By contrast, the caste or feudal society gave great scope to talent, but only if the talented man was born to high position. Relying on placement by birth, such societies gave much protection to the inept, but gained little from it. Their productive technology was not organized into sub-tasks or sub-units or carefully articulated job assignments, which would maximize the productivity of the less able. The less competent in high places could do more damage, and the inept in lower positions could not contribute as much, as in modern society.

Variation within Industrial Society. Evidently societies vary in their solutions to this problem, as do smaller units (sports teams, churches, and so forth) within each society. However, even with similar types of work organizations some variation is observable. In the French bureaucracy, for example, very little freedom of action is given to the outstanding, or for that matter even to the chief, and the lower echelons are still more controlled. On the other hand, from time to time an imaginative new organizational system is evolved by the very top men in the bureaucracy.[39]

In the Japanese system, entrance is granted to those who do well in competitive examinations, but of course that success is strongly determined by ascriptive criteria. Belonging to the right families guarantees better training for the tests.[40] Once hired, they move upward by seniority rather than merit, and people are rarely fired. However, the supervisor of a work unit gets credit for any ideas generated by people in his group, and precisely for that reason he need not attempt to stifle good ideas. Granted, the more able man receives little advantage in promotion, but he does receive group esteem and some of his talent is put to use. Individuals are protected, and there is a correspondingly high degree of group loyalty. One result is that the organization as a whole is much more productive and creative than the United States observer would predict from the simple statement that non-achievement factors play a large role in the Japanese factory and bureaucracy.

In the American bureaucracy, perhaps the worker can ob-

[39]Crozier, *op. cit.*, pp. 40 ff and 282 ff.

[40]See Herbert Passin, *Society and Education in Japan,* New York: Teachers College, Columbia University, 1965, especially Ch. 6; and Ezra F. Vogel, *Japan's New Middle Class: The Salary Man and his Family in a Tokyo Suburb,* Berkeley: University of California Press, 1963.

tain more individual credit for his contribution than would be likely under the Japanese system. Both factory and bureaucracy in the United States seem to change more easily than in France. The American system has become more decentralized, and more autonomous at the lower levels, than either the Japanese or the French. Superiors consult more easily with subordinates in the United States than in the other two countries. This pattern may increase somewhat the chances of obtaining an advantage from the contributions of the more able, but also yields less protection to the less competent.

CONCLUSION

So brisk a set of comparisons does not aim at a full answer to the question of optimum production or efficiency, but rather serves to illustrate the fact that apparently similar types of structure may give more or less protection to the inept, and more or less protection *from* the inept. The answer, if we were able to obtain it over the next few decades, would yield a still more useful by-product: how to create sets of social structures in different areas of action, to correspond more closely with our own values. In these relations, as in much of our social life, we may *will* some of the proximate social patterns without approving their ultimate result. If we knew better the full consequences of given arrangements for protecting the inept, we might decide to change these structures.

With reference to such values, I have ignored a number of issues that would have to be faced in a more extensive analysis. One, of course, is whether a society can or should reward equally those who are known to be less productive.[41] On a different level of values, though we may feel the less able performer ought not to be given more rewards, some of us may also assert that the performances properly to be rewarded are not those of automobile production and billboards, or even

[41]For an examination of some relevant arguments about this matter, see Melvin M. Tumin, "Some Unapplauded Consequences of Social Mobility in a Mass Society," *Social Forces*, 36 (October, 1957), pp. 32–37; and "Some Disfunctions of Institutional Imbalance," *Behavioral Science*, 1 (July, 1956), pp. 218–223; as well as "Rewards and Task Orientations," *American Sociological Review*, 20 (August, 1955), pp. 419–423.

moon-rockets, but the far less easily measurable performances of warmth and loving, truth—note that the problem here is not one of ineptitude but simply a lack of demand—beauty and taste, laughter, compassion, courage, generosity, or the support of variety in men and women.

We would, at the last, also have to examine not only our own values about the equality of opportunity, and the degradation of those who would inevitably fall behind,[42] but the more complex consequences for every sector or sub-system of the society. In doing so, we might have to take on a significant but nearly neglected task of an imaginative theory of society, the analysis and creation of utopias,[43] based on our widening and deepening knowledge of how social systems really operate. What kind of societies are in fact possible, other than those which have existed?

Perhaps, by ascertaining both our values and the possible organizations for achieving them, we might learn that the costs of many contemporary patterns are too great. I do not agree with the many critics in sociology who hold that our dominant theory is merely an extended Panglossian commentary, proving this is the best of all possible worlds. Doubtless, whatever is, is possible, and whatever is may have had to be, but we can, I believe, go beyond those powerful laws and demonstrate, as other sciences have before us, that many desirable but presently nonexistent arrangements *are* also possible.

[42]Michael Young, in his *The Rise of the Meritocracy, 1872–1933*, London: Pelican, 1963, implies that a pure system by merit could be inaugurated, and the principle of merit really accepted by the lower social strata. The dissidence that develops, in his satire, comes primarily from the proposal to return to placement by inheritance.

[43]Wilbert E. Moore, "The Utility of Utopias," *American Sociological Review*, 31 (December, 1966), pp. 765–722.

The Motives of Hamlet

by
Theodore Caplow

A great many dramatic situations can be cast in triadic form, since they involve the confrontation of a coalition and a closely related opponent. It remains to be seen whether analyzing a work of literature by means of triad theory contributes anything either to the theory or to our understanding of the drama.

Hamlet is an obvious choice for such an exercise, if only because of Shakespeare's explicit concern with the nature of human action: "For here lies the point:" says the Gravedigger, "if I drown myself wittingly, it argues an act; and an act hath three branches—it is to act, to do, and to perform." Although a distinguished Shakespearian critic once called the history of Hamlet criticism "a blot on the intellectual record of the race,"[1] hardly any writer of the past two centuries with a theory of human motivation has resisted the temptation to try it out on this inexhaustible text. No other piece of writing has provoked half as many hypotheses. An anonymous German scholar is quoted as saying that every essay on *Hamlet* has a good part and a bad; in the good part the author refutes all previous theories; and in the bad part he presents his own.

By virtue of its depth and breadth, Hamlet criticism covers every conceivable aspect of the play. The rosters of the University of Wittenberg have been combed to show that several Rosenkrantzes and Gyldnstjernes were enrolled there in the seventeenth century. The view from Krönberg Castle at sunrise has been checked against the versions of the ghost scene in the First and Second Quartos. The customs governing the burial of suicides in Denmark have been scrutinized.[2] Every

From Theodore Caplow, *Two Against One: Coalitions in Triads,* © 1968, pp. 114–127. Reprinted by permission of Prentice-Hall, Inc., Englewood Cliffs, New Jersey.

[1] Elmer Edgar Stoll, "Hamlet: An Historical and Comparative Study," *Research Publications of the University of Minnesota*, VIII, No. 5 (September 1919).

[2] Claud W. Sykes, "Alias William Shakespeare?" in C. C. H. Williamson, ed., *Readings on the Character of Hamlet* (London: George Allen & Unwin, 1950).

word in the saga of Amleth, written down by Saxo Grammaticus in the twelfth century and adapted by Belleforest in his *Histoires Tragiques* published in 1576, has been examined with exceeding care. Shakespeare's indebtedness to writings he might have read, such as Burton's *Anatomy of Melancholy* and Montaigne's *Apologie de Raimond Sebond* has been painstakingly parsed; and the influences of unknown works, like the lost Hamlet play possibly written by Thomas Kyd have been weighed with equal gravity.

More important for our present purpose, the personal relationships in *Hamlet* have been analyzed with a care unprecedented in literature or life. With regard to Hamlet's feelings about the Players, Claudius' sentiments towards Polonius, Ophelia's chastity, and the friendship between Hamlet and Horatio, every shred of evidence has been culled and compared, although, by some miracle, new evidence continues to be found, such as Wilson's recent discovery that the courtiers interpret the play-within-a-play as a threat by Hamlet to poison Claudius and not as a revelation of the elder Hamlet's murder.[3] The text is so fertile in such discoveries that some desperate critics have concluded that Shakespeare designed the play as an unsolvable puzzle.

The first scene, it will be remembered, takes place on the battlements of the royal castle. The sentries and Hamlet's friend Horatio see a ghost they recognize as Hamlet's father. The second scene introduces Claudius, the late King's brother, who has married Gertrude, the widowed Queen, and ascended the throne. Laertes, son of the King's minister Polonius, is given permission to return to France. Hamlet is chided for mourning his father too much and yields to the urging of the King and Queen not to return to school at Wittenberg. There follows the first soliloquy in which Hamlet complains about his mother's hasty and "incestuous" marriage with his uncle. He is interrupted by Horatio, who tells him about the ghost; they undertake to watch for it the same night. In the next scene, Laertes takes leave of his sister Ophelia and warns her against Hamlet's attentions. Their father, Polonius, overhearing the conversation, questions her about Hamlet and orders her to break off all contact with him; she agrees to do so. The same night, on the sentries' platform, the Ghost appears again, telling Hamlet that Claudius poisoned him as he slept in his orchard and accusing

[3] J. Dover Wilson, *What Happens in Hamlet* (Cambridge: The University Press, 1962).

Gertrude of indecent haste in marrying again and possibly of prior adultery with Claudius. He exhorts Hamlet to take revenge against Claudius, but warns him not to contrive anything against his mother. Hamlet swears his friends to absolute secrecy.

Between Acts I and II there is a lapse of time. As Act II opens, Polonius is sending a servant to spy upon Laertes' conduct in Paris. Then Ophelia enters to report that Hamlet, disordered in dress and appearance, had come to her room, stared, sighed, and gone away. Since her last appearance, she has rejected his letters and denied him access to her. Polonius goes to report the incident to the King.

The King and Queen receive Hamlet's old school fellows, Rosenkrantz and Guildenstern, who have been summoned to find out what afflicts Hamlet. Afterwards the King speaks with the Ambassadors returned from Norway. Polonius, showing the King a love letter from Hamlet to Ophelia, insists that Hamlet has been driven mad by Ophelia's coldness. A meeting between the lovers is arranged, with the King and Polonius hidden to overhear what is said. Hamlet baits Polonius in the fishmonger scene (according to one theory, because he has overheard the end of the previous conversation), then greets Rosenkrantz and Guildenstern, and makes them admit they have been sent for on his behalf. He learns that the "tragedians of the city" are on their way to Elsinore and presently they appear. At Hamlet's request, the First Player recites a long speech about the killing of Priam by Pyrrhus and the frenzy of Hecuba and the Players agree to stage a play called "The Murther of Gonzago" for the entertainment of the Court and to insert some new lines in it.

Hamlet is left alone for a long soliloquy in which he contrasts the Player's simulated grief for Hecuba with his own silence about his father, then reminds himself that he has no evidence against his uncle except the testimony of the Ghost who "may be a devil," and explains his plan to have the Players re-enact a murder similar to that of his father so that he can watch Claudius' reaction. Rosenkrantz and Guildenstern report to the King and Queen that they have not learned much from Hamlet and they convey his invitation to the play.

Meanwhile, the stage is set for Ophelia's meeting with Hamlet, spied on by the King and Polonius. Hamlet appears, delivers his famous soliloquy on suicide, and greets Ophelia, who begins the interview by returning his presents and complaining of unkindness. Hamlet upbraids her harshly and somewhat enigmatically. The King, convinced that Hamlet is neither in love nor mad, decides to send him away to England. Then, Polonius plans another interview, this one to be between Hamlet and the Queen, with himself concealed.

Hamlet briefs the Players on their evening's performance—and on the art of acting. He enlists Horatio to help watch Claudius at the critical moment so that later they may compare notes. As the play-within-a-play begins, there is more conversation among the principals, then a dumb show which recapitulates the murder of a king in a garden by a man who takes the crown for himself and seduces the queen. One of the major enigmas of *Hamlet* is that Claudius is unmoved by this almost literal re-enactment of his crime. The play-within-a-play proceeds. The Player Queen assures her husband in extravagant terms that she would not consider remarriage if he died. The real King and Queen are not seriously perturbed until "one Lucianus, nephew to the King" enters among the Players and begins to brew a vegetable poison. At this point, the King rises, Polonius stops the performance, and the entire Court sweeps away leaving Hamlet and Horatio behind. They agree that the Ghost's story has been verified. Almost at once, Rosenkrantz and Guildenstern return to say that the King is "marvelous distempered" and that Hamlet's mother has sent for him. Hamlet teases them mercilessly.

Rosenkrantz and Guildenstern are ordered to take Hamlet away to England. Left alone, the King attempts to pray and also tells the audience that the Ghost's accusations are true. Hamlet enters unseen, considers attacking Claudius but forbears to do it lest he send the King to Heaven by killing him "in the purging of his soul, when he is fit and seasoned for his passage." He then goes to his mother's chamber where Polonius has just hidden himself. Hamlet's entrance is so menacing that the Queen calls for help, Polonius echoes her cry, and Hamlet runs him through with a sword. Without much further attention to Polonius, he scolds the Queen for exchanging his father for his uncle. And although she seems remorseful, Hamlet's fury increases. The Ghost appears again, in a nightgown, visible to Hamlet but not to the Queen, and reminds Hamlet to whet his "almost blunted purpose" and in effect to be nicer to his mother. Hamlet continues to scold Gertrude but in a calm and reasonable tone to which she seems receptive. He urges her to break with Claudius: "Good night—but go not to my uncle's bed," and instructs her not to reveal that his madness is assumed. This much, at least, Gertrude promises, and they part on good terms, Hamlet tugging the corpse of Polonius towards the exit.

After an interlude of gruesome hide-and-seek the body is found, and Hamlet is shipped off to England in the custody of Rosenkrantz and Guildenstern, who carry secret letters ordering the English to execute him. As they depart, Hamlet encounters the Norwegian army on its way to an unnecessary war and contrasts "The imminent death of twenty thousand men/That for a fantasy and trick of fame/Go to their graves" with the slow progress of his own revenge.

Back at Elsinore, Ophelia goes mad and Laertes returns from France to raise a rebellion. He breaks in on the King and Queen and demands satisfaction for his father's death. The King calms him, deflects his anger to Hamlet, and promises to assist in his revenge. Meanwhile Horatio learns from a letter that Hamlet has escaped from his convoy and has returned to Denmark. The King has just begun to plot with Laertes when another letter announces Hamlet's imminent arrival. Then the King and Laertes plan the fencing match at which Hamlet is to be killed by a poisoned foil and a poisoned drink. They learn of Ophelia's drowning in the brook.

Act V begins with two clowns amusing each other with jokes and songs as they dig Ophelia's grave. Hamlet enters with Horatio, asks curious questions and discovers the unearthed skull of Yorick. His reflections on mortality are interrupted by the arrival of Ophelia's funeral procession, Laertes and Hamlet grapple in the grave and then Hamlet storms off. He tells Horatio how he had found the King's commission and had forged another ordering the immediate execution of Rosenkrantz and Guildenstern on their arrival in England. A courtier brings him Laertes' challenge to a fencing match attended by the King, Queen, "and all the State." The match begins. The King sets out the poisoned cup. Hamlet is winning when Laertes wounds him with the poisoned weapon, but in the scuffle they exchange rapiers and Laertes is poisoned also. The queen drinks the poisoned wine and dies, Laertes confesses his treachery, Hamlet stabs the King and forces the rest of the wine down his throat. Thus all the principals die, except for Horatio who remains alive to tell the story. Fortinbras comes in and Hamlet is eulogized.

Although there are more than two dozen speaking parts in Hamlet and all the minor personages are well-rounded, interpretation, like the play itself, fixes upon the central figure of the Prince. Most conceptions of him fall into three categories—the sick hero, the healthy hero, and the nonhero.[4]

Hamlet's illness is usually traced back to Henry Mackenzie, who wrote about 1789. This early criticism described Hamlet's illness as not very grave, although, according to Mackenzie, Hamlet shows "some temporary marks of a real disorder" and the delicacy of his feelings toward Ophelia approaches weakness.[5] In *Wilhelm Meister's Apprenticeship*, which first appeared in 1796, Hamlet's condition was described thus:

> A lovely, pure, noble, and most moral nature, without the strength of nerve which forms a hero, seeks to meet a burden which it cannot bear and must not pass away. All duties are holy for him; the present is too hard. Impossibilities have been required of him; not in themselves impossibilities, but such for him. He winds, and turns, and torments himself; he advances and recoils; is ever put in mind, ever puts himself in mind; at last does all but lose his purpose from his thoughts; yet still without recovering his peace of mind.[6]

This became the prevailing stage interpretation in the following century, and the sweet, nervous Hamlet, high-mindedly moping from one soliloquy to the next, is still with us.

At the end of the nineteenth century the patient took a turn for the worse. The magisterial Bradley, professor of poetry in the University of Oxford, diagnosed Hamlet as catatonic:

> . . . all this, and whatever else passed in a sickening round through Hamlet's mind, was not the healthy and right deliberation of a man with such task, but otiose thinking hardly deserving the name of thought, an unconscious weaving of pretexts for inaction, aimless tossings on a sick bed. . . .[7]

[4]Omitting a category of wider surmises, as that Hamlet was a woman or a symbol of the Roman Catholic Church.

[5]Henry Mackenzie, quoted in Williamson, *op. cit.*, pp. 24–27.

[6]Johann Wolfgang von Goethe, *Wilhelm Meister's Apprenticeship*, trans. Thomas Carlyle (New York: Collier Books, 1962), p. 236.

[7]A. C. Bradley, *Shakespearian Tragedy* (New York: The Macmillan Company, 1949), p. 123 (orig. pub. 1904).

From this it was only a short step to Freud's Hamlet, a neurotic "able to do anything except take vengeance on the man who did away with his father and took that father's place with his mother, the man who shows him the repressed wishes of his own childhood realized."[8] Freud was also quite sure that *Hamlet* reflected the poet's own experience, discovering that it was written soon after the deaths of Shakespeare's father and his young son, Hamnet, although later Freud "ceased to believe that the author of Shakespeare's works was the man from Stratford."[9] A much more elaborate psychoanalytic version was developed by Ernest Jones.[10]

In the measured judgment of T. S. Eliot, author of *The Cocktail Party* and other notable works for the stage, Shakespeare failed entirely with *Hamlet* because he undertook a subject too difficult for his talents.[11]

Hamlet the healthy hero has had a longer, less complex history. Stoll, who brought a great deal of factual evidence to the feverish world of Hamlet criticism,[12] showed that Hamlet was universally perceived to be a noble, gallant, and admirable figure for nearly two hundred years after the play first appeared. Popular and literary opinion found nothing wrong with Hamlet until the rise of romanticism. A comparison with other revenge plays of the sixteenth century suggests that the delayed execution of the revenge was an essential convention (otherwise there could be no play). The self-reproaches of the hero are equally conventional, reminding the audience that he takes his task seriously and does not lose sight of it during the postponements around which the dramatic action is staged. According to this interpretation, Hamlet has no real grounds for self-reproach. None of the other characters describe him as weak, timorous, or cowardly. The closing speeches—the author's opportunity to summarize—praise Hamlet more highly than any other Shakespearian hero. The peals of artillery at the end do not call to mind a frightened invalid. Stoll demonstrates by many Elizabethan examples that Hamlet's reluctance to kill the King at prayer lest he send his soul to Heaven was a perfectly normal sentiment for

[8]Sigmund Freud, *The Interpretation of Dreams,* trans. James Strachey (London: The Hogarth Press, Ltd., 1958), p. 65 (orig. pub. 1900).

[9]*Ibid.,* fn., p. 266.

[10]See his Essays in *Applied Psychoanalysis* (London and Vienna: International Psychoanalytical Press, 1923).

[11]T. S. Eliot, "Hamlet," in *Selected Essays* (New York: Harcourt, Brace & World, Inc., 1950), pp. 121–26.

[12]Stoll, *op. cit.*

an Elizabethan audience which would have been accustomed to the idea that revenge—at least stage revenge—should be directed against both body and soul. This is probably the crucial point in the choice between a morbid and a wholesome Hamlet, and we shall return to it a little later.

With the characteristic tendency of Hamlet criticism to fall into excesses, the twentieth-century revival of the healthy hero has led to such views as those of Grebanier,[13] whose Hamlet is so faultless that Ophelia must be presented as a psychopath to account for the trouble between them, and to the more intricate opinion of Dover Wilson[14] that Hamlet suffers from a mild type of emotional disorder while feigning a more serious syndrome. If Hamlet is given a clean bill of health, the play's mystery is shifted to the other characters. Does Polonius feign his dotage or is he really senile? Do the Ghost's passing references to adultery prove that Gertrude and Claudius had an affair before the murder? If so, how did the Ghost find out about it after his death?

An even greater effect of novelty can be achieved by making Hamlet the villain of the play. In Knight's *Wheel of Fire* Hamlet "is not of flesh or blood, he is a spirit of penetrating intellect and cynicism and misery, without faith in himself or anyone else, murdering his love of Ophelia, on the brink of insanity, taking delight in cruelty, torturing Claudius, breaking his mother's heart, a poison in the midst of the healthy bustle of the Court." In this fascinating version, Claudius, "a man kindly, confident, and fond of pleasure," courteous and dignified, a "true leader," is the hero. "Claudius, as he appears in the play, is not a criminal. He is—strange as it may seem—a good and gentle King, enmeshed by the chain of causality linking him with his crime. And this chain, he might, perhaps, have broken except for Hamlet, and all would have been well."[15]

For Salvador de Madariaga, Hamlet (whom he turned into a Spaniard with as little hesitation as that Herr Professor Borne who wrote "Hamlet *is* Germany") is a ruthless, egotistical killer on the model of Cesare Borgia. Less reputable scholars have revealed that the Prince was a syphilitic, a homosexual, or an impostor like Mark Twain's Pauper.

[13]Bernard Grebanier, *The Heart of Hamlet: The Play Shakespeare Wrote* (New York: Thomas Y. Crowell Company, 1960).

[14]Wilson, *op. cit.*

[15]G. Wilson Knight, *The Wheel of Fire: Interpretation of Shakespeare's Tragedy* (Cleveland: World Publishing Company, 1963), pp. 34, 35, and 38 (orig. pub. 1930).

It should be interesting to see whether triad theory kindles any new light here. The record exists to warn us against the dangers of taking the play too literally or not literally enough.

Triad theory deals with the tactical constraints that develop in every situation involving contention. The formation of a winning coalition in a triad is an attempt to halt contention by establishing peace within the coalition and securely subjugating the opponent, but this purpose cannot be accomplished as long as the opponent has some hope of luring either of the partners out of the existing coalition and into a new coalition with himself.

Suppose we think of Hamlet as a living man and visualize his problem in tactical terms. There is never any question of his ability to gain access to Claudius and stab him. Except for one passing reference, Shakespeare eliminated the Swiss guards who protected the King in earlier versions of the story. Let us suppose, then, that Hamlet had left the Ghost's presence to march to the King and cut his throat forthwith. As many commentators have pointed out, this would have dispensed with most of the play. And as Hamlet says, the Ghost's testimony is not conclusive:

> The spirit that I have seen
> May be a devil, and the devil hath power
> T'assume a pleasing shape, and perhaps
> Out of my weakness and my melancholy,
> As he is very potent with such spirits,
> Abuses me to damn me.

But these difficulties aside, we have only to imagine the aftermath of that decisive, unhesitating act to take most of the mystery out of Hamlet's indecision. Let us remember that there is no shred of demonstrable evidence to support the Ghost's story, and none is obtainable. The text seems to tell us that Gertrude is ignorant of the elder Hamlet's murder. So far as Hamlet—or the audience—can determine, there is no chance that witnesses to the crime will ever come forward. The exotic mode of poisoning[16] precludes a proof by autopsy. Hamlet, so far as he knows, will never be able to demonstrate to an impartial observer that his father was murdered or that

[16]Modern nit-picking has identified the poison as the alkaloid hyoscine in the plant *Hyoscyamus niger* and has pronounced the method of administering it plausible, although apparently untested.

Claudius was the murderer. In fact, Hamlet never *does* obtain any direct evidence about the murder. Claudius' reaction to the play-within-a-play is sufficient to convince Hamlet, and perhaps Horatio as well; it would hardly satisfy a jury. The commission issued to Rosenkrantz and Guildenstern to have Hamlet put to death in England provides him with demonstrable grounds for taking revenge on his own account, and the King's effort to poison Hamlet by one means or another lends support to the tale that Horatio eventually unfolds to the survivors. But if we did not have Claudius' confession in the prayer scene—addressed only to Heaven and the audience—there would be as much uncertainty about the murder of the elder Hamlet as now remains about Gertrude's adultery. Hamlet never entertains the hope that Claudius will make a public confession.

Hamlet's tactical problem is how to take his revenge on Claudius without himself being punished as a murderer. Were he to kill Claudius after the initial appearance of the Ghost or when he found him at prayer he could hardly hope to escape with his own life. To the Court of Elsinore and to the unseen populace whose presence is felt throughout the play the act would be abhorrent—regicide, almost parricide—a horror not to be excused or understood. Revenge for his father's murder is the only motive that might extenuate such a crime, keep Hamlet's life and honor intact, and leave him free to ascend the throne.

But it is unlikely that Hamlet's mere assertion would convince the onlookers of Claudius' guilt. And the evidence he might present would seem ridiculous—the testimony of a phantom, the King's boredom at a palace entertainment. The corroboration of Horatio—Hamlet's friend and follower—would be plainly worthless. There is only one witness whose testimony might save Hamlet after he killed Claudius, and whose opposition after the same event would certainly be his undoing. Hamlet's sole hope of surviving an act of revenge is to win his mother's support, or at least her neutrality. And this, to my mind, is the central action of the play—the contention within the Claudius-Gertrude-Hamlet triad as Hamlet attempts to dissolve the coalition of Claudius and Gertrude against himself.

Hamlet's role begins with a conversation among all three of them and ends in the same way. The initial power distribution is displayed in their first scene together as the King "beseeches" and the Queen "prays" Hamlet to give up his intention of going back to school in Wittenberg. Both of them seem to recognize that he is free to refuse. Hamlet ignores the King but yields to his mother's wish. At this time Claudius is more than affable—"be as ourself in Denmark"—and he celebrates Hamlet's decision by formal carousing and salutes of artillery.

There is no doubt for the moment that Claudius, the anointed King, is stronger than Hamlet, but the manner of his election is not very clear and research into the constitution of medieval Denmark does not help much. There seems to have been an elective procedure at one time, but the King's eldest son was generally the sole candidate, and, in any case, it is not certain that Shakespeare had the Danish constitution in mind. During his first appearance, Claudius refers to Gertrude as "Th'imperial jointress to this warlike state," suggesting that he—and possibly the elder Hamlet as well—held the crown through Gertrude, as did some husbands of English and Scottish queens. There is also a frank announcement that the councilors have played a part in arranging the succession, "nor have we herein barred your better wisdoms, which have freely gone with this affair along." Later on there will be repeated hints that public opinion has not entirely accepted the election of Claudius. Throughout the play Hamlet is, among other things, the potential leader of a coup d'état, and this may be why he is addressed with such circumspection by Claudius and Gertrude. Laertes, warning Ophelia about Hamlet's intentions, speaks of him as though he were already King:

> . . . his will is not his own;
> For he himself is subject to his birth.
> He may not, as unvalued persons do,
> Carve for himself, for on his choice depends
> The safety and health of this whole state
> And therefore must his choice be circumscrib'd
> Unto the voice and yielding of that body
> Whereof he is the head.

The King pursues his investigation of Hamlet's affliction with a growing suspicion that Hamlet threatens him and his crown. One modern scholar[17] attaches extraordinary importance to Hamlet's remark that the murderer in the play-within-a-play is "one Lucianus, nephew to the King,"

[17]J. Dover Wilson, *op. cit.*

interpreting this as a thinly veiled threat against Claudius' life by Hamlet, his nephew. Upon hearing the remark, the King loses no time in sending Rosenkrantz and Guilderstern back to Hamlet for further information, and this time Hamlet openly declares that he wants the crown.

> HAMLET: Sir, I lack advancement.
> ROSENKRANTZ: How can that be, when you have the voice of the King himself for your succession in Denmark?
> HAMLET: Ay, sir, but "while the grass grows"—the proverb is something musty.[18]

When this report is brought to Claudius, he mutters about his personal safety and begins to draft Hamlet's travel orders. After the death of Polonius, the King's apprehension of danger is even stronger, but he still speaks to Hamlet with circumspect politeness, and reminds his followers that Hamlet enjoys too much popular support to be attacked directly: "yet must not be put the strong laws on him; he's loved of the distracted multitude." Claudius is even more explicit about Hamlet's political strength in explaining to Laertes why Hamlet was not accused of murdering Polonius: "the other motive/Why to a public count I might not go/Is the great love the general gender bear him."

All that the King dares to do is hasten Hamlet's departure to England and secretly command his execution there. This attempt on his life becomes the fourth count in Hamlet's private indictment of Claudius, the first three being the murder of his father, the seduction of his mother, and the usurpation of the crown that should have been his.

> He that hath kill'd my king, and whor'd my mother;
> Popp'd in between th'election and my hopes;
> Thrown out his angle for my proper life,
> And with such coz'nage—is't not perfect conscience
> To quit him with his arm?

In the last scene of the play, Hamlet, dying, nominates Fortinbras to succeed him, as if he had always been the rightful King. As the play closes, Fortinbras reflects that "he was likely had he been put on, /To have prov'd most royally."

Until the play-within-a-play, Claudius and Gertrude always

---

[18]"While the grass grows, the horse starves."

confront Hamlet together and they speak with one voice, although with delicate differences of tone which tell us that Gertrude is genuinely concerned about her son while Claudius fears him. Nevertheless, they act jointly—urging Hamlet to stay at Court, sending for Rosenkrantz and Guildenstern, testing Polonius' theory that Hamlet is distracted by love, accepting the invitation to the play-within-a-play, and arranging the interview that follows it. Shakespeare clearly intends them to be a coalition whenever they face Hamlet. Business that does not involve the Prince, such as Laertes' petition and the negotiations with Norway, is handled by the King alone.

We begin, then, with a Type 5 triad in which Claudius is *A*, Gertrude is *B*, and Hamlet is *C*. The *AB* coalition, Claudius and Gertrude, dominates Hamlet easily, but a *BC* coalition, Gertrude and Hamlet, might be able to dominate Claudius. Hamlet's only way of accomplishing his revenge and surviving afterwards would be to persuade Gertrude to desert Claudius and draw her into a coalition with himself. The aftermath of his revenge would be largely determined by her reaction to this strategy. Hamlet can scarcely hope to escape punishment or seize the crown if his own mother accuses him of unprovoked regicide, which is precisely the reaction to be expected from her because of her solidary coalition with Claudius. Hamlet, melancholy and considering suicide as an escape, rails at himself as "a rogue and peasant slave" and "a dull and muddy-mettled rascal," but the act to which the Ghost urges him is impracticable until he can find some means of luring his mother out of the conservative coalition which renders him helpless to accomplish his revenge without losing his honor or leaving the ultimate advantage with Claudius.

The situation as it presents itself initially to Hamlet is bleak. He has trouble enough convincing himself of the Ghost's veracity and no hope of finding enough evidence to convince his mother. In addition, he suspects Gertrude of complicity in Claudius' crime, in which case, proof would be irrelevant and his chance of disrupting the coalition would be even slimmer.

Hamlet is unjust to Gertrude in at least two respects (perhaps because of his well-known oedipus complex). First, insofar as the audience can tell, she has not been an accomplice to the murder of Hamlet's father, knows nothing about it, and probably never finds out. Hamlet's accusation—just after he has stabbed Polonius—passes by her quite unnoticed:

QUEEN: O, what a rash and bloody deed is this!
HAMLET: A bloody deed—almost as bad, good mother,
   As kill a king, and marry with his brother.
QUEEN: As kill a king?
HAMLET: Ay, lady, it was my word.

She pays no attention whatever. A moment later she is still asking, "What have I done that thou dar'st wag thy tongue /In noise so rude against me?" Hamlet, abandoning the accusation of complicity in the murder, continues by complaining of her second marriage and her love for Claudius, but although he calls Claudius a murderer and a usurper, he does not mention adultery in his tirade.

Hamlet also seems to underestimate his mother's attachment to him, of which Claudius is so acutely aware. Even after he and Hamlet have fallen into open enmity, Claudius still feigns paternal tenderness in Gertrude's presence, and says to Laertes, "the Queen his mother /Lives almost by his looks."

By the time Hamlet goes to see his mother, the configuration of the triad has changed. Claudius knows—if Hamlet does not—that by commissioning Rosenkrantz and Guildenstern to arrange Hamlet's death, he has abandoned his coalition with Gertrude, who can never be expected to concur in her son's assassination. In the very next scene he accepts Polonius' offer to spy on Gertrude and Hamlet.

On his way to his mother's closet, Hamlet sees Claudius at prayer, draws his sword, but then hesitates and passes on. This scene certainly permits indecision to be taken as the theme of the play, no matter how plausible Hamlet's refusal to take the King at his spiritual best[19] may have appeared to Elizabethan audiences. Since the preceding scene, Hamlet has been rationally certain of Claudius' guilt, and just before his entrance, the last doubts of the audience are dispelled by the soliloquy in which Claudius confesses the murder. But I cannot find in Hamlet's hesitation the neurotic self-doubt that some critics have discerned, for he sounds almost arrogantly confident as he finishes with, "This physic but prolongs thy sickly days," and goes on his way to see his mother. At this point Hamlet does not yet suspect that Claudius is plotting

[19]Hamlet expresses a related sentiment in his very first appearance when he laments his mother's wedding without suspecting Claudius of anything more than undue haste: "Would I had met my dearest foe in heaven. Or even I had seen that day, Horatio!"

against him or that the Claudius-Gertrude coalition is beginning to dissolve.

Whether Gertrude has an inkling of these changes is uncertain. In the next scene she enters with Polonius, who advises her how to deal with Hamlet. We do not know if the advice is welcome. She tells him to withdraw and he hides behind the arras. We do not know from the text whether this is done with her knowledge, although the scene is usually played as if it were. Hamlet's main concern after he has killed Polonius is that the interview not be interrupted. He finds his mother unexpectedly receptive to his long tirade:

> O Hamlet, speak no more!
> Thou turn'st mine eyes into my very soul,
> And there I see such black and grained spots
> As will not leave their tinct.

When the Ghost leaves, Hamlet urges his mother to separate from Claudius and to form a coalition with himself. He warns her not to report their conversation to Claudius and especially not to reveal "That I essentially am not in madness, /But mad in craft." Her interests, he says in a complex metaphor, are the same as his own, and she will destroy herself if she violates his confidences. Gertrude agrees and swears silence; the rest of their talk is affectionate. She keeps her word and tells the King that Hamlet is raving mad, has killed Polonius in a fit, and grieves insanely over the body. Here Gertrude acts in concert with Hamlet against Claudius, and thereafter, so far as can be deduced from her few remaining speeches, she supports Hamlet quietly while Claudius plans Hamlet's assassination, first with Rosenkrantz and Guildenstern and then with the furious Laertes. Gertrude never supports Claudius again, except briefly when Laertes breaks in at the head of a mob. When, at the fencing match, she drinks the poisoned cup by mistake and is dying, her last words are directed to "my dear Hamlet."

Although Hamlet scolds himself in one more soliloquy ("How all occasions do inform against me. /And spur my dull revenge!"), he blames himself for delay, not indecision. There is no remaining trace of indecision in that speech or in any of his subsequent actions. After the interview with his mother, he is never again presented with an opportunity to kill the King until the last scene when he does so. But he shows no inner conflict, and he tells Horatio convincingly

that he intends to do the deed before the news about Rosenkrantz and Guildenstern arrives from England. The crushing
weight of the Claudius-Gertrude coalition has been lifted
from him. The documentary evidence he brings back—the
King's secret commission to have him killed in England—will
justify his rebellion to the Court and, for somewhat different
reasons, to Gertrude. When Hamlet gives his dying instruc-
tions to Horatio and nominates Fortinbras for the vacant
throne, he still shows the assurance that has marked all his
actions since the interview with his mother—his easy con-
temptuous handling of Rosenkrantz and Guildenstern, his
cheerful return to Elsinore, his behavior at the graveyard, and
his quarrel and reconciliation with Laertes.

If Gertrude is almost speechless throughout the latter half
of the play, it is because there is almost nothing she can say
either to Claudius, her deserted partner, or to Hamlet, with
whom she is now unhappily allied in the accomplishment of
her own ruin. "Wretched Queen adieu," he says, but saves the
remaining minutes of his life for Horatio and Fortinbras.

III.

SOCIAL GROUPS
AND SOCIAL SETTINGS

Most social interaction occurs in more or less structured social groups, not in fleeting encounters. Such groups differ in the impact they have on their members. Families, for example, are likely to be more far-reaching and consequential in their impact than, say, groups of neighbors in a housing project or trade-union locals. It is to this difference that one of the major ancestors of contemporary social psychology, Charles Horton Cooley, addressed himself when he coined the term "primary groups." By this term he meant to denote those groups, such as the family or children's intimate playgroups, that tend to have an enduring influence on the personality by virtue of long-lasting, intimate, face-to-face association among its members. He suggested that in such groups individuals learn to curb and bridle egotistic inclinations and propensities and to be drawn into cooperation and human companionship. It is in such contexts that we learn the meaning of the term "we" and are discouraged from purely self-enhancing behavior. Cooley, writing in the first quarter of this century, believed that in the long run such primary groups would prevail in America over tendencies toward atomization and privatization. We may no longer be so sure. In any case, Cooley has shown that a distinction between what he called "primary groups" and what others later called "secondary groups"—that is, groups not involving deep attachments among its members and hence providing only loose and fragile bonds—is central to studies of the human experience.

In a similar way, the distinction between *Gemeinschaft* (community) and *Gesellschaft* (society or association) introduced by the German sociologist Ferdinand Tönnies shortly before the turn of the century serves well to distinguish between the strong communal feelings characteristic of premodern, traditional social structures and modern associations that are based only on the partial involvement of their members.

Tönnies suggested that as modern history moved from the prevalence of communal structures to a predominance of associational types of relationships, modern people experienced a sense of loneliness, of lack of social supports. In the world we have lost, he suggested, the individual was safely enveloped in a protective cocoon of traditional social relations and life-styles; whereas today, in the words of the poet A.E. Housman, each of us feels "a stranger and afraid in a world I never made." There is, to be sure, some romanticism and nostalgia in Tönnies' picture, but he has, nevertheless, put his finger on a distinction that has served well to explain some crucial differences between the world of modernity and its traditional predecessors.

The other three papers in this chapter deal with general social settings rather than with specific group structures. In a recent and highly perceptive paper, Murray Melbin points to the key differentiation in social settings of people working in the usual daylight routines from those of the relatively exceptional people who are tied to nighttime schedules. He suggests that the night has become a new frontier, especially in urban areas, insofar as modern technologies have now made it possible to transcend the traditional separation between the day reserved for work and the night reserved for sleep. He suggests that nighttime social life in urban areas begins to resemble life on the frontier a century ago in that the nighttime social settings allow the emergence of novel styles of living and novel ways of responding to the challenges of work and of leisure.

While Melbin's paper highlights new settings made possible by technological changes that have obliterated the sharp distinction between night and day, W.F. Cottrell suggests, in a paper that is a minor classic, that changes in the technological environment have far-reaching effects on the ways people think, act, and experience reality. He focuses on inhabitants in the American Southwest who live in what used to be small railroad communities. The introduction of diesel locomotives has made many of these communities functionless, since diesel trains do not have to make as many stops for refueling as did steam locomotives. This technological change spelled obsolescence for many of these old railroad towns. Cottrell shows in instructive detail how such technological changes brought in their wake a decided change in outlook and attitudes in these communities. Feeling that what has been happening to them is "unjust," the inhabitants have largely abandoned their previous reliance on private initiative and sturdy self-help and now claim the aid of hitherto rejected governmental agencies to right this "injustice." They have moved from an individualistic to a collectivist image of the good society.

Everett Hughes, one of the deans of American sociology, in his seminal paper highlights a central sociological concept, that of social status—not by describing it, but by showing the dilemmas and contradictions to which it may give rise. By "status" he has in mind social positions that imply defined rights and duties for their incumbents. The term "father," for example, refers to a specific position in a network of family relations that creates the expectation that the holder will exercise certain rights over his children at the same time that he fulfills well-defined obligations toward them. In turn, he expects from them fulfillment of duties and the exercise of their own rights. Hughes now shows that contradictions may arise by virtue of the fact that people may occupy several positions, some of which may be low and some of which may be high in relation to their associates. Culturally, men usually rank higher than women in patriarchal societies, and this has a carryover in the occupational world, where status is supposed to be measured by achievement. What, then, is expected of one of the relatively rare women who has managed to attain the highly valued position of engineer, or what happens if a black person, usually treated as of low racial status, attains the highly valued position of physician? Hughes' highly perceptive paper shows how people in such positions, as well as the persons they interact with, manage to solve or at least make livable such dilemmas and contradictions of status.

Primary Groups

by
Charles Horton Cooley

By primary groups I mean those characterized by intimate face-to-face association and coöperation. They are primary in several senses, but chiefly in that they are fundamental in forming the social nature and ideals of the individual. The result of intimate association, psychologically, is a certain fusion of individualities in a common whole, so that one's very self, for many purposes at least, is the common life and purpose of the group. Perhaps the simplest way of describing this wholeness is by saying that it is a "we"; it involves the sort of sympathy and mutual identification for which "we" is the natural expression. One lives in the feeling of the whole and finds the chief aims of his will in that feeling.

It is not to be supposed that the unity of the primary group is one of mere harmony and love. It is always a differentiated and usually a competitive unity, admitting of self-assertion and various appropriative passions; but these passions are socialized by sympathy, and come, or tend to come, under the discipline of a common spirit. The individual will be ambitious, but the chief object of his ambition will be some desired place in the thought of the others, and he will feel allegiance to common standards of service and fair play. So the boy will dispute with his fellows a place on the team, but above such disputes will place the common glory of his class and school.

The most important spheres of this intimate association and coöperation—though by no means the only ones—are the family, the play-group of children, and the neighborhood or community group of elders. These are practically universal, belonging to all times and all stages of development; and are accordingly a chief basis of what is universal in human nature and human ideals. The best comparative studies of the

Reprinted by permission of Charles Scribner's Sons from *Social Organization* by Charles H. Cooley. Copyright 1909, Charles Scribner's Sons.

family, such as those of Westermarck[1] or Howard,[2] show it to us as not only a universal institution, but as more alike the world over than the exaggeration of exceptional customs by an earlier school had led us to suppose. Nor can anyone doubt the general prevalence of play-groups among children or of informal assemblies of various kinds among their elders. Such association is clearly the nursery of human nature in the world about us, and there is no apparent reason to suppose that the case has anywhere or at any time been essentially different.

As regards play, I might, were it not a matter of common observation, multiply illustrations of the universality and spontaneity of the group discussion and coöperation to which it gives rise. The general fact is that children, especially boys after about their twelfth year, live in fellowships in which their sympathy, ambition and honor are engaged even more often than they are in the family. Most of us can recall examples of the endurance by boys of injustice and even cruelty, rather than appeal from their fellows to parents or teachers—as, for instance, in the hazing so prevalent at schools, and so difficult, for this very reason, to repress. And how elaborate the discussion, how cogent the public opinion, how hot the ambitions in these fellowships.

Nor is this facility of juvenile association, as is sometimes supposed, a trait peculiar to English and American boys; since experience among our immigrant population seems to show that the offspring of the more restrictive civilizations of the continent of Europe form self-governing play-groups with almost equal readiness. Thus Miss Jane Addams, after pointing out that the "gang" is almost universal, speaks of the interminable discussion which every detail of the gang's activity receives, remarking that "in these social folk-motes, so to speak, the young citizen learns to act upon his own determination."[3]

Of the neighborhood group it may be said, in general, that from the time men formed permanent settlements upon the land, down, at least, to the rise of modern industrial cities, it has played a main part in the primary, heart-to-heart life of the people. Among our Teutonic forefathers the village community was apparently the chief sphere of sympathy and mu-

---

[1] The History of Human Marriage.
[2] A History of Matrimonial Institutions.
[3] Newer Ideals of Peace, 177.

tual aid for the commons all through the "dark" and middle ages, and for many purposes it remains so in rural districts at the present day. In some countries we still find it with all its ancient vitality, notably in Russia, where the mir, or self-governing village group, is the main theatre of life, along with the family, for perhaps fifty millions of peasants.

In our own life the intimacy of the neighborhood has been broken up by the growth of an intricate mesh of wider contacts which leaves us strangers to people who live in the same house. And even in the country the same principle is at work, though less obviously, diminishing our economic and spiritual community with our neighbors. How far this change is a healthy development, and how far a disease, is perhaps still uncertain.

Besides these almost universal kinds of primary association, there are many others whose form depends upon the particular state of civilization; the only essential thing, as I have said, being a certain intimacy and fusion of personalities. In our own society, being little bound by place, people easily form clubs, fraternal societies and the like, based on congeniality, which may give rise to real intimacy. Many such relations are formed at school and college, and among men and women brought together in the first instance by their occupations—as workmen in the same trade, or the like. Where there is a little common interest and activity, kindness grows like weeds by the roadside.

But the fact that the family and neighborhood groups are ascendant in the open and plastic time of childhood makes them even now incomparably more influential than all the rest.

Primary groups are primary in the sense that they give the individual his earliest and completest experience of social unity, and also in the sense that they do not change in the same degree as more elaborate relations, but form a comparatively permanent source out of which the latter are ever springing. Of course they are not independent of the larger society, but to some extent reflect its spirit; as the German family and the German school bear somewhat distinctly the print of German militarism. But this, after all, is like the tide setting back into creeks, and does not commonly go very far. Among the German, and still more among the Russian, peasantry are found habits of free coöperation and discussion almost uninfluenced by the character of the state; and it is a familiar and well-supported view that the village commune, self-governing as regards local affairs and habituated to discussion, is a very widespread institution in settled communities, and the continuator of a similar autonomy previously existing in the clan. "It is man who makes monarchies and establishes republics, but the commune seems to come directly from the hand of God."[4]

In our own cities the crowded tenements and the general economic and social confusion have sorely wounded the family and the neighborhood, but it is remarkable, in view of these conditions, what vitality they show; and there is nothing upon which the conscience of the time is more determined than upon restoring them to health.

These groups, then, are springs of life, not only for the individual but for social institutions. They are only in part moulded by special traditions, and, in larger degree, express a universal nature. The religion or government of other civilizations may seem alien to us, but the children or the family group wear the common life, and with them we can always make ourselves at home.

Gemeinschaft and Gesellschaft (Community and Society)

by
Ferdinand Tönnies

Human wills stand in manifold relation to one another. Every such relationship is a mutual action, inasmuch as one party is active or gives while the other party is passive or receives. These actions are of such a nature that they tend either towards preservation or towards destruction of the other will or life; that is, they are either positive or negative. This study will consider as its subject of investigation only the relationships of mutual affirmation. Every such relationship represents unity in plurality or plurality in unity. It consists of assistance, relief, services, which are transmitted back and forth from one party to another and are to be considered as expressions of wills and their forces. The group which is formed through this positive type of relationship is called an association (*Verbindung*) when conceived of as a thing of being which acts as a unit inwardly and outwardly. The relationship itself, and also the resulting association, is conceived of either as real and organic life—this is the essential characteristic of the *Gemeinschaft* (community)—or as imaginary and mechanical structure—this is the concept of *Gesellschaft* (society).

Through the application of these two terms we shall see that the chosen expressions are rooted in their synonymic use in the German language. But to date in scientific terminology they have been customarily confused and used at random without any distinction. For this reason, a few introductory remarks may explain the inherent contrast between these two concepts. All intimate, private, and exclusive living together, so we discover, is understood as life in Gemeinschaft (community). Gesellschaft (society) is public life—it is the world itself. In Gemeinschaft (community) with one's family, one

From *Gemeinschaft and Gesellschaft* by Ferdinand Toönes, trans. by Charles Loomis. New York: American Book Company, 1940. Reprinted with the permission of the publisher.

lives from birth on bound to it in weal and woe. One goes into Gesellschaft (society) as one goes into a strange country. A young man is warned against bad Gesellschaft (society), but the expression bad Gemeinschaft (community) violates the meaning of the word. Lawyers may speak of domestic (*häusliche*) Gesellschaft (society) thinking only of the legalistic concept of a social assocation, but the domestic Gemeinschaft (community) or home life with its immeasurable influence upon the human soul has been felt by everyone who ever shared it. Likewise, each member of a bridal couple knows that he or she goes into marriage as a complete Gemeinschaft (community) of life (*communio totius vitae*). A Gesellschaft (society) of life would be a contradiction in and of itself. One keeps or enjoys another's Gesellschaft (society or company) but not his Gemeinschaft (community) in this sense. One becomes a part of a religious Gemeinschaft (community); religious Gesellschaften (associations, or societies) like any other groups formed for given purposes, exist only in so far as they, viewed from without, take their places among the institutions of a political body or as they represent conceptual elements of a theory; they do not touch upon the religious Gemeinschaft as such. There exists a Gemeinschaft (community) of language, of folkways, or mores, or of beliefs; but, by way of contrast, Gesellschaft (society or company) exists in the realm of business, travel, or sciences. So of special importance are the commercial Gesellschaften (societies or companies), whereas, even though a certain familiarity and Gemeinschaft (community) may exist among business partners, one could indeed hardly speak of commercial Gemeinschaft (community). To make the word combination, "joint-stock Gemeinschaft," would be abominable. On the other hand, there exists a Gemeinschaft (community) of ownership in fields, forest, and pasture. The Gemeinschaft (community) of property between man and wife cannot be called Gesellschaft (society) of property. Thus many differences become apparent.

In the most general way, one could speak of a Gemeinschaft (community) comprising the whole of mankind, such as the church wishes to be regarded. But human Gesellschaft (society) is conceived as mere coexistence of people independent of each other. Recently, the concept of Gesellschaft as opposed to and distinct from the state has been developed. This term will also be used in this treatise, but can only derive its adequate explanation from the underlying contrast to the Gemeinschaft of the people.

Gemeinschaft (community) is old; Gesellschaft (society) is new as a name as well as a phenomenon. This has been recognized by an author who otherwise taught political science in all its aspects without penetrating to its fundamentals. "The entire concept of Gesellschaft (society) in a social and political sense," says Bluntschli (*Staatswörterbuch* IV), "finds its natural foundation in the folkways, mores, and ideas of the third estate. It is not really the concept of a people (*Volks-Begriff*) but the concept of the third estate . . . Its Gesellschaft has become the origin and expression of common opinions and tendencies . . . Wherever urban culture blossoms and bears fruits, Gesellschaft appears as its indispensable organ. The rural people know little of it." On the other hand, all praise of rural life has pointed out that the Gemeinschaft (community) among people is stronger there and more alive; it is the lasting and genuine form of living together. In contrast to Gemeinschaft, Gesellschaft (society) is transitory and superficial. Accordingly, Gemeinschaft (community) should be understood as a living organism, Gesellschaft (society) as a mechanical aggregate and artifact.

Night as Frontier

by
Murray Melbin

Humans are showing a trend toward more and more wakeful activity at all hours of day and night. The activities are extremely varied. Large numbers of people are involved. And the trend is worldwide. A unifying hypothesis to account for it is that night is a frontier, that expansion into the dark hours is a continuation of the geographic migration across the face of the earth. To support this view, I will document the trend and then offer a premise about the nature of time and its relation to space. Third, I will show that social life in the nighttime has many important characteristics that resemble social life on land frontiers.

THE COURSE OF EXPANSION

We were once a diurnal species bounded by dawn and dusk in our wakeful activity. Upon mastering fire, early humans used it for cooking and also for sociable assemblies that lasted for a few hours after darkness fell. Some bustle throughout the 24-hour cycle occurred too. Over the centuries there have been fires tended in military encampments, prayer vigils in temples, midnight betrothal ceremonies, sentinels on guard duty at city gates, officer watches on ships, the curing ceremonies of Venezuelan Indians that begin at sundown and end at sunrise, innkeepers serving travelers at all hours. In the first century A.D., Rome was obliged to relieve its congestion by restricting chariot traffic to the night hours (Mumford, 1961:217).

Yet around-the-clock activity used to be a small part of the

Reprinted from *American Sociological Review*, Vol. 43, No. 1, February 1978, pp. 3–22, with permission of the American Sociological Association and the author.

whole until the nineteenth century. Then the pace and scope of wakefulness at all hours increased smartly. William Murdock developed a feasible method of coal-gas illumination and, in 1803, arranged for the interior of the Soho works in Birmingham, England to be lighted that way. Other mills nearby began to use gas lighting. Methods of distributing coal-gas to all buildings and street lamps in a town were introduced soon after. In 1820 Pall Mall in London became the first street to be lit by coal-gas. Artificial lighting gave great stimulus to the nighttime entertainment industry (Schlesinger, 1933:105). It also permitted multiple-shift factory operations on a broad scale. Indeed by 1867 Karl Marx (1867:chap. 10, sec. 4) was to declare that night work was a new mode of exploiting human labor.

In the closing decades of the nineteenth century two developments marked the changeover from space to time as the realm of human migration in the United States. In 1890 the Bureau of the Census announced that the land frontier in America had come to an end, for it was no longer possible to draw a continuous line across the map of the West to define the edge of farthest advance settlement. Meanwhile, the search for an optimum material for lantern lights, capable of being repeatedly brought to a white heat, culminated in 1885 in the invention of the Welsbach mantle—a chemically impregnated cotton mesh. The use of the dark hours increased thereafter, and grew further with the introduction of electric lighting.

Here and there one may find documentation of the trend. During the First World War there was selective concern, expressed by Brandeis and Goldmark (1918) in *The Case Against Night Work for Women*, about the impact of off-hours work. A decade later the National Industrial Conference Board (1927) published a comprehensive survey with an account of the characteristics of the off-hours workers.

The most systematic evidence of steadily increasing 24-hour activity in the U.S. is the growth of radio and television broadcasting. Broadcasters authorize surveys to learn about the market that can be reached in order to plan programs and to set advertising rates. The number of stations active at given hours and the spread of those hours around the clock reflects these research estimates of the size of the wakeful population—the potential listeners. Table 1 shows trends in the daily schedule spanning the entire periods of commercial broadcasting for both radio and television. Although not shown in the table, television hours in Boston ended at 11:30 p.m. in 1949, and then widened to include the Late Show and then the Late Late Show in the intervening years until 1974. Each medium has moved increasingly to 24-hour programming and mirrors the growth in nighttime activity.

Table 1. Numbers of Radio and Television Stations and Their Hours of Broadcasting in Boston[a]

	The Span of Commercial Broadcasting									
	April 1929	April 1934	April 1939	April 1944	April 1949	April 1954	April 1959	April 1964	April 1969	April 1974
Radio										
Number of stations	7	7	8	7	8	14	15	20	26	27
Number of 24-hour stations	0	0	0	0	0	1	3	8	12	15
Percent of 24-hour stations						7%	20%	40%	46%	57%
Television										
Number of stations					2	4	4	4	5	7
Number of 24-hour stations					0	0	0	0	0	1
Percent of 24-hour stations										14%

[a] Sources: listings in Boston newspapers—*Globe, Herald, Record*, and *Traveler*—and the broadcasters themselves. If the content of a broadcaster's AM and FM radio programming or VHF and UHF television programming differs, that broadcast is counted as two stations.

In the present decade, for the first time, the U.S. Bureau of Labor Statistics (1976: Table 1) asked about the times of day that people worked. In 1976, of 75 million in the work force, 12 million reported they were on the job mainly after dark and 2.5 million of those persons worked a full shift beginning about midnight. Since these figures do not include *the clientele* that used such establishments as restaurants, hospital emergency wards, gambling rooms, and public transportation, these numbers are conservative estimates of how many people are up and about at night.

Today more people than ever are active outside their homes at all hours engaged in all sorts of activities. There are all-night supermarkets, bowling alleys, department stores, restaurants, cinemas, auto repair shops, taxi services, bus and airline terminals, radio and television broadcasting, rent-a-car agencies, gasoline stations. There are continuous-process refining plants, and three-shift factories, post offices, newspaper offices, hotels, and hospitals. There is unremitting provision of some utilities—electric supply, staffed turnpike toll booths, police patrolling, and telephone service. There are many emergency and repair services on-call: fire fighters, auto towing, locksmiths, suppliers of clean diapers, ambulances, bail bondsmen, insect exterminators, television repairers, plate glass installers, and funeral homes.

The trend of nighttime expansion is under way outside the United States as well. In Great Britain since the Second World War, the yearly increase in the percentage of the manual labor force on shifts in manufacturing has been about 1% a year, and greater increases have been noted in vehicle manufacture and in the chemical industry (Young and Willmott, 1973:175). Meier (1976:965) observes that Singapore is becoming one of the most intensive 24-hour cities. Data on around-the-clock activity in Peru, France, U.S.S.R. and eight other nations is provided in a volume on *The Use of Time* (Szalai, 1972:appendices).

SPACE AND TIME FRONTIERS AND SETTLEMENTS

Time, like space, is part of the ecological niche occupied by a species. Although every type exists throughout the 24-hour cycle, to reflect the way a species uses its niche we label it by *the timing of its wakeful life*. The terms diurnal and nocturnal refer to the periods the creatures are active. We improve our grasp of the ecology of a region by recognizing the nighttime activity of raccoons, owls and rats, as well as by knowing the spatial dispersion of these and other animals. The same area of a forest or meadow or coral reef is used incessantly, with diurnal and nocturnal creatures taking their active turns. We make geographic references to humans in a similar way. We refer to an island people or a desert people, or the people of arctic lands as a means of pointing out salient features of their habitats.

This similar treatment of time and space rests on the assumption that both of them are containers for living. Consider the dictionary definition of the word *occupy:* "2. To fill up (take time or space): *a lecture that occupied three hours*" (*American Heritage Dictionary*, 1970:908). Geographers study activities rather than physical structures to decide whether and how people occupy space (Buttimer, 1976:286). The mere presence of buildings and related physical structures in places like Machu-Pichu, Petra, and Zimbabwe do not make us believe they are habitations now. The once-boisterous mining centers in the American West that have become ghost towns are settlements no longer. Conversely, we say a farming region in which people are active is inhabited even though buildings are few. The presence of human-built structures is not the criterion for occupying a region, it is people and their activities.

Like rural settlements, the occupation of time need not be dense. For example, London Transport lists 21 all-night bus routes. On many of these routes "all-night" service means no more than once an hour. Yet, even though the bus does not pass during the intervening 59 minutes, the schedule is said to be continuous. If an active moment interacts with quiet moments around it, the entire period is taken as occupied.

Of course, no time has ever been used without also using it in some place. No space has ever been used without also using it some hours of the day. Space and time together form the container of life activity. We forget this in the case of former frontiers because expansion then occurred so dramatically across the land. Less notice was paid to the 16 hours of wakefulness because the daily use of time was rather constant as the surge of geographic expansion kept on over the face of the earth. As time use remained unchanged, it was disregarded in human ecological theory. In different eras, however, expansion may proceed more rapidly in either space or time. Recently expansion is taking place in time. Since people may exploit a niche by distributing themselves and their activities over more hours of the day just as they do by dispersing in space, a frontier could occur in the time dimension too.

A *settlement* is a stable occupation of space and time by people and their activities. A *frontier* is a pattern of sparse settlement in space or time, located between a more densely settled and a practically empty region. Below a certain density of active people, a given space-time region is a wilderness. Above that point and continuing to a higher level of density, the presence of people in activities will make that area a frontier. Above that second cutoff point the further denseness of active people turns the area into a fully inhabited region. In a given historical period the frontier's boundaries may be stable or expanding. When expanding, the frontier takes on the aspect of venturing into the unknown and is often accompanied by novelty and change.

SIMILARITIES BETWEEN LAND FRONTIERS AND TIME FRONTIERS

Two kinds of evidence would support the hypothesis of night as frontier. One is that the forces for expansion into the dark hours are the same as those resulting in expansion across the land. That is, a single causal explanation should account for the spread of people and their activities, whether in space or in time. I offered such an outline in another essay; it includes enabling factors, demand push, supply pull, and stabilizing feedback (Melbin, 1977). The other line of evidence is that the same important features of social life should be found both in time and in space frontiers. The rapid expansion in after-dark activity has been taking place mostly in urban areas. Therefore the culture of the contemporary urban nighttime should reveal the same patterns and moods found in former land frontiers.

I have chosen to review life in the U.S. West in the middle of the nineteenth century along with the present-day nighttime. Of course there were other land frontiers and the hypothesis should apply to all of them. However there are good reasons to begin by demonstrating it for the U.S. West. One is that the archives holding information about this westward flow are thorough, well organized, and readily available. Another reason is that the U.S. West has continuity with expansion into the night. The movement westward reached the California coast. California's main cities have since become areas of great activity in the dark hours, as if the flow across

Figure 1. Persons per Square Mile (and Percent Males per Square Mile) during the 1870–1880 Decade[a]

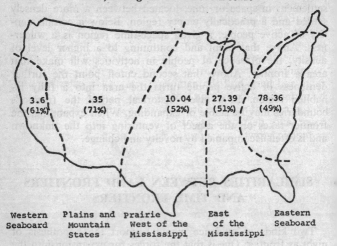

| Western Seaboard | Plains and Mountain States | Prairie West of the Mississippi | East of the Mississippi | Eastern Seaboard |

[a] Source: U.S. Bureau of the Census, 1975: Vol. 1, ser. A195–209.

the continent swerved into the nighttime rather than spilling into the sea.

Specifically, the land frontier to be discussed is the area west of the Mississippi River during the middle decades of the nineteenth century, about 1830–1880. The urban nighttime will be any major urban area during the stretch from about midnight to 7:30 a.m. during the decades of the 1960s and 1970s. Most of my examples will be findings from a recent study of Boston. There are many aspects in which social life at night is like the social life of other frontiers.

1. Advance Is in Stages. There is a succession of steps in colonizing any new region. People ventured into the western outskirts "in a series of waves . . . the hunter and the fur trader who pushed into the Indian country were followed by the cattle raiser and he by the pioneer farmer" (Turner, 1965:59; 1893:12, 19–20). Life styles were distinctive in each stage as well. The hunters and trappers did not dwell like the miners who followed, and they in turn lived differently from the pioneer farmers who came later (Billington, 1949:4–5). Although living conditions were generally crude then, there was a decided increase in comfort for the farmers settled in one place compared with the earlier-day trappers who were usually on the move.

There is also a succession of phases in settling the nighttime. Each stage fills the night more densely than before and uses those hours in a different way. First came isolated wanderers on the streets; then groups involved in production activities, the graveyard-shift workers. Still later those involved in consumption activities arrived, the patrons of all-night restaurants and bars, and the gamblers who now cluster regularly by midnight at the gaming table in resorts.

The rates of advance are unequal in both cases. Population gains and development are not unbroken. In the West economic growth was erratic. Periods of depression, dry seasons and other hardships drove many people to abandon their homesteads and move back east. Similarly, during the oil embargo of 1973–1974 there was some retreat from nighttime activity, as restaurants and auto service stations and other businesses cut back hours of serving the public.

2. Population Is Sparse and Also More Homogenous. At first only a few people venture into the new region. The frontier line in the U.S. West was drawn by the Census Bureau through an area of density of two to six inhabitants per square mile. The other side of the line was tabbed the "wilderness." The demographic composition of the western frontier was mostly vigorous young males with proportionately fewer females and aged persons than found in the populations of the eastern states (Riegel, 1947:624; Godkin, 1896:13; Dick, 1937:7, 232). This demographic picture fits the night as well. There are fewer people up and about and most of them are young males.

A crude comparison between a frontier line in the nineteenth-century West and a time interval in the twentieth-century nighttime is possible if the map of Figure 1 is scanned from right to left and the graph of Figure 2 is scanned from left to right. In this view both figures show similar graded densities. In Figure 2, the period after midnight until 7 a.m. is sparsest and stands in the same relation to the rest of the day as the region west of the Mississippi stands in relation to the East in Figure 1. The figures also show that the proportion of males in the population is higher on the frontiers. Just as this part of the total is largest in the Plains and Mountain States (71%), males comprise the largest part of the street population (89%) in the middle of the night.

Estimates of the ages of passersby were also made during

Figure 2. Females and Males Passing per Minute on the Streets of Central Boston[a]

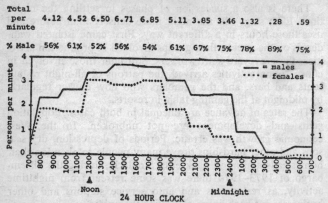

Total per minute	4.12	4.52	6.50	6.71	6.85	5.11	3.85	3.46	1.32	.28	.59
% Male	56%	61%	52%	56%	56%	54%	61%	67%	75%	78%	89%	75%

[a] The tallies were accomplished during field visits based on a stratified random sample in the city of Boston in 1974. Along with this personally, other measurements including the experiments described later in this section were carried out during these field visits. The 166 field visits (56 in early June, 56 in early September, and 54 in early December), each two hours long, were distributed among three sites: a shopping street, a residential street, and a transportation hub (62, 42, and 62 visits, respectively), each located one mile from the next along a line through the center city. In all, we made 456 five-minute tallies of people passing one-way at eight checkpoints.

The times of field visits were randomly selected from two-hour intervals around the 24-hour clock. I established 11 such intervals in this sampling frame for two reasons: certain times of day are clearly associated with certain kinds of activities, especially 0730–0929 as the morning rush hours and 1615–1814 as the evening rush hours. Given the two rush-hour spans placed as they are in the 24-hour period, and given the need for two-hour field visits in order to accomplish the experiments and other studies in the more comprehensive program of investigating activity around the clock, it was impossible to fit the remaining hours of the day neatly into two-hour intervals throughout the period. To insert 12 two-hour intervals into the period would force some of the strata to be out of phase with familiar time intervals in Boston. So 11 strata were established and the remaining scattered minutes left unsampled, as following: morning rush hour = 0730–0929; daytime = 0930–1129, 1130–1329 (1330–1344 omitted), 1345–1544 (1545–1614 omitted); evening rush hour = 1615–1814; evening = 1815–2014, 2015–2214, 2215–0014; and night = 0015–0214 (0215–0244 omitted), 0245–0444 (0445–0514 omitted), 0515–0714 (0715–0729 omitted). Thus the two longest phases (day and night) lose the unsampled minutes, 45 minutes from the daytime and 75 minutes at night. By removing these amounts from the sample, the day, evening and night phases are six hours each and the rush hours are two hours each. (It may be easier to design the

the field observations that yielded the data for Figure 2.[1] Whereas people of all ages were on the streets during the day, no one over 59 was seen between midnight and 5 a.m.; and from 2 to 5 a.m. no one over 41 was seen.

3. *There Is Welcome Solitude, Fewer Social Constraints, and Less Persecution.* The land frontier offered tranquillity, a place for relief from feelings of being hemmed in. "Fur traders . . . were psychological types who found forest solitudes more acceptable than the company of their fellow men" (Billington, 1949:4). It was appealing to escape into the wilderness, to leave deceit and disturbance, and vexing duties and impositions of the government behind (Robbins, 1960:148). " 'Oh, how sweet,' wrote William Penn from his forest refuge, 'is the quiet of these parts, freed from the troubles and perplexities of woeful Europe' " (Turner, 1893:262). Even later the West was "a refuge . . . from the subordination of youth to age" (Turner, 1932:25). The outer fringes offered escape from persecution too. Mormons and Hutterites both made their ways westward to avoid harassment from others.

In a parallel way, many have enjoyed the experience of walking at night along a street that is ordinarily jammed during the day. Individuals who are up and about then report a feeling of relief from the crush and anonymity of daytime city life. The calm of those hours is especially appealing to young people, who come to feel that they possess the streets. (A test of this proposition must of course control for the fear of criminal assault in the dark; I will discuss this further in items 7 and 8 below.) Also, a portion of the people out at night are those avoiding social constraints and perhaps persecution. Street people and homosexuals, for example, find

---

sample for 12 two-hour periods and then align the boundaries of each time stratum to local patterns in the analysis stage of the research. If this is done, records of measurement should be made to the minute.) The number of visits for the five phases of the day were: morning rush hour, 13; day, 47; evening rush hour, 11; evening, 48; and night, 47. The number counts for each time stratum were divided by the number of tally minutes for that stratum to equalize the sampling fractions across strata, and then doubled to provide two-way estimates.

Three teams of male and female researchers, with pairings reshuffled systematically across times of day and across sites, carried out these tallies and the experiments reported later in this section.

[1]A comparison of the age estimate made by an observer and the answer to an age query made of 696 passersby yielded a correlation (within two years) of .96 for the six observers, with the lowest coefficient for an observer being .93. Populations at these sites are somewhat younger than the city's census average.

more peace in the dark because surveillance declines. Some night owls are urban hermits. Some individuals who are troubled or stigmatized—such as the very ugly or obese—retreat from the daytime to avoid humiliation and challenge. They stay up later, come out when most others are gone, and are more secure as they hobnob with nighttime newsdealers and porters and elevator men. In this way the night affords an outlet. Like the West it serves an insulating function that averts possible tensions from unwanted encounters.

4. Settlements Are Isolated. Initially migration beyond the society's active perimeter is scattered. The land frontier settlements were small and apart from one another. There was little communication across districts and much went on in each in a self-sufficient way. People in the East did not think of the relevance of borderland activities for their own existence and the pioneers were indifferent to outside society (Billington, 1949:96, 746).

As the city moves through phases of the day it switches from coordinated actions to unconnected ones. Pockets of wakeful activity are separated from one another, are small scale compared to daytime events, and there is less communication between the pockets. The people of the daytime give little thought to those active in the dark and do not view them as part of the main community.

5. Government Is Initially Decentralized. Whatever high-level group may decide the laws and policies for a nation or a community, outside the purview of superiors there are subordinates who make decisions that would otherwise be the domain of the higher-ups or subject to their approval. As the land frontier moved farther from the national center of policy making, the interpretation of the law and judicial decisions were carried out by individuals who were rarely checked on and who rarely consulted with their superiors. Hollon (1973:96) notes that events took place "remote from the courts of authorities . . . [and] the frontiersmen not only enforced their own law, they chose which laws should be enforced and which should be ignored."

Today, although many organizations and cities are continually active, their primary administrators—directors, heads of departments, mayors—are generally on duty only during the daytime. At night they go to sleep and a similar decentralization of power follows. To some extent this is an explicit delegation of authority. But discretion is stretched for other reasons too. Night nurses decide not to wake up the doctor on duty because he gets annoyed at being disturbed for minor problems (Kozak, 1974:59). Shift supervisors choose not to bother the plant manager for similar reasons. Lesser officials make decisions that in the daytime are left for higher-ranking administrators. The style and content of the way the organization or the city is run at night changes accordingly. For example, for the same types of cases, decisions by police officers at night will be based less on professional role criteria and more on personal styles. This results in more extreme instances of being strict and lenient, arbitrary and humane.

6. *New Behavioral Styles Emerge.* Both land and time frontiers show more individualism because they are remote, the environment is unusual (compared with the centers of society), and others subjected to the same conditions are tolerant. Those who traveled to the western borders broke from ordinary society. The casual observance by others, the constituted authority, and the familiar settings and the norms they implied were gone. This left room for unconventional behavior. Easterners thought westerners were unsavory. The president of Yale College said, "The class of pioneers cannot live in regular society. They are too idle, too talkative, too passionate, too prodigal, and too shiftless to acquire either property or character" (cited in Turner, 1893:251). Another traveler in the same period wrote, "It is true there are worthless people here [in settlements hundreds of miles from any court of justice] and the most so, it must be confessed, are from New England" (Flint, 1826:402). He did go on to say that there were also many who were worthy.

Deviance was also *created* out west. Many pioneer wives lived on the plains for extended periods without ordinary social contacts, especially when their husbands left on journeys for days or weeks. These women often became withdrawn and untalkative, so shy and uneasy with strangers that they would run away when one approached (Humphrey, 1931:128). From the evidence at hand, these were normal, happy women in the cities when they were growing up, but they were affected by the frontier environment. On the western boundary people were used to this behavior on the part of lonely, isolated women and accepted it. In the eastern cities the same conduct would have been taken as odd.

There is also a popular image of the night as the haunt of weirdos and strange characters, as revealed in comments like "I don't know where they hide during the day but they sure come out after dark." Moreover, at night one can find people who, having lived normal lives, are exposed to unusual circumstances that draw them into unconventional behavior. Becker (1963:79, 97, 98) gives such an account of jazz musicians. They work late in the evening and then associate with very few daytime types in their recreation after midnight. The milieu harbors a deviant subculture that is tolerated and even expected.

7. *There Is More Lawlessness and Violence.* Both land frontier and the nighttime have reputations as regions of danger and outlawry. Interestingly, both do not live up to the myths about them, for the patterns of aggression are selective and localized.

On the one hand there is clear evidence of lawlessness and violence. Walter P. Webb observed that the West was lawless "because the law that was applied there was not made for the conditions that existed. . . . It did not fit the needs of the country, and could not be obeyed" (cited by Frantz and Choate, 1955:83). There was also a lack of policemen and law enforcement agencies were few (Riegel, 1947:627; Billington, 1949:480). There was violence in the gold fields (Hollon, 1974:211). In the cow towns, mining camps and boom towns in the early days, practically everyone carried guns. Fighting words, the ring of revolvers, and groans of pain were common sounds out there. Some western settlements were renowned for concentrations of gamblers and gougers and bandits, dance-hall girls and honky-tonks and bawdy houses. Horse thieving was widespread. The stage coach was held up many times. There was habitual fear of attack from either Indians or renegades. In the face of this, the people practiced constant watchfulness and banded together for self-protection (Billington, 1954:8; Doddridge 1912:103). Towns had vigilante groups. The covered wagons that crossed the plains were accompanied by armed convoys.

Yet the violence was concentrated in certain places; otherwise killings and mob law were remarkably infrequent. Such infamous towns as Tombstone and Deadwood, and the states of Texas and California had more than their share of gunfights (Frantz and Choate, 1955:83; Billington, 1949:63; Hollon, 1973:96). But the tumult in the cow towns was seasonal, and took place when the cowboys finally reached Abilene, Ellsworth, and Dodge City after the long drive. And the mayhem was selective. Flint (1826:401) wrote, "Instances of murder, numerous and horrible in their circumstances, have occurred in my vicinity . . . in which the drunkenness, brutality, and violence were mutual. . . . [Yet] quiet and sober men would be in no danger of being involved." W.T. Jackson (1973:79) adds, "Homicides and murders occurred so infrequently that when they did the community was shocked and outraged." Concerning violence, Hollon (1973:97–8) concludes that there was

> a natural tendency to exaggerate the truth and emphasize the exception . . . not a single shoot-out took place on main street at Dodge City or any of the other Kansas cow towns in the manner of the face-to-face encounter presented thousands of times on television.

Why, then, did the land frontier have the reputation of a "Wild West?" One reason may be that outlaw killers were drifters, so the same person may have contributed exploits over large areas. Another reason was boredom. The stories of violence persisted and spread because there was little to do or to read about in pioneer homes. The tedium of daily life was countered by exciting stories told and retold around the stove in the general store.

It is plausible that western desperados and nighttime muggers would have similar outlooks. Both believe there is less exposure, which improves their chances for succeeding at the risks they take. One relied on dry-gulching; the other uses the dark to set an ambush. Escape is easy because both could move from the scene of the crime into unpopulated areas and elude pursuers.

The nighttime has been noted also as a place of evil. It is thought of as crime-ridden and outside of ordinary social control. Medieval and Renaissance cities had no public illumination. Assaults by ruffians and thieves were so common after dark that wayfarers took to paying others to precede them through the streets carrying lighted torches. In the seventeenth century this escort-for-hire was called a "link-boy" in London, and a "falot" (lantern companion) in Paris. Deliveries of black market goods to stores, such as fuel oil to gasoline stations during the oil embargo of 1973–1974, was accomplished under cover of darkness. Lawlessness is possible then because police coverage is sparse (Boston *Globe*, 1977:1). In addition, the officers on duty make themselves unavailable by sleeping in their cars, an old custom in New York City where the practice is called "cooping" (*New York Times*, 1968). The same was informally reported to me about

Boston police as well; they are found snoozing in their police cars in the Arboretum by the early morning joggers.

In Boston today, carrying arms is more common at night. For fear of mugging or rape, escort services are provided on many college campuses for women returning to their dorms at night, or for women on the evening shift going from their places of work to the parking lot or subway station. An escort is provided for nurses at Boston City Hospital because of an increase in robberies in that area. And some apartment houses, with their sentries at the door, become vertical stockades to which people in the city retreat at night.

However, like the former West, lawlessness and violence at night are concentrated in certain hours in certain places and are otherwise uncommon. Fights reach their peak about midnight, as shown in Figure 3, but are least frequent from 2:30 to 11:00 a.m. The area of Boston in which many brawls and muggings take place, where prostitution is rampant and bars and lounges feature nude go-go dancers, is called the "combat zone." A large transient population of relatively young males come into the area to patronize the moviehouses featuring X-rated films and become drunk and aggressive in bars and on the streets. Although this description may approximate what was once reported of mining towns in the West, these combat zones do not function so after 2:30 a.m. or during the daytime. In the daytime the areas are parts of business districts. Many people shop at department stores nearby, or otherwise pass through and patronize eating places and businesses there. So the combat zone designation refers to these places only at certain hours and is not true for all the city all night.

8. There Is More Helpfulness and Friendliness. Hollon (1974:211–2) remarks that "For every act of violence during the frontier period, there were thousands of examples of kindness, generosity, and sacrifice. . . ." He quotes an English traveler who said, " 'Even the rough western men, the hardy sons of the Indian frontier, accustomed from boyhood to fighting for existence, were hospitable and generous to a degree hard to find in more civilized life.' "

Reports of life on the land frontier are replete with accounts of warmth toward strangers, of community house building and barn raisings, and of help for those in need (Darby, 1818:400; Frantz and Choate, 1955:64; Billington, 1949:96, 167; Riegel, 1947:81). "Neighbors were ready to lend anything they possessed. No man driving along with an

Figure 3. Number of Fights Reported and Percentage of People Awake at Those Times in the City of Boston

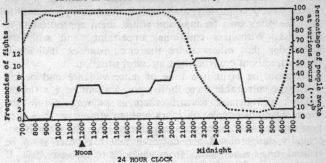

24 HOUR CLOCK

a Fights reported in emergency calls to telephone operators in the city of Boston, based on a 49-day (24-hour daily) sample made in 1974 (June, September, and December). The frequencies are adjusted for sampling variations over the 24 hours.
b Percentage of people awake is an estimate for Boston, and is based on a summary of 44 U.S. cities, reported in Szalai (1972:737).

empty wagon on a good road would pass another on foot without inviting him to ride" (Dick, 1937:512). Travelers returning from the outskirts said they were treated more kindly than they had been in the cities (Flint, 1826:402–03; Hollon, 1974:212).

At first these stories of openhanded western hospitality may seem inconsistent in the face of the high risks of thievery and violence. But the circumstances are actually related to one another. Dick (1937:510) observed that "As the isolated settlers battled against savage men, . . . and loneliness, they were drawn together in a fellowship." Billington (1972:166) added,

> Cooperation is normal within every in-group, but accentuates when the in-group is in conflict with an out-group and group solidarity is strengthened. This was the situation in frontier communities where conflicts with Indians, with raw nature, and with dominating Easterners heightened the spirit of interdependence.

That people want to affiliate under such conditions with others like themselves was demonstrated experimentally by Schachter (1959). He showed that the greater the risk people thought they were facing, the more anxious they were; and the more anxious they were, the more they wanted to be with others—even strangers—facing the same risk. Schachter (1959) concluded that being with others in the same boat served to reduce anxiety, and also provided an opportunity to appraise one's own feelings and adjust them appropriately to the risk. With less emotional uncertainty and with the knowledge that others share the circumstances, individuals feel better about confronting a stressful situation.

Because the night is a time of more violence and people feel more vulnerable then, those up and about have a similar outlook and behave toward others as pioneers did in the West. At night people are more alert to strangers when they pass on the street. Each tries to judge whether the other is potentially dangerous. Upon deciding that the other is to be trusted, one's mood shifts from vigilance to expansiveness. If not foe, then friend. Aware that they are out together in a dangerous environment, people identify with each other and become more outgoing. The sense of safety that spreads over those together at night in a diner or in a coffee shop promotes camaraderie there.

Also, on both frontiers people may be more hospitable because they have time to devote to strangers. Pioneers had plenty to do; yet often they had nothing to do. They were not closely synchronized in daily tasks as people were in the eastern cities, and the norm of punctuality was not emphasized. One man who grew up in the West

> . . . recalled the boredom he could never escape. . . .
> [T]he worst time of all was Sunday afternoon, when he
> had nothing to do. There were no newspapers to read
> and no books other than the family Bible, there was no
> one his age to talk with, and the nearest store was miles
> away. (Hollon, 1974:196)

In the city during the day, the mood of pressured schedules takes hold of folks and makes their encounters specific and short. The tempo slows markedly after midnight. The few who are out then hurry less because there are fewer places to rush to. Whereas lack of time inhibits sociability and helpfulness, available time clears the way for them.

I checked on these ideas by four tests of people's helpfulness and friendliness at various times in the 24-hour cycle. The tests are modest situations, not emergencies to which one has to respond under stress, but part of the common stream of social events. The ratings for degree of helpfulness and friendliness were established by asking sets of individuals to act as judges (ten judges for Test 3, six each for Tests 1, 2, and 4).

Test 1: Asking for directions. A male and female couple used a random sampling procedure on the street[2] to approach passersby and ask directions to a well-known location about a mile away. This is a familiar question, calling for little time and effort and one does not have to become personal in replying. Giving directions was scored one point. A nasty reaction—such as brushing by stiffly as if ignoring a panhandler, or turning and uttering an obscenity or a terse "Ask someone else," or quickly veering away from the speaker with apparent nonrecognition, or staring angrily and continuing to walk—was scored zero points. If the individual enlarged the scope of the encounter—such as by saying, in addition to giving directions, "Are you tourists here?" or "My son lives there," or "Do you need a ride? I have my car nearby"—it was scored two points. After each trial the two field researchers came to an agreement about the rating. Of 363 persons approached, 331 (91.2%) gave only directions, 21 (5.8%) enlarged the encounter, and 11 (3%) refused nastily.

[2]Tests 1, 2, and 3 reported in this section were carried out during each of the 166 field visits for which the sample is described in Figure 2n. A team of two researchers, always one male and one female, made a field visit. The male always asked for directions, but the two took turns attempting to secure interviews (Test 2). Tests 1, 2, and 3 were carried out in locations that were illuminated after dark, for example under a street lamp. Tests 1 and 2 both called for random sampling of passersby, and the procedure used the five-minute person-tally that contributed the data reported in Figure 2. This tally ascertained the density of the street population at that time of day, and this density number was used to set the sampling rate: if the number was greater than twenty-five, the fourth person passing from the direction would be chosen once the test was to start. If the count was from five to twenty-five, the third person would be chosen; if three or four, then the second person would be chosen; and if two or fewer passed during the five-minute tally then the first person from either direction would be selected. The members of the same group passing by were counted as one person; if the group was sampled the passerby nearest the researchers was approached. A maximum of three requests for directions and eight requests for interviews was to be made during each field visit. Sometimes the attempts were fewer—especially at night—because almost no one passed by during the segment of the field-visit schedule in which these attempts were to be made. The sampling was silently carried out by one researcher, who then by nudging or an equally subtle signal told the other whom to aproach. This minimized selection bias, for the researcher who was to carry out the test could not hesitate or overlook an unappealing passerby.

Test 2: Requesting a brief interview. A male and female couple followed a random selection procedure on the street (see fn. 2) to approach passersby and ask them to answer some questions in a survey being conducted about people who are in cities. This is a less common encounter but not unfamiliar in this land of frequent polls. One is asked to give time and trust to strangers, for the interview takes several minutes and the questions are personal—concerning feelings, employment, and living situation. A nasty refusal—such as an abrupt "Not from me [do you get an interview]!" or one of the reactions listed as nasty for Test 1 above—was scored zero points. A polite refusal—such as a plausible reason: "I'm sorry, I have an appointment" or equivalent delivered courteously—was scored one point. Consent was scored two points. Of 1,129 attempts, 175 (15.5%) refused nastily, 258 (22.9%) refused nicely, and 696 (61.6%) consented to the interview.

Test 3: Finding a lost key. A key found on the street is likely to be recognized as an object of value belonging to someone the finder does not know. Would the finder care enough about the stranger who lost it to send the key back? It is an anonymous situation. One does not have to become personal with the owner in order to return the key. This is a test of whether or not there is a difference in the rate of returning keys among people who pick them up at various hours and carry them away. The idea for using a key in such an experiment was developed by Forbes, TeVault, and Gromoll (1972). At the beginning of each of the field visits (see fn. 2), the researchers placed brightly colored aluminum keys in specific well-lighted locations on the streets at the sites. Each key had a tag attached listing the name and address of someone in a city ninety miles away (Northampton) and the request "Please return." We avoided locations near store entrances since the keys might be turned in to a clerk rather than mailed directly. The keys were color-coded and notch-coded, so that we could link each returned key with a particular interval of the 24-hour period. At the end of each two-hour visit the researchers made the rounds and retrieved every key that had not been carried away.

Overall, of 326 keys carried away, 220 (67.5%) were sent back. If the key was dropped in the mailbox (from which they were delivered to Northampton and postage due charges paid), it was scored one point; 154 (47.2%) were returned in this manner. The 38 keys (11.7%) that were returned in a stamped wrapper were scored two points each. Another 25 stamped and wrapped keys (7.7%) came with a personal note enclosed and were counted three points each. Three individuals (.9%) even telephoned Northampton to say that the key was in safe hands, and were scored four points each. The reactions reflect increased degrees of giving time and investing oneself in helping a stranger. The 106 keys (32.5%) not returned were scored zero points each.

Test 4: Being sociable in the supermarket. The supermarket checkout procedure is a microcosm of city street life. People who are mostly strangers to one another make limited contact in a brief, standardized situation. Research assistants, male and female couples, followed a stratified random sampling procedure[3] to visit three 24-hour supermarkets in different parts of Boston at various hours of the day and night. They posed as customers and noted the degree of sociability between single customers and clerks at the checkout counters. Sociability is defined as "showing warmth and expanding the scope of interaction with another." In this case, smiling was taken as showing warmth. The criterion for expanding the scope of the encounter was chatting about a topic other than the transaction—such as saying to the clerk, "Are you a high school student?" or "That's a nice shirt; where'd you get it?" or reporting general news. If the customer both smiled and chatted, the encounter was scored two points. If either happened alone it was rated one point, and zero points were scored if neither took place. (Interaction between customer and clerk showed a high degree of mutuality. When one was impassive the other was too, and when one was sociable the other responded in kind. That is why this simple scoring scheme was used rather than a tally that would have included the behavior of both parties.) To what extent do people

[3]The supermarket sample was similar to the sample for the experiments on Boston streets (see Fig. 2n). The same time intervals were listed in the sample frame and thirty visits were selected randomly (three, morning rush; seven, daytime; four, evening rush; seven, evening; and nine, night). The quota for nighttime visits was higher because fewer customers would be observed on each visit then. The observers were eleven pairs of students from my course on Social Interaction in the Fall, 1973; they were trained and rehearsed via earlier trials to reliability averaging .92 (between pairs of observers). One supermarket is a quarter-mile from the residential site for the street experiments; the other two markets are located in different parts of town. In each visit observers followed a systemmatically-varied visiting order among the three stores, for a total of 90 fifteen-minute observation periods.

Table 2. Aggregate Findings of Four Separate Tests for Helpfulness and Friendliness during Various Phases of the 24-Hour Daily Cycle, in Boston in 1974

Test	Time of Day					Analysis of Variance and Significance
	Morning rush hour 0730–0929	Daytime 0930–1614	Evening rush hour 1615–1814	Evening 1815–0014	Night 0015–0729	Σ
1. Give directions[a]	n=32*	n=115	n=27	n=123	n=66	n=363
	1.06	.97	1.07	1.00	[1.15]*	1.03
						F=4.917, p<.001
2. Consent to interview[b]	n=93	n=366	n=81	n=363	n=226	n=1129
	1.17	1.45	1.46	1.50	[1.55]	1.46
						F=4.531, p<.002
3. Return lost key[c]	n=29	n=113	n=26	n=94	n=64	n=326
	.93	1.00	1.04	[1.18]	.61(!)	.97
						F=3.972, p<.01
4. Be sociable with stranger[d]	n=68	n=212	n=161	n=179	n=132	n=752
	.24	.42	.29	.22	[.50]	.33
						F=5.250, p<.001

[a] Index based on zero points for nasty response and no directions given, one point for directions given only, two points for giving directions and expanding the scope of interaction as well; summed, and divided by number of trials (persons approached) within time period. Two of six judges differed in rating a courteous refusal—e.g., "I'm sorry, I don't know"—saying it is a common way to avoid getting involved. Hence polite refusals were omitted from the analysis. A check showed this made no difference. There were thirty instances of polite refusals, scattered over the times of day, and their inclusion (one point each) yielded the same ANOVA results as their exclusion.

[b] Index based on zero points for nasty refusal, one point for polite refusal, two points for consent; summed, and divided by number of trials (persons approached) within time period.

[c] Index based on zero points if key not returned, one point if returned unwrapped, two points if returned wrapped, three points if returned wrapped with message enclosed, four points if personal contact made by telephone; summed, and divided by number of trials (keys carried away) within time period.

[d] Index based on one point for smiling only, one point for chatting only, two points for both, zero points for neither; summed, and divided by number of cases (transactions observed at the checkout counter) within time period.

* n = number of trials; [ ] = highest mean score for test.

break through the confines of their roles in the supermarket checkout procedure to offer even the mildest sociability? Not much, for 562 (74.7%) of the 752 customers did not smile or talk about something other than the transaction. Smiling by itself occurred 98 times (13%), and only 66 (8.8%) both chatted and smiled.

To summarize, over 2,500 people were observed in various parts of central Boston throughout the 24-hour cycle and were rated on how they responded to four situations: giving directions when asked, consenting to be interviewed when asked, returning lost keys they found, and being sociable with strangers during the focused moment of paying for goods at a supermarket checkout counter. Four tests were used so that several different behaviors would help define and give face validity to what is being studied. While these do not cover the entire range of helpfulness and friendliness, showing some warmth, cooperating with another's modest appeal, and expanding the scope of interaction are the initial conditions of such relationships.

The samples of people among the tests are not the same. Tests 1 and 2 used a periodic selection of passersby following a random procedure adjusted to street population density. Test 3 focused only on persons who carried keys away. Test 4 involves only single customers at the checkout register in always-open supermarkets. Nevertheless, direct *time* comparisons are appropriate, for the tests are all based on random sampling designs for the same intervals around the clock. The issue for evaluating the hypothesis will be the sizes of the differences found among times of day within each test and the consistency of results by time of day across the four tests.

The results of the tests are shown in Table 2. There is impressive consistency for three of the tests, with nighttime scores being highest. Not only does nighttime show up best in these three cases, there is no other time of day consistently second best. In some instances the differences between nighttime and its nearest competitor are not statistically significant, even though the analysis of variance yields significant results when all times are compared. Although differences among hours are small in given instances, the cumulative effect of these practices would make a noticeable difference in the social mood at various times. The overall pattern supports the prediction that nighttime is a period of more helpfulness and friendliness than other portions of the day.

In that light the outcome of the key test is surprising. The night had by far the lowest rate of helpfulness. The lowest proportion of keys were returned (50%) and the least extra effort, beyond dropping keys unwrapped into the mailbox, was made then. This finding is so clear-cut and contrary to expectations that it must be significant. Its interpretation would benefit from information still to be presented, and I will postpone comment about its bearing on the frontier hypothesis until later.

The pattern of findings for all four tests does reject a rival hypothesis: *fear* determines people's conduct toward strangers at night. We know the night is viewed as a dangerous time to be outside one's home in the city (U.S. Office of Management and the Budget, 1974:58–9, 73). If fear of criminal assault dominated social behavior then, it should be greater in face-to-face encounters than for the passive, anonymous appeal to find a key tagged "Please return." We would expect people to be more guarded towards others at night, to shun approaches by strangers, but to be more helpful in the low-risk situation of dropping a lost key into the mailbox. Table 2 tells us that just the opposite happened. Nighttimers were more helpful and friendly towards strangers face to face. And yet, of the keys picked up, they returned the fewest.

9. Exploitation of the Basic Resource Finally Becomes National Policy. Westward expansion began long before anyone officially recognized the land frontier's possibilities for our society. It took years to realize even that the U.S. West was habitable. At one time the land west of the Missouri River was labeled on maps as the Great American Desert. Almost no one thought that some day many people would want to migrate and settle there (Hicks, 1948:508). Nor was the catch phrase "Manifest Destiny" applied to colonizing the West until 1845, centuries after the effort had been under way. In 1837 Horace Greeley introduced the slogan "Go West, Young Man, go forth into the Country." He looked upon such migration as a means of relief from the poverty and unemployment caused by the Panic of 1837. By 1854 Greeley was urging, "Make the Public Lands free in quarter-sections to Actual Settlers . . . and the earth's landless millions will no longer be orphans and mendicants" (cited in Smith, 1950:234–5). In 1862, with the passage of the Homestead Act, it became a deliberate policy of the U.S. government to use the western territory to help relieve the conditions of tenant farmers and hard-pressed city laborers. A member of Congress declared, in support of the Homestead Act, "I sustain this measure . . . because its benign operation will postpone for centuries, if it will not forever, all serious conflict between capital and labor in the older free states" (Smith, 1950:239). The policymakers finally saw the exploitation of western space as a means of solving social problems.

Similarly, in the first 150 years after Murdock's coal-gas illumination was introduced, there was no national consciousness in England or the United States about colonizing the nighttime. People went ahead, expanding their activities into the dark hours without declaring that a 24-hour community was being forged. Now in the 1970s policy makers have begun talking about cheap time at night the way they once spoke of cheap western land. V.D. Patrushev (1972:429) of the Soviet Union writes that "Time . . . is a particular form of national wealth. Therefore it is imperative to plan the most efficient use of it for all members of a society." Daniel Schydlowsky (1976:5), an economist who specializes in development in Latin America and who recently ended a three-year study there, has concluded that multiple-shift work would produce remarkable gains in reducing unemployment and improve the economies of overpopulated developing cities. His claim for the use of time echoes the attitudes of nineteenth century proponents of the use of western lands as a solution for those who were out of work.

The advocates of westward expansion also saw it as a way to draw off great numbers of people from the cities and forestall crowding there (Smith, 1950:8, 238). Today Dantzig and Saaty (1973:190–3) recommend dispersing activities around the clock as a means of reducing congestion. And Meier (1976:965) writes, "Scarce land and expensive human time can also be conserved by encouraging round-the-clock operation. . . . By such means people can live densely without stepping on each other's toes."

10. Interest Groups Emerge. As the U.S. frontier matured, the population became more aware of its own circumstances and organized to promote its own concerns. Turner (1893:207; 1965:54) remarked that the West felt a keen sense of difference from the East. He wrote:

> . . . [F]rom the beginning East and West have shown a sectional attitude. The interior of the colonies was disrespectful of the coast, and the coast looked down upon the upland folk. . . . [The westerners finally] became

self-conscious and even rebellious against the rule of the East. . . . [I]t resented the conception that it was merely an emanation from a rival North and South; that it was the dependency of one or another of the Eastern sections. . . . It took the attitude of a section itself. (1932:25–30)

Sections are geographically-based interest groups. One hundred years ago the West gave rise to such pressure groups and farm bloc organizations as the Greenback Party, the National Grange, and the Populists. The Granger movement, for example, grew with the westerners' problems with transportation in their region. There were no significant river or canal systems out west and so settlers were at the mercy of the railroads. But the rates in the newer regions of the West were far higher than those in the East, and it was protest against this disparity that aided the movement in the 1870s (Robbins, 1960:271).

The night also isolates a group from the main society. Antagonism may develop as daytimers deprecate the nighttimers and the latter resent the neglect shown by the others. People active after dark find their life style differing from that of daytime society, become aware of having a separate identity, and evolve into interest groups. New alignments in the tradition of sectionalism begin to emerge. This has already happened for two groups usually linked with the nighttime: homosexuals and prostitutes. The Gay Liberation Front is one nationwide organization devoted to the rights of homosexuals. Prostitutes also have a union. Appropriately they adopted the name of a creature renowned in the U.S. West for howling at night—the coyote. COYOTES (Call Off Your Old Tired Ethics) seek legislation to decriminalize their activities and protest courtroom discrimination against women who earn their living by prostitution (Boston *Globe*, 1976a).

An actual day vs. night contest has already been fought in Boston. The city's airport is flanked by residential neighborhoods and its afterdark activity became a nuisance to people wanting an undisturbed night's sleep. In 1976 dwellers in those neighborhoods, as private citizens and through two organized groups—Fair Share, and the Massachusetts Air Pollution and Noise Abatement Committee—made a concerted effort to stop airplane flights between 11 p.m. and 7 a.m. It led to counterarguments by the business community stressing the economic benefit of continuing the flights. The pro-nighttime group was a coalition among commercial interests, airline companies, unions, and airport employees holding jobs at night (some of whom lived in those very neighborhoods). This group argued that the curfew would result in the loss of thousands of jobs, millions of dollars in sales, and further would discourage business investment in the New England area. Joined by the governor, the mayor and many legislators, the coalition successfully won a decision from the Massachusetts Port Authority that the nighttime flights should be kept going. (Some proposals for noise reduction during the night accompanied the decision.) A month later, Eastern Airlines announced it was adding an airbus and expanding its staff at the airport "as a direct result of the recent decision . . . not to impose a night curfew at Logan [airport]." As one businessman put it, "The curfew decision was regarded as the shootout at the OK Corral" (Boston *Globe*, 1976b; 1976c).

DISCUSSION

The evidence bears out the hypothesis that night is a frontier. That nighttimers are *less* likely to return the keys they find also supports the idea. While the outcome of Test 3 seems to deny the claim that more help is given on a frontier, the lost-key experiment differs from the other tests in that it is the only one in which people do not meet face to face. It is a test of anonymous helpfulness. During the nighttime, strangers identify more readily with one another. A young man told me, "At 4 a.m. if someone sees you walking the streets at the same time he does, he must think, 'Gee, this guy must be part of the brethern, because no one else is awake at these times.'" However, if someone finds a key and does not know the owner, he would guess that everyone who passed that way is equally likely to have lost it. Nighttimers, knowing they are few, assume on the weight of numbers that the person who lost the key is a daytimer. In item ten above, I suggested that the feelings of nighttimers toward daytimers resembled the attitudes of westerners toward easterners a century ago. They perceive they are different and resent the neglect shown by the day people toward them. The nighttime in-group feels comradely within itself but indifferent or antagonistic toward the out-group (see Sumner, 1906:27). Whereas frontier people readily help others whom they meet on the frontier, their sense of difference from unknown day-timers leaves them less concerned about the others' plights and they do not return many lost keys.

I cannot think of an equally plausible rival explanation, compatible with the rest of the evidence, for this finding. This interpretation makes sense of the complete set of outcomes in Table 2 and fits the analysis in the preceding section. Revealing patterns stand out. One is the connection between violence and helpfulness and friendliness, a condition that emerges on the frontier because of fear there and solidarity among those who believe they share the dangers together. Another is the pairing of sectional attitudes and helpfulness, so that assistance is given selectively to those with whom the individuals identify.

The experiments confirm what we know about life on frontiers, but I did not explore wholly the causes of behavior here. The findings may be compared with research on helpfulness reported by Bryan and Test (1967), Feldman (1968), Latané and Darley (1970), Milgram (1970), Wispé and Freshley (1971), Darley and Batson (1973) and others. There is a problem of comparability because different times of day were not treated systematically in those studies. Yet some of the insights may work well together. The findings about available time, at least, agree with each other. Darley and Batson varied the degree to which their subjects were hurrying to an appointment when they came upon a person coughing, groaning, and apparently needing help. Of several possible influences that were measured, including what was in the subjects' thoughts at the moment (some of them were preparing to discuss the Good Samaritan parable!), only the degree of hurry was related to helping. A mere 10% of those who were late to their appointments stopped to help, whereas 63% of those who had ample time stopped to give aid to the crouching and suffering man.

CONCLUSION

What is the gain in thinking of night as a frontier? A single theoretical idea gives coherence to a wide range of events: the kind of people up and about at those hours, why they differ from daytimers in their behavior, the beginnings of political efforts by night people, the slow realization among leaders that public policy might be applied to the time resource. Even the variety of endeavors becomes understandable—from metal smelting plants to miniature golf courses, to mayor's complaint offices, to eating places, to computerized banking terminals that dispense cash. The niche is being expanded. Bit by bit, all of society migrates there. To treat this as a sequel to the geographic spread of past centuries is to summarize the move within familiar ecological concepts of migration, settlement, and frontier.

Though I have reviewed materials for one period in U.S. history, these conditions are features of all frontiers. They should apply to the Russians crossing the Urals, to the Chinese entering Manchuria during the Ch'ing dynasty, to the Boers settling South Africa, to Australians venturing into the Outback, to present-day Brazilians colonizing the Amazon interior, as well as to Americans migrating into the night. The patterns are confirmed by essays in Wyman and Kroeber's anthology on frontiers.

We should also consider the uniqueness of this new frontier. Each settlement beyond established boundaries has its own qualities. Here are some differences between the West and the night: (1) On the land frontier settlers lived rudely with few services at hand. At night a large portion of the total range of activities is services. (2) Utilities cost more on the western fringes; at night the fees for telephone calls, electricity, and airplane travel are lower. (3) While western settlements were in remote contact with the East, day and night are joined so that either can be affected quickly by events in the other. Twenty-four hour society is more constantly adjusting, more unstable. (4) Looking westward, pioneers saw no end to the possibilities for growth, but we know that expansion into the night can only go as far as the dawn. (5) The land frontier held promise of unlimited opportunity for individuals who ventured there. Miners and pioneers endured hardships because they lived for the future. They hoped to make their fortunes, or at least a better life. At night there are large numbers of unskilled, menial, and dirty tasks; but charwoman and watchman and hospital aide and porter are dead-end jobs. Many people so employed are immigrants or members of minority groups and this expanding margin of society is a *time ghetto*. The ghetto encloses more than minorities and immigrants, for ultimate control in 24-hour organizations remains with top management in the daytime. Policy making, important decisions, employee hiring, and planning are curtailed during off-hours. Since evening and night staffs are prevented from taking many actions that would lead to the recognition of executive ability, and since their performance is not readily observable by the bosses, all have poorer chances for advancement. (6) The western frontier's natural resources were so extensive that we became wasteful and squandered them. At night there is nothing new to exploit but time itself, so we maximize the use of fixed assets and become more frugal. (7) Migrating westward called for rather significant capital investment—outlays for a covered wagon, mining equipment, cattle, the railroad. There is little extra capital required for a move to the night. Instead, the incessant organization's need for more personnel reflects a swing toward more labor intensive operations. So the night frontier may appeal to developing countries with meager treasuries and teeming populations of unemployed.

This expansion is also unusual because it happens in time rather than in space. We change from a diurnal into an incessant species. We move beyond the environmental cycle—alternating day and night—in which our biological and social life evolved, and thus force novelty on these areas. (8) In the past a single set of minds shut down an enterprise one day and started it up on the next. It permitted easy continuity and orderly administration. For coverage around the clock, we introduce shifts of personnel. Several times a day another set of minds takes over the same activity and facilities. (9) A physiological upset is imposed on people who work at night and maintain ordinary recreation and social life on their days off. Each time they switch their active hours they undergo phase shifts in body rhythms such as heartbeat, temperature, and hormonal production. The several days' malaise that results was known to such workers long before air travel across time zones popularized the phrase "jet fatigue."

Ibsen's (1890: Act II) character, Eilert Lövborg, describes the two sections of the book he has written, "The first deals with the . . . forces of the future. And here is the second forecasting the probable line of development." We may believe we understand the forces, the conditions under which humans enlarge their niche, but what is the probable line of development? Forecasting is called for despite the difficulties of social prediction. We should consider the possibilities of an era in which unremitting activity is even more commonplace. What is the carrying capacity of the 24-hour day? What will happen when saturation occurs? Time will have extraordinary leverage as it gets used up, for time is a resource without direct substitute. It is unstretchable; we cannot do with it as we did with land by building up toward the sky and digging into the ground. Time is unstorable; we cannot save the unused hours every night for future need.

In his essay "The Frontier in American History," Frederick Jackson Turner (1893:38) reviewed the impact of the advance into western lands upon our society and remarked, "And now, four centuries from the discovery of America, at the end of a hundred years of life under the constitution, the frontier has gone." But it has not gone. During the era that the settlement of our land frontier was being completed, there began—into the night—a large-scale migration of wakeful activity that continues to spread over the world.

REFERENCES

American Heritage Dictionary of the English Language. Boston: Houghton Mifflin, 1970.

Becker, Howard. *Outsiders: Studies in the Sociology of Deviance.* New York: Free Press, 1963.

Billington, Ray Allen. *Westward Expansion.* New York: Macmillan, 1949.

Billington, Ray Allen. *The American Frontiersman.* London: Oxford University Press, 1954.

Billington, Ray Allen. "Frontier democracy: social aspects." pp. 160–84 in G.R. Taylor (ed.), *The Turner Thesis: Concerning the Role of the Frontier in American History.* 3rd ed. Lexington, Ma.: Heath, 1972.

Boston *Globe.* "Prostitutes speak of pride, but they are still victims." June 25: 1, 10, 1976a.

Boston *Globe.* "Dukakis decides to go against Logan curfew." August 12: 1, 20, 1976b.

Boston *Globe.* "Logan anti-noise plan offered." August 13: 35, 1976c.

Boston *Globe.* "Boston police today." April 4: 1, 3, 1977.

Brandeis, Louis D. and Josephine Goldmark. *The Case Against Night Work for Women.* Rev. ed. New York: National Consumers League, 1918.

Bryan, James H. and Mary Ann Test. "Models and helping: naturalistic studies in aiding behavior." *Journal of Personality and Social Psychology,* Vol. 6, pp. 400–7, 1967.

Buttimer, Anne. "Grasping the dynamism of lifeworld." *Annals of the Association of American Geographers,* Vol. 66, pp. 277–92, 1976.

Dantzig, George B. and Thomas L. Saaty. *Compact city*. San Francisco: Freeman, 1973.

Darby, William [1818]. "Primitivism in the lower Mississippi valley." In M. Ridge and R. A. Billington (Eds.), *America's Frontier Story*. New York: Holt, pp. 399–401, 1969.

Darley, John and C. Daniel Batson. "From Jerusalem to Jericho: a study of situational and dispositional variables in helping behavior." *Journal of Personality and Social Psychology*, Vol. 27, pp. 100–8, 1973.

Dick, Everett [1937]. *The Sod-House Frontier, 1854–1890*. New York: Appleton-Century, 1954.

Doddridge, Joseph [1912]. "Life in the old west." In M. Ridge and R. A. Billington (Eds.), *America's Frontier Story*. New York: Holt, pp. 101–6, 1969.

Feldman, Roy E. "Response to compatriot and foreigner who seek assistance." *Journal of Personality and Social Psychology*, Vol. 10, pp. 202–14, 1968.

Flint, Timothy [1826]. "Frontier society in the Mississippi valley." In M. Ridge and R. A. Billington (Eds.), *America's Frontier Story*. New York: Holt, pp. 401–3, 1969.

Forbes, Gordon, B., R. D. TeVault, and H. F. Gromoll. "Regional differences in willingness to help strangers: a field experiment with a new unobtrusive measure." *Social Science Research*, Vol. 1, pp. 415–9, 1972.

Frantz, J. B. and J. E. Choate. *The American Cowboy: The Myth and Reality*. Norman: University of Oklahoma Press, 1955.

Godkin, Edwin L. [1896]. "The frontier and the national character." In M. Ridge and R. A. Billington (Eds.), *America's Frontier Story*. New York: Holt, pp. 13–16, 1969.

Hicks, John D. *The Federal Union*. Boston: Houghton Mifflin, 1948.

Hollon, W. Eugene. "Frontier violence: another look." In R. A. Billington (Ed.), *People of the Plains and Mountains*. Westport, Ct.: Greenwood Press, pp, 86–100, 1973.

Hollon, W. Eugene. *Frontier Violence*. New York: Oxford University Press, 1974.

Humphrey, Seth K. *Following the Prairie Frontier*. Minneapolis: University of Minnesota Press, 1931.

Ibsen, Henrik [1890]. *Hedda Gabler*. Tr. E. Gosse and W. Archer. In J. Gassner (Ed.), *A Treasury of the Theatre*. New York: Simon and Schuster, pp. 42–74, 1950.

Jackson, W. Turrentine. "Pioneer life on the plains and in the mines." In R. A. Billington (Ed.), *People of the Plains and Mountains*. Westport, Ct.: Greenwood Press, pp. 63–85, 1973.

Kozak, Lola Jean. "Night people: a study of the social experiences of night workers." Michigan State University, *Summation*, Vol. 4, pp. 40–61, 1974.

Latané, Bibb and John Darley. *The Unresponsive Bystander*. New York: Appleton-Century, 1970.

Marx, Karl [1867]. *Capital*. New York: Modern Library, 1906.

Meier, Richard L. "A stable urban ecosystem." *Science*, Vol. 192, pp. 962–8, 1976.

Melbin, Murray. "The colonization of time." In T. Carlstein, D. Parkes, and N. Thrift (Eds.), *Timing Space and Spacing Time in Social Organization*. London: Arnold, 1977.

Milgram, Stanley. "The experience of living in cities." *Science*, Vol. 167, pp. 1461–8, 1970.

Mumford, Lewis. *The City in History*. New York: Harcourt Brace, 1961.

National Industrial Conference Board. *Night Work in Industry*. New York: National Industrial Conference Board, 1927.

New York Times. "Cooping: an old custom under fire." December 15: Sec. 4, 6E, 1968.

Patrushev, V. D. "Aggregate time-balances and their meaning for socio-economic planning." In A. Szalai (Ed.), *The Use of Time*. The Hague: Mouton, pp. 429–40, 1972.

Riegel, Robert E. *America Moves West*. New York: Holt, 1947.

Robbins, Roy M. *Our Landed Heritage*. Princeton: Princeton University Press, 1942.

Schachter, Stanley. *The Psychology of Affiliation*. Stanford: Stanford University Press, 1959.

Schlesinger, Arthur. *The Rise of the City: 1878–1895*. New York: Macmillan, 1933.

Schydlowsky, Daniel. "Multiple shifts would produce 'revolutionary results' for Latin American economy." Boston University, *Spectrum 4*, September 9, p. 5, 1976.

Smith, Henry Nash [1950]. *Virgin Land*. New York: Vintage, 1957.

Sumner, William Graham [1906]. *Folkways*. New York: New American Library, 1960.

Szalai, Alexander (Ed.). *The Use of Time*. The Hague: Mouton, 1972.

Turner, Frederick Jackson [1893]. *The Frontier in American History*. New York: Holt, 1920.

Turner, Frederick Jackson, *The Significance of Sections in American History*. New York: Holt, 1932.

Turner, Frederick Jackson [1965]. *America's Great Fontiers and Sections*. Unpublished essays edited by W. R. Jacobs. Lincoln: Nebraska University Press, 1969.

U. S. Bureau of the Census. *Historical Statistics of the United States*, Vol. 1: ser. A195-209. Washington, D.C.: U.S. Government Printing Office, 1975.

U. S. Bureau of Labor Statistics. *Current Population Survey*. Unpublished paper. May 12: Table 1. Washington, D.C., 1976.

U. S. Office of Management and Budget. *Social Indicators, 1973*. Washington, D.C.: U.S. Government Printing Office, 1974.

Wispé, Lauren G. and Harold B. Freshley. "Race, sex, and sympathetic helping behavior: the broken bag caper." *Journal of Personality and Social Psychology*, Vol. 17, pp. 59–64, 1971.

Wyman, Walker D. and Clifton B. Kroeber (Eds.). *The Frontier in Perspective*. Madison: University of Wisconsin Press, 1957.

Young, Michael and Peter Willmott [1973]. *The Symmetrical Family*. Harmondsworth, England: Penguin, 1975.

Death by Dieselization:
A Case Study in the Reaction
to Technological Change

by
W. F. Cottrell

In the following instance it is proposed that we examine a community confronted with radical change in its basic economic institution and to trace the effects of this change throughout the social structure. From these facts it may be possible in some degree to anticipate the resultant changing attitudes and values of the people in the community, particularly as they reveal whether or not there is a demand for modification of the social structure or a shift in function from one institution to another. Some of the implications of the facts discovered may be valuable in anticipating future social change.

The community chosen for examination has been disrupted by the dieselization of the railroads. Since the railroad is among the oldest of those industries organized around steam, and since therefore the social structure of railroad communities is a product of long-continued processes of adaptation to the technology of steam, the sharp contrast between the technological requirements of the steam engine and those of the diesel should clearly reveal the changes in social structure required. Any one of a great many railroad towns might have been chosen for examination. However, many railroad towns are only partly dependent upon the railroad for their existence. In them many of the effects which take place are blurred and not easily distinguishable by the observer. Thus, the "normal" railroad town may not be the best place to see the consequences of dieselization. For this reason a one-industry town was chosen for examination.

In a sense it is an "ideal type" railroad town, and hence

Reprinted from *American Sociological Review*, Vol. 16, No. 3, June 1951, pp. 358–65, with permission of the American Sociological Association and the author.

not complicated by other extraneous economic factors. It lies in the desert and is here given the name "Caliente" which is the Spanish adjective for "hot." Caliente was built in a break in an eighty-mile canyon traversing the desert. Its reason for existence was to service the steam locomotive. There are few resources in the area to support it on any other basis, and such as they are they would contribute more to the growth and maintenance of other little settlements in the vicinity than to that of Caliente. So long as the steam locomotive was in use, Caliente was a necessity. With the adoption of the diesel it became obsolescent.

This stark fact was not, however, part of the expectations of the residents of Caliente. Based upon the "certainty" of the railroad need for Caliente, men built their homes there, frequently of concrete and brick at the cost, in many cases, of their life savings. The water system was laid in cast iron which will last for centuries. Business men erected substantial buildings which could be paid for only by profits gained through many years of business. Four churches evidence the faith of Caliente people in the future of their community. A twenty-seven bed hospital serves the town. Those who built it thought that their investment was as well warranted as the fact of birth, sickness, accident and death. They believed in education. Their school buildings represent the investment of savings guaranteed by bonds and future taxes. There is a combined park and play field which, together with a recently modernized theatre, has been serving recreational needs. All these physical structures are material evidence of the expectations, morally and legally sanctioned and financially funded, of the people of Caliente. This is a normal and rational aspect of the culture of all "solid" and "sound" communities.

Similarly normal are the social organizations. These include Rotary, Chamber of Commerce, Masons, Odd Fellows, American Legion and the Veterans of Foreign Wars. There are the usual unions, churches, and myriad little clubs to which the women belong. In short, here is the average American community with normal social life, subscribing to normal American codes. Nothing its members had been taught would indicate that the whole pattern of this normal existence depended completely upon a few elements of technology which were themselves in flux. For them the continued use of the steam engine was as "natural" a phenomenon as any other element in their physical environment. Yet suddenly their life pattern was destroyed by the announcement that the railroad was moving its division point, and with it destroying the economic basis of Caliente's existence.

Turning from this specific community for a moment, let us examine the technical changes which took place and the reasons for the change. Division points on a railroad are established by the frequency with which the rolling stock must be serviced and the operating crews changed. At the turn of the century when this particular road was built, the engines produced wet steam at low temperatures. The steel in the boilers was of comparatively low tensile strength and could not withstand the high temperatures and pressures required for the efficient use of coal and water. At intervals of roughly a hundred miles the engine had to be disconnected from the train for service. At these points the cars also were inspected and if they were found to be defective they were either removed from the train or repaired while it was standing and the new engine being coupled on. Thus the location of Caliente, as far as the railroad was concerned, was a function of boiler temperature and pressure and the resultant service requirements of the locomotive.

Following World War II, the high tensile steels developed to create superior artillery and armor were used for locomotives. As a consequence it was possible to utilize steam at higher temperatures and pressure. Speed, power, and efficiency were increased and the distance between service intervals was increased.

The "ideal distance" between freight divisions became approximately 150 to 200 miles whereas it had formerly been 100 to 150. Wherever possible, freight divisions were increased in length to that formerly used by passenger trains, and passenger divisions were lengthened from two old freight divisions to three. Thus towns located at 100 miles from a terminal became obsolescent, those at 200 became freight points only, and those at three hundred miles became passenger division points.

The increase in speed permitted the train crews to make the greater distance in the time previously required for the lesser trip, and roughly a third of the train and engine crews, car inspectors, boilermakers and machinists and other service men were dropped. The towns thus abandoned were crossed off the social record of the nation in the adjustment to these technological changes in the use of the steam locomotive. Caliente, located midway between terminals about six hundred miles apart, survived. In fact it gained, since the less frequent stops caused an increase in the service required of the maintenance crews at those points where it took place. However, the introduction of the change to diesel engines projected a very different future.

In its demands for service the diesel engine differs almost completely from a steam locomotive. It requires infrequent, highly skilled service, carried on within very close limits, in contrast to the frequent, crude adjustments required by the steam locomotive. Diesels operate at about 35 per cent efficiency, in contrast to the approximately 4 per cent efficiency of the steam locomotives in use after World War II in the United States. Hence diesels require much less frequent stops for fuel and water. These facts reduce their operating costs sufficiently to compensate for their much higher initial cost.

In spite of these reductions in operating costs the introduction of diesels ordinarily would have taken a good deal of time. The change-over would have been slowed by the high capital costs of retooling the locomotive works, the long period required to recapture the costs of existing steam locomotives, and the effective resistance of the workers. World War II altered each of these factors. The locomotive works were required to make the change in order to provide marine engines, and the costs of the change were assumed by the government. Steam engines were used up by the tremendous demand placed upon the railroads by war traffic. The costs were recaptured by shipping charges. Labor shortages were such that labor resistance was less formidable and much less acceptable to the public than it would have been in peace time. Hence the shift to diesels was greatly facilitated by the war. In consequence, every third and sometimes every second division point suddenly became technologically obsolescent.

Caliente, like all other towns in similar plight, is supposed to accept its fate in the name of "progress." The general public, as shippers and consumers of shipped goods, reaps the harvest in better, faster service and eventually perhaps in lower charges. A few of the workers in Caliente will also share the gains, as they move to other division points, through higher wages. They will share in the higher pay, though whether this will be adequate to compensate for the costs of moving no one can say. Certain it is that their pay will not be adjusted to compensate for their specific losses. They will gain only as their seniority gives them the opportunity to work. These are those who gain. What are the losses, and who bears them?

The railroad company can figure its losses at Caliente fairly accurately. It owns 39 private dwellings, a modern clubhouse with 116 single rooms, and a twelve-room hotel with dining-room and lunch-counter facilities. These now become useless, as does much of the fixed physical equipment used for servicing trains. Some of the machinery can be used elsewhere. Some part of the roundhouse can be used to store unused locomotives and standby equipment. The rest will be torn down to save taxes. All of these costs can be entered as capital losses on the statement which the company draws up for its stockholders and for the government. Presumably they will be recovered by the use of the more efficient engines.

What are the losses that may not be entered on the company books? The total tax assessment in Caliente was $9,-946.80 for the year 1948, of which $6,103.39 represented taxes assessed on the railroad. Thus the railroad valuation was about three-fifths that of the town. This does not take into account tax-free property belonging to the churches, the schools, the hospital, or the municipality itself which included all the public utilities. Some ideas of the losses sustained by the railroad in comparison with the losses of others can be surmised by reflecting on these figures for real estate alone. The story is an old one and often repeated in the economic history of America. It represents the "loss" side of a profit and loss system of adjusting to technological change. Perhaps for sociological purposes we need an answer to the question "just who pays?"

Probably the greatest losses are suffered by the older "non-operating" employees. Seniority among these men extends only within the local shop and craft. A man with twenty-five years' seniority at Caliente has no claim on the job of a similar craftsman at another point who has only twenty-five days' seniority. Moreover, some of the skills formerly valuable are no longer needed. The boilermaker, for example, knows that jobs for his kind are disappearing and he must enter the ranks of the unskilled. The protection and status offered by the union while he was employed have become meaningless now that he is no longer needed. The cost of this is high both in loss of income and in personal demoralization.

Operating employees also pay. Their seniority extends over a division, which in this case includes three division points. The older members can move from Caliente and claim another job at another point, but in many cases they move leaving a good portion of their life savings behind. The younger men must abandon their stake in railroad employment. The loss may mean a new apprenticeship in another occupation, at a time in life when apprenticeship wages are not adequate to meet the obligations of mature men with families. A steam engine hauled 2,000 tons up the hill out of Caliente with the aid of two helpers. The four-unit diesel in command of one crew handles a train of 5,000 tons alone. Thus, to handle the same amount of tonnage required only about a fourth the man-power it formerly took. Three out of four men must start out anew at something else.

The local merchants pay. The boarded windows, half-empty shelves, and abandoned store buildings bear mute evidence of these costs. The older merchants stay, and pay; the younger ones, and those with no stake in the community will move; but the value of their property will in both cases largely be gone.

The bondholders will pay. They can't foreclose on a dead town. If the town were wiped out altogether, that which would remain for salvage would be too little to satisfy their claims. Should the town continue there is little hope that taxes adequate to carry the overhead of bonds and day-to-day expenses could be secured by taxing the diminished number of property owners or employed persons.

The church will pay. The smaller congregations cannot support services as in the past. As the church men leave, the buildings will be abandoned.

Homeowners will pay. A hundred and thirty-five men owned homes in Caliente. They must accept the available means of support or rent to those who do. In either case the income available will be far less than that on which the houses were built. The least desirable homes will stand unoccupied, their value completely lost. The others must be revalued at a figure far below that at which they were formerly held.

In a word, those pay who are, by traditional American standards, *most moral*. Those who have rasied children see friendships broken and neighborhoods disintegrated. The childless more freely shake the dust of Caliente from their feet. Those who built their personalities into the structure of the community watch their work destroyed. Those too wise or too selfish to have entangled themselves in community affairs suffer no such qualms. The chain store can pull down its sign, move its equipment and charge the costs off against more profitable and better located units, and against taxes. The local owner has no such alternatives. In short, "good citizens" who assumed family and community responsibility are the greatest losers. Nomads suffer least.

The people of Caliente are asked to accept as "normal" this strange inversion of their expectations. It is assumed that they will, without protest or change in sentiment, accept the dictum of the "law of supply and demand." Certainly they must comply in part with this dictum. While their behavior in part reflects this compliance, there are also other changes perhaps equally important in their attitudes and values.

The first reaction took the form of an effort at community self-preservation. Caliente became visible to its inhabitants as a real entity, as meaningful as the individual personalities which they had hitherto been taught to see as atomistic or nomadic elements. Community survival was seen as prerequisite to many of the individual values that had been given precedence in the past. The organized community made a search for new industry, citing elements of community organization themselves as reasons why industry should move to Caliente. But the conditions that led the railroad to abandon the point made the place even less attractive to new industry than it had hitherto been. Yet the effort to keep the community a going concern persisted.

There was also a change in sentiment. In the past the glib assertion that progress spelled sacrifice could be offered when some distant group was a victim of technological change. There was no such reaction when the event struck home. The change can probably be as well revealed as in any other way by quoting from the Caliente *Herald:*

> . . . (over the) years . . . (this) . . . railroad and its affiliates . . . became to this writer his ideal of a railroad empire. The (company) . . . appeared to take much more than the ordinary interest of big railroads in the development of areas adjacent to its lines, all the while doing a great deal for the communities large and small through which the lines passed.
>
> Those were the days creative of (its) enviable reputation as one of the finest, most progressive—and most human—of American railroads, enjoying the confidence and respect of employees, investors, and communities alike!
>
> One of the factors bringing about this confidence and respect was the consideration shown communities which

otherwise would have suffered serious blows when division and other changes were effected. A notable example was . . . (a town) . . . where the shock of division change was made almost unnoticed by installation of a rolling stock reclamation point, which gave (that town) an opportunity to hold its community intact until tourist traffic and other industries could get better established—with the result that . . . (it) . . . is now on a firm foundation. And through this display of consideration for a community, the railroad gained friends—not only among the people of . . . (that town) . . . who were perhaps more vocal than others, but also among thousands of others throughout the country on whom this action made an indelible impression.

But things seem to have changed materially during the last few years, the . . . (company) . . . seems to this writer to have gone all out for glamor and the dollars which glamorous people have to spend, sadly neglecting one of the principal factors which helped to make . . . (it) . . . great: that fine consideration of communities and individuals, as well as employees, who have been happy in cooperating steadfastly with the railroad in times of stress as well as prosperity. The loyalty of these people and communities seems to count for little with the . . . (company) . . . of this day, though other "Big Business" corporations do not hesitate to expend huge sums to encourage the loyalty of community and people which old friends of . . . (the company) . . . have been happy to give voluntarily.

Ever since the . . . railroad was constructed . . . Caliente has been a key town on the railroad. It is true, the town owed its inception to the railroad, but it has paid this back in becoming one of the most attractive communities on the system. With nice homes, streets and parks, good school . . . good city government . . . Caliente offers advantages that most big corporations would be gratified to have for their employees—a homey spot where they could live their lives of contentment, happiness and security.

Caliente's strategic location, midway of some of the toughest road on the entire system has been a lifesaver for the road several times when floods have wrecked havoc on the roadbed in the canyon above and below Caliente. This has been possible through storage in

Caliente of large stocks of repair material and equipment—and not overlooking manpower—which has thus become available on short notice.

. . . But (the railroad) or at least one of its big officials appearing to be almost completely divorced from policies which made this railroad great, has ordered changes which are about as inconsiderate as anything of which "Big Business" has ever been accused! Employees who have given the best years of their lives to this railroad are cut off without anything to which they can turn, many of them with homes in which they have taken much pride; while others, similarly with nice homes, are told to move elsewhere and are given runs that only a few will be able to endure from a physical standpoint, according to common opinion.

Smart big corporations the country over encourage their employees to own their own homes—and loud are their boasts when the percentage of such employees is favorable! But in contrast, a high (company) official is reported to have said only recently that "a railroad man has no business owning a home!" Quite a departure from what has appeared to be (company) tradition.

It is difficult for the Herald to believe that this official however "big" he is, speaks for the . . . (company) . . . when he enunciates a policy that, carried to the latter, would make tramps of (company) employees and their families!

No thinking person wants to stand in the way of progress, but true progress is not made when it is overshadowed by cold-blooded disregard for the loyalty of employees, their families, and the communities which have developed in the good American way through the decades of loyal service and good citizenship.

This editorial, written by a member of all the service clubs, approved by Caliente business men, and quoted with approbation by the most conservative members of the community, is significant of changing sentiment.

The people of Caliente continually profess their belief in "The American Way," but like the editor of the *Herald* they criticize decisions made solely in pursuit of profit, even though these decisions grow out of a clearcut case of technological "progress." They feel that the company should have based its decision upon consideration for loyalty, citizenship, and community morale. They assume that the company should regard the seniority rights of workers as important considerations, and that it should consider significant the effect of permanent unemployment upon old and faithful employees. They look upon community integrity as an important community asset. Caught between the support of a "rational" system of "economic" forces and laws, and sentiments which they accept as significant values, they seek a solution to their dilemma which will at once permit them to retain their expected rewards for continued adherence to past norms and to defend the social system which they have been taught to revere but which now offers them a stone instead of bread.

IMPLICATIONS

We have shown that those in Caliente whose behavior most nearly approached the ideal taught are hardest hit by change. On the other hand, those seemingly farthest removed in conduct from that ideal are either rewarded or pay less of the costs of change than do those who follow the ideal more closely. Absentee owners, completely anonymous, and consumers who are not expected to cooperate to make the gains possible are rewarded most highly, while the local people who must cooperate to raise productivity pay dearly for having contributed.

In a society run through sacred mysteries whose rationale it is not man's privilege to criticize, such incongruities may be explained away. Such a society may even provide some "explanation" which makes them seem rational. In a secular society, supposedly defended rationally upon scientific facts, in which the pragmatic test "Does it work?" is continually applied, such discrepancy between expectation and realization is difficult to reconcile.

Defense of our traditional system of assessing the costs of technological change is made on the theory that the costs of such change are more than offset by the benefits to "society as a whole." However, it is difficult to show the people of Caliente just why *they* should pay for advances made to benefit others whom they have never known and who, in their judgment, have done nothing to justify such rewards. Any action that will permit the people of Caliente to levy the costs of change upon those who will benefit from them will be morally justifiable to the people of Caliente. Appeals to the general welfare leave them cold and the compulsions of the price system are not felt to be self-justifying "natural laws" but are regarded as being the specific consequence of specific bookkeeping decisions as to what should be included in the costs of change. They seek to change these decisions through social action. They do not consider that the "American Way" consists primarily of acceptance of the market as the final arbiter of their destiny. Rather they conceive that the system as a whole exists to render "justice," and if the consequences of the price system are such as to produce what they consider to be "injustice" they proceed to use some other institution as a means to reverse or offset the effects of the price system. Like other groups faced with the same situation, those in Caliente seize upon the means available to them. The operating employees had in their unions a device to secure what they consider to be their rights. Union practices developed over the years make it possible for the organized workers to avoid some of the costs of change which they would otherwise have had to bear. Feather-bed rules, make-work practices, restricted work weeks, train length legislation and other similar devices were designed to permit union members to continue work even when "efficiency" dictated that they be disemployed. Members of the "Big Four" in Caliente joined with their fellows in demanding not only the retention of previously existing rules, but the imposition of new ones such as that requiring the presence of a third man in the diesel cab. For other groups there was available only the appeal to the company that it establish some other facility at Caliente, or alternatively a demand that "government" do something. One such demand took the form of a request to the Interstate Commerce Commission that it require inspection of rolling stock at Caliente. This request was denied.

It rapidly became apparent to the people of Caliente that they could not gain their objectives by organized community action nor individual endeavor but there was hope that by adding their voices to those of others similarly injured there might be hope of solution. They began to look to the activities of the whole labor movement for succor. Union strategy which forced the transfer of control from the market to government mediation or to legislation and operation was widely approved on all sides. This was not confined to those only who were currently seeking rule changes but was equally approved by the great bulk of those in the community who had been hit by the change. Cries of public outrage at their demands for make-work rules were looked upon as coming from those at best ignorant, ill-informed or stupid, and at worst as being the hypocritical efforts of others to gain at the workers' expense. When the union threat of a national strike for rule changes was met by government seizure, Caliente workers like most of their compatriots across the country welcomed this shift in control, secure in their belief that if "justice" were done they could only be gainers by government intervention. These attitudes are not "class" phenomena purely nor are they merely occupational sentiments. They result from the fact that modern life, with the interdependence that it creates, particularly in one-industry communities, imposes penalties far beyond the membership of the groups presumably involved in industry. When make-work rules contributed to the livelihood of the community, the support of the churches, and the taxes which maintain the schools; when feather-bed practices determine the standard of living, the profits of the business man and the circulation of the press; when they contribute to the salary of the teacher and the preacher; they can no longer be treated as accidental, immoral, deviant or temporary. Rather they are elevated into the position of emergent morality and law. Such practices generate a morality which serves them just as the practices in turn nourish those who participate in and preserve them. They are as firmly a part of what one "has a right to expect" from industry as are parity payments to the farmer, bonuses and pensions to the veterans, assistance to the aged, tariffs to the industralist, or the sanctity of property to those who inherit. On the other hand, all these practices conceivably help create a structure that is particularly vulnerable to changes such as that described here.

Practices which force the company to spend in Caliente part of what has been saved through technological change, or failing that, to reward those who are forced to move by increased income for the same service, are not, by the people of Caliente, considered to be unjustifiable. Confronted by a choice between the old means and resultant "injustice" which their use entails, and the acceptance of new means which they believe will secure them the "justice" they hold to be their right, they are willing to abandon (in so far as this particular area is concerned) the liberal state and the omnicompetent market in favor of something that works to provide "justice."

The study of the politics of pressure groups will show how widely the reactions of Caliente people are paralleled by those of other groups. Amongst them it is in politics that the decisions as to who will pay and who will profit are made. Through organized political force railroaders maintain the continuance of rules which operate to their benefit rather than for "the public good" or "the general welfare." Their defense of these practices is found in the argument that only so can their rights be protected against the power of other groups who hope to gain at their expense by functioning through the corporation and the market.

We should expect that where there are other groups similarly affected by technological change, there will be similar efforts to change the operation of our institutions. The case cited is not unique. Not only is it duplicated in hundreds of railroad division points but also in other towns abandoned by management for similar reasons. Changes in the location of markets or in the method of calculating transportation costs, changes in technology making necessary the use of new materials, changes due to the exhaustion of old sources of materials, changes to avoid labor costs such as the shift of the textile industry from New England to the South, changes to expedite decentralization to avoid the consequences of bombing, or those of congested living, all give rise to the question, "Who benefits, and at whose expense?"

The accounting practices of the corporation permit the entry only of those costs which have become "legitimate" claims upon the company. But the tremendous risks borne by the workers and frequently all the members of the community in an era of technological change are real phenomena. Rapid shifts in technology which destroy the "legitimate" expectations derived from past experience force the recognition of new obligations. Such recognition may be made voluntarily as management foresees the necessity, or it may be thrust upon it by political or other action. Rigidity of property concepts, the legal structure controlling directors in what they may admit to be costs, and the stereotyped nature of the "economics" used by management make rapid change within the corporation itself difficult even in a "free democratic society." Hence while management is likely to be permitted or required to initiate technological change in the interest of profits, it may and probably will be barred from compensating for the social consequences certain to arise from those changes. Management thus shuts out the rising flood of demands in its cost-accounting only to have them reappear in its tax accounts, in legal regulations or in new insistent union demands. If economics fails to provide an answer to social demands then politics will be tried.

It is clear that while traditional morality provides a means of protecting some groups from the consequences of technological change, or some method of meliorating the effects of change upon them, other large segments of the population are left unprotected. It should be equally clear that rather than a quiet acquiescence in the finality and justice of such arrangements, there is an active effort to force new devices into being which will extend protection to those hitherto expected to bear the brunt of these costs. A good proportion of these inventions increasingly call for the intervention of the state. To call such arrangements immoral, unpatriotic, socialistic or to hurl other epithets at them is not to deal effectively with them. They are as "natural" as are the "normal" reactions for which we have "rational" explanations based upon some prescientific generalization about human nature such as "the law of supply and demand" or "the inevitability of progress." To be dealt with effectively they will have to be understood and treated as such.

Dilemmas and
Contradictions of Status

by
Everett C. Hughes

It is doubtful whether any society ever had so great a variety of statuses or recognized such a large number of status-determining characteristics as does ours. The combinations of the latter are, of course, times over more numerous than the characteristics themselves. In societies where statuses[1] are well defined and are entered chiefly by birth or a few well-established sequences of training or achievement, the particular personal attributes proper to each status are woven into a whole. They are not thought of as separate entities. Even in our society, certain statuses have developed characteristic patterns of expected personal attributes and a way of life. To such, in the German language, is applied the term *Stand*.

Few of the positions in our society, however, have remained fixed long enough for such an elaboration to occur. We put emphasis on change in the system of positions which make up our social organization and upon mobility of the individual by achievement. In the struggle for achievement, individual traits of the person stand out as separate entities. And they occur in peculiar combinations which make for confusion, contradictions, and dilemmas of status.

I shall, in this paper, elaborate the notion of contradictions and dilemmas of status. Illustrations will be taken from professional and other occupational positions. The idea was put into a suggestive phrase by Robert E. Park when he wrote of the "marginal man." He applied the term to a special kind of case—the racial hybrid—who, as a consequence of the fact

Reprinted by permission of the publisher and the author from *The American Journal of Sociology*, Vol. 50, March 1945, pp. 353–59. Copyright 1945, University of Chicago Press.

[1]"Status" is here taken in its strict sense as a defined social position for whose incumbents there are defined rights, limitations of rights, and duties. See the *Oxford Dictionary* and any standard Latin lexicon. Since statuses tend to form a hierarchy, the term itself has—since Roman times—had the additional meaning of rank.

that races have become defined as status groups, finds himself in a status dilemma.

Now there may be, for a given status or social position, one or more specifically determining characteristics of the person. Some of them are formal, or even legal. No one, for example, has the status of physician unless he be duly licensed. A foreman is not such until appointed by proper authority. The heavy soprano is not a prima donna in more than temperament until formally cast for the part by the director of the opera. For each of these particular positions there is also an expected technical competence. Neither the formal nor the technical qualifications are, in all cases, so clear. Many statuses, such as membership in a social class, are not determined in a formal way. Other statuses are ill-defined both as to the characteristics which determine identification with them and as to their duties and rights.

There tends to grow up about a status, in addition to its specifically determining traits, a complex of auxiliary characteristics which come to be expected of its incumbents. It seems entirely natural to Roman Catholics that all priests should be men, although piety seems more common among women. In this case the expectation is supported by formal rule. Most doctors, engineers, lawyers, professors, managers, and supervisors in industrial plants are men, although no law requires that they be so. If one takes a series of characteristics, other than medical skill and license to practice it, which individuals in our society may have, and then thinks of physicians possessing them in various combinations, it becomes apparent that some of the combinations seem more natural and are more acceptable than others to the great body of potential patients. Thus a white, male, Protestant physician of old American stock and of a family of at least moderate social standing would be acceptable to patients of almost any social category in this country. To be sure, a Catholic might prefer a physician of his own faith for reasons of spiritual comfort. A few ardent feminists, a few race-conscious Negroes, a few militant sectarians, might follow their principles to the extent of seeking a physician of their own category. On the other hand, patients who identify themselves with the "old stock" may, in an emergency, take the first physician who turns up.[2]

---

[2] A Negro physician, driving through northern Indiana, came upon a crowd standing around a man just badly injured in a road accident. The physician tended the man and followed the ambulance which took him to the hospital. The hospital authorities tried to prevent the physi-

If the case is serious, patients may seek a specialist of some strange or disliked social category, letting the reputation for special skill override other traits. The line may be crossed also when some physician acquires such renown that his office becomes something of a shrine, a place of wonderful, last resort cures. Even the color line is not a complete bar to such a reputation. On the contrary, it may add piquancy to the treatment of a particularly enjoyed malady or lend hope to the quest for a cure of an "incurable" ailment. Allowing for such exceptions, it remains probably true that the white, male, Protestant physician of old American stock, although he may easily fail to get a clientele at all, is categorically acceptable to a greater variety of patients than is he who departs, in one or more particulars, from this type.

It is more exact to say that, if one were to imagine patients of the various possible combinations of these same characteristics (race, sex, religion, ethnic background, family standing), such a physician could treat patients of any of the resulting categories without a feeling by the physician, patient, or the surrounding social circle that the situation was unusual or shocking. One has only to make a sixteen-box table showing physicians of the possible combinations of race (white and Negro) and sex with patients of the possible combinations to see that the white male is the only resulting kind of physician to whom patients of all the kinds are completely accessible in our society (see Table 1).

One might apply a similar analysis to situations involving other positions, such as the foreman and the worker, the teacher and the pupil. Each case may be complicated by adding other categories of persons with whom the person of the given position has to deal. The teacher, in practice, has dealings not only with pupils but with parents, school boards, other public functionaries, and, finally, his own colleagues. Immediately one tries to make this analysis, it becomes clear

---

cian from entering the hospital for even long enough to report to staff physicians what he had done for the patient. The same physician, in answer to a Sunday phone call asking him to visit a supposedly very sick woman, went to a house. When the person who answered the door saw that the physician was a Negro, she insisted that they had not called for a doctor and that no one in the house was sick. When he insisted on being paid, the people in the house did so, thereby revealing their lie. In the first instance, an apparently hostile crowd accepted the Negro as a physician because of urgency. In the second, he was refused presumably because the emergency was not great enough.

Table 1*

Patient	Physician			
	White Male	White Female	Negro Male	Negro Female
White male..	....	....	....	....
White female.	....	....	....	....
Negro male..	....	....	....	....
Negro female.	....	....	....	....

* I have not used this table in any study of preferences but should be glad if anyone interested were to do so with selected groups of people.

that a characteristic which might not interfere with some of the situations of a given position may interfere with others.

I do not maintain that any considerable proportion of people do consciously put together in a systematic way their expectations of persons of given positions. I suggest, rather, that people carry in their minds a set of expectations concerning the auxiliary traits properly associated with many of the specific positions available in our society. These expectations appear as advantages or disadvantages to persons who, in keeping with American social belief and practice, aspire to positions new to persons of their kind.

The expected or "natural" combinations of auxiliary characteristics become embodied in the stereotypes of ordinary talk, cartoons, fiction, the radio, and the motion picture. Thus, the American Catholic priest, according to a popular stereotype, is Irish, athletic, and a good sort who with difficulty refrains from profanity in the presence of evil and who may punch someone in the nose if the work of the Lord demands it. Nothing could be farther from the French or French-Canadian stereotype of the good priest. The surgeon, as he appears in advertisements for insurance and pharmaceutical products, is handsome, socially poised, and young of face but gray about the temples. These public, or publicity, stereotypes—while they do not necessarily correspond to the facts or determine peoples' expectations—are at least significant in that they rarely let the person in the given position have any strikes against him. Positively, they represent someone's ideal conception; negatively, they take care not to shock, astonish, or put doubts into the mind of a public whose confidence is sought.

If we think especially of occupational status, it is in the colleague-group or fellow-worker group that the expectations concerning appropriate auxiliary characteristics are worked most intricately into sentiment and conduct. They become, in fact, the basis of the colleague-group's definition of its common interests, of its informal code, and of selection of those who become the inner fraternity—three aspects of occupational life so closely related that few people separate them in thought or talk.

The epithets "hen doctor," "boy wonder," "bright young men," and "brain trust" express the hostility of colleagues to persons who deviate from the expected type. The members of a colleague-group have a common interest in the whole configuration of things which control the number of potential candidates for their occupation. Colleagues, be it remembered, are also competitors. A rational demonstration that an individual's chances for continued success are not jeopardized by an extention of the recruiting field for the position he has or hopes to attain, or by some short-cutting of usual lines of promotion, does not, as a rule, liquidate the fear and hostility aroused by such a case. Oswald Hall found that physicians do not like one of their number to become a consultant too soon.[3] Consulting is something for the crowning, easing-off years of a career; something to intervene briefly between high power and high blood-pressure. He who pushes for such practice too early shows an "aggressiveness" which is almost certain to be punished. It is a threat to an order of things which physicians—at least, those of the fraternity of successful men—count upon. Many of the specific rules of the game of an occupation become comprehensible only when viewed as the almost instinctive attempts of a group of people to cushion themselves against the hazards of their careers. The advent of colleague-competitors of some new and peculiar type, or by some new route, is likely to arouse anxieties. For one thing, one cannot be quite sure how "new people"—new in

[3]Oswald Hall, "The Informal Organization of Medical Practice" (unpublished Ph.D dissertation, University of Chicago, 1944).

kind—will act in the various contingencies which arise to test the solidarity of the group.[4]

How the expectations of which we are thinking become embodied in codes may be illustrated by the dilemma of a young woman who became a member of that virile profession, engineering. The designer of an airplane is expected to go up on the maiden flight of the first plane built according to the design. He (sic) then gives a dinner to the engineers and workmen who worked on the new plane. The dinner is naturally a stag party. The young woman in question designed a plane. Her co-workers urged her not to take the risk—for which, presumably, men only are fit—of the maiden voyage. They were, in effect, asking her to be a lady rather than an engineer. She chose to be an engineer. She then gave the party and paid for it like a man. After food and the first round of toasts, she left like a lady.

Part of the working code of a position is discretion; it allows the colleagues to exchange confidences concerning their relations to other people. Among these confidences one finds expressions of cynicism concerning their mission, their competence, and the foibles of their superiors, themselves, their clients, their subordinates, and the public at large. Such expressions take the burden from one's shoulders and serve as a defense as well. The unspoken mutual confidence necessary to them rest on two assumptions concerning one's fellows. The first is that the colleague will not misunderstand; the second is that he will not repeat to uninitiated ears. To be sure that a new fellow will not misunderstand requires a sparring match of social gestures. The zealot who turns the sparring match into a real battle, who takes a friendly initiation too seriously, is not likely to be trusted with the lighter sort of comment on one's work or with doubts and misgivings; nor can he learn those parts of the working code which are communicated only by hint and gesture. He is not to be trusted, for, though he is not fit for stratagems, he is suspected of being prone to treason. In order that men may communicate freely and confidentially, they must be able to take a good deal of each other's sentiments for granted. They must feel easy about their silences as well as about their utterances. These factors

[4] It may be that those whose positions are insecure and whose hopes for the higher goals are already fading express more violent hostility to "new people." Even if so, it must be remembered that those who are secure and successful have the power to exclude or check the careers of such people by merely failing to notice them.

conspire to make colleagues, with a large body of unspoken understandings, uncomfortable in the presence of what they consider odd kinds of fellows. The person who is the first of his kind to attain a certain status is often not drawn into the informal brotherhood in which experiences are exchanged, competence built up, and the formal code elaborated and enforced. He thus remains forever a marginal man.

Now it is a necessary consequence of the high degree of individual mobility in America that there should be large numbers of people of new kinds turning up in various positions. In spite of this and in spite of American heterogeneity, this remains a white, Anglo-Saxon, male, Protestant culture in many respects. These are the expected characteristics for many favored statuses and positions. When we speak of racial, religious, sex, and ethnic prejudices, we generally assume that people with these favored qualities are not the objects thereof. In the stereotyped prejudices concerning others, there is usually contained the assumption that these other people are peculiarly adapted to the particular places which they have held up to the present time; it is a corollary implication that they are not quite fit for new positions to which they may aspire. In general, advance of a new group—women, Negroes, some ethnic groups, etc.—to a new level of positions is not accompanied by complete disappearance of such stereotypes but only by some modification of them. Thus, in Quebec the idea that French-Canadians were good only for unskilled industrial work was followed by the notion that they were especially good at certain kinds of skilled work but were not fit to repair machines or to supervise the work of others. In this series of modifications the structure of qualities expected for the most-favored positions remains intact. But the forces which make for mobility continue to create marginal people on new frontiers.

Technical changes also break up configurations of expected status characteristics by altering the occupations about which they grow up. A new machine or a new managerial device— such as the assembly line—may create new positions or break old ones up into numbers of new ones. The length of training may be changed thereby and, with it, the whole traditional method of forming the person to the social demands of a colleague-group. Thus, a snip of a girl is trained in a few weeks to be a "machinist" on a practically foolproof lathe; thereby the old foolproof machinist, who was initiated slowly into the skills and attitudes of the trade, is himself made a fool of in his own eyes or—worse—in the eyes of his wife, who hears that a neighbor's daughter is a machinist who makes nearly as much money as he. The new positions created by technical changes may, for a time, lack definition as a status. Both the technical and the auxiliary qualifications may be slow in taking form. The personnel man offers a good example. His title is perhaps twenty years old, but the expectations concerning his qualities and functions are still in flux.[5]

Suppose we leave aside the problems which arise from technical changes, as such, and devote the rest of this discussion to the consequences of the appearance of new kinds of people in established positions. Every such occurrence produces, in some measure, a status contradiction. It may also create a status dilemma for the individual concerned and for other people who have to deal with him.

The most striking illustration in our society is offered by the Negro who qualifies for one of the traditional professions. Membership in the Negro race, as defined in American mores or law, may be called a master status-determining trait. It tends to overpower, in most crucial situations, any other characteristics which might run counter to it. But professional standing is also a powerful characteristic—most so in the specific relationships of professional practice, less so in the general intercourse of people. In the person of the professionally qualified Negro these two powerful characteristics clash. The dilemma, for those whites who meet such a person, is that of having to choose whether to treat him as a Negro or as a member of his profession.

The white person in need of professional services, especially medical, might allow him to act as a doctor in an emergency. Or it may be allowed that a Negro physician is endowed with some uncanny skill. In either case, the white client of ordinary American social views would probably avoid any nonprofessional contacts with the Negro physi-

---

[5]The personnel man also illustrates another problem which I do not propose to discuss in this paper. It is that of an essential contradiction between the various functions which are united to one position. The personnel man is expected to communicate the mind of the workers to management and then to interpret management to the workers. This is a difficult assignment. The problem is well stated by William F. Whyte, in "Pity the Personnel Man," *Advanced Management,* October-December, 1944, pp. 154–58. The Webbs analyzed the similar dilemma of the official of a successful trade-union in their *History of Trade-Unionism* (rev. ed.; London: Longmans, Green, 1920).

cian.[6] In fact, one way of reducing status conflict is to keep the relationship formal and specific. This is best done by walking through a door into a place designed for the specific relationship, a door which can be firmly closed when one leaves. A common scene in fiction depicts a lady of degree seeking, veiled and alone, the address of the fortuneteller or the midwife of doubtful practice in an obscure corner of the city. The anonymity of certain sections of cities allows people to seek specialized services, legitimate but embarrassing as well as illegitimate, from persons with whom they would not want to be seen by members of their own social circle.

Some professional situations lend themselves more than others to such quarantine. The family physician and the pediatrician cannot be so easily isolated as some other specialists. Certain legal services can be sought indirectly by being delegated to some queer and unacceptable person by the family lawyer. At the other extreme is school teaching, which is done in full view of the community and is generally expected to be accompanied by an active role in community activities. The teacher, unlike the lawyer, is expected to be an example to her charges.

For the white colleagues of the Negro professional man the dilemma is even more severe. The colleague-group is ideally a brotherhood; to have within it people who cannot, given one's other attitudes, be accepted as brothers is very uncomfortable. Furthermore, professional men are much more sensitive than they like to admit about the company in which nonprofessionals see them. The dilemma arises from the fact that, while it is bad for the profession to let laymen see rifts in their ranks, it may be bad for the individual to be associated in the eyes of his actual or potential patients with persons, even colleagues, of so despised a group as the Negro. The favored way of avoiding the dilemma is to shun contacts with the Negro professional. The white physician or surgeon of assured reputation may solve the problem by acting as consultant to Negro colleagues in Negro clinics and hospitals.

For the Negro professional man there is also a dilemma. If he accepts the role of Negro to the extent of appearing content with less than full equality and intimacy with his white colleagues, for the sake of such security and advantage as can

[6]The Negro artist can be treated as a celebrity. It is within the code of social tufthunting that one may entertain, with a kind of affected Bohemian intimacy, celebrities who, on all counts other than their artistic accomplishments, would be beyond the pale.

be so got, he himself and others may accuse him of sacrificing his race. Given the tendency of whites to say that any Negro who rises to a special position is an exception, there is a strong temptation for such a Negro to seek advantage by fostering the idea that he is unlike others of his race. The devil who specializes in this temptation is a very insinuating fellow; he keeps a mailing list of "marginal men" of all kinds and origins. Incidentally, one of the by-products of American mores is the heavy moral burden which this temptation puts upon the host of Americans who have by great effort risen from (sic) groups which are the objects of prejudice.

There may be cases in which the appearance in a position of one or a few individuals of a kind not expected there immediately dissolves the auxiliary expectations which make him appear odd. This is not, however, the usual consequence. The expectations usually continue to exist, with modification and with exceptions allowed.

A common solution is some elaboration of social segregation. The woman lawyer may become a lawyer to women clients, or she may specialize in some kind of legal service in keeping with woman's role as guardian of the home and morals. Women physicians may find a place in those specialities of which only women and children have need. A female electrical engineer was urged by the dean of the school from which she had just been graduated to accept a job whose function was to give the "woman's angle" to design of household electrical appliances. The Negro professional man finds his clients among Negroes. The Negro sociologist generally studies race relations and teaches in a Negro college. A new figure on the American scene is the Negro personnel man in industries which have started employing Negro workers. His functions are to adjust difficulties of Negro workers, settle minor clashes between the races, and to interpret management's policies to the Negro as well as to present and explain the Negro's point of view to management. It is a difficult job. Our interest for the moment, however, is in the fact that the Negro, promoted to this position, acts only with reference to Negro employees. Many industries have had women personnel officials to act with reference to women. In one sense, this is an extension of the earlier and still existing practice of hiring from among a new ethnic group in industry a "straw boss" to look after them. The "straw boss" is the liaison officer reduced to lowest terms.

Another solution, which also results in a kind of isolation

if not in segregation, is that of putting the new people in the library or laboratory, where they get the prestige of research people but are out of the way of patients and the public. Recently, industries have hired a good many Negro chemists to work in their testing and research laboratories. The chemist has few contacts with the production organization. Promotion within the laboratory will put the Negro in charge of relatively few people, and those few will be of his own profession. Such positions do not ordinarily lead to the positions of corresponding importance in the production organization. They offer a career line apart from the main streams of promotion to power and prestige.

These solutions reduce the force of status contradiction by keeping the new person apart from the most troublesome situations. One of the consequences is that it adds new stories to the superstructure of segregation. The Negro hospital and the medical school are the formal side of this. The Negro personnel man and foreman show it within the structure of existing institutions. There are evidences that physicians of various ethnic groups are being drawn into a separate medical system of hospitals, clinics, and schools, partly because of the interest of the Roman Catholic church in developing separate institutions but also partly because of the factors here discussed. It is doubtful whether women will develop corresponding separate systems to any great extent. In all of these cases, it looks as if the highest point which a member of these odd groups may attain is determined largely by the number of people of his own group who are in a position to seek his services or in a position such that he may be assigned by other authority to act professionally with reference to them. On the other hand, the kind of segregation involved may lead professional people, or others advanced to special positions, to seek—as compensation—monopoly over such functions with reference to their own group.

Many questions are raised by the order of things here discussed. One is that of the place of these common solutions of status conflict in the evolution of the relations between the sexes, the races, and the ethnic groups of our society. In what circumstances can the person who is accepted formally into a new status, and then informally kept within the limits of the kind mentioned, step out of these limits and become simply a lawyer, foreman, or whatever? Under what circumstances, if ever, is the "hen doctor" simply a doctor? And who are the first to accept her as such—her colleagues or her patients?

Will the growth of a separate superstructure over each of the segregated bottom groups of our society tend to perpetuate indefintely the racial and ethnic division already existing, or will these superstructures lose their identity in the general organization of society? These are the larger questions.

The purpose of the paper, however, is not to answer these large questions. It is rather to call attention to this characteristic phenomenon of our heterogeneous and changing society and to suggest that it become part of the frame of reference of those who are observing special parts of the American social structure.

IV.

SOCIAL TYPES

SOCIOLOGICAL ANALYSIS has often utilized the notion of social type; in this respect it is perhaps in tune with "common-sense" notions about society. "Social type" refers to some salient characteristics of individuals who have distinct positions in society and are hence motivated to adopt special kinds of role behavior. This section introduces several such social types.

The German sociologist Georg Simmel provided a number of perceptive delineations of social types, among which his portrait of the stranger reprinted here is perhaps the most impressive. He argued that as we survey the social scene, we are likely to encounter persons who have only shallow roots in given societies and are therefore defined by more settled members of those societies as "strangers" as not being fully part of the community. Traders, from time immemorial, have had such characteristics; many Jews may be so defined either by themselves or by others. Strangers, Simmel suggests, may be conceived as people whose position in a group is crucially affected by the fact that they do not initially belong to it. They possess qualities that differentiate them from the group, that make them easy targets for the group's aggression and also carriers of highly valued contributions. The stranger, Simmel argues, is at the same time near and remote. Strangers are elements of a group, while at the same time they possess characteristics that differentiate them from that group. They may become scapegoats, but also they may become people to whom one has recourse when one requires judgments untainted by group traditions and group loyalties. Nearness and remoteness give the stranger a character of objectivity. Moreover, being inorganically appended to the group yet still an organic member of it, and being less bound to the concreteness of group living and group experience, the stranger develops abstract ways of thinking. In consequence, abstract thought, Simmel suggests, largely has its origin in the thought of strangers.

The stress on the contributions of strangers is further developed in an essay by the leader of the so-called Chicago School of sociology, Robert Park, who uses the term "marginal men." Park suggests that marginal people, such as those of mixed racial ancestry or migrants, develop a cosmopolitan bias in their behavior and attitudes that is much more difficult to achieve by persons not sharing this position. Such marginal men, he suggests, shun the pieties of traditional ways of life and hence tend to secularize relations that were hitherto sacred. Marginal men, to Park, are privileged carriers of the traditions of modernity, iconoclastic skeptics when it comes to ordinary customs, yet possessors of highly creative antennae when it comes to discerning novelty and innovative possibilities.

Orrin Klapp shows in his paper that the fool is a social type having a definable role and a special social status in group life. Those persons defined as fools depart from group norms and proprieties and are hence subject to the sanction of ridicule. Thus, fool-making, he argues, is a mechanism of social control that enforces proprieties and marks the boundaries between acceptable and reprehensible behavior.

Stanford M. Lyman demonstrates in his paper that even such apparently idiosyncratic behavior as gluttony is subject to social typification. A glutton is not the person who eats too much, but one who is described by others as such. Gluttony, while not proscribed by law, encounters some of the social sanctions and penalties that are ordinarily reserved for criminal behavior. Defined as excessive self-indulgence, it is seen as opposed to the demands of sociality; it is perceived as too egotistic for social toleration. It is perceived, as the author argues, as a sin against society, as emblematic of withdrawal from social obligations.

While competition between human beings may be as old as the hills, C. Wright Mills suggests that the competitive personality is a comparable newcomer on the human stage. The liberal-market society generally, and modern American society in particular, have given rise to a human type for whom competition on the market has become an overriding concern. Not content to compete in specific spheres, people compete all the time in all manner of situations, occupational, educational, or sexual. Such types, Mills suggests, operate in a "personality market." They practice the creative art of selling, but they do not sell goods as much as they sell themselves. The competitive personality, so Mills suggests, is predominantly found not among the consequential and the powerful, but among those who, in a bureaucratized world, are forced to engage in a kind of self-exploitation through marketing of the self. White-collar work as well as small entrepreneurship are the most fertile breeding grounds for competitive personality.

Murray Davis and Catherine Schmidt's paper "The Obnoxious and the Nice" deals, as they point out, with psychological rather than sociological types. Yet the authors display true sociological imagination in the way in which they describe how such typifications are applied to specific human beings and how such labels, once affixed, are likely to determine much of the life course of those so labeled. The obnoxious, they argue, are those who impose, or attempt to impose, their own self-definitions on unwilling others, whereas the nice are those who willingly acquiesce in the definitions others impose on them. What are the consequences, the authors ask, for people so defined and for the groups who engage in such defining? They suggest that this kind of typification forms part of a much larger class of typifying behaviors that inform much of the texture of social life by structuring the course of social interaction.

The final paper, by the editor, suggests how an apparently purely physiological impairment, castration of human males, has had in a number of social settings some important consequences for those afflicted by it, and also for the societies in which they lived. The very facts, the paper suggests, that eunuchs cannot have descendants and typically (at least in the case examined) had little or no connections with their families of origin made them preferred servants of Oriental rulers in the classical empires of the Far East and the Near East. Having no compelling ties to the community at large, it is argued, having no roots and no kin, they could be utilized by rulers of these societies as ideal instruments of reign. In such a manner, apparently purely physical impairments were transformed into the mark of a social type—a type, moreover, that served important functional requirements in the exercise of power.

The Stranger

by
Georg Simmel

If wandering is the liberation from every given point in
space, and thus the conceptional opposite to fixation at such a
point, the sociological form of the "stranger" presents the
unity, as it were, of these two characteristics. This phenomenon too, however, reveals that spatial relations are only the
condition, on the one hand, and the symbol, on the other, of
human relations. The stranger is thus being discussed here,
not in the sense often touched upon in the past, as the wanderer who comes today and goes tomorrow, but rather as the
person who comes today and stays tomorrow. He is, so to
speak, the *potential* wanderer: although he has not moved on,
he has not quite overcome the freedom of coming and going.
He is fixed within a particular spatial group, or within a
group whose boundaries are similar to spatial boundaries. But
his position in this group is determined, essentially, by the
fact that he has not belonged to it from the beginning, that
he imports qualities into it, which do not and cannot stem
from the group itself.

The unity of nearness and remoteness involved in every
human relation is organized, in the phenomenon of the
stranger, in a way which may be most briefly formulated by
saying that in the relationship to him, distance means that he,
who is close by, is far, and strangeness means that he, who
also is far, is actually near. For, to be a stranger is naturally
a very positive relation; it is a specific form of interaction.
The inhabitants of Sirius are not really strangers to us, at
least not in any sociologically relevant sense: they do not exist for us at all; they are beyond far and near. The stranger,
like the poor and sundry "inner enemies," is an element
of the group itself. His position as a full-fledged member involves both being outside it and confronting it. The following

Reprinted with permission of Macmillan Publishing Co., Inc. from
The Sociology of Georg Simmel, Kurt H. Wolff, trans. Copyright ©
1950, 1978, The Free Press, a Division of Macmillan Publishing Co.,
Inc.

statements, which are by no means intended as exhaustive, indicate how elements which increase distance and repel, in the relations of and with the stranger produce a pattern of coordination and consistent interaction.

Throughout the history of economics the stranger everywhere appears as the trader, or the trader as stranger. As long as economy is essentially self-sufficient, or products are exchanged within a spatially narrow group, it needs no middleman: a trader is only required for products that originate outside the group. Insofar as members do not leave the circle in order to buy these necessities—in which case *they* are the "strange" merchants in that outside territory—the trader *must* be a stranger, since nobody else has a chance to make a living.

This position of the stranger stands out more sharply if he settles down in the place of his activity, instead of leaving it again: in innumerable cases even this is possible only if he can live by intermediate trade. Once an economy is somehow closed, the land is divided up, and handicrafts are established that satisfy the demand for them, the trader, too, can find his existence. For in trade, which alone makes possible unlimited combinations, intelligence always finds expansions and new territories, an achievement which is very difficult to attain for the original producer with his lesser mobility and his dependence upon a circle of customers that can be increased only slowly. Trade can always absorb more people than primary production; it is, therefore, the sphere indicated for the stranger, who intrudes as a supernumerary, so to speak, into a group in which the economic positions are actually occupied—the classical example is the history of European Jews. The stranger is by nature no "owner of soil"—soil not only in the physical, but also in the figurative sense of a life-substance which is fixed, if not in a point in space, at least in an ideal point of the social environment. Although in more intimate relations, he may develop all kinds of charm and significance, as long as he is considered a stranger in the eyes of the other, he is not an "owner of soil." Restriction to intermediary trade, and often (as though sublimated from it) to pure finance, gives him the specific character of *mobility*. If mobility takes place within a closed group, it embodies that synthesis of nearness and distance which constitutes the formal position of the stranger. For the fundamentally mobile person comes in contact, at one time or another, with every individual, but is not organically connected, through established ties of kinship, locality, and occupation, with any single one.

Another expression of this constellation lies in the objectivity of the stranger. He is not radically committed to the unique ingredients and peculiar tendencies of the group, and therefore approaches them with the specific attitude of "objectivity." But objectivity does not simply involve passivity and detachment; it is a particular structure composed of distance and nearness, indifference and involvement. I refer to the discussion [in a preceding chapter of the book from which this is taken—Ed.] of the dominating positions of the person who is a stranger in the group; its most typical instance was the practice of those Italian cities to call their judges from the outside, because no native was free from entanglement in family and party interests.

With the objectivity of the stranger is connected, also, the phenomenon touched upon above, although it is chiefly (but not exclusively) true of the stranger who moves on. This is the fact that he often receives the most surprising openness—confidences which sometimes have the character of a confessional and which would be carefully withheld from a more closely related person. Objectivity is by no means nonparticipation (which is altogether outside both subjective and objective interaction), but a positive and specific kind of participation—just as the objectivity of a theoretical observation does not refer to the mind as a passive *tabula rasa* on which things inscribe their qualities, but on the contrary, to its full activity that operates according to its own laws, and to the elimination, thereby, of accidental dislocations and emphases, whose individual and subjective differences would produce different pictures of the same object.

Objectivity may also be defined as freedom: the objective individual is bound by no commitments which could prejudice his perception, understanding, and evaluation of the given. The freedom, however, which allows the stranger to experience and treat even his close relationships as though from a bird's-eye view, contains many dangerous possibilities. In uprisings of all sorts, the party attacked has claimed, from the beginning of things, that provocation has come from the outside, through emissaries and instigators. Insofar as this is true, it is an exaggeration of the specific role of the stranger: he is freer, practically and theoretically; he surveys conditions with less prejudice; his criteria for them are more general and more objective ideals; he is not tied down in his action by habit, piety, and precedent.[1]

Finally, the proportion of nearness and remoteness which gives the stranger the character of objectivity, also finds practical expression in the more *abstract nature* of the relation to him. That is, with the stranger one has only certain *more general* qualities in common, whereas the relation to more organically connected persons is based on the commonness of specific differences from merely general features. In fact, all somehow personal relations follow this scheme in various patterns. They are determined not only by the circumstance that certain common features exist among the individuals, along with individual differences, which either influence the relationship or remain outside of it. For, the common features themselves are basically determined in their effect upon the relation by the question whether they exist only between the participants in this particular relationship, and thus are quite general in regard to this relation, but are specific and incomparable in regard to everything outside of it—or whether the participants feel that these features are common to them because they are common to a group, a type, or mankind in general. In the case of the second alternative, the effectiveness of the common features becomes diluted in proportion to the size of the group composed of members who are similar in this sense. Although the commonness functions as their unifying basis, it does not make *these* particular persons interdependent on one another, because it could as easily connect everyone of them with all kinds of individuals other than the members of his group. This too, evidently, is a way in which a relationship includes both nearness and distance at the same time: to the extent to which the common features are general, they add, to the warmth of the relation founded on them, an element of coolness, a feeling of the contingency of precisely *this* relation—the connecting forces have lost their specific and centripetal character.

In the relation to the stranger, it seems to me, this constellation has an extraordinary and basic preponderance over the individual elements that are exclusive with the particular rela-

[1]But where the attacked make the assertion falsely, they do so from the tendency of those in higher position to exculpate inferiors, who, up to the rebellion, have been in a consistently close relation with them. For, by creating the fiction that the rebels were not really guilty, but only instigated, and that the rebellion did not really start with *them*, they exonerate themselves, inasmuch as they altogether deny all real grounds for the uprising.

tionship. The stranger is close to us, insofar as we feel between him and ourselves common features of a national, social, occupational, or generally human, nature. He is far from us, insofar as these common features extend beyond him or us, and connect us only because they connect a great many people.

A trace of strangeness in this sense easily enters even the most intimate relationships. In the stage of first passion, erotic relations strongly reject any thought of generalization: the lovers think that there has never been a love like theirs; that nothing can be compared either to the person loved or to the feelings for that person. An estrangement—whether as cause or as consequence it is difficult to decide—usually comes at the moment when this feeling of uniqueness vanishes from the relationship. A certain skepticism in regard to its value, in itself and for them, attaches to the very thought that in their relation, after all, they carry out only a generally human destiny; that they experience an experience that has occurred a thousand times before; that, had they not accidentally met their particular partner, they would have found the same significance in another person.

Something of this feeling is probably not absent in any relation, however close, because what is common to two is never common to them alone, but is subsumed under a general idea which includes much else besides, many *possibilities* of commonness. No matter how little these possibilities become real and how often we forget them, here and there, nevertheless, they thrust themselves between us like shadows, like a mist which escapes every word noted, but which must coagulate into a solid bodily form before it can be called jealousy. In some cases, perhaps the more general, at least the more unsurmountable, strangeness is not due to different and ununderstandable matters. It is rather caused by the fact that similarity, harmony, and nearness are accompanied by the feeling that they are not really the unique property of this particular relationship: they are something more general, something which potentially prevails between the partners and an indeterminate number of others, and therefore gives the relation, which alone was realized, no inner and exclusive necessity.

On the other hand, there is a kind of "strangeness" that rejects the very commonness based on something more general which embraces the parties. The relation of the Greeks to the Barbarians is perhaps typical here, as are all cases in which it is precisely general attributes, felt to be specifically and purely human, that are disallowed to the other. But "stranger," here, has no positive meaning; the relation to him is a non-relation; he is not what is relevant here, a member of the group itself.

As a group member, rather, he is near and far *at the same time,* as is characteristic of relations founded only on generally human commonness. But between nearness and distance, there arises a specific tension when the consciousness that only the quite general is common, stresses that which is not common. In the case of the person who is a stranger to the country, the city, the race, etc., however, this non-common element is once more nothing individual, but merely the strangeness of origin, which is or could be common to many strangers. For this reason, strangers are not really conceived as individuals, but as strangers of a particular type: the element of distance is no less general in regard to them than the element of nearness.

This form is the basis of such a special case, for instance, as the tax levied in Frankfort and elsewhere upon medieval Jews. Whereas the *Beede* [tax] paid by the Christian citizen changed with the changes of his fortune, it was fixed once for all for every single Jew. This fixity rested on the fact that the Jew had his social position as a *Jew,* not as the individual bearer of certain objective contents. Every other citizen was the owner of a particular amount of property, and his tax followed its fluctuations. But the Jew as a taxpayer was, in the first place, a Jew, and thus his tax situation had an invariable element. This same position appears most strongly, of course, once even these individual characterizations (limited though they were by rigid invariance) are omitted, and all strangers pay an altogether equal head-tax.

In spite of being inorganically appended to it, the stranger is yet an organic member of the group. Its uniform life includes the specific conditions of this element. Only we do not know how to designate the peculiar unity of this position other than by saying that it is composed of certain measures of nearness and distance. Althought some quantities of them characterize all relationships, a *special* proportion and reciprocal tension produce the particular, formal relation to the "stranger."

Migration and the Marginal Man

by
Robert E. Park

Migration as a social phenomenon must be studied not merely in its grosser effects, as manifested in changes in custom and in the mores, but it may be envisaged in its subjective aspects as manifested in the changed type of personality which it produces. When the traditional organization of society breaks down, as a result of contact and collision with a new invading culture, the effect is, so to speak, to emancipate the individual man. Energies that were formerly controlled by custom and tradition are released. The individual is free for new adventures, but he is more or less without direction and control. Teggart's statement of the matter is as follows:

> As a result of the breakdown of customary modes of action and of thought, the individual experiences a "release" from the restraints and constraints to which he has been subject, and gives evidence of this "release" in aggressive self-assertion. The overexpression of individuality is one of the marked features of all epochs of change. On the other hand, the study of the psychological effects of collision and contact between different groups reveals the fact that the most important aspect of "release" lies not in freeing the soldier, warrior, or berserker from the restraint of conventional modes of action, but in freeing the individual judgment from the inhibitions of conventional modes of thought. It will thus be seen (he adds) that the study of the *modus operandi* of change in time gives a common focus to the efforts of political historians, of the historians of literature and of ideas, of psychologists, and of students of ethics and the theory of education.[1]

Reprinted by permission of the publishers from the *American Journal of Sociology*, Vol. 33, May 1928, pp. 200–06, University of Chicago Press.

[1]Frederick J. Teggart, *Theory of History*, p. 196.

Social changes, according to Teggart, have their inception in events which "release" the individuals out of which society is composed. Inevitably, however, this release is followed in the course of time by the reintegration of the individuals so released into a new social order. In the meantime, however, certain changes take place—at any rate they are likely to take place—in the character of the individuals themselves. They become, in the process, not merely emancipated, but enlightened.

The emancipated individual invariably becomes in a certain sense and to a certain degree a cosmopolitan. He learns to look upon the world in which he was born and bred with something of the detachment of a stranger. He acquires, in short, an intellectual bias. Simmel has described the position of the stranger in the community, and his personality, in terms of movement and migration.

"If wandering," he says, "considered as the liberation from every given point in space, is the conceptual opposite of fixation at any point, then surely the sociological form of the stranger presents the union of both of these specifications." The stranger stays, but he is not settled. He is a potential wanderer. That means that he is not bound as others are by the local proprieties and conventions. "He is the freer man, practically and theoretically. He views his relation to others with less prejudice; he submits them to more general, more objective standards, and he is not confined in his action by custom, piety or precedents."

The effect of mobility and migration is to secularize relations which were formerly sacred. One may describe the process, in its dual aspect, perhaps, as the secularization of society and the individuation of the person. For a brief, vivid, and authentic picture of the way in which migration of the earlier sort, the migration of a people, has, in fact, brought about the destruction of an earlier civilization and liberated the peoples involved for the creation of a later, more secular, and freer society, I suggest Gilbert Murray's introduction to *The Rise of the Greek Epic*, in which he seeks to reproduce the events of the Nordic invasion of the Aegean area.

What ensued, he says, was a period of chaos:

A chaos in which an old civilization is shattered into fragments, its laws set at naught, and that intricate web of normal expectation which forms the very essence of human society torn so often and so utterly by continued disappointment that at last there ceases to be any normal expectation at all. For the fugitive settlers on the shores that were afterwards Ionia, and for parts too of Doris and Aeolis, there were no tribal gods or tribal obligations left, because there were no tribes. There were no old laws, because there was no one to administer or even to remember them; only such compulsions as the strongest power of the moment chose to enforce. Household and family life had disappeared, and all its innumerable ties with it. A man was now not living with a wife of his own race, but with a dangerous strange woman, of alien language and alien gods, a woman whose husband or father he had perhaps murdered—or, at best, whom he had bought as a slave from the murderer. The old Aryan husbandman, as we shall see hereafter, had lived with his herds in a sort of familiar connexion. He slew "his brother the ox" only under special stress or for definite religious reasons, and he expected his women to weep when the slaying was performed. But now he had left his own herds far away. They had been devoured by enemies. And he lived on the beasts of strangers whom he robbed or held in servitude. He had left the graves of his fathers, the kindly ghosts of his own blood, who took food from his hand and loved him. He was surrounded by the graves of alien dead, strange ghosts whose names he knew not, and who were beyond his power to control, whom he tried his best to placate with fear and aversion. One only concrete thing existed for him to make henceforth the centre of his allegiance, to supply the place of his old family hearth, his gods, his tribal customs and sanctities. It was a circuit wall of stones, a *Polis;* the wall which he and his fellows, men of diverse tongues and worships united by a tremendous need, had built up to be the one barrier between themselves and a world of enemies.[2]

It was within the walls of the *polis* and in this mixed company that Greek civilization was born. The whole secret of ancient Greek life, its relative freedom from the grosser superstitions and from fear of the gods, is bound up, we are told, with this period of transition and chaos, in which the older primitive world perished and from which the freer, more enlightened social order sprang into existence. Thought is emancipated, philosophy is born, public opinion sets itself up as an authority as over against tradition and custom. As Guyot puts it, "The Greek with his festivals, his songs, his poetry, seems to celebrate, in a perpetual hymn, the liberation of man from the mighty fetters of nature.[3]

What took place in Greece first has since taken place in the rest of Europe and is now going on in America. The movement and migration of peoples, the expansion of trade and commerce, and particularly the growth, in modern times, of these vast melting-pots of races and cultures, the metropolitan cities, has loosened local bonds, destroyed the cultures of tribe and folk, and substituted for the local loyalties the freedom of the cities; for the sacred order of tribal custom, the rational organization which we call civilization.

In these great cities, where all the passions, all the energies of mankind are released, we are in position to investigate the processes of civilization, as it were, under a microscope.

It is in the cities that the old clan and kinship groups are broken up and replaced by social organization based on rational interests and temperamental predilections. It is in the cities, more particularly, that the grand division of labor is effected which permits and more or less compels the individual man to concentrate his energies and his talents on the particular task he is best fitted to perform, and in this way emancipates him and his fellows from the control of nature and circumstance which so thoroughly dominates primitive man.

It happens, however, that the process of acculturation and assimilation and the accompanying amalgamation of racial stocks does not proceed with the same ease and the same speed in all cases. Particularly where people who come together are of divergent cultures and widely different racial stocks, assimilation and amalgamation do not take place so rapidly as they do in other cases. All our so-called racial problems grow out of situations in which assimilation and amalgamation do not take place at all, or take place very slowly. As I have said elsewhere, the chief obstacle to the cultural assimilation of races is not their different mental, but rather their divergent physical traits. It is not because of the mentality of the Japanese that they do not so easily assimilate as do the Europeans. It is because

[3]A. H. Guyot, *Earth and Man* (Boston, 1857), cited by Franklin Thomas, *The Environmental Basis of Society* (New York, 1911), p. 205.

the Japanese bears in his features a distinctive racial hallmark, that he wears, so to speak, a racial uniform which classifies him. He cannot become a mere individual, indistinguishable in the cosmopolitan mass of the population, as is true, for example, of the Irish, and, to a lesser extent, of some of the other immigrant races. The Japanese, like the Negro, is condemned to remain among us an abstraction, a symbol—and a symbol not merely of his own race but of the Orient and of that vague, ill-defined menace we sometimes refer to as the "yellow peril."[4]

Under such circumstances peoples of different racial stocks may live side by side in a relation of symbiosis, each playing a role in a common economy, but not interbreeding to any great extent; each maintaining, like the gypsy or the pariah peoples of India, a more or less complete tribal organization or society of their own. Such was the situation of the Jew in Europe up to modern times, and a somewhat similar relation exists today between the native white and the Hindu populations in Southeast Africa and in the West Indies.

In the long run, however, peoples and races who live together, sharing in the same economy, inevitably interbreed, and in this way if in no other, the relations which were merely co-operative and economic become social and cultural. When migration leads to conquest, either economic or political, assimilation is inevitable. The conquering peoples impose their culture and their standards upon the conquered, and there follows a period of cultural endosmosis.

Sometimes relations between the conquering and the conquered peoples take the form of slavery; sometimes they assume the form, as in India, of a system of caste. But in either case the dominant and the subject peoples become, in time, integral parts of one society. Slavery and caste are merely forms of accommodation, in which the race problem finds a temporary solution. The case of the Jews was different. Jews never were a subject people, at least not in Europe. They were never reduced to the position of an inferior caste. In their ghettos in which they first elected, and then were forced, to live, they preserved their own tribal traditions and their cultural, if not their political, independence. The Jew who left the ghetto did not escape; he deserted and became that ex-

[4] "Racial Assimilation in Secondary Groups," *Publications of the American Sociological Society,* vol. 8 (1914).

ecrable object, an apostate. The relation of the ghetto Jew to the larger community in which he lived was, and to some extent still is, symbiotic rather than social.

When, however, the walls of the medieval ghetto were torn down and the Jew was permitted to participate in the cultural life of the peoples among whom he lived, there appeared a new type of personality, namely, a cultural hybrid, a man living and sharing intimately in the cultural life and traditions of two distinct peoples; never quite willing to break, even if he were permitted to do so, with his past and his traditions, and not quite accepted, because of racial prejudice, in the new society in which he now sought to find a place. He was a man on the margin of two cultures and two societies, which never completely interpenetrated and fused. The emancipated Jew was, and is, historically and typically the marginal man, the first cosmopolite and citizen of the world. He is, par excellence, the "stranger," whom Simmel, himself a Jew, has described with such profound insight and understanding in his *Sociologie*. Most if not all the characteristics of the Jew, certainly his pre-eminence as a trader and his keen intellectual interest, his sophistication, his idealism and lack of historic sense, are the characteristics of the city man, the man who ranges widely, lives preferably in a hotel—in short, the cosmopolite. The autobiographies of Jewish immigrants, of which a great number have been published in America in recent years, are all different versions of the same story—the story of the marginal man; the man who, emerging from the ghetto in which he lived in Europe, is seeking to find a place in the freer, more complex and cosmopolitan life of an American city. One may learn from these autobiographies how the process of assimilation actually takes place in the individual immigrant. In the more sensitive minds its effects are as profound and as disturbing as some of the religious conversions of which William James has given us so classical an account in his *Varieties of Religious Experience*. In these immigrant autobiographies the conflict of cultures, as it takes place in the mind of the immigrant, is just the conflict of "the divided self," the old self and the new. And frequently there is no satisfying issue of this conflict, which often terminates in a profound disillusionment, as described, for example, in Lewisohn's autobiography *Up Stream*. But Lewisohn's restless wavering between the warm security of the ghetto, which he has abandoned, and the cold freedom of the outer world, in which he is not yet quite at home, is typical. A century earlier, Heinrich Heine, torn with the same conflicting loyalties, struggling to be at the same time a German and a Jew, enact-·ed a similar role. It was, according to his latest biographer, the secret and the tragedy of Heine's life that circumstance condemned him to live in two worlds, in neither of which he ever quite belonged. It was this that embittered his intellectual life and gave to his writings that character of spiritual conflict and instability which, as Browne says, is evidence of "spiritual distress." His mind lacked the integrity which is based on conviction: "His arms were weak"—to continue the quotation—"because his mind was divided; his hands were nerveless because his soul was in turmoil."

Something of the same sense of moral dichotomy and conflict is probably characteristic of every immigrant during the period of transition, when old habits are being discarded and new ones are not yet formed. It is inevitably a period of inner turmoil and intense self-consciousness.·

There are no doubt periods of transition and crisis·in the lives of most of us that are comparable with those which the immigrant experiences when he leaves home to seek his fortunes in a strange country. But in the case of the marginal man the period of crisis is relatively permanent. The result is that he tends to become a personality type. Ordinarily the marginal man is a mixed blood, like the Mulatto in the United States or the Eurasian in Asia, but that is apparently because the man of mixed blood is one who lives in two worlds, in both of which he is more or less of a stranger. The Christian convert in Asia or in Africa exhibits many if not most of the characteristics of the marginal man—the same spiritual instability, intensified self-consciousness, restlessness, and *malaise*.

It is in the mind of the marginal man that the moral turmoil which new cultural contacts occasion manifests itself in the most obvious forms. It is in the mind of the marginal man—where the changes and fusions of culture are going on—that we can best study the processes of civilization and of progress.

The Fool as a Social Type

by
Orrin E. Klapp

Among the collective labels which have an unusual power of assigning status is the epithet of "the fool." The fool represents a collective concept of a kind of person or conduct peculiarly ridiculous and inferior. Despite his low status, however, the fool is a symbol of fundamental importance, representing a role especially valued by the group. The fool is a social type found widely in folklore, literature, and drama. The role of the fool is institutionalized in comedy and in the professions of the clown and jester.[1] Everyone plays the fool at some time; fool-making is a continual social process; it is safe to say that every group must have a fool. Moreover, there is a tendency to dramatize social forces as a conflict of heroes and villains. In this human drama the fool also plays a part. Whereas the hero represents the victory of good over evil, the fool represents values which are rejected by the group: causes that are lost, incompetence, failure, and fiasco. So that, in a sense, fool-making might be called a process of history. Public figures who become classified as fools lose their chance of leadership. The label of "the fool" is, therefore, a propaganda device of special significance.

Our problem here is to define the fool as a social type. What is the role of the fool, what situations make fools, and what are the status and function of the fool in social organization? As a social type[2] the fool has certain definable char-

Reprinted by permission of the publishers and the author from *American Journal of Sociology*, Vol. 55, 1949–50, pp. 157–162, University of Chicago Press.

[1] See Stith Thompson, *Motif-Index of Folk-Literature* (Helsinki: Suomaleinen Tiedeakatemia, Academia Scientiarum Fennica, 1932–36), IV, 149–249; and O. M. Busby, *Development of the Fool in the Elizabethan Drama* (London: Oxford University Press, 1923). For a survey of the historical and institutional roles of the fool see Enid Welsford, *The Fool, His Social and Literary History* (London: Faber & Faber, Ltd., 1935); and Barbara Swain, *Fools and Folly during the Middle Ages and the Renaissance* (New York: Columbia University Press, 1932).

[2] For discussion of the concept and method of the social type, see Samuel M. Strong, "Social Types in a Minority Group: Formulation

acteristics, as to both personal traits and roles. The creation of a fool is accomplished by ascribing characteristics of the fool to a person through situations which "make a fool" of somebody or popular definitions which impute the character of a fool, that is, jokes and epithets. For purposes of investigation a fool is defined here as a person, real or imaginary, who is generally ridiculed and who occupies a distinctive status because of this.

TYPES OF FOOLS

The fool is distinguished from the normal group member by a deviation in person or conduct which is regarded as ludicrous and improper. He is usually defined as a person lacking in judgment, who behaves absurdly or stupidly. The antics of the fool, his ugliness, gracelessness, senselessness, or possible deformity of body represent departures from corresponding group norms of propriety. The fool is the antithesis of decorum, beauty, grace, intelligence, strength, and other virtues embodied in heroes; and, therefore, as a type is antiheroic. The deviation of the fool from the normal has three characteristics: It is an extreme exaggeration or deficiency; it is an evidence of weakness or irresponsibility; and it is an offense against propriety rather than against mores. With regard to the first of these, as the following examples will show, the role of the fool involves a striking exhibition of some incongruity or shortcoming. With respect to the second, the role of the fool inherently involves failure, weakness, or comic frustration. Because of his ineffectuality, the fool is regarded as incompetent and irresponsible. Despite his shortcomings, therefore, he is distinguished from the villain by the fact that his pranks involve no evil intent or are too stupid to be taken seriously. The fool is thus tolerated and is regarded with amusement rather than being punished. The types of fools described below are distinguished by the particular way in which they depart from group norms, whether by an excess or by a deficiency in respect to some virtue: (1) the antic fool, (2) the comic rogue, (3) the rash fool, (4) the clumsy

of a Method," *American Journal of Sociology*, XLVIII, (1923), 563–73; and "Negro-White Relations as Reflected in Social Types," *ibid.*, LII (1946), 23–30.

fool, (5) the deformed fool, (6) the simple fool, (7) the weak fool, (8) the comic butt, (9) the pompous fool, and (10) the mock hero.

The first three types deviate through excesses of conduct. The antic fool departs from decorum through impulsive or playful behavior, e.g., pranks, leaps, undignified postures, grimaces, mimicry, and other capers. He is the "cutup" or "life of the party." In the theatrical profession some of the epithets given to this role are "clowning" or "mugging." The comic rogue, or "scamp," is different from the antic fool in that his conduct departs from propriety specifically in the direction of forbidden behavior: "mischief" or criminality, e.g., impudent gestures, liberties, obscenities, or preposterous, burlesque villainies. His ineffectualness, lack of serious intent, or other weakness, however, prevents the group from taking him seriously. The rash fool, on the other hand, is characterized by immoderate extremes or lack of judgment in directions ordinarily approved by the group. His enthusiasm, however, is "recklessness"; his daring is "foolhardiness"; his bravery is "bravado." The rash fool is found in our society in the roles of the daredevil, the flagpole-sitter, the stunt flyer, and the youth with the "hot-rod" racer. He is found also in the prodigal or wastrel,[3] the person given to ruinous extremes in life or business. Finally, the rash fool is seen in the leader who gets "too far ahead of his time."

Other fool types depart from group norms through a deficiency in person or conduct. The clumsy fool shows a lack of grace or proficiency in situations requiring expertness and decorum, e.g., one who slips or falls into an awkward posture on a public occasion. The person who hobbles, limps, or is physically awkward more easily acquires this role. The deformed fool deviates in appearance from group norms of beauty, stature, posture, health, etc. He may be ugly, dwarfed, crippled, gigantic, animal-like, or subhuman in appearance. Deformity has the symbolic capacity to suggest various inappropriate roles of the fool. Artificial distortions through make-up are used to suggest the deformities of the fool, as, for instance, the large feet and bulbous nose of the clown. Any person who departs markedly from group norms of appearance is easily cast in the role of the fool. On the other hand, a demonstration of deficiency of intelligence or

[3]See David Malcomson, *Ten Heroes* (New York: Duell, Sloan & Pearce, 1941), pp. 115–40.

wit places a person in the category of the simple fool. He is classed as naïve, senseless, backward, or rustic. Among the roles which create the simple fool are ludicrous failure, comic frustration,[4] unintelligible behavior or utterances, and the quality of being easily taken advantage of. Another type of deficiency is found in the weak fool, the person lacking in aggressiveness, strength, or courage, e.g., the "sissy." Oversubmissive and overprotected personality types are caught in this appelation. So also is the person whose moral code, dress, background, etc., render him "too nice" for the world of practical affairs. The weak or oversubmissive fool, when his conduct becomes of serious consequence to the group, is called a coward, a type marginal to the villain or traitor.

The role of the comic butt is played particularly by deformed, weak, and simple fools. This may be defined as the regular recipience of group derision and abuse. The butt is persecuted because his appearance constantly draws derision or because he is too stupid, submissive, or cowardly to fight back. In appearance he may be bedraggled, drooping, forlorn, in patches, or he may present a picture of battered dignity, e.g., the comedy type of the hobo. As in the case of the comic-strip character, "Sad Sack," "everything happens to him." Despite his misfortunes, the comic butt is apparently indestructible. He survives blows, falls, and insults; and the onlookers laugh rather than pity.

Two fool roles are distinguished which involve pose or pretense to status. The great or pompous fool deviates from group standards through an excess of pride or presumption and a lack of competence. Persons of rank, age, or great size are particularly vulnerable to this role. They are deflated or "shown up" by revelation of pretense, defeat by a lesser rival, or a mistake, and thus made fools. Another pretender fool is found in the mock hero, a device commonly used in satirical literature. A mock hero is made by casting an ineffective person in the role or pose of the hero, e.g., by epithets applied to an ordinary person, such as "Crusader," "Sir Galahad," "Superman." Various devices reveal that the supposed hero is really a fool: he performs the gestures of the hero, but his weaknesses are apparent through his armor.

---

[4]E.g., American Indian folk fools dive for reflected food, shoot at enemy's reflection in water, eat medicines which physic them, etc.; see Stith Thompson, *Tales of North American Indians* (Cambridge, Mass.: Harvard University Press, 1920), pp. 364–65.

FOOL-MAKING SITUATIONS AND PROCESSES

As has been stated, certain collective processes and situations make fools. Fool-making situations are so constantly presented to the average person that he may be unable to avoid occasionally falling into the role.[5] Life is a continual process of fool-making. Popular humor, derision, and belittlement are constantly assigning this role. Consequently, because fool-ascription is a status descent, social relations are continually rendered unstable by fool-making. These processes and situations are of interest to those desirous of stabilizing or controlling political structure, e.g., through leadership or propaganda.

Fool-making situations are presented in the various institutions of comedy. These may be defined as those conditions which render it most likely that a person will act or appear as a fool. The profession of the clown embodies the perfected art of making a fool of one's self or others for public entertainment. To become a fool, one's appearance or conduct must be distorted from expectation in the direction of types such as those described above. Among the important fool-making situations may be itemized the following: (1) involuntary or deliberate distortion of appearance or dress from group norms, e.g., by a mustache or monocle; (2) antic or indecorous behavior in situations requiring proficiency and decorum, e.g., horseplay or a badly timed joke by a political candidate. Socrates was made a fool in Aristophanes' play, "The Clouds," by being lowered in a basket. The fool is also made by (3) absurd failures revealing weakness or frustration; (4) defeats by lesser rivals, e.g., being "shown up" in public debate; (5) unflattering comparisons with inferior persons, particularly with fools; (6) situations in which one is forced to make a bluff or to play an unfamiliar role, as, for instance, the youth who is trying to smoke like a man, the *nouveau riche* and his *faux pas* in "high society"; (7) lack of timing or insight, which causes one to play an inappropriate role, e.g., the "hero" who rushes on the stage too soon or too

---

[5]"All people are exposed to situations in which they must act as fools" (Kenneth Burke, *Attitudes toward History* [New York: New Republic, 1937], I, 52).

late; and (8) being made the butt of a joke which imputes any of the various roles of the fool.

Because fool-making is a collective imputation, it is not necessary, however, that a person actually have the traits or perform the role of the fool. A person is a fool when he is socially defined as a fool. All persons in public positions are exposed to popular humor. Among the social defining processes which assign the role of the fool are (1) jokes and popular humor, (2) name-calling, (3) literary and artistic satire, and (4) propaganda. No one, for instance, is so respected that no jokes or rumors will circulate about him. A ludicrous conception may be built up; the anecdote may become one of the imperishable stories which are part of his reputation.[6] Nicknames are also applied to public personages which help to characterize them and give the public a greater sense of familiarity with them. These epithets are often based upon some outstanding feature of the personality in question; the slightest idiosyncrasy may make him liable to jokes and epithets which assign the role of the fool. Satire may also distort his character through caricature, parody, burlesque, irony, etc. Finally, propaganda may exploit these spontaneous defining processes.

Despite the universality of fool-making processes, it is obvious that all persons who become thus characterized do not remain fools, that fools are selected. What makes a fool role stick? Among the factors responsible for permanent characterization as a fool we may particularly note (1) repeated performances or obvious personal traits which continually suggest the role of the fool; (2) a striking, conclusive, or colorful single exhibition which convinces the public that the person is irremediably a fool; (3) a story or epithet so "good" that it is continually repeated and remembered, making up an imperishable legend; and (4) failure to contradict a fool role by roles or stories of a different category.

ESCAPE FROM THE FOOL ROLE

Instances may be found in which persons popularly defined as fools have escaped from this role by actions or stories which allowed them to be redefined in terms of more favored

[6]B. A. Botkin has defined folklore as the "stuff that travels and the stuff that sticks" (*A Treasury of American Folklore* [New York: Crown Publishers, 1944]), p. xxiv.

social types. In general, however, it may be said that the longer a person has been characterized as a fool, the harder it is for him to redeem himself. The strategy of escape is to do something which causes people to take one seriously: aggressive actions[7] which cause one to be defined as a hero or exhibition of "human" traits which arouse sympathy.

Among the major routes of escape from the fool role are the following: (1) Avoidance of the imputation by "taking" a joke and "laughing it off" implies that there has been no injury, that the jibe is ineffectual or inapplicable. (2) A counter-joke or effective repartee "turns the tables" and makes the other a fool; "having the last word" or getting the best of a contest of wits has, in fact, the effect of defining the winner as a clever hero. (3) A similar strategy involves acceptance of the fool role and its use as a "ruse" or "trap" for a clever victory. This is embodied in the sage fool, the rustic wit, or pseudo-fool, who under a pose of simplicity hides unexpected sharpness. By defeating more pretentious opponents, he passes the fool role along. (4) Activity, aggressiveness, or "fight" may transform a fool into a hero, particularly when he picks a larger opponent or identifies himself with a social cause. By choice of a larger opponent there is a double chance of heroic status, since victory will make the person a "giant-killer," whereas defeat is no disgrace but may, on the contrary, cast him as a victim or martyr. (5) We must note also that the social pattern of the "Cinderella" operates as a powerful expectancy in American life, causing people to look hopefully at the "dark horse" or "underdog" for signs of a sudden rise to success. The person who is derided, clumsy, stupid, or made a fool, is a typical starting-point of the Cinderella theme. Any revelation of potentiality or unexpected merit may start this pattern of expectancy into operation. (6) Finally, by suffering or showing "human" traits which arouse sympathy, a person can escape from the fool role. Excessive persecution, e.g., "carrying a joke too far," tends to make a martyr out of the fool. Undue cruelty on the part of opponents, particularly if it is at the same time revealed that he has been injured, that he is human, has feelings, etc., will serve to evoke identification and shatter the definition of him as subhuman. Depiction of human traits by anecdotes of acts of kindness, showing his family life, etc., will perform the

[7] See O. E. Klapp, "Creation of Popular Heroes," *American Journal of Sociology*, LIV (1948), 135–41; and "The Folk Hero," *Journal of American Folklore*, LXII (1949), 17–25.

same function. If persecution occurs under conditions in which the fool can be identified with a popular cause, so that his sufferings are seen as sacrifices, conversion to the very powerful role of the martyr is possible.

STATUS AND FUNCTION OF THE FOOL

Whether professionalized as clown and jester or found in the butt of popular humor and village idiot, the position of the fool is distinctive. The various statuses of the fool include the household fool or court jester, the folk fool played by peasants, the folklore fool, the comic or dramatic fool, the professional clown or buffoon, and the village idiot. When established as part of social structure, the status of the fool has four characteristics. It is low, ridiculed, tolerated, and licensed. When not established as a formal status, it still persists as a social type or folklore conception in popular humor, particularly as comic butt and antic player of tricks. The status of the fool presents a paradox in that it is both depreciated and valued: It is at the same time despised and tolerated, ridiculed and enjoyed, degraded and privileged. Regarding the low status of the fool, we may note that he is at the nadir of the value system of the group. He is most lacking in honor and the recipient of all indignities.[8] The fool might be defined functionally as a ridiculed status. Being made a fool is a type of disgrace. Ascription of the fool role to any status is a descent. The fool is lacking in rights and responsibilities; nothing serious is demanded of him; the bauble of the fool symbolizes his incompetence, and nobody wants to follow him. His sole privilege is his "license." Despite his low status, however, the role of the fool is valued and appreciated. He enjoys a certain importance and popularity; he may have fame. His pranks and jokes are to his reputation what exploits are to the hero. He is, therefore, not a "nobody." He is appreciated through collective representations of his role, e.g., drama, fame, and folklore. The fact that the role is thus institutionalized in comedy and perpetuated in folklore suggests that the fool has important social functions.

[8]The importance of status is usually symbolized by honor; see Hans Speier, "Honor and Social Structure," *Social Research*, 11 (1935), 74–97; and O. E. Klapp, "Hero worship in America," *American Sociological Review*, XIV (1949), 53–62.

These social functions are to be found principally in certain contributions which the fool makes to group organization and discipline. Some of these may be noted: The fool upsets decorum by antics and eases routine by comic relief.[9] He also acts as a cathartic symbol for aggressions in the form of wit. He takes liberties with rank; and as butt or scapegoat receives indignities which in real life would be mortal insult or conflict-creating. But chiefly the social type of the fool functions as a device of status reduction and social control. Reduction of persons through the fool role is a continuous collective process of status adjustment. Fool ascription acts as a purging device, eliminating upstarts, pretenders, and incompetents from positions of influence. The fool also enforces propriety in conduct and thus acts as a mechanism of social control. Everybody avoids the role of the fool. Fear of ridicule may be as strong as fear of punishment or death. Social satire may be an effective control on political figures otherwise difficult to criticize. Group discipline is thus enhanced by the operation of ridicule as a sanction—as Bergson pointed out in his essay on laughter (1911)—the fool symbol functioning for propriety in a manner similar to that of the villain in the area of mores. Finally, the type of the fool functions in education, providing a negative example in literature and folklore, e.g., as an object-lesson for children in stories of Simple Simon, Humpty-Dumpty, etc. Thus the fool defines certain varieties of untrustworthy conduct. It operates as an avoidance symbol, discrediting leaders, movements, or individuals which show weaknesses in terms of group norms.

[9]Festivals are noted as "seasons of lawlessness and buffoonery when all revellers behaved foolishly." The "Feast of Fools" flourished in the cathedral towns of France during the fifteenth century: "It took the form of a complete reversal of ordinary custom. . . . The *baculus* or staff of office was delivered into the hands of one of the despised subdeacons who as 'bishop or Pope or King of Fools' led his fellows into the stalls of the higher clergy, to remain there and usurp their functions for the duration of the feast. This transference of authority was the signal for the most astonishing revels. As soon as the higher clergy shed their authority the ecclesiastical ritual lost its sanctity. Even the Mass was burlesqued. Censing was done with pudding and sausages. Sometimes an ass was introduced into church. . . . On these occasions solemn Mass was punctuated with brays and howls, and the rubrics of the 'office' direct that the celebrant instead of saying *Ite missa est* shall bray three times . . . and that the people shall respond in similar fashion. But . . . if local churches tolerated the Feast, it was ceaselessly combatted by the Church Universal" (Welsford, *op. cit.*, pp. 70, 200–201).

The Glutton

by
Stanford M. Lyman

The apparently voluntary character of food gluttony serves to point up why it is more likely to seem "criminal" than sick, an act of moral defalcation rather than medical pathology.[1] Although gluttony is not proscribed by the criminal law, it partakes of some of the social sanctions and moral understandings that govern orientations toward those who commit crimes. If, however, gluttony is a "crime," it would appear at first inspection to fall into that category of one without victims.[2] Gluttony supposedly injures only the person who overindulges his appetite, increasing his weight beyond normal proportions, slowing and marring his gait, reducing his motor speed and physical grace, and, if medical science is to be believed, shortening life itself. As a "victimless crime," gluttony is perhaps closer to suicide than any other crime of its type, for it not only facilitates an earlier death for the glutton but also creates a kind of living death for him as well. Deprived all too often of the admiration, companionship, and love of his nongluttonous peers, the overindulgent eater carries on an isolated, asocial existence. He not only consumes too much food; he is consumed by it.

However, it is precisely this overemphasis on consumption that renders gluttony ambiguous with regard to the number of its victims. Gluttony is an excessive *self*-indulgence. Even in its disrespect for the body it overvalues the ego that it slavishly satisfies. Such acts of overindulgence of self and individual constitute a resistance to—indeed a quiet rebellion against—the demands of sociality.[3] The glutton all too fre-

Reprinted by permission of the publishers from *The Seven Deadly Sins* by Stanford M. Lyman, St. Martin's Press, Inc., 1978.

[1]See Vilhelm Aubert and Sheldon S. Messinger, "The Criminal and the Sick," *Inquiry*, 1 (1958), 137–160; reprinted as chapter 1 of *The Hidden Society* by Vilhelm Aubert (Totowa, N.J.: Bedminster Press, 1965), pp. 25–54.

[2]See Edwin M. Schur, *Crimes Without Victims: Deviant Behavior and Public Policy* (Englewood Cliffs, N.J.: Prentice-Hall Spectrum, 1965).

[3]See Georg Simmel, "The Sociology of Sociability," trans. Everett C. Hughes, *American Journal of Sociology*, 55 (November 1949), 254–261.

quently eats alone and often; in the extreme case he concentrates his attention on obtaining and consuming more and more food. Dining becomes an obsession, the summum bonum of his existence, and gastronomic interests crowd out other aspects of existence, being, and relationship. Like the taboo against incest—or that against love marriage in clan-based societies, which in part stems from the fact that such intimacy is likely to withdraw too much of the services of the couple from the larger societal unit—gluttony's overindulgence of the self is too egoistic for societal toleration. The glutton has so greatly distorted the appropriate allocation of his duties to his ego and his society that, for the benefit of society and its needs for his services, he must be persuaded or coerced to desist in his indulgence. Gluttony in this sense becomes a sin against society. If the glutton is a "criminal," he can be charged not only with injuring himself and lowering his social esteem but also with insulting society by his withdrawal from it.

THE SOCIAL CONSTRUCTION OF GLUTTONY

Like all other designated socially identifiable practices, gluttony is recognized through interpretation. Indeed the glutton is recognizable as a dramatic type, noticeable because of his looks, manner, and habits. He exists not only as a type but as a character, performing a role that requires setting, props, scenario, and audience. Typically the glutton's is a supporting role, distinctive in its display of a deviant personality, contrastive in its visible departure from that of heroes and heroines, and all too often minor, removed, present only in a brief scene. The glutton performs only momentarily for our benefit; we need but to see him for a short time to apprehend his character, appreciate his problem, appropriate his humanity, and oppose his habit. As a performer in the drama of social reality, the glutton appears as a sinner—sometimes as sinister, more often as simple.[4]

Understanding the dramatic realization of gluttony requires an analysis of its special impositions on time, place, and man-

[4] For this term see Stanford M. Lyman and Marvin B. Scott, *The Drama of Social Reality* (New York: Oxford University Press, 1975).

ner. Let us begin with time.[5] Social time differs from clock time in the sense that the latter is but one measure of duration. Periods of time are defined by rates, pace, and tracks that connect the emptiness of duration to the continua and breaks of activity. These tracks of time are measures to all social phenomena. They are also elements in their evaluation. What are the temporal dimensions of gluttony? First note that gluttony might be noticed in the violation of regular mealtimes. In most cultures and societies and certainly in the Occident, eating is done according to a schedule and each meal varies in content and style according to its temporal place, for example, breakfast in the morning, lunch at midday, dinner after sundown. One sign of gluttony is a careless inattention to the temporal and food-specific occasions for eating. Foregoing both time and custom the glutton gorges himself on whatever satisfies his palate at whatever time he wishes. True, the glutton may observe the meal divisions that prevail, eating breakfast, lunch, and dinner, but he indicates his indifference to their singularity by overeating at each meal and eating between them. Some concession to his practice is recognized in the "between-meal snack," the variety of foods sold solely for consumption at times other than meals, and the late evening meal before retiring. These, however, pale into insignificance before the voracious appetite of the glutton. He is absorbed in his eating, forgetful of occasion and modesty, a master of the table, a slave of what is on it.

The seriousness of the glutton's nonobservance of mealtime is better understood if we speak of it in terms of the temporal aspects of gratification. It is a commonplace of the Protestant Ethic that its adherents are required to postpone fleshly gratification, awaiting the propriety of time and occasion. To be sure this ethical imperative is usually associated with the delay of marriage, the scheduling of sex, and the careful planning for leisure. But eating is one of the basic gratifications. Man as a feeder is expected to rise above the ever-hungry animal who is imagined to eat whenever food presents itself. The glutton's open disregard of the ethical commandment that he delay his satisfaction suggests his fall into sinfulness, lack of regard for his uniquely human nature, a descent into carnal pleasure.

[5]See Stanford M. Lyman and Marvin B. Scott, "On the Time Track," *A Sociology of the Absurd* (New York: Appleton-Century Crofts, 1970; reissued Pacific Palisades, Calif.: Goodyear Publishing, 1970), pp. 189–212.

Temporal dimensions of gluttony include more than timing for meals. They also embrace the pace at which he eats. Ordinary dining proceeds at a routinized rate which might be beyond the measure of all but the most precise clock but is easily observed nevertheless. While the shy and fastidious might eat too slowly, the glutton is characterized by the rapidity with which he devours his food. While others are halfway through their entrée, the glutton has emptied his plate and is ready for more. Indeed, as a social diner, the glutton threatens the occasion in a manner not dissimilar from that of the "rate-buster" on the factory assembly line. As one who eats faster than others, he makes an earlier claim on the portions of food left to be distributed to the gathering. In order to ensure equal apportionment the others will have to speed up, hold the glutton in check, or sullenly acquiesce to his disproportionate aggrandizement. Gluttony is a sin to society in that it voids the tacit guaranty of equal protection that undergirds sociability.

The glutton also is noticeable for his departure from the rules of place and territory that typically mark off meals.[6] Dining is territorial in that it usually proceeds at an appointed place, in the presence of others, and employing designated stations for each item of food and places for each diner. The glutton forgoes or forgets his place and violates the space of others. He may begin eating before the meal is served, going into the refrigerator for snacks before meals, getting at the food while it is still in the kitchen, or in an even more ravenous state, before it is fully cooked, reaching into frying pan or oven to snatch a morsel. At table he may spread beyond his place, taking over part of the space allotted to diners on either side or opposite him. "Imperialism" may characterize his table relations as he takes the bread and butter belonging to his neighbors, reaches to secure second and third helpings before others can offer them, and monopolizes dishes set before him but intended for further distribution. The glutton invades the kitchen backstage, raids the icebox, converts the public place at table to a private preserve, and in general eschews or obliterates the interaction territories that are also a part of social dining.

The glutton is also noticeable as a defiler of his own body space. His appetite threatens to engulf the space of others as he spreads out to take more than one person's ordinary allot-

---

[6]See Lyman and Scott, "Territoriality: A Neglected Sociological Dimension," *A Sociology of the Absurd*, pp. 89–110.

ment of territory. If he grows too large he may no longer fit into ordinary chairs, threaten by dint of his enormous weight to wreck the furniture, and require special arrangements in advance of his coming.[7] Here again we see another way in which the fat glutton burdens sociability. Precisely because his girth and weight call for precautions, he makes more demands on his friends and associates than others of normal size. Seemingly unmindful of the social consequences of his own size, he forces others to be conscious and careful for him. He is more present and better accounted for than others whose social and personal value may be greater than his own. As a potential threat to company and convenience, he may ultimately lose his place altogether, relegated to the back rooms, kitchens, and isolated eating places that will contain him.

Banishment from company is a territorial marker of the unrepentant glutton. Dropped from the invitational lists of his friends, denied access to those dining places where company and comportment are required, destined to seek ever after his cravings, he eats alone, in furtive places, sometimes without benefit of table, dishes, or utensils. Unable to await the setting of the table, eager to devour the food even before it is ready, he may seize it with his bare hands, tear at the meat with his teeth, devour huge chunks without bothering to chew. And in this disregard of utensil, setting, and mastication, his sin is revealed once more. He has sunk to his animal nature, indistinguishable from a dog or a coyote, gorging with tooth and claw. He has not only been banished from society but also given up his step on the ladder that places him above the beast and below the spirit.

From what we have already said, it becomes clear that the glutton is known by his manner. Dining is a delicate matter in a society that prides itself on moderation in all matters of the flesh. One must eat and yet not appear to be absorbed in the process. Indeed, given the choice of eating and attending to matters of business, politics, or education, the prudent and serious person might leave his food altogether. Often enough, popular films picture the central character deep in conversation over some serious matter while his food remains untouched, or jumping up from a hardly started meal to rush

---

[7] In the extreme he becomes a "freak," no longer suitable for ordinary social occasions but an object of curiosity, fear, or pity. See Frederick Drimmer, *Very Special People* (New York: Bantam, 1976), pp. 265–281.

off when a message arrives telling of trouble, or even of some significant commercial, political, or personal matter. Eating takes second place. But not to the glutton. To him eating takes precedence over all other matters. Stereotypes picture the glutton attending with more diligence to his cuisine than to his concerns. Reversing the social priorities he places his gustatorial welfare before his social obligations. '

The appropriate manner for eating is sociable. In the ideal case, the group gathered around the table engage in light conversation, break up what limited concentration they must employ for the act of eating by attending to the talk of their table mates. They observe proprieties, giving attention to the food only insofar as politeness requires, and consuming moderate amounts. The glutton is of a different manner. He lacks sociability. Rather than attend to the persons at the table, he engages the food. His concentration on eating subtracts from the occasion, and by that act of unsociable behavior invites rebuke or, more dangerously, emulation. Should others follow him into his kind of engagement with the cuisine, the glutton bids fair to threaten the social fabric. Usually, however, he lacks either the standing or the charisma to evoke a following. Failing to share himself with others, he fails to find others to share his habit with himself.

The glutton challenges the prevailing rule of fraternization in nearly every status group. As Max Weber has observed, "Fraternization at all times presupposes commensalism; it does not have to be actually practiced in everyday life, but it must be ritually possible."[8] The vicissitudes and breakthroughs of civilization into ever widening fraternizations, a topic central to Weber's sociology, need not detain us here. Suffice it to say that three processes—religious integration, establishment of more or less permanent national, racial, and ethnic sodalities, and the secularization of status, led in the Occident to the formation of large numbers of informal sociable gatherings, bonded together not by an oath of brotherhood but by a common style of life. These informal cliques, groups, and associations, in turn, indicate their exclusiveness by placing various kinds of social barriers around their own commensal occasions. Into such gatherings the glutton, possessing rights to participate on the basis of his status, nevertheless forfeits his dining privilege because of his mannerisms,

[8]Max Weber, "India: The Brahman and the Castes," *From Max Weber: Essays in Sociology*, ed. and trans. Hans Gerth and C. Wright Mills (New York: Oxford University Press, 1946), p. 402.

ugliness, aggression, and personal demands. The net result of this denial of commensal sociability is the occasional formation of specific places and the designation of special occasions where gluttons, otherwise denied an opportunity to socialize and gourmandize unmolested, can join together and enjoy the congregative spirit that prevails when outstanding differences have been muted.

Georg Simmel once pointed out that "Eating and drinking, the oldest and intellectually most negligible functions, can form a tie, often the only one, among very heterogeneous persons and groups."[9] Among gluttons, an outcast population, this sometimes occurs in the form of meetings at hideaway towns and certain restaurants, in which all the congregants, refugees from the diets to which they have been sentenced or from the dining tables of ordinary eaters, find solace and surcease, recognition and response, in joint and common participation at an orgiastic feast. Like criminals in their hideout, the gluttons can here throw caution to the winds. Stigma bearers on holiday, they can depart from the customary etiquette with which they ordinarily approach dining when under the scrutiny of others, denounce the fat-free, calorie-reduced diets that a slim-conscious society flaunts, and ridicule the exercises and health fads that promote the slim Greek body type. Durham, North Carolina, is one such gathering place.[10] Known as "Fat City" to the overweight people who migrate there, it is the location of the Kempner Clinic, a special dietary center for the chronically obese. Many of the enrollees, ostensibly present to undergo weeks or months of a strict, experimental regimen permitting only rice and fruit juice, in fact sneak off to the numerous fast-food stands that dot the area. Just outside Durham is a stretch of road known to the dieters as "Destruction Row" or "Sin Alley." Lined with short-order houses advertising roast beef sandwiches, Kentucky fried chicken, pizza, hamburgers, steaks, doughnuts, and ice cream, these roadside attractions become a classic temptation to patients just released from the clinic. Starved for months, the homeward-bound dieters pull their cars over, discuss the matter among themselves, agree finally that they are all in it together, and enter the fast-food

[9] Georg Simmel, "Fundamental Problems of Sociology: Individual and Society," *The Sociology of Georg Simmel*, trans. and ed. Kurt H. Wolff (Glencoe: The Free Press, 1950), p. 33.

[10] Burr Snider, "Fat City: Durham, North Carolina. Where the Obese Meet to Cheat," *Esquire*, 79 (March 1973), 112–114, 174–182.

establishments. Rabid, they move from place to place, eating everything, buying bags of food to take away, and eventually giving in completely to the gluttonous license to which their enforced diet entitles them. The roadside restaurants open up the opportunity for a sinful spree.

ABSOLUTION FROM THE SIN OF GLUTTONY: STRATEGIES OF EXCUSE AND JUSTIFICATION

The sin of gluttony is not so great that the sinner is without sources and resources of relief. All activities have value—in accordance with the evaluative label placed upon them. These labels in turn are subject to negotiation, debate, redesignation, and reevaluation. Hence acts that might be called sinful on one occasion can be matters of virtue on another. Even in the same situation an act need not evoke a single uniform evaluation. It might be praised or condemned, excused or justified. The sins are not absolute in their recognition, designation, or specification. For an act to become an example of sinfulness or virtue, it must partake of the vocabulary of motives, the rhetorics of right and wrong.

Precisely because gluttony falls along the line of acts of the will, it requires for its sinful designation an accurate imputation of motives.[11] Motives can only be inferred from behavior, but the range of behavior from which these inferences can be drawn is great and varied. In fact, gluttony itself requires a labeling of the acts of eating, an inference as to the motives behind these acts, an evaluation of the propriety of these motives, and a final designation of the entire process—act-connected-to-will—as a sin. Between each of these operations gapes a chasm of mystery and opportunity. The overeater, heavy drinker, and drug addict can relieve themselves of the charge of sinful gluttony by an artful employment of the rhetoric of exculpation, a clever exploitation of the vocabulary of motives, or even an accidental invocation of the redeeming words that bring redemption, forgiveness, or salvation.[12]

[11]See Robert M. MacIver, "The Imputation of Motives," *American Journal of Sociology*, 46 (July 1940), 1–12.

[12]C. Wright Mills, "Situated Actions and Vocabularies of Motives," *American Sociological Review*, 5 (December 1940), 904–913.

In general, the putative glutton can relieve himself of the accusation that he is a sinner by invoking an excuse or a justification.[13] If the former, the accused admits to the sinfulness, wrongfulness, badness, or evil of the charge but denies full responsibility; if the latter, the accused admits responsibility but denies the pejorative quality of the act in question. Excuses and justifications articulate a rhetoric of relief, a linguistic strategy for the release from sin.

Let us begin with excuses. Typically there are four model forms of excuse available to the putative glutton—the appeal to accidents, appeal to defeasibility, appeal to biological drives, and scapegoating. Employing any one or a combination of these, as in a sad tale, the accused sinner might carry off the sinful act without having to suffer the full burden of being a sinner.

Excuses that claim *accident* as the source of a charge of gluttony seek mitigation if not absolution from sin by pointing to recognized hazards of dining situations, the undeterrable claims of hunger's demand, and the inattention to controls that might have been operant. Since a gluttonous act might interrupt an otherwise normal eating regimen, the indulgence stands out, invites a searching motivational question, and leaves room for exculpatory maneuver. Since food habits vary among ethnic groups, cliques, and classes, a young man upon returning home from an evening out with friends of a different background than his own can claim that he did not intend to eat so much, did not know what he was getting into, had no idea how much his friends would invite him to eat, did not know that such foods or drinks are so filling and so forth. Or he might claim that because he had not eaten all day his hunger pangs overcame his will, that in responding to the demands of his stomach he overlooked the mistake he had made earlier in not eating properly during the day.

Appeals to *defeasibility* respond to recognized difficulties of personal control. They are central to the rhetoric of absolution of the glutton since they strike a blow at the heart of the charge of sinfulness—its willfulness. The putative glutton, by invoking the lack of freedom of his mind, indicating that he lacked either "knowledge" or control of his "will," relieves himself of the charge that he has entered into sin freely. Precisely because knowledge about nutrition and its effects is

[13]See Stanford M. Lyman and Marvin B. Scott, "Accounts," *American Sociological Review*, 33 (February 1968), 46–62; reprinted in Lyman and Scott, *Sociology of the Absurd*, pp. 111–144.

inexact and not widely understood, an individual can claim ignorance about the meaning, effect, amount, and kind of foods he ingests. Indeed as experts disagree about the physiological and nutritive effects of cholesterol, carbohydrates, and calories, individuals not only find it hard to follow a proper diet but also are in a position to invoke their understandable ignorance as an excuse for excess.

Impairment of the will is a more likely excuse. The individual claims that he is out of control. Some fat people claim that their corpulence dictates their lives. Sometimes derived from the "invalid" theory of obesity, the excuse claims that the desire to eat has overwhelmed all willful checks on it, and that the individual cannot help imbibing, cannot cope. Another "invalid" excuse refers the accusation from the center of the will to the physiological state. Appealing to recognized notions of glandular disorder, duodenal condition, or genetic heritage, the overeater denies personal responsibility, invites sympathy, and, where a medical problem is presented as still incurable, calls upon his accusers to indulge his excesses until research finds a way to relieve him. Finally, persons who are distraught, out of their mind with worry, beset with emotional and personal problems, can claim these departures from ordinary states of mind as excuses for their gorging.

Where temporary pathology or personal distraction cannot be employed, individuals can direct the cause of their overindulgence to *socialization*. Since modern thought tends to recognize that significant effects on habit, attitudes, and actions can be created in the earliest years of life, when the infant cannot control his situation, and since socialization practices can, in turn, be related to idiosyncrasy and subcultural variation, an individual is in a position to account for his gluttonous behavior by referring to his childhood experiences or national background. Hence, the adult individual who claims he is a food addict because his parents fed him whenever he cried as an infant exculpates his own indulgence while blaming his parents. A more benevolent excuse is that which invokes the dictates of culture and ethnicity, for example, the Jew who cannot help but overeat since his peers, family, and friends all encourage the morality of gastronomic pleasure.

Mention has already been made of the body and its inner workings. Ever with us but mysterious, *the body* invites exploitation as a resource for excuses. We have already noticed how putative gluttons can claim that aspects of their physiology, physique, or heritage force them to eat. These bodily drives can be expanded to include racial characteristics, anatomical developments, and somatic factors. The glutton's unfashionable body may be excused as a fateful gift of unkind nature, which has not only endowed some people with lovely bodies and a will to keep them so, but also cursed others with ugly fat that no effort or intention can make beautiful. Fatness can be its own excuse, a "viscerotonic" condition that demands growth and spread, dictates temperament, and does not give in to any external demands or internal pleas.[14]

Some people cannot excuse their indulgence to others but they can relieve their sinfulness to themselves. *Fantasy* here acts as a device to separate the self from its bodily frame and dictates. The corpulent individual sees himself not as obese and gluttonous but as thin, handsome, normal, and lovable. "Inside the fat man is a skinny one" goes the popular proverb. As a fantasized excuse the inner man substitutes for the real one, and taking priority over the latter, also excuses his defaults. If only the inner man could get out, could be recognized for what he is, the imputed state of sinfulness would be obviated.

When we turn to the realm of justifications we enter the kingdom of virtue regained. Whereas in all of the excuses there is an admission of wrongfulness, with justifications the accused denies that there is anything wrong in what he does. Justifications for gluttony do not deny that there is a sinful quality to voracious overeating. Rather, they distinguish between the generally impermissible and the particularly allowable. And in some instances they show that the apparently gluttonous act is not only acceptable but required.

Consider the claims of *occupations*.[15] Certain occupations are so centrally related to nutritive excess or gastronomic concentration that those who enter them are linked inextricably to a zealous regard for dietary excess. The gourmet whose profession as a journalistic food critic requires him to indulge continually in rich foods may overeat as part of his elected task. A man of enormous girth, he might wear his

[14]See William H. Sheldon, *The Varieties of Temperament* (New York: Harper and Brothers, 1942) and the discussion of temperament and body type in Tamotsu Shibutani, *Society and Personality: An Interactionist Approach to Social Psychology* (Englewood Cliffs, N.J.: Prentice-Hall, 1961), pp. 544–548.

[15]Notice that these claims might be an *excuse* if the individual employs them as countervailing his own intentions, ethics, desires, etc.

weight well, a badge of his endeavor and expertise. Questioned about his size and refusal to diet, he need only point to his occupation, its requirements and perquisites to relieve him of the charge of sinful intent. Other occupations may require activities that resemble gluttony but are not chargeable to its evil. The actor who is required to gain weight for a part, or who must never lose weight lest he lose his character type along with it, provides one example. Such well-known movie stars of an earlier era as S. Z. "Cuddles" Sakall, Fatty Arbuckle, and Sidney Greenstreet were primarily known for their girth, their manner of "wearing" their fat, and the characters that their physical appearance expressed. Each of these men would probably have lost much more than weight by dieting, but neither needed to bear a charge of gluttony in the face of his success and popularity. Similarly, such activities as espionage agent might require the cover of fat and the characterological masquerade of gluttony to disguise a perfectly laudable and patriotic service for one's country.

There also arise *situations and occasions* where indulgence seems to be warranted, and the prohibition on gluttony is temporarily set aside. Participation in these moral holidays requires no apology and may even be expected and encouraged. On a national level in the United States the Thanksgiving dinner and celebration constitute an easily recognized example. For others with only slightly less mass acceptability, consider the license given to overeating when "southern hospitality" prevails, the relaxation on the bans against intemperate drinking on New Year's Eve, or the latitude given to eating and drinking among soldiers about to go into battle. There may also be special situations that permit dietary excess. Prisoners sentenced to death are traditionally permitted to indulge their fancies in eating on the last night of their lives, but for those sentenced to hang, apprehensions about the indignity occasioned by loss of sphincter control while in the throes of strangulation sometimes inspire moderation or even abstinence. Finally, there are the modern versions of saturnalian role reversal, of which that carried on by body builders provides an excellent example of justified excess. According to Arnold Schwarzenegger, holder of the Mr. Universe and Mr. Olympia titles, body builders, who shun high-caloric foods for most of the week, enjoy having an occasional "food orgy": "That happens about once a week in California," he said. "We'll all get together and have a food orgy and eat for hours and have a good time. Our favorite dish is a mixture of ice cream, whipped cream, nuts, honey, and sugar. No one feels guilty, because all of us are there."[16]

Gluttony may also be justified because it is a tissue-related excess that allows nature to set its own limits. Overeaters occasionally report that their weight does not continue to increase indefinitely but reaches a plateau and then remains the same. Hence, they do not disregard the problems of weight but let nature take its course. A similar line of argument points out that excessive eating is not a problem or a social "crime" since satiation will set in for every human, and no one need worry about persons indulging beyond the point of satiety. Added to this latter justification is the recognition that the charge of gluttony varies according to situation, status, and society. A Buddhist monk might be unable to justify a request for a second cup of rice, while an American football player might be perfectly justified in eating two beefsteaks for dinner, and an anemic woman might find no shame in an extra glass of wine or a large rare beefsteak at dinner or between meals.

The glutton may, however, be bereft of excuses or justifications for his indulgence. Without any account to offer he may have to engage in information control and tension management to keep his sin a secret or mask his excess in subterfuge.

Anticipation of the difficulties involved in extricating oneself from the charge of overindulgence sometimes results in careful planning and the screening of one's habits. A fine example is presented in the film *Gone with the Wind*. Scarlett O'Hara, who is known to overeat, is to attend a gala ball and banquet at which she will be courted by all of the handsome beaux of the county. Her Negro "mammy," aware of how important it is for a southern belle to appear to be a dainty and delicate eater, prepares a special meal for Scarlett to eat just before she goes to the party so that, already filled, she will eat lightly or not at all while under the scrutiny of the gathered socialites. Gluttons who announce they are on diets may find that their flesh is weaker than their spirit. However, unwilling to admit defeat, they eat secretly and alone, while in the presence of peers and family they observe the proprieties of abstinence or moderation. In one remarkable instance a woman who had enrolled in the rice-and-fruit juice diet required at the Kempner Clinic, stole a turkey from the kitchen, hid it under her dressing gown, and devoured the whole bird during the late night hours. Her theft and dietary violation went undetected, and the next day, eleven pounds heavier, she baffled the doctors who weighed her and could not guess how such a large spontaneous gain could occur.[17]

Fear of being taken for a glutton can act as a deterrent to eating, but often enough it provokes an opposite reaction. For some people, anxiety is a goad to eating, so that the fear of overindulgence leads to raids on the refrigerator, devouring of snack foods, and mindless excesses at table. Moreover, anxiety often betrays the secret that provokes it. As the secret glutton widens his eyes. licks his lips, plays nervously with his utensils, and finally flinches at his first refusal of food, he gives himself away. Unable to control his expression of fear, he is undone by his eyes, mouth, finger, and voice. Although he has not sinned he has indicated his cravings, and this may be enough to evoke condemnation, or pity, for him.

THE SUBLIMATION OF GLUTTONY

Gluttony may not only be forgiven or justified, it may also be a diversion of energy from other sources or possible actions. From certain psychoanalytic perspectives as well as a common-sense point of view, overindulgence in food is interpreted as a deflection from sexual appetite. The sublimation may have a variety of etiologies, and its course may meander before eventually finding discharge in food excess. One possible scenario is that gluttony follows rejection by a love object, converting the libidinal energy into an introjective force that redirects the sensual longings, exchanges their content, and indeed may reverse their emotional valence. Unloved by the other, the individual may come to see himself as unlovable by anyone including himself. His body, however, in its normal form remains a potential object of love. When metamorphosed into something corpulent, gross, and grotesque, its outer appearance reveals his inner condition.

Moreover, once the person acquiesces in his fatness, develops a commitment and an attachment to the role that it contains, he may allow its energies and demands to deflect from all other possible activities, from social relations alto-

[17]Burr Snider, "Fat City," p. 182.

gether. Fatness becomes a justification for retreating from sociability.

> "See, when you're fat you don't have to take responsibility for anything but your fatness [according to a 350-pound man who has attended the Kempner Clinic for twelve years]. You don't have to go out and meet people and you don't have to take the chance of getting hurt that contact always poses. You can just stay in the dark and brood and fester. Nobody is particularly going to take the trouble to try to get to know a fat person. So the fat is a nice protection if you look at it that way. It's literally a nice thick wall insulating you from contact."[18]

But the sublimation of gluttony is not always so sad in its outcome. Consider the much-vaunted jolly fat man. To be sure, much of the argument behind the boasted joyfulness of the obese person is stereotype and misinformation. And many of the more oppressed members of the corpulent population bitterly denounce the situation in which they are expected to enliven every social gathering with their mirth and merriment. Yet much of the release from sin that comes to the glutton arises precisely from the fact that he is regarded as a harmless figure of fun, a cowardly lion of lovable proportions, a sinner who, although fallen from grace himself, nevertheless saves others by his insistence on bacchanalia and feast.

[18]Ibid., p. 174.

The Competitive Personality

by
C. Wright Mills

I

For liberals, competition has never been merely an impersonal mechanism regulating the economy of capitalism. It has been a guarantee of political freedom, a system for producing free individuals, and a testing field for heroes. These have been the alibis of the liberals for the hurt that competition has caused the people ground between the big sharp edges of its workings.

In every area of life, liberals have imagined independent individuals freely competing so that merit might win and character develop: in the free contractual marriage, the Protestant church, the voluntary association, the democratic state, as well as on the economic market. Competition is the way liberalism would integrate its historic era; it is also the central feature of liberalism's style of life.

The hero of liberalism has exemplified the ways of competition in every sphere of life, but it was in the economic sphere that his merit came out most clearly, and it was by virtue of his business career that he attained power and glory and even the legendary purity of which heroes are made.

As the worlds of monopoly spread out their grasp, the classic exemplar of liberalism, the old captain of industry, took on, at least in his cruder images, a somewhat bloated and overbearing shape. By the twentieth century he had been replaced in the business world by other types of economic men, among them the industrial rentier and the corporation executive, the little business and white-collar men, as well as a type we shall presently describe as the new entrepreneur. None of these have successfully filled the heroic place of the old, undivided captain of industry.

From *Power, Politics and People: The Collected Essays of C. Wright Mills*, edited by Irving Louis Horowitz. Copyright 1963 by the Estate of C. Wright Mills. Reprinted by permission of Oxford University Press, Inc.

The public image of the rentier is not that of a productively competitive man; he is either the stealthy miser or the lavish consumer. He doesn't live the business-wise life of competition, and even the liberal economists dislike his economic role. The corporation executive has never been a popular middle-class idol; he is too cold and high with impersonal power. On the engineering side, he is part of inexorable science, and no economic hero; and on the business side, he is correctly seen as part of the big finance.

It was the little man of business, with all his engaging human characteristics, who became the hero of liberalism in the early twentieth century. He has been seen as the somewhat woebegone inheritor of the old captain's tradition, even if only by default. The harder his struggle has become, the more sympathetic and the more heroized his image has been drawn; yet his plight has been a sad one, for he cannot live up to the heritage by which he is burdened.

The laws and planning of the Progressive Era, the muckraking, the square deals and new freedoms were, at least verbally, attempts to buck up the little businessman, that he might better live up to the carefully presented image of him. Much of the New Deal was dealt in his honor, lest he become a forgotten man. And in the decade after 1933, he became even more officially the hero of the liberal system; no less than 390 bills in his behalf were introduced for consideration by the Congress.

The Monographs and Hearings of the Temporary National Economic Committee are the last great scholarly and official monument to liberalism's little hero. Like other large attempts on behalf of things as they are imagined or hoped to be, the TNEC fetishizes competition and heroizes little business. But it does so under an enormous burden of fact. Only the necessary screen of political rhetoric, the peculiar structure of political representation, and the myopia induced by small-town life has kept this senatorial fetish and this heroic image alive. Now that the TNEC is well buried by war, we may treat it as a symbol,[1] having positive as well as negative references. For underneath its rhetoric and resting on its facts, we may dis-

[1]An excellent case study and partial summary of the Hearings has recently been written by David Lynch: *The Concentration of Economic Power*, Columbia University Press (New York, 1946). Some of the TNEC series have been brought up through the war in a publication of the Smaller War Plants: "Economic Concentration and World War II," U.S. Senate, 79th Congress, 2nd Session, Document No. 206 (Washington, 1946).

cern the present role of competition as well as some new
types of economic men and women, who are living a new
competitive life in the age of corporate bureaucracy.

What the million dollars' worth of TNEC facts demonstrate, no matter how they are arranged, is the detailed accuracy of Veblen's remark that competition is by no means
dead, only now it is chiefly "competition between the
businessman who controls production, on the one side, and
the consuming public, on the other side; the chief expedient
in this business-like competition being salesmanship and sabo-
tage." What the TNEC documents was already well supposed, but now the documentation is directly from the
mouths of the men who run things. In telling of the manner
in which competition has been hedged in by giant corporations, and by groups of smaller corporations acting collectively, they have made clear the locus of the big competition
and the masklike character of liberalism's rhetoric.

Yet for the benefit of their imaginary hero, the senators,
and their experts, have persisted in fetishizing this mask of
big business. They have proposed that the good old captains
of industry be given a rebirth with the full benefit of governmental midwifery.

Charles Beard has remarked that this proposal resembles
not a mouse creeping out of a mountain of fact but a mere
squeak. Yet it remains the best that the official liberal has to
say about the economic facts of life. In continuing to see
competition as salvation from complicated trouble, the priest-
like senators in charge of the ceremony naturally fall into the
old petty-bourgeois complaints; and the experts, perhaps for
the record, fall in with the senators. Now they are together in
the big volumes with their thin little wisdom. But their wisdom is nostalgic, and their offerings are dwarfed by the great
facts of the modern economy. Their mood ought to be the
mood of plight, but they have succeeded in setting up a
bright image of the little businessman, who could be rehabili-
tated as the hero of their system, if only competition were
once more to prevail.

II

This liberal hero, the little businessman, has a tendency to
forget the senatorial rhetoric put out in his behalf; he doesn't

seem to want to develop his character by free and open competition. Last year in six middle-sized cities, arbitrarily selected samples of little businessmen were asked if they thought "free competition was by and large a good thing." With authority and vehemence they all answered, Yes, of course, what do you mean? Then they were asked, "Here in this, your town?" Yes, they said, but now hesitating a little. Finally: How about here in this town in furniture, or groceries—or whatever the man's specific line was. Their answers were of two sorts: Yes, if it's fair competition, which turned out to mean something very simple and understandable: If it doesn't make me compete. The second type of answer also adds up to the brotherliness of the little businessmen, and their competitive opposition to the public: Well, you see, in certain lines, it's no good if there are too many businesses. You ought to kinda keep the other fellow's business in mind. The little businessman wants to become big, not by directly eating up the other fellow's business in competition, but by the indirect ways and means practiced by his own particular heroes—those already big. In the dream life of the little businessman, the sure fix is replacing the open market.

But if the little businessman is going back on his liberal spokesmen, he cannot really be blamed, for the liberal spokesmen, without knowing it, have also been going back on their little business hero. Only government, these spokesmen say, can save little business; they would *guarantee* by law the chances of the small business stratum. And if you guarantee a chance, it is no longer a chance; it is a sinecure. What this means is that all the private and public virtues that self-help, manly competition, and cupidity are supposed to foster would be denied the little businessman. The government would expropriate the very basis of political freedom and the flourishing of the free personality. If, as the chairman of the Smaller War Plants Corporation has said, "Democracy can only exist in a capitalistic system in which the life of the individual is controlled by supply and demand," then it is all over with democracy. However, the chairman adds, that to save capitalism, the government "must prevent small business from being shattered and destroyed." In the new way of salvation, inherited from the Progressive Era, the old faith in supply and demand is replaced by the hope of governmental aid and legalized comfort.

Big business doesn't have to compete and doesn't; little

business sometimes has to and always hates it; and all the while, liberal government is trying to ration out the main chance, thus helping to destroy the old meaning of competition as a style of life.

III

In the old style of life, the way up, according to the classic pattern of liberalism, was to establish a small business enterprise and to expand it by competition with other such enterprises. That was the economic cradle of the free personality and, given the equality of opportunity and of power that it assumed, the guarantee of political democracy. The new way up is the white-collar way: to get a job within a governmental or a business bureaucracy and to rise, according to the rules that prevail, from one prearranged step to another. For some 75 per cent of the urban middle class, the salaried employee component, this fate replaces heroic tactics on the open market.

Before each rung of the fixed ladders, the salaried employees may compete with one another, being in training for the next step; but their field of competition is too hedged in by bureaucratic regulation to give issue to the results expected from open competition across a free market. It is more likely to be seen as grubbing and backbiting: a bureaucracy is no testing field for heroes. The great, main chance of old becomes a series of small calculations, stretched out over the working lifetime of the individual. And these new middle classes are slowly beginning to give up their independence, in favor of a declaration of collective dependence: some 14 per cent of them are now in trade unions. They are beginning to dream of going up together, as members of modern businesslike unions.

This shift from business enterpriser to white-collar employee, along with the decline of the free farmer, is the master occupational change of twentieth-century social structure. It is a terrible blow at the old competitive life and at the personal and political consequences that the old pattern was supposed to have.

The white-collar man *enters* the public view as a tragic figure. He takes up where the little businessman ended; the powerless, little-man aspect engulfs whatever heroic features might be thought up for him. The white-collar people, it would seem, are not being heroized by the old middle class; indeed, they can only be heroized collectively, as they join unions or fight inflations or patiently live out their slow misery. As individuals, they are only insecure and tortured creatures, being pushed by forces or swallowed by movements that they do not understand, and that senators do not have to face. At the center of the picture is business bureaucracy with its trained managerial staff and its tamed white-collar mass. And it is within these structures of monopoly that the bulk of the middle-class men and women must make their prearranged ways.

IV

Yet, all this does not mean that the spirit of the old competition is entirely dead. There still remains an area where a type of go-gettem has found nourishment. If the agents of this new competition are not exactly the stuff of old-fashioned heroes, that is only because the conditions that prevail are so different; their initiative is being put to a harder test.

Against the unheroic backdrop of big business and the white-collar mass, within and between the bureaucratic patterns of success, a new type of entrepreneur has arisen. In contrast to the classic little businessman, who operated in a world opening up like a row of oysters under steam, the new entrepreneur must operate in a world in which all the pearls have already been grabbed up and are carefully guarded.

The only manner by which the new entrepreneur can express his initiative is by servicing the powers that be, in the hope of getting his cut. And he serves them by "fixing things," between one big business and another, between big business and government, and between business as a whole and the public. He gets ahead because men in power do not expect that things can be done legitimately, because these men know fear, because their spheres of operation are broader than their capacities to observe, and because they are personally not very bright.

As a competitor, the new entrepreneur is an agent of the bureaucracies he serves, and what he competes for is the good will and favor of those who run the business system. His chance exists because there are several of these bureaucracies, private and public, having complicated entanglements with one another and with the public. Unlike the little white-collar man, he does not often stay within any one corporate bureaucracy; his path zig-zags within and between bureaucracies, and he has made a well-worn path between big business and the regulatory agencies of the federal government.

He is a live wire, full of American know-how, and if he does not invest capital, his success is all the greater measure of his inherent worth, for this means that he is genuinely creative. Like the more heroic businessmen of old, he manages to get something for very little or nothing.

The new entrepreneur is very much at home in the "business services," in which bracket fall the commercial researcher and the public relations man, the advertising agencies, the labor relations expert, and the mass communication and entertainment industries. For the bright, young, educated man, these fields offer limitless opportunities, if he only has the initiative and the know-how, and if only the anxieties of the bureaucratic chieftains hold up.

The power of the old captain of industry rested, it is said, upon his engineering ability and upon his financial sharp dealing. The power of the present-day chieftain rests upon his control of the wealth piled up by the old captain and increased by a rational system of guaranteed tributes. The power of the new entrepreneur rests upon his personality and upon his skill in using it to manipulate the anxieties of the chieftain.

Now the concentration of power has modified the character and the larger meaning of competition. The competition in which these new entrepreneurs engage is not so much a competition for markets of commodities or services: it is a bright, anxious competition for the good will of the chieftain by means of personality. The "supply and demand" of the impersonal market does not decide the success or failure of the new entrepreneur; his success is decided by the personal decisions of intimately known chieftains of monopoly.

The new entrepreneur has this in common with the ordinary white-collar worker: the careers of both are administered by powerful others. The difference is that the toadying of the white-collar employee is small scale and unimaginative; he makes up the stable corps of the bureaucracy, and initiative is regimented out of his life. The new ulcered entrepreneur, running like Sammy, operates on the twin-faced edges of the several bureaucracies. He comes to the immediate attention of the men who make the big decisions as he services their fears and eagerly encourages their anxious whims.

Part of the frenzy of the new entrepreneur is due to the fact that in his life there are no objective criteria of success. For such types, the last criteria are the indefinite good will of the chieftains and the shifting symbols of status. Part of his frenzy may also be due to his apprehension that his function may disappear. For many of the jobs he has been doing for the chieftains are now a standardized part of business enterprise and no longer require the entrepreneurial flair, but can be performed by the cheaper and more dependable white-collar man. Besides, the new entrepreneur, with his lavish expense account, sometimes gets into the public eye as a fixer—along with the respectable businessman whose work he does—and even as an upstart and a crook. The same publics that idolize initiative become incensed when they find a grand model of success based, quite purely, upon it.

We may view the true scene of the new entrepreneur's operation as the personality market. Like the commodity market before it, the top levels of this market may well become an object to be administered rather than a play of free forces driven by crafty wile and unexampled initiative. Indeed, the new shape competition may take in this last remaining competitive market can already be seen. Its human meaning is displayed lower down the hierarchy, where bureaucratized business meets the public.

V

At this intersection, personality markets of a more stabilized sort have arisen. Three immediate conditions are needed: First, an employee must be part of a bureaucratic enterprise, in which his work is supervised by an authority over him. Second, it must be his regular business to contact a public from within this bureaucracy; he is thus the bearer of the firm's good name before anyone who cares to show up. Third, the public which he contacts must be anonymous, a mass of urban strangers.

One of the biggest of the several personality markets that may be isolated for study involves the salesperson in the metropolitan department store. Unlike the small independent merchant, the salesperson cannot haggle over prices. Prices are fixed by other employees of the bureaucracy. She cannot form her character by buying cheaply and selling wisely. Experts fix the market price; specialists buy the commodities which she is to sell. She cannot form her character by the promotional calculations and self-management of the classic heroes of liberalism or of the new entrepreneurs. There is only one area of her occupational life in which she is "free to act." That is the area of her own personality. She must make of her personality an alert, obsequious instrument whereby goods are distributed.

The white-collar worker, like the wage worker in a modern factory, is alienated from the tools and products of her labor; indeed, she does not even mix labor with raw stuff to produce things. The white-collar worker on a personality market must not only sell her time and energy; she must also "sell herself." In the normal course of her work, she becomes self-alienated. For, in the personality market, the personality itself, along with advertising, becomes the instrument of an alien purpose.

If there are not too many plant psychologists or personnel experts around, the factory worker is free to frown as he works. But not so the white-collar employee. She must put her personality into it. She must smile when it is the time to smile. An interviewer, working in the biggest store in the world, recently observed one of her experienced sales colleagues: "I have been watching her for three days now. She wears a fixed smile on her made-up face, and it never varies, no matter to whom she speaks. I never heard her laugh spontaneously or naturally. Either she is frowning or her face is devoid of any expression. When a customer approaches she immediately assumes her hard, forced smile. It amazes me because although I know that the smiles of most salesgirls are unreal, I've never seen such calculation given to the timing of a smile. I myself tried to copy such an expression, but I am unable to keep such a smile on my face if it is not sincerely and genuinely motivated."

In this market the human expressions are no longer expressions of private aspirations. For all the features of the character, especially the familial ones—the kindly gesture, tact, courtesy, the smile—now become expressions of the company's aspirations. They are the salaried mask of the individual, available by the week, designed to advance the competitive position of the store with the public. Year after year they are enforced by the store's bureaucratic discipline, including the "professional shopper" who reports to the personnel department. In due course, this life of alienation sets up its own traits in the personality, selected, constructed, and used as instruments in the competitive struggle of the employees within the store, and between the store and the consuming public. Such is the creative function of the new competition.

Yet the personality market, in one sense, is still subject to the old laws of supply and demand. When a "seller's market" exists and labor is hard to buy, the well-earned aggressions of the salespeople come out and jeopardize the good will of the buying public. When there is a "buyer's market" and jobs are hard to get, the salespeople must repress again and practice politeness. Thus the laws of supply and demand, as in an older epoch of capitalism, continue to regulate the intimate life-fate of the individual and the kind of personality that may be developed and displayed.

The old competition is dead, even if the old liberal alibis for it are now incarnate as fetishes. But new kinds of competition, making new kinds of people, have arisen.

Near the top of the new hierarchy are the new entrepreneurs, the bureaucratic fixers and the business experts; and at the bottom are the people on the personality markets. Somewhere in between, the little businessman struggles to gain the stable security of big business by having his tribute also guaranteed, and yet, in the *name* of competition, hoping somehow for the main chance.

Both of the newer types serve the bureaucracies, and both, in their own way, practice the creative art of selling. In a restricted market economy, salesmanship is truly praised as a creative act, but it is entirely too serious a matter to be trusted to mere creativity. The more alert chieftains are becoming aware of this. The really great opportunities for expropriation are in the field of the human personality itself. The fate of competition, and the character it will assume, depends upon the success or failure of the adventures of monopolists in this field.

The Obnoxious and the Nice

by
Murray S. Davis and
Catherine J. Schmidt

Sociology has continually been accused of not dealing with the texture of human life. Although it is not necessary for every science to be relevant, a science purporting to study society in its totality must include at least some concepts its members recognize as delineating important aspects of their world.

One set of sociological concepts many people deem too gross and distant from their lived experience are those for the social subgroups with whom they interact. They find little use for concepts like class, race, religion, age, and sex—the most commonly used sociological terms for categorizing people. At best, they apply these concepts to determine whether and how to initiate interaction with a stranger. But if their relation with the stranger becomes an ongoing one, his class, race, religion, age, and sex fade phenomenologically from their attention while his other attributes come to the fore. Since these other attributes are the most important determinants of interaction between acquaintances, and since acquaintances usually interact with greater frequency and intensity than strangers do, more refined concepts to categorize the social subgroups of these higher intimates are urgently needed.

Beyond the macrocategories of social structure listed above, there lie microcategories of social interactants. In the sociological literature the categorization of social interactants falls under the study of social types. Relative to other areas of sociological inquiry, this is a skimpy literature indeed.[1]

Reprinted from *Sociometry*, Vol. 40, No. 3, 1977, pp. 201–213, with permission of the American Sociological Association and the authors.

[1]According to their respective indexes, there were only six articles on types or typologies in the *American Sociological Review* (1936–1965) and only seven in the *American Journal of Sociology* (1895–1970). Four of these thirteen articles were by Orrin Klapp. Most of the rest concerned either typologies of nonhuman phenomena (like norms) or

Moreover, the most important investigators of social types—Simmel (the stranger, the miser, and the spendthrift), Thomas (the intellectual, the bohemian, and the philistine), Schutz (the stranger and the homecomer), and Orrin Klapp (heros, villains, and fools)—have focused on those most people experience infrequently. Those previously investigated social types appear only in extreme situations, not in everyday life.

Of the many types commonly encountered in everyday life, in this article we will investigate two: the obnoxious and the nice. The mid 1970's saw increased social recognition of these types in such popular television programs as *All in the Family* and *Maude* (obnoxious) as well as *The Waltons* and *The Mary Tyler Moore Show* (nice).

At first glance it seems that obnoxiousness and niceness are personality rather than social characteristics and hence characterize psychological rather than sociological types. But this distinction is blurred by the fact that no one can be obnoxious or nice alone—unlike more purely psychological types (melancholics, phlegmatics, neurotics, schizophrenics, etc.) which can exist by themselves. (Apparently solitary obnoxious or nice behavior—like leaving or cleaning up a mess—actually implies awareness of indirect interaction with others who will curse or praise it afterwards.) Thus what seemed solely personality traits are now seen manifested only in social interaction. Since it is more accurate to consider psychological and sociological types not as qualitatively distinct but rather as two ends of a continuum, we propose that both types be replaced by the more general classification of *social psychological type,* broadening the range of human types sociologists can investigate and emphasizing typing's effect on both self-conception and social behavior. Through this new concept, typing theory converges with labeling theory.

Our discussion of the obnoxious and the nice is based on our participant and nonparticipant observation of social behavior on the east coast, west coast, and midwest in academic and nonacademic settings; and on formal and informal inter-

---

theoretical discussions about the nature of typologies. Undoubtedly, types appear in many more articles, but the failure to index them as such makes them difficult to retrieve and indicates that those who compile indexes no longer believe "type" to be an important sociological tool. Although one of the first articles in *AJS* (Ross: 1896) dealt with types, interest in social types *per se*, relative to social settings and social processes, has declined markedly since.

views with those who said in effect that they regarded someone as obnoxious or nice. Quotations in parentheses are
typical.

I. OBNOXIOUS AND NICE BEHAVIORS

The Attack on the Individual's Self. Others consider a person's behavior *obnoxious* if it implies he is trying to impose
on them a self they do not want. They consider his behavior
nice if it implies he is allowing them to impose on him a self
he wants.[2] Both obnoxious and nice behaviors are "self-sacri-
ficing" behaviors; but the person who behaves obnoxiously
sacrifices others' selves whereas the person who behaves
nicely sacrifices his own.

Should a person impose one of his concrete self-embodi-
ments into the personal space delineated by the sense organs
of unwilling others, they will consider his behavior obnoxious.
Should he willingly allow them to impose theirs into his own
personal space, they will consider his behavior nice. In our
society there are several aspects of the body (and hence of
the self in one of its concrete forms) that can impose upon
the several sensory spaces.

One person's appearance may intrude upon others' visual

---

[2]Whether others interpret a particular behavior as obnoxious or nice
depends not only on this quality of the behavior but also on such characteristics of its context as: (a) *Cultural and historical environment*:
At all times and places obnoxious or nice behavior involves self-imposition, but the particular aspect of the self being imposed or imposed
upon varies with the society and times. (b) *Group background*: When
the behavior of everyone in a group is obnoxious or nice, the behavior
of no one in the group is interpreted as especially obnoxious or nice.
(c) *Performer's social category, especially age and sex*: Some social
categories are allowed or required to perform more self-imposing behaviors than others. The same behavior (e.g., breaking into a conversation) considered acceptable for the adult is often considered obnoxious
for the child. A man who refrains from imposing his self is considered
nice whereas a woman who imposes hers is considered obnoxious—at
least until recently. (d) *Performance's setting*: It is difficult for a performer intentionally to convince his audience to interpret any of his
behaviors as nice in some settings, like a riot or a war. It is easy for
him inadvertently to convince them to misinterpret many of his behaviors as obnoxious in other settings, like a funeral or a concert. (e) *Audience's mood*: In a bad mood, a person feels others are behaving
obnoxiously by trying to impose unwanted selves on him; in a good
mood, the same person feels they are behaving nicely by trying to ac-
commodate his own self-impositions.

space. His voice may intrude upon their auditory space. His physical bulk may intrude upon their proxemic space. His smell (including breath, body, and smoke) may intrude upon their olfactory space. Finally, his limbs or body may intrude upon their tactile space. (For a more extensive discussion of "the territories of the self," see Goffman, 1972:28–61.)

If a person is overly ugly, loud, fat, stinking, or grabby,[8] he is likely to be considered obnoxious unless he compensates for his particular intrusion on others by allowing them to intrude on him. For example, a fat person often compensates for his physical bulk by being "jolly," allowing others to intrude on his social self (see below) so they will ignore his intruding on their physical selves.

Linguistic usage confirms that most people regard these physically intrusive behaviors as obnoxious. For instance, they are less likely to describe someone as "beautiful and obnoxious" or "noisy and nice" than as "beautiful but obnoxious" or "noisy but nice." (For discussion of this in terms of attribution and consistency theory, see Heider, 1958.)

Just as bodies may intrude into others' sensory space, so objects may intrude into their property space. A person may feel that those parking *their* cars on *his* property are behaving obnoxiously but that those allowing him to park *his* car on *their* property are behaving nicely.

Someone can also cohere his self around one of his social roles. He may then impose a social role, and hence a social self, on others through an activity which Weinstein and Deutschberger (1963) call "altercasting." It is considered obnoxious for someone to impose on others a social self they do not wish to have. Conversely, it is considered nice for someone willingly to accept the social self others are trying to impose on him. One person often imposes a social self on another to transform his own self into its role reciprocal. For instance, whoever tells another to "get me a glass of water" implies that since the other is his servant, he must be a master. Obnoxious self-impositions are usually relatively low status, like ignoramus or stooge, demonstrating that the imposer is relatively high status, like cognoscente or comedian.

[8]There are two kinds of intrusions into tactile space a person may consider obnoxious: the mock friendly, and the mock hostile. "Making a pass" or "copping a feel" imply too much intimacy; "jabbing" and "goosing" imply too little. Obnoxious tactile intrusions are abrupt and pointed, like a "grab"; nonobnoxious ones are slow and diffuse, like a "caress." Anyone overly sensitive to tactile (and, by extension, other) intrusions is called "touchy."

Actually, one can experience any self-imposition, even a high-status role, as obnoxious if he feels manipulated ("Only intelligent people like yourself can appreciate this article.").

Self-imposition, both physical and social, can be a painful experience. Physical self-imposition overloads the sense receptors, especially those of the sensitive. Social self-imposition undermines the self-conception, especially that of the unself-confident. In fact, the term "obnoxious" itself is derived from the Latin root meaning "hurt" or "harm."

If obnoxious behavior shows a person is "disrespectful" of others' selves, nice behavior shows he is "respectful" of them. He will refrain from intruding on them and "apologize"—i.e., separate himself from his behavior—if he must ("I'm sorry I threw up on you. I couldn't help it."), and he will disregard, withstand, or minimize others' intrusions on his own self ("That's all right. It doesn't matter.")

A person may behave obnoxiously by evaluating old social selves negatively as well as by imposing new, low-status ones. He can lower another's status directly by being "critical": accusing him of possessing the same kind of self as members of a low-status group ("You're an idiot!"), or of associating with members of a low-status group ("Your girl friend must be a fool!"), or of acting like members of a low-status group ("I thought that book you're reading was intended for children!"). He can also lower another's status indirectly by "boastfully" upping his own: claiming the same kind of self as members of a high-status group ("I'm a genius!") or association with members of a high-status group ("My girl friend's a real intellectual!") or actions performed only by members of a high-status group ("It took me four hours and seventeen minutes to finish speed-reading my encyclopedia last night!"). On the other hand, a person may behave nicely by evaluating the selves of others positively: raising another's status directly by praising him, his associates, or his activities ("compliments"); or indirectly by humbly lowering his own ("modesty").

Obnoxious evaluatory behavior also involves expanding a criticism from one aspect of a person to the person as a whole as well as denying him the opportunity to put forward an "account" (Lyman and Scott, 1968) for his criticized action ("You've always done that! I don't want to hear any of your excuses!"). Nice evaluatory behavior also involves reducing a criticism's potential for applying to the person as a whole down to one of his inessential aspects, and putting forward an account for his misdeeds even before he need put one forward for himself ("It wasn't your fault. You couldn't help it.").

It is seen as obnoxious to publicize a person's temporary loss of status, maximizing its effects on him (for instance, by loudly complaining or facetiously applauding when a waitress spills food on a customer: "Look what you've done! My dress is ruined!"); it is seen as nice to conceal a person's temporary loss of status, minimizing its effect on him ("That's all right. No problem. It'll easily wash out.").

People find it obnoxious for someone to receive too little input from others as well as transmitting to much output to them. Whether the human faculty to receive input from others is called "verstehen" (Weber, 1947), "reciprocity of perspectives" (Schutz, 1962), "taking the role of the other" (Mead, 1934), or "reflexivity" (Garfinkle, 1967: Cicourel, 1973), its manifest lack is considered obnoxious.[4] If obnoxious behavior indicates atrophy of this receptive faculty, nice behavior indicates hypertrophy. Whoever behaves obnoxiously evinces ignorance of his interaction partners and indifference to their needs ("thoughtless"), whoever behaves nicely evinces interest in them and concern for their needs ("considerate").

A person may behave obnoxiously not only by imposing a self on others, but also by not allowing them to impose their selves back on him ("impoliteness"). One way he can negate their feedback is simply not to allow them to say anything. If it is considered normative to talk in "turns" (Goffman, 1972: 3–4n), it is considered obnoxious to "corner the turn": monopolizing the conversation through monologing long-windedly, increasing speed and volume and emotion as others try to take the floor, interrupting those just gaining the floor, and not paying attention to whoever finally holds the floor. (Especially obnoxious is manifest inattentativeness consisting of distracting side involvements, like looking out the window, shuffling papers, or even dozing off.) Another way he can negate their feedback is to give them no resources to say anything: dismissing their point of view while approaching the topic from scratch and speaking about it with finality ("What

[4]Previously, those treating this human faculty for receiving input from others have regarded it as universal. Universal it may be in all but the autistic; however, human beings are able to empathize with each other in different degrees, accounting for the ease of some interactions, the difficulty of others.

you've been saying is completely ridiculous! Let me tell you how it really is: . . .").

Conversely, a person may behave nicely by going out of his way to allow others to impose a self on him. He can accentuate their feedback by giving them more than equal opportunity to maintain the floor ("You go first."), by lowering his speed and volume and emotion whenever they raise theirs even slightly, by repressing his own contribution until they finish, and by encouraging them to continue through attention and agreement. (Especially nice is manifest attentiveness consisting of reinforcing main involvements, like eye contact, nods, and smiles.) He can also accentuate their feedback by giving them abundant resources for response: seeming to affirm their perspectives (even if disagreeing), to build on their assertions (even if not actually doing so), and to speak with tentativeness ("That's right! And furthermore . . . , though I'm not really sure about this. What do you think?").

People consider it obnoxious to ignore or distort negative feedback; nice to be sensitive to verbalized or, especially, nonverbalized criticism. They feel someone behaves obnoxiously when he is too "dense" to notice their nonverbal indications of disapproval (frowns, head shaking, etc.), forcing escalation to verbalized critiques, though even then he may not "get the point" that he should correct his shortcomings. On the other hand, the more subtle the critical cues to which someone responds, the nicer his behavior is regarded.

Microsocial control is manifested in the frowns of friends and admonitions of acquaintances. A person's interaction partners find obnoxious his failure to receive their negative feedback because his rigidity decreases their freedom, thus increasing their stress while interfering with the smooth oscillation of the interaction. Conversely, they find nice a person's sensitivity to their negative feedback because his flexibility increases their freedom, thus decreasing their stress while facilitating the smooth oscillation of the interaction.

In brief, if the best analogy for obnoxious behavior is garlic (which overpowers other foods' flavors), the best analogy for nice behavior is monosodium glutamate [Accent] (which accentuates other foods' flavors but is itself flavorless).

The Attack on the Group's Ethos. The group's ethos is similar to the individual's self in that both are vulnerable to disruption and both must be supported when threatened. Beyond any attack on members' particular selves, obnoxious behavior can attack their group's general ethos. Moreover, since the group ethos sustains a portion of its members' selves, should it break down, part of their selves collapse along with it, giving them a self interest to support their group's ethos.

It is considered obnoxious to impose one's physical presence on the group ethos, e.g., by entering a theater or a lecture noisily, especially after the performance that generates the ethos has begun. Conversely, it is considered nice to go out of one's way to refrain from doing so, e.g., by sitting in the back or literally tiptoeing to one's seat if one must arrive late.

Members who generated the group's original ethos feel that those trying to impose a new one are behaving obnoxiously (e.g., radicals who try to take over their meetings). Conversely, members feel that those actively helping generate the group ethos they want are behaving nicely (e.g., chairmen who try to obtain a consensus on how their meeting should proceed).

Members who have helped generate a group's ethos regard as obnoxious any behavior that evaluates it negatively—"booing" the group activities in general or "heckling" the group spokespersons in particular. They also consider manifest inattentiveness, like reading a joke book at a religious revival, obnoxious because it calls attention to oneself, away from the ethos. They regard as nice any behavior that evaluates their ethos positively—"applause" for the group activities or what may be called "negative heckling" ("Right on!" "You tell 'em, brother!" "Amen!") for the group spokespersons. They also consider it nice for someone to appear to "lose himself" in the spirit of the occasion.

When something goes wrong in the process of generating a group ethos, obnoxious behavior maximizes the devastation, nice behavior minimizes it. For example, when a popular colloquium presenter is having difficulty sustaining his desired definition of the situation, members of his audience will regard it as obnoxious to press him with difficult questions but nice to ask him easy ones or to try themselves to answer the tough ones others put to him. Those rescuing him sustain the group's shaky ethos and, through it, their own and everyone else's selves.

Finally, members feel it is doubly obnoxious for someone not only to threaten their group's ethos but also to ignore their warnings that he is doing so. At a popular play or lecture, the audience censures the noisy by shuffling, shushing, hissing, laughing, and groaning (in roughly that order) both for their noise and for their disregard of previous reproofs. On the other hand, they consider it nice for someone to show sensitivity to their feedback: quieting down as soon as they begin to rustle in their seats.

On the group level as well as individual level, people regard as obnoxious *behavioral invariants,* who act the same regardless of their interaction partners; and regard as nice *behavioral chameleons,* who adapt completely to each of them. Thus they criticize the "Ugly American" for maintaining his old style in a new culture whereas they praise those who "in Rome do as the Romans do" for adapting to new cultural patterns.

II. OBNOXIOUS AND NICE TYPES

Typing. Occasionally everyone engages in obnoxious or nice behavior,[5] but some get typed as obnoxious or nice persons. The transition from "doing" or "being" is too complex a question to consider here. Labeling theorists have discussed it at length, although usually confining themselves to those cases for which they can easily determine the tipping point— the point at which someone engaged in certain behaviors (breaking windows) comes into contact with an institution (courts, mental hospitals) which records him as a specific type of person (juvenile delinquent, schizophrenic). (But see Goffman, 1961: 127–169, for the more minor transition points in this institutionalizing "funnel.")

For those whose deviant interactions do not bring them into contact with certifying institutions, however, the precise mechanism of the transition from behavior to being is less clear. It seems, however, to involve a three-step process. First, a *particular behavior* becomes generalized to a person's *typical behavior* if he performs it in many situations ("What can you expect from him?"). Second, a *particular person* becomes generalized to a *particular type of person* if he performs one kind of behavior to the relative exclusion of other kinds ("He's just that kind of person."). Finally, a *particular typification* of the person becomes generalized to a *typical*

---

[5]The nebulous notion of "mood" influences how a person behaves as well how he perceives others' behavior. In a bad mood a person is more likely to impose his self on others obnoxiously; in a good mood the same person is more likely to accept others' self-impositions nicely.

typification of the person if his associate who first made the typification can convince all the rest of his associates of its appropriateness. In this way, an indexical (situated) behavior[6] is transformed through a psychic synechdoche (essential characterization)[7] into a transsituational, transbehavioral social-psychological type of person.

A person may or may not be aware of the way others are typing him (Klapp, 1962: 11–12). Those unaware of how others type them can do nothing about their typification. Such shortsightedness is especially critical for those typed as obnoxious. They are most likely to want to change their low-status characterization but least likely to discover it because of their insensitivity to feedback. (Those unaware of being typed as obnoxious are the opposite of those unaware of being typed as paranoid: the paranoid thinks others are persecuting him but they are not; the obnoxious thinks he is not persecuting others but he is.)

A person may or may not intend for others to type him in a certain way. Although most people in our society would prefer to be characterized as nice, a few would prefer to be known as obnoxious. The motto of the intentionally obnoxious characters of Celine, Genet, and Donleavy, for instance, seems to be "the meanness justifies the end." Some, like Norman Mailer, have even built careers out of being professionally obnoxious; others, like Dick Cavett, have built careers

---

[6]Indexical behaviors are those drawing their meaning only from the situation in which they occur (Garfinkle, 1967; Cicourel, 1973). Indexicality fades as typicality forms. Thus, from the phenomenological point of view, the indexical is a less useful concept than the typical. An individual is more likely to perceive his social world as a collection of typical situations than as a collection of particular situations. Indexicality exists only retrospectively as a *break-down concept*, coming to consciousness only when an individual is forced to analyze how he constructed a general type. The dispute over the relative significance of indexicality and typicality is one of the central issues between ethnomethodology and phenomenology.

[7]A psychic synechdoche is the characterization of a person as a whole by one of his attributes (see Simmel, 1950:58; Davis, 1973:170). Here a psychic synechdoche occurs whenever a person who behaves obnoxiously or nicely is characterized as an obnoxious or nice person. Note that the psychic synechdoche by which others characterize a person need not be the same one by which he characterizes himself. In keeping with the social psychological framework of this article, perhaps "socio-psychic synechdoche" would be a better term since it emphasizes both kinds of characterizers and characteristics: either a person or his social group can characterize himself as a whole by either his psychological or his social attributes.

out of being professionally nice. The intentionally obnoxious differ from the intentionally nice in where they locate a person's true self. The intentionally obnoxious try to undermine and break down a person's presented image because they believe he is most himself when his presented image is forced to fall off. The intentionally nice try to uphold and elaborate a person's presented image because they believe he is most himself when his presented image is allowed to unfold.

The extremity of one's behavior also affects how others type him. A person whose obnoxious behavior is extreme is as likely to be typed as mentally ill as to be typed as obnoxious, especially in our psychoanalytic age ("He's not just a bastard, he's really a psychotic."). A person who behaves extremely nicely may likewise be considered *pathologically nice*, especially if he continues to act against his own interests in order to acquiesce to others' self-impositions (see Laing, 1965). Others often regard an extremely obnoxious person as a sort of *situicidal maniac*, one whose mere presence in a social situation automatically seems to kill it; whereas they often regard an extremely nice person as a sort of *situational catatonic*, one who will remain in the social role or position others put him in just as many institutionalized catatonics remain in the physical stances or positions others place them in. (Anyone whose behavior fluctuates between extremely obnoxious and extremely nice is also likely to be typed as mentally ill rather than as obnoxious or nice. Like the normal person, his average behavior is neutral; unlike him, his distribution of behavior is an inverted curve.) On the normal–deviant continuum for social interactants, then, the obnoxious and (some say) the nice are the last extreme social psychological types before the mentally ill.

Post Typing. Those who type a person begin to interact with him in a new way. Before others type someone as an obnoxious person, they tried to challenge and correct his behavior. After they type him, however, they will give up trying to change him and will begin to treat him as a representative of an unattractive social psychological type—informally avoiding him, formally excluding him, and, if they can do neither, putting up with him (i.e., with his unwanted self-impositions).[8] Before typing someone as a nice person, others were

[8]The way Lemert (1962:8) suggests others interact with someone typed as paranoid is similar to the way others interact with someone typed as obnoxious: ". . . once perceptual reorientation takes place . . . interaction changes qualitatively . . . it becomes *spurious*, distinguished by patronizing, evasion, 'humoring,' guiding conversation

pleasantly surprised at his willingness to accept their self-impositions and rewarded him for each instance of nice behavior. After typing him, however, they will begin to treat him as a representative of an attractive social psychological type, often seeking him out for interaction; but they may also begin to take his niceness for granted, cease to reward him for it, and perhaps try to see how undesirable a self they can impose on him before he will no longer put up with it.

After others type a person, they will try to keep him true to type. Not only will they ritually elicit expected responses from him, they will disregard occasional occurrences of unexpected responses. They will dismiss a few obnoxious behaviors by someone typed as nice, considering him merely in a "bad mood." They will dismiss a few nice behaviors by someone typed as obnoxious, considering him merely in a "good mood." In short, they will try to retain the continuity of their typification even at the cost of losing the accuracy of their perception. If he continues to engage in behaviors anomolous to his type, however, they will be unable to maintain their typification of him. It will suddenly occur to them that he must have undergone a *transformative experience,* forcing them to retype him, though not necessarily in the opposite way. A person typed as nice who abruptly begins to behave obnoxiously will be retyped as "disturbed," "physically ill," "mentally ill," or even as "possessed" (as in *The Exorcist*). (Obnoxious people are seldom recategorized as possessed. Few would notice the difference.) A person typed as obnoxious who abruptly begins to behave nicely will be retyped as a "convert," as someone who "got religion" or "got mental health" overnight and who now "repents" for his past interactional sins or "accepts" his past personality problems (like Charles Colson, the government official who would have run over his grandmother to help Nixon before he ran into Jesus).

III. MICRO-TYPES AND MACRO-STRUCTURE

Stratification. Distinct from the macrostratification system in society based on class, status, and power, there is a micro-

into selected topics, underreaction, and silence, all calculated either to prevent intense interaction or to protect individual and group values by restricting access to them."

stratification system in groups based on interactive competence, physical attractiveness, and intelligence. Since those of relatively equal macrostatus tend to associate with one another, they make finer distinctions among themselves on the microstatus dimensions (often considering the latter even more significant than the former).

The most important of these microstratificational dimensions is interactive competence. On this *suaveness dimension,* the obnoxious rank near the bottom since others find them— literally—a pain to interact with; the nice always rank above the obnoxious since others usually find interaction with them a pleasure.

The relative status of the obnoxious and the nice in the group is often reversed in the society because the same personality trait that makes for obnoxiousness on the micro-level also makes for mobility on the macro-level. In those occupations where status is determined by individual achievement rather than by group acceptability, the more aggressive, imposing nature of the obnoxious will cause them to rise while the more passive, imposed-upon nature of the nice will cause them to fall. The obnoxious "don't let anyone stand in their way" whereas "nice guys finish last." The obnoxious can devote themselves primarily to work activities that produce mobility while the nice become bogged down in work chores that do not lead to advancement. In the academy, for instance, there are good reasons why "S.O.B.'s" seem to get more PhD's. Obnoxious faculty members who are "slave drivers" to their research assistants, "unprepared teachers" to their undergraduates, and "bad citizens" to their departments are rewarded with fewer students to talk to, fewer letters of recommendations to write, fewer committees to serve on, and fewer collegial papers to read—allowing them to devote more of their time and energy to such mobility-producing activities as research and publishing. Nice faculty members, however, are "exploited" by being assigned these nonmobility-producing, time- and energy-consuming tasks, which no one else will take but which they will not refuse. As far as macro-stratification is concerned, some people are "too nice for their own good."

Self-imposing, intrusive behavior is regarded as a "right" for those occupying high-status positions (e.g., a superior will not be considered obnoxious merely for telling his subordinates what to do). Conversely, those occupying low-status positions have the "duty" to allow their superiors to intrude and impose a self on them (e.g., a subordinate will not be considered nice merely for being compliant to his superior's dictates). Some desire high status because it allows them to get away with being obnoxious; others fear low status because it forces them to be nice too often to too many.

Members of rising low-status groups—Blacks, Jews, women, homosexuals—are often felt to behave obnoxiously by those who believe their actions claim higher status than they deserve. Conversely, members of falling high-status groups—Chekhov's nineteenth-century Russian aristocrats, Tennessee Williams' twentieth-century Southern aristocrats— are often portrayed as behaving with extreme nicety, perhaps because they fear their status claims are now too weak to sustain challenge. *Streetcar Named Desire* provides one of the best examples of the contact between a rising class (represented by brutish, demanding, earthy—and notably obnoxious— Stanley Kowalski) and a falling class (represented by delicate, acquiescent, artificial—and excessively nice— Blanche Dubois).

Integration. The effect of the obnoxious on the integration of groups is contradictory. On the one hand, his attack on the group ethos or members' selves may disrupt unity by forcing others to behave obnoxiously themselves—grabbing the floor, escalating their emotion, attacking not only the person who started it all but each other as well. The arrival of the obnoxious may reduce even the most cohesive collectivity to a micro-Hobbesian anarchy in which everyone is looking out for himself. On the other hand, his attack may intensify group unity. Instead of turning on each other, members may overcome their minor differences and turn, as a group, against him. Here, his seemingly disintegrative behavior actually integrates the group: present, he serves as a common focus of attention and purpose; absent, as one of conversation and concern.[9]

The nice, of course, integrate the group by absorbing its tensions, especially those created by the obnoxious. Unless some tensions are available for the nice to absorb, however, their receptive, acquiescent behavior may itself become disruptive of group unity—as any teacher of uninterested

---

[9]More institutionalized groups have even differentiated the social role of "bouncer" to deal with the disruptions of the obnoxious. By ejecting the group's irritant, the bouncer supports and strengthens the group's unity.

students discovers when he relinquishes his dominant lecturer role in favor of democratic group discussion.

The obnoxious who produce tension and the nice who consume tension generate one of the group's most important dynamic processes. (The movement of tensions from one place or part to another is the source of vitality in all organic and social units.) In the group the obnoxious and the nice confront each other like two teams—the one maximizing stress, the other minimizing it.[10] (Cf. the task and socioemotional group leaders discovered by Bales, 1953.) Although individually the active imposing obnoxious are more powerful than the passive imposed-upon nice, their relative power is usually balanced because the obnoxious dissipate their energy by fighting among themselves while the nice concentrate their energy by supporting one another. Self-imposers usually disagree about what selves to impose; self-imposees usually agree to acquiesce to whatever dominant selves are available. In this sense, nice people are all alike, but every obnoxious person is obnoxious in his own way (*pace* Tolstoy).

The ratio of the tension-producing obnoxious to the tension-consuming nice determines that elusive quality called "group tone." Too many stressers and too few relaxers give the group a *bad* tone. Too few stressers and too many relaxers, however, give the group not a *good* tone but a *boring* tone. A *good* group tone is given by a balance between the obnoxious stressers and the nice relaxers—though the difference in tone between a few extreme types and many moderate types remains to be explored.

Sometimes, strangely enough, groups encourage obnoxious behavior among their members both to indicate and to cause their integration. Victory celebrations, New Year's Eve parties, and car-honking wedding caravans obnoxiously impose group loudness on the auditory space of everyone in their vicinity.[11]

---

[10]It may be fruitful to develop a microsociology of literature analyzing the dynamics of novels or stories into those characters whose obnoxious behaviors create tensions and those characters whose nice behaviors absorb tensions. For example, much of the plot of Dostoyevski's *The Brothers Karamazov* is generated by Fyodor and Dmitri's obnoxious behaviors, which create the tensions that Alyosha's nice behaviors partially relax. And much of the action in Albee's *Who's Afraid of Virginia Woolf* is generated by George and Martha's obnoxious insults, which create the tensions that Nick and Honey's nice remarks unsuccessfully slacken.

[11]Our society has even developed a *technology of obnoxiousness* for these occasions. Horns and noisemakers are designed solely to enhance

The duty to be obnoxious to their communities is a fundamental article in the constitution of some groups. Motorcycle gangs, extremist political groups, fundamentalist religious sects, nineteenth-century Western outlaw bands, and early twentieth-century temperance groups all intend to attack their communities' ethos (though often strengthening it inadvertently by uniting other members against them—a common theme in Westerns). The charter of other groups—like Newcomer Clubs, Scout Troops, and Volunteer Associations—obliges them to be nice to support their communities' ethos. By attacking or supporting their community's ethos, obnoxious and nice groups affect its tension level. One need only compare communities where a stranger in town is greeted by the Hells Angels with those where he is greeted by Welcome Wagon. Although Durkheim (1951) suggested that the social tensions manifested in individual suicides are inherent in society as a whole, it may be more useful to see society as composed of tension-intensifying groups and tension-attenuating groups. One could then describe much of macro-social dynamics as the interchange of tension between these two types of groups, determining their society's "tone" in terms of their relative power.

IV. THE RELATION BETWEEN THE OBNOXIOUS AND THE NICE

Opposite as these two types seem, the obnoxious are sometimes transformed into the nice, the nice into the obnoxious—at least in part.

At the extremes, their relative status is reversed. If someone behaves obnoxiously enough, others will cease to take his behavior seriously and to see him as harmful. In fact, they may find extremely obnoxious behavior ludicrous, those who

---

their users' ability to be obnoxious. Obnoxiousness facilitation is a secondary purpose in other items, like muffler by-passes in hot-rods and motorcycles. Finally, obnoxiousness is an unintended consequence of still other technological innovations, such as smokestacks (as some industrial plants have recently found out) and stereos (as some apartment dwellers soon learn). Examples of a *technology of niceness* include visual and auditory shields like kleenex and soundproofing as well as feedback-enhancers like hearing aids.

engage in it amusing. They may begin to seek out these hy-
perobnoxious people even more than they do the bland, but
boring, nice. The outrageously obnoxious person, like Fal-
staff, W.C. Fields, Groucho Marx, or Don Rickles, may even
become the lovable fool, buffoon, pet, or mascot of the
group. (See Klapp, 1962, on the lovable harmlessness of
fools.)

Similarly, others may consider excessively nice people obsequious, and shun them because they are cognitively disorient-
ing. The obsequious, like the obnoxious, do not provide the
feedback necessary for someone to evaluate accurately his
own behavior, and consequently his own being. (See Cooley,
1964: 183-184, on the necessity of using others to construct a
"looking-glass self.") The obnoxious either fail to evaluate
others' self-expressions or evaluate them negatively. The obsequious always evaluate them positively regardless of merit. Of
all the obsequious characters in world literature, Shakespeare's Polonius is one of the most exasperating. Hamlet
makes fun of his excessively acquiescent niceness:

> HAMLET: Do you see yonder cloud that's almost in the
>   shape of a camel?
> POLONIUS: By the mass, and 'tis like a camel indeed.
> HAMLET: Methinks it is like a weasel.
> POLONIUS: It is backed like a weasel.
> HAMLET: Or like a whale?
> POLONIUS: Very like a whale.
>
> —*Hamlet*, Act III, scene ii

Mobility, either social or interpersonal, may also transform
the obnoxious into the nice, and vice versa. Status gainers often behave obnoxiously to the ex-peers they used to be nice
to: status losers often behave nicely to the ex-peers they used
to be obnoxious to. (At least this is the way their ex-peers are
likely to view their new behavior.) Intimates who split up often become more obnoxious to each other while becoming
nicer to others.

The obnoxious sometimes simulate niceness to entice a person into a relation with them, before suddenly intruding or
imposing an unwanted self on the person. Since the person
usually expects the obnoxious to be trying to intrude on or
impose selves continually, their *interaction bunt* catches him
off guard. Their seemingly compliant behavior may lead him
to trust them, before they suddenly turn on him. An extreme

version of this transformation is the theme of Alfred Hitchcock's movie *Psycho*, and other recent movies in which the nicest, most mild-mannered character turns out to be the axe murderer.

Some usually nice people feel a recurrent and uncontrollable urge to behave obnoxiously. Others find these *obnoxiholics* very attractive during their nice periods but very repulsive during their obnoxious episodes. Spouses of obnoxiholics, like spouses of alcoholics, must masochistically endure their continual switching between one kind of behavior and the other. The similarity between obnoxiholism and alcoholism is more than homonymic. Alcoholics frequently behave obnoxiously, intruding physical selves and imposing social selves with reckless abandon, while being insensitive to negative feedback about their behavior.

Nice compliant people may fantasize themselves behaving obnoxiously, at least at certain times to certain interaction partners. Robert Lewis Stevenson's *The Strange Case of Dr. Jekyll and Mr. Hyde* has continued to be popular in part because it portrays (in extreme form) a change of type that many nice people (who can't help always being nice) would occasionally like to undergo. Conversely, Dostoyevski's *Notes from Underground* maintains its popularity in part because it describes an obnoxious person (unable to avoid being obnoxious) who continually fantasizes himself behaving nicely.

The obnoxious and the nice are often attracted to each other because each type allows the other to behave in characteristic fashion: the one continually intruding and imposing a self, the other continually acquiescing to these self-impositions. (*Like* pairs of these psychological types, such as nice–nice or obnoxious–obnoxious, are sociologically less stable because neither partner provides the complementary interaction resources necessary for the other.) Comedy teams, such as Laurel and Hardy or Abbott and Costello, usually consist of one extremely obnoxious "funny man" and one extremely nice "straight man," the former madly intruding or imposing odd aspects of the self on the latter.

Although some nice people enjoy associating with the obnoxious, most do not. Unfortunately, they often find they must associate with them because, by definition, they are too nice to use the stronger forms of micro-social control necessary to shake off the obnoxious (who, as mentioned, are "hard of hearing" when it comes to negative feedback about their behavior or their presence). Unable to discontinue their relation effectively, the nice often discover they have polluted their social environment with too many obnoxious acquaintances. Eventually, however, extreme social pollution may force the nice either to "put their foot down" verbally telling their obnoxious acquaintances to go away, or to flee the area themselves.

If the social environment of the nice becomes filled with *interactional clutter*, the social environment of the obnoxious comes to consist of an *interactional vacuum*. Their social environment empties of interaction partners as each potential interactant goes out of his way to avoid them. Since the obnoxious cannot attract others into encounters (i.e., they are not "attractive" people), they must discover means to force them. One method of acquiring interaction partners that is used by the obnoxious is to achieve high status, a benefit of which is a continual supply of subordinates easily compelled to be "captive audiences." Another method is to do unnecessary favors for others—supplying them with objects or services they neither need nor want. The imposed role of "grateful recipient" obliges them to sustain encounters with their obnoxious benefactors. The obnoxious do favors to tie others to themselves; the nice find their having tied others to themselves an unfortunate consequence of their favors.

A third type—which we will call the charismatic—combines the best traits of both. Like the obnoxious, the charismatic impose selves on others. Unlike them, the charismatic impose selves that others desire, not selves that others dislike. Like the nice, the charismatic are sensitive to others' feedback about the selves they would like. Unlike them, the charismatic actively impose these wanted selves, rather than passively receive them. Charismatic political leaders, for example, persuade their constituents they are giving them what they really want.

The charismatic occupy the top position on both macro- and microstatus dimensions. In the macrostratificational system, the charismatic come to occupy a higher status than the obnoxious because they can be more successful in both individual achievement and corporate acceptability. In the microstratificational system, the charismatic come to occupy a higher status than the nice because they can be more successful in both determining what others want and actively seeming to give it to them. To describe someone as a "nice guy," therefore, is to damn him with faint praise, implying "He's acquiescent to everyone's wishes. That's his only virtue." An example from the Watergate Tapes (*Los Angeles Times*, August 6, 1974, p. 13):

> PRESIDENT: You've just not got to let Klein ever set up a meeting again. He doesn't have his head screwed on. You know what I mean. He just opens it up and sits there with egg on his face. He's just not our guy at all. . . . Absolutely, totally, unorganized.
>
> HALDEMAN: He's a very nice guy.
>
> PRESIDENT: People love him, but damn is he unorganized.

V. CONCLUSION

Obnoxious and nice types are important for sociologists to study because they disclose the rules of everyday interaction, not by breaking them violently, as mental patients do (Goffman, 1967: 80, 93), but by bending them slightly, thus revealing more subtle interaction rules than research on mental patients.

The obnoxious and the nice should also interest those concerned with social problems. As other social categories (race, sex, etc.) become more equal in the future, the nice will still be exploited while the obnoxious will still be avoided. In fact, discrimination against the obnoxious will intensify as discrimination against other social categories diminishes. One could interpret the present movement toward equalizing all social categories (save one) as the desire to eliminate all barriers that presently keep society from discriminating against a person solely because he is obnoxious. Truly the obnoxious are—and perhaps will remain—the last minority group to suffer discrimination. No professional spokesperson for human liberation has yet even claimed them for his own.

The obnoxious, the nice, and the charismatic are not the only social psychological types constituting the phenomenological fullness of our everyday reality. Each of us lives in the midst of a veritable social garden (or zoo) containing assholes, jerks, creeps, punks, schlemiels—to name only a few of the more visible varieties (or species) that surround us. Each of these types behaves differently and each type has a different sociological career. Perhaps a new field of *microdeviance* will be necessary to study the interactional characteristics of abnormal social psychological types.

The microprocesses involving these microtypes should also be investigated. The gravitation of the obnoxious to the nice, for instance, is but a small ripple in the great stirring of society, one often obscured by the larger waves of social movements. Yet it is these microsocial processes, accounting for a minute amount of the forces determining human behavior but enduring most persistently under various times and circumstances, that give everyday experience its fine texture. Long after larger social movements have run their course, the obnoxious will still be gravitating to the nice at their same small rate, even in the most utopian of future societies.

Finally, a renewed interest in social psychological types may overcome the ecological bias of much of micro-sociology. Symbolic interactionist and ethnomethodological field workers presently produce a distorted portrait of the social world by frequently treating impersonal settings—hospitals, classrooms, courtrooms, streets, etc.—but infrequently focusing on the social-psychological types that cross-cut them, those whose behavior remains the same regardless of their settings or how others interpret it. Certain social psychological types, like the obnoxious and the nice, suggest that the situation's effect on both the motivation and the interpretation of behavior is problematic. For this reason, we would like to reorient micro-sociology to bring these two analytical perspectives—the ecological and the typological—into better balance.

REFERENCES

Bales, Robert F. "The equilibrium problem in small groups." In Parsons, et al., Working Papers in the Theory of Action. New York: The Free Press, pp. 111–161, 1953.

Cicourel, Aaron. Cognitive Sociology: Language and Meaning In Social Interaction. New York: The Free Press, 1973.

Cooley, Charles. Human Nature and the Social Order. New York: Schocken, 1964.

Davis, Murray S. Intimate Relations. New York: The Free Press, 1973.

Durkheim, Emile. Suicide. New York: The Free Press, 1951.

Garfinkel, Harold. Studies in Ethnomethodology. Englewood Cliffs: Prentice-Hall, Inc., 1967.

Goffman, Erving. Asylums. Garden City: Doubleday, 1961.

Goffman, Erving. Interaction Ritual. Garden City: Doubleday, 1967.

Goffman, Erving. Relations in Public. New York: Harper & Row, 1972.

Heider, Fritz. *The Psychology of Interpersonal Relations.* New York: Wiley, 1958.

Klapp, Orrin. *Heroes, Villains, and Fools.* New York: Prentice Hall, 1962.

Lemert, E. "Paranoia and the dynamics of exclusion." *Sociometry,* Vol. 25, pp. 2–19, 1962.

Laing, R. D. *The Divided Self.* Baltimore: Penguin, 1965.

Lyman, S., and M. Scott. "Accounts." *American Sociological Review* Vol. 33 (February), pp. 46–62, 1968.

Mead, George H. *Mind, Self, and Society.* Chicago: The University of Chicago Press, 1934.

Ross, E. "Social control." *American Journal of Sociology,* Vol. 1 (March), pp. 513–535, 1896.

Schutz, Alfred. *Collected Papers I: The Problem of Social Reality.* The Hague: Nijhoff, 1962.

Simmel, Georg. *The Sociology of Georg Simmel.* New York: The Free Press, 1950.

Weber, Max. *The Theory of Social and Economic Organization.* New York: Oxford Press, 1947.

Weinstein, E., and P. Deutschberger. "Some dimensions of altercasting." *Sociometry,* Vol. 26, pp. 454–466, 1963.

The Political Eunuch

by
Lewis A. Coser

Eunuchs have been major instruments of imperial rule in most of the classical empires of the Far East and the Near East. In China and Byzantium, as well as in the Arab, Mesopotamian and Persian empires in particular, eunuchs held a variety of positions at the court, in government and in the army. In Persia after Xerxes "the eunuchs acquired a vast political authority and appeared then to have filled all the chief offices of state. They were the king's advisors in the palace, and his generals in the field. They superintended the education of the young princes, and found it easy to make them their tools."[1] In Ming China, "whole departments of eunuchs came into existence at court, and these were soon made use of for confidential business of the emperor's outside the palace."[2] They headed armies and, at times, controlled the bureaucracy, so that counselors could communicate with the emperor only through the intermediary of eunuchs.[3] In the earlier Han dynasty "they were established in the center of the governmental machine (and) soon obtained control of the civil service. . . ."[4] In fact, employment of eunuchs in top positions was so frequent in some Near-Eastern monarchies that the term eunuch sometimes, as in Hebrew, for example, lost its original meaning and was used as a synonym for court official or minister, regardless of whether these men were true eunuchs or not.[5]

This chapter will attempt a fundamental explanation of the

Reprinted with permission of Macmillan Publishing Co., Inc., from *Greedy Institutions* by Lewis A. Coser. Copyright ©1974 by The Free Press, a Division of Macmillan Publishing Co., Inc.

[1]George Rawlinson, *The Five Great Monarchies of the Ancient Eastern World*, New York: Dodd, Mead, 1881, Vol. 3, p. 221.

[2]Wolfram Eberhard, *A History of China*, Berkeley and Los Angeles: University of California Press, 1960, p. 253.

[3]Cf. Max Weber, *The Religion of China*, trans. and ed. by Hans Gerth, Glencoe, Ill.: The Free Press, 1951, p. 285.

[4]C. P. Fitzgerald, *China, A Cultural History*, New York: Frederick Praeger, 1954, p. 252.

[5]Peter Browe, S. J. *Zur Geschichte der Entmannung*, Breslau: Mueller and Seiffert, 1936, p. 38.

apparently surprising fact that men who are less than men have performed essentially similar political functions in a variety of different cultural settings. Similar structural requirements, I shall try to show, led to the recourse of political eunuchism.

Eunuchism originated in the need of masters of large harems to have dependable harem guards who could not be led into temptation and betray their masters. But this origin does not explain why eunuchs came to be used as preferred instruments of reign; as we have known ever since Durkheim, the origin of a phenomenon does not explain its persistence or its transformations.[6] In Byzantium, where the institution of the harem did not exist, "no office, however high, in Church or State (with the single exception of the imperial dignity itself) was withheld from the eunuchs on principle,"[7] and many of the leading Byzantine statesmen and generals were eunuchs. Although eunuchism originated in the needs of harem masters, it spread to non-harem areas because it served functions for the rulers of empires that went beyond those in which it originated.

Political eunuchism thrived under oriental despotism, where bureaucratic or protobureaucratic rule had already developed but where strong patrimonial elements were still prevalent. In such systems the Emperor wished to minimize his dependency on the bureaucracy, whose impersonal standards made it insufficiently pliable as an instrument of personal rule. He therefore required men who would owe him total allegiance. The tension between the need to rely on bureaucracy for purposes of centralization and the need for personal allegiance and dependence led to the creation of a new role, that of the political eunuch.

Eunuchs were typically recruited among young boys captured in slave raids or other military operations, or they were boys sold by peasants to agents of the palace. (In addition to boys castrated in their youth sometimes men punished by being castrated as adults were also used.) Once they had moved into the social circle of the court, these eunuchs typically lost contact with their families and their region of origin. They were, literally or figuratively, aliens.[8]

[6]Emile Durkheim, *The Rules of Sociological Method*, Glencoe, Ill.: The Free Press, 1950, p. 97.

[7]George Ostrogorsky, *History of the Byzantine State*, Oxford: Basil Blackwell, 1956, p. 221.

[8]J. K. Rideout, "The Rise of the Eunuchs during the T'ang Dynasty," *Asia Major*, I, pp. 53–72 and III, pp. 42–58.

Their ties to kinship and territorial units having been severed, having been "freed" from attachments to their families of orientation and being unable to found families of procreation, the eunuchs were ideally suited to perform a variety of political tasks for the emperor, on whom they depended as no men with competing familial or territorial loyalties could ever have depended. Xenophon put the matter with his customary shrewdness when he wrote about Cyrus: "He reflected . . . what sort of people he could have about him, who might be trusted [while he was eating, drinking or bathing]; and he came to the conclusion, that no man could ever be trusted who should love another more than the person that wanted his protection. Such men, therefore, as had sons or wives, that were agreeable to them, or youths that were objects of their affection, he deemed to be under a natural necessity of loving them best; but observing that eunuchs were destitute of all these ties, he thought that they would have the greatest affection for those that were able to enrich them"[9]—and give them honor and protection.

Medieval rulers used a celibate clergy, not only because of its literacy and learning, but also because men without families of procreation could give themselves more fully to the service of their masters than men whose loyalty was, as it were, divided between their families and their political masters. Yet loyalty to the Church would often interfere with loyalty to the king, as the tragedies of Becket and More testify. Moreover, while the celibate priest or monk had no family of procreation he did have a family of orientation and other kinsmen, which prevented him from giving exclusive allegiance to his political masters. Geographical removal of the clerical official from his region of origin might minimize such attachments, as it minimized them in the case of lay officials. Nevertheless, such officials, though temporarily uprooted, were yet conscious of having roots somewhere. In contrast, eunuchs were utterly alone. "Socially rootless, they owed everything they had and everything they were to their ruler; and their doglike devotion to him therefore resulted . . . consistently from their position. . . ."[10] Not only had the eunuch

---

[9]Xenophon, *The Cryopaedia*, trans. by J. S. Watson and Henry Dale, London: Bell and Daldy, 1870, p. 229. See the similar remarks by Herodotus, *The Histories of Herodotus*, trans. by G. C. Macaulay, London: Macmillan, 1904, Vol. 2, p. 275.

[10]Karl August Wittfogel, *Oriental Despotism*, New Haven: Yale University Press, 1963, p. 355. Wittfogel interprets political eunuchism in roughly the same manner I do here. I came across his remarks only

no territorial or kinship attachments, he was also an object of contempt and ridicule. It was therefore more important for him to be valued, recognized and protected by the ruler. Because he had no other groups of reference, the ruler—and his court—became for him the unique object of reference, the unique protector, the major point of repair. To quote Xenophon again, "Eunuchs, being objects of contempt to other men, are, for this reason in want of a master to protect them. . . ."[11]

What Georg Simmel said about the stranger applies with peculiar force to the eunuch: "He is not radically committed to the unique ingredients and peculiar tendencies of the group, and, therefore, approaches them with the specific attitude of 'objectivity' . . . whereas the relation to more organically connected persons is based on the commonness of specific differences . . ."[12] The very detachment of the eunuch-stranger from all group involvements makes for his "objectivity" vis-à-vis all subjects, and conversely for his nearness to the ruler. He is, hence, an ideal instrument of the ruler's subjectivity.[13]

---

after this paper had already been outlined, but I still profited a great deal from his erudite and perceptive discussion. See also, his *History of Chinese Society, Liao,* Philadelphia: The American Philosophical Society, 1949, p. 464. Cf. also, Keith Hopkins, "Eunuchs in Politics in the later Roman Empire," *Proceedings of the Cambridge Philological Society,* No. 189 (New Series, No. 9), 1963, pp. 62–80.

[11]Xenophon, *op. cit.,* p. 275.

[12]Georg Simmel, *The Sociology of Georg Simmel,* trans. by Kurt. H. Wolff, New York: The Free Press, 1950, pp. 404–405.

[13]In certain societies non-castrated slaves were also used as trusted instruments of rule. Cf., for example, the description of the power of court slaves among the Yoruba in M. Crowder's, *The Story of Nigeria,* London: Faber, 1962. Such slaves, being strangers to the society in which they found themselves after their capture, could be used to advantage by the rulers even though they were allowed to found families of their own.

Certain exceptions to the separation of the eunuch from his family of orientation must also be noted here. In Byzantium, "If one wished to ensure a successful career for one's son, one had him castrated. He might then easily become a governor, ambassador, prime minister, strategos, admiral or Patriarch." (René Guerdan, *Byzantium, Its Triumphs and Tragedy,* London: Allen and Unwin, 1956, p. 47.) "Even the nobelest parents were not above mutilating their sons to help their advancement . . ." (Steven Runcinam, *Byzantine Civilization,* New York: Longmans, Green, 1933, p. 203.) Since eunuchs could not wear the Imperial crown, nor transfer hereditary rights, they became the preferred public servants and castration was a step on the ladder of upward mobility—just as the taking of holy orders was in the

Bureaucratic officials, it stands to reason, were exceedingly distrustful of the eunuch system because it negated the emphasis on rationality, on disciplined and methodical behavior, which is the very essence of expert officialdom. The eunuchs were not bound by any rule and they could not be checked by bureaucratic superiors. Hence the constant struggle between the literati and the eunuch system in China without which, according to Max Weber, "Chinese history is most difficult to understand."[14] Throughout all the dynasties "energetic rules continually sought to shake off their bonds to the cultured status group of the literati with the aid of eunuchs and plebeian parvenus."[15] Whereas the literati attained their position through arduous examination procedures, eunuchs attained theirs through their power over women and children in the recesses of the harem and the court. They thrived under petticoat government, and, in contrast to the rationalism of the bureaucrats, were wont to utilize magic and superstition in the court intrigues through which they endeavored to gain power or influence. They practiced favoritism and particularism while the literati advocated universalistic standards.

Being in bodily attendance on the feminine household within the palace, the eunuchs exploited this position near the person of the ruler and his family. Their basis of operation was attendance on *persons*, while the bureaucratic official based his power upon his position in an *impersonal* system. They thrived on nearness, where bureaucrats cultivated distance. Even in Byzantium, though eunuchs occupied at times almost any state office, they almost invariably held a number of court functions, and these typically involved attendance on

---

Middle Ages. In such cases, obviously, eunuchs remained in touch with their families and were hence likely to use power and influence in their behalf. Similarly, in certain periods of Chinese history, such as during the Ming dynasty, educated eunuchs, recruited from the lower gentry, "accumulated great wealth, which they shared with their small gentry relatives. The rise of the small gentry class was therefore connected with the increased influence of the eunuchs at court." (Eberhard, *op. cit.*, p. 253.)

In these cases political eunuchism was, so to speak, sociologically incomplete. The eunuchs remained preferred instruments of rule, because they could have no issue, but being attached to kinsmen, they could not serve their masters with the same unalloyed devotion as did the eunuchs who were totally without social roots. In these cases, though eunuchs were used by the monarch as a device for control, they would very often tend to develop into somewhat independent foci of strength.

[14] Weber, *op. cit.*, p. 138.

[15] *Ibid.*, p. 139. See also Otto Franke, *Geschichte des Chinesischen Reiches*, Berlin: Walter de Gruyter, 1936, esp. Vol. 2, *passim*.

the person of the ruler; such offices as head of the imperial wardrobes, imperial steward of the household, head of the imperial kitchens, were nearly always staffed by eunuchs. The *paracoemomenus,* who slept near the imperial bed and was usually the emperor's most trusted confident, was likewise usually a eunuch,[16] as were the commander of the imperial bodyguard and the bodyguard himself.[17]

A eunuch's power over a ruler often stemmed from his having been in attendance on him ever since his childhood. "When the heir to the throne," Fitzgerald writes of China, "as was often the case in the second century A.D., was a boy born and bred in the palace, under the care and in the company of eunuchs from his childhood, the Emperor became the plaything of these servitors, who knew his foibles, [and] colored all he ever learned of the outside world."[18] Rulers who had grown up in the harem and had known mainly eunuchs as trusted attendants, were wont in later years to rely on these men in whom they had put an early trust. It stands to reason that they tended to regard the members of the regular civil service with a certain lack of confidence. These men represented the coldness of impersonal rule. The eunuchs they knew personally; the bureaucracy, even though devoted to the emperor, would appear to them as alien representatives of impersonal forces.

Antagonism between emperor and bureaucracy had other sources as well. Although the bureaucracy claimed to be devoted to the rulers, it also developed tendencies toward autonomy. In its early stages, it fully identified with the king, but "Later, when the bureaucracy had developed into a somewhat autonomous body with its traditions, conflicts with the rulers tended to arise . . . The bureaucracy developed, to some extent, an ideology emphasizing its own autonomy, and its direct ethical, professional (and sometimes even legal) responsibility for implementing the society's values and goals . . ."[19] Wherever this occurred, reliance on eunuchs offered the ruler a way of escaping bureaucratic pressures and a means of asserting independence. At times, as during the late Han period of Chinese history, "as tools of the emperor or of

[16]Ostrogorsky, *op. cit.,* p. 221. See also R. Guilland's series of studies in *Revue des Etudes Byzantines* I, pp. 197–238, II, pp. 185–225 and III, pp. 179–214.

[17]Ostrogorsky, *op. cit.,* p. 35.

[18]Fitzgerald, *op. cit.,* p. 251.

[19]S. N. Eisenstadt, *The Political Systems of Empires,* New York: The Free Press, 1963, p. 159.

his wives or in-laws, they temporarily exerted an almost unlimited control over the bureaucracy."[20] Under the Ming emperors they "were in charge of special agencies for
supervising the metropolitan officials and commoners."[21]
"When . . . eunuchs controlled appointments to government
posts, long established practices of bureaucratic administration were eliminated and the court, i.e., the emperor and his
tools, the eunuchs, could create a rule by way of arbitrary decisions, a despotic rule."[22] At other times the bureaucracy asserted itself again and subjected court and emperor to its
rules and regulations—often slaughtering its adversaries
among the eunuchs.

While eunuchs thus often served as the preferred tool of
the ruler in his attempt to free himself from the control of his
own instruments, the eunuchs were more generally used
against anybody who threatened to develop autonomous
power. Wherever aristocratic or gentry cliques threatened the
court, eunuchs were preferred as a counterweapon. In Ming
China "the emperors used the eunuchs as a tool to counteract
the power of gentry cliques and thus to strengthen their personal power."[23] In China generally, "Eunuchs were used . . .
as a powerful weapon for checking the influence in politics of
the tenacious Chinese family system."[24] In Byzantium, the
employment of eunuchs provided a "great weapon against the
feudal tendency for power to be concentrated in the hands of
a hereditary nobility."[25] "They gave the Emperor a governing
class he could trust,"[26] because they represented the very antithesis of the principle of inheritance upon which any aristocratic status group necessarily rests. They were trustworthy
since they could never covet hereditary power. They could be
safely charged, e.g., with the leadership of armies since they
were naturally incapable of aspiring to the throne.[27] Their
very position rested upon the rejection of aristocratic
principles just as it made them consistent opponents of
bureaucratic principles. They were hence the appropriate

[20]Wittfogel, *Oriental Despotism, op. cit.,* p. 356.

[21]*Ibid.,* p. 357.

[22]Eberhard, *op. cit.,* p. 253.

[23]*Ibid.*

[24]Owen Lattimore, *Inner Asian Frontiers of China,* New York: American Geographical Society, 1951, p. 377.

[25]Runcinam, *op. cit.,* p. 204.

[26]*Ibid.*

[27]George Finlay, *History of the Byzantine Empire,* Edinburgh: Black-
wood, 1853, Vol. 1, p. 460.

instruments of any ruler who wished to escape the control of both gentry and bureaucracy while using them for his own purposes.[28]

Sociological theory tends too frequently to focus attention exclusively on the dominant norms and patterns of behavior and to disregard the tensions and dysfunctions that full adherence to those norms might entail. I have attempted here to document the emergence of mechanisms that mitigated the impact of a dominant mode of administration—impersonal bureaucracy—by the parallel reintroduction of elements of personal dependence. It remains to indicate that political eunuchism is not the only mechanism that might be used for such purposes and that functional alternatives to this pattern exist.

In situations where power holders utilize an administrative staff organized on bureaucratic principles and where, at the same time, they claim the total allegiance of those who serve them, a structural problem arises. The very principle of bureaucracy precludes personal fealty and dependence. Such dependence is also weakened by the tendency inherent in a bureaucratic apparatus toward at least partial autonomy from power holders. If the latter wish to maximize the advantages provided by impersonal bureaucratic organization and by personal loyalties as well, they must overcome the incompatibility between impersonal and personal principles of administration.

One means to this end consists of overcoming the role segmentation inherent in the notion of bureaucratic office. Bureaucratic administration rests on the assumption that only a segment of the officeholder's personality is involved in his bureaucratic tasks while the rest remains "free" for other involvements. Office holders whose other foci of loyalty are eliminated can therefore give their total allegiance to the organization they serve.

The notion of "total allegiance" accounts for the fact that most Utopias since Plato's have been hostile to the family. Whether Utopian authors limited their emphasis to the allegiance of specialized office holders, as in the case of Catholic

---

[28]The eunuchs were not the only instruments used to control the bureaucracy and to counteract familistic or aristocratic tendencies. Other devices were the continuous creation of new titles and offices. It should also be kept in mind, as Keith Hopkins (personal communication, February 9, 1965) has pointed out to me, that at times the eunuchs attempted to form an interest group of their own, and so endeavored to free themselves to some extent from the powers of the ruler.

priests, or whether they wished to maximize the loyalty of all citizens, they saw in both cases that total allegiance to the state could be achieved only if family ties did not detract from such loyalty. Opposition to the family in the early years of the Russian revolution, as well as during the Nazi regime a decade or two later, served similar concerns.[29]

In the "perfectionist" Oneida community, according to one of Noyes' followers, "they who have wives should be as though they had none." "Each male member is the husband of all the females, and each female the wife of every man." "This was the crucial test of man's love for his fellow men; without that love he was unfit for community life."[30] The exclusive attachment of two persons was regarded as selfish and "idolatrous," and it was usually broken up by "mutual criticism" of the members of the community.[31] As Philip Slater has convincingly argued, libidinal withdrawal threatens every community, but especially one that is built upon total immersion of the personality in the community. "We may hypothesize," says Slater, "that the more totalitarian the collectivity, in terms of making demands upon the individual to involve every area of his life in collective activity, the stronger will be the prohibition against dyadic intimacy."[32]

Celibacy, eunuchism and promiscuity, manifestly opposed sexual practices from the point of view of cultural patterning, may fulfill essentially similar social functions. They assure that a person's total loyalty and affective involvement remain within the group and at the disposal of the leadership.

[29]Cf. Lewis A. Coser, "Some Aspects of Soviet Family Policy," *The American Journal of Sociology*, 56 (March 1951), pp. 424–37.

[30]Allan Estlack, *The Oneida Community*, London: George Redway, 1900, p. 35 and p. 87.

[31]Mark Holloway, *Heavens on Earth*, New York: Library Publishers, 1951, pp. 185–186.

[32]Philip E. Slater, "On Social Regression," *American Sociological Review*, 28 (June 1963), p. 349 and *passim*.

V.

WORK AND LEISURE

MOST CLASSIC AUTHORS in the sociological tradition, writing in the age of the Industrial Revolution and after, focused much of their attention on the impact on the human condition of the new industrial mode of production. Their assessments differed widely. Some chose to focus on the potential for the liberation and the perfectibility of the human race that increased productivity and the rationalization of the work process could bring about; others pointed to the alienation and degradation of workers in the huge factories that began to dot the landscape in the first half of the nineteenth century.

Henri de Saint-Simon, that erratic genius whose visions inspired the early writings of August Comte as well as that of many technocrats of a later age, chose to stress the fact that the future of humankind rested with the new industrial classes and that the vestigial noble elites were but drones that hampered the full development of productive forces. His delightfully ironic portrayal of the differential importance of these classes opens this chapter.

Karl Marx, though also optimistic about the ultimate impact of modern industry, was most critical of its immediate consequences. His portrayal of the alienation of the worker in modern capitalist society has been unsurpassed by any subsequent writings. The few pages reprinted here show the force and persuasiveness of his argument.

Marx expected that after the overthrow of capitalism, industrial production would be based on associations of producers freed from the fetters of capitalist domination and the dictates of the market. He did not bother to describe in any detail the socialist society that he looked forward to. But others among his socialist contemporaries, among them the utopian socialist Charles Fourier, addressed themselves directly to concrete problems that would arise in socialist societies. In the lovely little essay here reprinted, he addresses the perennial question: Who will do the dirty work in the good society? His answer was as delightful as it was whimsical. In the socialist colonies that he envisaged, little children would do the dirty work, since it is well known that kids just love to play with dirt.

Writing roughly a century after these early commentators on the Industrial Revolution, the American sociologist and economist Thorstein Veblen argued in his influential *The Theory of the Leisure Class* that ever since the institution of private property, humankind has been divided between those who toil and those who manage to appropriate enough of the products of such toil so that they can live a life of leisure. He saw the leisure class as removed from the discipline of production and hence wholly devoted to an unremitting competition among its members for invidious distinctions through conspicuous consumption and pecuniary emulation. His savage portrait of the lifestyles of the upper classes has inspired much subsequent cultural criticism of the ways of the rich. A few of his most mordant pages are included here.

The remaining paper is meant to give a sample, inadequate though it must necessarily be, of current work in the sociology of work and leisure. In his paper on the relations between the cabdriver and his fare, Fred Davis shows the imbalance and instability in the relations between the two. The vagaries of tipping, he argues, account for much of that instability. Where relations between work and client are not contractually stabilized, a large element of chance opens the way for various manipulative strategies so that relations between server and served tend to be narrowly calculative.

Who Contributes to Society?

by
Henri de Saint-Simon

Suppose that France suddenly lost fifty of her best physicists, chemists, physiologists, mathematicians, poets, painters, sculptors, musicians, writers; fifty of her best mechanical engineers, civil and military engineers, artillery experts, architects, doctors, surgeons, apothecaries, seamen, clockmakers; fifty of her best bankers, two hundred of her best business men, two hundred of her best farmers, fifty of her best ironmasters, arms manufacturers, tanners, dyers, miners, clothmakers, cotton manufacturers, silk-makers, linen-makers, manufacturers of hardware, of pottery and china, of crystal and glass, ship chandlers, carriers, printers, engravers, goldsmiths, and other metal-workers; her fifty best masons, carpenters, joiners, farriers, locksmiths, cutlers, smelters, and a hundred other persons of various unspecified occupations, eminent in the sciences, fine arts, and professions; making in all the three thousand leading scientists, artists, and artisans of France.[1]

These men are the Frenchmen who are the most essential producers, those who make the most important products, those who direct the enterprises most useful to the nation, those who contribute to its achievements in the sciences, fine arts and professions. They are in the most real sense the flower of French society; they are, above all Frenchmen, the most useful to their country, contribute most to its glory, increasing its civilization and prosperity. The nation would become a lifeless corpse as soon as it lost them. It would immediately fall into a position of inferiority compared with

From Henri de Saint-Simon, *Social Organization, The Science of Man*, ed. Felix Markham (New York: Harper & Row, Oxford: Basil Blackwell, 1952), pp. 72–75. Reprinted by permission of the publishers. Extract first published in 1819.

[1]Artisan usually means an ordinary workman. To avoid circumlocution, I mean by this expression all those who are concerned with material production, viz., farmers, manufacturers, merchants, bankers, and all the clerks and workmen employed by them.

the nations which it now rivals, and would continue to be inferior until this loss had been replaced, until it had grown another head. It would require at least a generation for France to repair this misfortune; for men who are distinguished in work of positive ability are exceptions, and nature is not prodigal of exceptions, particularly in this species.

Let us pass on to another assumption. Suppose that France preserves all the men of genius that she possesses in the sciences, fine arts and professions, but has the misfortune to lose in the same day Monsieur the King's brother, Monseigneur le duc d'Angoulême, Monseigneur le duc de Berry, Monseigneur le duc d'Orléans, Monseigneur le duc de Bourbon, Madame la duchesse d'Angoulême, Madame la duchesse de Berry, Madame la duchesse d'Orléans, Madame la duchesse de Bourbon, and Mademoiselle de Condé. Suppose that France loses at the same time all the great officers of the royal household, all the ministers (with or without portfolio), all the councillors of state, all the chief magistrates, marshals, cardinals, archbishops, bishops, vicars-general, and canons, all the prefects and sub-prefects, all the civil servants, and judges, and, in addition, ten thousand of the richest proprietors who live in the style of nobles.

This mischance would certainly distress the French, because they are kind-hearted, and could not see with indifference the sudden disappearance of such a large number of their compatriots. But this loss of thirty-thousand individuals, considered to be the most important in the State, would only grieve them for purely sentimental reasons and would result in no political evil for the State.

In the first place, it would be very easy to fill the vacancies which would be made available. There are plenty of Frenchmen who could fill the function of the King's brother as well as can Monsieur; plenty who could take the place of a Prince as appropriately as Monseigneur le duc d'Angoulême, or Monseigneur le duc d'Orléans, or Monseigneur le duc de Bourbon. There are plenty of Frenchwomen who would be as good princesses as Madame la duchesse d'Angoulême, or Madame la duchesse de Berry, or Mesdames d'Orléans, de Bourbon, and de Condé.

The ante-chambers of the palace are full of courtiers ready to take the place of the great household officials. The army has plenty of soldiers who would be as good leaders as our present Marshals. How many clerks there are who are as good as our ministers? How many administrators who are capable of managing the affairs of the departments better than the existing prefects and sub-prefects? How many barristers who are as good lawyers as our judges? How many vicars as expert as our cardinals, archbishops, bishops vicars-general, and canons? As for the ten thousand aristocratic landowners, their heirs would need no apprenticeship to do the honours of their drawingrooms as well as they.

The prosperity of France can only exist through the effects of the progress of the sciences, fine arts and professions. The Princes, the great household officials, the Bishops, Marshals of France, prefects and idle landowners contribute nothing directly to the progress of the sciences, fine arts and professions. Far from contributing they only hinder, since they strive to prolong the supremacy existing to this day of conjectural ideas over positive science. They inevitably harm the prosperity of the nation by depriving, as they do, the scientists, artists, and artisans of the high esteem to which they are properly entitled. They are harmful because they expend their wealth in a way which is of no direct use to the sciences, fine arts, and professions: they are harmful because they are a charge on the national taxation, to the amount of three or four hundred millions under the heading of appointments, pensions, gifts, compensations, for the upkeep of their activities which are useless to the nation.

These suppositions underline the most important fact of present politics: they provide a point of view from which we can see this fact in a flash in all its extent; they show clearly, though indirectly, that our social organization is seriously defective: that men still allow themselves to be governed by violence and ruse, and that the human race (politically speaking) is still sunk in immorality.

The scientists, artists, and artisans, the only men whose work is of positive utility to society, and cost it practically nothing, are kept down by the princes and other rulers who are simply more or less incapable bureaucrats. Those who control honours and other national awards owe, in general, the supremacy they enjoy, to the accident of birth, to flattery, intrigue and other dubious methods.

Those who control public affairs share between them every year one half of the taxes, and they do not even use a third of what they do not pocket personally in a way which benefits the citizen.

These suppositions show that society is a world which is upside down.

The nation holds as a fundamental principle that the poor should be generous to the rich, and that therefore the poorer classes should daily deprive themselves of necessities in order to increase the superfluous luxury of the rich.

The most guilty men, the robbers on a grand scale, who oppress the mass of the citizens, and extract from them three or four hundred millions a year, are given the responsibility of punishing minor offences against society.

Ignorance, superstition, idleness and costly dissipation are the privilege of the leaders of society, and men of ability, hard-working and thrifty, are employed only as inferiors and instruments.

To sum up, in every sphere men of greater ability are subject to the control of men who are incapable. From the point of view of morality, the most immoral men have the responsibility of leading the citizens towards virtue; from the point of view of distributive justice, the most guilty men are appointed to punish minor delinquents.

Alienated Labor

by
Karl Marx

The worker becomes poorer the more wealth he produces,
the more his production increases in power and extent. The
worker becomes a cheaper commodity the more commodities
he produces. The *increase in value* of the world of things is
directly proportional to the *decrease in value* of the human
world. Labor not only produces commodities. It also produces itself and the worker as a *commodity*, and indeed in
the same proportion as it produces commodities in general.

This fact simply indicates that the object which labor produces, its product, stands opposed to it as an *alien thing,* as a
power independent of the producer. The product of labor is
labor embodied and made objective in a thing. It is the *objectification* of labor. The realization of labor is its objectification. In the viewpoint of political economy this realization of
labor appears as the *diminution* of the worker, the objectification as the *loss of and subservience to the object,* and the appropriation as *alienation* [*Entfremdung*], as externalization
[*Entäusserung*].

So much does the realization of labor appear as diminution
that the worker is diminished to the point of starvation. So
much does objectification appear as loss of the object that the
worker is robbed of the most essential objects not only of life
but also of work. Indeed, work itself becomes a thing of
which he can take possession only with the greatest effort and
with the most unpredictable interruptions. So much does the
appropriation of the object appear as alienation that the more
objects the worker produces, the fewer he can own and the
more he falls under the domination of his product, of capital.

All these consequences follow from the fact that the
worker is related to the *product of his labor* as to an *alien*

From *Writings of the Young Marx on Philosophy and Society,* translated and edited by Loyd D. Easton and Kurt Guddat. Copyright ©1967
by Loyd D. Easton and Kurt H. Guddat. Reprinted by permission of
Doubleday & Company, Inc.

object. For it is clear according to this premise: The more the worker exerts himself, the more powerful becomes the alien objective world which he fashions against himself, the poorer he and his inner world become, the less there is that belongs to him. It is the same in religion. The more man attributes to God, the less he retains in himself. The worker puts his life into the object; then it no longer belongs to him but to the object. The greater this activity, the poorer is the worker. What the product of his work is, he is not. The greater this product is, the smaller he is himself. The *externalization* of the worker in his product means not only that his work becomes an object, an *external* existence, but also that it exists *outside him* independently, alien, an autonomous power, opposed to him. The life he has given to the object confronts him as hostile and alien. . . .

Up to now we have considered the alienation, the externalization of the worker only from one side: his *relationship to the products of his labor*. But alienation is shown not only in the result but also in the *process of production*, in the *producing activity* itself. How could the worker stand in an alien relationship to the product of his activity if he did not alienate himself from himself in the very act of production? After all, the product is only the résumé of activity, of production. If the product of work is externalization, production itself must be active externalization, externalization of activity, activity of externalization. Only alienation—and externalization in the activity of labor itself—is summarized in the alienation of the object of labor.

What constitutes the externalization of labor?

First is the fact that labor is *external* to the laborer—that is, it is not part of his nature—and that the worker does not affirm himself in his work but denies himself, feels miserable and unhappy, develops no free physical and mental energy but mortifies his flesh and ruins his mind. The worker, therefore feels at ease only outside work, and during work he is outside himself. He is at home when he is not working and when he is working he is not at home. His work, therefore, is not voluntary, but coerced, *forced labor*. It is not the satisfaction of a need but only a *means* to satisfy other needs. Its alien character is obvious from the fact that as soon as no physical or other pressure exists, labor is avoided like the plague. External labor, labor in which man is externalized, is labor of self-sacrifice, of penance. Finally, the external nature of work for the worker appears in the fact that it is not his own but another person's, that in work he does not belong to himself but to someone else. In religion the spontaneity of human imagination, the spontaneity of the human brain and heart, acts independently of the individual as an alien, divine or devilish activity. Similarly, the activity of the worker is not his own spontaneous activity. It belongs to another. It is the loss of his own self.

The result, therefore, is that man (the worker) feels that he is acting freely only in his animal functions—eating, drinking, and procreating, or at most in his shelter and finery—while in his human functions he feels only like an animal. The animalistic becomes the human and the human the animalistic.

To be sure, eating, drinking, and procreation are genuine human functions. In abstraction, however, and separated from the remaining sphere of human activities and turned into final and sole ends, they are animal functions.

We have considered labor, the act of alienation of practical human activity, in two aspects: (1) the relationship of the worker to the *product of labor* as an alien object dominating him. This relationship is at the same time the relationship to the sensuous external world, to natural objects as an alien world hostile to him; (2) the relationship of labor to the *act of production in labor*. This relationship is that of the worker to his own activity as alien and not belonging to him, activity as passivity, power as weakness, procreation as emasculation, the worker's *own* physical and spiritual energy, his personal life—for what else is life but activity—as an activity turned against him, independent of him, and not belonging to him. *Self-alienation*, as against the alienation of the *object*, stated above. . . .

A direct consequence of man's alienation from the product of his work, from his life activity, and from his species-existence, is the *alienation of man* from *man*. When man confronts himself, he confronts *other* men. What holds true of man's relationship to his work, to the product of his work, and to himself, also holds true of man's relationship to other men, to their labor, and the object of their labor.

Who Will Do the Dirty Work?

by
Charles Fourier

Fresh souls, especially those of the young, possess an energy in the exercise of patriotic virtues which is not found in people of the world, who are ready to waver and tack about to obtain a sinecure.

In view of this, it is at once evident that the fathers are inferior to the children in the exercise of the virtues called patriotic.

Association knows how to profit by this inclination of youth to devotion to society; it knows how to employ childhood in positions where the father would be remiss; among others, in positions involving repugnant labour.

This repugnance is today overcome by the inducement of money; but it will be overcome by attraction, in an order of things in which pleasure will be the prime mover in the social mechanism.

The *régime* of attraction would fail utterly, unless it succeeded in attaching powerful baits to repellent kinds of labour, which can only be carried on in civilisation by the inducement of wages.

Some mercantile champion will object, that if Harmony is so immensely rich, as shown by the tables given of the thirty-fold relative increase, it could appropriate a large amount to the remuneration of repugnant labour. Such will be the case in emasculated (partial) association, which cannot develop the great springs of attraction; but in complete Harmony not a farthing will be appropriated to the payment of unclean labour: it would be subversive of the entire mechanism of high attraction, which should conquer the very strongest feelings of repugnance by *esprit de corps*.

Why is childhood selected for the chief *rôle* in the mechanism of general amity? It is because children, among the affective passions, are devoted to honour and friendship.

From Charles Fourier, *Design for Utopia, Selected Writings of Charles Fourier*, Schocken Books: New York, 1971. First published in 1901.

Neither love nor the family-feeling divert them from those sentiments: it is among them, therefore, that we ought to find friendship in all its purity, and to give it the noblest spur, that of social unitary charity, preventing, thereby, the debasement of the lower classes, through the encroachment of abject duties, and maintaining amity between the rich and the poor.

In the different chapters treating of the Series, I have demonstrated that if there were a single kind of labour which was despised, considered ignoble and degrading for the class that engaged in it, the inferior duties would soon sink into disrepute in every branch of industry, in the stables, the kitchen, rooms, workshops, etc.: the debasement would spread from one sort of labour to another; the contempt for labour would be gradually revived, and the result be that, as in civilisation, those people would be termed *comme il faut* who do nothing, are good for nothing. Then the time would come when this wealthy class would no longer take any part in the industrial Series, and would disdain to entertain any social relations with the classes of the poor.

It is the part of childhood to preserve the social body from this evil, undertaking as a body all duties held in disdain, by labouring for a mass and not for an individual (except attending the sick, which can only be entrusted to a body of mature persons, that of the infirmaries; however, the Little Hordes will take part by doing the dirty work).

It is to that age only we can turn to have the repugnant part of labour performed, by means of indirect attraction.

The love of dirt which prevails in children is only an uncultivated germ, like wild fruit; it must be refined by applying to it two forces—that of the *unitary religious spirit* and that of *corporative honour*. Supported by these two impulses, repugnant occupations will become games, having IN-DIRECT COMPOSITE attraction. This condition, set forth in the preceding chapter, is found to be satisfied by the two allurements I have just indicated.

For a long time I committed the error of censuring this comical peculiarity of children, and of endeavouring to have it disappear in the mechanism of the passionate Series; that was acting like a Titan, who wishes to change the work of God. I achieved no success until I adopted the attitude of planning in agreement with attraction; seeking to utilise the inclinations of childhood, such as Nature has created them. This calculation gave me the corporation which I have just described; it practises corporatively the only branch of charity remaining in Harmony; there are no longer any poor to be succoured, any captives to be ransomed and delivered from prison; there is nothing, therefore, left for children but to take up the domain of unclean labour—charity of high statesmanship, since it preserves from contempt the lowest industrial classes, and in the end the intermediate classes. It establishes, thus, the *fraternity* dreamed of by the philosophers, the spontaneous drawing together of all classes.

If, in such an order, the masses are refined, upright, above want, the great can no longer entertain a feeling of mistrust or of contempt for them. A friendly enthusiasm, therefore, is aroused in all the industrial groups, where the masses necessarily mingle with the great. Thus the dream is realised, which wishes to make all mankind a family of brothers.

This precious union would cease the moment one class of labour were held in disdain, disparaged: for instance, if there were paid boot-blacks in Harmony, those children, and consequently their parents, would be counted an inferior class, not admissible in a committee of the Series, in which the rich are members.

If that kind of service is accounted ignoble, the Little Hordes take charge of it and ennoble it. For the rest, it is rarely necessary to clean one's shoes in Harmony, thanks to the covered ways.

They are always up and about at 3 o'clock in the morning, cleaning the stables, attending to the animals, working in the slaughter-houses, where they are on the watch to see that no unnecessary suffering be ever inflicted upon the animals put to death.

The Little Hordes have, as one of their duties, the incidental repairing of the highways, that is, the daily maintenance of the surface-roads. The highways, in Harmony, are regarded as salons of unity; and, consequently, the Little Hordes, by virtue of their unitary charity, watch over the cleanliness and the ornamentation of the roadways.

It is to the *amour propre* of the Little Hordes that Harmony will be beholden for having, the world over, highways more sumptuous than the walks of our flower-gardens. They will be lined with trees and shrubs, even flowers, and watered up to the side-walk.

If a post-route sustain the slightest damage, the alarm is sounded instantly, and a tocsin of the tower of order apprises the Argot, who proceeds, by the light of torches if necessary, to make provisional ~pairs, and to hoist an accident-signal over the place, for fear that the damage may not be noticed by some travellers, and give rise to an accusation against the canton of having bad "*sacripants*." It would likewise be accused of having bad "*chenapans*,"[1] if a vicious reptile, serpent or viper, were discovered, or a croaking of frogs heard, in proximity to the high-roads.

In spite of their labour being the most difficult, through lack of *direct* attraction, the Little Hordes receive the lowest remuneration of all the Series. They would not accept anything if it were "becoming" in association to accept no share; they take only the smallest; that does not, however, prevent any of their members from obtaining the largest shares in other occupations: but in virtue of their being philanthropic unitary bodies, they have as their law the *indirect* contempt of riches, and devotion to repugnant labour, which they perform as a point of honour.

I have already remarked that indications of charitable devotion to abject duties are found even among monarchs, and that on Holy Thursday sovereigns are seen washing the feet of a dozen poor people—a duty by which the monarch thinks himself honoured, on account of the abjectness of the service. Now, when there shall be a corporation of high degree, devoted to the exercise of all the abject duties, none of these will in reality be such; without this condition, no binding together of the rich class and the poor.

If it is demonstrated that the religious spirit engenders a devotion to general charity, such as is found among the Redemptorist Fathers and other societies, all that need be done is to make use of this inclination, in accordance with the exigencies of the new order; and even should the corporation of the Little Hordes not appear to be the most efficacious arrangement, it would be none the less certain *that the principle of industrial charity, only alloyed with the religious spirit*, exists among us; and if I have erred in the application, the use, the customs and laws of the body of unitary charity, the critics ought to exert themselves to make better use of an impulse whose existence they cannot dispute; to invent a sect better able to do away with the obstacle of industrial disgust for unclean labour.

However, the Harmonians, more judicious than we in the

---

[1] In the vocabulary of Fourier, each one of the Little Hordes has a *nom de guerre*, according with the species of labour to which it devotes itself, and among these names there figure those of "*sacripants*" and "*chenapans*."

theory and the practice of charity, will not apply that virtue to useless ceremonies, such as washing the feet of the poor, which they could very well do themselves, or employing a confessor with an income of 50,000 francs to detach a criminal from the gallows. When there shall no longer exist either beggars or people to be hanged, they can no longer serve for calculations of ostentatious charity. All those practices, laudable as to intention and as examples, are only the abortions of a charitable policy. It ought to be applied to effect the drawing together of the classes at the extremes, whom nothing can conciliate in civilisation, because that order is a failure.

Pecuniary Emulation

by
Thorstein Veblen

Wherever the institution of private property is found, even in a sightly developed form, the economic process bears the character of a struggle between men for the possession of goods. It ·has been customary in economic theory, and especially among those economists who adhere with least faltering to the body of modernized classical doctrines, to construe this struggle for wealth as being substantially a struggle for subsistence. Such is, no doubt, its character in large part during the earlier and less efficient phases of industry. Such is also its character in all cases where the "niggardliness of nature" is so strict as to afford but a scanty livelihood to the community in return for strenuous and unremitting application to the business of getting the means of subsistence. But in all progressing communities an advance is presently made beyond this early stage of technological development. Industrial efficiency is presently carried to such a pitch as to afford something appreciably more than a bare livelihood to those engaged in the industrial process. It has not been unusual for economic theory to speak of the further struggle for wealth on this new industrial basis as a competition for an increase of the comforts of life—primarily for an increase of the physical comforts which the consumption of goods affords.

The end of acquisition and accumulation is conventionally held to be the consumption of the goods accumulated— whether it is consumption directly by the owner of the goods or by the household attached to him and for this purpose identified with him in theory. This is at least felt to be the economically legitimate end of acquisition, which alone it is incumbent on the theory to take account of. Such consumption may of course be conceived to serve the consumer's physical wants—his physical comfort—or his so-called higher wants—spiritual, æsthetic, intellectual, or what not; the latter

From Thorstein Veblen, *The Theory of the Leisure Class*, Macmillan. First published in 1899.

class of wants being served indirectly by an expenditure of goods, after the fashion familiar to all economic readers.

But it is only when taken in a sense far removed from its naïve meaning that consumption of goods can be said to afford the incentive from which accumulation invariably proceeds. The motive that lies at the root of ownership is emulation; and the same motive of emulation continues active in the further development of the institution to which it has given rise and in the development of all those features of the social structure which this institution of ownership touches. The possession of wealth confers honor; it is an invidious distinction. Nothing equally cogent can be said for the consumption of goods, nor for any other conceivable incentive to acquisition, and especially not for any incentive to the accumulation of wealth.

It is of course not to be overlooked that in a community where nearly all goods are private property the necessity of earning a livelihood is a powerful and ever-present incentive for the poorer members of the community. The need of subsistence and of an increase of physical comfort may for a time be the dominant motive of acquisition for those classes who are habitually employed at manual labor, whose subsistence is on a precarious footing, who possess little and ordinarily accumulate little; but it will appear in the course of the discussion that even in the case of these impecunious classes the predominance of the motive of physical want is not so decided as has sometimes been assumed. On the other hand, so far as regards those members and classes of the community who are chiefly concerned in the accumulation of wealth, the incentive of subsistence or of physical comfort never plays a considerable part. Ownership began and grew into a human institution on grounds unrelated to the subsistence minimum. The dominant incentive was from the outset the invidious distinction attaching to wealth, and, save temporarily and by exception, no other motive has usurped the primacy at any later stage of the development.

Property set out with being booty held as trophies of the successful raid. So long as the group had departed but little from the primitive communal organization, and so long as it still stood in close contact with other hostile groups, the utility of things or persons owned lay chiefly in an invidious comparison between their possessor and the enemy from whom they were taken. The habit of distinguishing between the interests of the individual and those of the group to which he belongs is apparently a later growth. Invidious comparison between the possessor of the honorific booty and his less successful neighbors within the group was no doubt present early as an element of the utility of the things possessed, though this was not at the outset the chief element of their value. The man's prowess was still primarily the group's prowess, and the possessor of the booty felt himself to be primarily the keeper of the honor of his group. This appreciation of exploit from the communal point of view is met with also at later stages of social growth, especially as regards the laurels of war.

But so soon as the custom of individual ownership begins to gain consistency, the point of view taken in making the invidious comparison on which private property rests will begin to change. Indeed, the one change is but the reflex of the other. The initial phase of ownership, the phase of acquisition by naïve seizure and conversion, begins to pass into the subsequent stage of an incipient organization of industry on the basis of private property (in slaves); the horde develops into a more or less self-sufficing industrial community; possessions then come to be valued not so much as evidence of successful foray, but rather as evidence of the prepotence of the possessor of these goods over other individuals within the community. The invidious comparison now becomes primarily a comparison of the owner with the other members of the group. Property is still of the nature of trophy, but, with the cultural advance, it becomes more and more a trophy of successes scored in the game of ownership carried on between the members of the group under the quasi-peaceable methods of nomadic life.

Gradually, as industrial activity further displaces predatory activity in the community's everyday life and in men's habits of thought, accumulated property more and more replaces trophies of predatory exploit as the conventional exponent of prepotence and success. With the growth of settled industry, therefore, the possession of wealth gains in relative importance and effectiveness as a customary basis of repute and esteem. Not that esteem ceases to be awarded on the basis of other, more direct evidence of prowess; not that successful predatory aggression or warlike exploit ceases to call out the approval and admiration of the crowd, or to stir the envy of the less successful competitors; but the opportunities for gaining distinction by means of this direct manifestation of superior force grow less available both in scope and frequency.

At the same time opportunities for industrial aggression, and for the accumulation of property by the quasi-peaceable methods of nomadic industry, increase in scope and availability. And it is even more to the point that property now becomes the most easily recognized evidence of a reputable degree of success as distinguished from heroic or signal achievement. It therefore becomes the conventional basis of esteem. Its possession in some amount becomes necessary in order to have any reputable standing in the community. It becomes indispensable to accumulate, to acquire property, in order to retain one's good name. When accumulated goods have in this way once become the accepted badge of efficiency, the possession of wealth presently assumes the character of an independent and definitive basis of esteem. The possession of goods, whether acquired aggressively by one's own exertion or passively by transmission through inheritance from others, becomes a conventional basis of reputability. The possession of wealth, which was at the outset valued simply as an evidence of efficiency, becomes, in popular apprehension, itself a meritorious act. Wealth is now itself intrinsically honorable and confers honor on its possessor. By a further refinement, wealth acquired passively by transmission from ancestors or other antecedents presently becomes even more honorific than wealth acquired by the possessor's own effort; but this distinction belongs at a later stage in the evolution of the pecuniary culture and will be spoken of in its place.

Prowess and exploit may still remain the basis of award of the highest popular esteem, although the possession of wealth has become the basis of commonplace reputability and of a blameless social standing. The predatory instinct and the consequent approbation of predatory efficiency are deeply ingrained in the habits of thought of those peoples who have passed under the discipline of a protracted predatory culture. According to popular award, the highest honors within human reach may, even yet, be those gained by an unfolding of extraordinary predatory efficiency in war, or by a quasi-predatory efficiency in statecraft; but for the purpose of a commonplace decent standing in the community these means of repute have been replaced by the acquisition and accumulation of goods. In order to stand well in the eyes of the community, it is necessary to come up to a certain, somewhat indefinite, conventional standard of wealth; just as in the earlier predatory stage it is necessary for the barbarian man to come up to the tribe's standard of physical endurance, cunning and skill at arms. A certain standard of wealth in one case, and of prowess in the other, is a necessary condition of reputability, and anything in excess of this normal amount is meritorious.

Those members of the community who fall short of this, somewhat indefinite, normal degree of prowess or of property suffer in the esteem of their fellowmen; and consequently they suffer also in their own esteem, since the usual basis of self-respect is the respect accorded by one's neighbors. Only individuals with an aberrant temperament can in the long run retain their self-esteem in the face of the disesteem of their fellows. Apparent exceptions to the rule are met with, especially among people with strong religious convictions. But these apparent exceptions are scarcely real exceptions, since such persons commonly fall back on the putative approbation of some supernatural witness of their deeds.

So soon as the possession of property becomes the basis of popular esteem, therefore, it becomes also a requisite to that complacency which we call self-respect. In any community where goods are held in severalty it is necessary, in order to ensure his own peace of mind, that an individual should possess as large a portion of goods as others with whom he is accustomed to class himself; and it is extremely gratifying to possess something more than others. But as fast as a person makes new acquisitions, and becomes accustomed to the resulting new standard of wealth, the new standard forthwith ceases to afford appreciably greater satisfaction than the earlier standard did. The tendency in any case is constantly to make the present pecuniary standard the point of departure for a fresh increase of wealth; and this in turn gives rise to a new standard of sufficiency and a new pecuniary classification of one's self as compared with one's neighbors. So far as concerns the present question, the end sought by accumulation is to rank high in comparison with the rest of the community in point of pecuniary strength. So long as the comparison is distinctly unfavorable to himself, the normal, average individual will live in chronic dissatisfaction with his present lot; and when he has reached what may be called the normal pecuniary standard of the community, or of his class in the community, this chronic dissatisfaction will give place to a restless straining to place a wider and ever-widening pecuniary interval between himself and this average standard. The invidious comparison can never become so favorable to the individual making it that he would not gladly rate himself still higher relatively to his competitors in the struggle for pecuniary reputability.

In the nature of the case, the desire for wealth can scarcely be satiated in any individual instance, and evidently a satiation of the average or general desire for wealth is out of the question. However widely, or equally, or "fairly," it may be distributed, no general increase of the community's wealth can make any approach to satiating this need, the ground of which is the desire of everyone to excel everyone else in the accumulation of goods. If, as is sometimes assumed, the incentive to accumulation were the want of subsistence or of physical comfort, then the aggregate economic wants of a community might conceivably be satisfied at some point in the advance of industrial efficiency; but since the struggle is substantially a race for reputability on the basis of an invidious comparison, no approach to a definitive attainment is possible.

What has just been said must not be taken to mean that there are no other incentives to acquisition and accumulation than this desire to excel in pecuniary standing and so gain the esteem and envy of one's fellowmen. The desire for added comfort and security from want is present as a motive at every stage of the process of accumulation in a modern industrial community; although the standard of sufficiency in these respects is in turn greatly affected by the habit of pecuniary emulation. To a great extent this emulation shapes the methods and selects the objects of expenditure for personal comfort and decent livelihood.

Besides this, the power conferred by wealth also affords a motive to accumulation. That propensity for purposeful activity and that repugnance to all futility of effort which belong to man by virtue of his character as an agent do not desert him when he emerges from the naïve communal culture where the dominant note of life is the unanalyzed and undifferentiated solidarity of the individual with the group with which his life is bound up. When he enters upon the predatory stage, where self-seeking in the narrower sense becomes the dominant note, this propensity goes with him still, as the pervasive trait that shapes his scheme of life. The propensity for achievement and the repugnance to futility remain the underlying economic motive. The propensity changes only in the form of its expression and in the proximate objects to which it directs the man's activity. Under the regime of indi-

vidual ownership the most available means of visibly achieving a purpose is that afforded by the acquisition and
accumulation of goods; and as the self-regarding antithesis
between man and man reaches fuller consciousness, the
propensity for achievement—the instinct of workmanship—
tends more and more to shape itself into a straining to excel
others in pecuniary achievement. Relative success, tested by
an invidious pecuniary comparison with other men, becomes
the conventional end of action. The currently accepted legitimate end of effort becomes the achievement of a favorable
comparison with other men; and therefore the repugnance
to futility to a good extent coalesces with the incentive of
emulation. It acts to accentuate the struggle for pecuniary
reputability by visiting with a sharper disapproval all shortcoming and all evidence of shortcoming in point of pecuniary
success. Purposeful effort comes to mean, primarily, effort directed to or resulting in a more creditable showing of accumulated wealth. Among the motives which lead men to
accumulate wealth, the primacy, both in scope and intensity,
therefore, continues to belong to this motive of pecuniary
emulation.

In making use of the term "invidious," it may perhaps be
unnecessary to remark, there is no intention to extol or depreciate, or to commend or deplore any of the phenomena
which the word is used to characterize. The term is used in a
technical sense as describing a comparison of persons with a
view to rating and grading them in respect of relative worth
or value—in an aesthetic or moral sense—and so awarding
and defining the relative degrees of complacency with which
they may legitimately be contemplated by themselves and by
others. An invidious comparison is a process of valuation of
persons in respect of worth.

The Cabdriver and His Fare: Facets of a Fleeting Relationship[1]

by
Fred Davis

Even in an urban and highly secularized society such as ours, most service relationships, be they between a professional and his client or a menial and his patron, are characterized by certain constraints on too crass a rendering and consuming of the service.[2] That is to say, in the transaction, numerous interests besides that of simply effecting an economic exchange are customarily attended to and dealt with. The moral reputation of the parties,[3] their respective social standing, and the skill and art with which the service is performed[4] are but a few of the non-instrumental values which are usually incorporated into the whole act.

Tenuous though such constraints may become at times, particularly in large cities where anonymous roles, only segmentally related, occur in great profusion, it is at once evident that for them to exist at all something approximating a community must be present. Practitioners and clients must be sufficiently in communication for any untoward behavior to stand a reasonable chance of becoming known, remarked

Reprinted by permission of the publishers and the author from *American Journal of Sociology*, Vol. 65, 1959–60, pp. 158–65. Copyright 1959, 1960 by University of Chicago.

[1]This article is based largely on notes and observations made by me over a six-month period in 1948 when I worked as a cabdriver for one of the larger taxicab firms in Chicago. I am greatly indebted to Erving Goffman, Everett C. Hughes, and Howard S. Becker for their comments and criticisms.

[2]Talcott Parsons, *The Social System* (Glencoe, Ill.: Free Press, 1951), pp. 48–56.

[3]Erving Goffman, *The Presentation of Self in Everyday Life* (Edinburgh: University of Edinburgh Social Science Research Centre, 1956), pp. 160–62.

[4]Everett C. Hughes, *Men and Their Work* (Glencoe, Ill.: Free Press. 1958), pp. 88–101.

upon, remembered, and, in extreme cases, made public. And, whereas the exercise of sanctions does not necessarily depend on a community network[5] that is closely integrated (or one in which there is a total identity of values and interests), it does depend on there being some continuity and stability in the relationships that make up the network, so that, at minimum, participants may in the natural course of events be able to identify actions and actors to one another.[6]

It is mainly, though not wholly, from this vantage point that big-city cabdriving as an occupation is here discussed, particularly the relationship between cabdriver and fare and its consequences for the occupational culture.[7] Approximating in certain respects a provincial's caricature of the broad arc of social relations in the metropolis, this relationship affords an extreme instance of the weakening and attenuation of many of the constraints customary in other client-and-patron-oriented services in our society. As such, its analysis can perhaps point up by implication certain of the rarely considered preconditions for practitioner-client relations found in other, more firmly structured, services and professions.

In a large city like Chicago the hiring of a cab by a passenger may be conceived of in much the same way as the random collision of particles in an atomic field. True, there are some sectors of the field in which particles come into more frequent collision than others, for example, downtown, at railroad depots, and at the larger neighborhood shopping centers. But this kind of differential activity within the field as a whole provides little basis for predicting the coupling of any two specific particles.

To a much more pronounced degree than is the case in other client-and-patron-oriented services, the occupation of cabdriver provides its practitioners with few, if any, regularities by which to come upon, build up, and maintain a steady

---

[5]Because it better delineates the boundaries and linkages of informal sanctioning groups found in large cities, the term "network" is used here to qualify the more global concept of "community." See Elizabeth Bott, *Family and Social Network* (London: Tavistock, 1957), pp. 58–61.

[6]Robert K. Merton, "The Role Set: Problems in Sociological Theory," *British Journal of Sociology*, VIII, No. 2 (June, 1957), 114.

[7]Parallel studies of this aspect of occupational culture are: Hughes, *op. cit.*, pp. 42–55; Howard S. Becker, "The Professional Dance Musician and his Audience," *American Journal of Sociology*, LVII (September, 1951), 136–44; Ray Gold, "Janitors versus Tenants: A Status-Income Dilemma," *American Journal of Sociology*, LVII (March, 1952), 486–93.

clientele. The doctor has his patients, the schoolteacher her pupils, the janitor his tenants, the waitress her regular diners; and in each case server and served remain generally in some continuing or renewable relationship. By contrast, the cabdriver's day consists of a long series of brief contacts with unrelated persons of whom he has no foreknowledge, just as they have none of him, and whom he is not likely to encounter again.

Furthermore, by virtue of the differential spatial, social, and organizational arrangements of the community, it is also likely that the clients of these other practitioners will, in some manner at least, know one another and be related to one another in ways that often transcend the simple circumstance of sharing the same services: they may also be friends, kin, neighbors, or colleagues. For this reason the clientele of most practitioners is something more than an aggregate of discrete individuals; it is, as well, a rudimentary social universe and forum to which the practitioner must address himself in other than purely individual terms.[8]

The cabdriver, by comparison, has no such clientele. He has no fixed business address, and his contacts with passengers are highly random and singular. To a striking degree he is a practitioner without reputation because those who ride in his cab do not comprise, except perhaps in the most abstract sense, anything approximating a social group. They neither know nor come into contact with one another in other walks of life, and, even if by chance some do, they are unaware of their ever having shared the services of the same anonymous cabdriver. Even were the driver deliberately to set out to build up a small nucleus of steady and favored passengers, the time-space logistics of his job would quickly bring such a scheme to nought. Unable to plot his location in advance or to distribute time according to a schedule, he depends on remaining open to all comers wherever he finds himself. Much more so than other classes of service personnel, cabdrivers are both the fortuitous victims and the beneficiaries of random and highly impersonal market contingencies.

This set of circumstances—fleeting, one-time contact with a heterogeneous aggregate of clients, unknown to one another—exerts an interesting influence on the role of cabdriver.

Unable, either directly through choice or indirectly through

[8]Merton, *op. sit.*, pp. 110–12.

location, to select clients, the cabdriver is deprived of even minimal controls. His trade therefore exposes him to a variety of hazards and exigencies which few others, excepting policemen, encounter as frequently; for example: stick-ups, belligerent drunks, women in labor, psychopaths, counterfeiters, and fare-jumpers. Unlike the policeman's, however, his control over them is more fragile.

Nor, incidentally, is the cabdriver's social status or level of occupational skill of much help in inducing constraint in fares. Patently, his status is low, in large part precisely because, unlike the professional and other practitioners commanding prestige, he can hardly be distinguished from his clients in task-relevant competence. Not only is the operation of a motor car a widely possessed skill, but a large proportion of fares have, for example, a very good idea of the best routes to their destination, the rules and practices of the road, and the charges for a trip. Though they are rarely as adept or sophisticated in these matters as the cabdriver, the discrepancy is so small that many think they know the driver's job as well as he does. Periodically, a cabdriver will boldly challenge a difficult and critical passenger to take over the wheel himself. Others, wishing to impress on the fare that theirs is a real service requiring special talent and skill, will resort to darting nimbly in and out of traffic, making neatly executed U-turns and leaping smartly ahead of other cars when the traffic light changes.

Goffman[9] speaks of a category of persons who in some social encounters are treated as if they were not present, whereas in fact they may be indispensable for sustaining the performance. He terms these "non-persons" and gives as an example a servant at a social gathering. Although cabdrivers are not consistently approached in this way by fares, it happens often enough for it to become a significant theme of their work. Examples are legion. Maresca[10] tells of the chorus girl who made a complete change from street clothing into stage costume as he drove her to her theater. More prosaic instances include the man and wife who, managing to suppress their anger while on the street, launch into a bitter quarrel the moment they are inside the cab; or the well-

[9]Goffman, *op. cit.*, p. 95.

[10]James V. Maresca, *My Flag Is Down* (New York: E. P. Dutton & Co., 1945). Essentially the same incident is related by an unidentified cabdriver on the documentary recording of Tony Schwartz, *The New York Taxi Driver* (Columbia Records, ML5309, 1959).

groomed young couple who after a few minutes roll over on the back seat to begin petting; or the businessman who loudly discusses details of a questionable business deal. Here the driver is expected to, and usually does, act as if he were merely an extension of the automobile he operates. In actuality, of course, he is acutely aware of what goes on in his cab, and, although his being treated as a non-person implies a degraded status, it also affords him a splendid vantage point from which to witness a rich variety of human schemes and entanglements.

The fleeting nature of the cabdriver's contact with the passenger at the same time also makes for his being approached as someone to whom intimacies can be revealed and opinions forthrightly expressed with little fear of rebuttal, retaliation, or disparagement. And though this status as an accessible person is the product of little more than the turning inside-out of his non-person status—which situation implies neither equality nor respect for his opinion—it nevertheless does afford him glimpses of the private lives of individuals which few in our society, apart from psychiatrists and clergy, are privileged to note as often or in such great variety. It is probably not a mistaken everyday generalization that big-city cabdrivers, on their part, feel less compunction about discussing their own private lives, asking probing questions, and "sounding off" on a great many topics and issues than do others who regularly meet the public, but less fleetingly.[11]

In cabdriving, therefore, propriety, deference, and "face" are, in the nature of the case, weaker than is the case in most other service relationships. This absence contributes to a heightened preoccupation with and focusing on the purely instrumental aspect of the relationship which for the driver is the payment he receives for his service. This perhaps would be less blatantly the case were it not for the gratuity or tip. For the non-cab-owning company driver, the sum collected in tips amounts roughly to 40 per cent of his earnings. Considering, for example, that in Chicago in the late forties a hardworking cabdriver, who worked for ten hours a day, six days a week, would on the average take home approximately seventy-five dollars a week including tips, the importance of tipping can readily be appreciated. For the family man who

[11]Cf. Schwartz, *op. cit.* In fact, these characteristic qualities, with a work-adapted, bitter-sweet admixture of cynicism and sentimentality, comprise the core of the personality widely imputed to cabdrivers by the riding public. Cf. Hughes, *op. cit.* pp. 23–41.

drives, tips usually represent the difference between a subsistence and a living wage. Also, tips are, apart from taxes, money "in the clear," in that the driver does not have to divide them with the company as he does his metered collections.[12] Sum for sum, therefore, tips represent greater gain for him than do metered charges.

It would probably be incorrect to hold that pecuniary considerations are the sole ones involved in the cabdriver's attitude toward the tip. Yet in such tip-sensitive occupations as cabdriving, waitering, and bellhopping to suggest[13] that the tip's primary significance is its symbolic value as a token of affection or appreciation for a service well performed would be even wider of the mark. Vindictive caricatures abound among cabdrivers, as they do among waiters, waitresses, and bellhops, of the "polite gentleman" or "kind lady" who with profuse thanks and flawless grace departs from the scene having "stiffed" (failed to tip) them. In occupations where the tip constitutes so large a fraction of the person's earnings, the cash nexus, while admittedly not the only basis upon which patrons are judged, is so important as to relegate other considerations to a secondary place. Will the fare tip or will he "stiff"? How much will he tip? The answers remain in nearly every instance problematic to the end. Not only is there no sure way of predicting the outcome, but in a culture where the practice of tipping is neither as widespread nor as standardized as in many Continental countries, for example, the driver cannot in many cases even make a guess.

No regular scheme of work can easily tolerate so high a degree of ambiguity and uncertainty in a key contingency. Invariably, attempts are made to fashion ways and means of greater predictability and control; or, failing that, of devising formulas and imagery to bring order and reason in otherwise inscrutable and capricious events. In the course of a long history a rich body of stereotypes, beliefs, and practices[14] has grown up whose function is that of reducing uncertainty, increasing calculability, and providing coherent explanations.

A basic dichotomy running through the cabdriver's concept

[12] In Chicago in 1948 the company driver's share of the metered sum was 42½ per cent. Since that time the proportion has been increased slightly.

[13] Cf. William F. Whyte, *Human Relations in the Restaurant Industry* (New York: McGraw-Hill Book Co., 1948), p. 100.

[14] Cf. here and in the section to follow the pertinent remarks of Hughes on "guilty knowledge" developed by those in a service occupation with reference to their clientele. Hughes, *op. cit.*, pp. 81–82.

of his client world is of regular cab users and of non-cab users, the latter referred to as "jerks," "slobs," "yokels," "public transportation types," and a host of other derogatory terms. The former class, though viewed as quite heterogeneous within itself, includes all who customarily choose cabs in preference to other forms of local transportation, are conversant with the cab-passenger role, and, most of all, accept, if only begrudgingly, the practice of tipping. By comparison, the class of non-cab users includes that vast aggregate of persons who resort to cabs only in emergencies or on special occasions, and are prone too often to view the hiring of a cab as simply a more expensive mode of transportation.

Take, for example, the familiar street scene following a sudden downpour or unexpected breakdown in bus service, when a group of individuals cluster about a bus stop, several of whom dart from the curb now and then in hope of hailing a cab. Such persons are almost by definition non-cab users or they would not be found at a bus stop in the rain; nor would they be keeping an eye out for a possible bus. A potential fare in this predicament is to the cabdriver a foul-weather friend, and drivers are on occasion known to hurtle by in spiteful glee, leaving the supplicant standing.

He who hires a cab only on special occasions, frequently to impress others or, perhaps, himself alone, is another familiar kind of non-cab user. Writing of his experiences as a London cabdriver, Hodge relates a by no means uncommon encounter:

> But tonight is different. Perhaps the Pools have come up for once. Anyhow, he's got money. He signals me with exaggerated casualness from the cinema entrance. . . . She steps in daintily, the perfect lady, particularly where she puts her feet. As soon as she's safely inside, he whispers the address . . . and adds, as one man of the world to another, "No hurry, driver." Then he dives in with such utter *savoir faire, comme il faut,* and what not, that he trips over the mat and lands face first on the back seat.[15]

Perhaps the most obvious kind of non-user is the person who, after hailing a cab, will ask the driver some such question as, "How much will it cost to take me to 500 Elm

[15]Herbert Hodge, "I Drive a Taxi," *Fact*, No. 22 (January, 1939), pp. 28–29.

Street?" By this simple inquiry this person stands revealed as one who takes a narrow view of cab travel and from whom not much, if anything, can be expected by way of tip. On the other hand, regular cab users demonstrate in a variety of ways that for them this is a customary and familiar mode of travel. The manner in which they hail a cab, when and how they announce their destination, the ease with which they enter and exit, how they sit—these, and more, though difficult to describe in precise detail, comprise the Gestalt.

There exists among drivers an extensive typology of cab users, the attributes imputed to each type having a certain predictive value, particularly as regards tipping. Some of the more common and sharply delineated types are:

The Sport. The cabdriver's image of this type combines in one person those attributes of character which he views as ideal. While the Sport's vocation may be any one of many, his status derives more from his extra-vocational activities, e.g., at the race track, prize fights, ball games, popular restaurants, and bars. He is the perennial "young man on the town." Gentlemanly without being aloof, interested without becoming familiar, he also is, of course, never petty. Most of all, his tips are generous, and even on very short rides he will seldom tip less than a quarter. A favorite success story among cabdrivers describes at length and in fine detail the handsome treatment accorded the driver on an all-night tour with a Sport.[16]

The Blowhard. The Blowhard is a false Sport. While often wearing the outer mantle of the Sport, he lacks the real Sport's casualness, assured manners, and comfortable style. Given to loquaciousness, he boasts and indiscriminately fabricates tales of track winnings, sexual exploits, and the important people he knows. Often holding out the promise of much by way of tip, he seldom lives up to his words.

The Businessman. These are the staple of the cab trade, particularly for drivers who work by day. Not only are they the most frequently encountered; their habits and preferences are more uniform than those of any other type: the brisk effi-

---

[16] As in the past, the Sport still serves as something of a hero figure in our culture, particularly among the working classes. A type midway between the Playboy and the Bohemian, his unique appeal rests perhaps on the ease and assurance with which he is pictured as moving between and among social strata, untainted by upper-class snobbishness, middle-class conventionality and lower-class vulgarity. In *The Great Gatsby*, Fitzgerald gives us a penetrative exposition of the myth of the Sport and its undoing at the hands of the class system.

ciency with which they engage a cab, their purposefulness and disinclination to partake of small talk. Though not often big tippers, they are thought fair. Thus they serve as something of a standard by which the generosity or stinginess of others is judged.

The Lady Shopper. Although almost as numerous as businessmen, Lady Shoppers are not nearly as well thought of by cabdrivers. The stereotype is a middle-aged woman, fashionably though unattractively dressed, sitting somewhat stiffly at the edge of her seat and wearing a fixed glare which bespeaks her conviction that she is being "taken for a ride." Her major delinquency, however, is undertipping; her preferred coin is a dime, no more or less, regardless of how long or arduous the trip. A forever repeated story is of the annoyed driver, who, after a grueling trip with a Lady Shopper, hands the coin back, telling her, "Lady, keep your lousy dime. You need it more than I do."[17]

Live Ones.[18] Live Ones are a special category of fare usually encountered by the cabdriver who works by night. They are, as a rule, out-of-town conventioneers or other revelers who tour about in small groups in search of licentious forms of entertainment: cabarets, burlesques, strip-tease bars, pick-up joints, etc. As often as not, they have already had a good deal to drink when the cabdriver meets them, and, being out-of-towners they frequently turn to him for recommendations on where to go. In the late forties an arrangement existed in Chicago whereby some of the more popular Near North Side and West Madison Street "clip joints" rewarded cabdrivers for "steering" Live Ones to their establishments. Some places paid fifty cents "a head"; others a dollar "for the load." As do the many others who regularly cater to Live Ones—e.g., waitresses, bartenders, female bar companions (B-girls), night-club hosts and hostesses, entertainers, prostitutes—cabdrivers often view them as fair game. And while their opportunities for pecuniary exploitation are fewer and more limited than those open, for example, to B-girls and night-

---

[17]The stereotype of women as poor tippers is widely shared by other tip-sensitive occupations. Cf. Frances Donovan, *The Woman Who Waits* (Boston: Badger, 1920).

[18]The term "Live Ones" is employed in a variety of pursuits as apparently diverse as retail selling, night-club entertainment, traveling fairs, and panhandling. Generally, it designates persons who are "easy touches," eager to succumb to the oftentimes semifraudulent proposals of the operator. Cf. W. Jack Peterson and Milton A. Maxwell, "The Skid Row Wino," *Social Problems,* V (Spring, 1958), 312.

club proprietors, many drivers feel less inhibited about padding charges and finagling extras from Live Ones than they do from other fares. Often extravagant in their tips because of high spirits and drink, Live Ones are also frequently careless and forget to tip altogether. Knowing that Live Ones are out to "blow their money" anyway, many drivers believe they are justified in seeing to it that they are not deprived of a small portion.

Although the cab driver's typology of fares stems in a large part from the attempt to order experience, reduce uncertainty, and further calculability of the tip, it is questionable of course as to how accurate or efficient it is. For, as has often been remarked, stereotypes and typologies have a way of imparting a symmetry and regularity to behavior which are, at best, only crudely approximated in reality. Too often it happens, for example, that a fare tabbed as a Sport turns out to be a Stiff (non-tipper), that a Blowhard matches his words with a generous tip, or that a Lady Shopper will give fifteen or even twenty cents. The persistence of the typology therefore has perhaps as much to do with the cabdriver's a posteriori reconstructions and rationalizations of fare behavior as it does with the typology's predictive efficiency.

To protect and insure themselves against an unfavorable outcome of tipping, many drivers will, depending upon circumstances, employ diverse tactics and stratagems (some more premeditated than others) to increase the amount of tip or to compensate for its loss should it not be forthcoming. Certain of these are listed below. It should be understood however, that in the ordinary instance the driver makes no attempt to manipulate the fare, believing resignedly that in the long run such means bear too little fruit for the effort and risk.

Making Change. Depending on the tariff and the amount handed him, the driver can fumble about in his pockets for change, or make change in such denominations as often to embarrass a fare into giving a larger tip than he had intended. The efficacy of this tactic depends naturally on the determination and staying power of the fare, qualities which many fares are averse to demonstrate, particularly when it comes to small change.

The Hard-Luck Story. This is usually reserved for young persons and others who, for whatever reason, evidence an insecure posture vis-à-vis the driver. Typically, the hard-luck story consists of a catalogue of economic woes, e.g., long and hard hours of work, poor pay, insulting and unappreciative passengers, etc. In "confiding" these to the fare, the driver pretends to esteem him as an exceptionally sympathetic and intelligent person who, unlike "the others," can appreciate his circumstances and act accordingly. Most drivers, however, view the hard-luck story as an unsavory form of extortion, beneath their dignity. Furthermore, while it may work in some cases, its potential for alienating tips is probably as great as its success at extracting them.

Fictitious Charges. The resort to fictitious and fraudulent charges occurs most commonly in those cases in which the driver feels that he has good reason to believe that the fare will, either through malice or ignorance, not tip and when the fare impresses him as being enough of a non-cab user as not to know when improper charges are being levied. Once, when I complained to a veteran cabdriver about having been "stiffed" by a young couple, newly arrived in Chicago, to whom I had extended such extra services as carrying luggage and opening doors, I was told: "Wise up kid! When you pick up one of these yokels at the Dearborn Station carrying a lot of cheap straw luggage on him, you can bet ninety-nine times out of a hundred that he isn't going to tip you. Not that he's a mean guy or anything, but where he comes from, they never heard of tipping. What I do with a yokel like that is to take him to where he's going, show him what the fare is on the meter, and tell him that it costs fifteen cents extra for each piece of luggage. Now, he doesn't know that there's no charge for hand luggage, but that way I'm sure of getting my tip out of him."

The "Psychological" Approach. Possibly attributing more art to their trade than is the case, some drivers are of the opinion that a cab ride can be tailored to fit a passenger in much the same way as can a suit of clothes. One cabdriver, boasting of his success at getting tips, explained: "In this business you've got to use psychology. You've got to make the ride fit the person. Now, take a businessman. He's in a hurry to get someplace and he doesn't want a lot of bullshit and crapping around. With him you've got to keep moving. Do some fancy cutting in and out, give the cab a bit of a jerk when you take off from a light. Not reckless, mind you, but plenty of zip. He likes that.[19] With old people, it's just the opposite. They're more afraid than anyone of getting hurt or

[19]Cf. Hodge, *op. cit.,* p. 17.

killed in a cab. Take it easy with them. Creep along, open doors for them, help them in and out, be real folksy. Call them 'Sir' and 'Ma'am' and they'll soon be calling you 'young man.' They're suckers for this stuff, and they'll loosen up their pocketbooks a little bit."

In the last analysis, neither the driver's typology of fares nor his stratagems further to any marked degree his control of the tip. Paradoxically, were these routinely successful in achieving predictability and control, they would at the same time divest the act of tipping of its most distinguishing characterisics—of its uncertainty, variability, and of the element of revelation in its consummation. It is these—essentially the problematic in human intercourse[20]—which distinguish the tip from the fixed service charge. And though another form of remuneration might in the end provide the cabdriver with a better wage and a more secure livelihood, the abrogation of tipping would also lessen the intellectual play which uncertainty stimulates and without which cabdriving would be for many nothing more than unrelieved drudgery.

That the practice of tipping, however, expressively befits only certain kinds of service relationships and may under slightly altered circumstances easily degenerate into corruption or extortion is demonstrated, ironically enough, by the predicament of some cabdrivers themselves. To give an example: In the garage out of which I worked, nearly everyone connected with maintenance and assignment of cabs expected tips from drivers for performing many of the routine tasks associated with their jobs, such as filling a tank with gas, changing a tire, or adjusting a carburetor. Although they resented it, drivers had little recourse but to tip. Otherwise, they would acquire reputations as "stiffs" and "cheapskates," be kept waiting interminably for repairs, and find that faulty and careless work had been done on their vehicles. Particularly with the dispatcher did the perversion of the tipping system reach extortionate proportions. His power derived from the assignment of cabs; to protect themselves from being assigned "pots" (cabs that would break down in the middle of the day), drivers tipped him fifty cents at the beginning of every week. Since nearly every driver tipped the dispatcher and since there were more drivers than good cabs, a certain number of drivers would still be assigned "pots." Some, wishing to insure doubly against this would then raise the bribe to a dollar and a half a week, causing the others to follow suit

[20]Cf. Donovan, *op. cit.*, p. 262.

in a vicious spiral. If little else, this shows how the tip—as distinguished from the gift, honorarium, inducement, or bribe—depends for its expressive validity on there not being a too close, long sustained, or consequential relationship between the parties to a service transaction.

Among service relationships in our society, that between the big city cabdriver and his fare is, due to the way in which they come into contact with each other, especially subject to structural weakness. The relationship is random, fleeting, unrenewable, and largely devoid of socially integrative features which in other client and patron oriented services help sustain a wider range of constraints and controls between the parties to the transaction. (Much the same might be said of such service occupations as waitress, bellhop and hotel doorman, the chief difference being, however, that these operate from a spatially fixed establishment, which in itself permits of greater identifiability, renewability, and hence constraint in one's relationship to them.) As a result, the tendency of the relationship is to gravitate sharply and in relatively overt fashion toward those few issues having to do with the basic instrumental terms of the exchange. The very fact of tipping, its economic centrality and the cab culture's preoccupation with mastering its many vagaries reflect in large part the regulative imbalance inherent in the relationship.

By inference, this analysis raises anew questions of how to account for the many more formidable and apparently more binding practitioner-client constraints found in other personal service fields, in particular the professions. To such matters as career socialization, colleague groups, socially legitimated skill monopolies, and professional secrecy there might be added a certain safe modicum of continuity, stability, and homogeneity of clientele.[21] For, given too great and random a circulation of clients among practitioners, as might occur for example under certain bureaucratic schemes for providing universal and comprehensive medical service, the danger is that informal social control networks would not come into being in the community, and, as in big-city cabdriving, relations between servers and served would become reputationless, anonymous, and narrowly calculative.

[21] William J. Goode, "Community within a Community: The Professions," *American Sociological Review*, XXII, No. 2 (April, 1957), 198-200, and Eliot Freidson, "Varieties of Professional Practice," draft version of unpublished paper, 1959.

VI.

AGE AND SEX

...based on age and sex, since these ... be purely biological categories. But as the selections in this chapter should
make clear, this is far from being the case. In fact, sociologists have made some of their most significant contributions
... precisely these areas. Age and sex may be biologically de-
... mined factors, but the way they are dealt with and responded to depends on the way a society and its culture are
organized. Being importantly tied to the survival and reproduction of members of society and indirectly to the organization
of social values, age and sex are everywhere subject to considerable regulation.

Kingsley Davis, in his essay on parent-youth conflict, takes
another modern classic argument. ... conflict
may exist in every society, but that they assume major proportions in the modern age, an age that is characterized by
rapid change, in more traditional societies, the rotation of
... are bound similar to those of ... however. The rate of
change have a way, ... the world that children grow into will
... early resemblance of their fathers and mothers. But in rapidly changing societies, children must respond in the context
of their orientation to challenges and ideals that were
largely absent in the parents' generations. If parents and children live, in effect, in fairly different cultural environments.
Davis argues, accentuated conflicts between them are likely to
... the rule rather than the exception. Moreover, such conflict may be highly beneficial to the younger generation,
since they allow it to cut loose from the guidance of their
parents, thus enabling the young to strike new/out paths in
a world of modernity that the parental generation cannot fol-
... to generations accustomed to reject and appreciate.

From Philip Slater's paper on the American college sorority
takes what in effect is an obverse perspective from that of
Kingsley Davis, while Davis focuses on social change, Slater
stresses social continuity, but since any social formation is

361

IT MIGHT APPEAR at first blush that sociologists would have little to say on age and sex, since these seem to be purely biological categories. But as the selections in this chapter should make clear, this is far from being the case. In fact, sociologists have made some of their most significant contributions in precisely these areas. Age and sex may be biologically determined factors, but the way they are dealt with and responded to depends on the way a society and its culture are organized. Being directly tied to the survival and reproduction of members of society, and indirectly to the transmission of social values, age and sex are everywhere subject to control and regulation.

Kingsley Davis, in a paper on parent-youth conflicts that is another modern classic, argues persuasively that such conflicts may appear in every society, but that they assume major proportions in the modern age, an age that is characterized by rapid change. In more traditional societies, the routines of today are largely similar to those of yesteryear. The rate of change being slow, the world that children grow into will largely resemble that of their fathers and mothers. But in rapidly changing societies, children must respond in the course of their maturation to challenges and stimuli that were largely absent in the parental generations. If parents and children live, in effect, in fairly different cultural environments, Davis argues, accentuated conflicts between them are likely to be the rule rather than the exception. Moreover, such conflicts may be highly beneficial to the younger generation, since they allow it to cut loose from the guidance of their parents, thus enabling the young to define their own paths in a world of modernity that the parental generation either fails to perceive or is accustomed to reject and depreciate.

John Finley Scott's paper on the American college sorority takes what, in effect, is an obverse perspective from that of Kingsley Davis. While Davis focuses on social change, Scott stresses social continuity; but since any social formation is subject to both forces, these papers are complementary. Scott argues that sororities, though often disesteemed by academics, fulfill important conservative functions in society by helping to assure the continuity of class and ethnic differentiations and hierarchies. If there were no social control over courtship, Scott argues, the chance would be high that persons of very different class or ethnic origins would mate. One need not accept the values of ethnic and class divisions to realize that this lifting of social control would do much to lessen them. Hence, controls are called for through arrangements that simultaneously discourage "improper" marriages and encourage "proper" ones. Organizations such as college sororities perform these functions by facilitating endogamy (in-marriage) in a milieu where opportunities and temptations for exogamy (out-marriage) are fairly powerful.

The varieties of sexual customs and sexual mores have probably fascinated trained as well as untrained observers from time immemorial. The relativity of sexual standards, be it between different societies or within them, has been noted especially in a modern age where such varieties have become visible and can no longer be covered up by the upholders of one particular standard of sexual orthodoxy. Denis Diderot, the great French 18th-century *philosophe*, in his delightful *Supplement to Bougainville's Voyages*, from which a few pages are here reprinted, highlights the notion of cultural relativism in his imaginary and whimsical discussion of the differences in sexual customs between the cultures of Tahiti and of the West. One need not accept his notion that Tahitian culture is somehow more rational than our own to find his argument as to the relativity of moral and sexual standards still quite persuasive.

William Foote Whyte, best known to students as the author of a classic study of an urban neighborhood, *Street Corner Society*, focuses in the paper reprinted here on the sexual attitudes and standards of sexual behavior in a slum. Slums are often pictured as breeding grounds of promiscuity and disorganization—areas lacking social standards. Whyte shows that, common-sensical impressions to the contrary, slums have their own sexual codes, as binding as those of the middle-class suburbs, but widely different from them in a specific content. Male slum dwellers, Whyte shows, classify women into "good girls" (virgins) and three categories of nonvirgins.

For each category, there is an appropriate form of behavior supported by social sanctions. Even in slums, contrary to the fond beliefs of those going slumming, sex is not to be had for the asking.

The Sociology of
Parent-Youth Conflict

by
Kingsley Davis

It is in sociological terms that this chapter attempts to frame and solve the sole question with which it deals, namely: Why does contemporary Western civilization manifest an extraordinary amount of parent-adolescent conflict?[1] In other cultures, the outstanding fact is generally not the rebelliousness of youth, but its docility. There is practically no custom, no matter how tedious or painful, to which youth in primitive tribes or archaic civilizations will not willingly submit.[2] What, then, are the peculiar features of our society which give us one of the extremest examples of endemic filial friction in human history?

Our answer to this question makes use of constants and variables, the constants being the universal factors in the parent-youth relation, the variables being the factors which

Reprinted from *American Sociological Review*, Vol. 5, No. 4, August 1940, pp. 523-535, with permission of the American Sociological Association and the author.

[1]In the absence of statistical evidence, exaggeration of the conflict is easily possible, and two able students have warned against it. E. B. Reuter, "The Sociology of Adolescence," and Jessie R. Runner, "Social Distance in Adolescent Relationships," both in *Amer. J. Sociol.*, November 1937, 43: 415-416, 437. Yet sufficient nonquantitative evidence lies at hand in the form of personal experience, the outpour of literature on adolescent problems, and the historical and anthropological accounts of contrasting societies to justify the conclusion that in comparison with other cultures ours exhibits an exceptional amount of such conflict. If this chapter seems to stress conflict, it is simply because we are concerned with this problem rather than with parent-youth harmony.

[2]Cf. Nathan Miller, *The Child in Primitive Society*, New York, 1928; Miriam Van Waters, "The Adolescent Girl Among Primitive Peoples," *J. Relig. Psychol.*, 1913, 6: 375-421 (1913) and 7: 75-120 (1914); Margaret Mead, *Coming of Age in Samoa*, New York, 1928 and "Adolescence in Primitive and Modern Society," 169-188, in *The New Generation* (ed. by V. F. Calverton and S. Schmalhausen), New York, 1930; A. M. Bacon, *Japanese Girls and Women*, New York and Boston, 1891 and 1902.

differ from one society to another. Though one's attention, in explaining the parent-youth relations of a given milieu, is focused on the variables, one cannot comprehend the action of the variables without also understanding the constants, for the latter constitute the structural and functional basis of the family as a part of society.

THE RATE OF SOCIAL CHANGE

The first important variable is the rate of social change. Extremely rapid change in modern civilization, in contrast to most societies, tends to increase parent-youth conflict, for within a fast-changing social order the time-interval between generations, ordinarily but a mere moment in the life of a social system, become historically significant, thereby creating a hiatus between one generation and the next. Inevitably, under such a condition, youth is reared in a milieu different from that of the parents; hence the parents become old-fashioned, youth rebellious, and clashes occur which, in the closely confined circle of the immediate family, generate sharp emotion.

That rapidity of change is a significant variable can be demonstrated by three lines of evidence: a comparison of stable and nonstable societies;[3] a consideration of immigrant families; and an analysis of revolutionary epochs. If, for example, the conflict is sharper in the immigrant household, this can be due to one thing only, that the immigrant family generally undergoes the most rapid social change of any type of family in a given society. Similarly, a revolution (an abrupt form of societal alternation), by concentrating great change in a short span, catapults the younger generation into power—a generation which has absorbed and pushed the new ideas, acquired the habit of force, and which accordingly, dominates those hangovers from the old regime, its parents.[4]

---

[3] Partially done by Mead and Van Waters in the works cited above.

[4] Soviet Russia and Nazi Germany are examples. See Sigmund Neumann, "The Conflict of Generations in Contemporary Europe from Versailles to Munich," Vital Speeches of the Day, August 1, 1939, 5: 623–628. Parents in these countries are to be obeyed only so long as they profess the "correct" (i.e., youthful, revolutionary) ideas.

THE BIRTH-CYCLE, DECELERATING SOCIALIZATION, AND PARENT-CHILD DIFFERENCES

Note, however, that rapid social change would have no power to produce conflict were it not for two universal factors: first, the family's duration; and second, the decelerating rate of socialization in the development of personality. "A family" is not a static entity but a process in time, a process ordinarily so brief compared with historical time that it is unimportant, but which, when history is "full" (i.e., marked by rapid social change), strongly influences the mutual adjustment of the generations. This "span" is basically the birth-cycle—the length of time between the birth of one person and his procreation of another. It is biological and inescapable. It would, however, have no effect in producing parent-youth conflict, even with social change, if it were not for the additional fact, intimately related and equally universal, that the sequential development of personality involves a constantly decelerating rate of socialization. This deceleration is due both to organic factors (age—which ties it to the birth-cycle) and to social factors (the cumulative character of social experience). Its effect is to make the birth-cycle interval, which is the period of youth, the time of major socialization, subsequent periods of socialization being subsidiary.

Given these constant features, rapid social change creates conflict because *to* the intrinsic (universal, inescapable) differences between parents and children it adds an extrinsic (variable) difference derived from the acquisition, at the same stage of life, of differential cultural content by each successive generation. Not only are parent and child, at any given moment, in different stages of development, but the content which the parent acquired at the stage where the child now is, was a different content from that which the child is now acquiring. Since the parent is supposed to socialize the child, he tends to apply the erstwhile but now inappropriate content (see Diagram). He makes this mistake, and cannot remedy it, because, due to the logic of personality growth, his basic orientation was formed by the experiences of his own childhood. He cannot "modernize" his point of view, because *he* is the product of those experiences. He can change in superficial ways, such as learning a new tune, but he cannot change (or *want* to change) the initial modes of thinking upon which his subsequent social experience has

Figure 1. The Birth-Cycle, Social Change, and Parent-Child Relations at Different Stages of Life*

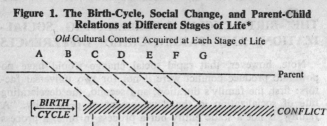

Old Cultural Content Acquired at Each Stage of Life

New Cultural Content at Each Stage

*Because the birth-cycle interval persists throughout their conjoint life, parent and child are always at a different stage of development and their relations are always therefore potentially subject to conflict, e.g., when the parent is at stage *D*, the child is at stage *B*. But social change adds another source of conflict, for it means that the parent, when at the stage where the child now is, acquired a different cultural content from that which the child must now acquire at that stage. This places the parent in the predicament of trying to transmit old content no longer suited to the offspring's needs in a changed world. In a stable society, *B* and *B'* would have the same cultural content. In a changing society, they do not, yet the parent tries to apply the content of *A, B, C*, etc., to the corresponding stages in the child's development, *A', B', C'*, etc., which supposedly and actually have a different content. Thus, a constant (the birth-cycle) and a variable (social change) combine to produce parent-youth conflict.

Though the birth-cycle remains absolutely the same, it does not remain relatively the same, because it occupies, as time goes on, a successively smaller percentage of the total time lived. Furthermore, because of the decelerating rate of socialization, the difference in the total amount of cultural content as between parent and child becomes less pronounced. After the period of adolescence, for example, the margin is reduced to a minimum, which explains why a minimum of conflict is achieved after that stage.

been built. To change the basic conceptions by which he has learned to judge the rightness and reality of all specific situations would be to render subsequent experience meaningless, to make an empty caricature of what had been his life.

Although, in the birth-cycle gap between parent and offspring, astronomical time constitutes the basic point of disparity, the actual sequences, and hence the actual differences significant for us, are physiological, psychosocial, and sociological—each with an acceleration of its own within, but to some degree independent of, sidereal time, and each containing a divergence between parent and child which must be taken into account in explaining parent-youth conflict.

PHYSIOLOGICAL DIFFERENCES

Though the disparity in chronological age remains constant through life, the precise physiological differences between parent and offspring vary radically from one period to another. The organic contrasts between parent and *infant*, for example, are far different from those between parent and adolescent. Yet whatever the period, the organic differences produce contrasts (as between young and old) in those desires which, at least in part, are organically determined. Thus, at the time of adolescence the contrast is between an organism which is just reaching its full powers and one which is just losing them. The physiological need of the latter is for security and conservation, because as the superabundance of energy diminishes, the organism seems to hoard what remains.

Such differences, often alleged (under the heading of "disturbing physiological changes accompanying adolescence") as the primary cause of parent-adolescent strife, are undoubtedly a factor in such conflict, but, like other universal differences to be discussed, they form a constant factor present in every community, and therefore cannot in themselves explain the peculiar heightening of parent-youth conflict in our culture.

The fact is that most societies avoid the potential clash of old and young by using sociological position as a neutralizing agent. They assign definite and separate positions to persons of different ages, thereby eliminating competition between them for the same position and avoiding the competitive emotions of jealousy and envy. Also, since the expected behavior of old and young is thus made complementary rather than identical, the performance of cooperative functions as accomplished by different but mutually related activities suited to the disparate organic needs of each, with no coercion to behave in a manner unsuited to one's organic age. In our culture, where most positions are *theoretically* based on accomplishment rather than age, interage competition arises, superior organic propensities lead to a high evaluation of youth (the so-called "accent on youth"), a disproportionate lack of opportunity for youth manifests itself, and consequently, arrogance and frustration appear in the young, fear and envy, in the old.

PSYCHOSOCIAL DIFFERENCES: ADULT REALISM VERSUS YOUTHFUL IDEALISM

The decelerating rate of socialization (an outgrowth both of the human being's organic development, from infant plasticity to senile rigidity, and of his cumulative cultural and social development), when taken with rapid social change and other conditions of our society, tends to produce certain differences of orientation between parent and youth. Though lack of space makes it impossible to discuss all of these ramifications, we shall attempt to delineate at least one sector of difference in terms of the conflict between adult realism (or pragmatism) and youthful idealism.

Though both youth and age claim to see the truth, the old are more conservatively realistic than the young, because on the one hand they take Utopian ideals less seriously and on the other hand take what may be called operating ideals, if not more seriously, at least more for granted. Thus, middle-aged people notoriously forget the poetic ideals of a new social order which they cherished when young. In their place, they put simply the working ideals current in the society. There is, in short, a persistent tendency for the ideology of a person as he grows older to gravitate more and more toward the status quo ideology, unless other facts (such as a social crisis or hypnotic suggestion) intervene.[5] With advancing age, he becomes less and less bothered by inconsistencies in ideals. He tends to judge ideals according to whether they are widespread and hence effective in thinking about practical life, not according to whether they are logically consistent. Furthermore, he gradually ceases to bother about the *untruth* of his ideals, in the sense of their failure to correspond to reality. He assumes through long habit that, though they do not correspond perfectly, the discrepancy is not significant. The reality of an ideal is defined for him in terms of how many people accept it rather than how completely it is mirrored in actual behavior.[6] Thus, we call him, as he approaches middle age, a realist.

The young, however, are idealists, partly because they take

[5]See Footnote 11 for necessary qualifications.
[6]When discussing a youthful ideal, however, the older person is quick to take a dialectical advantage by pointing out not only that this ideal af-

working ideals literally and partly because they acquire ideals not fully operative in the social organization. Those in authority over children are obligated as a requirement of their status to inculcate ideals as a part of the official culture given the new generation.[7] The children are receptive because they have little social experience—experience being systematically kept from them (by such means as censorship, for example, a large part of which is to "protect" children). Consequently, young people possess little ballast for their acquired ideals, which therefore soar to the sky, whereas the middle-aged, by contrast, have plenty of ballast.

This relatively unchecked idealism in youth is eventually complicated by the fact that young people possess keen reasoning ability. The mind, simply as a logical machine, works as well at sixteen as at thirty-six.[8] Such logical capacity, combined with high ideals and an initial lack of experience, means that youth soon discovers with increasing age that the ideals it has been taught are true and consistent are not so in fact. Mental conflict thereupon ensues, for the young person has not learned that ideals may be useful without being true and consistent. As a solution, youth is likely to take action designed to remove inconsistencies or force actual conduct into line with ideals, such action assuming one of several typical adolescent forms—from religious withdrawal to the militant support of some Utopian scheme—but in any case consisting essentially in serious allegiance to one or more of the ideal moral systems present in the culture.[9]

---

fronts the aspirations of the multitude, but that it also fails to correspond to human behavior either now or (by the lessons of history) probably in the future.

[7] See amusing but accurate article, "Fathers Are Liars," *Scribner's Magazine*, March, 1934.

[8] Evidence from mental growth data which point to a leveling off of the growth curve at about age sixteen. For charts and brief explanations, together with references, see F. K. Shuttleworth, *The Adolescent Period*, Monographs of the Society for Research in Child Development, III, Serial No. 16 (Washington, D.C., 1938), Figs. 16, 230, 232, 276, 285, 308.

Maturity of judgment is of course another matter. We are speaking only of logical capacity. Judgment is based on experience as well as capacity; hence, adolescents are apt to lack it.

[9] An illustration of youthful reformism was afforded by the Laval University students who decided to "do something about" prostitution in the city of Quebec. They broke into eight houses in succession one night, "whacked naked inmates upon the buttocks, upset beds and otherwise proved their collegiate virtue. . . ." They ended by "shoving the few remaining girls out of doors into the cold autumn night." *Time*, October 19, 1936.

A different, usually later reaction to disillusionment is the cynical or sophomoric attitude; for, if the ideals one has imbibed cannot be reconciled and do not fit reality, then why not dismiss them as worthless? Cynicism has the advantage of giving justification for behavior that young organisms crave anyway. It might be mistaken for genuine realism if it were not for two things. The first is the emotional strain behind the "don't care" attitude. The cynic, in his judgment that the world is bad because of inconsistency and untruth of ideals, clearly implies that he still values the ideals. The true realist sees the inconsistency and untruth, but without emotion; he uses either ideals or reality whenever it suits his purpose. The second is the early disappearance of the cynical attitude. Increased experience usually teaches the adolescent that overt cynicism is unpopular and unworkable, that to deny and deride all beliefs which fail to cohere or to correspond to facts, and to act in opposition to them, is to alienate oneself from any group,[10] because these beliefs, however unreal, are precisely what makes group unity possible. Soon, therefore, the youthful cynic finds himself bound up with some group having a system of working ideals, and becomes merely another conformist, cynical only about the beliefs of other groups.[11]

[10]This holds only for expressed cynicism, but so close is the relation of thought to action that the possibility of an entirely covert cynic seems remote.

[11]This tentative analysis holds only insofar as the logic of personality development in a complex culture is the sole factor. Because of other factors, concrete situations may be quite different. When, for example, a person is specifically trained in certain rigid, other-worldly, or impractical ideals, he may grow increasingly fanatical with the years rather than realistic, while his offspring, because of association with less fanatical persons, may be more pragmatic than he. The variation in group norms within a society produces persons who, whatever their orientation inside the group, remain more idealistic than the average outsider, while their children may, with outside contacts, become more pragmatic. Even within a group, however, a person's situation may be such as to drive him beyond the everyday realities of that group, while his children remain undisturbed. Such situations largely explain the personal crises that may alter one's orientation. The analysis, overly brief and mainly illustrative, therefore represents a certain degree of abstraction. The reader should realize, moreover, that the terms "realistic" and "idealistic" are chosen merely for convenience in trying to convey the idea, not for any evaluative judgments which they may happen to connote. The terms are not used in any technical epistemological sense, but simply in the way made plain by the context. Above all, it is not implied that ideals are "unreal." The ways in which they are "real"

While the germ of this contrast between youthful idealism and adult realism may spring from the universal logic of personality development, it receives in our culture a peculiar exaggeration. Social change, complexity, and specialization (by compartmentalizing different aspects of life) segregate ideals from fact and throw together imcompatible ideologies while at the same time providing the intellectual tools for discerning logical inconsistencies and empirical errors. Our highly elaborated burden of culture, correlated with a variegated system of achieved vertical mobility, necessitates long years of formal education which separate youth from adulthood, theory from practice, school from life. Insofar, then, as youth's reformist zeal or cynical negativism produces conflict with parents, the peculiar conditions of our culture are responsible.

SOCIOLOGICAL DIFFERENCES:
PARENTAL AUTHORITY

Since social status and office are everywhere partly distributed on the basis of age, personality development is intimately linked with the network of social positions successively occupied during life. Western society, in spite of an unusual amount of interage competition, maintains differences of social position between parent and child, the developmental gap between them being too clear-cut, the symbiotic needs too fundamental, to escape being made a basis of social organization. Hence, parent and child, in a variety of ways, find themselves enmeshed in different social contexts and possessed of different outlooks. The much publicized critical attitude of youth toward established ways, for example, is partly a matter of being on the outside looking in. The "established ways" under criticism are usually institutions (such as property, marriage, profession) which the adolescent has not yet entered. He looks at them from the point of view of the outsider (especially since they affect him in a restrictive manner), either failing to imagine himself finding satisfaction in such patterns or else feeling re-

and "unreal" to observer and actor are complex indeed. See T. Parsons, *The Structure of Social Action*, 396. New York, 1937, and V. Pareto, *The Mind and Society*, III: 1300–1304, New York, 1935.

sentful that the old have in them a vested interest from which he is excluded.

Not only is there differential position, but also *mutually* differential position, status being in many ways specific for and reciprocal between parent and child. Some of these differences, relating to the birth-cycle and constituting part of the family structure, are universal. This is particularly true of the super- and subordination summed up in the term *parental authority*.

Since sociological differences between parent and child are inherent in family organization, they constitute a universal factor potentially capable of producing conflict. Like the biological differences, however, they do not in themselves produce such conflict. In fact, they may help to avoid it. To understand how our society brings to expression the potentiality for conflict, indeed to deal realistically with the relation between the generations, we must do so not in generalized terms but in terms of the specific "power situation." Therefore, the remainder of our discussion will center upon the nature of parental authority and its vicissitudes in our society.

Because of his strategic position with reference to the new-born child (at least in the familial type of reproductive institution), the parent is given considerable authority. Charged by his social group with the responsibility of controlling and training the child in conformity with the mores and thereby insuring the maintenance of the cultural structure, the parent, to fulfill his duties, must have the privileges as well as the obligations of authority, and the surrounding community ordinarily guarantees both.

The first thing to note about parental authority, in addition to its function in socialization, is that it is a case of authority within a primary group. Simmel has pointed out that authority is bearable for the subordinate because it touches only one aspect of life. Impersonal and objective, it permits all other aspects to be free from its particularistic dominance. This escape, however, is lacking in parental authority, for since the family includes most aspects of life, its authority is not limited, specific, or impersonal. What, then, can make this authority bearable? Three factors associated with the familial primary group help to give the answer: (1) the child is socialized within the family, and therefore knowing nothing else and being utterly dependent, the authority of the parent is internalized, accepted; (2) the family, like other primary groups, implies identification, in such sense that one person understands and responds emphatically to the sentiments of the other, so that the harshness of authority is ameliorated;[12] (3) in the intimate interaction of the primary group control can never be purely one-sided; there are too many ways in which the subordinated can exert the pressure of his will. When, therefore, the family system is a going concern, parental authority, however, inclusive, is not felt as despotic.

A second thing to note about parental authority is that while its duration is variable (lasting in some societies a few years and in others a lifetime), it inevitably involves a change, a progressive readjustment, in the respective positions of parent and child—in some cases an almost complete reversal of roles, in others at least a cumulative allowance for the fact of maturity in the subordinated offspring. Age is a unique basis for social stratification. Unlike birth, sex, wealth, or occupation, it implies that the stratification is temporary, that the person, if he lives a full life, will eventually traverse all of the strata having it as a basis. Therefore, there is a peculiar ambivalence attached to this kind of differentiation, as well as a constant directional movement. On the one hand, the young person, in the stage of maximum socialization, is, so to speak, *moving into* the social organization. His social personality is expanding, i.e., acquiring an increased amount of the cultural heritage, filling more powerful and numerous positions. His future is before him, in what the older person is leaving behind. The latter, on the other hand, has a future before him only in the sense that the offspring represents it. Therefore, there is a disparity of interest, the young person placing his thoughts upon a future which, once the first stages of dependence are passed, does not include the parent, the old person placing his hopes vicariously upon the young. This situation, representing a *tendency* in every society, is avoided in many places by a system of respect for the aged and an imaginary projection of life beyond the grave. In the absence of such a religio-ancestral system, the role of the aged is a tragic one.[13]

Let us now take up, point by point, the manner in which

[12]House slaves, for example, are generally treated much better than field slaves. Authority over the former is of a personal type, while that over the latter (open in the form of a foreman-gang organization) is of a more impersonal or economic type.
[13]Sometimes compensated for by an interest in the grandchildren, which permits them partially to recover the role of the vigorous parent.

Western civilization has affected this *gemeinschaftliche* and processual form of authority.

1. Conflicting Norms. To begin with, rapid change has, as we saw, given old and young a different social content, so that they possess conflicting norms. There is a loss of mutual identification, and the parent will not "catch up" with the child's point of view, because he is supposed to dominate rather than follow. More than this, social complexity has confused the standards *within* the generations. Faced with conflicting goals, parents become inconsistent and confused in their own minds in rearing their children. The children, for example, acquire an argument against discipline by being able to point to some family wherein discipline is less severe, while the parent can retaliate by pointing to still other families wherein it is firmer. The acceptance of parental attitudes is less complete than formerly.

2. Competing Authorities. We took it for granted, when discussing rapid social change, that youth acquires new ideas, but we did not ask how. The truth is that, in a specialized and complex culture, they learn from competing authorities. Today, for example, education is largely in the hands of professional specialists, some of whom, as college professors, resemble the sophists of ancient Athens by virtue of their work of accumulating and purveying knowledge, and who consequently have ideas in advance of the populace at large (i.e., the parents). By giving the younger generation these advanced ideas, they (and many other extrafamilial agencies, including youth's contemporaries) widen the intellectual gap between parent and child.[14]

3. Little Explicit Institutionalization of Steps in Parental Authority. Our society provides little explicit institutionalization of the progressive readjustments of authority as between parent and child. We are intermediate between the extreme of virtually permanent parental authority and the extreme of very early emancipation, because we encourage release in late adolescence. Unfortunately, this is a time of enhanced sexual desire, so that the problem of sex and the problem of emancipation occur simultaneously and complicate each other. Yet

[14] The essential point is not that there are other authorities—in every society there are extrafamilial influences in socialization—but that, because of specialization and individualistic enterprise, they are *competing* authorities. Because they make a living by their work and are specialists in socialization, some authorities have a competitive advantage over parents who are amateurs or at best merely general practitioners.

even this would doubtless be satisfactory if it were not for the fact that among us the exact time when authority is relinquished, the exact amount, and the proper ceremonial behavior are not clearly defined. Not only do different groups and families have conflicting patterns, and new situations arise to which old definitions will not apply, but the different spheres of life (legal, economic, religious, intellectual) do not synchronize, maturity in one sphere and immaturity in another often coexisting. The readjustment of authority between individuals is always a ticklish process, and when it is a matter of such close authority as that between parent and child it is apt to be still more ticklish. The failure of our culture to institutionalize this readjustment by a series of well-defined, well-publicized steps is undoubtedly a cause of much parent-youth dissension. The adolescent's sociological exit from his family, via education, work, marriage, and change of residence, is fraught with potential conflicts of interest which only a definite system of institutional controls can neutralize. The parents have a vital stake in what the offspring will do. Because his acquisition of independence will free the parents of many obligations, they are willing to relinquish their authority; yet, precisely because their own status is socially identified with that of their offspring, they wish to insure satisfactory conduct on the latter's part and are tempted to prolong their authority by making the decisions themselves. In the absence of institutional prescriptions, the conflict of interest may lead to a struggle for power, the parents fighting to keep control in matters of importance to themselves, the son or daughter clinging to personally indispensable family services while seeking to evade the concomitant control.

4. *Concentration within the Small Family.* Our family system is peculiar in that it manifests a paradoxical combination of concentration and dispersion. On the one hand, the unusual smallness of the family unit makes for a strange intensity of family feeling, while on the other, the fact that most pursuits take place outside the home makes for a dispersion of activities. Though apparently contradictory, the two phenomena are really interrelated and traceable ultimately to the same factors in our social structure. Since the first refers to that type of affection and antagonism found between relatives, and the second to activities, it can be seen that the second (dispersion) isolates and increases the intensity of the affectional element by sheering away common activities and the extended kin. Whereas ordinarily the

sentiments of kinship are organically related to a number of common activities and spread over a wide circle of relatives, in our mobile society they are associated with only a few common activities and concentrated within only the immediate family. This makes them at once more instable (because ungrounded) and more intense. With the diminishing birth rate, our family is the world's smallest kinship unit, a tiny closed circle. Consequently, a great deal of family sentiment is directed toward a few individuals, who are so important to the emotional life that complexes easily develop. This emotional intensity and situational instability increase both the probability and severity of conflict.

In a familistic society, where there are several adult male and female relatives within the effective kinship group to whom the child turns for affection and aid, and many members of the younger generation in whom the parents have a paternal interest, there appears to be less intensity of emotion for any particular kinsman and consequently less chance for severe conflict.[15] Also, if conflict between any two relatives does arise, it may be handled by shifting mutual rights and obligations to another relative.[16]

5. *Open Competition for Socioeconomic Position.* Our emphasis upon individual initiative and vertical mobility, in contrast to rural-stable regimes, means that one's future occupation and destiny are determined more at adolescence than at birth, the adolescent himself (as well as the parents) having some part in the decision. Before him spread a panorama of possible occupations and avenues of advancement, all of them fraught with the uncertainties of competitive vicissitude. The youth is ignorant of most of the facts. So is the parent, but less so. Both attempt to collaborate on the future, but because of previously mentioned sources of friction, the collaboration is frequently stormy. They evaluate future possibilities differently, and since the decision is uncertain yet important, a clash of wills results. The necessity of choice at adolescence extends beyond the occupational field to practi-

---

[15]Margaret Mead, *Social Organization of Manua*, 84, Honolulu, Bernice P. Bishop Museum Bulletin 76, 1930. Large heterogeneous households early accustom the child to expect emotional rewards from many different persons. D. M. Spencer, "The Composition of the Family as a Factor in the Behavior of Children in Fijian Society," *Sociometry* (1939), 2: 47–55.

[16]The principle of substitution is widespread in familism, as shown by the wide distribution of adoption, levirate, sororate, and classificatory kinship nomenclature.

cally every phase of life, the parents having an interest in each decision. A culture in which more of the choices of life were settled beforehand by ascription, where the possibilities were fewer and the responsibilities of choice less urgent, would have much less parent-youth conflict.[17]

6. *Sex Tension.* If until now we have ignored sex taboos, the omission has represented a deliberate attempt to place them in their proper context with other factors, rather than in the unduly prominent place usually given them.[18] Undoubtedly, because of a constellation of cultural conditions, sex looms as an important bone of parent-youth contention. Our morality, for instance, demands both premarital chastity and postponement of marriage, thus creating a long period of desperate eagerness when young persons practically at the peak of their sexual capacity are forbidden to enjoy it. Naturally, tensions arise—tensions which adolescents try to relieve, and adults hope they will relieve, in some socially acceptable form. Such tensions not only make the adolescent intractable and capricious, but create a genuine conflict of interest between the two generations. The parent, with respect to the child's behavior, represents morality, while the offspring reflects morality *plus* his organic cravings. The stage is thereby set for conflict, evasion, and deceit. For the mass of parents, toleration is never possible. For the mass of adolescents, sublimation is never sufficient. Given our system of morality, conflict seems well nigh inevitable.

Yet it is not sex itself but the way it is handled that causes conflict. If sex patterns were carefully, definitely, and uniformly geared with nonsexual patterns in the social structure, there would be no parent-youth conflict over sex. As it is, rapid change has opposed the sex standards of different groups and generations, leaving impulse only chaotically controlled.

The extraordinary preoccupation of modern parents with the sex life of their adolescent offspring is easily understandable. First, our morality is sex-centered. The strength of the impulse which it seeks to control, the consequent stringency of its rules, and the importance of reproductive institutions for society, make sex so morally important that being moral and being sexually discreet are synonymous. Small wonder,

[17]M. Mead, *Coming of Age in Samoa,* 200 ff.
[18]Cf., e.g., L. K. Frank, "The Management of Tensions," *Amer. J. Sociol.,* March 1928, 33: 706–722; M. Mead, *op. cit.,* 216–217, 222–223.

then, that parents, charged with responsibility for their children and fearful of their own status in the eyes of the moral community, are preoccupied with what their offspring will do in this matter. Moreover, sex is intrinsically involved in the family structure and is therefore of unusual significance to family members *qua* family members. Offspring and parent are not simply two persons who happen to live together; they are two persons who happen to live together because of past sex relations between the parents. Also, between parent and child there stand strong incest taboos, and doubtless the unvoiced possibility of violating these unconsciously intensifies the interest of each in the other's sexual conduct. In addition, since sexual behavior is connected with the offspring's formation of a new family of his own, it is naturally of concern to the parent. Finally, these factors taken in combination with the delicacy of the authoritarian relation, the emotional intensity within the small family, and the confusion of sex standards, make it easy to explain the parental interest in adolescent sexuality. Yet because sex is a tabooed topic between parent and child,[19] parental control must be indirect and devious, which creates additional possibilities of conflict.

SUMMARY AND CONCLUSION

Our parent-youth conflict thus results from the interaction of certain universals of the parent-child relation and certain variables the value of which are peculiar to modern culture. The universals are (1) the basic age or birth-cycle differential between parent and child, (2) the decelerating rate of socialization with advancing age, and (3) the resulting intrinsic differences between old and young on the physiological, psychosocial, and sociological planes.

Though these universal factors tend to produce conflict between parent and child, whether or not they do so depends upon the variables. We have seen that the distinctive general features of our society are responsible for our excessive

[19]"Even among the essentially 'unrepressed' Trobrianders the parent is never the confidant in matters of sex." Bronislaw Malinowski, *Sex and Reproduction in Savage Society*, 36 (note), London, 1927, p. 36n. Cf. the interesting article, "Intrusive Parents," *The Commentator*, September 1938, which opposes frank sex discussion between parents and children.

parent-adolescent friction. Indeed, they are the same features which are affecting *all* family relations. The delineation of these variables has not been systematic, because the scientific classification of whole societies has not yet been accomplished; and it has been difficult, in view of the interrelated character of societal traits, to seize upon certain features and ignore others. Yet certainly the following four complex variables are important: (1) the rate of social change; (2) the extent of complexity in the social structure; (3) the degree of integration in the culture; and (4) the velocity of movement (e.g., vertical mobility) within the structure and its relation to the cultural values.

Our rapid social change, for example, has crowded historical meaning into the family time-span, has thereby given the offspring a different social content from that which the parent acquired, and consequently has added to the already existent intrinsic differences between parent and youth, a set of extrinsic ones which double the chance of alienation. Moreover, our great societal complexity, our evident cultural conflict, and our emphasis upon open competition for socioeconomic status have all added to this initial effect. We have seen, for instance, that they have disorganized the important relation of parental authority by confusing the goals of child control, setting up competing authorities, creating a small family system, making necessary certain significant choices at the time of adolescence, and leading to an absence of definite institutional mechanisms to symbolize and enforce the progressively changing stages of parental power.

If ours were a simple rural-stable society, mainly familistic, the emancipation from parental authority being gradual and marked by definite institutionalized steps, with no great postponement of marriage, sex taboo, or open competition for status, parents and youth would not be in conflict. Hence, the presence of parent-youth conflict in our civilization is one more specific manifestation of the incompatibility between an urban-industrial-mobile social system and the familial type of reproductive institutions.[20]

---

[20]For further evidence of this incompatibility, see the writer's "Reproductive Institutions and the Pressure for Population," (*Brit.*) *Sociol. Rev.*; July 1937, 29: 289–306.

The American College Sorority: Its Role in Class and Ethnic Endogamy

by
John Finley Scott

All who study higher education in America sooner or later encounter college sororities. They are visible centers of the rites of feminine adolescence—rites so amusing and so seemingly trivial that academicians tend not to give them serious attention. But "sorority membership" as an antecedent variable has earned the more serious respect of many research workers who study the behavior of college students.[1] Sororities are most common at the large campuses of public land-grant schools; formally, they are private associations providing (where college administrations permit) separate dormitory facilities for female students, sharply distinguished from other such facilities by "Greek-letter" names, a strict and invidious policy of recommendatory and invitational

Reprinted from *American Sociological Review*, Vol. 30, No. 3, June 1965, pp. 514–27, with permission of the American Sociological Association and the author.

[1]For recent research reporting the effect of sorority affiliation see Rose K. Goldsen, Morris Rosenberg, Robin M. Williams, Jr., and Edward A. Suchman, *What College Students Think*, Princeton: Van Nostrand, 1960, Ch. 3; Martin Trow and Burton Clark, "Determinants of College Student Subculture" (unpublished paper, Center for the Study of Higher Education, University of California, Berkeley, 1960); Hanan C. Selvin and Warren O. Hagstrom, "The Empirical Classification of Formal Groups," *American Sociological Review*, 28 (1963), pp. 399–411; and the particularly informative study by Frances Potter Gamble, "Effects of Campus Living Groups on Academic Value and Performance," unpublished M.A. Thesis, University of California, Berkeley (1961). For a good popular account, see David Boroff, *Campus U.S.A.*, New York: Harper, 1958, esp. pp. 90ff. See also Robert F. Winch, "Courtship in College Women," *American Journal of Sociology*, 55 (1949), p. 275, and *idem, The Modern Family*, New York: Holt, Rinehart and Winston, 1952, pp. 489–493 (based on unpublished work by J. D. Ray).

membership, and substantial control by organized adult "alumnae" rather than the college.

The basic research problem here is that sororities are known only by their effects. There is little public record of their internal structure and little more on their relation to the environing society. Then too sororities, when academicians do take note of them, are usually seen as alien to the values of liberal education.[2] Thus they have been mainly studied as an exercise in academic morality, and only so that they might thereby be better deplored. Especially is this the case regarding their membership criteria in such categories of ascribed status as religion and "race." Sociological explanation of these criteria is thereby neglected.[3] *Tout comprendre,*

---

[2] Probably a representative current indictment is that of Walter D. Weir, "The Fraternity System and a Changing University," *Banta's Greek Exchange* 49, (1961), pp. 186–189: ". . . too often the fraternities—and to a lesser extent, the sororities—have failed to come to terms with the central aim of a university: the development and dissemination of knowledge; the timewasting propensities of fraternities, and particularly of the sororities, demonstrate sheer genius in the art of organizing trivia; the rigid separation between the academic and the social, which fraternities and sororities tend to insist upon, empties both phases of life of meaning; too often the fraternity system encourages the complacent acceptance of pious platitudes for gospel truth and pursues surface values; the fraternity system seems to encourage the status quo and takes little cognizance of the swelling idealism of this college generation" (p. 187).

[3] Here see several articles in *Social Problems*, 2 (1955), "A Symposium on Segregation and Integration in College Fraternities." Most of these papers simply demonstrate that fraternity and sorority membership criteria exclude "minority groups." The major sociological work on the topic is Alfred McClung Lee, *Fraternities Without Brotherhood*, Boston: Beacon Press, 1955. As informative as this book is on fraternity and sorority history and policy, its explanatory value is sacrificed to its moral concern and its author's apparent belief that status ascription is obsolete or primitive. Norms of ascriptive groups are not mentioned except as "tribalistic prejudices" (see, e.g., p. 130).

Campaigns against status ascription in general are quixotic, because some ascription is essential for socialization (see Kingsley Davis, "The Child and the Social Structure," *Journal of Educational Sociology*, 14 (1940), esp. pp. 217–223; also his *Human Society*, New York: Macmillan, 1948, pp. 97ff.). Indeed, Ralph Linton suggested that most statuses are in fact ascribed, in *The Study of Man*, New York: Appleton-Century, 1936, p. 113. Status ascription occurs concretely in many different guises. In the form of partial or "fluid ascription" it is a potent motive in parenthood, recently exemplified in the flight of the urban middle classes to class-homogeneous suburbs and in the recent resistance of otherwise "liberal" New Yorkers to racial integration of public schools, when such integration threatens the schools' capacity to *c'est tout pardonner;* thus the moralist cannot venture to explain what he only wants to condemn.

Sororities claim to be secret societies and in many respects they are: their mystery is designed, their structure hidden, their liaisons discreet. What is this peculiar institution? Why is it what it is? In answering these questions my proximate concern is to explain a parochial and now embattled institution; ultimately I want to show more generally how control of marital choice by ascriptive groups,[4] a topic most thoroughly studied and most clearly understood in simple and agrarian societies, can be adapted to the conditions imposed by such modern institutions as mass higher education.[5] The sorority may expire, but the motives behind it will persist: thus it provides an interesting introduction to some of the variables involved in the relation between the ancient institutions of kinship and novel forms of industrial social organization.

Even with this abstract and generalizing concern, however, the analysis rests on concrete details. Here then is a brief note of what sororities are *not*, because so many common beliefs about them, influenced by their mystery and circumlocu-

---

reinforce a familially-ascribed stratified status. Many academicians who sincerely believe in "equal opportunity" still provide for their own children an ascribed and unequal access to elite education.

[4] Since anthropologists studied kinship first, they invented the terminology for it; not surprisingly it fits their purposes better than those of sociologists. Most kinship terms refer to face-to-face groups in small societies and are difficult to apply to groups larger than this but still based on some aspect of kinship. As used in this paper, an *ascriptive group* is one of any size whose members are mainly recruited on an ascriptive basis and who in turn prefer to restrict membership in this group to those who gain it by inheritance or descent, i.e., familial ascription. Concrete examples in complex societies are social classes or strata (because even in achievement-oriented industrial societies the placement of persons in the various strata largely accomplished by familial ascription), "ethnic groups," and solidary racial groups or castes. It also includes the "descent group," "inheritance group" and the men in the exogamous "clan" (see Morris Zelditch, Jr., "Family, Marriage and Kinship," in Robert E. L. Faris (ed.), *Handbook of Modern Sociology*, New York: Rand McNally, 1964, pp. 716–717.) Talcott Parsons' term "ascriptive solidarity" appears to be equivalent to my "ascriptive group," though Parsons does not define his term. See his introduction to Part Two, Section A, in Parsons, Edward Shils, Kaspar D. Naegele, and Jesse R. Pitts (eds.), *Theories of Society*, New York: Free Press of Glencoe, 1961, Vol. I, pp. 267–268.

[5] Excepting studies of the impact of sex roles on public school teaching (see Burton Clark's fine summary in "Sociology of Education" [in Faris, *op. cit.*, pp. 753–756]), little research has related kinship variables to education.

tion, are in fact largely wrong, and if believed render implausible the explanation that follows. Sororities are much more than a simple feminine counterpart to the more wide-spread college fraternity; less variable in their form, they differ from fraternities mainly because marriage is a profoundly more important determinant of social position for women than for men and because the norms associated with marriage correspondingly bear stronger sanctions for women than for men. Though what is called "youth culture" shapes much sorority activity, recruitment, membership, and activities are only narrowly governed by college-age members; effective control rests with parent-age "alumnae." Though many college women wish to join sororities and many more affect sorority manners, conduct, and dress, recruitment and the maintenance of membership are chronic organizational problems. The prototypical sorority is not so much the servant of youthful interests as it is an organized agency for controlling them; dominated by ascriptive groups and concerned to maintain their norms, it operates at a physical remove from these groups and in a larger and frequently hostile institutional setting.

In this paper I do not outline the structure of sororities completely, but instead consider on a more abstract or theoretical level some of the variables that relate kinship to other social processes, especially as regards the choice of marital partners. From the combination of these variables that obtains in higher education in industrial society, it is possible to derive the idea or "model" of an organization designed to maintain the norms of ascriptive groups in the face of opposition from other parts of the society. This hypothetical organization corresponds remarkably well to sororities as they exist in fact.

The factors or variables that account for the evolution of the sorority are:

1. The relation between kinship institutions and those of higher education;
2. Rules of mate selection that inhere in the persistence of strata and ethnic groups;
3. Hypergamy and its derivative "Brahmin problem;"
4. Love;
5. The social heterogeneity of tax-supported colleges; and
6. The bargaining advantage for women of timely marriage and the institutionalization of feminine youth.

These variables do not account for all that goes on in concrete sororities, but they do account for much that is otherwise difficult to explain.

KINSHIP AND HIGHER EDUCATION

Structural differentiation in industrial societies has evolved a system of education wherein the more technical and cognitive aspects of socialization are removed from the control of family and ascriptive groups and assigned to special agents. Nowhere has this differentiation gone further than in the United States, and nowhere are the societal "substructures" relating kinship institutions and education more specialized.[6]

Familial and extra-familial agents of socialization are inherently disposed to conflict.[7] Even when their teaching is complementary they still compete for the child's limited attention. The potential for conflict increases as the content of what is taught diverges, being realized most fully in "higher education." No prior stage in formal education is so sharply set off from familial socialization; this is signalled by the frequent separation of the student's residence from that of his family of orientation. And while higher education may complement socialization by ascriptive groups, simply passing on the same culture in a more specialized way (and indeed

---

[6]The plausible exception is, of course, the U.S.S.R. For a valuable interpretation of such data as were available in the West before 1959, see Alex Inkeles and Raymond A. Bauer, *The Soviet Citizen*, Cambridge: Harvard University Press, 1959. Interview data from refugees suggest that educational opportunities, as in the West, can be predicted by ascribed stratum position ("father's occupation;" see pp. 136–138), in spite of the explicit contrary "policy of the Soviet regime to favor . . . the laboring class and impede. . . . the members of the 'former exploiting classes'" (p. 144). Soviet marriage is largely stratum- and ethnic-endogamous (p. 196, table 50), with some evidence of the Brahmin problem in the higher strata (p. 198).

[7]The general nature of the conflict was first suggested, though not in terms of structural variables, by Willard Waller in *The Sociology of Teaching*, New York: Wiley, 1932, pp. 68ff. For a structural account, see Talcott Parsons, "The School Class as a Social System: Some of its Functions in American Society," *Harvard Educational Review*, 29 (1959) pp. 297–318. He stresses the importance in public education of "an achievement criterion . . . [which] is not simply a way of affirming a previously determined ascriptive status" (p. 300). Parsons does not explicitly mention the potential conflict here, though he does list some ways in which it is avoided *(loc. cit.)*.

many regional and religio-ethnic colleges do little more than this) higher education is both theoretically and factually important not where it complements the values of ascriptive groups but where it challenges them. University education is literally universal in the variety of ways in which it celebrates excellence in achievement; necessarily it thereby threatens the persistence of ascription. Where kinship, based on nuclear families, tends to suppress competition, higher education must select and place persons who are already approximate ascribed equals. It therefore encourages competition explicitly in its curricular matters and implicitly in its extra-curricular ones as well (including courtship on the campus).

But higher education can serve ascriptive interests as well as threaten them. All families ascribe their social and economic status to their children; this process fundamentally connects the family to the system of stratification. But the many technical positions in industrial societies require that pure ascription be reinforced by learned (and therefore achieved) skills. Education and especially higher education are perhaps the most efficient general way to impart these skills. When a family desires upward mobility of the children, achievement has to be the principal basis for the increment in status, and the importance of education is thereby increased.[8] Finally, higher education is not only a means of mobility, but becomes a symbol of what it facilitates, so that the degrees conferred by colleges and universities, as well as other visible indicators of college attendance, come to be valuable in themselves,[9] and higher education is thus respected as a sym-

[8]This is more directly true for men, whose status depends more on occupational performance. More women move up in the class system by hypergamy than by work, and physical beauty is a salient (and sociologically neglected) factor in accounting for which women move up through marriage and which do not. Even so, hypergamy still involves some achievement: figure and face may be inherited, but straightened teeth, exercise, clothing and dietary control of the figure, and grooming of the face, depend on some form of achievement. And other skills, not erotically significant, figure in hypergamy. Though hardly the same skills useful for masculine stratum mobility they can still be learned through higher education. Academicians tend not to assess the modal orientation of women to college realistically, perhaps because to do so would undermine factual assumptions underlying the ideals of "liberal education." For an argument that the facts do not confirm the ideal see Howard S. Becker, "What Do They Really Learn at College?", *Transaction*, 1 (May, 1964), pp. 14–17; more generally see Ralph H. Turner, "Some Aspects of Women's Ambition," *American Journal of Sociology*, 70 (1964), pp. 271–285.

[9]Sorority affiliation, because it is associated with higher education, is

bol of status even by persons who may strongly depreciate its instrumental value. Effective familial ascription to higher strata comes therefore to mean "sending the children to college," despite the risks it also entails.

Now, from the point of view of ascriptive groups the "ideal" college would reinforce ascription where it needed to be reinforced, without threatening it otherwise. To such an "ideal" college kinship groups could, for example, delegate control over the technical details of education, but they would retain control over the less technical processes more likely to be undone by educational "universalism" and vital to their own interests, such as mate selection, religious or ethnic ritual, and symbolic representation of class position. In practice, ascriptive groups have countered the general threat at the colleges they cannot control as primary institutions, by inaugurating or coöpting (where possible) ancillary secondary institutions. A dormitory, for example, because of the time students spend in it, can often influence behavior more than the formal curriculum of the primary institution itself. So long as children live at home, the family of orientation exercises control over them simply because they spend so much time there; and thus the collegiate break in familial residence is a salient threat to familial control. This is why ascriptive groups have invested so much in the operation and defense of residence halls catering to their own members, and of which the college sorority is the most extreme example.

ENDOGAMY

Familial ascription in industrial societies, just as in nonindustrial ones, involves a principle of endogamy, a norm of marriage within some particular group. A status can be

---

thus rendered desirable in itself. This has inspired a host of imitative "adult sororities" similar in Greek-letter nomenclature but otherwise dissimilar, and for which a college education is not required. The names are actually the initial letters of the organization's motto, rendered in classical Greek. At the time the Greek-letter groups were founded, all college students could be expected to know Greek, but no one else would; and thus its use served both to advance fraternal secrecy and conspicuously to signal the educational status of the member. Today, however, the motto has to be transliterated even to be uttered at secret meetings by rote, and every "manual for pledges" has a pronouncing Greek alphabet on the back cover.

taught to children more thoroughly when both parents occupy it to begin with. Two forms of endogamy bear on sororities: ethnic endogamy and stratum or class endogamy. As for the first, sororities are differentiated along ethnic lines; the stronger the desire for endogamy by the ethnic group, the more complete the differentiation. The best examples are the Jewish sororities, because among all normatively endogamous American ethnic groups only the Jews so far have made much use of higher education.[10] Stratum or class endogamy, however, is more pervasive; and it is additionally important because it is also respected by those committed to norms of ethnic endogamy.[11] Norms of endogamy generally apply more strongly to women than to men because a man derives his status from an occupational position (whether gained by ascription or achievement) and confers that status on his

[10]The relevance of Jewish fraternal organizations has been little noted in the literature on collegiate fraternities and sororities. Thus Ian C. Ross, in "Group Standards Concerning the Admission of Jews to Fraternities at the University of Michigan," *(Social Problems, loc. cit.)* deals only with exclusion of Jews from gentile groups and fails to note the apparently far more complete (at least in sororities) exclusion of gentiles from Jewish groups. But Jewish solidarity, including a norm of ethnic endogamy, is vastly more than a short-run response to gentile exclusiveness (this being Lee's interpretation, in *op. cit.*, pp. ix, 10, and 38). For a more accurate historical perspective on Jewish endogamy and the reciprocal character of Jewish-gentile segregation, see Jacob Katz, *Exclusiveness and Tolerance*, New York: Schocken Books, 1962, pp. 11, 22, 42. For more recent evidence on the force of Jewish norms of endogamy, see John E. Meyer, *Jewish-Gentile Courtship*, New York: Free Press, 1961, Chs. 7–8, and Milton R. Barron, *People Who Intermarry*, Syracuse, N.Y.: Syracuse University Press, 1946, pp. 21–33.

Jewish endogamy is maintained at a physical remove from parents in higher education by two general mechanisms: 1) the avoidance (especially by women) of colleges where Jewish enrollment is slight, and 2) through special Jewish youth organizations which serve as settings for potentially endogamous introductions and courtship, and of which the Jewish sorority system is the best example. These sororities mirror the gentile system and actively cooperate with the latter through the National Panhellenic Council on general sorority concerns.

[11]When norms of ethnic and stratum endogamy interact, unless the stratum is also a caste (thus precluding achieved mobility) the maintenance of either norm is more difficult. For Jewish parents the most desirable potential son-in-law will be both of high status and of Jewish descent. But not all high-status men are Jewish and not all Jewish men are of high status. In emphasizing one norm the risk is run of violating the other. This dilemma is not unappreciated, and parents prefer to remove their daughters from the sorority system altogether if entry cannot be gained into the one or two "decent" or highest-status Jewish sororities.

wife, whereas a woman leaves her antenuptial status to assume that conferred by her husband.[12] In industrial societies women can gain a tolerable status by their own occupational achievements, but such a status, as every college girl knows, is still stigmatized as secondary and inferior to that conferred by a husband. This stigma motivates marriage, preserves the equivalence of stratum level between parents that status ascription to progeny requires, and facilitates employment of women in positions less prestigeful than their husbands'.

A variety of organizations and activities can reinforce behavior appropriate to a particular stratum or ethnic group, but only a few can maintain control over mate selection. Especially in their routine activities, sororities too reinforce much that is class-specific but not very important to the control of courtship. But without the latter they could not count on the long-run support from interested ascriptive groups that they now command. The specifically feminine skills appropriate to middle- or higher-class women still largely require marriage to a man of similarly high status for their exercise: if spinsterhood or unfitting marriage is the price of learning them their achievement is empty and meaningless.

HYPERGAMY AND THE "BRAHMIN PROBLEM"

Stratum mobility through marriage occurs widely, being effectively prohibited only in racial caste systems.[13] The movement of a woman through marriage to a stratum higher than that to which she was born is named *hypergamy*, and to a

[12]Marriage can be a means of occupational mobility for men, as in the folklore on "marrying the boss's daughter." But this is far less common than mobility through marriage for women, and besides it is no exception to the principle that men acquire status by occupation. He who marries the boss's daughter is then promoted to assistant boss or an equivalent position, the better to confer an appropriate status back on his wife.

[13]Kingsley Davis, "Intermarriage in Caste Societies," *American Anthropologist*, 43 (1941), pp. 186–188. The present paper owes much to Davis' several articles on kinship, both for substantive points of analysis and for its method of explanation. Specially relevant to sororities is his "The Sociology of Parent-Youth Conflict," *American Sociological Review*, 5 (1940), pp. 525–535. Much of what Davis says about parent-youth conflict applies more generally to conflict between generations and between age-graded statuses, and applies, *mutatis mutandis*, to conflict between sorority "actives" and alumnae.

lower one, *hypogamy*. Especially in industrial societies, norms of stratum endogamy (as distinct from the practice) seldom exist as such except where they reinforce stronger norms of ethnic endogamy; instead they reflect the emphasis on mobility that prevails in these societies. A social class is not the same kind of ascriptive group as a caste: though both rely mainly or wholly on ascription for recruitment, a caste ascribes the *same* status, whereas members of a mobility-oriented class desire to ascribe a *higher* status. This means that hypergamy rather than class endogamy is to be sought, and hypogamy avoided. The reasons for this are clear. First, mobility from low status to high is widely desired. Second, industrial societies encourage and facilitate mobility. Primarily they do so for men, stressing the possibility of achieving highly ranked positions in the labor force. But in these societies the typical family is small, and given its function of instilling strong generalized motives for achievement, it has neither the inclination nor the resources (compared with large families in simple societies) for much differential socialization by sex. Emphasis on the rewards given to the higher strata, and on the use of efficient means for entering those strata, though addressed mainly to sons, will hardly be lost on daughters. Third, stratum mobility through marriage is simply easier than stratum mobility through work. And it is made easier still by such differential socialization as persists in industrial societies, whereby women are relatively well trained in the strategems of attracting men and relatively poorly motivated (as compared with men) to compete for and maintain a well-rewarded position. So efficient is hypergamy as a means of improving one's status that it comes to be institutionalized as an aspiration of both parents and daughters (though more unequivocally for parents than for daughters).[14] Available data suggest that sororities facilitate hypergamy rather than stratum endogamy as such.[15]

---

[14]Evidence of hypergamy in the U.S. is presented by Richard Centers, "Marital Selection and Occupational Strata," *American Journal of Sociology*, 54 (1949), pp. 530–535. Just what the hypergamy rate is (compared with that of class endogamy) depends on how narrowly "classes" are defined. Using seven classes, Centers found that for over half the women marriage involved a change from the antenuptial class (based on "father's occupation"). In the higher strata hypogamy was more common; in the lower (where there are more people), hypergamy prevailed.

For a good general discussion of the relation between social class and marital choice see Harry M. Johnson, *Sociology: A Systematic Introduction*, New York: Harcourt Brace, 1960, Ch. 18.

Marriage always involves an element of exchange and hypergamy figures in the exchange.[16] It gives men of higher status a marketing advantage, since they have a more valuable status to confer; but it also disadvantages women of high antenuptial status. I call this the *Brahmin problem*. It occurs in courtship bargaining with respect to any valuable status or attribute that cannot be reciprocally conferred between marital partners. Generally the most valuable of these statuses and attributes are related to stratum level, but not all of them are: handsomeness and beauty, wit, kindness, intelligence, if not equally distributed among different strata, are at least in no society the monopoly of any one, and this provides motives for marriage across stratum boundaries. Yet a man's status, if high, is valuable enough in exchange to offset greatly his personal defects, because he can confer it; whereas the high status to which a woman may be born is not so valuable in exchange, because she is relatively unable to confer it.[17] Because her status is valuable to her and to her parents,

---

[16]Survey data in Gamble, *op. cit.*, show that even in "high-prestige" sororities a minority of girls have college-educated parents; of three classes a minority are "upper class" by birth (pp. 40–43). The pattern is even stronger in the highest-prestige Jewish sorority, where daughters of entrepreneurs strongly outnumber daughters of professionals (p. 20).

[16]Cf. William J. Goode, *World Revolution and Family Patterns,* New York: The Free Press of Glencoe, 1963: "*All* courtship systems are market or exchange systems. They differ from one another with respect to *who* does the buying and selling, which characteristics are more or less valuable in that market, and how open or explicit the bargaining is. In a conjugal family system mutual attraction in both courtship and marriage acquires a higher value. Nevertheless, the elders do not entirely lose control" (p. 7). Goode then anticipates the present explanation of the sorority. "Youngsters are likely to marry only those with whom they fall in love, and they fall in love only with the people they meet. Thus, the focus of parental controls is one of who is allowed to meet whom at parties, in the school and neighborhood, and so on." The sorority is one such "focus of parental control." Goode also summarizes comparative evidence and analyzes marital control more generally (*op. cit.*, pp. 28–35).

[17]Status conferral from wife to husband is not completely absent. See Becker, *op. cit.*, p. 14: a woman can learn before marriage skills that will enhance her husband's "status-as-consumer," and because in a rapidly changing society dimensions of stratification (e.g. status-as-producer vs. status-as-consumer) can be somewhat independent in the short run. Some achievements in the wifely role are class-specific, referring to standards of consumption, to information and wit in conversation, recreational skills, competence in the arts, and so on. Skills of this sort are, therefore, valuable in courtship exchange. But the class-specific attributes that a man contributes to a marriage—income,

she prefers to marry a man whose status is at least equally high, but for these men she must compete to some extent against women from all strata.[18] Further, except in societies where the status of women is low generally, women born to high strata are disadvantaged by a peculiar pattern of what may be called "class-specific vanity;" for they expect to receive in courtship the same extravagant favors and attention that their well-situated parents have made available to them.[19] But men who court them are seldom wholly insensitive to vanity, and where inter-stratum contact is frequent they often discover that the favors, including the prospect of marriage,

---

power, occupational prestige—remain primary, and those that his wife contributes remain secondary, because the woman's contribution presumes the availability of the man's.

[18]Davis, referring to India, notes that "the women of higher castes, being unable to marry down, suffer a deadly competition from their lower-caste sisters . . ." ("Intermarriage in Caste Societies," *op. cit.*, p. 385). See also Aileen D. Ross, *The Hindu Family in its Urban Setting*, Toronto, University of Toronto, 1961, pp. 260ff. For relevant U.S. data see Ernest Havemann and Patricia Salter West, *They Went to College*, New York: Harcourt Brace, 1952, pp. 53ff. College women generally have a lower marriage rate, college men a higher one.

The competition can be deadly on other grounds too. Besides social class, reciprocity of status conferral fails (at least in western societies) with regard to height and age, disadvantaging tall and old women. The college sorority specializes in relieving the Brahmin problem with regard to stratum or ethnic endogamy; but outside of higher education are similar sororities of the old and the tall, which try to provide access to even older and taller men.

[19]A middle- or upper middle-class American girl grows up in a family where resources are high and fertility is low, thus making much available to each child. Because nubility is a desirable status in which older women tend vicariously to participate, the daughter receives much attention from her mother, and for related and other reasons she is also favored during this period by her father. The mother may think nothing of spending several hundred dollars annually on her daughter's wardrobe, while the father will with the same equanimity spend several hundred hours each year personally chauffeuring her to adolescent *fétes*, ballet school, summer camp, etc., rather than expose her to the status contamination of public transport and (as he imagines and rationalizes) the risk of sexual assault. The daughter tends to regard these rewards not as the accidental and ascribed result of relations to particular persons—her parents—but as due to her generally. She may, for example, expect a law student who is courting her to spend several hours driving her to the airport just at the time he is facing semester examinations on which his occupational future crucially depends. Thus few men in competitive curricula can afford to court girls who are vain, class-specifically or otherwise. Implications for the future of sororities in a setting of increasingly competitive higher education are clear.

of lower-status women can be had for a smaller investment of their own scarce time, money, and emotion. Higher-strata women are therefore often indisposed for the potentially sanguinary competition they must face anyway. The Brahmin problem is inherent in hypergamy, and it is important because of the structures that have grown up to contend with it.

Some possible solutions—each of which has been used by the higher strata of some society—are female infanticide, spinsterhood, polygyny, and dowries and groom-service fees. Except for spinsterhood, all of these are structurally incompatible with industrial organization, and even spinsterhood, though apparently more common in industrial societies than in simple ones, is disesteemed. Further, since family institutions in industrial societies have many functions besides solving the Brahmin problem, the solution must be economical, and applicable where it will be most effective—namely, where the most suitable men are likely to be met, and at an age where they are disposed to marry. Both of these criteria imply concentration on the institutions of higher education, for here are found both men born to higher strata and men moving into them. The campus presents an excellent marriage market, though (because it also facilitates hypogamy) a risky one; and consequently in societies where substantial proportions of the population go to college, courtship and marriage are as much a part of what happens there as is the formal curriculum.

Within the college population, one way to relieve the Brahmin problem to some degree is to maximize encounters with men who are themselves mobile, who aspire to a group to which they do not yet belong. More than others, these men will value the symbolic reassurance provided by social contact with girls whose skills are those of the class to which they aspire; they will be tempted less than others, then, by charms that women of all strata possess. Since college fraternities are filled with men who aspire to stratum mobility, their members, indisposed to hypergamy, are the sorority girls' most convenient suitors.

LOVE[20]

The emotions called "love" characteristically fail to guarantee respect for any prior classification of the persons involved, including classification into strata or ethnic groups. Lovable traits vary among societies but in none are they distributed solely according to any principle of ascribed status. The theoretical importance of love derives from its capacity to motivate exogamy in the face of some norm of endogamy; if the norm is to prevail, then love must be controlled. No organization can prevent its members from falling in love; indeed sororities use love to motivate timely marriage. Their distinctive office is to see that their nubile participants fall in love only with men who qualify as desirable mates under the principle of endogamy involved.

Love is also important to the educational setting and to sororities because it appeals most strongly to adolescents. It tempts the young into exogamy and hypogamy; the burden of normative control is thus left to the old.

HETEROGENEITY OF PUBLIC EDUCATION

The general factors mentioned so far do not by themselves account for sororities. Imagine a system of higher education in which admission policies were such that free mate selection within each college would be in complete accord with the appropriate principles of endogamy. Thus young members of endogamy-seeking ethnic groups would all attend ethnically segregated schools, while women aspiring to hypergamy would choose schools where they might meet men above their own stratum, but never below it. This system would be ideal so far as endogamy is the object, and many actual schools approach it. In that system the maintenance of endogamy would not require special independent secondary organiza-

---

[20]This section summarizes William Goode's concise and excellent discussion in "The Theoretical Importance of Love," *American Sociological Review*, 24 (1959) pp. 38–47.

tions, and class-and religion-specific schools are in fact relatively devoid of them.[21]

A large and growing proportion of American college enrollment, however, is in tax-supported colleges and universities, where the cost of attendance is relatively low and admission and matriculation are competitively based on ability.[22] These schools draw students from many strata and ethnic groups: from the relatively poor, because they can afford nothing else; and to a considerable extent from more affluent groups (especially in the American west and midwest) because their academic reputations often compete with those of private schools. But the variety of students exacerbates the Brahmin problem. Those parents who are afflicted with it and choose to enroll their daughters in public schools are motivated to devise some way to restrict interstratum and interethnic contact in college, generally in residential proximity to other women and crucially in courtship encounters with men.

The total costs of rather expensive sorority residence, together with the nominal tuition at a public school, are usually much less than dormitory residence would be at a class-specific private school with its high tuition. Then, too, many girls, whose parents hope they will marry "the right kind of

[21]Pertinent here is the history of sororities at a private, reputable, and expensive western university, where they were summarily abolished about 20 years ago following the poignant suicide of a rejected rushee. Yet the pattern of female enrollment changed little after the sororities' demise, and class endogamy was unaffected, because the university's admissions policies (including a very high sex ratio) and the high monetary costs of attendance were themselves sufficient to minimize the risk of hypogamous love.

At eastern "elite" private schools the trend has been for independant secondary organizations to lose control of students' residence and to lose strength generally. They have not been strongly defended by the ascriptive groups whose interests they served because these interests are now served well enough by the character of the school as a whole. Even when private schools are not co-educational, dating tends to be limited to a physically and socially proximate school of the other sex; the entire school serves the function which at public colleges must be handled by specialized groups. Religion-specific schools are noted for a monolithic character in which independent secondary organizations are not tolerated; note the Roman Catholic church's ban on membership in "secret societies which it does not directly or indirectly control." See Noel P. Gist, "Secret Societies," *The University of Missouri Studies,* 15 (1940, entire), p. 150.

[22]In 1949, 49.3 per cent of 2.45 million college students were enrolled in public schools; in 1961 both figures had risen, to 60.5 per cent of 3.89 million students. U.S. Office of Education, *Digest of Educational Statistics,* Washington: Government Printing Office, 1962, p. 86.

man," lack the intellectual fortitude (because they learn the techniques for hypergamy instead)[23] to meet the increasingly severe performance standards of high-status private colleges, even if their parents could afford the tuition. Co-educational schools of high repute, whether public or private, are characterized by a high sex ratio (a preponderance of men); those of low repute by a low sex ratio; and the social strata represented by the students are consistent with the academic reputation. Thus the disposition of nubile girls to feminine charm, which brings them profound rewards, and their indisposition to abstract thought, excludes many of them from one fine source of high-status men, private schools of high prestige; they must instead rely on what can be found at the less selective public schools.

Sorority girls attend tax-supported schools and benefit from their capacity to reinforce a familially ascribed status with marketable technical skills (e.g., educated conversation and taste, as well as occupational training, should employment be contemplated after marriage), while the organizations in which they reside vastly reduce the potential for interstratum and interethnic contact and the corollary risk of exogamous love. It is at the great state universities, free, open, and competitive, that the sorority system is most fully developed.

But the relative scarcity of high status men at the public schools, and the relative surplus of low-status women, are still to be contended with. Although sororities can do little about the first problem, they can do quite a bit about the second by establishing and maintaining the belief that, at least at particular colleges, dating opportunities are severely curtailed for girls who are not sorority members. Thus many high school girls, fearing that they will not be invited into sorority membership at a particular college, enroll at other colleges where sororities are absent or are thought to be less dominant.[24] Since these girls will generally be unsophisticated, unattractive, or of lower-class or sub-ordinated ethnic descent, less afflicted with general or class-specific vanity and thus easier to

[23]See Turner, *op. cit.*, pp. 271–273.

[24]Thus in questionnaires I distributed in 1963 and 1964 among undergraduate women at the University of California at Davis, the modal response (about 30 per cent) to the open-ended question "Why did you choose to come to Davis?" was "no sororities," and their absence was mentioned together with other factors in another 20 per cent of the responses. More intensive interviewing suggested that the belief that sororities dominate social life at certain other campuses is widely and strongly held among high school girls.

court, the Brahmin problem is relieved at the school with the strong sorority system to the extent that they are frightened away from it.

IMPORTANCE OF TIMELY MARRIAGE

Even given all the preceding conditions, however, an exogamy-deterring alternative to the sorority can still be imagined: postponement of the time of marriage until the risk of college-inspired exogamous love is past. This might be called an "Irish Solution to the Brahmin Problem," in view of Eire's late age at marriage since the potato famine. Yet women are constrained, if they contemplate marriage at all, to be timely about it. Whether endogamous or exogamous, arranged or romantic, marriage is an exchange in which (among other things) the sexual attractiveness of women is offered in return for status and support from men. Men can confer status and extend support for relatively many years; women are sexually attractive for relatively few. Since youth and nubile beauty are such important aspects of women's exchange in marriage, the problem of avoiding an undesirable marriage cannot be solved by postponing marriage indefinitely. Demographically, late marriage is associated with a high proportion of spinsters; this is the price the Irish have paid for late marriage.[25]

Among all the age-graded statuses through which a woman passes, the period of nubility is the most rewarded; indeed, the rewards are so great relative to other periods that "feminine youth" is not simply an abstract age-graded status but a veritable institution, consciously recognized, celebrated in folklore and literature, the object of anticipatory socialization of female children and a time to which later memories return.[26] This situation favors the sororities, for they are explic-

[25]See Kingsley Davis and Judith Blake, "Social Structure and Fertility: An Analytic Framework," in Seymour M. Lipset and Neil J. Smelser (eds.), Sociology: The Progress of a Decade, Englewood Cliffs, N.J.: Prentice-Hall, 1961, p. 363.

[26]Cf. Talcott Parsons, "Age and Sex in the Social Structure of the United States," in Parsons, Essays in Sociological Theory (1st. ed.), Glencoe, Ill.: The Free Press, 1949, pp. 226–227. Parsons interprets the institutionalization of feminine youth differently, in terms of maximum chances for future achievement—"a certain romantic nostalgia for the time when the fundamental choices were still open" (p. 226)—rather than in terms of maximum immediate reward.

itly designed to maximize the rewards of nubility, to enhance with symbol and ceremony a highly valued yet ephemeral status, quite apart from the services they offer to endogamy. As the youthful condition is cherished, so stands to be also its organizational expression.

SORORITIES: A BRIEF DESCRIPTION[27]

Given the conditions just reviewed, an organization can be imagined whose purpose it would be to encourage the timely marriage of women in conformity with norms of endogamy or hypergamy in the face of exceptional risks of exogamous or hypogamous love, by restricting heterosexual encounters to the appropriate groups. This set of conditions seems too complex as a "latent function" ever to be made manifest.

[27]My data are necessarily incomplete. The "secret society" aspect of sorority organization requires the use of indirect and risky methods of research. Sorority members are required by the National Panhellenic Council not to provde *any* information about their organizations, and this rule has foiled more than one attempt at survey study. Then too sororities have been besieged by critics for several decades; their silence has been historically warranted by the fact that most information on sororities has been collected by persons who sought their abolition or fundamental reorganization. See Lee and also *Social Problems, opera cit.*

I thus collected most of my data by "ethnographic" procedures, including intensive and unstructured interviews with fraternity and sorority members selected solely for their cooperativeness and their access to relevant information, and with college deans and administrative officers. I read sorority magazines and student publications, and gained some access to confidential sorority and "Panhellenic" memoranda. The confidential materials contained little not implicit in "external" evidence. They do reveal the sorority system to be well organized, and its leaders not unsophisticated about the problems they face. I also conducted some limited "participant-observation" in suitable service roles ("party photographer").

For more comprehensive data, the best extant source is Gamble, *op. cit.* Her use of survey material is good, but the best parts of her discussion of sororities are also ethnographic. Both Gamble's essay and my own work draw heavily on the unique and valuable material presented in the incomplete (and now apparently lost) work of Meredith Luther Friedman, 1956–60.

The data of Gamble and Friedman, as well as most of my own, were collected at a western state university whose admission standards and academic reputation make it and its sorority system highly unrepresentative. This particular campus, however, is a bellwether of trends that are spreading throughout public higher education.

Yet in fact it is the *consciously* designed (if largely un-acknowledged) purpose of sororities; the difference be-tween sociological and lay conceptions is not so much a mat-ter of latency *v.* manifestation as one of terminology. The threat to endogamy and the conditions of its maintenance are more or less well understood by those who control soror-ities—their middle-aged "alumnae." These women know per-fectly well that a young girl probably will not meet the right kind of man unless she goes to college, but that if left to her-self at a large school she may fall in love with the wrong kind, that the best way to assure marriage to one of the right kind of men is to arrange for meaningful encounters with lots of them, and that marriage must not be put off too long. The problem in more technical and general terms is that of maintaining the norms of the ascriptive group at the critical point when the person moves by marriage from his family of orientation to his family of procreation. Although the homi-letical tone appropriate to her era avoids the problems of courtship control, a founder of one of the great national so-rorities posed the general issue well enough:

> . . . In taking a girl out of the crowd and making her
> a permanent member of a small group, the sorority is
> rendering her an inestimable service. It is providing her
> during her college course with family affiliations and
> with the essential elements of a home—sympathetic in-
> terest, wise supervision, disinterested advice. Incidentally
> society itself is benefited. The corner stone of the social
> structure is the family, and it is not altogether wise that
> college girls, or college boys for that matter, should cut
> lose from youth's anchorage and drift far from home
> moorings during four long years. There is a danger, and
> a very grave danger, that four years' residence in a dor-
> mitory will tend to destroy right ideals of home life and
> substitute in their stead a belief in the freedom that
> comes from community living. . . . Culture, broad,
> liberalizing. humanizing culture, we cannot get too much
> of, unless while acquiring it we are weaned from home
> and friends, from ties of blood and kindred.[28]

Because endogamy and other familial interests seem less important to girls than to their parents, an organization dedi-

[28]Sarah Ida Shaw Martin (Mrs. William Holmes Martin), *The Soror-ity Handbook* (11th ed.), Boston: privately published, 1931, pp. 41–42.

cated to maintaining them at the expense of other activities will have problems of recruitment, especially if it is at least partly voluntary. Sororities indeed have such a problem. The folklore of student life stresses that many who wish to live in sororities are not invited into them. This is true enough, but it obscures the equally true point that many whom the sororities want as members do not wish to join. Recruitment thus depends on a number of special techniques.

First, parents often pressure daughters to join sororities; many girls join only because parents insist. Second, sororities do their most effective recruiting not among college students, but at high schools, where a picture of college life can be drawn for prospective recruits who cannot readily test it by direct experience.[29] Sororities are claimed to have a monopoly on all that is pleasant; especially are they claimed to have cornered all masculine attention. Although the extent to which these claims are true varies among colleges—depending in part on the heterogeneity of student culture—their effect depends on the extent to which they are believed, and (as noted above) apparently they are believed even where they are largely false. Third, in all respects save those that increase the risk of exogamy sorority life is not only represented but is in fact made as attractive as possible to prospective recruits. This is why the "subculture" of the sorority, especially in its public manifestations, often seems so studiously adolescent and, by adult standards, trivial. Its prospective members are mainly pre-college girls, who seldom understand, and often fear, much of their future collegiate role, and as a result the sorority must be oriented more to the world of the high school where it solicits than to that of the college where it resides. Just as girls tend to flock to the "party schools" of low academic repute, avoiding those that emphasize scholarship, and to seek less competitive courses and departments within the school,[30] so historically the most effective way to recruit pre-college girls has been to maintain

[29]At present, the more direct experience a girl has had with opportunities for social life at a particular campus, the less likely she is to join its sororities. At the main campus studied, only a small proportion of sorority girls join after their first semester at the school. At other campuses where sorority membership must be preceded by a semester's residence at the school, recruitment is severely handicapped, with chapter houses (especially those of low prestige) reduced to taking in non-affiliated boarders to pay the costs of running the property.

[30]For partial confirmation of this assertion regarding fields of study, see U.S. Office of Education, *op. cit.*, pp. 95 and 100; also Turner, *op. cit.*, pp. 272–273.

sorority life as one of fun and frolic with an abundance of masculine attention. For that life to prevail the rigors of scholarship must necessarily be reduced to the minimum required for continued attendance at the school.

Institutionalized hedonism, as a solution to problems of recruitment, poses other problems of membership retention. The sorority does not serve the interests of youth, but those of an earlier generation; and it maintains a number of rules that are issues of conflict between sorority alumnae and active members just as, in the home, they are issues between parents and children. Not surprisingly, therefore, sorority life is regularly reported even by its partisans among undergraduate women to involve a great deal of constraint.[31] Parental standards are enforced to a degree unmatched in other collegiate living groups, with regard to public conduct, when escorted by men, and for dress "appropriate for a young lady." An elaborate calendar of parliamentary activities, committee meetings, confrontations with alumnae, and community projects such as student theatrical routines, must be carried out;[32] the pressure to meet young men at social "exchanges", picnics, parties, co-operative building of floats for parades, etc., sometimes exceeds even the widespread desire to meet them; crowding is sometimes severe; the noise level is high; the esoteric rituals grow tedious and sophomoric; and most forms of privacy do not exist. Thus sororities are rather carefully designed to be far easier to enter, when the pleasures of membership are anticipated and youthful enthusiasm is high, than they are to leave later on, when alternatives to sororities

[31]My data suggest, and Gamble's data show, a high rate of disaffection, especially remarkable in view of the homogeneity among sorority members produced by alumnae attention to "background" and by active members to "personality." Some disaffection and withdrawal comes simply from an increase in members' sophistication in spite of the sorority's efforts to prevent it. A girl whose reference group is shifting to one composed of adults will, to the extent of the shift, come to dislike the proximity of adolescents. Here especially recruitment and retention policies tend to be opposed. Another source of disaffection is an instrumental attitude toward the sorority as a means of meeting men: once a suitable man is met the sorority has served its purpose and membership is discontinued.

[32]As Weir (op. cit., p. 187) comments on the same phenomenon: ". . . one wonders how the girls ever find the time to escape at all from their houses into the classroom." That, of course, is just the point of the activities: they keep the "broad liberalizing culture" of the classroom from interfering with the "ties of blood and kindred." (Martin, loc. cit.)

have been discovered and their constraints have been directly experienced.

In short, the sorority protects its members against the stratum-dissolving standards of the larger university, and its potential for hypogamous love, simply by dominating their collegiate life. Time is encompassed completely, especially for the novitiates or "pledges," by compulsory activities planned in advance, so that little energy or time remains for events where inappropriate men might be encountered. The control is relaxed somewhat for accepted members, who by then have adequately learned the standards and taboos.

Sorority girls are especially limited in their opportunities to meet varieties of men.[33] The typical arrangement is for each sorority to maintain traditional liaisons with one or more fraternities, matched closely on a basis of ethnicity or class level. Encounters and courtship are facilitated by parties and exchanges between sororities and fraternities, and by the untiring efforts of intermediaries, or "fixer-uppers," who arrange social engagements, or "dates," between those who might not otherwise meet, and on behalf of men too timid or unskilled to essay them directly. The efforts of the fixer-uppers greatly reduce the inconvenience, and more saliently the anxiety, in dating, and thus effectively raise its rate above what it would be otherwise.[34] The control achieved in simple or traditional

---

[33] Freshman sorority girls are often restricted to the chapter house on week-day nights by some fixed early hour (such as 7 p.m.); though designed to encourage study, this also narrows the range of men they meet. Students generally report that many acquaintances are begun at such places as the campus library; a sorority freshman, on the other hand, has very little time to spend in the library and meets men only at the "exchange," etc., which the sorority sponsors and whose invitation list they control.

[34] Probably the importance of intermediaries even in supposedly "free" American dating and courtship has been underestimated, and the large number of young persons who do little or no dating overlooked. In a society where marriage is not arranged by elders, high marriage rates require high dating rates. But dating is often ruthlessly competitive, and, in a society that celebrates erotic appeal yet makes much of premarital celibacy, it first excites and then frustrates that one strong primary drive whose reward might otherwise sustain it. Under these circumstances only a few will find dating intrinsically rewarding; for many, anxiety and frustration tend to extinguish the activity unless it is reinforced extrinsically by various mechanisms and agents.

The Japanese *nakohdo*, go-between, continues to function in an industrializing society under conditions where direct familial arrangement of marriage is increasingly unworkable but dating as such is still uncommon. See Ezra Vogel, "The Go-Between in a Developing Society: The Case of the Japanese Marriage Arranger," *Human Organiza-*

societies by parental arrangement of marriages is achieved in industrial society by these go-betweens, who in the case of the sorority operate within an organization controlled by interested ascriptive groups. The result is largely the same: marriage is timely, its rate is high, and exogamous and hypogamous combinations of partners are avoided. Then too the style and occasions of sorority dating tend to be expensive and time-consuming, and this discourages the attentions of poor and low-status men.

No organization with the characteristics described could depend for internal control on consensus among its active members; sororities are therefore effectively controlled by their alumnae. Control derives from alumnae ownership of the chapter house and from assumption of *in loco parentis* power over active members, most of whom are legal minors. But the principal basis for control is the recommendatory requirement for membership: no girl can be invited to join a sorority without recommendations (typically) from two or more alumnae. This procedure helps maintain standards of deportment, class position, reputations for sexual morality, and so on; and direct inheritance of membership, from mother to daughter, is given special consideration. This together with the active members' practical preference for congenial and accommodative persons who can be tolerated in constant interaction in close quarters effectively excludes from membership headstrong, enterprising, and innovative girls who, were they members, might be catalysts for organizational change. This is why sorority girls are so compliant in the face of alumnae dominance, and why, to academicians who often value novelty in ideas and a mild irreverence toward bourgeois conventions, they seem so consistently bland and uninteresting as students.

Although the day-to-day governing of the sorority is formally democratic, informally it is not. The broad outline of regulations is fixed by the national association, and much of the communication from national headquarters to local chapters, and from alumnae to active members, consists of

---

tion, 20 (1961), pp. 112–120; reprinted in part in William J. Goode (ed.), *Readings on the Family and Society*, Englewood Cliffs, N.J.: Prentice-Hall, 1964, pp. 71–82. And apparently the *shatchen* still practices in Jewish communities together with a great deal of informal but intensive match-making by kith and kin. See the newspaper advertisements cited in William M. Kephart, *The Family, Society, and the Individual*, Boston: Houghton, Mifflin, 1961, p. 333.

efforts to explain and defend points of policy which are chronic sources of youthful complaint. The actual offices of control are filled by an elaborate process of coöptation of active members by alumnae and housemothers (who are appointed by alumnae). The ratio of officers to members is high, and the more demanding offices, or those entrusted to enforce unpopular standards, tend to be rewarded by special privileges or extra living space. And deviance on small matters, when discreet, is relatively unpunished; this draws attention from more important controls and provides a sense of independence to the deviants, keeps down the withdrawal rate, and permits for the sorority an economy of sanctions, the better that it can deploy those at its command against more serious transgressions.

To keep high the rate of engagement and marriage, sororities rely heavily on emotionally potent ceremonies and rituals to sanctify matrimony. Exposure to and dating of the right man are not enough; if endogamy is to be maintained the dates must lead to engagements and the engagements to marriage. Thus the sorority subculture, especially as sustained by the alumnae, define all dating encounters as prolegomena to marriage. Housemothers and alumnae do what they can to discourage truly casual and spontaneous dating and to encourage structured and organized involvement. "Pinning"—a pre-engagement relationship signifying reciprocal commitment and sexual prerogative—is solemnized by an elaborate ritual, often involving the participation of many students, witnessed by all the sorority sisters and attended, in its classic form, by a choir of fraternity men singing outside the sorority. This serves to reinforce progress toward engagement at its weakest point and to hinder withdrawal from the "pinned" commitment. The special status of the pinned and engaged is ceremonially reinforced in other ways too: where sorority functions are recorded in college newspapers, much attention is given to pinnings and engagements.

Sororities also encourage hypergamy by teaching a repertory of class-specific activities, especially where their members are from families of relatively low status (sororities are elaborately ranked among themselves, in ways correlative to stratification in their host society). Thus the lower-ranked sororities carefully teach the manners thought appropriate to the higher strata; e.g., "how to drink like a lady," always to order and sour mixed drinks, etc. Since the higher-ranked sororities are the reference groups for the lower (members of the latter being mainly girls who had hoped to be invited to join the former), in regard to distinctive sorority characteristics the lower sororities tend to be *plus royaux que le roi.*

Blissful Isles

by
Denis Diderot

In the sharing of Bougainville's crew among the Tahitians,
the almoner was allotted to Orou; they were about the same
age, thirty-five to thirty-six. Orou had then only his wife and
three daughters, called Asto, Palli, and Thia. They undressed
the almoner, bathed his face, hands and feet, and served him
a wholesome and frugal meal. When he was about to go to
bed, Orou, who had been absent with his family, reappeared
and presenting to him his wife and three daughters, all naked,
said: "You have eaten, you are young and in good health; if
you sleep alone you will sleep badly, for man needs a companion beside him at night. There is my wife, there are my
daughters; choose the one who pleases you best. But if you
wish to oblige me you will give preference to the youngest of
my daughters, who has not yet had any children." The
mother added: "Alas! But it's no good complaining about it;
poor Thia! it is not her fault."

The almoner answered that his religion, his office, good
morals and decency would not allow him to accept these offers.

Orou replied: "I do not know what this thing is that you
call 'religion'; but I can only think ill of it, since it prevents
you from tasting an innocent pleasure to which nature, the
sovereign mistress, invites us all; prevents you from giving existence to one of your own kind, from doing a service which
a father, mother, and children all ask of you, from doing
something for a host who has received you well, and from
enriching a nation, by giving it one more citizen. I do not
know what this thing is which you call your 'office' but your
first duty is to be a man and to be grateful. I do not suggest
that you should introduce into your country the ways of
Orou, but Orou, your host and friend, begs you to lend your-

Reprinted from *Diderot Interpreter of Nature*, translated by Jean
Stewart and Jonathan Kemp, International Publishers, New York, 1943,
by permission of the publishers.

self to the ways of Tahiti. Whether the ways of Tahiti are better or worse than yours is an easy question to decide. Has the land of your birth more people than it can feed? If so your ways are neither worse nor better than ours. But can it feed more than it has? Our ways are better than yours. As to the sense of decency which you offer as objection, I understand you; I agree that I was wrong, and I ask your pardon. I do not want to injure your health; if you are tired, you must have rest; but I hope that you will not continue to sadden us. See the care you have made appear on all these faces; they fear lest you should have found blemishes on them which merit your disdain. But when it is only the pleasure of doing honour to one of my daughters, amidst her companions and sisters, and of doing a good action, won't that suffice you? Be generous!"

The Almoner: It's not that: they are all equally beautiful; but my religion! my office!

Orou: They are mine and I offer them to you; they are their own and they give themselves to you. Whatever may be the purity of conscience which the thing 'religion' and the thing 'office' prescribe, you can accept them without scruple. I am not abusing my authority at all; be sure that I know and respect the rights of the individual.

Here the truthful almoner agrees that Providence had never exposed him to such violent temptation. He was young, he became agitated and tormented; he turned his eyes away from the lovely suppliants, and then regarded them again; he raised his hands and eyes to the sky. Thia, the youngest, clasped his knees and said: "Stranger, do not distress my father and mother, do not afflict me. Honour me in the hut, among my own people; raise me to the rank of my sisters, who mock me. Asto, the eldest, already had three children; the second, Palli, has two; but Thia has none at all. Stranger, honest stranger, do not repulse me; make me a mother, make me a child that I can one day lead by the hand, by my side, here in Tahiti; who may be seen held at my breast in nine months' time; one of whom I shall be so proud and who will be part of my dowry when I go from my parents' hut to another's. I shall perhaps be more lucky with you than with our young Tahitians. If you will grant me this favour I shall never forget you; I shall bless you all my life. I shall write your name on my arm and on your son's; we shall pronounce it always with joy. And when you leave these shores, my good wishes will go with you on the seas till you reach your own land."

The candid almoner said that she clasped his knees, and gazed into his eyes so expressively and so touchingly; that she wept; that her father, mother and sisters withdrew; that he remained alone with her, and that, still saying, "my religion, my office," he found himself the next morning lying beside the young girl, who overwhelmed him with caresses, and who invited her parents and sisters, when they came to their bed in the morning, to join their gratitude to hers. Asto and Palli, who had withdrawn, returned bringing food, fruits and drink. They kissed their sister and made vows over her. They all ate together.

Then Orou, left alone with the almoner, said to him:

"I see that my daughter is well satisfied with you and I thank you. But would you teach me what is meant by this word 'religion' which you have repeated so many times and so sorrowfully?"

The almoner, after having mused a moment answered:

"Who made your hut and the things which furnish it?"

Orou: I did.

The Almoner: Well then, we believe that this world and all that it contains is the work of a maker.

Orou: Has he feet, hands and a head then?

The Almoner: No.

Orou: Where is his dwelling-place?

The Almoner: Everywhere.

Orou: Here too?

The Almoner: Here.

Orou: We have never seen him.

The Almoner: One doesn't see him.

Orou: That's an indifferent father, then! He must be old, for he will at least be as old as his work.

The Almoner: He does not age. He spoke to our ancestors, gave them laws, prescribed the manner in which he wished to be honoured; he ordered a certain behaviour as being good, and he forbade them certain other actions as being wicked.

Orou: I follow you; and one of the actions he forbade them, as wicked, was to lie with a woman or a girl? Why, then, did he make two sexes?

The Almoner: That they might be united; but with certain requisite conditions, after certain preliminary ceremonies in consequence of which the man belongs to the woman and only to her; and the woman belongs to the man, and only to him.

Orou: For their whole lives?

The Almoner: For the whole of their lives.

Orou: So that if it happened that a woman should lie with a man other than her husband, or a husband with another woman . . . but that couldn't happen. Since the maker is there and this displeases him, he will know how to prevent them doing it.

The Almoner: No; he lets them do it, and they sin against the law of God (for it is thus we call the great maker) against the law of the country; and they commit a crime.

Orou: I should be sorry to offend you by what I say, but if you would permit me, I would give you my opinion.

The Almoner: Speak.

Orou: I find these singular precepts opposed to nature and contrary to reason, made to multiply crimes and to plague at every moment this old maker, who has made everything, without help of hands, or head, or tools, who is everywhere and is not seen anywhere, who exists today and tomorrow and yet is not a day older, who commands and is not obeyed, who can prevent and yet does not do so. Contrary to nature because these precepts suppose that a free, thinking and sentient being can be the property of a being like himself. On what is this law founded? Don't you see that in your country they have confused the thing which has neither consciousness nor thought, nor desire, nor will; which one picks up, puts down, keeps or exchanges, without injury to it, or without its complaining, have confused this with the thing which cannot be exchanged or acquired, which has liberty, will, desire, which can give or refuse itself for a moment or for ever, which laments and suffers, and which cannot become an article of commerce, without its character being forgotten and violence done to its nature; contrary to the general law of existence? In fact. nothing could appear to you more senseless than a precept which refuses to admit that change which is a part of us, which commands a constancy which cannot be found there and which violates the liberty of the male and female by chaining them for ever to each other; more senseless than a fidelity which limits the most capricious of enjoyments to one individual: than an oath of the immutability of two beings made of flesh: and all that in the face of a sky which never for a moment remains the same, in caverns which threaten destruction, below a rock which falls to powder, at the foot of a tree which cracks, on a stone which rocks? Believe me, you have made the condition of man worse than that of animals. I do not know what your great maker may be; but I rejoice that he has never spoken to our forefathers, and I wish that he may never speak to our children; for he might tell them the same foolishness, and they commit the folly of believing it. Yesterday, at supper, you mentioned 'magistrates' and 'priests,' whose authority regulates your conduct; but, tell me, are they the masters of good and evil? Can they make what is just to be unjust and unjust, just? Does it rest with them to attribute good to harmful actions, and evil to innocent or useful actions? You could not think it, for, at that rate, there would be neither true nor false, good nor bad, beautiful nor ugly; or at any rate only what pleased your great maker, your magistrates and your priests to pronounce so. And from one moment to another you would be obliged to change your ideas and your conduct. One day someone would tell you, on behalf of one of your three masters, to kill, and you would be obliged by your conscience to kill; another day, "steal," and you would have to steal; or "do not eat this fruit" and you would not dare to eat it; "I forbid you this vegetable or animal" and you would take care not to touch them. There is no good thing that could not be forbidden you, and no wickedness that you could not be ordered to do. And what would you be reduced to, if your three masters, disagreeing among themselves, should at once permit, enjoin and forbid you the same thing, as I believe must often happen. Then, to please the priest you must become embroiled with the magistrate; to satisfy the magistrate you must displease the great maker; and to make yourself agreeable to the great maker you must renounce nature. And do you know what will happen then? You will neglect all of them, and you will be neither man, nor citizen nor pious; you will be nothing; you will be out of favour with all the kinds of authorities, at odds even with yourself, tormented by your heart, persecuted by your enraged masters; and wretched as I saw you yesterday evening when I offered my wife and daughters to you, and you cried out, "But my religion, my office!"

Do you want to know what is good and what is bad in all times and in all places? Hold fast to the nature of things and of actions; to your relations with your fellows; to the influence of your conduct on your individual usefulness and the general good. You are mad if you believe that there is any-

thing, high or low in the universe, which can add to or sub-
tract from the laws of nature. Her eternal will is that good
should be preferred to evil, and the general good to the individual good. You may ordain the opposite but you will not
be obeyed. You will multiply the number of malefactors and
the wretched by fear, punishment and remorse. You will de-
prave consciences; you will corrupt minds. They will not
know what to do or what to avoid. Disturbed in their state of
innocence, at ease with crime, they will have lost their guiding star."

A Slum Sex Code

by
William Foote Whyte

Respectable middle-class people have very definite standards of sex behavior. They are inclined to assume that behavior which does not conform to these standards is unorganized and subject to no set of ethics. It is my purpose to point out that, in one particular area commonly thought to be characterized by laxness of sex behavior, there is an elaborate and highly developed sex code. A study of the social and sex life of the slum will also yield certain clues as to the nature of the process of assimilation of an alien people into American society.

My information is based upon a three-and-a-half-year study of the Italian slum district of "Cornerville" in "Eastern City." By discussions with a number of men in corner gangs, in which I was a participant observer, I was able to learn the sex code of the slum, as it appears to the corner boys.

The story must be told against a background of local social life. In peasant Italy, as in other peasant societies, the family group undertook to regulate the social annd sexual relations of the children. Marriages were arranged by the parents of the couple, and no young man was allowed to visit a girl's home unless he had been accepted as her suitor. The influence of this system is still to be observed in Cornerville. Parents try to keep a strict watch upon their daughters. In most cases they are unable to arrange the marriages for their children, but they retain control over the home. The corner boy knows that if he once visits a girl in her home it will be assumed by her parents (and by everyone else) that he intends to marry her. Consequently, until he is completely sure of his own intentions, the corner boy remains outside of the house. He even hesitates to make a date with a girl, for if he does take her out alone it is assumed that he is her "steady."

Reprinted by permission of the publishers and the author from *American Journal of Sociology*, Vol. 49, 1943–44, pp. 24–31, University of Chicago Press.

Dances given by local clubs mark the high point of the social activities. Except for those who are "going steady," groups of men and groups of girls go separately to the dances. The man chooses his girl for each dance and, at the conclusion of the number, leaves her with her friends. There is no cutting in. When the dance is over, the men and women go home separately. Parties in a girl's home, picnics, evenings at the bowling alleys, and other social activities all tend to take this group form.

When a man centers his attention upon one girl, he arranges to meet her on the street corner. Good girls are not expected to "hang" on the corner, but the men consider it perfectly respectable for them to keep appointments on the corner. Most parents object to this practice more or less strongly and try to insist that the man shall come to the home. The insistence of the parents and the reluctance of the corner boy place the girl in a difficult position. Of course, she herself may not wish to give the relationship the permanent form which a visit to the home would involve. If they work outside of the home, most girls are able to insist upon some right to govern their own social relations; but this always involves friction with the parents, its seriousness depending upon the strength of parental control and the strenuousness of the daughter's efforts to gain independence.

The sex life of the corner boy begins when he is very young. One of them writes:

In Cornerville children ten years of age know most all the swear words and they have a good idea of what the word "lay" means. Swearing and describing of sex relations by older people and by the boys that hang on the corner are overheard by little children and their actions are noticed and remembered. Many of the children when they are playing in the streets, doorways and cellars actually go through the motions which pertain to the word "lay." I have seen them going through these motions, even children under ten years of age.

Most all the boys that I know and all my friends carry safes [condoms]. Most boys start carrying safes when they are of high school age.

Safes are purchased from necktie salesmen as cheap as a dozen for fifty cents. Some boys buy them and then make a profit by selling them to the boys at school. You can get them in some of the stores around here.

The sex play of young boys is relatively unregulated. The code of sex behavior crystallizes only as the corner boys reach maturity.

Relations between corner boys and women cannot be described in uniform terms, since there are tremendous variations in behavior, depending upon the category in which the woman is placed and the man's qualifications for access to women of various categories. The local classification of women is explicit or implicit in corner-boy attitudes and behavior may be represented in the three categories shown in the accompanying tabulation. The most highly valued type of woman is placed at the top of each category.

Sex Experience	Physical Attractiveness	Social- and Ethnic-Group Position
1. "Good girls"	Beautiful	1. Superior groups
2. "Lays"		2. Italian nonslum
a) One-man girls	to	3. Italian slum
b) Promiscuous		
c) Prostitutes	ugly	

One evening the corner boys were discussing a beautiful girl in the neighborhood. Danny said that he would take three months in any jail in the country, even Alcatraz, for the privilege of being in bed with her for eight hours. Doc said that Danny felt this way because the girl was a virgin. Danny agreed but added: "I would take one week in any jail even if she was a lay; that's how good I think she is." The difference between three months and one week strikingly illustrates the different valuations placed upon "good girls" and "lays." Doc explained the desirability of a virgin in this way: "No one has been there before. You are showing her the way. It's a new discovery. . . . We all say we would like to lay a virgin, but we really wouldn't."

The corner-boy code strongly prohibits intercourse with a virgin. Thus the most desirable of women is also the most inaccessible. A good girl may submit to a limited amount of kisses and caresses without compromising her reputation. She must not be a "teaser" (one who attempts to excite the man as much as possible without granting him sexual access). The virginity of a "teaser" is thought to be only a technicality, and if she is raped it serves her right. Otherwise a girl's virginity must be protected.

"Good girls" are the kind that one marries. A man who takes her virginity from a "good girl," seriously affecting her marriageability, will marry her because he is responsible. The man who seeks to evade his responsibility, especially if he has made the girl pregnant, may be forced into marriage by the priest and the girl's parents. The alternative is going to jail and being held liable for the support of the child to the age of twenty-one.

While strong legal and institutional sanctions uphold virginity, corner boys do not abide by the code simply from fear of the consequences of violation. They have strong sentiments supporting the sanctity of virginity. It is felt that only the lowest type of man would have intercourse with a virgin.

If the ban on intercourse with virgins were never violated, the only nonvirgins would be girls who had had sex relations with men outside of the district. This is obviously not the case. Several stories indicate that some early-adolescent boys and girls introduce each other to sex activity. The young boy who has never had intercourse himself does not feel so strongly the protective attitude toward virgins that he will assume later. There are a few local men who break the rule, but the danger of entanglements within the district is so great that most such activity must be confined to outsiders. In any case a corner boy cannot admit having "laid" a virgin without incurring the scorn of his fellows.

The corner boys believe that a man's health requires sexual intercourse at certain intervals. "Good girls" are not available for this purpose, and even casual social relations with them are likely to lead to commitments and responsibilities that the man is not prepared to assume. The corner boy has much more freedom, and much less responsibility in dealing with "lays"; freedom increases and responsibility decreases as he establishes relations lower down in this class.

From the standpoint of prestige and social advantage, the ideal girl in the "lay" class is the one who will have sexual relations with only one man in one period, but there are great risks involved in such a relationship. As one corner boy said:

> If you go with a girl too long, even if she lays, you're bound to get to like her. That's human nature. I was going out with a girl, and I was banging her every date. After about four months, I saw I was really getting fond of the girl, so I dropped her just like that.

While a man should marry only a good girl, he may become attached to the one-man girl and allow his emotions to override his judgment. Furthermore, if it is not widely known that the girl is a "lay" and she consequently enjoys a good reputation, her family will be able to exert a good deal of pressure to force a marriage. If he makes her pregnant, marriage is hardly to be avoided.

The promiscuous girl is less desirable socially, but there is also less risk in having relations with her. Only pregnancy can impose a responsibility; and, since the identity of the father is difficult to prove, such entanglements may frequently be avoided.

In practice it is hard to distinguish between these two types of "lays," because the promiscuous girl usually tries to pass herself off as a one-man "lay" and one-man girls are constantly slipping into the lower category. Nevertheless, there is a real distinction in the mind of the corner boy, and he acts differently according to his conception of the girl's sexual status. He talks freely about the promiscuous girl and is glad to share her with his friends. He keeps the higher type of "lay" to himself, says little about his relations with her, and treats her with more respect. The reputation of the one-man "lay" is not, however, permanently protected. If she breaks off with the corner boy and takes up with another man, the corner boy is likely to boast openly that he had her first.

The professional prostitute or "hustler" is the least desirable of women. I have heard some men advocate having relations with prostitutes on the ground that no social risk is involved; but generally the corner boys feel that to go to a house of prostitution would be to admit that they could not "pick up" any girls. One corner boy expressed his opinion in this way:

> I never go to a whore house. What do you get out of that? It's too easy. You just pay and go in and get it. Do you think the girl gets any fun out of that? . . . I like to take a girl out and bull her into it [persuade her]. Then when you lay her, you know she's enjoying it too. . . . And after you're through, you feel that you have accomplished something.

Another had this to say:

> You might pay a hustler a dollar and that's all there is to it, it's a business proposition. If you pick up a girl, you may spend three to five dollars on food and drinks,

but I'd rather do that any time. . . . You figure, the other way, it's just a business proposition. When you go out with a girl that ain't a hustler, you figure, she must like you a little anyway or she wouldn't go out with you. A hustler will take any man she can get, but this girl is just for you tonight anyway. You take her out, have something to eat and drink, you go for a ride, you begin muggin' her up, then you get in there. . . . That's the way I like to do it. You're staking out new territory. You get the feeling you really done something when you get in there.

The corner boys make a distinction between a house of prostitution and a "line-up." In a line-up one of the men brings a prostitute to some room in the district and allows his friends to have intercourse with her, each man paying the girl for the privilege. While this is a commercial arrangement, nevertheless, it is handled by the boys themselves, and some who would not think of going to a house of prostitution are willing to participate with their friends in a line-up.

The code not only differentiates different types of women in corner-boy attitudes; it also involves strikingly different behavior with women of the different categories, as the following stories indicate.

Danny had picked up a "hustler" and taken her to his gambling joint on the understanding that she would receive a dollar a man. When she was finished, he handed her an envelope containing the bills. She had counted the bills when he pretended to be alarmed and snatched the envelope away from her, replacing it in his pocket. She protested. Danny handed her another envelope of the same size which contained only slips of paper. She was satisfied and went away without looking into the envelope. Danny felt that he had played a clever trick upon the girl.

Doc told me another story about Danny:

There are some noble things down here, Bill. . . . You take Danny's wife, as we call her. She goes to church all the time—what a good kid she is, and she's nice looking too. She goes for Danny. She wants to marry him. Now she goes for him so much that he could probably belt her if he wanted to. But he doesn't want to marry her. He hasn't a job to support a wife. So he stays away from her. . . . Then take Al Mantia. He was a hound. He was after women all the time. One time he and Danny went out with a girl—she said she was a virgin. She had one drink, and she was a little high. They were up in a room, and they had her stripped—stripped! She still said she was a virgin, but she wanted them to give her a belt. But they wouldn't do it. . . . Can you imagine that, Bill? There she was stripped, and they wouldn't do anything to her. . . . The next day she came around and thanked both of them. They can't be such bad fellows if they do that.

The Danny who spared the virgin is the same Danny who cheated the "hustler." In one case the code imposed a strong responsibility; in the other case no responsibility was involved.

The physical-attractiveness criterion needs little comment, for here the corner boys are simply evaluating women in much the same terms as those used by men everywhere in their society. The only significant local variation is found in the strong preference for blondes in sexual relationships. Most of the local Italian girls tend to have black hair and olive complexions. While a good example of this type may appear strikingly attractive to the outsider, the corner boys are more impressed by blonde hair and a fair skin.

In the social- and ethnic-group category, the most desirable woman for nonmarital sex relations is the girl of old American-stock background, preferably blonde, who has a higher status than the corner boy. Once I was walking through the aristocratic section of Eastern City with a corner boy when we passed a tall and stately blonde, fashionably dressed, and very attractive. My companion breathed deeply as he said: "The old Puritan stock! . . . The real McCoy! Wouldn't I like to give her a belt."

The attraction of the native stock is not confined to the lower-class Italian. Mario Martini was born in Cornerville, but as he became successful in business he moved out to a fashionable suburb. He married an Italian girl and raised a family, sending his children to private school. He had many business relations and some social relations with upper-class Yankees. He made a practice of hiring only girls of native background for his secretarial work, and on some of his business trips he would take one of these girls along—for sexual as well as secretarial purposes. One of Martini's former secretaries, who told me this story, was a girl of rather plain

features, which emphasizes the prestige of the native background even for a man who was as successful as Mario Martini.

If an old-stock American girl is not accessible, then a socially superior member of an ethnic group living outside of
Cornerville is the next best thing. There is little prestige involved in having relations with a Cornerville "lay," unless she
is especially attractive on a physical basis.

The three categories so far discussed give us a rating scale
in terms of feminine desirability. There is one important factor which limits access to certain women, however desirable
they may be in terms of these categories. We must consider
the social ties between the man and the woman. The incest
taboo operates in Cornerville, as elsewhere, to prohibit access
to females of certain specified familial ties. While marriages
may be contracted beyond these incest limits, the corner-boy
code also prohibits nonmarital access to relatives who are not
blood relations (for example, the brother-in-law's cousin) and
to relatives of friends. A corner boy described such a case to
me. He was careful to explain that his friend, the girl's
cousin, knew that she was a "lay" and would have been glad
to have him enjoy himself. Furthermore, the girl was chasing
after him so that she was practically forcing the sex relationship upon him. When he was about to have intercourse, he
thought of his friend, and, as he says, "I couldn't do a thing."
It is only with an outsider, with someone who is not related
to him or to a friend, that the corner boy feels free to have
sexual relations.

The three categories of "Sex Experience," "Physical Attractiveness," and "Social- or Ethnic-Group Position" are not,
of course, the product of any individual's evaluation. They
represent, implicitly, the standards of the group—the corner
gang. The standards are being continually defined in action
and in group discussion. The corner boys are continually talking over the girls that they know and others that they have
observed in terms of all these categories. Consequently, a
high degree of consensus tends to arise in placing the individual girl in her position in each category. The men then know
how they are supposed to act in each case; and the observer,
equipped with this conceptual scheme, is able to predict how,
as a general rule, the men will attempt to act.

One feature of this classificatory scheme should be noted.
The standards for marriage and for nonmarital sex relations
are quite different. For nonmarital sex relations the ideal girl

is a one-man "lay," blonde and fair skinned, belonging to a socially superior old-stock group, and having no familial connection with the corner boy or any of his friends. For marriage, preference is for the virgin of Italian extraction and having some family connection with friends or relatives of ego. (The girl fitting this description would usually, but not always, be a dark brunette.)

Different sorts of evaluation are involved in the two cases. The corner boy thinks of casual sex relations in terms of personal prestige as well as physical satisfaction. If he were able to persuade an attractive blonde to drive down to his corner and pick him up in an expensive-looking car, he could make a great impression upon his fellows. Wives are thought of in terms of long-run compatibility and utility. Corner boys express their preference for a wife of Italian extraction because "she would understand my ways," "she would know how to cook for me," and "I could trust her more than the others"; "the Italian women make faithful wives; it's their upbringing."

The corner boy's relations with the opposite sex are not determined simply by his evaluation of feminine desirability. He must possess certain qualifications in order to gain access to the most desirable women. Talk is important. The man who can talk entertainingly and "bull the girl to her ears" gains in prestige with his fellows, as well as in his social opportunities. However, talk is not enough. Social position, money, and possession of a car weigh heavily in the balance. It is a common complaint of the corner boys that the most desirable women are most difficult of access because they demand more in position, money, and a car than most corner boys can provide. I once asked a corner boy if it was necessary to have a car in order to pick up a girl for sexual purposes. He answered:

> No, you can take her up to a room. . . . But no nice girl will go up to a man's room. If you take her out in the car, that's all right. If she goes up to your room with you, she's really a bum.

Under the influence of a car, a ride in the country, drinks, and heavy petting, a girl can allow a man to have sexual intercourse with her without any premeditation on her part. But if he suggests to her that they go to a room she can no longer pretend that she does not know what he is about. By consenting, she stamps herself as the kind of girl who goes to rooms with men. Even the most promiscuous like to maintain the pretense that they do it seldom and never in such a premeditated fashion. Thus the man with a car is generally able to have intercourse with a more desirable class of women than are available to the man who must rely upon rented rooms.

If the observer can classify the corner boy in terms of these criteria and classify the women within his social orbit in terms of the categories described above, then the individual's social and sexual behavior becomes still more subject to close prediction. No invariable rules can be set up, for the corner boy's code, like all other codes, is sometimes violated; but the discussion so far should clearly indicate that the relations between the sexes in the slums are subject to definite rules of behavior. The corner boys, while deviating from respectable middle-class standards, lead an organized sex life.

Our discussion has been confined to pre-marital sex and social relations. Little change is required in order to apply our conclusions to the post-marital behavior of the corner boy. The wife is expected to be completely faithful, and even the slightest flirtations are seriously regarded. The husband is expected to be a good provider and to have an affection for his wife and children. Nevertheless, the field of sexual adventure is not barred to him, and he endeavors to keep this quite separate from his married life. While the wives object, the men see nothing wrong in extra-marital sex relations, as long as they are not carried to the extremes of an open scandal or serious neglect of the family. Within these limits, the married man looks upon the feminine world just as he did before marriage.

While the slum sex code has now been described in outline form, it remains for us to consider the effect of this code and of the behavior it involves upon some of the broader social processes.

It is not easy for the Cornerville girl to maintain a good reputation if she has social relations with Cornerville men. Once I went to a dance outside of the district with two corner boys and three girls. It was late when we drove back to Cornerville. The driver stopped the car just outside of the district, and all the girls and one of the men got out to walk home. Later I asked why the girls had not been driven home. The driver answered:

Well, you know, Bill, the people of Cornerville are very suspicious people. They can make up a story about nothing at all. . . . If the girls came home alone, people would talk. If we all drove up in a car at one o'clock in the morning, they would wonder what we had been doing. . . . If the three of them walk home with Nutsy, then people will say, "Well, they have been in good company."

It is not only the older generation which gossips about the girls. The corner gang is continually defining and redefining reputations. Not even the "good girl" is safe from suspicion, and her local field of action is sharply circumscribed if she does not want to commit herself to marriage at an early age. As we have seen, the one-man "lay" cannot afford to have her "boy friend" in Cornerville because, if the relationship broke down, her reputation could be destroyed.

While social life outside of Cornerville has a great appeal to most girls, those who center their activities beyond the local boundaries seem to fit largely into two categories that represent the top and the bottom of Cornerville feminine society. There are a number of "good girls" who work outside of the district and use contacts made in this way in order to move into superior social circles. Then there are the "lays," who find greater freedom elsewhere. Most of the "good girls," being limited by their backgrounds, are unable to build up a social life outside of Cornerville. They have a romantic picture of a non-Cornerville, non-Italian of superior educational and economic status who will some day come along and marry them. While the social restrictions of Cornerville weigh particularly heavily upon the girls and influence many of them to wish for an escape through marriage outside the district, most marriages are contracted within Cornerville or between Cornerville and adjoining districts of similar social background. Nevertheless, the character of Cornerville social life operates to withdraw a significant number of local women from the orbit of the corner boys.

This situation is recognized by the corner boys. One of them commented:

There are lots of lays in Cornerville. You take Market Street from Norton Street down; nine out of ten of those girls will lay. But they won't lay for a Cornerville fellow. You know why? Because they figure if they lay for me,

I'll tell my friends the girls lay, and they'll want to lay her, and it'll get around. . . . Can you beat it, Bill, they're all around us yet we can't get them.

My informant was disgruntled over his failure to "get" Cornerville girls, and his 90 per cent figure is not to be taken seriously. If these girls actually did go outside of the district, he was in no position to know their sexual status, and any estimate can be no more than a guess. Probably the percentage of "lays" among local girls is very small. In any case, the fact remains that Cornerville men find most local girls barred to them except for marriage. In this situation they also must look outside of Cornerville for social and sexual satisfactions. The men, with their highly organized and localized corner gangs, tend to be even more restricted than the women in their social movements, and only a minority are able to operate at all effectively outside of Cornerville. However, even that minority contributes toward changing the social structure of Cornerville and Eastern City.

The restrictions of the peasant Italian family mores, plus the close watch kept upon their behavior, tend to push some of the young Italian girls out of Cornerville. Finding local fields restricted, some of the young men follow the girls in reaching for outside social contacts. This operates to stimulate intermarriage, illegitimate births out of interethnic sex relations, and social mobility. The study of the assimilation of the Italian population would be incomplete if we did not analyze the social and sex life of the slums in these terms.

VII.

CRIME AND DEVIANCE

IT IS NOT SURE whether, as the Bible has it, the poor will always be with us, but it is certain that crime and deviance can never be eradicated from any society, no matter what its particular structure. In fact, as the French sociologist Emile Durkheim argued forcefully, crime is normal in any society; even a society of saints would not be without some who deviate from the straight path. However, although crimes and deviance are to be found in any social structure, this does not mean that amount of deviance and criminality will not vary between societies or between different periods in the same society. Nor does this imply that the crime or types of deviants will not change.

This section opens with a well-known paper by the contemporary sociologist Daniel Bell, provocatively titled "Crime as an American Way of Life." Far from being exempt from societal trends, crime, Bell argues, follows them. As American society became more "organized," as the American businessman became more "civilized" and less "buccaneering," the American racketeer followed suit. As huge corporations replaced family capitalism, the criminal enterprise also became more "institutionalized." Nowadays, rationalization is the watchword of industry, and also of organized crime. What is perhaps even more startling, Bell contends, is that ethnic participation in major crime has varied over time in conjunction with immigration trends. At one time hegemony over crime was held by the newly arrived and discriminated-against Irish immigrants. At a later point, Jews were among the major racketeers. At present much organized crime is under the control of Italians. As each of these immigrant groups made its way up the social structure through upward mobility, its crime rates tended to fall, and a next generation of immigrants, still largely excluded from the ladder to success, took its place. The exploitation of illegitimate opportunities fell to those who still found it hard to exploit legitimate ones.

This pattern may now change, Bell argues, but up until the recent past, patterns of crime followed the lines of ethnic succession, so that crime, like "ordinary" social mobility, was an American way of life.

Common sense would seem to suggest that the definition of crime and the criminal is unambiguous. Anyone who breaks the law, it suggests, is a criminal. In fact, the matter is far more difficult. Whether someone is said to have committed a crime or is labeled a criminal depends not only upon objective facts, but on subjective definitions. A youngster who steals from a discount store in Harlem is labeled a juvenile delinquent, but an identical act committed by a middle-class suburban youngster may be called a "behavior disorder." What has been discussed in an earlier chapter under the heading of variant social definitions is of particular relevance in the area of deviance and crime.

Egon Bittner's study of the police on skid-row illustrates the force of social definitions. Basing his conclusions on close observation of the behavior of patrolmen on skid-row, Bittner finds that these men do not treat every suspicious person in the same way. Some obnoxious behavior by one person may be tolerated, while objectively similar behavior may lead to arrest for another. Patrolmen, it turns out, have a peculiar conception of the social order of skid-row that determines the procedure they use to control it. They wish to reduce the aggregate total of trouble in the area and are not concerned about evaluating cases according to strict standards of merit or equity. When it comes to action to be taken, they "play it by ear," rather than adhering to strict rules. Whether someone is arrested hence depends at least as much on subjective definitions as on objective circumstances.

Common sense often assumes that criminals and deviants are, as it were, a breed basically different from ordinary citizens. Often such opinions are based on the erroneous belief that differences between deviants and the upholders of law and order are based on biological or genetic factors. The fact is, however, that crime or deviance, like any other human behavior, is largely learned by interaction with others. Thieves, prostitutes, or embezzlers are not born as such; they are made through association with others who have previously engaged in such activities.

In a highly suggestive paper, Everett Hughes argues, using Nazi Germany as an example, that one of the effects of separating the activities of those who do "dirty work" from the behavior of "good people" is to exonerate the good people from responsibility for the dirty work done in their midst. In fact, Hughes argues, the good people in Nazi Germany gave the mandate to do what they perceived to be dirty work—the building and maintenance of concentration camps, for example—to a special category of people, so that they themselves would remain untainted and unblemished. The good people, Hughes argues, gave unconscious orders to the Nazis to go beyond anything they themselves would care to do or even to acknowledge. There is then, he suggests, a definite division of labor between good people and those doing their dirty work. Responsibility for dirty work turns out to be a more complicated matter than is usually assumed.

Crime as an American Way of Life: A Queer Ladder of Social Mobility

by
Daniel Bell

In the 1890's the Reverend Dr. Charles Parkhurst, shocked at the open police protection afforded New York's bordellos, demanded a state inquiry. In the Lexow investigation that followed, the young and dashing William Travers Jerome staged a set of public hearings that created sensation after sensation. He badgered "Clubber" Williams, First Inspector of the Police Department, to account for wealth and property far greater than could have been saved on his salary; it was earned, the Clubber explained laconically, through land speculation "in Japan." Heavy-set Captain Schmittberger, the "collector" for the "Tenderloin precincts"—Broadway's fabulous concentration of hotels, theaters, restaurants, gaming houses, and saloons—related in detail how protection money was distributed among the police force. Crooks, policemen, public officials, businessmen, all paraded across the stage, each adding his chapter to a sordid story of corruption and crime. The upshot of these revelations was reform—the election of William L. Strong, a stalwart businessman, as mayor, and the naming of Theodore Roosevelt as police commissioner.

It did not last, of course, just as previous reform victories had not lasted. Yet the ritual drama was re-enacted. Thirty years ago the Seabury investigation in New York uncovered the tin-box brigade and the thirty-three little McQuades. Jimmy Walker was ousted as Mayor and in came Fiorello LaGuardia. Tom Dewey became district attorney, broke the industrial rackets, sent Lucky Luciano to jail, and went to the governor's chair in Albany. Then reform was again swallowed up in the insatiable maw of corruption until in 1950

Kefauver and his committee counsel Rudolph Halley threw a new beam of light into the seemingly bottomless pit.

How explain this repetitious cycle? Obviously the simple moralistic distinction between "good guys" and "bad guys," so deep at the root of the reform impulse, bears little relation to the role of organized crime in American society. What, then, does?

THE QUEER LADDER

Americans have had an extraordinary talent for compromise in politics and extremism in morality. The most shameless political deals (and "steals") have been rationalized as expedient and realistically necessary. Yet in no other country have there been such spectacular attempts to curb human appetites and brand them as illicit, and nowhere else such glaring failures. From the start America was at one and the same time a frontier community where "everything goes," and the fair country of the Blue Laws. At the turn of the century the cleavage developed between the Big City and the small-town conscience. Crime as a growing business was fed by the revenues from prostitution, liquor, and gambling that a wide-open urban society encouraged and that a middle-class Protestant ethos tried to suppress with a ferocity unmatched in any other civilized country. Catholic cultures have rarely imposed such restrictions and have rarely suffered such excesses. Even in prim and proper Anglican England, prostitution is a commonplace of Piccadilly night life, and gambling is one of the largest and most popular industries. In America the enforcement of public morals has been a continuing feature of our history.

Some truth may lie in Max Scheler's generalization that moral indignation is a peculiar fact of middle-class psychology and represents a disguised form of repressed envy. The larger truth lies perhaps in the brawling nature of American development and in the social character of crime. Crime, in many ways, is a Coney Island mirror, caricaturing the morals and manners of a society. The jungle quality of the American business community, particularly at the turn of the century, was reflected in the mode of "business" practiced by the coarse gangster elements, most of them from new immigrant families, who were "getting ahead," just as Horatio Alger had urged. In the older, Protestant tradition the intensive acquisitiveness, such as that of Daniel Drew, was rationalized by a compulsive moral fervor. But the formal obeisance of the ruthless businessman in the workaday world to the church-going pieties of the Sabbath was one that the gangster could not make. Moreover, for the young criminal, hunting in the asphalt jungle of the crowded city, it was not the businessman with his wily manipulation of numbers but the "man with the gun" who was the American hero. "No amount of commercial prosperity," once wrote Teddy Roosevelt, "can supply the lack of the heroic virtues." The American was "the hunter, cowboy, frontiersman, the soldier, the naval hero"—and in the crowded slums, the gangster. He was a man with a gun, acquiring by personal merit what was denied him by complex orderings of stratified society. And the duel with the law was the morality play par excellence: the gangster, with whom ride our own illicit desires, and the prosecutor, representing final judgment and the force of the law.

Yet all this was acted out in a wider context. The desires satisfied in extra-legal fashion were more than a hunger for the "forbidden fruits" of conventional morality. They also involved, in the complex and ever shifting structure of group, class, and ethnic stratification, which is the warp and woof of America's "open" society, such "normal" goals as independence through a business of one's own, and such "moral" aspirations as the desire for social advancement and social prestige. For crime, in the language of the sociologists, has a "functional" role in the society, and the urban rackets—the illicit activity organized for continuing profit, rather than individual illegal acts—is one of the queer ladders of social mobility in American life. Indeed, it is not too much to say that the whole question of organized crime in America cannot be understood unless one appreciates (1) the distinctive role of organized gambling as a function of a mass-consumption economy; (2) the specific role of various immigrant groups as they, one after another, became involved in marginal business and crime; and (3) the relation of crime to the changing character of the urban political machines.

GATSBY'S MODEL

As a society changes, so does, in lagging fashion, its type of crime. As American society became more "organized," as the American businessman became more "civilized" and less "buccaneering," so did the American racketeer. And just as there were important changes in the structure of business enterprise, so the "institutionalized" criminal enterprise was transformed too.

In the America of the last fifty years the main drift of society has been toward the rationalization of industry, the domestication of the crude self-made captain of industry into the respectable man of manners, and the emergence of a mass-consumption economy. The most significant transformation in the field of "institutionalized" crime in the 1940's was the increasing importance of gambling as against other kinds of illegal activity. And, as a multi-billion-dollar business, gambling underwent a transition parallel to the changes in American enterprise as a whole. This parallel was exemplified in many ways: in gambling's industrial organization (e.g., the growth of a complex technology such as the national racing-wire service and the minimization of risks by such techniques as lay-off betting); in its respectability, as was evidenced in the opening of smart and popular gambling casinos in resort-towns and in "satellite" adjuncts to metropolitan areas; in its functional role in a mass-consumption economy (for sheer volume of money changing hands, nothing has ever surpassed this feverish activity of fifty million American adults); in the social acceptance of the gamblers in the important status world of sport and entertainment, i.e., "café society."

In seeking to "legitimize" itself, gambling had quite often actually become a force against older and more vicious forms of illegal activity. In 1946, for example, when a Chicago mobster, Pat Manno, went down to Dallas, Texas, to take over gambling in the area for the Accardo-Guzik combine, he reassured the sheriff as follows: "Something I'm against, that's dope peddlers, pickpockets, hired killers. That's one thing I can't stomach, and that's one thing the fellows up there—the group won't stand for, things like that. They discourage it, they even go to headquarters and ask them why they don't do something about it."

Jimmy Cannon once reported that when the gambling raids started in Chicago the "combine" protested that, in upsetting existing stable relations, the police were only opening the way for ambitious young punks and hoodlums to start trouble. Nor is there today, as there was twenty or even forty years ago, prostitution of major organized scope in the United States. Aside from the fact that manners and morals have changed, prostitution *as an industry* doesn't pay as well as gambling. Besides, its existence threatened the tacit moral acceptance and quasi-respectability that gamblers and gambling have secured in the American way of life. It was, as any operator in the field might tell you, "bad for business."

The criminal world of the 1940's, its tone set by the captains of the gambling industry, is in startling contrast to the state of affairs in the decade before. If a Kefauver report had been written then, the main "names" would have been Lepke and Gurrah, Dutch Schultz, Jack "Legs" Diamond, Lucky Luciano, and, reaching back a little further, Arnold Rothstein, the czar of the underworld. These men (with the exception of Luciano, who was involved in narcotics and prostitution) were in the main "industrial racketeers." Rothstein, the model for Wolfsheim the gambler in F. Scott Fitzgerald's *The Great Gatsby,* had a larger function: he was, as Frank Costello became later, the financier of the underworld, the pioneer big businessman of crime who, understanding the logic of co-ordination, sought to *organize* crime as a source of regular income. His main interest in this direction was in industrial racketeering, and his entry was through labor disputes. At one time, employers in the garment trades hired Legs Diamond and his sluggers to break strikes, and the Communists, then in control of the cloakmakers union, hired one Little Orgie to protect the pickets and beat up the scabs; only later did both sides learn that Legs Diamond and Little Orgie were working for the same man, Rothstein.

Rothstein's chief successors, Lepke Buchalter and Gurrah Shapiro, were able, in the early thirties, to dominate sections of the men's and women's clothing industries, of painting, fur dressing, flour trucking, and other fields. In a highly chaotic and cutthroat industry such as clothing, the racketeer, paradoxically, played a stabilizing role by regulating competition and fixing prices. When the NRA came in and assumed this function, the businessman found that what had once been a quasi-economic service was now pure extortion, and he began to demand police action. In other types of racketeering, such as the trucking of perishable foods and waterfront loading, where the racketeers entrenched themselves as middlemen—taking up, by default, a service that neither shippers nor truckers wanted to assume—a pattern of accommodation was roughly worked out, and the rackets assumed a quasi-legal veneer. On the waterfront, old-time racketeers perform the necessary function of loading—but at an exorbitant price—and this monopoly was recognized by both the union and the shippers, and tacitly by the government.

But in the last decade and a half, industrial racketeering has not offered much in the way of opportunity. *Like American capitalism itself, crime shifted its emphasis from production to consumption.* The focus of crime became the direct exploitation of the citizen as consumer, largely through gambling. And while the protection of these huge revenues was inextricably linked to politics, the relation between gambling and "the mobs" became more complicated.

BIG-BUSINESS BOOKIES

Although it never showed up in the gross national product, gambling in the last decade was one of the largest industries in the United States. The Kefauver Committee estimated it as a $20 billion business. This figure has been picked up and widely quoted, but in truth no one knows what the gambling "turnover" and "take" actually is, nor how much is bet legally (parimutuel, etc.) and how much illegally. In fact, the figure cited by the committee was arbitrary and was arrived at quite sloppily. As one staff member said: "We had no real idea of the money spent. . . . The California crime commission said twelve billion. Virgil Peterson of Chicago estimated thirty billion. We picked twenty billion as a balance between the two."

If comprehensive data is not available, we do know, from specific instances, the magnitude of many of the operations. Some indication can be seen from these items culled at random:

James Carroll and the M & G syndicate did a $20 million

annual business in St. Louis. This was one of the two large books in the city.

The S & G syndicate in Miami did a $26 million volume yearly; the total for all books in the Florida resort reached $40 million.

Slot machines were present in 69,786 establishments in 1951 (each paid $100 for a license to the Bureau of Internal Revenue); the usual average is three machines to a license, which would add up to 210,000 slot machines in operation in the United States. In legalized areas, where the betting is higher and more regular, the average gross "take" per machine is $50 a week.

The largest policy wheel (i.e., "numbers") in Chicago's "Black Belt" reported taxable net profits for the four-year period from 1946 through 1949, after sizable deductions for "overhead," of $3,656,968. One of the large "white" wheels reported in 1947 a gross income of $2,317,000 and a net profit of $205,000. One CIO official estimated that perhaps 15 per cent of his union's lower-echelon officials are involved in the numbers racket (a steward, free to roam a plant, is in a perfect situation for organizing bets).

If one considers the amount of dollars bet on sports alone—an estimated six billion on baseball, a billion on football pools, another billion on basketball, six billion on horse racing—then Elmo Roper's judgment that "only the food, steel, auto, chemical, and machine-tool industries have a greater volume of business" does not seem too farfetched.

While gambling has long flourished in the United States, the influx of the big mobsters into the industry—and its expansion—started in the thirties, when repeal of Prohibition forced them to look about for new avenues of enterprise. (The change, one might say crudely, was in the "democratization" of gambling. In New York of the 1860's, 1870's, and 1880's, one found elegant establishments where the wealthy men of the city, bankers, and sportsmen gambled. The saloon was the home of the worker. The middle class of the time did not gamble. In the changing mores of America, the rise of gambling in the 1930's and 1940's meant the introduction of the middle class to gambling and casinos as a way of life.) Gambling, which had begun to flower under the nourishment of rising incomes, was the most lucrative field in sight. To a large extent the shift from bootlegging to gambling was a mere transfer of business operations. In the East, Frank Costello went into slot machines and the operation of a number of ritzy gambling casinos. He also became the "banker" for the Erickson "book," which "laid off" bets for other bookies. Joe Adonis, similarly, opened up a number of casinos, principally in New Jersey. Across the country, many other mobsters went into bookmaking. As other rackets diminished and gambling, particularly horse-race betting, flourished in the forties, a struggle erupted over the control of racing information.

Horse-race betting requires a peculiar industrial organization. The essential component is time. A bookie can operate only if he can get information on odds up to the very last minute before the race, so that he can "hedge" or "lay off" bets. With racing going on simultaneously on many tracks throughout the country, this information has to be obtained speedily and accurately. Thus, the racing wire is the nerve ganglion of race betting.

The racing-wire news service got started in the twenties through the genius of the late Moe Annenberg, who had made a fearful reputation for himself as Hearst's circulation manager in the rough-and-tough Chicago newspaper wars. Annenberg conceived the idea of a telegraphic news service which would gather information from tracks and shoot it immediately to scratch sheets, horse parlors, and bookie joints. In some instances, track owners gave Annenberg the rights to send news from tracks; more often, the news was simply "stolen" by crews operating inside or near the tracks. So efficient did this news distribution system become, that in 1942, when a plane knocked out a vital telegraph circuit which served an Air Force field as well as the gamblers, the Continental Press managed to get its racing wire service for gamblers resumed in fifteen minutes, while it took the Fourth Army, which was responsible for the defense of the entire West Coast, something like three hours.

Annenberg built up a nationwide racing information chain that not only distributed wire news but controlled sub-outlets as well. In 1939, harassed by the Internal Revenue Bureau on income tax and chivvied by the Justice Department for "monopolistic" control of the wire service, the tired and aging Annenberg simply walked out of the business. He did not sell his interest or even seek to salvage some profit; he simply gave it up. Yet, like any established and thriving institution, the enterprise continued, though on a decentralized basis. James Ragen, Annenberg's operations manager and likewise a veteran of the old Chicago circulation wars, took over the national wire service through a dummy friend and renamed it the Continental Press Service.

The salient fact is that in the operation of the Annenberg and Ragen wire service, formally illegal as many of its subsidiary operations may have been (i.e., in "stealing" news, supplying information to bookies, etc.), gangsters played no part. It was a business, illicit, true, but primarily a business. The distinction between gamblers and gangsters, as we shall see, is a relevant one.

In 1946, the Chicago mob, whose main interest was in bookmaking rather than in gambling casinos, began to move in on the wire monopoly. Following repeal, the Capone lieutenants had turned, like Lepke, to labor racketeering. Murray ("The Camel") Humphries muscled in on the teamsters, the operating engineers, and the cleaning-and-dyeing, laundry, and linen-supply industries. Through a small-time punk, Willie Bioff, and union official George Browne, Capone's chief successors, Frank ("The Enforcer") Nitti and Paul Ricca, came into control of the motion-picture union and proceeded to shake down the movie industry for fabulous sums in order to "avert strikes." In 1943, when the government moved in and smashed the industrial rackets, the remaining big shots, Charley Fischetti, Jake Guzik, and Tony Accardo, decided to concentrate on gambling, and in particular began a drive to take over the racing wire.

In Chicago, the Guzik-Accardo gang, controlling a sub-distributor of the racing-news service, began tapping Continental's wires. In Los Angeles, the head of the local distribution agency for Continental was beaten up by hoodlums working for Mickey Cohen and Joe Sica. Out of the blue appeared a new and competitive nationwide racing information and distribution service, known as Trans-American Publishing, the money for which was advanced by the Chicago mobs and Bugsy Siegel, who, at the time, held a monopoly of the bookmaking and wire-news service in Las Vegas. Many books pulled out of Continental and bought information from the new outfit; many hedged by buying from both. At the end of a year, however, the Capone mob's wire had lost about $200,000. Ragen felt that violence would erupt and went to the Cook County district attorney and told him that his life had been threatened by his rivals. Ragen knew his competitors. In June, 1946, he was killed by a blast from a shotgun.

Thereafter, the Capone mob abandoned Trans-American and got a "piece" of Continental. Through their new control of the national racing-wire monopoly, the Capone mob began to muscle in on the lucrative Miami gambling business run by the so-called S & G syndicate. For a long time S & G's monopoly over bookmaking had been so complete that when New York gambler Frank Erickson bought a three months' bookmaking concession at the expensive Roney Plaza Hotel, for $45,000, the local police, in a highly publicized raid, swooped down on the hotel; the next year the Roney Plaza was again using local talent. The Capone group, however, was tougher. They demanded an interest in Miami bookmaking and, when refused, began organizing a syndicate of their own, persuading some bookies at the big hotels to join them. Florida Governor Warren's crime investigator appeared—a friend, it seemed, of old Chicago dog-track operator William Johnston, who had contributed $100,000 to the Governor's campaign fund—and began raiding bookie joints, but only those that were affiliated with S & G. Then S & G, which had been buying its racing news from the local distributor of Continental Press, found its service abruptly shut off. For a few days the syndicate sought to bootleg information from New Orleans, but found itself limping along. After ten days' war of attrition, the five S & G partners found themselves with a sixth partner, who, for a token "investment" of $20,-000, entered a Miami business that grossed $26,000,000 in one year.

GAMBLERS AND GUYS

While Americans made gambling illegal, they did not in their hearts think of it as wicked—even the churches benefited from the bingo and lottery crazes. So they gambled—and gamblers flourished. Against this open canvas, the indignant tones of Senator Wiley and the shocked righteousness of Senator Tobey during the Kefauver investigation rang oddly. Yet it was probably this very tone of surprise that gave the activity of the Kefauver Committee its piquant quality. Here were some senators who seemingly did not know the facts of life, as most Americans did. Here, in the person of Senator Tobey, was the old New England Puritan conscience poking around in industrial America, in a world it had made but never seen. Here was old-fashioned moral indignation, at a time when cynicism was rampant in public life.

Commendable as such moralistic fervor was, it did not make for intelligent discrimination of fact. Throughout the Kefauver hearings, for example, there ran the presumption that all gamblers were invariably gangsters. This was true of Chicago's Accardo-Guzik combine, which in the past had its fingers in many kinds of rackets. It was not nearly so true of many of large gamblers in America, most of whom had the feeling that they were satisfying a basic American urge for sport and looked upon their calling with no greater sense of guilt than did many bootleggers. After all, Sherman Billingsley did start out as a speakeasy proprietor, as did the Kreindlers of the "21" Club; and today the Stork Club and the former Jack and Charlie's are the most fashionable night and dining spots in America (one prominent patron of the Stork Club: J. Edgar Hoover).

The S & G syndicate in Miami, for example (led by Harold Salvey, Jules Levitt, Charles Friedman, Sam Cohen, and Edward [Eddie Luckey] Rosenbaum), was simply a master pool of some two hundred bookies that arranged for telephone service, handled "protection," acted as bankers for those who needed ready cash on hard-hit books, and, in short, functioned somewhat analogously to the large factoring corporations in the textile field or the credit companies in the auto industry. Yet to Kefauver, the S & G men were "slippery and arrogant characters. . . . Salvey, for instance, was an old-time bookie who told us he had done nothing except engage in bookmaking or finance other bookmakers for twenty years." When, as a result of committee publicity and the newly found purity of the Miami police, the S & G syndicate went out of business, it was, as the combine's lawyer told Kefauver, because the "boys" were weary of being painted "the worst monsters in the world." "It is true," Cohen acknowledged, "that they had been law violators." But they had never done anything worse than gambling, and "to fight the world isn't worth it."

Most intriguing of all were the opinions of James J. Carroll, the St. Louis "betting commissioner," who for years had been widely quoted on the sports pages of the country as setting odds on the Kentucky Derby winter book and the baseball pennant races. Senator Wiley, speaking like the prosecutor in Camus's novel, *The Stranger*, became the voice of official morality:

SENATOR WILEY: Have you any children?

MR. CARROLL: Yes, I have a boy.

SENATOR WILEY: How old is he?

MR. CARROLL: Thirty-three.

SENATOR WILEY: Does he gamble?

MR. CARROLL: No.

SENATOR WILEY: Would you like to see him grow up and become a gambler, either professional or amateur?

MR. CARROLL: No. . . .

SENATOR WILEY: All right. Is your son interested in your business?

MR. CARROLL: No, he is a manufacturer.

SENATOR WILEY: Why do you not get him into the business?

MR. CARROLL: Well, psychologically a great many people are unsuited for gambling.

Retreating from this gambit, the Senator sought to pin Carroll down on his contributions to political campaigns:

SENATOR WILEY: Now this morning I asked you whether you contributed any money for political candidates or parties, and you said not more than $200 at one time. I presume that does not indicate the total of your contributions in any one campaign, does it?

MR. CARROLL: Well, it might, might not, Senator. I have been an "againster" in many instances. I am a reader of *The Nation* for fifty years and they have advertisements calling for contributions for different candidates, different causes. . . . They carried an advertisement for George Norris; I contributed, I think, to that, and to the elder LaFollette.

Carroll, who admitted to having been in the betting business since 1899, was the sophisticated—but not immoral!—counterpoint to moralist Wiley. Here was a man without the stigmata of the underworld or underground; he was worldly, cynical of official rhetoric, jaundiced about people's motives; he was an "againster" who believed that "all gambling legislation originates or stems from some group or some individual seeking special interests for himself or his cause."

Asked why people gamble, Carroll distilled his experiences of fifty years with a remark that deserves a place in American social history: "I really don't know how to answer the question," he said. "I think gambling is a biological necessity for certain types. I think it is the quality that gives substance to their daydreams."

In a sense, the entire Kefauver materials, unintentionally, seem to document that remark. For what the committee revealed time and time again was a picture of gambling as a basic institution in American life, flourishing openly and accepted widely. In many of the small towns, the gambling joint is as open as a liquor establishment. The town of Havana, in Mason County, Illinois, felt miffed when Governor Adlai Stevenson intervened against local gambling. In 1950, the town had raised $15,000 of its $50,000 budget by making friendly raids on the gambling houses every month and having the owners pay fines. "With the gambling fines cut off," grumbled Mayor Clarence Chester, "the next year is going to be tough."

Apart from the gamblers, there were the mobsters. But what Senator Kefauver and company failed to understand was that the mobsters, like the gamblers, and like the entire gangdom generally, were seeking to become quasi-respectable and establish a place for themselves in American life. For the mobsters, by and large, had immigrant roots, and crime, as the pattern showed, was a route of social ascent and place in American life.

THE MYTH OF THE MAFIA

The mobsters were able, where they wished, to "muscle in" on the gambling business because the established gamblers were wholly vulnerable, not being able to call on the law for protection. The senators, however, refusing to make any distinction between a gambler and a gangster, found it convenient to talk loosely of a nationwide conspiracy of "illegal" elements. Senator Kefauver asserted that a "nationwide crime syndicate does exist in the United States, despite the protestations of a strangely assorted company of criminals, self-serving politicians, plain blind fools, and others who may be honestly misguided, that there is no such combine." The Senate committee report states the matter more dogmatically: "There is a nationwide crime syndicate known as the Mafia. . . . Its leaders are usually found in control of the most lucrative rackets in their cities. There are indications of a centralized direction and control of these rackets. . . . The Mafia is the cement that helps to bind the Costello-Adonis-Lansky syndicate of New York and the Accardo-Guzik-Fischetti syndicate of Chicago. . . . These groups have kept in touch with Luciano since his deportation from the country."

Unfortunately for a good story—and the existence of the Mafia would be a whale of a story—neither the Senate Crime Committee in its testimony, nor Kefauver in his book, presented any real evidence that the Mafia exists as a functioning organization. One finds police officials asserting before the Kefauver committee their *belief* in the Mafia; the Narcotics Bureau *thinks* that a world-wide dope ring allegedly run by Luciano is part of the Mafia; but the only other "evidence" presented—aside from the incredulous responses both of Senator Kefauver and Rudolph Halley when nearly all the Italian gangsters asserted that they didn't know about the Mafia—is that certain crimes bear "the earmarks of the Mafia."

The legend of the Mafia has been fostered in recent years largely by the peephole writing team of Jack Lait and Lee Mortimer. In their *Chicago Confidential*, they rattled off a series of names and titles that made the organization sound like a rival to an Amos and Andy Kingfish society. Few serious reporters, however, give it much credence. Burton Turkus, the Brooklyn prosecutor who broke up the "Murder, Inc." ring, denies the existence of the Mafia. Nor could Senator Kefauver even make out much of a case for his picture of a national crime syndicate. He is forced to admit that "as it exists today [it] is an elusive and furtive but nonetheless tangible thing," and that "its organization and machinations are not always easy to pinpoint."[1] His "evidence" that many

[1] The accidental police discovery of a conference of Italian figures, most of them with underworld and police records, in Apalachin, New York, in November 1957, revived the talk of a Mafia. *Time* magazine assigned a reporter, Serrell Hillman, to check the story, and this is what he reported: "I spent some two weeks in New York, Washington and Chicago running down every clue to the so-called Mafia that I could find. I talked to a large number of Federal, state and local law enforcement authorities; to police, reporters, attorneys, detectives, non-profit civic groups such as the Chicago Crime Commission. Nobody from the F.B.I. and Justice Department officials on down, with the exception of a couple of Hearst crime reporters—always happy for the sake of a street sale to associate the 'Mafia' with the most routine bar-

gangsters congregate at certain times of the year in such places as Hot Springs, Arkansas, in itself does not prove much; people "in the trade" usually do, and as the loquacious late Willie Moretti of New Jersey said, in explaining how he had met the late Al Capone at a race track, "Listen, well-charactered people you don't need introductions to; you just meet automatically."

Why did the Senate Crime Committee plump so hard for its theory of a Mafia and a national crime syndicate? In part, they may have been misled by their own hearsay. The Senate committee was not in the position to do original research, and its staff, both legal and investigative, was incredibly small. Senator Kefauver had begun the investigation with the attitude that with so much smoke there must be a raging fire. But smoke can also mean a smoke screen. Mob activities is a field in which busy gossip and exaggeration flourish even more readily than in a radical political sect.

There is, as well, in the American temper, a feeling that "somewhere," "somebody" is pulling all the complicated strings to which this jumbled world dances. In politics the labor image is "Wall Street" or "Big Business"; while the business stereotype was the "New Dealers." In the field of crime, the side-of-the-mouth low-down was "Costello."

The salient reason, perhaps, why the Kefauver Committee was taken in by its own myth of an omnipotent Mafia and a

---

room shooting—and the Narcotics Bureau believed that a Mafia exists as such. The Narcotics Bureau, which has to contend with a big problem in dope-trafficking, contends that a working alliance operates between an organized Mafia in Italy and Sicily and a U.S. Mafia. But the Bureau has never been able to submit proof of this, and the F.B.I. is skeptical. The generally held belief is that there is no tightly knit syndicate, but instead a loose "trade association" of criminals in various cities and areas, who run their own shows in their own fields but have matters of mutual interest to take up (as at the Appalachian conference). At any rate, nobody has ever been able to produce specific evidence that a Mafia is functioning."

In early 1959, Fredric Sondern, Jr., an editor of the *Reader's Digest*, published a best-selling book on the Mafia, *Brotherhood of Evil*, but a close reading of Mr. Sondern's text indicates that his sources are largely the files of the Narcotics Bureau, and his findings little more than a rehash of previously publicized material. (For a devastating review of the book, see the *Times Literary Supplement*, London, June 12, 1959, p. 351.) Interestingly enough, in May, 1959, Alvin Goldstein, a former assistant district attorney in New York, who had prosecuted racketeer Johnny Dio, conducted a crime survey of California for Governor Pat Brown and reported that he found no evidence of the existence of a Mafia in California.

despotic Costello was its failure to assimilate and understand three of the more relevant sociological facts about institutionalized crime in its relation to the political life of large urban communities in America, namely: (1) the rise of the American Italian community, as part of the inevitable process of ethnic succession, to positions of importance in politics, a process that has been occurring independently but also simultaneously in most cities with large Italian constituencies— New York, Chicago, Kansas City, Los Angeles; (2) the fact that there are individual Italians who play prominent, often leading roles today in gambling and in the mobs; and (3) the fact that Italian gamblers and mobsters often possessed "status" within the Italian community itself and a "pull" in city politics. These three items are indeed related—but not so as to form a "plot."

THE JEWS . . . THE IRISH . . . THE ITALIANS

The Italian community has achieved wealth and political influence much later and in a harder way than previous immigrant groups. Early Jewish wealth, that of the German Jews of the late nineteenth century, was made largely in banking and merchandising. To that extent, the dominant group in the Jewish community was outside of, and independent of, the urban political machines. Later Jewish wealth, among the East European immigrants, was built in the garment trades, though with some involvement with the Jewish gangster, who was typically an industrial racketeer (Arnold Rothstein, Lepke and Gurrah. etc.). Among Jewish lawyers, a small minority, such as the "Tammany lawyer" (like the protagonist of Sam Ornitz's *Haunch, Paunch and Jowl*), rose through politics and occasionally touched the fringes of crime. Most of the Jewish lawyers, by and large the communal leaders, climbed rapidly, however, in the opportunities that established and legitimate Jewish wealth provided. Irish immigrant wealth in the northern urban centers, concentrated largely in construction, trucking, and the waterfront, has, to a substantial extent, been wealth accumulated in and through political alliance, e.g., favoritism in city contracts.

Control of the politics of the city thus has been crucial for the continuance of Irish political wealth. This alliance of Irish immigrant wealth and politics has been reciprocal; many noted Irish political figures lent their names as important window-dressing for business corporations (Al Smith, for example, who helped form the U.S. Trucking Corporation, whose executive head for many years was William J. McCormack, the alleged "Mr. Big" of the New York waterfront), while Irish businessmen have lent their wealth to further the careers of Irish politicians. Irish mobsters have rarely achieved status in the Irish community, but have served as integral arms of the politicians, as strong-arm men on election day.

The Italians found the more obvious big-city paths from rags to riches pre-empted. In part this was due to the character of the early Italian immigrant. Most of them were unskilled and from rural stock. Jacob Riis could remark in the nineties, "the Italian comes in at the bottom and stays there." These dispossessed agricultural laborers found jobs as ditch-diggers, on the railroads as section hands, along the docks, in the service occupations, as shoemakers, barbers, garment workers, and stayed there. Many were fleeced by the "padrone" system; a few achieved wealth from truck farming, wine growing, and marketing produce; but this "marginal wealth" was not the source of coherent and stable political power.

Significantly, although the number of Italians in the United States is about a third as high as the number of Irish, and of the thirty million Catholic communicants in the United States, about half are of Irish descent and a sixth of Italian, there is not one Italian bishop among the hundred Catholic bishops in this country or one Italian archbishop among the 21 archbishops. The Irish have a virtual monopoly. This is a factor related to the politics of the American church; but the condition also is possible because there is not significant or sufficient wealth among Italian Americans to force some parity.

The children of the immigrants, the second and third generation, became wise in the ways of the urban slums. Excluded from the political ladder—in the early thirties there were almost no Italians on the city payroll in top jobs, nor in books of the period can one find discussion of Italian political leaders—and finding few open routes to wealth, some turned to illicit ways. In the children's court statistics of the 1930's, the largest group of delinquents were the Italian; nor were there any Italian communal or social agencies to cope with these problems. Yet it was, oddly enough, the quondam racketeer, seeking to become respectable, who provided one of the major supports for the drive to win a political voice for Italians in the power structure of the urban political machines.

This rise of the Italian political bloc was connected, at least in the major northern urban centers, with another important development which tended to make the traditional relation between the politician and the protected or tolerated illicit operator more close than it had been in the past. This is the fact that the urban political machines had to evolve new forms of fund-raising, since the big business contributions, which once went heavily into municipal politics, now—with the shift in the locus of power—go largely into national affairs. (The ensuing corruption in national politics, as recent Congressional investigations show, is no petty matter; the scruples of businessmen do not seem much superior to those of the gamblers.) One way that urban political machines raised their money resembled that of the large corporations which are no longer dependent on Wall Street: by self-financing—that is, by "taxing" the large number of municipal employees who bargain collectively with City Hall for their wage increases. So the firemen's union contributed money to O'Dwyer's campaign.

A second method was taxing the gamblers. The classic example, as *Life* reported, was Jersey City, where a top lieutenant of the Hague machine spent his full time screening applicants for unofficial bookmaking licenses. If found acceptable, the applicant was given a "location," usually the house or store of a loyal precinct worker, who kicked into the machine treasury a high proportion of the large rent exacted. The one thousand bookies and their one thousand landlords in Jersey City formed the hard core of the political machine that sweated and bled to get out the votes for Hague.

A third source for the financing of these machines was the new, and often illegally earned, Italian wealth. This is well illustrated by the career of Costello and his emergence as a political power in New York. Here the ruling motive has been the search for an entree—for oneself and one's ethnic group—into the ruling circles of the big city.

Frank Costello made his money originally in bootlegging. After repeal, his big break came when Huey Long, desperate for ready cash to fight the old-line political machines, invited Costello to install slot machines in Louisiana. Costello did, and he flourished. Together with Dandy Phil Kastel, he also opened the Beverly Club, an elegant gambling establishment just outside New Orleans, at which have appeared some of the top entertainers in America. Subsequently, Costello invested his money in New York real estate (including 79 Wall Street, which he later sold), the Copacabana night club, and a leading brand of Scotch whiskey.

Costello's political opportunity came when a money-hungry Tammany, starved by lack of patronage from Roosevelt and LaGuardia, turned to him for financial support. The Italian community in New York has for years nursed a grievance against the Irish and, to a lesser extent, the Jewish political groups for monopolizing political power. They complained about the lack of judicial jobs, the small number—usually one—of Italian congressmen, the lack of representation on the state tickets. But the Italians lacked the means to make their ambition a reality. Although they formed a large voting bloc, there was rarely sufficient wealth to finance political clubs. Italian immigrants, largely poor peasants from southern Italy and Sicily, lacked the mercantile experience of the Jews and the political experience gained in the seventy-five-year history of Irish immigration.

During the Prohibition years, the Italian racketeers had made certain political contacts in order to gain protection. Costello, always the compromiser and fixer rather than the muscle-man, was the first to establish relations with Jimmy Hines, the powerful leader of the West Side in Tammany Hall. But his rival, Lucky Luciano, suspicious of the Irish and seeking more direct power, backed and elected Al Marinelli for district leader on the Lower West Side. Marinelli in 1932 was the only Italian leader inside Tammany Hall. Later, he was joined by Dr. Paul Sarubbi, a partner of gangster Johnny Torrio in a large, legitimate liquor concern. Certainly, Costello and Luciano represented no "unified" move by the Italians as a whole for power; within the Italian community there are as many divisions as in any other group. What is significant is that different Italians, for different reasons and in various fashions, were achieving influence for the first time. Marinelli became county clerk of New York and a leading power in Tammany. In 1937, after being blasted by Tom Dewey, then running for district attorney, as a "political ally of thieves . . . and big-shot racketeers," Marinelli was removed from office by Governor Lehman. The subsequent conviction by Dewey of Luciano and Hines, and the election of LaGuardia, left most of the Tammany clubs financially weak and foundering. This was the moment Costello made his move. In a few years, by judicious financing, he controlled a bloc of "Italian" leaders in the Hall—as well as some Irish on the upper West Side and some Jewish leaders on the East Side—and was able to influence the selection of a number of Italian judges. The most notable incident, revealed by a wire tap on Costello's phone, was the "Thank you, Francisco" call in 1943 by Supreme Court judge nominee Thomas Aurelio, who gave Costello full credit for his nomination.

It was not only Tammany that was eager to accept campaign contributions from newly rich Italians, even though some of these *nouveaux riches* had "arrived" through bootlegging and gambling. Fiorello LaGuardia, the wiliest mind that melting-pot politics has ever produced, understood in the early thirties where much of his covert support came from. (So, too, did Vito Marcantonio, an apt pupil of the master: Marcantonio has consistently made deals with the Italian leaders of Tammany Hall—in 1943 he supported Aurelio and refused to repudiate him even when the Democratic party formally did.) Joe Adonis, who had built a political following during the late twenties, when he ran a popular speakeasy, aided LaGuardia financially to a considerable extent in 1933. "The Democrats haven't recognized the Italians," Adonis told a friend. "There is no reason for the Italians to support anybody but LaGuardia; the Jews have played ball with the Democrats and haven't gotten much out of it. They know it now. They will vote for LaGuardia. So will the Italians."

Adonis played his cards shrewdly. He supported LaGuardia, but also a number of Democrats for local and judicial posts, and became a power in the Brooklyn area. His restaurant was frequented by Kenny Sutherland, the Coney Island Democratic leader; Irwin Steingut, the Democratic minority leader in Albany; Anthony DiGiovanni, later a councilman; William O'Dwyer, and Jim Moran. But, in 1937, Adonis made the mistake of supporting Royal Copeland against LaGuardia, and the irate Fiorello finally drove Adonis out of New York.

LaGuardia later turned his ire against Costello, too. Yet Costello survived and reached the peak of his influence in 1942, when he was instrumental in electing Michael Kennedy leader of Tammany Hall. Despite the Aurelio fiasco, which first brought Costello into notoriety, he still had sufficient power in the Hall to swing votes for Hugo Rogers as Tammany leader in 1948. In those years many a Tammany leader came hat-in-hand to Costello's apartment or sought him out on the golf links to obtain the nomination for a judicial post.

During this period, other Italian political leaders were also coming to the fore. Generoso Pope, whose Colonial Sand and Stone Company began to prosper through political contacts, became an important political figure, especially when his purchase of the two largest Italian-language dailies (later merged into one), and of a radio station, gave him almost a monopoly of channels to Italian-speaking opinion of the city. Through Generoso Pope, and through Costello, the Italians became a major political force in New York.

That the urban machines, largely Democratic, have financed their heavy campaign costs in this fashion rather than having to turn to the "moneyed interests" explains in some part why these machines were able, in part, to support the New and Fair Deals without suffering the pressures they might have been subjected to had their source of money supply been the business groups.[2] Although he has never publicly revealed his political convictions, it is likely that Frank Costello was a fervent admirer of Franklin D. Roosevelt and his efforts to aid the common man. The basic measures of the New Deal, which most Americans today agree were necessary for the public good, would not have been possible without the support of the "corrupt" big-city machines.

THE "NEW" MONEY—AND THE OLD

There is little question that men of Italian origin appeared in most of the leading roles in the high drama of gambling and mobs, just as twenty years ago the children of East European Jews were the most prominent figures in organized crime, and before that individuals of Irish descent were similarly prominent. To some extent statistical accident and the tendency of newspapers to emphasize the few sensational figures gives a greater illusion about the domination of illicit activities by a single ethnic group than all the facts warrant. In

[2]This is an old story in American politics. Theodore Allen, a gambler and saloon keeper, whose American Mabille was an elegant music hall and bordello (he once told a Congressional investigating committee that he was the wickedest man in New York), gave Republican Boss Thurlow Weed a campaign contribution of $25,000 for the re-election of Abraham Lincoln in 1864.

many cities, particularly in the South and on the West Coast, the mob and gambling fraternity consisted of many other groups, and often, predominantly, of native white Protestants. Yet it is clear that in the major northern urban centers there was a distinct ethnic sequence in the modes of obtaining illicit wealth and that, uniquely in the case of the recent Italian elements, the former bootleggers and gamblers provided considerable leverage for the growth of political influence as well. A substantial number of Italian judges sitting on the bench in New York today are indebted in one fashion or another to Costello; so too are many Italian district leaders—as well as some Jewish and Irish politicians. And the motive in establishing Italian political prestige in New York was generous rather than scheming for personal advantage. For Costello it was largely a case of ethnic pride. As in earlier American eras, organized illegality became a stepladder of social ascent.

To the world at large, the news and pictures of Frank Sinatra, for example, mingling with former Italian mobsters could come somewhat as a shock. Yet to Sinatra, and to many Italians, these were men who had grown up in their neighborhoods and who were, in some instances, bywords in the community for their helpfulness and their charities. The early Italian gangsters were hoodlums—rough, unlettered, and young (Al Capone was only twenty-nine at the height of his power). Those who survived learned to adapt. By now they are men of middle age or older. They learned to dress conservatively. Their homes are in respectable suburbs. They sent their children to good schools and sought to avoid publicity.[8] Costello even went to a psychiatrist in his effort to overcome a painful feeling of inferiority in the world of manners.

As happens with all "new" money in American society, the rough and ready contractors, the construction people, trucking entrepreneurs, as well as racketeers, polished up their manners and sought recognition and respectability in their own ethnic as well as in the general community. The "shanty" Irish became the "lace curtain" Irish, and then

[8]Except at times by being overly neighborly, like Tony Accardo, who, at Yuletide 1949, in his elegant River Forest home, decorated a 40-foot tree on his lawn and beneath it set a wooden Santa and reindeer, while around the yard, on tracks, electrically operated skating figures zipped merrily around while a loudspeaker poured out Christmas carols. The next Christmas, the Accardo lawn was darkened; Tony was on the lam from Kefauver.

moved out for wider recognition. Sometimes acceptance came first in established "American" society, and this was a certificate for later recognition by the ethnic community, a process well illustrated by the belated acceptance in established Negro society of such figures as Sugar Ray Robinson and Joe Louis, as well as leading popular entertainers.

Yet, after all, the foundation of many a distinguished older American fortune was laid by sharp practices and morally reprehensible methods. The pioneers of American capitalism were not graduated from Harvard's School of Business Administration. The early settlers and founding fathers, as well as those who "won the West" and built up cattle, mining, and other fortunes, often did so by shady speculations and a not inconsiderable amount of violence. They ignored, circumvented, or stretched the law when it stood in the way of America's destiny and their own—or were themselves the law when it served their purposes. This has not prevented them and their descendants from feeling proper moral outrage when, under the changed circumstances of the crowded urban environments, latecomers pursued equally ruthless tactics.

THE EMBOURGEOISEMENT OF CRIME

Ironically, the social development which made possible the rise to political influence sounds, too, the knell of the rough Italian gangster. For it is the growing number of Italians with professional training and legitimate business success that both prompts and permits the Italian group to wield increasing political influence; and increasingly it is the professionals and businessmen who provide models for Italian youth today, models that hardly existed twenty years ago. Ironically, the headlines and exposés of "crime" of the Italian "gangsters" came years after the fact. Many of the top "crime" figures had long ago forsworn violence, and even their income, in large part, was derived from legitimate investments (real estate in the case of Costello, motor haulage and auto dealer franchises in the case of Adonis) or from such quasi-legitimate but socially respectable sources as gambling casinos. Hence society's "retribution" in the jail sentences for Costello and Adonis was little more than a trumped-up morality that disguised a social hypocrisy.

Apart from these considerations, what of the larger context

of crime and the American way of life? The passing of the
Fair Deal signalizes, oddly, the passing of an older pattern of
illicit activities. The gambling fever of the past decade and a
half was part of the flush and exuberance of rising incomes,
and was characteristic largely of new upper-middle-class rich
having a first fling at conspicuous consumption. These upper-
middle-class rich, a significant new stratum in American life
(not rich in the nineteenth-century sense of enormous wealth,
but largely middle-sized businessmen and entrepreneurs of the
service and luxury trades—the "tertiary economy" in Colin
Clark's phrase—who by the tax laws have achieved sizable
incomes often much higher than the managers of the super-
giant corporations), were the chief patrons of the munificent
gambling casinos. During the war decade when travel was
difficult, gambling and the lush resorts provided important
outlets for this social class. Now they are settling down,
learning about Europe and culture. The petty gambling, the
betting and bingo which relieve the tedium of small-town life,
or the expectation among the urban slum dwellers of winning
a sizable sum by a "lucky number" or a "lucky horse," goes
on. To quote Bernard Baruch: "You can't stop people from
gambling on horses. And why should you prohibit a man
from backing his own judgment? It's another form of personal initiative." But the lush profits are passing from gambling as the costs of co-ordination rise. And in the future it is
likely that gambling, like prostitution, winning tacit acceptance as a necessary fact, will continue on a decentralized,
small entrepreneur basis.

But passing, too, is a political pattern, the system of political "bosses" which in its reciprocal relation provided "protection" for, and was fed revenue from, crime. The collapse of
the "boss" system was a product of the Roosevelt era. Twenty
years ago Jim Farley's task was simple; he had to work only
on some key state bosses. Now there is no such animal. New
Jersey Democracy was once ruled by Frank Hague; now
there are five or six men each "top dog," for the moment, in
his part of the state or faction of the party. Within the urban
centers, the old Irish-dominated political machines in New
York, Boston, Newark, and Chicago have fallen apart. The
decentralization of the metropolitan centers, the growth of
suburbs and satellite towns, the breakup of the old ecological
patterns of slum and transient belts, the rise of functional
groups, the increasing middle-class character of American
life, all contribute to this decline.

With the rationalization and absorption of some illicit activities into the structure of the economy, the passing of an older generation that had established a hegemony over crime, the general rise of minority groups to social position, and the breakup of the urban boss system, the pattern of crime we have discussed is passing as well. Crime, of course, remains as long as passion and the desire for gain remain. But the kind of big, organized city crime, as we have known it for the past seventy-five years, was based on more than these universal motives. It was based on certain characteristics of the American economy, American ethnic groups, and American politics. The changes in all these areas means that, in the form we have known it, it too will change.

The Police on Skid-Row:
A Study of Peace Keeping

by
Egon Bittner

The prototype of modern police organization, the Metropolitan Police of London, was created to replace an antiquated and corrupt system of law enforcement. The early planners were motivated by the mixture of hardheaded business rationality and humane sentiment that characterized liberal British thought of the first half of the nineteenth century.[1] Partly to meet the objections of a parliamentary committee, which was opposed to the establishment of the police in England, and partly because it was in line with their own thinking, the planners sought to produce an instrument that could not readily be used in the play of internal power politics but which would, instead, advance and protect conditions favorable to industry and commerce and to urban civil life in general. These intentions were not very specific and had to be reconciled with the existing structures of governing, administering justice, and keeping the peace. Consequently, the locus and mandate of the police in the modern polity were ill-defined at the outset. On the one hand, the new institution was to be a part of the executive branch of government, organized, funded, and staffed in accordance with standards that were typical for the entire system of the executive. On the other hand, the duties that were given to the police or-

Reprinted from *American Sociological Review*, Vol. 32, No. 5, October 1967, pp. 699–715, with permission of the American Sociological Association and the author.

[1] The bill for a Metropolitan Police was actually enacted under the sponsorship of Robert Peel, the Home Secretary in the Tory Government of the Duke of Wellington. There is, however, no doubt that it was one of the several reform tendencies that Peel assimilated into Tory politics in his long career. Cf. J. L. Lyman, "The Metropolitan Police Act of 1829," *Journal of Criminal Law, Criminology and Police Science*, 55 (1964), 141–154.

ganization brought it under direct control of the judiciary in its day-to-day operation.

The dual patronage of the police by the executive and the judiciary is characteristic for all democratically governed countries. Moreover, it is generally the case, or at least it is deemed desirable, that judges *rather than* executive officials have control over police use and procedure.[2] This preference is based on two considerations. First, in the tenets of the democratic creed, the possibility of direct control of the police by a government in power is repugnant.[3] Even when the specter of the police state in its more ominous forms is not a concern, close ties between those who govern and those who police are viewed as a sign of political corruption.[4] Hence, mayors, governors, and cabinet officers—although the nominal superiors of the police—tend to maintain, or to pretend, a hands-off policy. Second, it is commonly understood that the main function of the police is the control of crime. Since the concept of crime belongs wholly to the law, and its treatment is exhaustively based on considerations of legality, police procedure automatically stands under the same system of review that controls the administration of justice in general.

By nature, judicial control encompasses only those aspects of police activity that are directly related to full-dress legal prosecution of offenders. The judiciary has neither the authority nor the means to direct, supervise, and review those activities of the police that do not result in prosecution. Yet such other activities are unavoidable, frequent, and largely within the realm of public expectations. It might be assumed

[2]Jerome Hall, "Police and Law in a Democratic Society," *Indiana Law Journal*, 28 (1953), 133–177. Though other authors are less emphatic on this point, judicial control is generally taken for granted. The point has been made, however, that in modern times judicial control over the police has been asserted mainly because of the default of any other general controlling authority, cf. E. L. Barrett, Jr., "Police Practice and the Law," *California Law Review*, 50 (1962), 11–55.

[3]A. C. German, F. D. Day and R. R. J. Gallati, *Introduction to Law Enforcement*, Springfield, Ill.: C. C. Thomas, 1966; "One concept, in particular, should be kept in mind. A dictatorship can never exist unless the police system of the country is under the absolute control of the dictator. There is no other way to uphold a dictatorship except by terror, and the instrument of this total terror is the secret police, whatever its name. In every country where freedom has been lost, law enforcement has been a dominant instrument in destroying it" (p. 80).

[4]The point is frequently made; cf. Raymond B. Fosdick, *American Police Systems*, New York: Century Company, 1920; Bruce Smith, *Police Systems in the United States*, 2nd rev. ed., New York: Harper, 1960.

that in this domain of practice the police are under executive control. This is not the case, however, except in a marginal sense.[5] Not only are police departments generally free to determine what need be done and how, but aside from informal pressures they are given scant direction in these matters. Thus, there appear to exist two relatively independent domains of police activity. In one, their methods are constrained by the prospect of the future disposition of a case in the courts; in the other, they operate under some other consideration and largely with no structured and continuous outside constraint. Following the terminology suggested by Michael Banton, they may be said to function in the first instance as "law officers" and in the second instance as "peace officers."[6] It must be emphasized that the designation "peace officer" is a residual term, with only some vaguely presumptive content. The role, as Banton speaks of it, is supposed to encompass all occupational routines not directly related to making arrests, without, however, specifying what determines the limits of competence and availability of the police in such actions.

Efforts to characterize a large domain of activities of an important public agency have so far yielded only negative definitions. We know that they do not involve arrests; we also know that they do not stand under judicial control, and that they are not, in any important sense, determined by specific executive or legislative mandates. In police textbooks and manuals, these activities receive only casual attention, and the role of the "peace officer" is typically stated in terms suggesting that his work is governed mainly by the individual officer's personal wisdom, integrity, and altruism.[7] Police departments generally keep no records of procedures that do not involve making arrests. Policemen, when asked, insist that they merely use common sense when acting as "peace officers," though they tend to emphasize the elements of experience and practice in discharging the role adequately. All this ambiguity is the more remarkable for the fact that peace keeping tasks, i.e., procedures not involving the formal legal

[5]The executive margin of control is set mainly in terms of budgetary determinations and the mapping of some formal aspects of the organization of departments.

[6]Michael Banton, *The Policeman in the Community,* New York: Basic Books, 1964, pp. 6–7 and 127 ff.

[7]R. Bruce Holmgren, *Primary Police Functions,* New York: William C. Copp, 1962.

remedy of arrest, were explicitly built into the program of the modern police from the outset.[8] The early executives of the London police saw with great clarity that their organization had a dual function. While it was to be an arm of the administration of justice, in respect of which it developed certain techniques for bringing offenders to trial, it was also expected to function apart from, and at times in lieu of, the employment of full-dress legal procedure. Despite its early origin, despite a great deal of public knowledge about it, despite the fact that it is routinely done by policemen, no one can say with any clarity what it means to do a good job of keeping the peace. To be sure, there is vague consensus that when policemen direct, aid, inform, pacify, warn, discipline, roust, and do whatever else they do without making arrests, they do this with some reference to the circumstances of the occasion and, thus, somehow contribute to the maintenance of the peace and order. Peace keeping appears to be a solution to an unknown problem arrived at by unknown means.

The following is an attempt to clarify conceptually the mandate and the practice of keeping the peace. The effort will be directed not to the formulation of a comprehensive solution of the problem but to a detailed consideration of some aspects of it. Only in order to place the particular into the overall domain to which it belongs will the structural determinants of keeping the peace in general be discussed. By structural determinants are meant the typical situations that policemen perceive as *demand conditions* for action without arrest. This will be followed by a description of peace keeping in skid-row districts, with the object of identifying those aspects of it that constitute a *practical skill*.

Since the major object of this paper is to elucidate peace keeping practice as a skilled performance, it is necessary to make clear how the use of the term is intended.

Practical skill will be used to refer to those methods of doing certain things, and to the information that underlies the use of the methods, that *practitioners themselves* view as proper and efficient. Skill is, therefore, a stable orientation to work tasks that is relatively independent of the personal

---

[8]Cf. Lyman, *op. cit.*, p. 153; F. C. Mather, *Public Order in the Age of the Chartists*, Manchester: Manchester University Press, 1959, chapter IV. See also Robert H. Bremer, "Police, Penal and Parole Policies in Cleveland and Toledo," *American Journal of Economics and Sociology*, 14 (1955), 387–398, for similar recognition in the United States at about the turn of this century.

feelings and judgments of those who employ it. Whether the exercise of this skilled performance is desirable or not, and whether it is based on correct information or not, are specifically outside the scope of interest of this presentation. The following is deliberately confined to a description of what police patrolmen consider to be the reality of their work circumstances, what they do, and what they feel they must do to do a good job. That the practice is thought to be determined by normative standards of skill minimizes but does not eliminate the factors of personal interest or inclination. Moreover, the distribution of skill varies among practitioners in the very standards they set for themselves. For example, we will show that patrolmen view a measure of rough informality as good practice vis-a-vis skid-row inhabitants. By this standard, patrolmen who are "not rough enough," or who are "too rough," or whose roughness is determined by personal feelings rather than by situational exigencies, are judged to be poor craftsmen.

The description and analysis are based on twelve months of field work with the police departments of two large cities west of the Mississippi. Eleven weeks of this time were spent in skid-row and skid-row-like districts. The observations were augmented by approximately one hundred interviews with police officers of all ranks. The formulations that will be proposed were discussed in these interviews. They were recognized by the respondents as elements of standard practice. The respondents' recognition was often accompanied by remarks indicating that they had never thought about things in this way and that they were not aware how standardized police work was.

STRUCTURAL DEMAND CONDITIONS OF PEACE KEEPING

There exist at least five types of relatively distinct circumstances that produce police activities that do not involve invoking the law and that are only in a trivial sense determined by those considerations of legality that determine law enforcement. This does not mean that these activities are illegal but merely that there is no legal directive that informs the acting policeman whether what he does must be done or how it is to be done. In these circumstances, policemen act as all-purpose and terminal remedial agents, and the confronted problem is solved in the field. If these practices stand under any kind of review at all, and typically they do not, it is only through internal police department control.

1. Although the executive branch of government generally refrains from exercising a controlling influence over the direction of police interest, it manages to extract certain performances from it. Two important examples of this are the supervision of certain licensed services and premises and the regulation of traffic.[9] With respect to the first, the police tend to concentrate on what might be called the moral aspects of establishments rather than on questions relating to the technical adequacy of the service. This orientation is based on the assumption that certain types of businesses lend themselves to exploitation for undesirable and illegal purposes. Since this tendency cannot be fully controlled, it is only natural that the police will be inclined to favor licensees who are at least cooperative. This, however, transforms the task from the mere scrutiny of credentials and the passing of judgments, to the creation and maintenance of a network of connections that conveys influence, pressure, and information. The duty to inspect is the background of this network, but the resulting contacts acquire additional value for solving crimes and maintaining public order. Bartenders, shopkeepers, and hotel clerks become, for patrolmen, a resource that must be continuously serviced by visits and exchanges of favors. While it is apparent that this condition lends itself to corrupt exploitation by individual officers, even the most flawlessly honest policeman must participate in this network of exchanges if he is to function adequately. Thus, engaging in such exchanges becomes an occupational task that demands attention and time.

Regulation of traffic is considerably less complex. More than anything else, traffic control symbolizes the autonomous authority of policemen. Their commands generally are met with unquestioned compliance. Even when they issue citations, which seemingly refer the case to the courts, it is common practice for the accused to view the allegation as a finding against him and to pay the fine. Police officials emphasize that it is more important to be circumspect than legalistic in traffic control. Officers are often reminded that a large segment of the public has no other contact with the po-

[9] Smith, *op. cit.*, pp. 15ff.

lice, and that the field lends itself to public relations work by the line personnel.[10]

2. Policemen often do not arrest persons who have committed minor offenses in circumstances in which the arrest is technically possible. This practice has recently received considerable attention in legal and sociological literature. The studies were motivated by the realization that "police decisions not to invoke the criminal process determine the outer limits of law enforcement."[11] From these researches, it was learned that the police tend to impose more stringent criteria of law enforcement on certain segments of the community than on others.[12] It was also learned that, from the perspective of the administration of justice, the decisions not to make arrests often are based on compelling reasons.[13] It is less well appreciated that policemen often not only refrain from invoking the law formally but also employ alternative sanctions. For example, it is standard practice that violators are warned not to repeat the offense. This often leads to patrolmen's "keeping an eye" on certain persons. Less frequent, though not unusual, is the practice of direct disciplining of offenders, especially when they are juveniles, which occasionally involves inducing them to repair the damage occasioned by their misconduct.[14]

The power to arrest and the freedom not to arrest can be used in cases that do not involve patent offenses. An officer can say to a person whose behavior he wishes to control, "I'll let you go this time!" without indicating to him that he could not have been arrested in any case. Nor is this always deliberate misrepresentation, for in many cases the law is sufficiently ambiguous to allow alternative interpretations. In short, not to make an arrest is rarely, if ever, merely a decision not to act; it is most often a decision to act alternatively. In the case of minor offenses, to make an arrest often is merely one of several possible proper actions.

[10]Orlando W. Wilson, "Police Authority in a Free Society," *Journal of Criminal Law, Criminology and Police Science,* 54 (1964), 175–177.

[11]Joseph Goldstein, "Police Discretion Not to Invoke the Criminal Process," *Yale Law Journal,* 69 (1960), 543.

[12]Jerome Skolnick, *Justice Without Trial,* New York: Wiley, 1966.

[13]Wayne LaFave, "The Police and Nonenforcement of the Law," *Wisconsin Law Review* (1962), 104–137 and 179–239.

[14]Nathan Goldman, *The Differential Selection of Juvenile Offenders for Court Appearance,* National Research and Information Center, National Council on Crime and Delinquency, 1963, pp. 114 ff.

3. There exists a public demand for police intervention in matters that contain no criminal and often no legal aspects.[15] For example, it is commonly assumed that officers will be available to arbitrate quarrels, to pacify the unruly, and to help in keeping order. They are supposed also to aid people in trouble, and there is scarcely a human predicament imaginable for which police aid has not been solicited and obtained at one time or another. Most authors writing about the police consider such activities only marginally related to the police mandate. This view fails to reckon with the fact that the availability of these performances is taken for granted and the police assign a substantial amount of their resources to such work. Although this work cannot be subsumed under the concept of legal action, it does involve the exercise of a form of authority that most people associate with the police. In fact, no matter how trivial the occasion, the device of "calling the cops" transforms any problem. It implies that a situation is, or is getting, out of hand. Police responses to public demands are always oriented to this implication, and the risk of proliferation of troubles makes every call a potentially serious matter.[16]

4. Certain mass phenomena of either a regular or a spontaneous nature require direct monitoring. Most important is the controlling of crowds in incipient stages of disorder. The specter of mob violence frequently calls for measures that involve coercion, including the use of physical force. Legal theory allows, of course, that public officials are empowered to use coercion in situations of imminent danger.[17] Unfortunately, the doctrine is not sufficiently specific to be of much help as a rule of practice. It is based on the assumption of the adventitiousness of danger, and thus does not lend itself readily to elaborations that could direct the routines of early detection and prevention of untoward developments. It is interesting that the objective of preventing riots by informal

[15]Elaine Cumming, Ian Cumming and Laura Edell, "Policeman as Philosopher, Guide and Friend," *Social Problems*, 12 (1965), 276–286.

[16]There is little doubt that many requests for service are turned down by the police, especially when they are made over the telephone or by mail, cf. LaFave, *op. cit.*, p. 212, n. 124. The uniformed patrolman, however, finds it virtually impossible to leave the scene without becoming involved in some way or another.

[17]Hans Kelsen, *General Theory of Law and State*, New York: Russell & Russell, 1961, pp. 278–279; H. L. A. Hart, *The Concept of Law*, Oxford: Clarendon Press, 1961; pp. 20–21.

means posed one of the central organizational problems for the police in England during the era of the Chartists.[18]

5. The police have certain special duties with respect to persons who are viewed as less than fully accountable for their actions. Examples of those eligible for special consideration are those who are under age[19] and those who are mentally ill.[20] Although it is virtually never acknowledged explicitly, those receiving special treatment include people who do not lead "normal" lives and who occupy a pariah status in society. This group includes residents of ethnic ghettos, certain types of bohemians and vagabonds, and persons of known criminal background. The special treatment of children and of sick persons is permissively sanctioned by the law, but the special treatment of others is, in principle, opposed by the leading theme of legality and the tenets of the democratic faith.[21] The important point is not that such persons are arrested more often than others, which is quite true, but that they are perceived by the police as producing a special problem that necessitates continuous attention and the use of special procedures.

The five types of demand conditions do not exclude the possibility of invoking the criminal process. Indeed, arrests do occur quite frequently in all these circumstances. But the concerns generated in these areas cause activities that usually do not terminate in an arrest. When arrests are made, there exist, at least in the ideal, certain criteria by reference to which the arrest can be judged as having been made more or less properly, and there are some persons who, in the natural course of events, actually judge the performance.[22] But for actions not resulting in arrest there are no such criteria and no such judges. How, then, can one speak of such actions as

[18]Mather, op. cit.; see also, Jenifer Hart, "Reform of the Borough Police, 1835–1856." English History Review, 70 (1955), 411–427.

[19]Francis A. Allen, The Borderland of Criminal Justice, Chicago: University of Chicago Press, 1964.

[20]Egon Bittner, "Police Discretion in Emergency Apprehension of Mentally Ill Persons," Social Problems, 14 (1967), 278–292.

[21]It bears mentioning, however, that differential treatment is not unique with the police, but is also in many ways representative for the administration of justice in general; cf. J. E. Carlin, Jan Howard and S. L. Messinger, "Civil Justice and the Poor," Law and Society, 1 (1966), 9–89; Jacobus tenBroek (ed.) The Law of the Poor, San Francisco: Chandler Publishing Co., 1966.

[22]This is, however, true only in the ideal. It is well known that a substantial number of persons who are arrested are subsequently released without ever being charged and tried, cf. Barret, op. cit.

necessary and proper? Since there does not exist any official answer to this query, and since policemen act in the role of "peace officers" pretty much without external direction or constraint, the question comes down to asking how the policeman himself knows whether he has any business with a person he does not arrest, and if so, what that business might be. Furthermore, if there exists a domain of concerns and activities that is largely independent of the law enforcement mandate, it is reasonable to assume that it will exercise some degree of influence on how and to what ends the law is invoked in cases of arrests.

Skid-row presents one excellent opportunity to study these problems. The area contains a heavy concentration of persons who do not live "normal" lives in terms of prevailing standards of middle-class morality. Since the police respond to this situation by intensive patrolling, the structure of peace keeping should be readily observable. Needless to say, the findings and conclusions will not be necessarily generalizable to other types of demand conditions.

THE PROBLEM OF KEEPING THE PEACE IN SKID-ROW

Skid-row has always occupied a special place among the various forms of urban life. While other areas are perceived as being different in many ways, skid-row is seen as completely different. Though it is located in the heart of civilization, it is viewed as containing aspects of the primordial jungle, calling for missionary activities and offering opportunities for exotic adventure. While each inhabitant individually can be seen as tragically linked to the vicissitudes of "normal" life, allowing others to say "here but for the Grace of God go I," those who live there are believed to have repudiated the entire role-casting scheme of the majority and to live apart from normalcy. Accordingly, the traditional attitude of civic-mindedness toward skid-row has been dominated by the desire to contain it and to salvage souls from its clutches.[23]

[23]The literature on skid-row is voluminous. The classic in the field is Nels Anderson, *The Hobo*, Chicago: University of Chicago Press, 1923. Samuel E. Wallace, *Skid-Row as a Way of Life*, Totowa, New Jersey: The Bedminster Press, 1965, is a more recent descriptive account and contains a useful bibliography. Donald A. Bogue, *Skid-Row*

The specific task of containment has been left to the police. That this task pressed upon the police some rather special duties has never come under explicit consideration, either from the government that expects control or from the police departments that implement it. Instead, the prevailing method of carrying out the task is to assign patrolmen to the area on a fairly permanent basis and to allow them to work out their own ways of running things. External influence is confined largely to the supply of support and facilities, on the one hand, and to occasional expressions of criticism about the overall conditions, on the other. Within the limits of available resources and general expectations, patrolmen are supposed to know what to do and are free to do it.[24]

Patrolmen who are more or less permanently assigned to skid-row districts tend to develop a conception of the nature of their "domain" that is surprisingly uniform. Individual officers differ in many aspects of practice, emphasize different concerns, and maintain different contacts, but they are in fundamental agreement about the structure of skid-row life. This relatively uniform conception includes an implicit formulation of the problem of keeping the peace in skid-row.

In the view of experienced patrolmen, life on skid-row is fundamentally different from life in other parts of society. To be sure, they say, around its geographic limits the area tends to blend into the surrounding environment, and its population always encompasses some persons who are only transitionally associated with it. Basically, however, skid-row is perceived as the natural habitat of people who lack the capacities and commitments to live "normal" lives on a sustained basis. The presence of these people defines the nature of social reality in the area. In general, and especially in casual encounters, the presumption of incompetence and of the disinclination to be "normal" is the leading theme for the interpretation of all ac-

in American Cities, Chicago: Community and Family Center, University of Chicago, 1963, contains an exhaustive quantitative survey of Chicago skid-row.

[24]One of the two cities described in this paper also employed the procedure of the "round-up" of drunks. In this, the police van toured the skid-row area twice daily, during the mid-afternoon and early evening hours, and the officers who manned it picked up drunks they sighted. A similar procedure is used in New York's Bowery and the officers who do it are called "condition men." Cf. Bowery Project, Bureau of Applied Social Research, Columbia University, Summary Report of a Study Undertaken under Contract Approved by the Board of Estimates, 1963, mimeo., p. 11.

tions and relations. Not only do people approach one another in this manner, but presumably they also expect to be approached in this way, and they conduct themselves accordingly.

In practice, the restriction of interactional possibilities that is based on the patrolman's stereotyped conception of skid-row residents is always subject to revision and modification toward particular individuals. Thus, it is entirely possible, and not unusual, for patrolmen to view certain skid-row inhabitants in terms that involve non-skid-row aspects of normality. Instances of such approaches and relationships invariably involve a personal acquaintance and the knowledge of a good deal of individually qualifying information. Such instances are seen, despite their relative frequency, as exceptions to the rule. The awareness of the possibility of breakdown, frustration, and betrayal is ever-present, basic wariness is never wholly dissipated, and undaunted trust can never be fully reconciled with presence on skid-row.

What patrolmen view as normal on skid-row—and what they also think is taken for granted as "life as usual" by the inhabitants—is not easily summarized. It seems to focus on the idea that the dominant consideration governing all enterprise and association is directed to the occasion of the moment. Nothing is thought of as having a background that might have led up to the present in terms of some compelling moral or practical necessity. There are some exceptions to this rule, of course: the police themselves, and those who run certain establishments, are perceived as engaged in important and necessary activities. But in order to carry them out they, too, must be geared to the overall atmosphere of fortuitousness. In this atmosphere, the range of control that persons have over one another is exceedingly narrow. Good faith, even where it is valued, is seen merely as a personal matter. Its violations are the victim's own hard luck, rather than demonstrable violations of property. There is only a private sense of irony at having been victimized. The overall air is not so much one of active distrust as it is one of irrelevance of trust; as patrolmen often emphasize, the situation does not necessarily cause all relations to be predatory, but the possibility of exploitation is not checked by the expectation that it will not happen.

Just as the past is seen by the policeman as having only the most attenuated relevance to the present, so the future implications of present situations are said to be generally devoid of prospective coherence. No venture, especially no joint venture, can be said to have a strongly predictable future in line with its initial objectives. It is a matter of adventitious circumstance whether or not matters go as anticipated. That which is not within the grasp of momentary control is outside of practical social reality.

Though patrolmen see the temporal framework of the occasion of the moment mainly as a lack of trustworthiness, they also recognize that it involves more than merely the personal motives of individuals. In addition to the fact that everybody *feels* that things matter only at the moment, irresponsibility takes an *objectified* form on skid-row. The places the residents occupy, the social relations they entertain, and the activities that engage them are not meaningfully connected over time. Thus, for example, address, occupation, marital status, etc., matter much less on skid-row than in any other part of society. The fact that present whereabouts, activities, and affiliations imply neither continuity nor direction means that life on skid-row lacks a socially structured background of accountability. Of course, everybody's life contains some sequential incongruities, but in the life of a skid-row inhabitant every moment is an accident. That a man has no "address" in the future that could be in some way inferred from where he is and what he does makes him a person of *radically reduced visibility*. If he disappears from sight and one wishes to locate him, it is virtually impossible to systematize the search. All one can know with relative certainty is that he will be somewhere on some skid-row and the only thing one can do is to trace the factual contiguities of his whereabouts.

It is commonly known that the police are expert in finding people and that they have developed an exquisite technology involving special facilities and procedures of sleuthing. It is less well appreciated that all this technology builds upon those socially structured features of everyday life that render persons findable in the first place.

Under ordinary conditions, the query as to where a person is can be addressed, from the outset, to a restricted realm of possibilities that can be further narrowed by looking into certain places and asking certain persons. The map of whereabouts that normally competent persons use whenever they wish to locate someone is constituted by the basic facts of membership in society. Insofar as membership consists of status incumbencies, each of which has an adumbrated future that substantially reduces unpredictability, it is itself a guarantee of the order within which it is quite difficult to get lost. Membership is thus visible not only now but also as its own projection into the future. It is in terms of this prospective availability that the skid-row inhabitant is a person of reduced visibility. His membership is viewed as extraordinary because its extension into the future is *not* reduced to a restricted realm of possibilities. Neither his subjective dispositions, nor his circumstances, indicate that he is oriented to any particular long-range interests. But, as he may claim every contingent opportunity, his claims are always seen as based on slight merit or right, at least to the extent that interfering with them does not constitute a substantial denial of his freedom.

This, then, constitutes the problem of keeping the peace on skid-row. Considerations of momentary expediency are seen as having unqualified priority as maxims of conduct; consequently, the controlling influences of the pursuit of sustained interests are presumed to be absent.

THE PRACTICES OF KEEPING THE PEACE IN SKID-ROW

From the perspective of society as a whole, skid-row inhabitants appear troublesome in a variety of ways. The uncommitted life attributed to them is perceived as inherently offensive; its very existence arouses indignation and contempt. More important, however, is the feeling that persons who have repudiated the entire role-status casting system of society, persons whose lives forever collapse into a succession of random moments, are seen as constituting a practical risk. As they have nothing to foresake, nothing is thought safe from them.[25]

The skid-row patrolman's concept of his mandate includes

[25] An illuminating parallel to the perception of skid-row can be found in the more traditional concept of vagabondage. Cf. Alexandre Vexliard, *Introduction a la Sociologie du Vagabondage*, Paris: Librarie Marcel Riviere, 1956, and "La Disparition du Vagabondage comme Fleau Social Universel," *Revue de L'Instut de Sociologie* (1963), 53–79. The classic account of English conditions up to the 19th century is C. J. Ribton-Turner, *A History of Vagrants and Vagrancy and Beggars and Begging*, London: Chapman and Hall, 1887.

an awareness of this presumed risk. He is constantly attuned to the possibility of violence, and he is convinced that things to which the inhabitants have free access are as good as lost. But his concern is directed toward the continuous condition of peril *in the area* rather than *for society in general*. While he is obviously conscious of the presence of many persons who have committed crimes outside of skid-row and will arrest them when they come to his attention, this is a peripheral part of his routine activities. In general, the skid-row patrolman and his superiors take for granted that his main business is to keep the peace and enforce the laws *on skid-row*, and that he is involved only incidentally in protecting society at large. Thus, his task is formulated basically as the protection of putative predators from one another. The maintenance of peace and safety is difficult because everyday life on skid-row is viewed as an open field for reciprocal exploitation. As the lives of the inhabitants lack the prospective coherence associated with status incumbency, the realization of self-interest does not produce order. Hence, mechanisms that control risk must work primarily from without.

External containment, to be effective, must be oriented to the realities of existence. Thus, the skid-row patrolman employs an approach that he views as appropriate to the *ad hoc* nature of skid-row life. The following are the three most prominent elements of this approach. First, the seasoned patrolman seeks to acquire a richly particularized knowledge of people and places in the area. Second, he gives the consideration of strict culpability a subordinate status among grounds for remedial sanction. Third, his use and choice of coercive interventions is determined mainly by exigencies of situations and with little regard for possible long range effects on individual persons.

The Particularization of Knowledge. The patrolman's orientation to people on skid-row is structured basically by the presupposition that if he does not know a man personally there is very little that he can assume about him. This rule determines his interaction with people who live on skid-row. Since the area also contains other types of persons, however, its applicability is not universal. To some such persons it does not apply at all, and it has a somewhat mitigated significance with certain others. For example, some persons encountered on skid-row can be recognized immediately as outsiders. Among them are workers who are employed in commercial and industrial enterprises that abut the area, persons who come for the purpose of adventurous "slumming," and some patrons of second-hand stores and pawn shops. Even with very little experience, it is relatively easy to identify these people by appearance, demeanor, and the time and place of their presence. The patrolman maintains an impersonal attitude toward them, and they are, under ordinary circumstances, not the objects of his attention.[26]

Clearly set off from these outsiders are the residents and the entire corps of personnel that services skid-row. It would be fair to say that one of the main routine activities of patrolmen is the establishment and maintenance of familiar relationships with individual members of these groups. Officers emphasize their interest in this, and they maintain that their grasp of and control over skid-row is precisely commensurate with the extent to which they "know the people." By this they do not mean having a quasi-theoretical understanding of human nature but rather the common practice of individualized and reciprocal recognition. As this group encompasses both those who render services on skid-row and those who are serviced, individualized interest is not always based on the desire to overcome uncertainty. Instead, relations with service personnel become absorbed into the network of particularized attention. Ties between patrolmen, on the one hand, and businessmen, managers, and workers, on the other hand, are often defined in terms of shared or similar interests. It bears mentioning that many persons live *and* work on skid-row. Thus, the distinction between those who service and those who are serviced is not a clearcut dichotomy but a spectrum of affiliations.

As a general rule, the skid-row patrolman possesses an immensely detailed factual knowledge of his beat. He knows, and knows a great deal about, a large number of residents. He is likely to know every person who manages or works in the local bars, hotels, shops, stores, and missions. Moreover, he probably knows every public and private place inside and out. Finally, he ordinarily remembers countless events of the past which he can recount by citing names, dates and places with remarkable precision. Though there are always some threads missing in the fabric of information, it is continuously woven and mended even as it is being used. New facts,

[26]Several patrolmen complained about the influx of "tourists" into skid-row. Since such "tourists" are perceived as seeking illicit adventure, they receive little sympathy from patrolmen when they complain about being victimized.

however, are added to the texture, not in terms of structured categories but in terms of adjoining known realities. In other words, the content and organization of the patrolman's knowledge is primarily idiographic and only vestigially, if at all, nomothetic.

Individual patrolmen vary in the extent to which they make themselves available or actively pursue personal acquaintances. But even the most aloof are continuously greeted and engaged in conversations that indicate a background of individualistic associations. While this scarcely has the appearance of work, because of its casual character, patrolmen do not view it as an optional activity. In the course of making their rounds, patrolmen seem to have access to every place, and their entry causes no surprise or consternation. Instead, the entry tends to lead to informal exchanges of small talk. At times the rounds include entering hotels and gaining access to rooms or dormitories, often for no other purpose than asking the occupants how things are going. In all this, patrolmen address innumerable persons by name and are in turn addressed by name. The conversational style that characterizes these exchanges is casual to an extent that by nonskid-row standards might suggest intimacy. Not only does the officer himself avoid all terms of deference and respect but he does not seem to expect or demand them. For example, a patrolman said to a man radiating an alcoholic glow on the street, "You've got enough of a heat on now; I'll give you ten minutes to get your ass off the street!" Without stopping, the man answered, "Oh, why don't you go and piss in your own pot!" The officer's only response was, "All right, in ten minutes you're either in bed or on your way to the can."

This kind of expressive freedom is an intricately limited privilege. Persons of acquaintance are entitled to it and appear to exercise it mainly in routinized encounters. But strangers, too, can use it with impunity. The safe way of gaining the privilege is to respond to the patrolman in ways that do not challenge his right to ask questions and issue commands. Once the concession is made that the officer is entitled to inquire into a man's background, business, and intentions, and that he is entitled to obedience, there opens a field of colloquial license. A patrolman seems to grant expressive freedom in recognition of a person's acceptance of his access to areas of life ordinarily defined as private and subject to coercive control only under special circumstances. While patrolmen accept and seemingly even cultivate the rough *quid pro quo* of informality, and while they do not expect sincerity, candor, or obedience in their dealings with the inhabitants, they do not allow the rejection of their approach.

The explicit refusal to answer questions of a personal nature and the demand to know why the questions are asked significantly enhances a person's chances of being arrested on some minor charge. While most patrolmen tend to be personally indignant about this kind of response and use the arrest to compose their own hurt feelings, this is merely a case of affect being in line with the method. There are other officers who proceed in the same manner without taking offense, or even with feelings of regret. Such patrolmen often maintain that their colleagues' affective involvement is a corruption of an essentially valid technique. The technique is oriented to the goal of maintaining operational control. The patrolman's conception of this goal places him hierarchically above whomever he approaches, and makes him the sole judge of the propriety of the occasion. As he alone is oriented to this goal, and as he seeks to attain it by means of individualized access to persons, those who frustrate him are seen as motivated at best by the desire to "give him a hard time" and at worst by some darkly devious purpose.

Officers are quite aware that the directness of their approach and the demands they make are difficult to reconcile with the doctrines of civil liberties, but they maintain that they are in accord with the general freedom of access that persons living on skid-row normally grant one another. That is, they believe that the imposition of personalized and far-reaching control is in tune with standard expectancies. In terms of these expectancies, people are not so much denied the right to privacy as they are seen as not having any privacy. Thus, officers seek to install themselves in the center of people's lives and let the consciousness of their presence play the part of conscience.

When talking about the practical necessity of an aggressively personal approach, officers do not refer merely to the need for maintaining control over lives that are open in the direction of the untoward. They also see it as the basis for the supply of certain valued services to inhabitants of skid-row. The coerced or conceded access to persons often imposes on the patrolman tasks that are, in the main, in line with these persons' expressed or implied interest. In asserting this connection, patrolmen note that they frequently help people to obtain meals, lodging, employment, that they direct them to welfare and health services, and that they aid them in various other ways. Though patrolmen tend to describe such services mainly as the product of their own altruism, they also say that their colleagues who avoid them are simply doing a poor job of patrolling. The acceptance of the need to help people is based on the realization that the hungry, the sick, and the troubled are a potential source of problems. Moreover, that patrolmen will help people is part of the background expectancies of life on skid-row. Hotel clerks normally call policemen when someone gets so sick as to need attention; merchants expect to be taxed, in a manner of speaking, to meet the pressing needs of certain persons; and the inhabitants do not hesitate to accept, solicit, and demand every kind of aid. The domain of the patrolman's service activity is virtually limitless, and it is no exaggeration to say that the solution of every conceivable problem has at one time or another been attempted by a police officer. In one observed instance, a patrolman unceremoniously entered the room of a man he had never seen before. The man, who gave no indication that he regarded the officer's entry and questions as anything but part of life as usual, related a story of having had his dentures stolen by his wife. In the course of the subsequent rounds, the patrolman sought to locate the woman and the dentures. This did not become the evening's project but was attended to while doing other things. In the densely matted activities of the patrolman, the questioning became one more strand, not so much to be pursued to its solution as a theme that organized the memory of one more man known individually. In all this, the officer followed the precept formulated by a somewhat more articulate patrolman: "If I want to be in control of my work and keep the street relatively peaceful, I have to know the people. To know them I must gain their trust, which means that I have to be involved in their lives. But I can't be soft like a social worker because unlike him I cannot call the cops when things go wrong. I am the cops!"[27]

The Restricted Relevance of Culpability. It is well known that policemen exercise discretionary freedom in invoking the law. It is also conceded that, in some measure, the practice

[27]The same officer commented further, "If a man looks for something, I might help him. But I don't stay with him till he finds what he is looking for. If I did, I would never get to do anything else. In the last analysis, I really never solve any problems. The best I can hope for is to keep things from getting worse."

is unavoidable. This being so, the outstanding problem is whether or not the decisions are in line with the intent of the law. On skid-row, patrolmen often make decisions based on reasons that the law probably does not recognize as valid. The problem can best be introduced by citing an example.

A man in a relatively mild state of intoxication (by skid-row standards) approached a patrolman to tell him that he had a room in a hotel, to which the officer responded by urging him to go to bed instead of getting drunk. As the man walked off, the officer related the following thoughts: Here is a completely lost soul. Though he probably is no more than thirty-five years old, he looks to be in his fifties. He never works and he heardly ever has a place to stay. He has been on the street for several years and is known as "Dakota." During the past few days, "Dakota" has been seen in the company of "Big Jim." The latter is an invalid living on some sort of pension with which he pays for a room in the hotel to which "Dakota" referred and for four weekly meal tickets in one of the restaurants on the street. Whatever is left he spends on wine and beer. Occasionally, "Big Jim" goes on drinking sprees in the company of someone like "Dakota." Leaving aside the consideration that there is probably a homosexual background to the association, and that it is not right that "Big Jim" should have to support the drinking habit of someone else, there is the more important risk that if "Dakota" moves in with "Big Jim" he will very likely walk off with whatever the latter keeps in his room. "Big Jim" would never dream of reporting the theft; he would just beat the hell out of "Dakota" after he sobered up. When asked what could be done to prevent the theft and the subsequent recriminations, the patrolman proposed that in this particular case he would throw "Big Jim" into jail if he found him tonight and then tell the hotel clerk to throw "Dakota" out of the room. When asked why he did not arrest "Dakota," who was, after all, drunk enough to warrant an arrest, the officer explained that this would not solve anything. While "Dakota" was in jail "Big Jim" would continue drinking and would either strike up another liaison or embrace his old buddy after he had been released. The only thing to do was to get "Big Jim" to sober up, and the only sure way of doing this was to arrest him.

As it turned out, "Big Jim" was not located that evening. But had he been located and arrested on a drunk charge, the fact that he was intoxicated would not have been the real reason for proceeding against him, but merely the pretext. The point of the example is not that it illustrates the tendency of skid-row patrolmen to arrest persons who would not be arrested under conditions of full respect for their legal rights. To be sure, this too happens. In the majority of minor arrest cases, however, the criteria the law specifies are met. But it is the rare exception that the law is invoked merely because the specifications of the law are met. That is, compliance with the law is merely the outward appearance of an intervention that is actually based on altogether different considerations. Thus, it could be said that patrolmen do not really enforce the law, even when they do invoke it, but merely use it as a resource to solve certain pressing practical problems in keeping the peace. This observation goes beyond the conclusion that many of the lesser norms of the criminal law are treated as defeasible in police work. It is patently not the case that skid-row patrolmen apply the legal norms while recognizing many exceptions to their applicability. Instead, the observation leads to the conclusion that in keeping the peace on skid-row, patrolmen encounter certain matters they attend to by means of coercive action, e.g., arrests. In doing this, they invoke legal norms that are available, and with some regard for substantive appropriateness. Hence, the problem patrolmen confront is not which drunks, beggars, or disturbers of the peace should be arrested and which can be let go as exceptions to the rule. Rather, the problem is whether, when someone "needs" to be arrested, he should be charged with drunkeness, begging, or disturbing the peace. Speculating further, one is almost compelled to infer that virtually any set of norms could be used in this manner, provided that they sanction relatively common forms of behavior.

The reduced relevance of culpability in peace keeping practice on skid-row is not readily visible. As mentioned, most arrested persons were actually found in the act, or in the state, alleged in the arrest record. It becomes partly visible when one views the treatment of persons who are not arrested even though all the legal grounds for an arrest are present. Whenever such persons are encountered and can be induced to leave, or taken to some shelter, or remanded to someone's care, then patrolmen feel, or at least maintain, that an arrest would serve no useful purpose. That is, whenever there exist means for controlling the troublesome aspects of some person's presence in some way alternative to an arrest, such means are preferentially employed, provided, of course, that the case at hand involves only a minor offense.[28]

The attention of the relevance of culpability is most visible when the presence of legal grounds for an arrest could be questioned, i.e., in cases that sometimes are euphemistically called "preventive arrests." In one observed instance, a man who attempted to trade a pocket knife came to the attention of a patrolman. The initial encounter was attended by a good deal of levity and the man willingly responded to the officer's inquiries about his identity and business. The man laughingly acknowledged that he needed some money to get drunk. In the course of the exchange it came to light that he had just arrived in town, traveling in his automobile. When confronted with the demand to lead the officer to the car, the man's expression became serious and he pointedly stated that he would not comply because this was none of the officer's business. After a bit more prodding, which the patrolman initially kept in the light mood, the man was arrested on a charge involving begging. In subsequent conversation the patrolman acknowledged that the charge was only speciously appropriate and mainly a pretext. Having committed himself to demanding information he could not accept defeat. When this incident was discussed with another patrolman, the second officer found fault not with the fact that the arrest was made on a pretext but with the first officer's own contribution to the creation of conditions that made it unavoidable. "You see," he continued, "there is always the risk that the man is testing you and you must let him know what is what. The best among us can usually keep the upper hand in such situations without making arrests. But when it comes down to the wire, then you can't let them get away with it."

Finally, it must be mentioned that the reduction of the significance of culpability is built into the normal order of skid-row life, as patrolmen see it. Officers almost unfailingly say, pointing to some particular person, "I know that he knows

---

[28]When evidence is present to indicate that a serious crime has been committed, considerations of culpability acquire a position of priority. Two such arrests were observed, both involving checkpassers. The first offender was caught *in flagrante delicto*. In the second instance, the suspect attracted the attention of the patrolman because of his sickly appearance. In the ensuing conversation the man made some remarks that led the officer to place a call with the Warrant Division of his department. According to the information that was obtained by checking records, the man was a wanted checkpasser and was immediately arrested.

that I know that some of the things he 'owns' are stolen, and that nothing can be done about it." In saying this, they often claim to have knowledge of such a degree of certainty as would normally be sufficient for virtually any kind of action except legal proceedings. Against this background, patrolmen adopt the view that the law is not merely imperfect and difficult to implement, but that on skid-row, at least, the association between delict and sanction is distinctly occasional. Thus, to implement the law naively, i.e., to arrest someone *merely* because he committed some minor offense, is perceived as containing elements of injustice.

Moreover, patrolmen often deal with situations in which questions of culpability are profoundly ambiguous. For example, an officer was called to help in settling a violent dispute in a hotel room. The object of the quarrel was a supposedly stolen pair of trousers. As the story unfolded in the conflicting versions of the participants, it was not possible to decide who was the complainant and who was alleged to be the thief, nor did it come to light who occupied the room in which the fracas took place, or whether the trousers were taken from the room or to the room. Though the officer did ask some questions, it seemed, and was confirmed in later conversation, that he was there not to solve the puzzle of the missing trousers but to keep the situation from getting out of hand. In the end, the exhausted participants dispersed, and this was the conclusion of the case. The patrolman maintained that no one could unravel mysteries of this sort because "these people take things from each other so often that no one could tell what 'belongs' to whom." In fact, he suggested, the terms owning, stealing, and swindling, in their strict sense, do not really belong on skid-row, and all efforts to distribute guilt and innocence according to some rational formula of justice are doomed to failure.

It could be said that the term "curb-stone justice" that is sometimes applied to the procedures of patrolmen in skid-rows contains a double irony. Not only is the procedure not legally authorized, which is the intended irony in the expression, but it does not even pretend to distribute deserts. The best among the patrolmen, according to their own standards, use the law to keep skid-row inhabitants from sinking deeper into the misery they already experience. The worst, in terms of these same standards, exploit the practice for personal aggrandizement or gain. Leaving motives aside, however, it is easy to see that if culpability is not the salient consideration leading to an arrest in cases where it is patently obvious, then the practical patrolman may not view it as being wholly out of line to make arrests lacking in formal legal justification. Conversely, he will come to view minor offense arrests made solely because legal standards are met as poor craftsmanship.

The Background of Ad Hoc *Decision Making.* When skid-row patrolmen are pressed to explain their reasons for minor offense arrests, they most often mention that it is done for the protection of the arrested person. This, they maintain, is the case in virtually all drunk arrests, in the majority of arrests involving begging and other nuisance offenses, and in many cases involving acts of violence. When they are asked to explain further such arrests as the one cited earlier involving the man attempting to sell the pocket knife, who was certainly not arrested for his own protection, they cite the consideration that belligerent persons constitute a much greater menace on skid-row than any place else in the city. The reasons for this are twofold. First, many of the inhabitants are old, feeble, and not too smart, all of which makes them relatively defenseless. Second, many of the inhabitants are involved in illegal activities and are known as persons of bad character, which does not make them credible victims or witnesses. Potential predators realize that the resources society has mobilized to minimize the risk of criminal victimization do not protect the predator himself. Thus, reciprocal exploitation constitutes a preferred risk. The high vulnerability of everybody on skid-row is public knowledge and causes every seemingly aggressive act to be seen as a potentially grave risk.

When, in response to all this, patrolmen are confronted with the observation that many minor offense arrests they make do not seem to involve a careful evaluation of facts before acting, they give the following explanations: First, the two reasons of protection and prevention represent a global background, and in individual cases it may sometimes not be possible to produce adequate justification on these grounds. Nor is it thought to be a problem of great moment to estimate precisely whether someone is more likely to come to grief or to cause grief when the objective is to prevent the proliferation of troubles. Second, patrolmen maintain that some of the seemingly spur-of-the-moment decisions are actually made against a background of knowledge of facts that are not readily apparent in the situations. Since experience not only contains this information but also causes it to come to mind, patrolmen claim to have developed a special sensitivity for qualities of appearances that allow an intuitive grasp of probable tendencies. In this context, little things are said to have high informational value and lead to conclusions without the intervention of explicitly reasoned chains of inferences. Third, patrolmen readily admit that they do not adhere to high standards of adequacy of justification. They do not seek to defend the adequacy of their method against some abstract criteria of merit. Instead, when questioned, they assess their methods against the background of a whole system of *ad hoc* decision making, a system that encompasses the courts, correction facilities, the welfare establishment, and medical services. In fact, policemen generally maintain that their own procedures not only measure up to the workings of this system but exceed them in the attitude of carefulness.

In addition to these recognized reasons, there are two additional background factors that play a significant part in decisions to employ coercion. One has to do with the relevance of situational factors, and the other with the evaluation of coercion as relatively insignificant in the lives of the inhabitants.

There is no doubt that the nature of the circumstances often has decisive influence on what will be done. For example, the same patrolman who arrested the man trying to sell his pocket knife was observed dealing with a young couple. Though the officer was clearly angered by what he perceived as insolence and threatened the man with arrest, he merely ordered him and his companion to leave the street. He saw them walking away in a deliberately slow manner and when he noticed them a while later, still standing only a short distance away from the place of encounter, he did not respond to their presence. The difference between the two cases was that in the first there was a crowd of amused bystanders, while the latter case was not witnessed by anyone. In another instance, the patrolman was directed to a hotel and found a father and son fighting about money. The father occupied a room in the hotel and the son occasionally shared his quarters. There were two other men present, and they made it clear that their sympathies were with the older man. The son was whisked off to jail without much study of the relative merits of the conflicting claims. In yet another case, a middle-aged woman was forcefully evacuated from a bar even after the bartender explained that her loud behavior was merely a response to goading by some foul-mouth youth.

In all such circumstances, coercive control is exercised as a means of coming to grips with situational exigencies. Force is used against particular persons but is incidental to the task. An ideal of "economy of intervention" dictates in these and similar cases that the person whose presence is most likely to perpetuate the troublesome development be removed. Moreover, the decision as to who is to be removed is arrived at very quickly. Officers feel considerable pressure to act unhesitatingly, and many give accounts of situations that got out of hand because of desires to handle cases with careful consideration. However, even when there is no apparent risk of rapid proliferation of trouble, the tactic of removing one or two persons is used to control an undesirable situation. Thus, when a patrolman ran into a group of four men sharing a bottle of wine in an alley, he emptied the remaining contents of the bottle into the gutter, arrested one man—who was no more and no less drunk than the others—and let the others disperse in various directions.

The exigential nature of control is also evident in the handling of isolated drunks. Men are arrested because of where they happen to be encountered. In this, it matters not only whether a man is found in a conspicuous place or not, but also how far away he is from his domicile. The further away he is, the less likely it is that he will make it to his room, and the more likely the arrest. Sometimes drunk arrests are made mainly because the police van is available. In one case a patrolman summoned the van to pick up an arrested man. As the van was pulling away from the curb the officer stopped the driver because he sighted another drunk stumbling across the street. The second man protested saying that he "wasn't even half drunk yet." The patrolman's response was "OK, I'll owe you half a drunk." In sum, the basic routine of keeping the peace on skid-row involves a process of matching the resources of control with situational exigencies. The overall objective is to reduce the total amount of risk in the area. In this, practicality plays a considerably more important role than legal norms. Precisely because patrolmen see legal reasons for coercive action much more widely distributed on skid-row than could ever be matched by interventions, they intervene not in the interest of law enforcement but in the interest of producing relative tranquility and order on the street.

Taking the perspective of the victim of coercive measures, one could ask why he, in particular, has to bear the cost of keeping the aggregate of troubles down while others, who are equally or perhaps even more implicated, go scot-free. Patrolmen maintain that the *ad hoc* selection of persons for attention must be viewed in the light of the following consideration: Arresting a person on skid-row on some minor charge may save him and others a lot of trouble, but it does not work any real hardships on the arrested person. It is difficult to overestimate the skid-row patrolman's feeling of certainty that his coercive and disciplinary actions toward the inhabitants have but the most passing significance in their lives. Sending a man to jail on some charge that will hold him for a couple of days is seen as a matter of such slight importance to the affected person that it could hardly give rise to scruples. Thus, every indication that a coercive measure should be taken is accompanied by the realization "I might as well, for all it matters to him." Certain realities of life on skid-row furnish the context for this belief in the attenuated relevance of coercion in the lives of the inhabitants. Foremost among them is that the use of police authority is seen as totally unremarkable by everybody on skid-row. Persons who live or work there are continuously exposed to it and take its existence for granted. Shopkeepers, hotel clerks, and bartenders call patrolmen to rid themselves of unwanted and troublesome patrons. Residents expect patrolmen to arbitrate their quarrels authoritatively. Men who receive orders, whether they obey them or not, treat them as part of life as usual. Moreover, patrolmen find that disciplinary and coercive actions apparently do not affect their friendly relations with the persons against whom these actions are taken. Those who greet and chat with them are the very same men who have been disciplined, arrested, and ordered around in the past, and who expect to be thus treated again in the future. From all this, officers gather that though the people on skid-row seek to evade police authority, they do not really object to it. Indeed, it happens quite frequently that officers encounter men who welcome being arrested and even actively ask for it. Finally, officers point out that sending someone to jail from skid-row does not upset his relatives or his family life, does not cause him to miss work or lose a job, does not lead to his being reproached by friends and associates, does not lead to failure to meet commitments or protect investments, and does not conflict with any but the most passing intentions of the arrested person. Seasoned patrolmen are not oblivious to the irony of the fact that measures intended as mechanisms for distributing deserts can be used freely because these measures are relatively impotent in their effects.

SUMMARY AND CONCLUSIONS

It was the purpose of this paper to render an account of a domain of police practice that does not seem subject to any system of external control. Following the terminology suggested by Michael Banton, this practice was called keeping the peace. The procedures employed in keeping the peace are not determined by legal mandates but are, instead, responses to certain demand conditions. From among several demand conditions, we concentrated on the one produced by the concentration of certain types of persons in districts known as skid-row. Patrolmen maintain that the lives of the inhabitants of the area are lacking in prospective coherence. The consequent reduction in the temporal horizon of predictability constitutes the main problem of keeping the peace on skid-row.

Peace keeping procedure on skid-row consists of three elements. Patrolmen seek to acquire a rich body of concrete knowledge about people by cultivating personal acquaintance with as many residents as possible. They tend to proceed against persons mainly on the basis of perceived risk, rather than on the basis of culpability. And they are more interested in reducing the aggregate total of troubles in the area than in evaluating individual cases according to merit.

There may seem to be a discrepancy between the skid-row patrolman's objective of preventing disorder and his efforts to maintain personal acquaintance with as many persons as possible. But these efforts are principally a tactical device. By knowing someone individually the patrolman reduces ambiguity, extends trust and favors, but does not grant immunity. The informality of interaction on skid-row always contains some indications of the hierarchical superiority of the patrolman and the reality of his potential power lurks in the background of every encounter.

Though our interest was focused initially on those police procedures that did not involve invoking the law, we found that the two cannot be separated. The reason for the connection is not given in the circumstance that the roles of the "law officer" and of the "peace officer" are enacted by the same person and thus are contiguous. According to our observations, patrolmen do not act alternatively as one or the other, with certain actions being determined by the intended objective of keeping the peace and others being determined by the duty to enforce the law. Instead, we have found that *peace keeping occasionally acquires the external aspects of law enforcement.* This makes it specious to inquire whether or not police discretion in invoking the law conforms with the intention of some specific legal formula. The real reason behind an arrest is virtually always the actual state of particular social situations, or of the skid-row area in general.

We have concentrated on those procedures and considerations that skid-row patrolmen regard as necessary, proper, and efficient relative to the circumstances in which they are employed. In this way, we attempted to disclose the conception of the mandate to which the police feel summoned. It was entirely outside the scope of the presentation to review the merits of this conception and of the methods used to meet it. Only insofar as patrolmen themselves recognized instances and patterns of malpractice did we take note of them. Most of the criticism voiced by officers had to do with the use of undue harshness and with the indiscriminate use of arrest powers when these were based on personal feelings rather than the requirements of the situation. According to prevailing opinion, patrolmen guilty of such abuses make life unnecessarily difficult for themselves and for their co-workers. Despite disapproval of harshness, officers tend to be defensive about it. For example, one sergeant who was outspokenly critical of brutality, said that though in general brutal men create more problems than they solve, "they do a good job in some situations for which the better men have no stomach." Moreover, supervisory personnel exhibit a strong reluctance to direct their subordinates in the particulars of their work performance. According to our observations, control is exercised mainly through consultation with superiors, and directives take the form of requests rather than orders. In the background of all this is the belief that patrol work on skid-row requires a great deal of discretionary freedom. In the words of the same sergeant quoted above, "a good man has things worked out in his own ways on his beat and he doesn't need anybody to tell him what to do."

The virtual absence of disciplinary control and the demand for discretionary freedom are related to the idea that patrol work involves "playing by ear." For if it is true that peace keeping cannot be systematically generalized, then, of course, it cannot be organizationally constrained. What the seasoned patrolman means, however, in saying that he "plays by ear" is that he is making his decisions while being attuned to the realities of complex situations about which he has immensely detailed knowledge. This studied aspect of peace keeping generally is not made explicit, nor is the tyro or the outsider made aware of it. Quite to the contrary, the ability to discharge the duties associated with keeping the peace is viewed as a reflection of an innate talent of "getting along with people." Thus, the same demands are made of barely initiated officers as are made of experienced practitioners. Correspondingly, beginners tend to think that they can do as well as their more knowledgeable peers. As this leads to inevitable frustrations, they find themselves in a situation that is conducive to the development of a particular sense of "touchiness." Personal dispositions of individual officers are, of course, of great relevance. But the license of discretionary freedom and the expectation of success under conditions of autonomy, without any indication that the work of the successful craftsman is based on an acquired preparedness for the task, is ready-made for failure and malpractice. Moreover, it leads to slipshod practices of patrol that also infect the standards of the careful craftsman.

The uniformed patrol, and especially the foot patrol, has a low preferential value in the division of labor of police work. This is, in part, at least, due to the belief that "anyone could do it." In fact, this belief is thoroughly mistaken. At present, however, the recognition that the practice requires preparation, and the process of obtaining the preparation itself, is left entirely to the practitioner.

Good People and Dirty Work

by
Everett C. Hughes

> ". . . une secte est le *noyau* et le *levain* de
> toute foule. . . . Etudier la foule c'est juger un
> drame d'après ce qu'on voit sur la scène;
> étudier la secte c'est le juger d'après ce qu'on
> voit dans les coulisses."
> —S. Sighele, *Psychologie des sectes*
> Paris, 1898. Pp. 62, 63, 65.[1]

The National Socialist Government of Germany, with the
arm of its fanatical inner sect, the S.S., commonly known as
the Black Shirts or Elite Guard, perpetrated and boasted of
the most colossal and dramatic piece of social dirty work the
world has ever known. Perhaps there are other claimants to
the title, but they could not match this one's combination of
mass, speed and perverse pride in the deed. Nearly all
peoples have plenty of cruelty and death to account for. How
many Negro Americans have died by the hands of lynching
mobs? How many more from unnecessary disease and lack of
food or of knowledge of nutrition? How many Russians died
to bring about collectivization of land? And who is to blame

Reprinted by permission of the publisher from *Social Problems*, Vol.
10, No. 1, Summer 1962, pp. 3–11. Copyright 1962 by Society for the
Study of Social Problems.
[1]". . . a sect is the nucleus and the yeast of every crowd. . . .
To study a crowd is to judge by what one sees on the stage; to study
the sect is to judge by what one sees backstage." These are among the
many passages underlined by Robert E. Park in his copy, now in my
possession, of Sighele's classic work on political sects. There are a
number of references to this work in the Park and Burgess *Introduction to the Science of Sociology*, Chicago, University of Chicago Press,
1921, 1969. In fact, there is more attention paid to fanatical political
and religious behavior in Park and Burgess than in any later sociological work in this country. Sighele's discussion relates chiefly to the anar-
chist movement of his time. There have been fanatical movements since.
The Secret Army Organization in Algeria is but the latest.

if there be starving millions in some parts of the world while wheat molds in the fields of other parts?

I do not revive the case of the Nazi *Endlösung* (final solution) of the Jewish problem in order to condemn the Germans, or make them look worse than other peoples, but to recall to our attention dangers which lurk in our midst always. Most of what follows was written after my first postwar visit to Germany in 1948. The impressions were vivid. The facts have not diminished and disappeared with time, as did the stories of alleged German atrocities in Belgium in the first World War. The fuller the record, the worse it gets.[2]

Several millions of people were delivered to the concentration camps, operated under the leadership of Heinrich Himmler with the help of Adolf Eichmann. A few hundred thousand survived in some fashion. Still fewer came out sound of mind and body. A pair of examples, well attested, will show the extreme of perverse cruelty reached by the S.S. guards in charge of the camps. Prisoners were ordered to climb trees; guards whipped them to make them climb faster. Once they were out of reach, other prisoners, also urged by the whip, were put to shaking the trees. When the victims fell, they were kicked to see whether they could rise to their feet. Those too badly injured to get up were shot to death, as useless for work. A not inconsiderable number of prisoners were drowned in pits full of human excrement. These examples are so horrible that your minds will run away from them. You will not, as when you read a slightly salacious novel, imagine the rest. I therefore thrust these examples upon you and insist that the people who thought them up could, and did, improvise others like them, and even worse, from day to day over several years. Many of the victims of the camps gave up the ghost (this Biblical phrase is the most apt) from a combination of humiliation, starvation, fatigue

[2] The best source easily available at that time was Eugen Kogon's *Der SS Staat. Das System der Deutschen Konzentrationslager*, Berlin. Verlag der Frankfurter Heft, 1946. Many of my data are from his book. Some years later H. G. Adler, after several years of research, wrote *Theresienstadt, 1941–1945. Das Antlitz einer Zwangsgemeinschaft* (Tübingen, J. C. B. Mohr, 1955), and still later published *Die Verheimlichte Wahrheit, Theresienstädter Dokumente* (Tübingen, J. C. B. Mohr, 1958), a book of documents concerning that camp in which Czech and other Jews were concentrated, demoralized and destroyed. Kogon, a Catholic intellectual, and Adler, a Bohemian Jew, both wrote out of personal experience in the concentration camps. Both considered it their duty to present the phenomenon objectively to the public. None of their statements has ever been challenged.

and physical abuse. In due time, a policy of mass liquidation in the gas chamber was added to individual virtuosity in cruelty.

This program—for it was a program—of cruelty and murder was carried out in the name of racial superiority and racial purity. It was directed mainly, although by no means exclusively, against Jews, Slavs and Gypsies. It was thorough. There are few Jews in the territories which were under the control of the Third German Reich—the two Germanies, Holland, Czechoslovakia, Poland, Austria, Hungary. Many Jewish Frenchmen were destroyed. There were concentration camps even in Tunisia and Algiers under the German occupation.

When, during my 1948 visit to Germany, I became more aware of the reactions of ordinary Germans to the horrors of the concentration camps, I found myself asking not the usual question, "How did racial hatred rise to such a high level?" but this one, "How could such dirty work be done among and, in a sense, *by* the millions of ordinary, civilized German people?" Along with this came related questions. How could these millions of ordinary people live in the midst of such cruelty and murder without a general uprising against it and against the people who did it? How, once freed from the regime that did it, could they be apparently so little concerned about it, so toughly silent about it, not only on talking with outsiders—which is easy to understand—but among themselves? How and where could there be found in a modern civilized country the several hundred thousand men and women capable of such work? How were these people so far released from the inhibitions of civilized life as to be able to imagine, let alone perform, the ferocious, obscene and perverse actions which they did imagine and perform? How could they be kept at such a height of fury through years of having to see daily at close range the human wrecks they made and being often literally spattered with the filth produced and accumulated by their own actions?

You will see that there are here two orders of questions. One set concerns the good people who did not themselves do this work. The other concerns those who did do it. But the two sets are not really separate; for the crucial question concerning the good people is their relation to the people who did the dirty work, with a related one which asks under what circumstances good people let the others get away with such actions.

An easy answer concerning the Germans is that they were not so good after all. We can attribute to them some special inborn or ingrained race consciousness, combined with a penchant for sadistic cruelty and unquestioning acceptance of whatever is done by those who happen to be in authority. Pushed to its extreme, this answer simply makes us, rather than the Germans, the superior race. It is the Nazi tune, put to words of our own.

Now there are deep and stubborn differences between peoples. Their history and culture may make the Germans especially susceptible to the doctrine of their own racial superiority and especially acquiescent to the actions of whoever is in power over them. These are matters deserving of the best study that can be given them. But to say that these things could happen in Germany simply because Germans are different—from us—buttresses their own excuses and lets us off too easily from blame for what happened there and from the question whether it could happen here.

Certainly in their daily practice and expression before the Hitler regime, the Germans showed no more. if as much, hatred of other racial or cultural groups than we did and do. Residential segregation was not marked. Intermarriage was common, and the families of such marriages had an easier social existence than they generally have in America. The racially exclusive club, school and hotel were much less in evidence than here. And I well remember an evening in 1933 when a Montreal business man—a very nice man, too—said in our living room, "Why don't we admit that Hitler is doing to the Jews just what we ought to be doing?" That was not an uncommon sentiment, although it may be said in defense of the people who expressed it, that they probably did not know and would not have believed the full truth about the Nazi program of destroying Jews. The essential underlying sentiments on racial matters in Germany were not different in kind from those prevailing throughout the western, and especially the Anglo-Saxon, countries. But I do not wish to over-emphasize this point. I only want to close one easy way out of serious consideration of the problem of good people and dirty work, by demonstrating that the Germans were and are about as good and about as bad as the rest of us on this matter of racial sentiments and, let us add, their notions of decent human behaviour.

But what was the reaction of ordinary Germans to the persecution of the Jews and to the concentration camp mass torture and murder? A conversation between a German school teacher, a German architect and myself gives the essentials in a vivid form. It was in the studio of the architect, and the occasion was a rather casual visit, in Frankfurt am Main in 1948.

The architect: "I am ashamed for my people whenever I think of it. But we didn't know about it. We only learned about all that later. You must remember the pressure we were under; we had to join the party. We had to keep our mouths shut and do as we were told. It was a terrible pressure. Still, I am ashamed. But you see, we had lost our colonies, and our national honour was hurt. And these Nazis exploited that feeling. And the Jews, they *were* a problem. They came from the east. You should see them in Poland; the lowest class of people, full of lice, dirty and poor, running about in their Ghettos in filthy caftans. They came here, and got rich by unbelievable methods after the first war. They occupied all the good places. Why, they were in the proportion of ten to one in medicine and law and government posts!"

At this point the architect hesitated and looked confused. He continued: "Where was I? It is the poor food. You see what misery we are in here, Herr Professor. It often happens that I forget what I was talking about. Where was I now? I have completely forgotten."

(His confusion was, I believe, not at all feigned. Many Germans said they suffered losses of memory such as this, and laid it to their lack of food.)

I said firmly: "You were talking about loss of national honour and how the Jews had got hold of everything."

The architect: "Oh, yes! That was it! Well, of course that was no way to settle the Jewish problem. But there *was* a problem and it had to be settled someway."

The school teacher: "Of course, they have Palestine now."

I protested that Palestine would hardly hold them.

The architect: "The professor is right. Palestine can't hold all the Jews. And it was a terrible thing to murder people. But we didn't know it at the time. But I am glad I am alive now. It is an interesting time in men's history. You know, when the Americans came it was like a great release. I really want to see a new ideal in Germany. I like the freedom that lets me talk to you like this. But, unfortunately that is not the general opinion. Most of my friends really hang on to the old ideas. They can't see any hope, so they hang on to the old ideas."

This scrap of talk gives. I believe, the essential elements as well as the flavor of the German reaction. It checks well with formal studies which have been made, and it varies only in detail from other conversations which I myself recorded in 1948.

One of the most obvious points in it is unwillingness to think about the dirty work done. In this case—perhaps by chance, perhaps not—the good man suffered an actual lapse of memory in the middle of this statement. This seems a simple point. But the psychiatrists have shown that it is less simple than it looks. They have done a good deal of work on the complicated mechanisms by which the individual mind keeps unpleasant or intolerable knowledge from consciousness, and have shown how great may, in some cases, be the consequent loss of effectiveness of the personality. But we have taken collective unwillingness to know unpleasant facts more or less for granted. That people can and do keep a silence about things whose open discussion would threaten the group's conception of itself, and hence its solidarity, is common knowledge. It is a mechanism that operates in every family and in every group which has a sense of group reputation. To break such a silence is considered an attack against the group; a sort of treason, if it be a member of the group who breaks the silence. This common silence allows group fictions to grow up; such as, that grandpa was less a scoundrel and more romantic than he really was. And I think it demonstrable that it operates especially against any expression, except in ritual, of collective guilt. The remarkable thing in present-day Germany is not that there is so little reference to something about which people do feel deeply guilty, but that it is talked about at all.

In order to understand this phenomenon we would have to find out who talks about the concentration camp atrocities, in what situations, in what mood, and with what stimulus. On these points I know only my own limited experiences. One of the most moving of these was my first post-war meeting with an elderly professor whom I had known before the Nazi time; he is an heroic soul who did not bow his head during the Nazi time and who keeps it erect now. His first words, spoken with tears in his eyes, were:

"How hard it is to believe that men will be as bad as they say they will. Hitler and his people said: 'Heads will roll,' but how many of us—even of his bitterest opponents—could really believe that they would do it."

This man could and did speak, in 1948, not only to the likes of me, but to his students, his colleagues and to the public which read his articles, in the most natural way about the Nazi atrocities whenever there was occasion to do it in the course of his tireless effort to reorganize and to bring new life into the German universities. He had neither the compulsion to speak, so that he might excuse and defend himself, nor a conscious or unconscious need to keep silent. Such people were rare; how many there were in Germany I do not know.

Occasions of another kind in which the silence was broken were those where, in class, public lecture or in informal meetings with students, I myself had talked frankly of race relations in other parts of the world, including the lynchings which sometimes occur in my own country and the terrible cruelty visited upon natives in South Africa. This took off the lid of defensiveness, so that a few people would talk quite easily of what happened under the Nazi regime. More common were situations like that with the architect, where I threw in some remark about the atrocities in response to Germans' complaint that the world is abusing them. In such cases, there was usually an expression of shame, accompanied by a variety of excuses (including that of having been kept in ignorance), and followed by a quick turning away from the subject.

Somewhere in consideration of this problem of discussion versus silence we must ask what the good (that is, ordinary) people in Germany did know about these things. It is clear that the S.S. kept the more gory details of the concentration camps a close secret. Even high officials of the government, the army and the Nazi party itself were in some measure held in ignorance, although of course they kept the camps supplied with victims. The common people of Germany knew that the camps existed; most knew people who had disappeared into them; some saw the victims, walking skeletons in rags, being transported in trucks or trains or being herded on the road from station to camp or to work in fields or factories near the camps. Many knew people who had been released from concentration camps; such released persons kept their counsel on pain of death. But secrecy was cultivated and supported by fear and terror. In the absence of a determined and heroic will to know and publish the truth, and in the absence of all the instruments of opposition, the degree of knowledge was undoubtedly low, in spite of the fact that all knew that something both stupendous and horrible was going on; and in spite of the fact that Hitler's *Mein Kampf* and the utterances of his aides said that no fate was too horrible for the Jews and other wrong-headed or inferior people. This must make us ask under what conditions the will to know and to discuss is strong, determined and effective; this, like most of the important questions I have raised, I leave unanswered except as answers may be contained in the statement of the case.

But to return to our moderately good man, the architect. He insisted over and over again that he did not know, and we may suppose that he knew as much and as little as most Germans. But he also made it quite clear that he wanted something done to the Jews. I have similar statements from people of whom I knew that they had had close Jewish friends before the Nazi time. This raises the whole problem of the extent to which those pariahs who do the dirty work of society are really acting as agents for the rest of us. To talk of this question one must note that, in building up his case, the architect pushed the Jews firmly into an out-group; they were dirty, lousy and unscrupulous (an odd statement from a resident of Frankfurt, the home of old Jewish merchants and intellectual families long identified with those aspects of culture of which Germans are most proud). Having dissociated himself clearly from these people, and having declared them a problem, he apparently was willing to let someone else do to them the dirty work which he himself would not do, and for which he expressed shame. The case is perhaps analogous to our attitude toward those convicted of crime. From time to time, we get wind of cruelty practiced upon the prisoners in penitentiaries or jails; or, it may be, merely a report that they are ill-fed or that hygienic conditions are not good. Perhaps we do not wish that the prisoners should be cruelly treated or badly fed, but our reaction is probably tempered by a notion that they deserve something, because of some dissociation of them from the in-group of good people. If what they get is worse than what we like to think about, it is a little bit too bad. It is a point on which we are ambivalent. Campaigns for reform of prisons are often followed by counter-campaigns against a too high standard of living for prisoners and against having prisons run by softies. Now the people who run prisons are our agents. Just how far they do or could carry out our wishes is hard to say. The minor prison guard, in boastful justification of some of his more questionable practices, says, in effect: "If those reformers and those big shots upstairs had to live with these birds as I do, they would soon change their fool notions about running a prison." He is suggesting that the good people are either naive or hypocritical. Furthermore, he knows quite well that the wishes of his employers, the public, are by no means unmixed. They are quite as likely to put upon him for being too nice as for being too harsh. And if, as sometimes happens, he is a man disposed to cruelty, there may be some justice in his feeling that he is only doing what others would like to do, if they but dared; and what they would do, if they were in his place.

There are plenty of examples in our own world which I might have picked for comparison with the German attitude toward the concentration camps. For instance, a newspaper in Denver made a great scandal out of the allegation that our Japanese compatriots were too well fed in the camps where they were concentrated during the war. I might have mentioned some feature of the sorry history of the people of Japanese background in Canada. Or it might have been lynching, or some aspect of racial discrimination. But I purposely chose prisoners convicted of crime. For convicts are formally set aside for special handling. They constitute an out-group in all countries. This brings the issue clearly before us, since few people cherish the illusion that the problem of treating criminals can be settled by propaganda designed to prove that there aren't any criminals. Almost everyone agrees that something has to be done about them. The question concerns what is done, who does it, and the nature of the mandate given by the rest of us to those who do it. Perhaps we give them an unconscious mandate to go beyond anything we ourselves would care to do or even to acknowledge. I venture to suggest that the higher and more expert functionaries who act in our behalf represent something of a distillation of what we may consider our public wishes, while some of the others show a sort of concentrate of those impulses of which we are or wish to be less aware.

Now the choice of convicted prisoners brings up another crucial point in inter-group relations. All societies of any great size have in-groups and out-groups; in fact, one of the best ways of describing a society is to consider it a network of smaller and larger in-groups and out-groups. And an in-group is one only because there are out-groups. When I refer to *my* children I obviously imply that they are closer to me than other people's children and that I will make greater efforts to buy oranges and cod-liver oil for them than for others' children. In fact, it may mean that I will give them cod-liver oil if I have to choke them to get it down. We do our own dirty work on those closest to us. The very injunction that love my neighbor as myself starts with me; if I don't love myself and my nearest, the phrase has a very sour meaning.

Each of us is a center of a network of in- and out-groups. Now the distinctions between *in* and *out* may be drawn in various ways, and nothing is more important for both the student of society and the educator than to discover how these lines are made and how they may be redrawn in more just and sensible ways. But to believe that we can do away with the distinction between *in* and *out*, *us* and *them* in social life is complete nonsense. On the positive side, we generally feel a greater obligation to in-groups; hence less obligation to out-groups; and in the case of such groups as convicted criminals, the out-group is definitely given over to the hands of our agents for punishment. That is the extreme case. But there are other out-groups toward which we may have aggressive feelings and dislike, although we give no formal mandate to anyone to deal with them on our behalf, and although we profess to believe that they should not suffer restrictions or disadvantages. The greater their social distance from us, the more we leave in the hands of others a sort of mandate by default to deal with them on our behalf. Whatever effort we put on reconstructing the lines which divide in and out-groups, there remains the eternal problem of our treatment, direct or delegated, of whatever groups are considered somewhat outside. And here it is that the whole matter of our professed and possible deeper unprofessed wishes comes up for consideration; and the related problem of what we know, can know and want to know about it. In Germany, the agents got out of hand and created such terror that it was best not to know. It is also clear that it was and is easier to the conscience of many Germans not to know. It is, finally, not unjust to say that the agents were at least working in the direction of the wishes of many people, although they may have gone beyond the wishes of most. The same questions can be asked about our own society, and with reference not only to prisoners but also to many other groups upon whom there is no legal or moral stigma. Again I have not the answers. I leave you to search for them.

In considering the question of dirty work we have eventually to think about the people who do it. In Germany, these were the members of the S.S. and of that inner group of the S.S. who operated the concentration camps. Many reports have been made on the social backgrounds and the personalities of these cruel fanatics. Those who have studied them say that a large proportion were *gescheiterte Existenzen,* men or women with a history of failure, of poor adaptation to the demands of work and of the classes of society in which they had been bred. Germany between wars had large numbers of such people. Their adherence to a movement which proclaimed a doctrine of hatred was natural enough. The movement offered something more. It created an inner group which was to be superior to all others, even Germans, in their emancipation from the usual bourgeois morality; people above and beyond the ordinary morality. I dwell on this, not as a doctrine, but as an organizational device. For, as Eugen Kogon, author of the most penetrating analysis of the S.S. and their camps, has said, the Nazis came to power by creating a state within a state; a body with its own counter-morality and its own counter-law, its courts and its own execution of sentence upon those who did not live up to its orders and standards. Even as a movement it had inner circles within inner circles; each sworn to secrecy as against the next outer one. The struggle between these inner circles continued after Hitler came to power; Himmler eventually won the day. His S.S. became a state within the Nazi state, just as the Nazi movement had become a state within the Weimar state. One is reminded of the oft quoted but neglected statement of Sighele: "At the center of a crowd look for the sect." He referred, of course, to the political sect; the fanatical inner group of a movement seeking power by revolutionary methods. Once the Nazis were in power, this inner sect, while becoming now the recognized agent of the state and, hence, of the masses of the people, could at the same time dissociate itself more completely from them in action, because of the very fact of having a mandate. It was now beyond all danger of interference and investigation. For it had the instruments of interference and investigation in its own hands. These are also the instruments of secrecy. So the S.S.

could and did build up a powerful system in which they had the resources of the state and of the economy of Germany and the conquered countries from which to steal all that was needed to carry out their orgy of cruelty luxuriously as well as with impunity.

Now let us ask, concerning the dirty workers, questions similar to those concerning the good people. Is there a supply of candidates for such work in other societies? It would be easy to say that only Germany could produce such a crop. The question is answered by being put. The problem of people who have run aground (*gescheiterte Existenzen*) is one of the most serious in our modern societies. Any psychiatrist will, I believe, testify that we have a sufficient pool or fund of personalities warped toward perverse punishment and cruelty to do any amount of dirty work that the good people may be inclined to countenance. It would not take a very great turn of events to increase the number of such people, and to bring their discontents to the surface. This is not to suggest that every movement based on discontent with the present state of things will be led by such people. That is obviously untrue; and I emphasize the point lest my remarks give comfort to those who would damn all who express militant discontent. But I think study of militant social movements does show that these warped people seek a place in them. Specifically, they are likely to become the plotting, secret police of the group. It is one of the problems of militant social movements to keep such people out. It is of course easier to do this if the spirit of the movement is positive, its conception of humanity high and inclusive, and its aims sound. This was not the case of the Nazi movement. As Kogan puts it: "The SS were but the arch-type of the Nazis in general."[3] But such people are sometimes attracted for want of something better, to movements whose aims are contrary to the spirit of cruelty and punishment. I would suggest that all of us look well at the leadership and entourage of movements to which we attach ourselves for signs of a negativistic, punishing attitude. For once such a spirit develops in a movement, punishment of the nearest and easiest victim is likely to become more attractive than striving for the essential goals. And, if the Nazi movement teaches us anything at all, it is that if any shadow of a mandate be given to such people, they will—having compromised us—make it larger and larger. The

[3]*Ibid.*, p. 316.

processes by which they do so are the development of the power and inward discipline of their own group, a progressive dissociation of themselves from the rules of human decency prevalent in their culture, and an ever-growing contempt for the welfare of the masses of people.

The power and inward discipline of the S.S. became such that those who once became members could get out only by death; by suicide, murder or mental breakdown. Orders from the central offices of the S.S. were couched in equivocal terms as a hedge against a possible day of judgment. When it became clear that such a day of judgment would come, the hedging and intrigue became greater; the urge to murder also became greater, because every prisoner became a potential witness.

Again we are dealing with a phenomenon common in all societies. Almost every group which has a specialized social function to perform is in some measure a secret society, with a body of rules developed and enforced by the members and with some power to save its members from outside punishment. And here is one of the pardoxes of social order. A society without smaller, rule-making and disciplining powers would be no society at all. There would be nothing but law and police; and this is what the Nazis strove for, at the expense of family, church, professional groups, parties and other such nuclei of spontaneous control. But apparently the only way to do this, for good as well as for evil ends, is to give power into the hands of some fanatical small group which will have a far greater power of self-discipline and a far greater immunity to outside control than the traditional groups. The problem is, then, not of trying to get rid of all the self disciplining, protecting groups within society, but one of keeping them integrated with one another and as sensitive as can be to a public opinion which transcends them all. It is a matter of checks and balances, of what we might call the social and moral constitution of society.

Those who are especially devoted to efforts to eradicate from good people, as individuals, all those sentiments which seem to bring about the great and small dirty work of the world, may think that my remarks are something of an attack on their methods. They are right to this extent; that I am insisting that we give a share of our effort to the social mechanisms involved as well as to the individual and those of his sentiments which concern people of other kinds.

VIII.

SOCIOLOGICAL
WHIMSY

IN CONSONANCE WITH the title of this book, and in order to show through example that sociologists are not necessarily humorless creatures, this collection closes with two instances of sociological whimsy.

At the height of the Cold War, the Harvard sociologist David Riesman wrote a sociological fantasy called "The Nylon War." The well-known sociological notion of relative deprivation, which holds that people are stirred into protest and feel alienated not so much by their level of absolute deprivation but in relation to the standards of others with whom they compare themselves, lies at the heart of this paper. If this is indeed the case, Riesman argued, then efforts to subvert the Russian system of government might be powerfully enhanced were we to show to the Russian population at large how superior the living standards of Americans are compared to their own. What better way to do this, he argued, tongue in cheek, than to send bombers over Russia which would drop not atom bombs, but Sears Roebuck catalogs, nylon stockings, and other consumer goods unknown to the Russians. This would result in massive defections among large sectors of the Russian population. Who knows, perhaps, it would topple the Russian government, or at least force it to make major concessions to the oppressed population.

Warren Hagstrom's "What Is the Meaning of Santa Claus?" is a deliberate spoof of the thoughtways of the sociological community. With various approaches and methods of sociology passing in review, the author suggests how each would be most likely to tackle the problems of establishing the meaning of Santa Claus. Depicting scholarly battles between Clauseologists and Positivists, between historical and behavioral approaches, between Marxists and Durkheimians, Hagstrom clearly has a very good time, and so, I hope, will his readers.

The Nylon War
by
David Riesman

Today—August 1, 1951—the Nylon War enters upon the third month since the United States began all-out bombing of the Soviet Union with consumers' goods, and it seems time to take a retrospective look. Behind the initial raid of June 1 were years of secret and complex preparations, and an idea of disarming simplicity: that if allowed to sample the riches of America, the Russian people would not long tolerate masters who gave them tanks and spies instead of vacuum cleaners and beauty parlors. The Russian rulers would thereupon be forced to turn out consumers' goods, or face mass discontent on an increasing scale.

The Nylon War was conceived by an army colonel—we shall call him "Y"—whose name cannot yet be revealed. Working with secret funds which the Central Intelligence Agency had found itself unable to spend, Y organized shortly after World War II the so-called "Bar Harbor Project," the nucleus of which, some five years later, became "Operation Abundance," or, as the press soon dubbed it, the "Nylon War." After experiments with rockets and balloons, it was concluded that only cargo planes—navigating, it was hoped, above the range of Russian radar—could successfully deliver the many billion dollars' worth of consumer goods it was planned to send. Nevertheless, when Y and his group first broached their plans to a few selected congressional leaders in the winter of 1948 they were dismissed as hopelessly academic. America had neither the goods nor the planes nor the politics to begin such an undertaking. But in the fall of 1950, with the country bogged down in a seemingly endless small-scale war in Korea, Y's hopes revived. For one thing, the cargo planes needed for the job were beginning to become available.

Reprinted with permission of Macmillan Publishing Co., Inc., from *Individualism Reconsidered* by David Riesman. Copyright 1954 by The Free Press, a Corporation.

Moreover, a certain amount of overordering by the armed services, panicky over Korea, had created a stockpile of consumer goods. More important, the Administration, having locked up all known and many suspected Communists in one of the old camps for Japanese aliens, had still not convinced the country that it was sufficiently anti-Soviet, though at the same time many Americans wanted peace but did not dare admit it. A plan which, in fact and in presentation, took attention away from alleged Far Eastern bungling, and which was both violently anti-Soviet and pro-peace, appeared to offer the possibility of restoring the Administration's tottering position in the country.

This is not the place to recount the political maneuverings that preceded Truman's success in securing a two-billion-dollar initial appropriation from Congress, nor the Potomac maneuverings that led to the recruitment of top-flight production and merchandising talent from civilian life. Our story begins with Truman going before Congress to secure authority to "bring the benefits of American technology to less fortunate nations" by round-the-clock bombing, the day after the news of the first raids hit the American public.

The planners of the Bar Harbor Project had staked American prestige, their professional futures, and the lives of six thousand airmen on the belief that the Soviets would not know of these first flights nor meet them with armed resistance. When the opening missions were accomplished without incident, permitting Truman to make his appeal, Washington was immensely relieved; but when the second wave of planes met with no resistance either, Washington was baffled. It was at first assumed that the Soviet radar network had again simply failed to spot the high-flying planes—cruising at 48,000 feet and self-protected from radar by some still presumably secret device. We now know that what actually happened was a division of opinion in the Kremlin—we can piece the story together from intelligence reports and from clues in *Pravda*. A faction, led by foreign-trade chief Mikoyan, maintained that the scheme was a huge hoax, designed to stampede Russia into a crusade against a fairy tale—and so to make her the laughing stock of the world. He counseled, wait and see. And, indeed, it *was* a fairy tale for secret-police boss Beria, who argued that the raids had never taken place, but that reports of them had been faked by some Social Democratic East Germans who had somehow gotten access to the communications networks. When this idea was exploded, Beria counseled shooting the planes down, on the ground that they were simply a screen spying out plants for an atomic attack. Stalin himself believed with repentant economist Varga that American capitalism had reached so critical a point that only through forcible gifts overseas could the Wall Street ruling clique hope to maintain its profits and dominance. Coupled with these divisions of opinion, which stalemated action, was the fear in some quarters that America might welcome attacks on its errand-of-mercy planes as a pretext for the war of extermination openly preached by some only mildly rebuked American leaders.

At any rate, the confusion in the Politburo was more than mirrored by the confusion in the target cities caused by the baptismal raids. Over 600 C-54s streamed high over Rostov, and another 200 over Valdivostok, dropped their cargoes, and headed back to their bases in the Middle East and Japan. By today's standard these initial forays were small-scale—200,-000 pairs of nylon hose, 4,000,000 packs of cigarettes, 35,000 Toni wave kits, 20,000 yo-yos, 10,000 wrist watches, and a number of odds and ends from PX overstock. Yet this was more than enough to provoke frenzied rioting as the inhabitants scrambled for a share. Within a few hours after the first parcels had fallen, the roads into the target cities were jammed. Roadblocks had to be thrown up around the cities, and communications with the outside were severed. The fast-spreading rumors of largesse from above were branded "criminally insane," and their source traced to machinations of the recently purged "homeless cosmopolitan Simeon Osnavitch (Rosenblum)."

But the propaganda of the deed proved stronger than the propaganda of the word. As Odessa, Yakutsk, Smolensk, and other cities became targets of aggressive generosity, as Soviet housewives saw with their own eyes American stoves, refrigerators, clothing, and toys, the Kremlin was forced to change its line and, ignoring earlier denials, to give the raids full but negative publicity. David Zaslavsky's article in the June 10 *Izvestia* heralded the new approach. Entitled "The Mad Dogs of Imperialism Foam at the Mouth," he saw the airlift as harbinger of America's economic collapse. "Unable because of the valiant resistance of the peace-loving democracies to conquer foreign markets, America's Fascist plutocracy is now reduced to giving away goods. . . ." Taking another line, *Red Star* argued that to accept American consumer goods would make stalwart Russians as decadent as rich New Yorkers.

However, the Russian poeple who could get access, either directly or through the black market that soon arose, to American goods seemed not to fear decadence. Again, there was a change of line. Falling back on a trick learned during Lend-Lease, it was claimed that the goods were Russian-made, and *Pravda* on June 14 stated that the Toni wave kit had been invented by Pavlov before World War I. However, Colonel Y's staff had anticipated this altogether routine reaction. On June 17, the target cities of that day—Kiev, Stalingrad, Magnitogorsk—received their wares wrapped in large cartoons of Stalin bending over, in a somewhat undignified pose, to pick up a dropped Ansco camera. This forced still another switch of line. On June 20, Beria went on the air to announce that the Americans were sending over goods poisoned by atomic radiation, and all papers and broadcasts caried scare stories about people who had died from using Revlon or Schick shavers. And indeed booby traps (planted by the MVD) succeeded in killing a number of overeager citizens. For a while, this permitted specially recruited Party members to gather up the goods and take them to headquarters for alleged deradiation.

But here something unexpected occurred. We know from a few people who managed to escape to the West that a number of Party elements themselves became disaffected. Asked to turn in all American goods, they held on to some possessions secretly—there was a brisk underground trade in fake Russian labels. Sometimes wives, having gotten used to the comforts of Tampax and other disappearing items, would hide them from their more ascetic husbands; children of Party members cached pogo sticks and even tricycles. Thus it came about that when Party members were ordered to join "decontamination" squads the depots were re-entered at night and portable items taken. By the beginning of July, all attempts to deceive the people had only made matters worse; things were getting out of hand.

Faring badly in the "war," the Kremlin turned to diplomacy. On July 5, at Lake Success, Malik described the airlift as "an outrage remindful of Hitlerite aggression" and, invoking Article 39 of the UN Charter, he called on the Security Council to halt the "shameful depredations of the American warmongers." Austin replied that "these gifts are no more or less than a new-fashioned application of ancient principles," and the Russian resolution was defeated, 9–2. The next step occurred in Washington, when Ambassador Panyushkin handed Secretary Acheson a sharply worded note warning that "should these present outrages continue, the U.S.S.R. will have no recourse but to reply in kind."

Seattle was the first American city to learn the meaning of the Soviet warnings as on July 15, a hundred Russian heavy bombers (presumably from bases in the Kuriles) left behind them 15,000 tins of caviar, 500 fur coats, and 80,000 copies of Stalin's speeches on the minorities question. When the Russian planes came, followed in by American jets, many were apprehensive, but as the counterattack had been anticipated it proved possible to prevent incidents in the air and panic on the ground. Since then, Butte, Minneapolis, Buffalo, and Moscow, Idaho, have been added to the list of America's front-line cities. But in quantity and quality the counteroffensive has been unimpressive. Searing vodka, badly styled mink coats (the only really selling item), undependable cigarette lighters—these betray a sad lack of know-how in production and merchandising. In an editorial, "Worse than Lend-Lease," the New York *Daily News* has charged that the Nylon War gives the Soviets free lessons in the secrets of America's success, but truly conservative papers like the *Herald-Tribune* see the comparative showing of Americans and Russians as a world demonstration of the superiority of free enterprise.

It is clear, at any rate, that free enterprise has not suffered much of a jolt—nor, indeed, has the mounting inflation been much reduced—by the Russian campaign. To be sure, the massive air-borne shipments of caviar have made luxury grocers fear inventory losses, and Portugal, heavily dependent on the American anchovy market, has been worried. But these pinpricks are nothing to what is now becoming evident on the Russian side—namely the imminent collapse of the economy. For the homeland of centralized economic planning is experiencing its own form of want in the midst of plenty. Soviet consumers, given a free choice between shoddy domestic merchandise and air-lift items, want nothing to do with the former and in a score of fields Russian goods go unwanted as the potential buyer dreams of soon owning an American version. Soviet housewives, eager to keep up with American-supplied "Joneses," pester their local stores, often to the point of creating local shortages—indeed, the American refrigerators have created demands, not only for electricity, but also for many foods which can now be stored (and hoarded).

Much of this disruption is the result of careful planning by the Bar Harbor Project's Division of Economic Dislocation. The Division, for example, early began studies of Russian power distribution, and saw to the landing of 60-cycle radios, shavers, toasters, milking machines, in 60-cycle areas; 25-cycle appliances in 25-cycle areas, and so on, especially with an eye to areas of power shortage or competition with critical industries. In co-operation with GE, methods were worked out by which the Russian donees could plug their appliances, with appropriate transformers, directly into high-voltage or street power lines; thus simply shutting off house current could not save the Russian utilities from overload. Similarly, drawing on the American monopolistic practice of tie-in sales, goods were dropped whose use demanded other items in short supply—oil ranges, for instance, were dropped throughout the Baku fields. Of course, mistakes were made, and in one or two cases bottlenecks in the Russian economy were relieved, as when some containers were salvaged to repair a tin shortage of which the planners had not been advised.

But it is not only on the production end that the raids have been disruptive. Last Friday's raid on Moscow—when 22,000 tons of goods were dropped—may be taken as an illustration. For the first time General Vandenberg's airmen tackled—and successfully solved—the knotty engineering problem of dropping jeeps (complete with 150 gallons of gasoline and directions in simple Russian). So skillfully was the job done that half the three hundred vehicles parachuted down landed directly on the Kremlin's doorstep—in the center of Red Square. The raid was given wide advance publicity through the Voice and leaflets and when the great day came Moscow's factories were deserted as people fought for roof-top perches; in addition, an estimated 250,000 collective farmers swarmed into the city. In fact, as people drift from place to place hoping that their ship may fly in, the phrase "rootless cosmopolite" at last assumes real meaning. Economists, talking learnedly of "multipliers," calculate that Russian output is dropping 3 per cent a month.

The Kremlin has reacted in the only way it knows, by a series of purges. Serge Churnik, erstwhile head of the cigarette trust, is on trial for "deliberate wrecking and economic treason." Bureaucrats live in terror lest their region or their industry be next disrupted by the American bombardment, and they waiver between inactivity and frantic Stakhanovite shows of activity. These human tragedies testify to the growing fear in the Politburo concerning the long-run consequences of the American offensive. The tangible proofs of American prosperity, ingenuity, and generosity can no longer be gainsaid; and the new official line that Wall Street is bleeding America white in order to create scarcity and raise prices at home, while "believed," has little impact against the ever mounting volume, and fascinating variety, of goods and rumors of goods. Can the capitalistic gluttons of privilege be such bad fellows if we, the Russians, are aided by them to enjoy luxuries previously reserved for the dachas of novelists and plant managers? In an article in *New Statesman and Nation*, Geoffrey Gorer has recently contended that the airlift serves to revive primitive Russian "orality," and that the image of America can no longer be that of a leering Uncle Sam or top-hatted banker but must soon become amiably matronly. It is thoughts along this line that most worry the Politburo although, of course, the MVD sees to it that only a tiny fraction of the mounting skepticism expresses itself openly or even in whispered jokes. But what is the MVD to do about a resolution of the All-Workers Congress of Tiflis that "Marxist-Leninist-Stalinist democracy demands that party cadres install officials who can cope with the mounting crisis"?

Translated into plain talk, this means that the Russian people, without saying so in as many words, are now putting a price on their collaboration with the regime. The price—"goods instead of guns." For Russia's industrial plant, harassed by the rapidly growing impact of Operation Abundance, cannot supply both, let alone carry on the counteroffensive against America. Intelligence reports speak of scheduled production cutbacks varying from 25 per cent on tanks to 75 per cent on artillery; it is symptomatic that washing machines, designed to compete with the American Bendixes which are being dropped in ever increasing numbers, will soon start rolling off the assembly lines of the great Red October Tank Works—after its former manager had been shot for asserting that conversion to peacetime production could not be achieved in less than two years.

Meanwhile, diplomatic moves are under way—so, at least, the Alsop brothers report—to liquidate the Nylon War. It is obvious why the Russian leaders are prepared to make very considerable concessions in the satellite countries, in China, and in Indo-China in order to regain the strategic initiative in their domestic affairs. But on the American side the willingness of many to listen to Russian overtures is based on the success, rather than the failure, of the campaign. One sees a repetition of 1940 as the Washington *Times-Herald* and the *Daily Compass* join hands in attacking Operation Abundance, the former calling it "an international WPA," the latter arguing "you can't fight ideas with goods." Addressing the Stanford Alumni Club of Los Angeles, Herbert Hoover spoke for millions in observing that the monthly cost of the airlift has already exceeded the entire federal budget for the year 1839. Still another tack has been taken by senators who want the airlift to continue, but with different targets; some, insisting that charity begins at home, have wanted free goods landed on their districts; others have supported the claims of Japan, the Philippines, or Franco. Still others fear that many of the air-lift items could be reconverted in some way for use by the Russian war machine; they are especially opposed to the jeep delivery program, despite reports it is wreaking havoc with the Russian road system as well as with the gasoline supply. And the House Committee on Un-American Activities has charged that trade secrets are being delivered to Russian spies by Red homosexual officials and professors disguised as plane pilots.

These are the obvious enemies, and against them stand some obvious friends of the Nylon War. Both AFL and CIO, now in their eighth round of wage increases, vigorously support the program, though it is rumored that the Railroad Brotherhoods have done so only in return for a fact-finding board's support of a fourteen-hour week. Farmers have become reconciled by the promise that bulk agricultural products will soon move over the aerial transmission belt—in part to encourage the wanderings of Russian farmers. The business community is divided, with the CED, Juan Trippe, and Baruch leading the supporters of the airlift.[1] But it

---

[1] It goes without saying that there are many fights within pressure groups as to *what* the airlift shall carry—and ideological considerations are not confined to the Soviet side. Thus, the Committee against Juvenile Delinquency has registered strong protests against sending comic books. More serious issues revolve around the Planned Parenthood League's campaign to get contraceptives included in the air-lift items. In addition to humanitarian arguments, the claim is made that this will reverse the demographic trend now so favorable to Russia; the League's slogan is "Give them the tools and they will do the job."

would be a mistake to assume that support of Operation Abundance springs only from hopes of material gain. The renewed fight against oppression and want, the excitement of following the raids in maps and betting pools, the ridiculousness of the Russian response—all these things have made many millions of Americans less anxious than they have been since the days in October 1950 when it seemed as if the Korean War would be quickly concluded.

Indeed, it is just this loss of tension which has given rise to much of the covert opposition to the Nylon War, as distinguished from the overt opposition already discussed. On the one hand, certain leaders are frightened that the Russian dictatorship may indeed be overthrown—as Colonel Y in his more optimistic moments had ventured to hope. This is thought to raise the possibility of all sorts of chaotic movements developing in Central and Eastern Europe, and even further west—Franco, for instance, feels threatened at the loss of his "enemy," and has offered to act as mediator in the Nylon War. On the other hand, it has become increasingly difficult for American politicians to frighten the American public about Russia: the once-feared monolith now appears as almost a joke, with its crude poster-and-caviar reprisals, its riots over stockings, soap, Ronsons, and other gadgets which Americans regard in matter-of-fact fashion. The sharp drop in war sentiment in the United States has resulted in psychological and even actual unemployment for a number of people.

What do the coming months hold? It is significant that this depends almost entirely on the outcome of the American domestic struggle: the Nylon War has altered the whole power-complex which, as the Korean War dragged on, still heavily favored Russia. It is now Russia, not America, whose resources are overcommitted, whose alliances are overstrained. In fact, Mao's visit to Moscow at the end of July seems to have been attended with apprehension lest he ask America to cut Red China in on Operation Abundance—at a price, of course. The possibility that this may redound to the credit of the Truman Administration in the 1952 campaign is not the least of the nightmares haunting many Americans, and at this writing it is impossible to predict whether the opponents of the program will win out.

Meanwhile, Operation Abundance marches on, solving

Walter Lippmann predicts a Rome-Moscow axis if the League should win out.

technical problems of incredible complexity. The latest move is the perfection of an ordering system whereby Russians can "vote" for the commodities they most want, according to a point system, by the use of radio-sending equipment, battery-run, with which we have provided them. The commodities available will be described over the Voice of America—now for the first time having something to "sell"—by Sears Roebuck-type catalogues, and by dropped samples in the case of soft goods. The method making it impossible for the Russian government effectively to jam this two-way communication of distributor and consumer is still the great secret of the Nylon War.

What Is the Meaning of Santa Claus?

by
Warren O. Hagstrom

What is the meaning of Santa Claus? A simple and naïve answer to this question would be something like the following: "Santa Claus is a fat man with a white beard in a red suit who brings gifts at Christmas and rides in a sleigh drawn by reindeer and—who either exists or doesn't exist." This is the kind of answer a child might give. More sophisticated children (among whom I include many of my readers) might answer the question of the meaning of Santa Claus either in terms of *Clauseology* or *Positivism*.

CLAUSEOLOGY AND POSITIVISM

The Clauseologist position is that Santa Claus exists but that his essential nature ("meaning") cannot be empirically ascertained. The empirical phenomena associated with Santa are likely to be illusory and deceptive. It is instead necessary to rely on nonempirical methods of investigation, of which there are two types: inner experience and revealed sources. I cannot report here my inner experiences of Santa Claus, since it has been so long since I've had any *genuine* experiences of this type. In any case, sorting the genuine from the spurious Claus-experiences is one of the major problems of the Clauseologist. Another major problem is collecting authentic revealed sources and reconciling apparent inconsistencies among them. Thus, works like Clement C. Moore's "A Night Before Christmas" can certainly be accepted as part of the revealed canon; and I believe that Jean de Brunhof's *Babar and*

Reprinted from *The American Sociologist*, Vol. 1, 1966, pp. 248–254, with permission of the American Sociological Association and the author.

Father Christmas can likewise be accepted as authentic. The latter source, however, suggests that Santa is known as Father Christmas (Père Noël), that he lives in Prjmneswe, Bohemia, and that he uses a flying machine instead of a reindeer-drawn sleigh. Such minor inconsistencies with American stories do not discourage the Clauseologist, who is able to detect temporal change, symbolism, and consistency among apparent inconsistencies. The Clauseologist, however, will reject from his revealed canon works like "Yes, Virginia, there is a Santa Claus," by Francis Church. Such works of higher criticism, by giving metaphorical interpretations to Santa, concede the essential elements of belief.

The Positivist (19th century version) accept the Clauseologist's definition of Santa Claus but rejects the use of nonempirical methods. Belief in Santa Claus is defined as erroneous; and the problem of the Positivist is to discover how such erroneous beliefs arise. The Positivist, arguing that all beliefs arise by inference from experiences, finds the meaning of Santa in false inferences from actual experiences. An Animist, following E. B. Tylor and Herbert Spencer, might say that the child, confronted with the experience of receiving gifts from anonymous donors, and given many images and even dreams of Santa, makes the logical, if false, inference that Santa brings these gifts.[1] Such inferential processes undoubtedly exist. One boy, at age 4, lived in a family in which gifts were opened Christmas Eve after lying under the Christmas tree for some days. He inferred that Santa brings the gifts to the department stores and can be seen in such places; parents then pick up gifts there in the stores. He was unable to convince friends of this interpretation, and was somewhat disturbed by his failure to do so; but he would not accept cultural relativism as an explanation of the differences.

The Naturism of Max Müller is a variety of Positivism which finds the origin of figures like Santa in natural phenomena. Children, like primitive men, tend to personalize the abstract forces of nature.[2] Santa, or Father Frost as he is known in the Soviet Union, is then likely to be a representative of the benevolent aspects of midwinter—the Winter Sol-

[1] Note the sympathetic reference to Tylor's theories in Renzo Sereno, "Some Observations on the Santa Claus Custom," *Psychiatry,* XIV (1951), 387–96, at 396.

[2] The best evidence on this is from Jean Piaget. See his *The Language and Thought of the Child* (London: Routledge & Kegan Paul, Ltd., 1926).

stice heralding the return of the sun. While small children may find it difficult to conceptualize the winter solstice, they find it easy to conceptualize Santa Claus. (Ask any child questions about the two phenomena.)

The social scientist can accept neither Clauseology nor Positivism. Since he relies on empirical evidence, he cannot accept the results of Clauseological investigations—nor can he reject them, for that matter. The scientific reasons for rejecting the Positivist interpretation are more complex and can only be hinted at here.[3] Three reasons may be mentioned. First, the Positivist theories do not account for the "sacred" aspects of Santa Claus; as we shall see below, Santa may be profaned, and Positivist theories cannot account for this. Second, if Santa is an expression of natural forces, "it is hard to see how it has maintained itself, for it expresses them in an erroneous manner"[4]—as any eight-year-old knows. Third, it seems unlikely that beliefs in Santa and similar figures, of immense importance in history and in family relations, can be merely illusory; the persistence of the beliefs implies a social meaning and a social function.

HISTORICAL APPROACHES

The naïve historian finds the meaning of anything in its origins: The meaning of the oak is to be found in the acorn. The more sophisticated historian looks for the unique characteristics of anything in its origins and history; while the meaning of oaks in general cannot be interpreted in terms of acorns in general, the characteristics of *this* oak is to be found in its acorn, and subsequent experiences. Since the historian does not present empirical generalizations (or does so only implicitly and in a simpleminded fashion), the historical meaning of Santa is an incomplete meaning from the point of view of the scientist. Nevertheless, the work of the historian can suggest and delimit problems for the scientist and provide evidence for general hypotheses.

Historians find, in brief, that Santa Claus is a thoroughly

[3]See Emile Durkheim, *The Elementary Forms of the Religious Life*, trans. J. W. Swain (London: George Allen & Unwin, 1915), Chapters II and III; and Talcott Parsons, *The Structure of Social Action* (New York: The Free Press, 1937), the argument summarized on pp. 728 ff.
[4]Durkheim, *op. cit.*, p. vi.

American figure who appears for the first time in the early 19th century. The alleged descent from Saint Nicholas, Bishop of Myra and patron saint of children (as well as maidens, lovers, merchants, sailors, robbers, and scholars) is mythical.[5] Saint Nicholas does play a role similar to Santa Claus in the Netherlands, but he neither looks like Santa nor acts like him—he is a much more punitive figure and appears on December 6th—and there is no direct historical connection between him and Santa. The early Dutch settlers of America were Calvinists and hagiophobic in the extreme.[6] The attribution of Santa to the Dutch was made by Clement Moore, who wrote " 'Twas the Night Before Christmas" in 1822, and by other early 19th century American writers who created a mythical and sentimental picture of Dutch life in America a century earlier.[7] Washington Irving is perhaps the best known member of this group. Our current picture of Santa was not provided until 1863, when the political cartoonist Thomas Nast published his first drawing of Santa.

This American Santa Claus is quite different not only from Saint Nicholas but from the mythical Christmas or midwinter figure found in other cultures. He is not involved in ceremonies of role reversal, like the Saturnalia celebrated by the ancient Romans in late December—Santa is no relative of the Lord of Misrule, or the Boy Bishop of the Western Middle

[5]A few items about Saint Nicholas may be of interest, however. He is alleged to have played an important role in establishing Trinitarian doctrine at the Council of Nicaea, where he died of a stroke after vanquishing his opponents in the midst of debate (A.D. 345?). See John Shlien, "Santa Claus: The Myth in America," *Human Development Bulletin*, No. 6, Spring, 1953, Committee on Human Development (Chicago: University of Chicago), 27–32. Christmas itself became established as an important holiday only at this time; previously Epiphany, the commemoration of Jesus's baptism or enlightenment, had been the more important holiday. Christmas, by emphasizing the divinity of Jesus from conception and birth and by de-emphasizing any later enlightenment, is a kind of Trinitarian and anti-Unitarian holiday. Ludwig Jekels has suggested that Christmas and Trinitarianism may represent a resoluton of the Oedipus problem: The Trinitarians elevated the Son to a level with the Father. Why did they do this in the fourth century A.D.? Because, says Jekels, on the one hand they were still a rebellious minority, resentful of the Emperor father figure, and, on the other, they felt powerful enough to partly displace authority figures. "On the Psychology of the Festival of Christmas," *International Journal of Psychoanalysis*, XVII (1936), 57–72.

[6]Eric R. Wolf, "Santa Claus: Notes on a Collective Representation," in *Process and Pattern in Culture*, ed. Robert A. Manners (Chicago: Aldine Publishing Company, 1964), pp. 147–55, at pp. 147 ff.

[7]*Ibid.*

Ages.[8] Santa has no connection with the Latin Three Kings; and he "would not be seen dead in the company of light-bringing and gift-bearing female spirits, such as the Swedish Santa Lucia, the Russian Babushka, or Befana, the Italian witch."[9] Thus, when Santa Claus appears in person in department stores in Paris, Rome, and Lima, he is almost certainly diffusing from the United States.[10] This diffusion suggests some interesting questions that can only be noted in this paper. Although some Italians oppose Santa as an alien, Santa rites sometimes coexist with Befana rites, which occur in January. Santa may also coexist with the Three Kings in Mexico or Peru. Is there a differentiation of functions in such cases, with Santa bringing gifts in the nuclear family and Befana or the Three Kings bringing them in the extended family? If so, when Befana or the Three Kings decline in relative importance, as they appear to, is this symptomatic of a change in the importance of the extended family? Santa evidently does not displace the Jultomten of Sweden; does this imply the functional equivalence of Santa and the Jultomten? When Peruvians adopt Santa Claus, does this represent a desire to appear like United States citizens; or does Santa fill a need in the evolving Peruvian family system that cannot be filled by traditional figures such as the Three Kings?

Santa Claus is originally American; and in the United States his acceptance by minority groups probably facilitates and indicates the assimilation of minority groups into the larger American community.[11] But why does he exist only in American and other areas that have become Americanized? What is his *meaning* for Americans?

---

[8]The Protestant Reformation put a stop to these practices. It has, however, been suggested that providing gifts for children originated as a form of bribery in such role-reversal ceremonies, something like our own tricks-or-treats on Halloween. See Wolf, "Santa Claus," p. 148.

[9]*Ibid.*

[10]Sereno, "Santa Claus Custom," pp. 387 ff.

[11]Eric Wolf says there is no Negro Santa Claus (*op. cit.*, p. 153), something which might appear to inhibit the assimilation of Negroes. However, Wolf is mistaken. Department stores in the Negro areas of Chicago have used Negro Santas, although one store owner pointed out "Now that we've used both white and black it doesn't seem to matter which he is—the children think it's Okay." And there are some Negro Santas on Christmas cards. See Shlien, "Myth in America," p. 30.

APPROACHES IN THE BEHAVIORAL SCIENCES

Although behavioral scientists have unjustly neglected the study of Santa Claus, theories developed for other reasons can be applied to him very neatly.

Psychoanalysis. Psychoanalysts have written surprisingly little about Santa Claus; and as a result I have been compelled to concoct my own half-baked theory instead of using someone else's. Richard Sterba,[12] however, has suggested the obvious place to start from by noting that Santa Claus, "no doubt, is a father representative." However, he goes on to suggest that Santa Claus and the rest of Christmas is an "acting out of childbirth in the family." There is a period of "expecting" involving much secrecy, a Christmas rush involving great "labor," the exhibition and admiration of presents, and the obvious sexual symbolism of having Santa come down the chimney and through the fireplace. This last suggests that Santa is not entirely masculine, as does his fat belly and bag of gifts (is he pregnant?).[13] Sterba's theory implies the hypothesis that Santa Claus should be especially significant when the facts of childbirth are kept secret from children and should be less significant when children are well informed. This can be tested and is probably true. (There is no Santa Claus in the Trobriand Islands.) However, like many psychoanalytic explanations, Sterba's unduly neglects interpersonal relations and is incapable of explaining many variations within and among cultures. To generate better explanations, it is necessary to use neo-Freudian or post-Freudian theories.

Young children have ill-formed personifications of their parents. On the one hand, they may not clearly distinguish fathers and mothers, and, on the other, they may distinguish between a "good Mother" and a "bad Mother."[14] It is not

[12]Richard Sterba, "On Christmas," *Psychoanalytic Quarterly,* XIII (1944), 79–83.

[13]This argument would probably be attractive to Bruno Bettelheim, who has argued elsewhere that many male initiation rites in primitive societies involve a symbolic acquisition of female sexual characteristics and stem from masculine envy of female sexuality. See his *Symbolic Wounds* (New York: The Free Press, 1954).

[14]See Tamotsu Shibutani, *Society and Personality* (Englewood Cliffs, N.J.: Prentice-Hall, Inc., 1961); and Harry S. Sullivan, *The Interper-*

easy to construct a consistent image of a parent. Children's myths often clearly differentiate images of consistently good parents from images of consistently bad parents. The prevalence of witches, goblins, and giants allows children to express hostility and anxiety toward parent figures which they are not allowed to express toward their actual parents.[15] But why Santa Claus? Isn't it permissible to express affection toward the real father? No, for two reasons. First, the real father doesn't deserve the affection. Santa represents a wish-fulfilling fantasy. Second, the real father tends to reject excessive affection because it is associated with excessive dependency. Fathers are relatively incompetent nurturant figures and confine affection from children within limits, so that children will be unable to make dependent demands on them. Thus, Santa is a consistently benevolent father image toward whom affectionate and dependent feelings may be expressed.[16]

This approach suggests that Santa beliefs are especially likely to be salient when the child finds it difficult to construct a consistent image of his father. This is especially likely to be so in American society, where fathers and mothers both express affection toward children and where they both order children about, but where the father tends to be more punitive and less affectionate than the mother.[17] Fathers in other societies tend to be more consistently authoritative and more distant emotionally,[18] so that there is less cause for children to respond intensely to images like Santa Claus. The relative

---

sonal Theory of Psychiatry (New York: W. W. Norton & Company, Inc., 1953).

[15]On the prevalence of witches and bogey-men, see Beatrice Whiting, ed., *Six Cultures: Studies of Child Rearing* (New York: John Wiley & Sons, Inc., 1963).

[16]One of my critics has argued that I have here followed a persistent tendency of psychoanalytic thinkers in emphasizing the nuclear family to the neglect of the extended family in discussing child socialization. This critic points out that many of Santa's characteristics are more befitting a grandfather figure or an uncle figure than a father figure; grandfathers and uncles often play the role of Santa in family ceremonies. I believe American grandfathers and uncles are seldom salient figures in child socialization, although I might be wrong; we lack good data on this point.

[17]See Charles E. Bowerman and Glen H. Elder, Jr., "Variations in Adolescent Perception of Family Power Structure," *The American Sociological Review*, XXIX (1964), 551–67.

[18]See B. Whiting, *Six Cultures;* and E. C. Devereux, Jr., U. Bronfenbrenner, and G. J. Suci, "Patterns of Parent Behavior in the United States of America and the Federal Republic of Germany," *International Social Science Journal*, XIV (1962), 488–506.

"dedifferentiation"[19] of parental roles in American families not only makes Santa an appropriate figure, it has also led to the increasingly frequent appearance of *Mrs*. Santa Claus.[20]

Although the figure of Santa Claus may have an important psychological meaning for children, this is only a small part of his meaning in society. "Children don't make culture," and if Santa beliefs persist it is because they have meaning for adults as well as children—or, rather, because they have meaning for adults in their relations to children.

Marxism. On the one hand, belief in Santa is an ideology of parents to facilitate the control of children, and, on the other, it is an expression of the distress of children. On the former, Friedrich Engels might have written, religion

> . . . became more and more the exclusive possession of the ruling classes, and these apply it as a mere means of government, to keep the lower classes within bounds. Moreover, each of the different classes uses its own appropriate religion: the landed nobility—Catholic Jesuitism or Protestant orthodoxy; the liberal and radical bourgeoisie—rationalism; parents—Santa Claus; and it makes little difference whether these ladies and gentlemen themselves believe in their respective religions or not.[21]

On the latter, Karl Marx might have written,

> The belief in Santa Claus is at the same time the *expression* of real distress and the *protest* against real distress. Belief in Santa is the sigh of the oppressed children, the heart of a heartless world, just as it is the spirit of an unspiritual situation. It is the *opium* of childhood. The abolition of Santa Claus as the *illusory* happiness of children is required for their *real* happiness. The demand

---

[19]Philip E. Slater, "Parental Role Differentiation," *The American Journal of Sociology*, LXVII (1961), 296–308.

[20]One wonders what the Bishop of Myra would have had to say about her.

[21]Engels, "Ludwig Feuerbach and the End of Classical German Philosophy," in Marx and Engels: *Basic Writings on Politics and Philosophy*, L. S. Feuer (Garden City, N.Y.: Doubleday Anchor Books, 1959), p. 240.

to give up the illusions about their condition is the *demand to give up a condition which needs illusions.*[22]

Parents use the belief in Santa Claus to control children, to induce children to defer demands for gratification to Christmas and to make it appear that Santa, not the parents, causes the deprivation of children.

Although Marx and Engels didn't make the above statements, they might have. Numerous later writers on Santa Claus have expressed themselves in such a vein. For example, Eric Wolf writes,

> A long time ago Marx criticized the 'commodity fetishism' of Smith and his followers, their tendency to conceptualize the dance of commodities as a reality independent of the social relations that make up the market. In Santa Claus, this commodity fetishism has found an appropriate collective representation. . . . [As] God has been replaced by society, so the word of God has been replaced by the morality of the market place that governs the production and distribution of goods. Of this morality Santa Claus is both emblem and agent.[23]

Renzo Sereno has presented a similar argument, adding that the adult emphasis on the exchange of commodities at Christmas stems from their feelings of loneliness and worthlessness. Sereno not only argues that children are the "innocent victims" of Santa Claus beliefs, but that they are unwilling victims. He argues that children are distressed by Santa and anxious in his presence, and that adults can recall only unhappiness in their own childhood experiences with Santa.[24]

These arguments have serious weaknesses, which will be discussed below. However, there is some indirect corroborating evidence. While there have been no systematic studies of Santa Claus as a child control device, belief in God has

[22]Marx, "Toward the Critique of Hegel's Philosophy of Right," in *ibid.*, p. 263.

[23]Wolf, "Santa Claus," pp. 153 and 154.

[24]Sereno, "Santa Claus Custom," pp. 389–92. Sereno conducted interviews about Santa beliefs in central Illinois; the credibility of his work must be qualified by his admission that, "My investigation required no intensive interviews, because in most cases the candor of the adults matched the candor of children," *Ibid.*, p. 391.

been studied in this way. Clyde Z. Nunn reports a study[25] in which a good sample of adults in eastern Tennessee were asked, "Do you tell your child that God will punish him if he is bad?" In 27 per cent of 367 families both parents said they did, and either father or mother did in an additional 40 per cent. The data show a slight tendency for parents affiliated with sectarian religions to use this "coalition with God" as a child control device more frequently than parents associated with denominational religions, except in the lower income groups.

Nunn's data suggest that parents are most likely to attempt to form a coalition with God when their power is hampered in other respects. Thus, a coalition with God is most likely to be attempted when family income is low and when the mother is employed outside the home; if only one parent attempts to form a coalition with God, the mother is most likely to do so when the child is more affectionate to the father than to her, and the father is most likely to do so when the child is more affectionate to the mother.

Children tend to believe parents who tell them they will be punished by God for misbehavior. Thus, a considerably larger proportion of children who were told this by their parents than of those who were not, responded affirmatively to the question, "Do you believe God punishes you when you get angry?" Believing this, they also tend to blame themselves more when they do get angry. There is also a slight tendency for children whose parents form a coalition with God to believe that "A child should obey his parents without question" more than other children.

This study deserves to be replicated for such figures as Santa Claus and bogey-men; and it deserves to be elaborated to other areas of personality. Casual observation suggests considerable variation in the degree to which Santa is used as a child control device, in the degree to which parents tell children that rewards from Santa are contingent upon good behavior. (This variation is limited in two ways. First, the idea that Santa's behavior is contingent on good behavior is prevalent in the larger culture and manifested in such songs as "Santa Claus is coming to town." Children may acquire the belief from other sources than their parents. Second, *in fact* Santa's rewards are generally not contingent upon good behavior; parents who assert otherwise are bluffing.) We need

---

[25]Clyde Z. Nunn, "Child-Control through a Coalition with God,'" *Child Development*, XXXV (1964), 417–32.

information on the social determinants of these aspects of the behavior of Santa Claus.

Nunn suggests that the parental coalition with God produces *compliance* to rules on the child's part (and self-blame for noncompliance) but that it does not produce inner *commitment* to rules. It is also possible that parental coalitions with God or Santa generate anxiety and a sense of inner worthlessness in children; the child cannot rely on the unconditional support of his parents or other figures, and he is rewarded not for what he is but for what he does. This is an as yet untested hypothesis. Even if true, it is likely to be true only of a minority of American Santa Clauses. Santa Claus is generally a benevolent figure, and not only children but their parents regard him as such. Parents do not use Santa in a cynical fashion but tend to accept him themselves. This fact is a critical weakness of Marxist approaches. Engels to the contrary notwithstanding, it does make a difference if parents believe in Santa Claus.

Durkheim. Santa Claus satisfies Emile Durkheim's definition of a religious object: the distinction between the sacred and the profane is made with regard to him, belief in him is closely related to a set of rites, and these rites are acted out in an organized social group, the family.

The sacred character of Santa Claus may explain Sereno's observations of apparently negative reactions by children to him. The sacred is often approached with awe and anxiety, not with informality and glee. This does not imply that the sacred is negatively valued. In the absence of systematic data, some observations of John Shlien[26] can be used to support the idea that Santa is a sacred figure.

1. During the second World War, the coal miners went on strike shortly before Christmas. A news commentator dramatized his announcement of the event by saying, "John L. Lewis just shot Santa Claus." Within an hour NBC network offices received 30,000 phone calls from frantic children and their parents. A little boy in Texas drank a bottle of castor oil in despair. NBC put Morgan Beatty on the air with an interview of Santa, who said reassuringly, "John L. Lewis just missed me." This reassured everyone except John L. Lewis, who called this the foulest blow of all. Evidently some children do have strong positive sentiments toward Santa.

[26] Shlien, "Myth in America," pp. 29–31.

2. In 1948, *Time* magazine published a picture of several hooded and robed members of the Ku Klux Klan surrounding an elderly negro couple to whom they had just presented a radio as a Christmas present. The Grand Dragon of the Klan, in Santa Claus costume, stood front and center holding the hands of the old Negroes. *Time* called it "The most incongruous picture of the week"; and when Shlien showed the photographs to his professional acquaintances, one turned away in disgust and said it made him want to spit, and another said, "It's a perversion. . . . There is such a thing as the Devil." "That which is sacred is shown to be so if it is capable of being profaned by misuse or by contact with its opposite."[27]

3. Shlien performed a kind of experiment in which a plate of chocolate squares, fruit, animals, and Santa Clauses (all of chocolate) were placed before three different groups.[28] Among eleven 4 and 5 year old nursery school children, only one ate a Santa Claus, and she had an older brother. In a group of nine seven- and 8 year olds, all ate the Santa Claus. And, at a bridge party of twelve young parents, only one person ate a Santa Claus, and his wife criticized him for it. There is evidently a curvilinear relation between age and acceptance of Santa Claus. (It is likely that Sereno interviewed mostly 7 to 9 year old children.)

Santa Claus is a sacred figure. Like the totemic figures of the Australian aborigines which were analyzed by Durkheim, eating him or his representations is taboo. Like the Australian totems, he does not represent natural objects but a social group. Groups need such representation, since they are real but often invisible; the group exists even when its members are dispersed. Unlike Australian totems, Santa Claus does not represent the total society or the clan; however, he represents the group most important to small children, the nuclear family. Santa Claus beliefs and rituals represent the family and serve to enhance its solidarity.

To derive testable hypotheses from these statements, it is necessary to go beyond the theories of Durkheim. This can be done best by following the lead of Durkheim's associate Marcel Mauss[29] and considering the most important ritual as-

[27]*Ibid.*, p. 29.

[28]David Schmitt has suggested to me that this technique could be generalized into a larger class of "projective eating" tests.

[29]Mauss, *The Gift: Forms and Functions of Exchange in Archaic Societies,* trans. Ian Cunnison (New York: The Free Press, 1954).

sociated with Santa Claus, gift-giving. The exchange of gifts (and, in an attenuated form, cards) is one way in which the solidarity of American extended families is maintained. It is not the economic value of these gifts that is important, but their symbolic value; the gifts symbolize positive familial sentiments, sentiments that are often latent (not affecting overt behavior) but which are nevertheless important.[30] Gifts are freely given, and by definition they are not given in expectation of a return gift. But, implicitly, reciprocity is expected, either in the form of a gift or in the form of feelings of gratitude and deference.[31] If reciprocity is not extended, feelings are hurt or hostility is aroused; in any event, the social relation is broken. Gift-giving is obviously capable of abuse, and gifts may be given in the conscious expectation of a return and in the absence of favorable sentiments. Most people can make the distinction, however, between a gift and a bribe. Some of the condemnation of the "commercialism" of Christmas rests on just this feeling that alleged exchanges of "gifts" are often forms of barter or bribery. Recognition of this in no way weakens the importance of gift-giving for the maintenance of solidarity in families and similar groups.

Gifts exchanged between adults are generally acknowledged publicly. It is almost necessary that they be so acknowledged if they are to perform the functions described above. The problem of Santa Claus is that he is associated with anonymous gift-giving. Santa does not stay around to be thanked for his gifts, and parents are enabled to give gifts, not in their own names, but in his. Why? The Marxist answer would be that the parent prevents his children from bugging him for gifts all year long by the assertion that he is incapable of giving any and that the children must rely on another figure, Santa Claus (who is, fortunately, in league with the parent). (Santa Claus may also be a scapegoat if a child's wishes are denied.) There may be something to this, but why should the parent make any gift at all in this case? It seems more likely that the parent expresses a real affection toward his children in the form of the anonymous gift. An acknowledged gift always carries the possible suspicion of an

---

[30]Sociologists will notice a revision of Durkheim here. The exchange of commodities, which Durkheim felt to be especially important for organic solidarity, turns out to be important for maintaining mechanical solidarity when it takes the form of gift-exchange.

[31]Cf. Alvin W. Gouldner, "The Norm of Reciprocity," *The American Sociological Review,* XXV (1960), 161–78.

expectation of reward—especially when the gift is made to a child, who may be unable to distinguish between the explicit denial of an expectation of reciprocity and the implicit acceptance of a norm of reciprocity. The anonymous gift is much less likely to arouse such suspicions, on the part of the donor as well as others. Thus, whenever we place a high value on the possession of certain positive sentiments we are likely to value the anonymous gift. Some of the attraction of many Christmas stories resides in this—stories like "The Juggler of Tours," or the dispatch of the reformed Scrooge of an unacknowledged turkey to the Cratchit family.

Christmas rites permit the expression of positive sentiments in extended and nuclear families. Santa Claus, by accepting responsibility for our gifts, allows us to express morally uncontaminated sentiments toward children. He is an especially important figure in American families because of the great emotional importance of the small family group for Americans. Santa Claus is likely to become important in other Western societies to the extent that their family systems become more like the American—to the extent that the power of extended families loses importance, and to the extent that the nuclear family becomes the center of the emotional life of all its members.

Needed Research. The behavioral science approaches to Santa Claus that have been presented here need not be inconsistent with one other. It is conceivable that Santa Claus can be simultaneously a benevolent father figure, a child-control technique, and a symbolic representation of affection in small family groups. Santa's very complexity may account in part for his importance as a cultural figure. However, the apparent compatibility of these theories is also a sign of their weakness. They are not stated in a form that will permit their refutation. Additional work of a theoretical nature would be valuable, either to provide a genuine synthetic theory or to generate hypotheses, the test of which would make it possible to reject one theory while retaining others.

Some needed empirical research has been suggested on the preceding pages. We need to know the conditions leading parents to form a coalition with a Santa Claus threatening to withhold rewards from children who misbehave; and we need to know the consequences of this Santa belief. We need studies like those reported by Shlien to show the extent to which Santa Claus is regarded in a sacred light. And we need to know which types of families in other societies are most likely to adopt the American Santa Claus system of beliefs and rites.

It is unlikely that studies of the distribution of Santa Claus beliefs in American society would be interesting in terms of the theories stated above. It seems likely that the most important determinant of these beliefs among young children is the religion of their parents. Parents of strict orthodox beliefs—obviously orthodox Judaism but also orthodox Christianity—and parents who are militant atheists are probably most likely to reject Santa Claus. The middle ranges of religiosity are probably most likely to be associated with belief in Santa.

The age at which children cease to believe in Santa, and the process by which disbelief develops, does deserve study. The presence or absence of older siblings is probably an important determinant of age of disbelief. Whatever the age, disbelief may have consequences for child behavior. Does the child feel taken in by his parents, and does he tend as a result of disbelief to question the legitimacy of his parents' authority? Or does he feel guilty for not believing as he is expected to? (A nine-year-old subject pretended to believe in Santa Claus, perhaps so that he would not disillusion his parents.) Or is disbelief a functional "belief" in its own right, enabling the child to identify himself as a more mature and sophisticated figure, one who can accept the symbolic meaning of gifts in the manner of an adult? Contrary to the beliefs of Clauseologists and Positivists, the meaning of Santa Claus does not depend solely on his existence or non-existence. The question, "Does Santa Claus exist?" may be misleading. As George Herbert Mead said, "Reality is itself a social process."

Selected Additional Readings

GENERAL INTRODUCTIONS:

1. Berger, Peter L. *Invitation to Sociology: A Humanistic Perspective*. New York: Anchor Books, 1963. A delightfully written and lucidly argued introduction. A little gem.
2. Gerth, Hans, & C. Wright Mills. *Character and Social Structure*. New York: Harcourt Brace Jovanovich, Inc., 1953. A successful attempt to join the approaches of Marx and Mead.
3. Goode, William J. *Principles of Sociology*. New York: McGraw-Hill, 1977. An innovative and provocative general text.
4. Light, Donald, & Suzanne Keller. *Sociology*, 2nd ed. New York: Knopf, 1978. Probably the best among standard introductions.
5. Williams, Robin. *American Society*, 3rd ed. New York, Knopf, 1978. Focused on a sociological scrutiny of American society.

SOME MAJOR CLASSICAL WORKS:

1. Cooley, Charles H. *Social Organization*. New York: Schocken, 1964.
2. Durkheim, Emile. *Suicide*. New York: The Free Press, 1951.
3. Mannheim, Karl. *Ideology and Utopia*. New York: Harcourt Brace Jovanovich, 1936.
4. Marx, Karl. *Selected Writings in Sociology and Social Philosophy*, newly translated by T. B. Bottomore. New York: McGraw-Hill, 1964.
5. Mills, C. Wright, & Hans Gerth, eds. *From Max Weber*. New York: Oxford University Press, 1946.
6. Park, Robert E. *Human Communities*. New York: The Free Press, 1952.
7. Simmel, Georg. *The Sociology of Georg Simmel*. Wolff,

Kurt H., ed. & translator. New York: The Free Press, 1950.

8. Strauss, Anselm, ed. *George H. Mead on Social Psychology.* Chicago: The University of Chicago Press, 1964.

9. Toennies, Ferdinand. *Community and Society.* New York: American Book Co., 1957.

10. Veblen, Thorstein. *The Theory of the Leisure Class.* New York: Modern Library, 1934.

SOME MAJOR HISTORIES OF SOCIOLOGICAL THOUGHT:

1. Aron, Raymond. *Main Currents in Sociological Thought,* 2 vols. New York: Basic Books, 1965.

2. Coser, Lewis A. *Masters of Sociological Thought: Ideas in Historical and Social Context,* 2nd ed. New York: Harcourt Brace Jovanovich, 1977.

3. Hughes, H. Stuart. *Consciousness and Society.* New York: Vintage, 1961.

4. Nisbet, Robert. *The Sociological Tradition.* New York: Basic Books, 1966.

5. Parsons, Talcott. *The Structure of Social Action.* New York: The Free Press, 1949.

OTHER WORKS BY CONTRIBUTORS TO THIS VOLUME:

1. Bell, Daniel. *The Coming of Post-Industrial Society.* New York: Basic Books, 1973.

2. ———*The Cultural Contradictions of Capitalism.* New York: Basic Books, 1976.

3. Coser, Lewis A. *The Functions of Social Conflict.* New York: The Free Press, 1956.

4. Coser, Rose Laub. *Training in Ambiguity: Learning Through Doing in a Mental Hospital.* New York: The Free Press, 1979.

5. Davis, Kingsley. *Human Society.* New York: Macmillan, 1950.

6. Goffman, Erving. *Asylums: Essays on the Social Situation of Mental Patients and Other Inmates.* New York: Anchor, 1961.

7. ——— *Presentation of Self in Everyday Life.* New York: Anchor, 1959.

8. Goode, William J. *The Celebration of Heroes: Prestige as a Control System.* Berkeley: The University of California Press. 1978.

9. Hagstrom, Warren. *The Scientific Community.* New York: Basic Books, 1965.

10. Hughes, Everett C. *The Sociological Eye*, 2 vols. Chicago: Alvine, 1974.

11. Lazarsfeld, Paul F., & Wagner Thielens. *The Academic Mind*. New York: The Free Press, 1958.

12. Levi-Strauss, Claude. *The Elementary Structures of Kinship*. Boston: Beacon, 1970.

13. Lyman, Stanford, & Marvin Scott. *The Drama of Social Reality*. New York: Oxford University Press, 1975.

14. Lynd, Robert S., & Helen M. *Middletown*. New York: Harcourt Brace Jovanovich, 1959.

15. ———— *Middletown in Transition: A Study in Cultural Conflicts*. New York: Harcourt Brace Jovanovich, 1964.

16. Merton, Robert K. *Social Theory and Social Structures*, rev. ed. New York: The Free Press, 1968.

17. Riesman, David. *The Lonely Crowd*. New Haven: Yale University Press, 1961.

18. Whyte, William F. *Street Corner Society*. Chicago: The University of Chicago Press, 1943.

SOCIAL RESEARCH METHODS:

1. Junker, Buford. *Field Work: An Introduction to the Social Sciences*. Chicago: The University of Chicago Press, 1962.

2. Lazarsfeld, Paul F., & Elihu Katz. *The Language of Social Research*. New York: The Free Press, 1965.